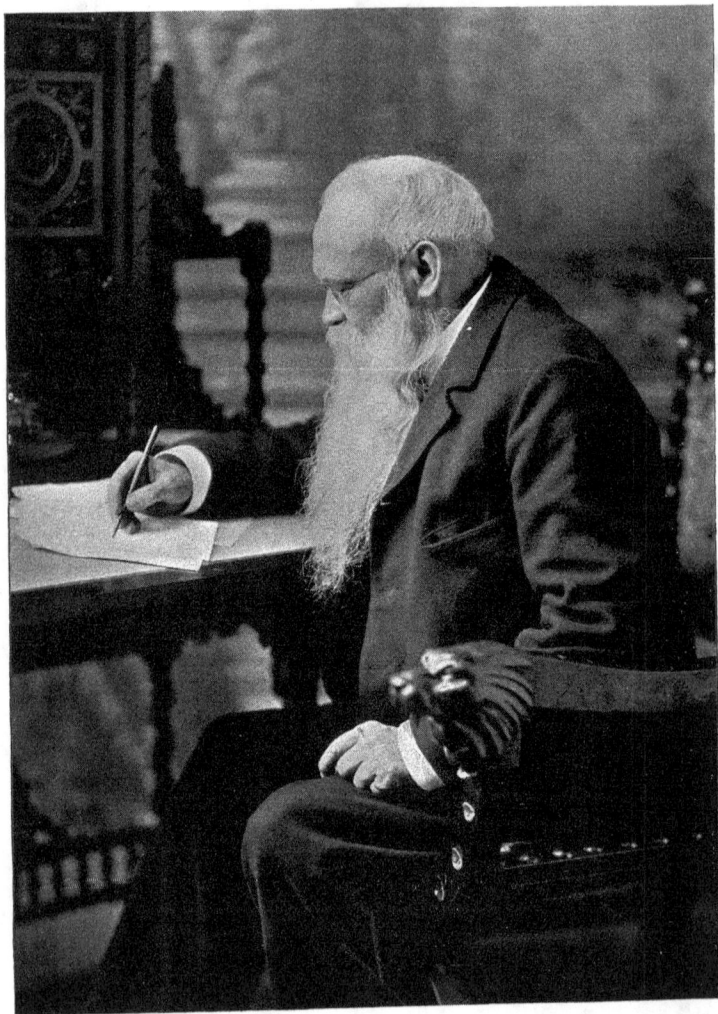

James E. Greenleaf

GENEALOGY
of the
GREENLEAF FAMILY

By birth the name alone descends;
Your honor on yourself depends.
—Gay

Compiled by
James Edward Greenleaf

HERITAGE BOOKS
2008

HERITAGE BOOKS

AN IMPRINT OF HERITAGE BOOKS, INC.

Books, CDs, and more—Worldwide

For our listing of thousands of titles see our website
at
www.HeritageBooks.com

A Facsimile Reprint
Published 2008 by
HERITAGE BOOKS, INC.
Publishing Division
100 Railroad Ave. #104
Westminster, Maryland 21157

International Standard Book Numbers
Paperbound: 978-1-55613-227-8
Clothbound: 978-0-7884-7163-6

CONTENTS.

ILLUSTRATIONS.

PREFACE.

THE custom of prefacing books with introductory remarks, or explanations,—which the author desires to bring to the notice of the reader,—is a pleasant way of saying, "Pause, before you pass the threshold of this house: it contains many things which you should behold understandingly; and although the door stands wide open for you to enter therein, a cordial greeting awaits you, the guests are already assembled, and you are to take possession, I stand here to make the transfer, and we will, if you please, enter together. As we wander about its hospitable halls, let us view kindly any imperfections we may discover, the better to enjoy the work as a whole." With this metaphor, I frankly state that the sense of freedom as we enter the door is to me refreshing: because of the opportunity it gives for *personal* expression,—a feeling of latitude, enough to set forth all that is required for a clear understanding by the reader of my aim and purpose in preparing this book, and that he may know the path I took in the intricate labyrinth of research; and also to know of some of those to whom I owe and sincerely render my acknowledgments.

My copy of the "Genealogy of the Greenleaf family, by Jonathan Greenleaf, of Brooklyn, N. Y., printed for the use of the family, 1854," has, in the handwriting of my honored father, the late Rev. P. H. Greenleaf, D.D., the inscription, "James Edward Greenleaf, from his Affect. Father, June, 1854." The perusal of its pages awakened an interest which led me to the habit of gathering, from time to time, all items of family interest that would come in my way. These fragments, whether of history, or data of birth, marriage or death, being carefully preserved, necessarily formed a large accumulation in the forty years which now have passed.

How and when to utilize them for family use has been an interesting problem. The busy life of an active man in daily toil and struggle,—the experience of most of us,—gave me no opportunity to enter upon the task of compiling and putting in proper order all the material I had, and adding thereto by a systematic research matter for a "full, reliable, and complete" work; and therefore, content with what I had, I bided my time, in patient anticipation. At last the way was opened, in a truly unexpected manner, through the door of an illness, which compelled me to abandon business for a time. I commenced late in September, 1892, "assembling the rank and file, and calling the roll of those present and absent." By Jan. 1, 1893, the material was in an orderly condition; I was then looking to an early publication of the book. I sent a circular in July of that year to some eight hundred of our family, who are scattered throughout the length and breadth of the land. The replies showed appreciation of the idea, and readiness to co-operate and render assistance in the fulfillment of the enterprise.

Gladly would I publish a list of these correspondents, as a tribute of gratitude, if I could by so doing give expression to my sentiments to *all* who have aided in many ways, as by searching records of the archives of town, counties, and state, etc.

Miss Marion Constance, daughter of Dr. Richard Cranch Greenleaf, of Lenox, Mass., kindly sent me photographs from portraits which have enabled me to give the illustrations of the early ancestors, and which add so much to the interest of the book.

To Levi Greenleaf, Attorney and Counsellor at Law, formerly of Lewiston, now of Portland, Maine, I am especially indebted for assistance in presenting the descendants of Joseph, the son of Stephen, son of Stephen, Jr., a branch omitted from Chart XXIII. of the book published in 1854, and of which my collection was fragmentary, unconnected, and seemingly hopelessly obscure. He has generously given largely of his valuable time, and most faithfully pursued and followed out to a conclusion the various, and somewhat at times mythlike, clues in the line of genealogical chains, until at last is presented a record of rare fullness and completion.

The venerable and honored John Greenleaf, of Wiscasset, Maine, was one of my first correspondents with reference to this branch of the family. Another, whose kind assistance I shall ever hold in felicitous regard, is the Rev. Ebenezer Greenleaf Parsons, son of Captain Jotham and Olive (Greenleaf) Parsons, and now residing in Derry, N. H., to whom my grateful acknowledgments are given for the elaborate record of the descendants of Olive and Thankful, daughters, and Ebenezer, son of Stephen and Mary (Knight) Greenleaf.

Clement A. Greenleaf, of Indiana, aided me materially, besides giving information of his own family by sending a large collection of names and addresses throughout the South and West as far as the Pacific Slope.

To Marshall W. Wood, A.M., M.D., Major and Surgeon United States Army, I am indebted for the very interesting sketch of Major-General Daniel Gooking.

These and many more kind friends have increased the numbers whose record the pages of the Genealogy bears. It is a vast throng. A clergyman who called on me and saw the well-laden desk, chairs, yes, and floor, too, covered with leaves of record, remarked, "Well, sir, with such surroundings, and the shades of the departed they must call forth to appear before you, you are not likely to feel lonesome," — a sentiment with which I was in hearty accord; and if ever a person may be said to desire an interview with those who have gone hence,— to lift the veil and ask for this, that, or the other member of the family to come forth and explain,—it is the genealogist who is in a strait for reconcilation of conflicting returns he has received; and he who comes forward in time of need, is really a friend indeed. At one such period I received reply to a letter of inquiry which led to a correspondence with Mr. William F. J. Boardman, of Hartford, Conn. Mr. Boardman married Jane Maria, daughter of Dr. Charles and Electa (Toocker) Greenleaf. I cannot convey by writing the appreciation I have of his letters, without prolixity, which would pass beyond limits of indulgence. Let it suffice that I am indebted to him greatly for suggestions, timely, and of much value, in developing the *ideal* which I had set up as my *standard* for accuracy in data and correctness in statement of historical fact, also for family records of the descendants of Dr. Daniel Greenleaf in the line of Dr. Charles, of Chart XVI.

In the summer of 1893, my brother, Lieut.-Col. Charles R. Greenleaf, Deputy Surgeon General United States Army, went abroad by order of the Secretary of War as a delegate to represent the United States at the Medical Congress. On his return, being in England, he visited Ipswich, for the purpose of examining the records of the parish of " St. Mary la Tours," where he found the date of baptism of our common ancestor, Edmund Greenleaf, and of Enoch, his son. It is there that the names of other children of Edmund may be found; and had time permitted, it is possible that further investigation might have revealed the earlier history of our ancestors when they came over from France, and perhaps a glimpse of whence they fled from their cruel persecutors. These are beyond my power to disclose, for the present, at least.

In the summer of 1894 my nephew, Prof. Ernest A. Congdon, of the Drexel Institute, Philadelphia, while in London, England, made research in the archives of State papers, 1534–1674, examining among others the "Calendar," of 4 volumes (Colonial), and the "Calendar" of State papers, 44 volumes, 1635–1668 (Domestic). These and all previous researches by their negative value give strength to the tradition of the HUGUENOT ORIGIN OF THE FAMILY; but it remains for the future historian or antiquary to supply the authentic record of descent. This I had hoped to have done, and had prepared a paper on the Huguenots, which, to incorporate in these pages with our present incomplete information, would appear premature and out of place. So, likewise, I regard the subject of "FAMILY COAT OF ARMS."

At least three are claimed in different branches of our family. To give copies of these, and not state the grounds upon which the claims are based, would be unsatisfactory. I have therefore concluded to rest the subject on a descriptive statement, quoting from a "note" on page 115 of the Genealogy of our family, by Rev. Jonathan Greenleaf, D.D.

"The Hon. William Greenleaf, once of Boston, and then of New Bedford, being in London about the year 1760, obtained from an office of Heraldry a device said to be the Arms of the family, which he had painted, and the painting is now (1854) in the possession of his granddaughter, Mrs. Ritchie, of Roxbury, Mass. The field is white (argent), bearing a chevron between three leaves (vert). The crest is a dove standing on a wreath of green and white, holding in its mouth three green leaves. The helmet is that of a warrior (visor down) : a garter below, but no motto."

Another branch of the family claims for its "Coat of Arms" that referred to by Heralds as belonging to the name *Greenlees.* "A fleur-de-lis vert, between three mullets gu, within a bordure engr. of the last. Crest: a sprig growing out of a mount proper. Motto, *Vivesco;*" but, "the only book of Heraldry known to contain the name of Greenleaf (spelt with an e final) is " Robson's British Herald," where it is stated that the arms are the same with those of the family of Green*land*, and are thus emblazoned : "He beareth argent, three saltiers, vert: Crest, a dexter arm, couped and embowed, holding a bomb, fired proper." It is this latter which is claimed by my branch of the family, and which was engraved upon the seal worn by my grandfather, the late Hon. Simon Greenleaf, and which I have upon my own seal ring.

It was my good fortune to receive, by the kindness of the daughters of my great uncle, the Rev. Jonathan Greenleaf, D.D., his book of records, and the letters received by him relating to the data from which his genealogy was compiled—many of which bear a date later than that of the publication, and down to 1860. I have carefully read all of these and have registered in a book kept for the purpose, numbering each letter to correspond with the register number, and recording against the same the subject-matter of the letter, for reference. These letters clearly indicate his intention to publish a later and more complete edition, and they explain many omissions and errors of the book of 1854. For example : regarding the family of Joseph, son of Stephen, to which I have referred, he made repeated efforts to obtain records of that family, but in vain, for various reasons,—unanswered letters, incorrect data, etc. ; and this illustrates a trying feature in the experience of the genealogist.

The paper on which this work is printed was made by the Holyoke Paper Co., Holyoke, Mass., of which O. H. Greenleaf is President, and O. S. Greenleaf is Treasurer.

A list of some of the authorities consulted in the preparation of this work, and from which some extracts have been taken.

GENEALOGIES.

Appleton, Binney, Treat, Coffin, Walworth's Hyde family, Clark, Wentworth, Whiting, Wilders, Willard, Chauncey, Cushman, Cutler, Dimond or Dimon, Phillips, Preble, Prentiss, Reed, Hunt, Little, Mason, John Leigh or Lee, Tuttle, Rawlins or

Rollins, Thurston, Wadsworth family for 250 years, Ingraham, Perkins, Spofford, Kip, Goode, Virginia genealogies by Horace Edwin Hayden, M.A., 1891.

HISTORIES.

Hingham, Cape Cod, Lexington, Mass.; Bradford, Vt.; Medford, Oxford, Haverhill, Mass.; Norway, Paris, Industry, Maine; Lancaster, Mass., by Hon. H. S. Nourse, A.M.; Newbury, Mass. (Mrs. E. Vale Smith, Coffin, Cushing, Mrs. Emery), Washington, N. H. Huguenots in the Nipmuck Country. Huguenot Refugees and their descendants in Great Britain and Ireland. History of the Huguenots (Browning, Weiss, Smiles, Poole). Emigration of the Huguenots to America. *The Virginia Magazine of History and Biography* (published quarterly), Vol. I., June, 1894. Old churches and families of Virginia.

MISCELLANEOUS.

Annual Register of Colonial Wars; Bridgeman's Granary Burial Ground; Hinman's Historical Collection of the part sustained by Connecticut in the War of Revolution; American Annual Register Records of the Colony of Massachusetts Bay, 1630–1810 (for the first fifty years, printed); History of the Law, The Courts, and the Lawyers of Maine; The Huguenot Society of America; The Commemoration of the Bi-centenary of the Edict of Nantes; Report of a French Protestant Refugee in Boston; Roll of the Huguenots: representing the coats of arms borne by the principal Huguenot families at the date of their settling in England (with a Key, containing a brief account of the refugees); New England Historical and Genealogical Register from January 1847 to 1894; Virginia Historical Collections, New Series: Richmond, 1886–1888; Articles on Virginia, by R. A. Brock, 1876–1878; a collection of clippings from the *Standard*, Vols. I., II., III.

INTRODUCTION.

SO much of interest is associated with the home of the *Common Ancestor of the Greenleaf* family, and of others of the early ancestry, it seems fitting that sketches of the history, reminiscences, and other incidents relating to their first abiding place in New England should form a part of these Annals.

A few extracts from the historians, whose works have given much voluminous details, and from manuscripts and traditions verbally handed down through the generations, will give a fair idea of the "Ould Newberry" town,—its origin, growth, religious and business life.

It was characteristic of the body of religious men and women from whom the family descend, to hold in peculiar veneration, and to honorably cherish and treasure up, every material of historic and genealogical research, to regard with favor *the tenacity of tradition;* and it is but natural for us to contemplate and keep fresh in mind the great trials and triumphs through which these our early ancestors passed, and their influence in developing the country. It was the motto of their ancestors, the Huguenots, that "Every man's work shall be made manifest, for the day shall declare it"; and it was this inborn element of mind and character that for over two centuries has been leading their descendants to deeds of patriotism and industry in developing the resources in the maturing of their homes, and of their share of the American Republic.

To their rude church in the clearing they devoted their first labors. Here was kindled a pure spiritual light that has shed its sacred cheer upon many a home.

> "Scarce steal the winds that sweep the woodland tracks,
> The larch's perfume from the settler's axe,
> Ere like a vision of the morning air,
> His slight-framed steeple marks the house of prayer."
>
> .   .   .   .
>
> "It sheds the raindrops from its shingled eaves,
> Ere its green brothers once have changed their leaves."

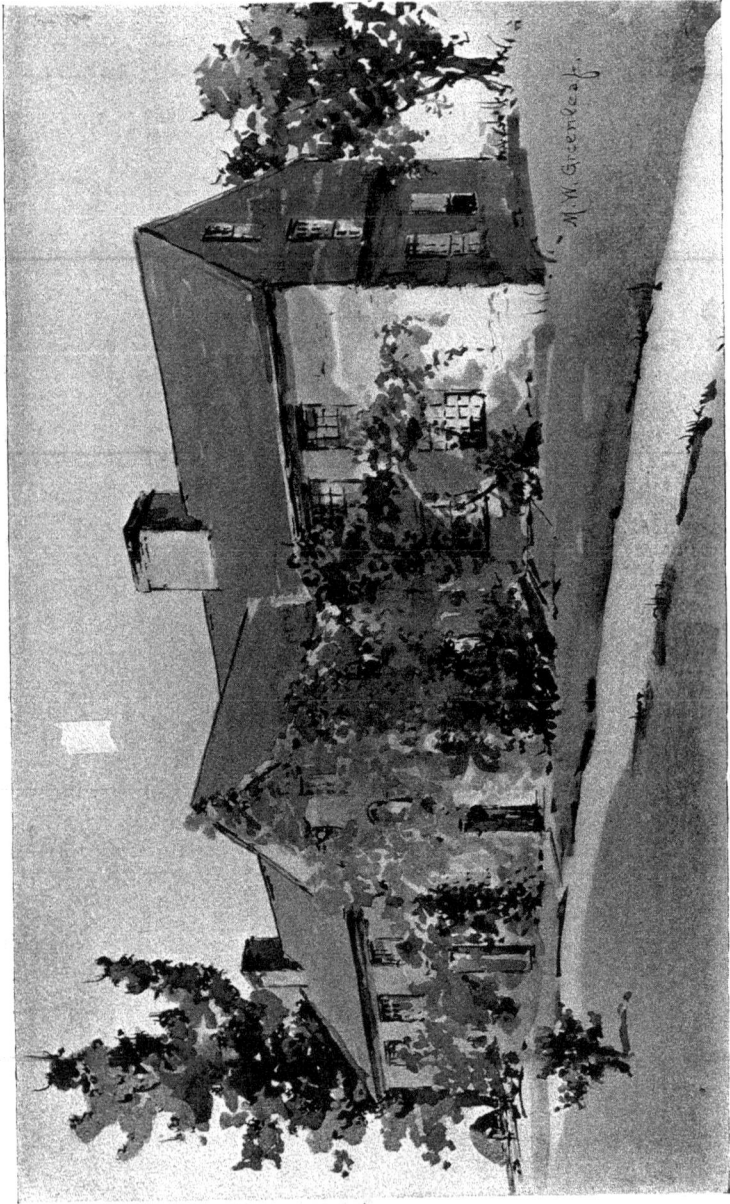

Old Garrison House, 1640-42, Newbury, Mass.

Built for refuge from Indians.   It is still standing, 1896.

NEWBURY, MASS.

1635.

IN the year 1633 eight ships, with passengers, arrived in New England. In 1634 twenty-two ships arrived,—six coming in May, fifteen in June, and one in November. These ships brought large numbers of passengers, who soon found places to settle. "On one of the ships that arrived in May came Mr. Thomas Parker, a minister, and a company with him, being about one hundred, [and] went to sit down at Agawam, and divers others of the newcomers." The plantation at Agawam was, from the first year of its being raised to a township (August, 1634), so filled with inhabitants that some of them presently swarmed out into another place a little farther eastward.

Mr. Parker was at first called to Ipswich, but choosing to accompany some of his countrymen, removed with them and settled at Newbury. Capt. Edward Johnson, in his "Wonder Working Providence," written in 1651, states that "Messrs. Parker and Noyes *began* to build the tenth church at a place called Newberry in the latter end of the year 1634," which would, by the Puritan reckoning, be the Spring of the year. The year with our Puritan forefathers began on the twenty-fifth of March, and not on the first of January. Not satisfied with renouncing all rites and ceremonies not in their opinion clearly warranted by the Bible, they attempted a reformation in the calendar, by repudiating the names of the months and of the days of the week, as of heathenish origin, and altogether unsuitable to be used by Christians. In order, however, to accommodate all those who did not desire this reformation, a double date was used between January first and March twenty-fifth. Thus twelfth mo. 1634-5 meant either February, the twelfth month, 1634, or February, the second month, 1635, according to the different opinions of the reader. "The latter end" of 1634 might mean, and probably did mean, the time between January first and March twenty-fifth, which would then be considered as the beginning of 1635.

The town of Newbury was originally one of the largest towns in the county.

Ould Newberry, as it was anciently called, was settled, incorporated, and paid its first tax, in the spring of 1635. It derives its name from Newbury, a town in Berkshire, England, situated in the south part of the county on the river Kennet, fifty-six miles west from London. It was so named in honor of the Rev. Thomas Parker, who had for some time preached in Newbury, England, before his arrival in America. Till its incorporation, in 1635, it was called by its Indian name, Quascacunquen; a name which the natives gave, not to the whole territory (as the word signifies " a waterfall "), but to " the falls," on what is now called the river Parker, on whose banks the first settlers fixed their habitations.

As different dates have been assigned by different persons for the first settlement of the town, some placing it in 1633, and others in 1634, and others in 1635, Mr. Joshua Coffin, in his " History of Newbury," gives his authority for the statement that no permanent settlement was here made till early in the spring of 1635. Governor Winthrop, in his " History of New England," Vol. I. page 160, states: " At this General Court (May, 1635) some of the *chief* of Ipswich desired leave to remove to Quascacunquen, to *begin* a town there, which was granted them, and it was named Newberry."

In the division of land throughout the town, the following are the names of the most wealthy of the grantees; and their wealth can be very easily estimated by the number of acres of land which was granted them.

This was according to the rule agreed upon in London, in 1629, by the " assistants of the company " who settled in Massachusetts. They gave to each adventurer two hundred acres of land for every fifty he put into the common stock, and so in proportion. " Such adventurers as send over any person, were to have fifty acres for each person whom they send." Every person who " transported himself and family to New England at his own expense, should have fifty acres."

To each of the first settlers was granted a house lot of at least four acres, with a suitable quantity of salt and fresh meadow.

Mr. Richard Dummer . .	1080	Mr. James Noyes	120
Mr. Henry Sewall	630	Mr. Thomas Parker . . .	90
Mr. John Clark	540	*Capt. Edmund Greenleaf* .	122
Mr. John Woodbridge . .	237	Mr. James Browne	159
Mr. Edward Rawson . . .	581	Mr. Edward Woodman . .	120
Mr. John Kent, Jr.	134	Mr. Nicholas Easton . . .	89
Mr. William Moody . . .	92	Mr. Stephen Kent	84
Mr. John Merrill	96	Mr. Stephen Dummer . .	386
Mr. John Cutting	220	Mr. Nicholas Holt	80

To the other grantees the number of acres varied from ten to eighty; many of the later settlers obtained the principal part of their land by purchase, such for instance as George Little, Robert Adams, Capt. William Gerrish, Richard Dole, Mr. John, Mr. Richard, and Mr. Percival Lowle, and others.

The town was thirteen miles long, and about six miles broad in the widest place, and contained about thirty thousand acres, of which nearly two thousand were covered with water.

1636.

The first water mill erected in Newbury was built at "the falls," on the river Parker, by Messrs. Dummer and Spencer, in accordance with the grant from the General Court, and an agreement with the town in 1635.

The first white male child born in Newbury was Joshua Woodman, son of Mr. Edmund Woodman. He died the 30th of May, 1703, in his sixty-seventh year.

1638.

June 15th.—"The court having left it to the liberty of particular townes to take, order, and provide, according to their discretion, for the bringing of armes to the meetinghouse, it is for the present thought fitt and ordered that the town being divided in four several equal parts, sayd part shall bring compleat armes according to the direction of those whom the town hath appointed to oversee the busynesse in order and manner as followeth; namely, John Pike, Nicholas Holt, John Baker, and *Edmund Greenleafe* being appointed as overseers of the busynesse, are ordered to follow this course, namely: They shall give notice to the party of persons under their severall divisions to bring their armes compleat one Sabbath day in a month and the lecture day following, in order successively one after another, and the persons aforementioned shall cause every person under their severall divisions to stand sentinell at the doores all the time of the publick meeting every one after another either by himself in person or by a sufficient substitute to be allowed by the overseer of the ward. And, further, it is ordered that the sayd overseers shall diligently mark and observe any that shall be defective in this respect, having lawfull warning, and they together with the Surveyour of the armes shall collect or distrain twelve pence for every default, according as hath been thought fitt by order of the court in this case provided."

Trumbull thus alludes to this practice of the early settlers in Connecticut, as well as Massachusetts :—

> " So once, for fear of Indian beating,
> Our grandsires bore their guns to meeting;
> Each man equipped on Sunday morn
> With psalm book, shot, and powder-horn,
> And looked in form, as all must grant,
> Like th' ancient true church militant,
> Or fierce, like modern deep divines,
> Who fight with quills and porcupines."

1639.

June.—Edmund Greenleaf was ordered to be Ensign for Newbury.

1641.

The General Court desired "the elders would make a catechism for the instruction of youth in the grounds of religion." In compliance with this desire, Mr. James Noyes, of Newbury, composed "a short catechism for the use of the children." A copy of this work which was reprinted in 1714 may be found in "Coffin's History of Newbury," Appendix B.

1648.

July 15th.—Lieut. Edmund Greenleaf is allowed to keep an ordinary in Newbury.

1670.

May 11th.—The court having left it to the care of the Major General to make temporary provision for military officers at Newbury, who did appoint Archelaus Woodman, Lieutenant, and *Stephen Greenleaf*, Ensign, confirms their appointment.

1675.

On the 24th of June was shed the first English blood in what was afterwards called Philip's War. On that day nine

Englishmen were murdered in Swanzy by the Indians, as they were returning from the meetinghouse, it being the day appointed as a day of humiliation and prayer throughout Plymouth County, who, being thus unexpectedly involved in trouble, sent to the other colonies for assistance. August 5th, *Stephen Greenleaf* and others from Newbury, Mass., with fourteen days' provisions marched against the Indians. (Town Records.)

1676.

March.—Stephen Greenleaf and five others (Selectmen) report to a court held at Boston measures of protection. (Coffin's History, p. 118.)

1680.

January 5th.—The town granted liberty to Ensign (Stephen) Greenleaf and Mr. (Daniel) Davison to build a wharf.

1686.

Stephen Greenleaf captain in militia.

1689.

May 6th.—Thomas Noyes and *Stephen Greenleaf* chosen to go to Boston as Committee of Safety, representing the town.

1690.

August 7th.—Military order concerning arms and ammunition. "These ar in his majesty's name to require all the soldiers belonging to this toune to bring their arms and ammunition to ye meeting house every Saboth day and at all other publick meetings, and also they ar required to carry their arms and ammunition with them into meadows and places where they worke, and if any man doe refuse or neglect his dewty as above expressed he shall pay five shillings for every such neglect."

October.—Captain *Stephen Greenleaf*, Lieut. James Smith, Ensign William Longfellow, Sergeant Increase Pilsbury, William Mitchell, Jabez Musgrave of Newbury and four more were cast away and drowned.

"This year," Robert Pike, of Salisbury, thus writes, "Captain Pierce, Captain Noyes, Captain *Greenleaf*, and Lieutenant Moores, with the rest of the gentlemen of Newbury, whose assistance next under God was the means of preservation of our tounes of Salisbury and Amesbury in the day of our distress by the Assaults of the enemy.

"*First:* I give you my hearty thanks for your readiness to adventure yourselves in that service, as always you have been ready to do and so forth.

"*Second*, to request the like favor of you upon the like occasion, if any such be offered.

"*Third:* That no *dunt*,* which is common pay in the country, may hinder any advised man from doing thayr duty, which is the advice that I give to myself, which you cannot but think have and shall have as much *dunt* as I can bear and so forth."

This year Essex soldiers were divided into three regiments.

1695.

October 7th.—On the afternoon of this day five Indians attacked and plundered the house of John Brown, who lives on the westerly side of Turkey Hill, and "captivated" nine persons; only one person of the family escaped to tell the tale. On the same day Col. Daniel Pierce sent a letter to Colonel Appleton and Colonel Wade of Ipswich asking for military force to "range the woods toward Andover, Rowley, and Bradford," in pursuit of the Indians.

October 8th, 5 A. M.—Colonel Appleton writes to Colonel Gednay, directing that several companies "range the woods with all possible speed toward Bradford and Andover, and so toward Merrimack River, so that if it might be ye enemy may be found and destroyed, which spoyle our people." Three hours after this, Col. Thomas Wade writes from Ipswich: "Honored Sir,—Just now Captain Wicom brings information that the last night Captain *Greenleaf*, with a party of men met with the enemy by the river side, have redeemed all the captives but one, which they doubt is killed. Three of the Indians got into a canoe and made escape, and the other two ran into the woods. Captain *Greenleaf* is wounded in the side and arm, how much we know not."

1696.

February 28th.—A rate was made for payment of building and finishing the west end meetinghouse and ministry house.

---

* "I hae a guid braid sword,
I'll take *dunts* frae naebody."—*Burns.*

The expense was twenty-two pounds and three shillings in money, and two hundred and eighteen pounds eighteen shillings and two pence in pay. This was due from sixty-four persons. Of this number *Tristram Greenleaf* and twenty-three others objected to the continuance of the meetinghouse on the plains, and wished to have it removed to Pipe Stave Hill. The contest, thus commenced, continued for many years with an obstinacy and bitterness to which the annals of Newbury furnish no parallel. Its result we shall see hereafter.

March 1st.—The town granted to *Stephen Greenleaf* four or five rods on the flats from Watts' cellar spring to Ensign Greenleaf's, and Mr. Davison's grant from high-water mark to low-water mark, to build a wharf and a place to build vessels upon.

March 5th.—Captain *Greenleaf* petitions the General Court, relating the affair of the Indians on October 7th previous; describes his wounds as " Shot through the wrist between the bones," also "a large wound in his side, which wounds have been very painful and costly in the cure of them ; have utterly taken away the use of his left hand, and wholly taken him from his employment; and prays they would make him such compensation as shall seem fit."

March 6th.—Read and voted that there be paid out of the province treasury to the petitioner the sum of forty pounds.

The coat which Captain *Greenleaf* wore in his pursuit of the Indians is still preserved by his descendants, together with the bullet which was extracted from his wound.

This is said to be the only instance in which the Indians either attacked, " captivated," or killed any of the inhabitants of Newbury.

1697.

March.—Laid out to *Stephen Greenleaf* a " parcel of flats and rocks lying on Merrimac River near Watts' cellar, bounded northerly by the river, easterly by Major Davison's grant, southerly by the common land of Newbury, and the westerly bound comes within about fifteen foot of the spring."

1698.

November. — This year Ezra Cottle commenced shipbuilding at or near the foot of Chandler's Lane (Federal Street), where Mr. William Johnson built.

In 1764 Newbury was divided into two towns, Newbury
and Newburyport.   In 1771, a province valuation was taken,
and in 1781 a valuation was taken by the State in which Newbury and Newburyport stood thus : —

Newbury.	Newburyport.	
750	875	Polls ratable.
10	7	Polls supported by the town.
75	51	Polls not supported by the town.
437	430	Dwelling houses.
36	60	Shops, separate or adjoining other buildings.
26	38	Tan houses, slaughter-houses, etc.
393	210	Barns.
14	45	All other buildings of £5 value and upwards.
1450	113½	Acres of tillage land.
2380	86¾	Acres of English and upland mowing.
10802	113½	Acres of pasturage.
192	7176	Tons of vessels of 5 tons burthen and upwards.
£592	£74131	Stock in trade.
341	146	Horses and mares, 3 years old and upwards.
562	30	Oxen, 4 years old and upwards.
1468	1741	Cows, 4 years old and upwards.
645	160	Swine, 6 months old and upwards.
318	5149	Ounces of silver plate.
£57726	£24668	Debts due to any persons.
———	£2825	Monies on hand.

Newburyport also in 1781 had ten distill and sugarhouses,
three rope walks, thirty-nine warehouses, and eighty-seven thousand nine hundred superficial feet of wharf.   Newbury, also, in
1781 had sixteen grist, saw, fulling, and slitting mills, one thousand one hundred and six acres of fresh meadow, three thousand
one hundred and sixty-seven acres of salt marsh, made one thousand four hundred and thirteen barrels of cider, had eight hundred and fifty-two acres of wood land, three hundred and three
acres of unimproved land, and thirty-five acres of land unim-
provable, had ten colts two years old, fourteen colts one year
old, three hundred and one neat cattle three years old, three hundred and ninety two years old, three hundred and fifty-five one
year old, and two thousand three hundred and seventy-six sheep
and goats.

In 1819 West Newbury was set off and incorporated as a
separate town.

In 1796 Dr. Dwight thus writes : " Newburyport lies on
the southern shore of the Merrimac.   The town is built on a

declivity of unrivalled beauty. The slope is easy and elegant, the soil rich, the streets clean and sweet; and the verdure, wherever it is, exquisite. The streets are either parallel, or right angled to the river; the southern shore of which bends here towards the southeast. There are few towns of equal beauty in this country. The houses taken collectively make a better appearance than those of any other town in New England. Many of them are particularly handsome, their appendages also unusually neat.

"From the tower of the church belonging to the fifth congregation, a noble prospect is presented to the spectator.

"On the west and south spreads an extensive champaign* country, ornamented with good farmers' houses, orchards, and cultivated fields, and varied by a number of beautiful hills.

"Behind them rise, remotely, two mountains, finely connecting the landscape with the sky. On the north flows the Merrimac, visible about four miles, exhibiting two islands in its bosom near the point where it first appears, and joining the ocean between two sandbanks, on which are erected two movable lighthouses. On the north shore stand the towns of Salisbury and Amesbury. Behind this the country rises gradually, parted into a variety of eminences; one of them, which from its appropriation by the savages is called Powow Hill, particularly handsome. Over all these ascends, at the distance of twenty-five miles, the round summit of Agamenticus. Northeastward, the Isles of Shoals appear at the distance of eight leagues, like a cloud in the horizon. Eastward the Ocean spreads illimitably. At a small distance from the shore Plum Island, a wild and fantastic sand beach, is thrown up by the joint power of winds and waves into the thousand wanton figures of a snowdrift. Immediately beneath is the town itself, which with its churches and beautiful houses, its harbor and shipping, appears as the proper center of this circle of scenery, and leaves on the mind a cheerfulness and brilliancy strongly resembling that which accompanies a delightful morning in May.

"Newbury contains five parishes, in which are five congregations and a Society of Friends. It is all settled in plantations, formed especially along the Merrimac, of excellent land under good cultivation. The surface is generally pleasant, and re-

* A flat, open country.

markably so on the borders of the river from some of the eminences." These eminences, of which the doctor speaks, are principally in West Newbury, and are called Pipe-Stave, Crane-Neck, Archelaus, Old-town, and Indian Hills. Newbury has the honor of having the first incorporated academy in the State, the first toll bridge, the first chain bridge, the first incorporated woolen factory. The first vessel that displayed the American flag in the river Thames was the "Count de Grasse," commanded by Captain Nicholas Johnson, of Newburyport, and the first United States ship of war, the "Adams" was built at Newburyport.

Captain Nicholas Johnson was the third son of Eleazer and Elizabeth (Pierce) Johnson, of Newburyport. He was born Nov. 4, 1752, and married, Dec. 12, 1776, Mary Perkins. Their children were Nicholas, Anne Greenleaf, Mary, Elizabeth, Sarah, Philip, Abel, Benjamin Greenleaf, and Henry. His father, Eleazer, was born in 1720, and lived to 1792. He was in the prime of life when the oppression of the colonies commenced, and his sons were old enough to be participators in the Revolutionary struggle. William Johnson, his great grandfather, was born in Charlestown, Mass., in 1671, and removed to Newbury in 1698, and married Martha Pierce, on the Pierce—or Pearce —farm, later as the Pettingill, and now known as the Little farm, and succeeded in business his relative and associate, Thomas Johnson, who was the first shipbuilder in Newburyport. His first vessel being of thirty tons; his yard being located "southeasterly from Chandler Lane (Federal Street)," as William Chandler testifies in court in 1700. At the date of his coming there, there were but two houses on the whole of Water Street below, though it had been a public street more than fifty years. One of these houses is the "old Johnson house," said to have been built about 1648.

The ship carpenters were among the most active of the patriots, and Eleazer Johnson was one of their leaders. He was a man above the ordinary size, with black hair, a black, flashing eye, and dark complexion, firm set, and remarkable for his strength. It was said of him that he could carry timber over the bows of a vessel against any four men of his yard. Such have been the physical characteristics of the Johnson family, accompanied with great strength of mind, great patriotism, and great industry; and therefore for more than two hundred years they have been marked men in the town, of superior intelligence, wealth, and influence.

As an interesting reminiscence of those stirring times in the history of "Ould Newberry,"—for these old towns of Newbury, Newburyport, and West Newbury alike cling to the dear name of "Ould Newberry,"—is related of the ship carpenters, and their devotion to their pastor, the Rev. Mr. Parsons, who was among the most active in defense of liberty, that at a meeting on Sunday, at the close of one of his sermons, he called for volunteers to step forward in the church for the formation of a military company. The company was at once formed. On a previous occasion, in the year that the Powder House was built, 1754, the town voted that the bill granting " an excise on distilled spirits was an infringement on the natural rights of Englishmen"; for this vote, all the carpenters in town held up their hands; they knew when eleven and four o'clock came in the yards (an allowance of grog was given them). Next after came the stamp oppression, and here again they were united; and from these shipyards, more than elsewhere, came the processions that marched about the town with fife and drum, calling upon every man to answer the question, "Stamp, or no stamp." If the answer was "Stamp," they knocked him down, hissed him, or otherwise showed their displeasure; if "No stamp," the answer was, "Fall in. Join us." No neutrals were allowed. Eleazer Johnson was in the head ranks of this semi-rebellion.

Of the destruction of the tea in Newburyport, it is related that it was stored in the Powder House for safe keeping. Eleazer Johnson standing one day upon the timber of his yard, called his men about him, and after a few patriotic words gave the order, "All who are ready to join, knock your adzes from their handles, shoulder the handles, and follow me." Every adz in the yard was knocked off, and that stout, athletic man, who would have marched through a regiment of " Red Coats " had they stood in his way, taking his broad axe as an emblem of leadership and for use, marched at the head of the company to the Powder House. There that well tried axe opened a way through the door, and each man shouldered his chest of tea, and again fell into line. They marched direct to the market, and then, in single file around the old meetinghouse, where the pump now is, when Johnson's axe opened his chest, and box and tea were on the ground together. Each man as he came up did the same; then, with his own hand Johnson lighted the pile and burned it to ashes; and on that spot, without disguise, the ship carpenters of Newburyport destroyed the first tea that was destroyed in America.

Twice in Newburyport was resistance to the tea imposition made; once by burning it in Federal Street, and again in the market.

Newburyport held a meeting December 23d, and Newbury December 29, 1772, and chose committees, the former of twelve persons, the latter of sixteen, "to take under consideration our public grievances" and "the infringement of our rights and liberties," and to report, and so forth. In both meetings allusion was made to the able pamphlet "received from Boston" and of their proceedings at a meeting November 20th.

1773.

January 1st.—The town "voted that *Captain Jonathan Greenleaf*, our representative, be acquainted that it is the desire and expectation of this town that he will persevere with steadiness and resolution in conjunction with his brethren in the honorable House of Representatives to use his utmost endeavors to procure a full and complete redress of all our publick grievances, and to do everything in his power in order that the present and succeeding generations may have the full enjoyment of all those privileges and advantages, which naturally and necessarily result from our glorious constitution."

December 9th.—At a numerous (informal) meeting of the people of Newburyport and others, a committee of five was chosen, who reported the following, which was accepted: "We have taken into consideration the late proceedings of the town of Boston relating to the importation of tea by the East India Company into America, and do acquiesce in their proceedings and are determined to give them all the assistance in our power *even at the risque of our lives and fortune.*"

On December 16, 1773, were moored at Griffins Wharf, in Boston, three British ships with cargoes of tea. About ninety citizens of Boston, partly disguised as Indians, poured the three ships' cargoes, three hundred and forty chests in all, into the sea, and made the world ring with the exploit of the Boston Tea Party.

> "No! ne'er was mingled such a draught,
> In palace, hall or arbor,
> As freemen brewed, and tyrants quaffed,
> That night in Boston harbor!"

Philip Johnson, born 1743, the oldest son of Eleazer Johnson, was a volunteer in the Revolutionary War, and was engaged in the battle of Bunker Hill; and at the close of the war he returned to the business of his father, living in what is called the "Johnson house," below Ship Street, and working in the old yard opposite. He was distinguished as a builder, and there is now in possession of the family a beautiful and valuable silver tankard, evidence of the consideration in which he was held by merchant contractors. It bears this inscription: "Presented by Heard and Amory (of Boston) to Mr. Philip Johnson, as a token of their respect for his fidelity in building the ship "Pomona," in 1795."

William Pierce Johnson, born 1745, the second son, married, October, 1770, Sarah Greenleaf, born May 31, 1753 (daughter of Hon. *Jonathan Greenleaf*); like all his brothers was brought up to the use of the axe, the saw, and the mallet, but afterwards left them for the waters. He was successful as a shipmaster, and when the war of '76 commenced he was in one of the French West Indies Islands in the Brig "American Hero,"—a very appropriate name for the times, the commander, and the business he entered upon. Hearing that war existed, he immediately loaded his vessel with arms and ammunition and sailed for Boston, which port he reached in safety, to the great joy of patriots who were in want of such a cargo, *the first material aid they had received.*

In 1798 he built the wharf that has since borne his name; after the building of which he did a very profitable business. His vessels were constantly arriving from Honduras with mahogany and other woods; from the West Indies with coffee, sugar, molasses, and rum; from the "Straits" with brandy, fruits, soap, olive oil, etc.; from the north of Europe with hemp and iron; and he, first in the history of Newburyport, had a freighting ship, named the "Industry," principally employed in carrying tobacco from the James River to Europe. Had he lived, he was in a way to become very wealthy; but when less than sixty years old, apparently in perfect health, and without any premonition, he died, sitting in a chair, in his own house. As it was, he left an estate of about $120,000. The town mourned his loss. It is doubtful if he left behind one merchant more intelligent, upright, liberal minded, and accomplished, as a gentleman, than himself. His personal appearance was indicative of his whole nature,—tall, well proportioned, athletic, commanding, and powerful. At the time of his death he weighed two hundred and sixty-five pounds, and was strong in proportion to his size. It was customary formerly, more than now, for men to pride themselves on their ability to lift, run, wrestle, etc. Mr. Bartlett, Capt. William Millbury, and Captain Johnson were each of them giants in strength, and each was a little jealous of the other. Their boasts of strength would frequently lead to trials of their power; one of which was in raising fifty-six pound weights. Mr. Bartlett and Captain Millbury could lift seventeen. Captain Johnson raised eighteen, and was pronounced the strongest man in town.

Nicholas Johnson, born 1752, the third son of Eleazer, and whom we have referred to as commanding the ship "Count de Grasse," under letter of marque in the Revolutionary War, was the first to hoist the American flag in the Thames River after Independence. The Stars and Stripes, seen at the British metropolis for the first time, caused quite a commotion, and hundreds and thousands of Englishmen came down to see the vessel. Capt. Nicholas Johnson superintended the construction of the Government ship "Warren," at Salisbury, Mass., which vessel sailed from Newburyport, under the command of Timothy Newman, who had been an Algerine captive, and who died on board at Havana the following year. Among the children of Capt. Nicholas Johnson were Nicholas, associated in business with Capt. J. N. Cushing, who married his sister Elizabeth, Jan. 3, 1815; and Henry Johnson, who was the second mayor of Newburyport. Joseph Johnson, born 1754, the fourth son of Eleazer, was also a shipmaster, and died very suddenly at his residence at the foot of Ship Street. Among his children were Eleazer, on High Street, a sea captain for many years, and afterwards president of the Mechanics Bank.

Of the children of Capt. William Pierce Johnson, who married *Sarah Greenleaf*, there were six,—Mary, Catharine, William Pierce, Sarah, Eleazer and Jonathan (twins). William Pierce Johnson married, first, Henrietta Tracy; second, Sarah Waite. By the first marriage he had three children,—William Pierce, Margaret Laughton, and Edward Augustus. Margaret Laughton Johnson married the Rev. *Patrick Henry Greenleaf* (son of Hon. Simon), April, 1829.

The twins, Eleazer and Jonathan Greenleaf Johnson, born Nov. 12, 1790, were noted men in Newburyport, and were worthy descendants of their ancestry; genial, polite, and honorable in all their intercourse with others. In stature large, they were, like their father, powerfully built, and of strong and massive form, and of striking likeness to him and each other. Few people have lived or could live in a community and be more intimately connected with the town and its people. Capt. Eleazer Johnson for forty years, save one, held the office of town and city clerk, during the entire period from the 28th of March, 1831, until the date of his death, Feb. 27, 1870. He had previously filled the office of selectman and overseer of the poor; the greater part of his life having been as a public officer of the town and city. From this standpoint he gazed upon a whole generation as they came and went. He watched the human wave rolling onto the shore; heard its dash; and saw it receding into the fathomless abyss. He took the names of that whole generation as they were born; he signed the certificates of their marriages; he recorded their deaths. It was but half of his life, but the whole of theirs; and all through it he was the same genial, pleasant, and noble specimen of a man. He had a kind word for the young and old; a friendly greeting for the rich and poor; and in turn was the object of their confidence and respect.

The other twin, the doctor, bore the name of their maternal grandfather, Hon. *Jonathan Greenleaf*, who, like the Johnsons, was distinguished for patriotism and statesmanship. The doctor's life was one of untiring industry and devotion to his profession, and one of kind words and kind acts, which had strongly attached the people to him. For fifty-five years they had seen him on the streets, ever on foot,—for he seldom used a carriage,—with a smile, and a bow, and a pleasant word for high or low, rich or poor, old or young. They loved the man that forgot himself in heat or cold, in sunshine or storm, by day or night, for their health and comfort, never asking to be excused even when years began to weigh heavily upon him; and never inquiring whether there was to be material recompense for his labors. They had met him in their homes when the house was to be gladdened by a new voice,—a new object to love,—or when affliction, and sorrow, and death were crossing the threshold; but whether they were in gladness or grief, he was the unchanged friend in sympathy to perform his duty and to help them in the way of life. They had come to know and love him, and the announcement of his sickness and of his death gave anxiety and sorrow to many a heart, and especially among the poor. He died Sept. 9, 1868.

During the periods of apprehension and excitement which were preparing the people for the arduous conflict before them, they found opportunities for amusement, peculiar to their situation. "Many cases like the following might be given, which I relate," says Mr. Coffin, in his history of Newbury, "on the testimony of an eyewitness, Mr. Caleb Greenleaf of Haverhill, and the public papers." February 15, 1774, one Holland Shaw, having been detected in stealing a shirt, was immediately taken before a sort of extempore court, convened for the occasion, and was sentenced as follows; namely, "that he parade through the public streets of the town, accompanied by the town-crier with his drum." The sentence was forthwith put into execution. The town-crier, William Douglass, with his brass-barrelled drum, and the thief with the shirt, headed the procession, which took up its line of march. The paper of that day informs us "that he was compelled to proclaim his crime, and produce the evidence, which was the shirt, with the sleeves tied round his neck, the other part on his back." The proclamation which he was compelled to utter with a loud voice was, "I stole this shirt, which is tied round my neck, from Mr. Joseph Coffin's house in Salisbury, and I am very sorry for it." Having been thus marched through the principal streets, and satisfied the demands of this new court of justice, he was dismissed, and never after that night was he seen in Newburyport.

Another person who had stolen some salt fish, was compelled to make atonement for the offense by parading through the streets, holding a salt fish in his hands above his head, and proclaiming his crime in a similar manner, "I stole this fish, and five quintals more."

An English sailor was also marched round the town with a pair of stolen breeches tied round his neck, informing the people what he had, and how he obtained them.

1774.

October 3.—The town of Newburyport met, and gave instructions to Captain *Jonathan Greenleaf*, their representative, of the most determined and decided character. The following is an extract: "Armed ships and armed men are the arguments to compel our obedience, and the more than implicit language that these utter is that we must submit or die. But God grant that neither of these may be our unhappy fate. We design not madly to brave our own destruction, and we do not thirst for the blood of others, but reason and religion demand of us that we guard our invaluable rights at the risque of both," and so forth.

October 24th.—The town of Newburyport held a meeting, and "Voted, that all the inhabitants be desired to furnish themselves with arms and ammunition, and have bayonets fixed to their guns, as soon as may be."

November 5th.—The last public celebration of "Pope Day," so called from the discovery of the "Gunpowder Plot," Nov. 5, 1605, occurred this year. The celebration went off with a great flourish. In the daytime companies of little boys might be seen, in various parts of the town, with their little popes dressed up in the most grotesque and fantastic manner, which they carried about, some on boards and some on little carriages, for their own and others' amusement. But the great exhibition was reserved for the night, in which young men, as well as boys, participated. They first constructed a huge vehicle, forty feet long, eight or ten feet wide, and five or six feet high from the lower to the upper platform, on the front of which they erected a paper lantern, capacious enough to hold, in addition to the lights, five or six persons. Behind that, as large as life, sat the mimic pope, and several other personages—monks, friars, and so forth. Last, but not least,

stood an image of what was designed to be a representation
of Old Nick himself, furnished with a pair of huge horns,
holding in his hand a pitchfork, and otherwise accoutered
with all the frightful ugliness that their ingenuity could devise.
Their next step, after they had mounted their ponderous vehicle on four wheels, chosen their officers, captain, first and
second lieutenants, and purser, was to place a boy under the
platform, to elevate and move round, at proper intervals, the
movable head of the pope, attached to ropes on the front part of
the machine, and take their line of march through the principal
streets of the town. Sometimes, in addition to the images of
the pope and his company, there might be found, on the same
platform, half a dozen dancers and a fiddler, whose

> "Hornpipes, jigs, strathspeys and reels,
> Put life and mettle in their heels,"

together with a large crowd, who made up a long procession.

December 28th.—Town of Newburyport chose Tristram
Dalton, Esquire, Captain *Jonathan Greenleaf*, and Mr.
Stephen Cross, "to represent this town in the provincial con-
gress to be held at Cambridge, in February next."

In 1774, the right granted in the time of William and Mary
for the inhabitants to choose persons as jurymen was taken
away, and all jurymen, grand and petty, were returnable to
the sheriff only,—the creature of the royal governor's appointment, thus insuring, in every case between the government and
the people, a packed jury, ready to express the will of the
governor; and as if this was not enough, it was further ordained
"that on motion of either of the parties, a cause or action
might be tried in any other county than that where the
action was first brought." All this and much more of the
same nature was enforced by fines and penalties, laying the
whole province at the complete mercy of the governor and
his minions.

In view of these dangerous innovations a town meeting was
called in August, and it was unanimously voted to answer to a
proposal from the Committee of Safety, at Marblehead, "that
in the opinion of this town the situation of our public affairs
claims the attention of every true friend of his country, and
demands an exertion of their utmost abilities to preserve it from

that infamy and ruin that now stare us in the face; wherefore, we do most earnestly concur in the proposal for a county meeting, and accordingly appoint Tristram Dalton, Esq., Mr. Jonathan Jackson, Captain *Jonathan Greenleaf*, Messrs. Stephen Cross, and John Broomfield, a committee on the part of this town, to meet with the committees of the other towns in this county, when and where shall be judged most convenient, in order that they may from time to time deliberate, propose, and pursue all such measures as may have the most probable tendency to serve the interests of the community, in this time of difficulty and danger; this Committee to continue until the further order of this town, and to have a reasonable allowance for their services.

Voted *nem. con.*   STEPHEN SEWALL,
Attest: a true copy.   *Town Clerk.*"

The delegates appointed by Newburyport to meet with those from other towns in the county of Essex, met at Ipswich, on the 6th and 7th of September.

Among the final resolves were the following:—

"*Resolved*,—That the Act of Parliament, entitled 'An Act for the better regulating the Government of the Province of the Massachusetts Bay, in New England,' being a most dangerous infraction of our constitutional and charter rights, and tending to a total subversion of the government of the province, and destruction of our liberties; and having been with uncommon zeal, with arbitrary exertions, and military violence attempted to be carried into execution, and this zeal and violence still continuing: from the sacred regard, the inviolable attachment we owe to those rights which are essential to, and distinguish us as, Englishmen and freemen, and from a tender concern for the peace of this country, we are bound to pursue all reasonable measures by which any attempts to enforce immediate obedience to that Act may be defeated.

"That the Judges, Justices, and other civil officers in this county, appointed agreeable to the charter and the laws of the province, are the only civil officers in the county whom we may lawfully obey. That no authority whatever can remove those officers, except that which is constituted pursuant to the charter and those laws. That it is the duty of these officers to continue in the execution of their respective trusts as if the aforementioned Act of Parliament had never been made. And that while they thus continue, untainted by any official misconduct, in conformity to said Act, we will vigorously support them therein, to the utmost of our power, indemnify them in their persons and property, and to their lawful doings yield a ready obedience.''

It having been intimated that the next court to be held in Newburyport would not be permitted to sit, it was resolved by the delegates of Essex County, who met at Ipswich, ''that all the judges and other officers held their commissions agreeably to the charter and the laws of the province,'' and therefore ought to be sustained by the county; that it was the duty of the officers to continue their functions the same as if the late Act of Parliament had never passed; and that while they continue '' untainted by any official misconduct, the county will support them.''

And the people of Newburyport fulfilled their part of the above resolve at a town meeting held September 28th, Jonathan Greenleaf being moderator. It was voted that '' the determination of the county delegates expressed in their late meeting at Ipswich ought to be adhered to, and the court supported in the exercise of their constitutional authority, and accordingly we will, as far as in our power, support them. But if any officers of the court presume to act under the new and oppressive regulations, they must cease to expect support from us.''

The court was held, and the county and town resolutions carried out by the people as confidently as if those addresses had been legal legislative Acts.

One Nathan Brown, of Newburyport, having accepted a commission as undersheriff, grounded on the late offensive Act of Parliament, was waited upon by the committee of the town and informed that he had thus incurred the displeasure of his fellow-citizens. He made a formal and public renunciation of his commission, promising in future to maintain the old charter privileges, and in no case to accept an office from the new administration.

The following Committee of Safety and Correspondence was appointed by the town, Sept. 23, 1774:—

Hon. *Benjamin Greenleaf.*	Capt. *Jonathan Greenleaf.*
Patrick Tracy, Esq.	Dr. Micajah Sawyer.
Dr. John Sprague.	Mr. David Moody.
William Atkins, Esq.	Mr. John Bromfield.
Capt. James Hudson.	Mr. John Stone.
Mr. Edmund Bartlett.	Major William Coffin.
Mr. Ralph Cross, Jr.	Capt. Thomas Thomas.
Tristram Dalton, Esq.	Capt. Joseph Huse.
Mr. Edward Harris.	Capt. Samuel Batchelor.
Mr. Enoch Titcomb, Jr.	Mr. Moses Nowell.
Capt. Jacob Boardman.	Mr. Jonathan Jackson.
Mr. William Teel.	Mr. Richard Titcomb.
Mr. Samuel Tufts.	Mr. John Herbert.
Capt. Moses Rogers.	Mr. Moses Frazier.
Mr. Jonathan Marsh.	Capt. Nicholas Tracy.

The town was divided into military lines. Every male over sixteen years of age was required to appear " complete in arms and ammunition," either under officers commanding independent companies, or in one of the four existing companies belonging to the town. These were required to meet for practice in the military art, such persons only to be excepted whom the field officer " judged unfit or unable."

The people were now preparing in earnest for the coming struggle, and were providing themselves with arms and ammunition. The Committee of Safety of Newburyport reported in November " that the people throughout the town were well supplied with arms, and those few who were deficient were resolved immediately to obtain them." During the winter the town was thoroughly canvassed, and every man capable of bearing arms was enrolled in one of the regular or independent companies.

By the spring of 1775 the town was put in a state of thorough preparation for war. The Committee of Safety had divided the whole town into four military districts, having their alarm posts, etc. The harbor was protected by sinking piers in the channel, not obstructing the whole passage, but in such a way that it would be difficult for strangers to find the passage. A fort was also built on Salisbury shore, called " Fort Merrimac," and, shortly after, another on Plum Island. These harbor defenses cost £2,433, 8s. 2½d. Military stores, and even provisions, were laid up; heavy cannon purchased; arms provided for such as wished to enlist in the Provincial Service, and needed such assistance, and arrangements were made for supplying their families during their absence; and the Committee of Safety was authorized to incur "any expense which the safety of the town or county required."

About this time came the news of the seizure of the public stores at Concord, by the British troops, or "regulars," as those stationed in Boston were generally called, and of the Battle of Lexington. A company at once marched from Newburyport to Lexington, having left the town at eleven o'clock at night, that no time might be lost in offering their assistance.

It was now perceived that peace was impossible. General Gage with his troops had already invested Boston, and the ministers from their pulpits joined their persuasions to the general voice of the town, and treated their hearers to patriotic and political addresses, as well as dispensing religious instruction.

Rev. Jonathan Parsons made an appeal at the close of one of his sermons for volunteers, and a volunteer company was immediately formed, with Ezra Lunt as captain. On the 9th of May ensuing, this company was provided with accouterments by the town; and that they used them right well, Bunker Hill soon after witnessed.

> They left the plough in the corn,
>   They left the steer in the yoke,
> And away from mother and child that morn,
>   And the maiden's first kiss, they broke.
> In the shower of the deadly shot,
>   In the lurid van of the war,
> Sternly they stood—but they answered not
>   To the hireling's wild hurrah.
>
> But still as the brooding storm,
>   Ere it dashes ocean to foam,
> The strength of the free was in every arm,
>   And every heart on its home.
> Of their pleasant homes they thought,
>   They prayed to their fathers' God;
> But forward they went, till their dear blood bought
>   The broad, free land they trod.
>   .   .   .   .
>   Fast fled morn's shadows gray,
>   And with the breaking day,
>   Our hearts grew still;

But ere that ruddy beam
Tinged Mystic's silent stream,
Flashed the red cannons' gleam
By Bunker Hill.

.   .   .   .

We from our fort's low crest,
Our muskets down at rest,
    Glance in a row ;
There, not a drumbeat stirred,
But " Steady ! "—all we heard—
" Keep your fire, wait the word,
    Then, boys, aim low ! "

.   .   .   .

" Fire, fire ! " the order came—
Heavens ! what a burst of flame !
True every marksman's aim.

.   .   .   .

Broken, they fly the hill ;
Our shot, with right good will,
    Follows them fast.

.   .   .   .

Our chief, from rank to rank,
And Putnam on our flank,
    Marked how we stood ;
Stark, grimly calm, was there,
Pomeroy with silvery hair,
Knowlton, none braver were,
    Chester, as good.

These verses were written by the late Hon. George Lunt.

The commission under which Captain Perkins led his men
on the 17th of June, is dated at Watertown, May 19, 1775,
and is signed by Joseph Warren, president. His company were
mostly enlisted ten days before. The names of the company
are as follows :—

Benjamin Perkins, Captain.
Joseph Whittemore, First Lieut.
Stephen Jenkins, Second Lieut.
William Stickney, Ensign.
Samuel Foster, First Sergt.
Amos Pearson, Second Sergt.

Thomas Frothingham, Third Sergt.
Thomas Wescomb, Fourth Sergt.
John Brazier, Drummer.
Richard Hale, Drummer.
Isaac Howard, Fifer.
John West Folsom, Fifer.

PRIVATES.

Jonathan Carter.
Edward Swain.
Jeremiah Smith.
Moses Wickes.
Benjamin E. Knapp.
Benjamin Perkins.
Moses Pidgeon.
Daniel Pike.
Edmund Rogers.
Nathaniel Godfrey.
Thomas Boardman.
Samuel Coffin.
Zebulon Titcomb.
Joseph Somersby.
Samuel Harris.
Jacob Knapp.
John Cook.
Thomas Wyatt.
Abraham Toppan.
John Brett.
Jonathan Norton.
Moses Newman.

Thomas Haynes.
Aaron Davis.
Abiel Kent.
Joseph Mitchell.
Patrick Harrington.
Joseph Noyes.
Charles Butler.
John Coffin.
Joseph Knight.
John Murray.
Joseph Pettingell.
Philip Johnson.
Isaac Frothingham.
John Dillaway.
Charles Jarvis.
Stephen Wyatt.
John Kettle.
Josiah Teal.
Paul Stevens.
Joseph Davis.
Thomas Merrill.
Benjamin Eaton.
Samuel Nelson.

Joseph Stickney.
William Connor.
Solomon Aubin.
Joseph Somersby, 2d.
Nicholas Titcomb.
Silas Parker.
Moses Carr.
Amos Hale.
Makepeace Colby.
Jacob Foss.
Jacob Willard.
Simeon Noyes.
Patrick Tracy.
William Page.
Benjamin Cotton.
Daniel Lane.
Shadrick Ireland.
Daniel Somersby.
Benjamin H. Toppan.
Benjamin McClanning.
Michael Titcomb.
William Elliot.

On the morning of June 17th, when Captain Perkins reached Charlestown Neck with his men, he found it was commanded by the shot from the " Glasgow," man-of-war, and also by two floating batteries, which kept up a heavy cross fire on the American troops who attempted to pass. Finding it growing rather warm, he threw away his wig, ordered his men to follow in single file, and made the passage without loss.

From a pamphlet* published by Col. Samuel Swett, of Boston (son of the late Dr. J. Barnard Swett, of Newburyport), it appears that three of this company were wounded; and as two of these, and one of Frye's regiment, belonging to Newburyport, were called to give some evidence concerning the conduct of General Putnam in that battle, and thus incidentally state the position of their respective companies on the ground, the following extracts appear :—

Philip Bagley, well known as the Deputy Sheriff of Newburyport for over thirty years, was attached to Frye's regiment.

*Historical and Topographical Sketch of Bunker Hill, with a plan.

He says: "Went over night; fought at the breastwork till they turned the corner of the rail fence, and began to rake the whole breastwork; the shot were very thick."

Philip Johnson, of Newburyport, of Captain Perkins' company, stated before Ebenezer Mosely, Esq. : "Was at the rail fence; while there, just before the action began, saw General Putnam on horseback; very near him, and distinctly heard him say: 'Men, you know you are all good marksmen; you can take a squirrel from the tallest tree. *Don't fire till you see the whites of their eyes.*' Immediately after the first retreat of the British, General Putnam rode up and said : 'Men, you have done well, but next time you will do better; *aim at the officers.*' The balls were flying as thick as peas."

In the report made to Congress by the "Committee for Massachusetts," the report says : "The artillery advanced towards the open space between the breastwork and rail fence; this ground was defended by some brave Essex troops, covered only by scattered trees. With resolution and deadly aim they poured the most destructive volleys on the enemy. The (enemy's) cannon, however, turned the breastwork, enfiladed the line, and sent the balls through the open gateway, or sally port, directly into the redoubt, under cover of which the troops at the breastwork were compelled to retire. Capt. Ezra Lunt's company was ordered up to cover the retreat of these exhausted troops, whose ammunition was now all expended. His company did good service, and with the aid of others forming this devoted rear guard, effectually kept the enemy at bay till the retreat was accomplished; but many of them were killed or wounded."

A return of Capt. Ezra Lunt's Company in the Seventh Regiment Foot, Col. Moses Little, eight months' service, 1775.

ENTERED SERVICE MAY 2D.

Ezra Lunt, Captain.	Moses Kimball, Corporal.
Paul Lunt, Lieutenant.	Christopher Pilsbury, Corporal.
Nathaniel Montgomery.	William Coker, Corporal.
Robert Fowle, Sergeant Major.	Bishop Norton, Drum.
Nathaniel Mitchell, Sergeant.	Benjamin Pearson, Fife.
John McLarty, Sergeant.	Daniel Ela.
Edward Moore, Sergeant.	Enoch Pierce.
Timothy Palmer, Sergeant.	Parker Chase.
William Holliday, Corporal.	Michael Casswel.

Moses Mooers.
Nathaniel Smith.
John Perry.
Robert Marshall.
John Smith.
Samuel Stickney.
Moses Rogers.
John Chase.
Abraham Knowlton.
Timothy Cowdry.
David Pearson.
David Rogers.
Nathaniel Warner.
Richard Hannel.
Samuel Lancaster.
Thomas Hammond.
Caleb Haskell.
William Shackford.

Thomas Gould.
Enoch Richardson.
Moses Cross.
Nathaniel Babson.
Jonathan Stickney.
John Sleeper.
Moses George.
Thomas Bolter.
Joseph Carr.
John Goodhue.
Jack True.
Mayo Greenleaf.
John Carr Roberts.
Enoch Foot.
Jesse Emery.
Bartholomew Spooner.
Moses Merril.
John Shackford.

The detachment under Arnold destined for the siege of Quebec encamped at Newburyport for several days, awaiting the transports which were to convey them to the Kennebec. Here an addition was made to their numbers. Among others who joined them was the Rev. Samuel Spring (afterwards pastor of the Third Religious Society of Newburyport), who accompanied the expedition in the capacity of chaplain; they embarked on the morning of September 19th. The detachment consisted of ten companies of musketmen and three companies of riflemen, amounting to eleven hundred men, on board ten transports, sailed for Kennebec,—fifty leagues from Newburyport.

General Arnold was entertained while here by Messrs. Nathaniel Tracy and Tristram Dalton, whose mansions were well accustomed to the presence of distinguished guests.

Newburyport early engaged in privateering, by which for a while her merchants retrieved the losses they had voluntarily encountered by agreeing to the Non-importation Act, by which their staple business of building ships for the British was destroyed. But, eventually, little was gained, the size of the vessels being ill adapted to cope with the heavy ships of the British navy. Many of them, after successful and daring cruises, were finally captured; while many more became a prey to the elements. The clearances of twenty-two vessels are recorded as having left Newburyport with a thousand or more men, who never returned. One of this unfortunate class was the " Yankee Hero," a privateer of about eighteen guns, commanded by James Tracy, for some time successful; but on one of her cruises she encountered the British frigate "Milford," a heavy vessel, much too superior in force to have been voluntarily engaged; and, notwithstanding her immense superiority, Captain Tracy engaged her, and fought desperately for two hours before he surrendered. On being exchanged, and returning home, he was furnished with another privateer of the same name, and of twenty guns, manned with one hundred and seventy men, including some fifty young volunteers from the first families of Newburyport and vicinity. She sailed from the port, and neither vessel, officers, nor crew, were heard of more.

The first privateer fitted out in the United States sailed from this port, and was owned by Nathaniel Tracy, Esq. (a relative of Capt. James Tracy, of the " Yankee Hero"), the first of whose fleet sailed in August, 1775. From that time to 1783, Mr. Tracy was the principal owner of one hundred and ten merchant vessels, having an aggregate tonnage of fifteen thousand six hundred and sixty, which with their cargoes were valued at $2,733,300. Twenty-three of the above vessels were under letters of marque, and mounted two hundred and ninety-eight carriage guns, and registered one thousand six hundred and eighteen men. Of this one hundred and ten sail, but thirteen were left at the end of the war; all the rest were taken by the enemy or lost. During this same period Mr. Tracy was also the principal owner of twenty-four cruising ships, the combined tonnage of which was six thousand three hundred and thirty, carrying three hundred and forty guns, six, nine, and twelve pounders, and navigated by two thousand eight hundred men. When it is considered that these were in addition to the letter of marque vessels, it exhibits Mr. Tracy rather as a naval than a " merchant" prince. Of these twenty-four cruisers, only one remained at the close of the war. But they had not been idle, nor were they ignobly surrendered. These ships captured from the enemy one hundred and twenty sail, amounting to twenty-three thousand three hundred and sixty tons, which, with their cargoes, were sold for three million nine hundred and fifty thousand specie dollars (one hundred and sixty-seven thousand two hundred and nineteen dollars Mr. Tracy devoted to the army and other public demands) ;

and with these prizes were taken two thousand two hundred and twenty-five men, prisoners of war.*

Nathaniel Tracy was the son of Patrick Tracy, who was born in Ireland in 1711, and died in Newburyport Feb. 28, 1789.

On the large monument in St. Paul's churchyard is the following :—

"Underneath lie the remains of Patrick Tracy, Esquire, who departed this life February 28, 1789, aged 78 years. In various and strongly contrasted scenes of life he eminently shone a man, a citizen, and a Christian. His firm expectation of another existence moderated his temper in Prosperity, supported him in Adversity, and enabled him to triumph in Death."

He was a very prosperous and princely merchant. By his second marriage he had three children, Nathaniel, John, and Hannah.

Mr. Tracy married first Hannah Carter, of Hampton, Mass., Jan. 25, 1742. She was born 1718, and died March 27, 1746. He married second, Hannah Gookin, of Newbury, Mass., July 25, 1749. She was born 1723, and died Aug. 20, 1756. He married third, Mary, widow of Michael Dalton; born, 1711, died, Dec. 10, 1791.

Nathaniel graduated at Harvard College in 1769, and after leaving the University settled as a merchant in Newburyport, his birthplace, in company with Hon. Jonathan Jackson, his brother-in-law, an accomplished gentleman and thorough merchant. He married a lady of one of the first families of the State. She was of great personal beauty, and the daughter of the illustrious patriot of the Revolution, Col. Lee, of Marblehead.

Mr. Tracy was soon known for the variety, extent, and success of his business. At the commencement of the Revolution he was foremost among the Sons of Liberty, and staked his fortune, his fame, and life on the event of the contest. So Midas-like did he appear to accumulate his riches, that he seemed justified in lavishing vast sums to maintain his establishment in the most sumptuous manner. His stables were famed for con-

* The above account is taken from a memorial addressed to Congress by a gentleman who was part owner and concerned with Mr. Tracy. It was published at the time of the application to Congress, in the New York papers, and republished in the Newburyport *Herald*, Dec. 4, 1826.

taining the most spirited horses and finest equipages of the day, and the grounds were the most beautiful in Essex County. In front of the mansion were ornamental trees which he imported from England. The garden in the rear was stocked with the choicest fruit trees, also imported. There were fine fish ponds. Throughout the whole there was displayed an air of aristocratic taste and luxurious habit, rivaling the establishments of the Dutch burgomasters of an earlier date ; so that it was literally a wonder of the times.

He had an admirable farm in Newbury, and another in Medford. He was also the owner of the Vassal house, known in later days as the Longfellow or Craigie house, in Cambridge, Mass., which General Washington made his headquarters while staying there. He was a gentleman of polished manners and high character and standing, contributing very greatly by his public spirit toward the improvement of his native town. "Every one," says a writer in *Echoes From Old Essex* (reprinted in Newburyport *Herald*, July 18, 1874), "was found around him who could bring tongue, pen, sword, wealth, or influence into the cause of liberty and independence. The magnitude of his commercial relations, his patriotic sacrifices in the cause of his country, the munificence and hospitality of his establishments, his patronage to deserving individuals, threw around him a Medicean splendor, which attracted the gaze and reached the hearts of citizen and stranger. Such a man, and the necessity for such a one, will never probably again occur in this country."

But the sun whose beams were so gorgeous, and waked into life and action such a busy creation, was soon to suffer an eclipse, and be forever shorn of its original brightness. The British, who were mortified and vexed at losing so much valuable property by American cruisers, made such efforts toward the close of the war that most of the American armed vessels and merchantmen were swept from the ocean. The days of adversity began now to thicken on his calendar as rapidly as the days of prosperity once did ; and misfortune followed misfortune, until at last he was stripped of his vast wealth, and he retired to his farm in Newbury, which had been secured to his family by his father, and avoided the world during the rest of his remaining days. During his prosperity he was universally loved and honored, and in his adversity he retained the esteem of his fellow-citizens. The man who did so much good, and at such a period, freely and heartily merits of his country a splendid monument and an ample page in her annals.

John Tracy was a man of education, excellent disposition, and gentlemanly manners. In the Revolutionary War he commanded an independent military company in Newburyport, and served in General Sullivan's army in Rhode Island as aide-de-camp to General Glover. For many years he was one of the port inspectors. Thomas Jefferson was an intimate friend of Mr. Tracy's, and wrote some poetry concerning him. He was a guest of Mr. Tracy for some time with his eldest daughter and a female slave, and they embarked with Mr. Tracy in his ship "Ceres" for England, where Mr. Jefferson debarked and Mr. Tracy sailed for Portugal. The Marquis de Chastellux, the Vicompte de Vaudreuil, M. de Montesquieu, and the famous Talleyrand, visited Newburyport in 1780 with a letter of introduction to Mr. John Tracy; but before it was delivered Mr. Tracy and Colonel Wigglesworth called to invite them to pass the evening with Mr. Tracy.

The Marquis de Chastellux writes of this visit: " This colonel remained with me till Mr. Tracy finished his business, when he came with two handsome carriages, well equipped, and conducted me and my aide-de-camps to his country house. (This was the mansion on High Street, above the former Dexter House.) I went by moonlight to see the garden, which is composed of different terraces. There is likewise a hothouse and a number of young trees. The house is handsome and well finished, and everything breathes that air of magnificence accompanied with simplicity which is only to be found among merchants. The evening passed rapidly by the aid of agreeable conversation and a few glasses of punch. At ten o'clock an excellent supper was served. We drank good wine; Miss Lee (Mrs. Tracy's cousin) sung, and prevailed upon Messrs. de Vaudreuil and Talleyrand to sing also. Towards midnight the ladies withdrew, but we continued drinking Madeira and Xery. Mr. Tracy, according to the custom of the country, offered us pipes, which were accepted by M. de Talleyrand and M. de Montesquieu; the consequence of which was that they became intoxicated, and were led home, where they were happy to get to bed. As to myself, I remained perfectly cool, and continued to converse on trade and politics with Mr. Tracy."

The brothers Nathaniel and John Tracy were associated in business interests, and they resided, each, in one of the two companion houses on High Street, next in grandeur to the house built for Nathaniel by his father, Patrick Tracy, on State Street, known as the "Tracy" house, and now the Public Library. Their houses were thronged by men of letters, officers, naval and military, merchants, foreigners, and statesmen.

Colonel John Tracy, born April 19, 1753, married May 2, 1775, Margaret, daughter of Henry Laughton of Boston, born March 12, 1755, died Nov. 8, 1806. He died May 1, 1815, in Newburyport. His children were: [1]John, born March 4, 1776, died Nov. 27, 1781. [2]Henry Laughton, born Sept., 1777. [3]Nathaniel, born June 19, 1779, died at sea. [4]Margaret, born March 22, 1781, died June 25, 1843. [5]Mary, born March 22, 1781, married Capt. Christopher Bassett, born May 11, 1774, died March 13, 1848. Mary died Jan. 27, 1854. [6]Henrietta, born June 28, 1782, married William Pierce Johnson, Jan. 18, 1807; and their daughter, Margaret Laughton Johnson, born Jan. 20, 1809, married Patrick Henry, son of Hon. *Simon Greenleaf.* Henrietta Tracy died July 8, 1812. [7]John, born Jan. 2, 1786, died 1822, in Matanzas. [8]Elizabeth Farris, born Dec. 14, 1791, married March, 1818, Henry Loring, born Nov. 19, 1792. He died June 11, 1866. She died Aug. 15, 1828. Mr. Loring was a merchant long and well known in Boston, and of the firm of Fairbanks, Loring & Company, wholesale hardware dealers. Their trade extended around the world. He was a typical gentleman of the "old school." His father, Joseph Loring, born Feb. 17, 1752, was a captain in Gridley's Brigade, and was in the trenches at the Battle of Bunker Hill. His wife, Nancy True, born Sept. 29, 1756, sat all the 17th of June on the top of a house on Copp's Hill, Boston, and saw the entire battle. Of the children of Henry Loring and his wife, Henrietta Tracy, born Dec. 15, 1818, married James Henry Carleton, Lieutenant First United States Dragoons. She died at Fort Gibson, Indian Territory, October 16, 1842. Ann, born Nov. 9, 1820, resides at Newburyport, Mass. Elizabeth Farris, born May 28, 1822, died Dec. 26, 1871. Henry, born May 31, 1824, died November, 1862. He had been Adjutant Nineteenth Indiana Volunteers. Mary Wyer, born July 5, 1827, married Charles Frederic Crehore, M.D. Henry Loring married, second, Mary Middleton Lovell, at Newton Centre, Mass., Dec. 8, 1829. ⁹Catherine Deblois, born Nov. 12, 1794, married George Titcomb, born Feb. 21, 1785. He died Dec. 4, 1863. She died March 13, 1875. He was son of Enoch, born 1752, died Aug. 13, 1814; son of Henry, born 1723, died 1785; son of Joseph, born 1698, died 1779; son of William, born 1659, died 1740; son of Captain William, born 1620, died Sept. 24, 1676. Mr. George Titcomb was a noted teacher in Newburyport, and well known among present citizens of that city as "Master Titcomb." The family lived fifty-four years in the same house, at No. 19 Market Street. Of their daughters, Mrs. Geo. W. Hale resides in Taunton, Mass., Mrs. J. F. Hodgkins and the Misses Margaret T. and Selina J. Titcomb still reside in Newburyport.

Among the first settlers of Newbury was Captain William Titcomb, born 1620, died Sept. 24, 1676, who emigrated from Newbury, Berkshire County, in England, in 1635. His grandson, Colonel Moses Titcomb, was distinguished in the expedition against Louisburg in 1745, and afterwards commanded a regiment at Crown Point in 1755, where he was killed while reconnoitering the enemy's post.

Another of the descendants of William Titcomb, Captain Michael Titcomb, son of Joseph, belonged to Washington's bodyguard. Two others: Enoch Titcomb, born 1752, died Aug. 13, 1814, was an ardent Whig, and served as Brigade Major at Rhode Island among the troops commanded by General Sullivan. Afterwards he held different town offices for many years. At the age of forty he was member of the Legislature, and continued in office either as Representative or Senator until the infirmities of age obliged him to retire into private life. He was for a long time Justice of the Peace and Notary Public. He was esteemed for his piety, integrity, and good sense. He died in 1814, aged 62.

Jonathan Titcomb, born 1722, was distinguished as an ardent Whig during the Revolution. He commanded a regiment of militia, under General Sullivan, upon the Rhode Island expedition, and afterwards became a Brigadier General.

In 1774–75 he was a member of the Committee of Safety, and belonged to the first General Court after the British evacuated Boston. Subsequently he represented the town in General

Court for several years, and was chosen to the convention for framing the constitution of the State.

He was appointed by Washington first Naval Officer, 1789, for this district, which place he held until 1812. He died in 1817, at the advanced age of 89.

Monday, Jan. 15, 1776. The Brig " Sukey," Captain Engs, ninety tons, from Ireland, was taken by the " Washington" privateer, and brought into Newburyport, laden with provisions, destined for Boston. On the morning of the same day the British ship " Friends," Captain Bowie, of London, bound for Boston, appeared off Newbury bar. As she lay off and on several miles from the land, showing English colors, and tacking often, the wind being easterly, with appearance of a storm, it was conjectured by sóme persons who observed her from town, that the captain had mistaken Ipswich Bay for that of Boston, which was then in possession of the British, and that she had lost her bearings, they immediately planned a scheme for her capture ; accordingly, seventeen persons embarked in three whaleboats under command of Capt. Offin Boardman (who married Sarah, daughter of Timothy and Susanna Greenleaf) ; as they approached the ship, being satisfied by the movements that they were right in their conjectures, they determined to offer their services as pilots. For this purpose they rowed within hailing distance, hailed the ship, enquiring where she was bound and where she hailed from. The captain replied, "From London, bound to Boston ;" and then asked what land was in sight, and where the boats came from. Captain Boardman replied, " We are from Boston ; do you want a pilot?" And his offer being accepted by the unsuspicious stranger, the ship was hove to, and Captain Boardman soon stood on the quarter deck of the " Friends." He carried no arms in sight, and after shaking hands with the captain, entered into conversation with him, asking the news from London, etc., while his companions from the three boats, seventeen in all, quietly mounted the ship's gangway, and now stood guard by the same. Seeing they were all ready, Captain Boardman threw off his assumed character of pilot, and to the astonishment and chagrin of the late master, ordered the English flag to be struck and neither crew nor commander making any resistance, the order was instantly executed. The ship had four carriage guns, and a crew of about the same number as the captors, but taken wholly by surprise, and at the moment unprepared, they fell an easy prey to the shrewd management of the little party; though it must be confessed that three boats in company, containing seventeen men, might reasonably have been suspected of carrying others than pilots. Thus by a stratagem, the morality of which one of the party afterwards seriously questioned,* a valuable ship and cargo was secured, and in the course of a few hours brought up to the wharf, when she was found to contain fifty-two chaldrons of coal, eighty-six butts and thirty hogsheads of porter, twenty hogsheads of vinegar and sixteen hogsheads of sauerkraut, besides live stock, for which the British troops in Boston were at that moment suffering.

"The names of this party have not all been preserved; but in addition to Captain Boardman, there were Mr. William Bartlett, Enoch Hale, John Coombs, Joseph Stanwood, Gideon Woodwell, Johnson and Cutting Lunt. These two vessels, the Brig "Sukey" and the ship "Friends," were the first prizes brought into Newburyport.

February 16.— The "Yankee Hero" took and brought into Newburyport a bark of three hundred tons, loaded with coal, pork, and flour.

March 1.— She brought in the brig "Nelly," from White Haven, bound to Boston, having two hundred tons coal and ten tons potatoes.

In 1779 we have the first intimation of the town's improving the streets by planting trees. March 9th Nathaniel Tracy was empowered to plant trees on High Street, where the old ropewalk stood (near Frog Pond). The town, under all the disadvantages of the times, continued to grow; and in 1781 the inconveniences arising from want of suitable building lots induced several public-spirited gentlemen, owning land in the vicinity, to give to the town "sufficient to lay out a regular, handsome street, four rods wide, half way between Fish and Queen Streets"; and thus Green Street originated. The names of the donors were: Nathaniel Tracy, *Benjamin Greenleaf*, Enoch, Joshua, and Richard Titcomb, Stephen Sewall, Stephen and Mary Hooper, Nathaniel, Parker A., Stephen A., and Nathaniel, Jr., Atkinson, and the guardians of the heirs of Benjamin Frothingham.

*William Bartlett, Esq.

For the eight years, reckoning from the battle of Lexington to the proclamation of peace, Newburyport raised for the extraordinary expenses of the town, the payment of bounties, and providing for all those exigencies that were dependent on the war, the sum of £504,500. The usual current expenses of the town per annum, previous to the breaking out of hostilities, had been but £750; making (for the eight years) £498,500 to be set down as war expenses—in dollars, 2,492,500. £17,000, or $85,000, are specified as having been raised in gold and silver, and as some of the debts were also paid in coin, it is impossible to determine exactly what the real cost was; but when we consider that much was also done in providing provisions for the army and clothing for the soldiers, the sum becomes, considering the size and ability of the town, truly enormous.

In this year the business of chaise-making was introduced into Newbury by James Burgess. The first regular builders were *Nathaniel* and *Abner Greenleaf*. In Belleville, the business was commenced by *Samuel Greenleaf*, in 1792.

The winter of 1780 was unusually severe. For forty days, including the month of March, there was no perceptible thaw on the southerly side of any house; and so deep and hard was the snow, that loaded teams passed over walls and fences in any direction.

March.—The Constitution of Massachusetts was framed. The first article in the declaration of rights is, "All men are born free and equal." This was inserted with the intent, and for the purpose, of entirely abolishing slavery.

Prior to the Revolution, several slaves had sued their masters for detaining them in slavery; one in Cambridge in 1770, and one in Newburyport, Cæsar against his master, *Richard Greenleaf*, in September, 1773. In all these cases the courts decided in favor of the slave. In 1781 a case occurred in Worcester, in which the Supreme Federal Court decided that slavery was abolished by the Constitution.

May 19th.—This day is the most remarkable in the memory of man for darkness, which began about twenty minutes before eleven o'clock A. M., and lasted the whole day, though not equally dark all the time. It was the darkest from about twelve to one o'clock. Candles were lighted up in the houses; the birds, having sung their evening songs, disappeared and became silent; the fowls retired to roost; the cocks were crowing all around, as at break of day. Everything bore the appearance and gloom of night.

March 12, 1781.—Newburyport "voted that the Selectmen be directed to cause the bells to be rung at one of the clock in the day and at nine of the clock at night during the ensuing year."

September 3, 1783.—On this day a treaty of peace was signed at Paris between Great Britain and the United States, by David Hartley and John Adams, Esquires, and on October 13th Congress issued a proclamation for disbanding the army.

1784.—The bridge over the river Parker, which was built in 1758, under the direction of Mr. Ralph Cross, was this year repaired. It is eight hundred and seventy feet long, twenty-six feet wide, has nine solid piers and eight wooden arches.

December 6, 1786.—A slight shock of an earthquake at 4.15 P. M. This year is rendered memorable by an insurrection in the western part of Massachusetts, headed by Daniel Shays. One company, fifty-five in all, commanded by Capt. Edward Longfellow, went from Newbury.

1787.—"The west wind blew steadily from November 30, 1786 to March 20th of this year, with only four slight interruptions." This year the Hessian fly, so destructive to wheat, made its first appearance in New England, entering Connecticut from New York.

April 4, 1787.—"This day there was a ' spinning match ' at the house of the Rev. Mr. Murray, to whom were given two hundred and thirty-six skeins of thread and yarn. The meeting was in the parsonage house, every apartment of which," says the *Essex Journal,* "was full. The music of the spinning wheel resounded from every room. It was truly a pleasing sight,—some spinning, some reeling, some carding the cotton, some combing the flax. The labors of the day were concluded about five o'clock."

In the fall of 1789, Washington, then recently elected to the presidential chair, conceiving it his duty to become as fully acquainted as possible with the country over which he had been called to preside, availed himself of the first interim of public duties to make a tour through those States with which he was least acquainted. On his way through Massachusetts to New

Hampshire he visited Newburyport, on Friday, the 1st of November, remaining until Saturday morning. Every preparation was made to give the first President a worthy reception. The Hon. Tristram Dalton and Major-General Titcomb, with other distinguished gentlemen from Newburyport, had met and accompanied him from Ipswich, with an escort of two companies of cavalry. On approaching the boundaries of the town, the *cortège* was met (on High Street, near Bromfield) by the militia and artillery companies of Newburyport, the procession which was to escort him through the town, and a company of young men who had prepared an Ode of Welcome* to the chief magistrate of the country.

After the firing of a Federal salute by the artillery company the Ode was sung, and proved an affecting, as it was a novel, feature in the receptions given to the President on his tour. Washington was moved even to tears by this unexpected and interesting mode of welcome; additional effect being given to the words by the accompaniment of the military and other instrumental music, appropriately joining in the sentiments expressed. The procession embraced, in addition to the military, all the town officers, professional men, manufacturers, tradesmen, sea-captains and mariners, with all the children of the public schools,† each having a quill in his hand. The procession conducted the President through High to State Street, to the mansion of Nathaniel Tracy, Esq., where he remained through the day and evening. On his arrival there he was greeted with an

*He comes! he comes! the Hero comes!
Sound, sound your trumpets, beat your drums.
From port to port let cannons roar;
He's welcome to New England's shore.
Welcome, welcome, welcome, welcome,
Welcome to New England's shore!

Prepare! prepare! your songs prepare,
Loud, loudly rend the echoing air;
From pole to pole his praise resound,
For virtue is with glory crowned.
Virtue, virtue, virtue, virtue,
Virtue is with glory crowned.

† These contained boys only; there were four hundred and twenty in the procession. Female public schools were not established at this time.

address written by John Quincy Adams,* to which he made the following reply :—

Gentlemen : The demonstrations of respect and affection which you are pleased to pay to an individual whose highest pretension is to rank as your fellow-citizen, are of a nature too distinguished not to claim the warmest return that gratitude can make. . . . In visiting the town of Newburyport I have obeyed a favorite inclination, and I am much gratified by the indulgence. In expressing a sincere wish for its prosperity and the happiness of its inhabitants, I do but justice to my own sentiments and their merits.

In the evening a *feu de joie* was fired by the militia companies, and a display of fireworks terminated the public demonstrations of joy felt by the community at the privilege of entertaining so illustrious a guest. Washington had entered the town over the Parker River bridge, advancing through Newbury, old town, to High Street. On leaving the next morning he was escorted as far as the boundary line of New Hampshire, where he was met by the chief magistrate of that State, General Sullivan, and four companies of light horse.

The Marine Society of Newburyport had prepared a beautiful barge, in which the President was carried across the Merrimac from a point opposite Amesbury.

November 16th.—This has been a day of much animation, for carriages and foot people have been constantly passing to see a whale, which some fishermen found at sea and towed up to Oldtown Bridge. It was about sixty feet long.

1790.—According to the census this year Newbury had five hundred and thirty-eight houses, seven hundred and twenty-three families, and three thousand nine hundred and seventy-two inhabitants.

Newburyport had six hundred and sixteen houses, nine hundred and thirty-nine families, and four thousand eight hundred and thirty-seven inhabitants. At this time the town owned six ships, forty-five brigantines, thirty-nine schooners, and twenty-eight sloops. Total, eleven thousand eight hundred and seventy tons.

From May 25, 1790, to November 19, 1791, the number of vessels cleared from Newburyport was one hundred and seventy-nine. In the Newburyport *Herald* of January 12, 1791, an account is given of the establishment of Sunday schools in Philadelphia by some benevolent persons in the city, with this comment,

* Copy of this address is on page 263, Coffin's History of Newburyport.

NEWBURY. 39

"Pity their benevolence did not extend so far as to afford them tuition on days when it is lawful to follow such pursuits, and not thereby lay a foundation for the profanation of the Sabbath."

November 26, 1792.—On this day Essex Merrimac bridge was opened for the public. "It consisted, in fact, of two bridges resting on Deer Island in the midst of the river." It was, when finished, one thousand and thirty feet long, thirty-four wide, height of arch above high-water mark thirty-seven feet, and contained six thousand tons of timber.

March, 1793.—A codfish was sold in Newburyport weighing ninety-eight pounds, five feet and a half in length, and girth at the thickest place three feet four inches.

July 4th.—"This day," says the *Essex Journal*, "Timothy Dexter delivered an Oration at Essex Merrimac bridge, which, for elegance of Style, propriety of Speech, and force of Argument, was truly Ciceronian!!"

Timothy Dexter found a biographer and artist to preserve his memory, in Samuel Lorenzo Knapp, LL.D., of Newburyport; a practicing lawyer, who was particularly distinguished as a *belles-lettres* scholar, and who wrote on various subjects. He writes: "Whatever were the faults of Dexter, he was a pecuniary benefactor of the town, and also for a long series of years held an office in it; viz., 'Informer of Deer!'"

"He has," says Mrs. E. Vale Smith, "generally been considered a fool, with a slight mixture of the knave; but nearly every act of his apparent folly may be traced to one overpowering passion, uncontrolled by any natural or cultivated taste, though combined with considerable shrewdness; this passion was vanity, so inordinate as to lead him into all sorts of absurdities. To be an object of attention to the present, and of remembrance to succeeding generations, in his adopted town, was the central idea of his life, around which all others revolved, and were subordinate."

Says Mrs. Sarah Anna Emery, in her "Reminiscences of a Nonagenarian," p. 251: "For years the chief wonder of the place was Lord Timothy Dexter, his hairless dog, and his images. This man was born in Malden, in 1743, and died in Newburyport, Oct. 26, 1806. He came to Newburyport in early manhood, and married a Miss Frothingham, from the old Frothingham mansion, on the corner of High and Olive Streets.

In a short time he obtained a large fortune by taking advantage
of the markets and by lucky adventures. His first successful
speculation was buying up Continental notes when depreciated,
and selling them when a prospect of redemption had raised their
value. His speculation in Mittens, Warming-pans, Whalebone
and the like, were widely known. An example of his folly is
his sending a cargo of Warming-pans (a covered pan of brass,
with a long ladle. Hot coals being placed in the pans, they
were used for warming beds), and woolen mittens to the West
Indies, which turned out a profitable speculation ; the Warming-
pans being bought for ladles, to be used on the Sugar estates in
the straining of Syrup, and the mittens sold at a heavy advance
to a vessel bound to the Baltic. Query : Was it folly,—or
shrewd management?''

His house and grounds on High Street, nearly opposite his
wife's maiden home, he embellished, after his own design, with
wooden statues. These figures were remarkable specimens in
wood carving. The figures of Washington, Adams, and Jefferson, over the front door, were excellent, the other figures, and
the eagle upon the cupola, were lifelike and in good proportion. He built a tomb in the garden, had a mock funeral,
acted his part as corpse, and afterwards beat his wife because
she did not weep while following him to the grave.

Dexter owned a farm in Chester, and consequently styled
himself Earl of Chester. He erected handsome buildings on
this estate, and these were decorated with several images, which
were a wonder in that region for a long time. Determined to
rank among those whose names never die, Dexter wrote a book,
entitled, ''A Pickle for the Knowing Ones,''—a sufficiently
original production to obtain its author's aim. Punctuation was
omitted till the last page, which was closely covered with the
various marks, the readers being directed to '' pepper and salt
it as they please.''

One of the most important rights affecting personal liberty,
was obtained by Newburyport in 1794. This was procured by
the passage of an act incorporating the several religious societies
then existing, and enlarging the liberty of the individual by per-
mitting him to attend what place of worship he chose, without
being liable to be taxed for the support of a ministry with which
he had no sympathy. It seems almost incredible that the de-

scendants of the Pilgrims in Newburyport never acquired this essential of religious liberty till more than a century after their settlement here; yet such is the fact. It was not until 1834 that the Legislature of Massachusetts passed an act distinctly releasing all persons from the liability to pay taxes for the support of religious worship.

1796.—Exeunt pounds and *enter* dollars! By the town records, for the first time, appears this insignia of American Independence, used in the estimates of the annual town expenses. There had been, previous to the introduction of the Continental bills, but one other considerable change in the currency of Massachusetts; the English money being in common circulation from the first settlement of the country, except during a period of forty-eight years, from 1702 to 1750, when a paper currency was introduced into New England by the Colonial Government, bearing on the face of the bills the promise of future redemption; which promises were met, like those of the Continental Congress, only with new emissions. The consequences were the same, though the necessities of the case were not. The money, which is now known as " old tenor," sunk in value so as to compare with coin, which was distinguished as " lawful money" in Massachusetts, seven and one-half to one; in some other parts of New England even lower.

The " old tenor" currency was a monetary invention introduced to meet the expenses of the French war; and in 1750 Parliament reimbursed Massachusetts for her exertions during that war by sending over a large sum of money, all in silver.*

* A dirge, set to the tune of Chevy Chace, was written by one Joseph Green, of Boston " on the death of Mr. 'Old Tenor,'" in which he shows the good which " Old Tenor" had done in his life. A verse or two of the ballad runs thus :—

> Led on by him, our soldiers bold
> Against the foe advance;
> And took, in spite of wet and cold,
> Strong Cape Breton from France.

> The merchants, too,—those topping folks,—
> To him owe all their riches;
> Their ruffles, lace, and scarlet cloaks,
> And eke their velvet breeches.

> . . . .

> In Senate he like Cæsar fell,
> Pierced through with many a wound;
> He sunk, ah! doleful tale to tell,
> The members sitting round!

Commerce, religion, and education were the staple objects
of solicitude at this period, and by the following extract the early
interest in the education of the young by Newburyport appears
in the *Essex Journal*, Newburyport, 1793 : " Notwithstanding
the smallness of this town when compared with Boston, there
are two more public schools here than there are in that place.
Such is the opinion of the inhabitants of this town with regard
to the necessity of well educating the rising generation, that they
cheerfully support nine public and several private schools."

In the political horizon of Massachusetts there appeared
with the incoming century a group of men who, from their
learning and personal weight of character, it was soon seen, were
to exert a large influence in the history of the State ; they were
known as the " Essex Junta," and among them was Theophilus
Parsons (Judge), John Lowell (Judge), Rev. Thomas Cary,
Hon. Jonathan Jackson, Nathaniel Tracy, Hon. *Jonathan
Greenleaf*, William Coombs, and others,—men who were
prominent citizens of Newburyport; and with these were
associated the most active Federalists of the county.   The origin
of this " political corps," so designated, it is said by one of
Napoleon's great marshals (Soult), was that these men of the
" Junta," enlightened and firm statesmen, who were fervent and
sincere in their attachment to the cause of liberty, patriots without
stain or reproach, but who feared that the people, after the
struggle for their independence was over, would be remiss and
backward in forming good constitutions and making wholesome
laws for the tranquility and prosperity of the country.   These
sound politicians frequently saw each other, and expressed their
fears and anxieties, and of course were constantly suggesting
among themselves some hints and plans to prevent the anticipated
evil.   They moved the people to form a constitution, which is
substantially the same we now live under.   They guarded it by
the most scrupulous caution against every partiality for royalty ;
an abjuration is made by them in renunciation and denial of every
kindred feeling, affection, or allegiance to Great Britain, or any
principalities, potentates, or powers which must be repeated in
the form of an oath by every one who holds an office under it.
The " Essex Junta " was a powerful watchword in the mouths
of those who wished for no law or order, for it alarmed the
timid, the jealous, and the ignorant, and to them the name was

made to represent all that was hateful in aristocracy and monarchy. These friends of their country struggled on until a constitution and laws were made and in operation, in defiance of obloquy and opposition. The memory of these men at this day is fragrant with honor and pride in boasting of them as our countrymen, and that we are descendants of some of these beacon lights in the night of anarchy, and firm pillars in the temple of freedom. It is for this reason that a few sketches of those with whom we claim kinship by blood or marriage, or both, are introduced in these notes, for they were men—our ancestors—who were on the stage, and actors in those important days when all they had or hoped was put on the point of the sword and risked on the event of the battle. These are just, but scanty epitaphs, and deserve their proper niche in the temple of their country's fame. May they radiate upon these pages their talents and virtues, to inspire in the hearts of their children that love of devotion to the cause of their country's welfare which can only come to those of pure and truthful hearts, filled with love and charity toward our fellow-man, and a deep and abiding faith and trust in an overruling Providence to guide, guard, and protect those who in sincerity look to Him.

Hon. *Jonathan Greenleaf* was born in Newbury, in July, 1723, and died on May 24, 1807, at the age of eighty-four years. With the gift of fine natural talents, a genteel person, a courteous demeanor, bland and conciliatory manners, with a peculiar tact for public life, he filled many important offices for a long series of years with honor to himself and advantage to his country. He understood better than most other men the signs of the times, and knew precisely when to advance and when to retreat, what the people would bear and when they would become restive. He used such gentle and delicate persuasions to overcome his opponents and to cheer his friends, that the populace gave him the appellation of "Silver-tongue."

In troublesome times, that which was projected by other great luminaries, his address and perseverance carried into effect. In every "storm of state" he was seen on the billows in a political lifeboat, pouring oil on the waves to calm their rage, and dexterously managing to gain the point proposed.

Mr. Greenleaf was placed on the first "Committee of Correspondence and Safety" appointed in Newburyport, and was for many years a representative from this town to the General Court.

Judge Theophilus Parsons was the third son of the Rev. Moses Parsons, of Byfield parish, Newbury. He was born on the 24th of February, 1750. He was early placed at Dummer Academy, of which the celebrated Master Moody was then principal. He was graduated at Harvard College in 1769; he then entered as a law student with Theophilus Bradbury, and in 1777 commenced practice in Newburyport, having already obtained the reputation of a "young man of great talent and remarkable acquirements." It was at this interesting epoch that the Legislature of Massachusetts formed the constitution which they submitted to the people for their consideration. It contained many defects, and a general movement was made to prevent its adoption, in which Essex County took the lead, and Mr. Parsons was elected as a delegate to meet with gentlemen from the other towns of the county at Ipswich. Here he was placed on a committee to prepare a report on the subject, and he then drafted the famous paper known as the "Essex Result." In 1779-80 a convention was called for the purpose of drafting a new constitution, and to this body Mr. Parsons was also a delegate, and one of the most active and influential members. In 1789 the Massachusetts convention met in Boston to consult upon the adoption of the Federal Constitution, then submitted to the several States for their adhesion. In this convention met a host of distinguished statesmen, and to this body Mr. Parsons was also a delegate. Learning, wit, satire, and argument combined made his influence pre-eminent, as his genius deserved that it should be. One of the members, a clergyman, having remarked " that no angel presided at the formation of the instrument, for that the name of God was not in it," Parsons reminded him that by the same rule of judgment there was no Divinity in one of the books of the Old Testament, referring the astonished clergyman to the book of Esther, which contains no mention of the name of the Deity. A large share of the effort which secured the final majority in favor of the adoption of the Constitution may fairly be attributed to Mr. Parsons. In 1801 he was appointed Attorney-General of the United States, but declined accepting his commission. In 1806 Chief Justice Dana resigned his office, and he was nominated by Governor Strong, and accepted the appointment. He died in Boston, October 13, 1813.

The Hon. Jonathan Jackson in early life settled as a merchant, spent his most efficient days, and reared his children, in Newburyport; and was before, during, and after the Revolution an Essex man. He was born in Boston, and married Hannah, daughter of Patrick Tracy, Esq., and sister of Nathaniel and John Tracy. He was "a man of whom the world knew much, but knew too little." As a patriot, he combined the qualities which form the estimable citizen, and rendered him useful as a statesman. He took an early and zealous part in the Revolution, and devoted much of his time to the public service. His zeal for civil liberty in the early part of his life was enthusiastic, but his penetrating mind early suspected danger from pure Democratic institutions, and he was anxious to have such modifications made in our National Constitution as would secure the permanence, as well as the fullness, of our liberties. The views which he entertained on this subject may be known by the draft of a Constitution prepared by delegates from the County of Essex, in forming which Mr. Jackson bore a considerable share. Before the adoption by the State of the Federal Constitution, Mr. Jackson published a pamphlet on the subject, replete with understanding, foresight, and patriotism, approving of the Constitution, to which, and to the policy of Washington, he remained firmly and invariably attached.

From the constant exercise of that politeness which is formed of courtesy, philanthropy, and delicacy of taste, he was uniformly considered as the "*arbiter elegantiarum*" in the refined society in which he moved. But useful as he was to the State in his public capacity, the beautiful symmetry and integrity of his private life, his urbanity and refinement, his intellectual endowments, and his moral piety, overshadowed and eclipsed his public reputation. As the beau ideal of a gentleman, he retained the supremacy among that galaxy of worthies which formed the intellectual and social life of Newburyport. He was a member of the Continental Congress in 1780, Marshal of the District of Massachusetts under Washington, first Inspector, and afterwards Supervisor, of the Internal Revenue, Treasurer of the Commonwealth for five years, and at the time of his death was Treasurer of Harvard College.

His eldest son, Charles Jackson, born 1775, in Newburyport, graduated at Cambridge, and having studied law with Theophilus

Parsons, commenced practice in his native town. He rapidly rose to distinction at the bar, and having removed to Boston, was, on the death of Theodore Sedgwick, made Judge of the Supreme Court of Massachusetts.

His second son, Dr. James Jackson, was of equal reputation in the medical profession, with his brother in that of the law.

Patrick Tracy Jackson, the youngest son of Hon. Jonathan Jackson, was born at Newburyport, Aug. 14, 1780. He received his early education in the public schools of his native town, and afterwards at Dummer Academy. When about fifteen years of age he was apprenticed to Mr. William Bartlett. He soon secured the esteem and confidence of Mr. Bartlett, who intrusted to him, when under twenty years of age, a cargo of merchandise for St. Thomas, with authority to take the command of the vessel from the captain if he should see occasion.

His career as a free man commenced very nearly on the first day of the present century, and it has been one of remarkable record in enterprise, activity, and commercial prominence. A large experience from several voyages made to India enabled him, in 1808, to make a successful commencement in mercantile business at Boston. He had the support, in this, of his brother-in-law, Francis C. Lowell, and his invaluable counsels. He entered largely into business, and his credit was unbounded. He continued in the India and Havana trade till the breaking out of the war in 1812, after which he engaged in the manufacture of cotton. It would be very interesting to follow him in this new industry, but the limits of these sketches will not permit. His career therein was characterized by the same broad, expansive, and thoroughly systematic methods and views which led to his success in the mercantile world, and with like results. As one example of this, his mill at Waltham was probably the first one in the world that combined all the operations necessary for converting the raw cotton into finished cloth. In 1813 Messrs. Lowell and Jackson associated themselves with other intelligent merchants of Boston, and obtained a charter under the name of the "Boston Manufacturing Company," with a capital of $100,000. After the death of Mr. Lowell, in 1817, Mr. Jackson devoted himself to the manufacturing business exclusively. In

1821 he conceived the idea of possessing himself of the whole power of the Merrimac at Chelmsford, by the purchase of the Pawtucket Canal, and, aware of the necessity of secrecy in order to secure it at a reasonable price, he undertook it single-handed. It was necessary to purchase not only all the canal stock, but the farms on both sides of the river which controlled the water power; and it was not until he had accomplished all that was material for his purpose, that he offered a share in the project to a few of his former colleagues. Such was the beginning of Lowell, a city which was named in honor of his friend, and which he lived to see, as it were, completed. In 1825 that portion of Chelmsford which he had purchased and built up was incorporated under the name of Lowell.

In 1830 Mr. Jackson, in unison with Mr. Boott, entered into the then untried project of obtaining a charter for a railroad in New England, and he deliberately and satisfactorily solved the doubts in his own mind, and those of others, before he commenced the work. The road was graded for a double track. It was opened in 1835. Its success is too well known to require recapitulation here. The brilliant issue of this business greatly enhanced Mr. Jackson's previous reputation, and no great enterprizes of a public nature were brought forward without the sanction of his opinion. During the last years of his life he was treasurer and agent of the Great Falls Manufacturing Company, in Somersworth. He died at his seaside residence, in Beverly, Sept. 12, 1847.

The records of the various churches and religious societies show the exercise of a praiseworthy liberality, corresponding with the state of the town: In August, 1806, at one time, a collection of nine hundred and fifty dollars was taken up "to aid in printing the Bible in the Indian languages."

One of the most pleasing charitable institutions was instituted in 1803; namely, the establishment of an asylum for female orphans. The original fund procured by subscription was about fifteen hundred dollars. During the first twenty years of its existence this association provided for over fifty orphan girls.

Newburyport was among the first towns which opened subscriptions to build a National Washington monument, and liberal sums were subscribed here in 1802, and so sanguine were her citizens of a hearty response on this subject that they decided

none should give more than ten dollars; and if more than
enough was collected throughout the country, which was then
thought probable, it was agreed to devote it "to building a
national university." Perhaps one of the most convincing proofs
of the advance of society, was the steadily increasing support
given to the permanent newspaper established here, which the
editor did not fail, at regular intervals, to announce; the subscription list and improvements in the paper keeping pace with
each other. Among the various enterprises and events of this
period it is interesting to note the following : 1794, Newburyport
Library in operation; by-laws passed by the town against
smoking in the streets, and forbidding owners of water-fowl to
allow them to frequent Frog Pond; act passed incorporating the
several religious societies then existing in the town, viz., Rev.
Thomas Carey's, Rev. J. Murray's, Rev. Samuel Spring's, Rev.
C. W. Milton's, Rev. Edward Bass's, and amending the mode of
taxation; State survey of Newburyport ordered and taken; an
organ placed in the church in Market Square; 1795, great
change took place in the harbor bar; Pleasant, Harris, Broad,
and Essex Streets laid out; 1797, Lime, Beck, Ship, and
Spring Streets laid out; night watch appointed; town presents patriotic address to President on difficulties with France;
1798, citizens of Newburyport propose to build a ship for the
United States; June 1st she was completed, named "Merrimac," and launched Oct. 12, 1798.

Washington died Dec. 14, 1799. Funeral ceremonies observed in Newburyport, eulogy by Robert T. Paine, Jan. 2, 1800.

1800.—Capt. Edmund Bartlett gave fourteen hundred dollars
to improve the Mall, which then received the name of "Bartlett's
Mall." Town, with the aid of voluntary subscriptions, purchased the land on which Rev. T. Carey's church stood (now
Market Square), for eight thousand dollars. Market Square laid
out. Four stages employed (on a daily line) between Boston and
Newburyport. Circulating library in operation, with fifteen hundred volumes. Washington Street laid out. A religious library
established. Mackerel fishing commenced. Labrador fishery
commenced by Newburyport vessels about 1799–1800.

1802.—The road from Newburyport line to Essex Merrimac bridge laid out and completed by town of Newbury. Spring
and Roberts Streets laid out.

1803.—Active fire society organized.   Stone jail built.

1805.—Newburyport Social Library instituted.   Turnpike opened for public travel.   Charter Street laid out.   Plum Island turnpike and bridge open to the public.

1807.—Newburyport Academy incorporated.   Ninety men raised in anticipation of war, by order of the President.

September 21st.—Newburyport " voted that the generous donation made to the town by the late Mr. Timothy Dexter of two thousand dollars, the interest of which he directed the overseers of the poor annually to distribute to such of the poor of the town as are the most necessitous, who are not in the workhouse, is an act of benevolence, which the town accept, and acknowledge with gratitude and thankfulness." Embargo, December 29th.   Newburyport Mechanic Association formed.

1808.—Additional acts of embargo, in winter.   Town petition United States to suspend embargo, August.   Another address to President United States on embargo, October.   Dr. Spring preached (Thanksgiving) against embargo.

1809.—Town memorialize State Legislature on distressed state of the country, January.   Soup houses for relief of poor established in winter.   Merrimac Bible Society instituted. Embargo repealed; non-intercourse act substituted, March.

1810.—Athenæum incorporated.   Essex Merrimac bridge rebuilt, being the first in New England with chain draw. Several branches of business flourishing during this period have since died out.   Ten or twelve distilleries* and a brewing† establishment gave employment to a large number of persons, while the manufacture of cordage was one of the most important interests dependent on our mercantile success ; sugar refining was also a profitable business, and in the manufacture of gold beads and silver buckles large capitals were invested, and combs and horn buttons were made in considerable quantities.   The comb business was revived in 1853.

But the great contrast between the present time and the social era that passed away with the first decade of the nineteenth century, was the degree of style and fashion observed by

---

* In the procession which escorted Washington on his entrance to Newburyport through the town, the " distillers marched as a distinct body."

† Robert Laird's beer, porter, and ale were famed throughout the country.

the wealthy. Every family of any pretension kept their family carriage, footman and coachman, and ladies their own saddle horses.

The deep wine cellars under some of the old mansions broadly hint of the stores of port and Burgundy which once filled their now dreary depths, while vessel after vessel arriving direct with rich silks, velvets, and laces from France, enabled our grandmothers to appear in costumes which would awaken the envy of many a modern belle.

A wedding *cortége* of about 1808 is thus referred to in a private letter: "The bride and bridegroom arrived yesterday. Mr. ——'s splendid new carriage was drawn by six white horses. They had four outriders, and all the horses were decked with white favors. His footmen and coachmen are put into new liveries," etc.

With the incoming nineteenth century, garments were more in conformity with present fashions, which took precedence of three-cornered hats, long coats with immense pocket folds and cuffs, but without collars, to which men of the eighteenth century prided themselves, with their buttons of pure silver, or plated, of the size of a half dollar, presenting a great superfluity of coat and waistcoat when contrasted with the short nether garments styled "breeches," or "small clothes," which reached only to the knee, being there fastened with large silver buckles, which ornament was also used in fastening the straps of shoes. The gentlemen quite equaled the ladies at this period in the amount of finery and the brilliancy of colors in which they indulged. A light-blue coat with large fancy buttons, a white satin embroidered waistcoat, red velvet breeches, silk stockings, and buckled shoes, with a neckcloth or scarf of finely embroidered cambric, or figured stuff, the ends hanging loose, the better to show the work, and liberal bosom and wrist-ruffles (the latter usually fastened with gold or silver buckles), was considered a proper evening dress for a gentleman of any pretension to fashion. The clergy and many other gentlemen commonly wore black silk stockings, and others contented themselves with gray woolen. The boots had a broad fold of white leather turned over the top, with tassels dangling from either side. The clergy frequently wore silk or stuff gowns and powdered wigs. The ladies usually wore black silk or satin bonnets, long-waisted and narrow-skirted dresses for the street, with long, tight sleeves, and in the house, sleeves reaching to the elbow, finished with an immensely broad frill, high-heeled shoes, and always, when in full dress, carried a profusely ornamented fan. The excessively long waists, toward the close of this period, were exchanged for extremely short ones; so short that the belt or waist was inhumanly contrived to come at the broadest part of the chest. But no fashion of dress was so permanent as other customs clinging to particular eras. Anciently, as now, fashions were changed more or less extensively every few years, though certain broad characteristics remained long enough to give a specific character to the costuming of the eighteenth century.

But not only in dress and social customs is there now a marked difference; the whole style of architecture has changed since then. The large three-story, square houses on High, State, Green, and a few other streets, with their commodious carriage ways and large garden lots, are the most permanent and impressive remains of the past commercial prosperity. These capacious dwellings look down on a new age, and a comparatively diminutive style of building; neat and comfortable enough, but with contracted surroundings, and on a scale which suggests small means, and which is devoid of all imposing architectural effect. But with all the profuseness of expenditure among the wealthier class, we do not find that the laboring people were depressed, or suffered any abridgment of comforts. All classes participated in the prosperity which the business enterprise of the merchants imparted to the place. All might find employment who would work, and the labor market partook of the general buoyancy.

Modern improvements have dispensed with the necessity of many things which went to make up the grandeur of those old times; and the wider diffusion and greater equalization of wealth, compensate for the pleasing pageantry of the past, while the increased attention to female education is a step forward worth all that is left behind.

It was not the purpose of the compiler of these reminiscences of Newbury and Newburyport to bring such notes further down than the period to which we have just referred, but a glimpse, in passing, will stir the patriotic heart, as we recall the general response to an appeal made in the winter of 1840, for funds to complete the Bunker Hill Monument. Extensive arrangements were made to hold a fair at Quincy Hall, in Boston, to aid in the object. A meeting was held at Market Hall in Newburyport, July 24th, and a committee of gentlemen and ladies was appointed to procure aid for the "fair," and in September, four hundred and fifty dollars in money and articles were contributed.

Miss Lucy Hooper, of Newburyport, wrote a poetical answer to the appeal, of which the following is an extract:—

> We are coming! we are coming!
>   We have heard the thrilling call;
> We are coming from the hillside—
>   We are coming from the hall!
> We are coming! we are coming!
>   High thoughts our bosoms fill;
> One watchword wakens every heart—
>   The name of Bunker Hill!
> There Freedom's fire was lighted,
>   And its flame was broad and high,
> Till a wakened and a rescued land
>   Sent up its battle cry!
> "Old Massachusetts! dost thou need,
>   To gem thy 'lordly crown,'
> Aught richer than that battlefield
>   Which tells of thy renown?
> Home of the Pilgrim Sires, who crossed
>   The waste and trackless sea!
> Was it not meet that on thy soil
>   The first brave strife should be?
> Dear to thy children in thy home,
>   Dear to thine exiles far,
> To Freedom's sons, in every age,
>   It shines a beacon star!"
> .   .   .   .
> We are coming! we are coming!
>   That thy martyrs brave and free,
> In the record of the future
>   Shall e'er be linked with thee;
> That upon thy glory never
>   One dimming shade may fall;
> We are coming from the hillside,
>   We are coming from the hall!

THE OLD POWDER HOUSE.

Newburyport.—A few rods distant from Pierce's farm, more recently known as the Little farm, stands an ancient stone house, built about 1660 or 1670, used in the early days of Newbury to store the town's powder, a portion of which on one occasion exploded and blew out a side of the house, lodging a woman, a negro slave of Mr. Pierce, bed and all, in the branches of a large apple tree. From this Pierce family was descended Franklin Pierce, President of the United States; Benjamin Pierce of Hillsboro being descended from Benjamin Pierce of Newbury, who is buried in Byfield Parish, Newbury, and by his epitaph, like his descendant a "pillar i' th' State he was."

DUMMER ACADEMY.

Though situated in the parish of Byfield, Newbury, it has been the resort of Newburyport youth from its first institution to the present time, and is, therefore, properly placed among those educational influences which have given character to the young men of the town. It was founded by William Dummer, Lieutenant Governor of the Province of Massachusetts, who, at his decease, devised his whole estate in Newbury for the endowment of a free grammar school and the erection of a schoolhouse. The estate consisted of a farm, upon which the schoolhouse was built. It was first opened in 1763, just one year before the incorporation of Newburyport. The execution of the will was originally committed to Nathaniel Dummer, Thomas Foxcroft, and Charles Chauncey; but in 1782, the latter gentleman being the only executor living, the Legislature appointed a board of trustees to manage the fund, and the following gentlemen were incorporated as "Trustees of Dummer Academy": Jeremiah Powell, *Benjamin Greenleaf, Jonathan Greenleaf,* Rev. Joseph Willard (President of Harvard College), Rev. Charles Chauncey, Rev. Moses Parsons, Rev. John Tucker, Rev. Thomas Cary, Samuel Moody (the Preceptor), William Powell, Dr. Micajah Sawyer, Dummer Jewett, Samuel Osgood, Nathaniel Tracy, and Richard Dummer,—nearly all Newburyport men.

Governor Dummer descended from William Dummer, one of the fathers of the Colony. He emigrated in 1635, and was chosen a member of the Court of Assistants, in which he served for several years, after which he retired to his estate in Newbury, and greatly contributed by his wealth and liberality to the growth of Byfield Parish. His farm descended in his family to William Dummer, who was appointed Lieutenant Governor of the Province in 1716.

Dummer has always ranked high as a classical school, and during the first half century of its existence there were constantly more applicants for admission than could be accommodated. Mr. Samuel Moody's fame as a teacher greatly assisted the reputation of the Academy. He was succeeded by Rev. Isaac Smith, Dr. Benjamin Allen, Rev. Abiel Abbott, Hon. Samuel Adams, Nehemiah Cleaveland, Dr. Jonathan Greenleaf Johnson (in 1854), and others.

CHURCHES.

The ecclesiastical history of Newburyport and vicinity presents some peculiar features, which can best be shown in a general sketch of the successive churches formed and their connection with each other and their parent root, The First Church in Newbury.

This was for sixty-three years the only church in Newbury. In 1698 a church in what was called the west precinct of Newbury was organized, with the Rev. Samuel Belcher as the minister. The district being widely, though not thickly settled, the inhabitants were divided among themselves regarding the location of their meetinghouse, making it impossible that all could be accommodated by having the meetinghouse near their own dwellings. At a meeting of the parish it was finally voted to have the meetinghouse on Pipe Stave Hill, while a respectable minority refused to coincide with this vote, and proceeded to the erection of a building for the better accommodation of themselves and their families on what is called the Plains, where the original parish meetinghouse stood. Difficulties arising among themselves relative to taxes for the support of the minister, and other differences, the result was that twenty-two of the residents of the plains declared themselves for the Church of England and the Protestant Episcopal Church, the present representative of which is St. Paul's, originated in Newbury about the year 1712. The Rev. Henry Lucas arrived from England and took charge of the parish in the summer of 1715, and was succeeded after his death, which occurred in August, 1720, by the Rev. Matthias Plant (in 1722). A few years afterwards it was proposed to build a church nearer to the business center of the town, and the frame of St. Paul's was raised in 1738, the church on the Plains being known as Queen Anne's Chapel. St. Paul's was not used for public service till 1740. Upon the decease of Mr. Plant, April 2, 1753, he was succeeded by his late assistant, Rev. Edward Bass (afterwards the first Bishop of Massachusetts, in 1796), who continued to officiate once a month in Queen Anne's Chapel until 1766, when public service in that building was abandoned, part of the congregation uniting with St. Paul's, and others returning to the Congregational form, which their fathers had abandoned. Thus deserted, the edifice went to decay, and finally fell down through feebleness and the weight of years. The bell, which had been presented to the church by the Bishop of London, was hung in the belfry of the Bellville meetinghouse.

From the records of baptisms in the First Church in Newbury, the following names of the Greenleaf family appear: Mary, Dec. 17, 1676; Elizabeth, Jan. 10, 1677; Daniel, Feb. 22, 1679; Stephen, Sept. 10, 1682; Moses, Feb. 29, 1697; Samuel, May, 1697; Mary, Sept. 12, 1697; Sarah, Sept. 26, 1697; Rebecca, Feb. 24, 1699; Henry, Aug. 5, 1705; Richard, 1710; Mary, 1712; Elizabeth, 1713; Enoch, 1713; Martha, 1714; Deborah, 1716; Joanna, 1716; Samuel, 1718; Timothy, 1719; Eleazer, April 30, 1720; Elizabeth, Jan. 25, 1721–22; Caleb, April, 1722; Stephen, March, 1725; Oliver, Oct., 1727.

The First Church in Newburyport was the third in Newbury, being organized in 1725, and the Rev. John Lowell settled as pastor the year succeeding. Its history is one of peculiar interest, presenting in its early records the simple idea of a primitive church, intent only on fulfilling their appointed work of making themselves and the world better.

As early as 1726 we find organized within the church a voluntary association of twenty-four persons who, having taken " into serious consideration the decaying and languishing state of religion," subscribed their names to six articles, by which they agreed to meet once a month, " none to absent themselves unless on some extraordinary occasion ; and first to redress in themselves and families any irregularities, and next to admonish their neighbors of the same." Under date of Jan. 2, 1727, they voted to request the " honorable justice to see that the ferrymen in and about Newbury carry no one over the ferries on the Lord's day," and a month later agreed to a measure much neglected by the churches in those days; namely, "to visit the young communicants of the church, and endeavor to counsel and advise them to continue in the sincere practice of those duties that are encumbent on them by their public profession of Christ." On

one occasion they appointed a committee "to converse withe ye
wife of ———, concerning the disturbance she gives him when
he is going to perform family prayers."

The First Presbyterian Church was formed on the 3d of
January, 1746, by nineteen persons who had formally withdrawn from the first parish in Newbury, a young graduate of
Harvard University, Joseph Adams, officiating as their pastor.
By the advice of "Whitefield," the new church (the "Separa-
tists," as they were called) extended an invitation to the Rev.
Jonathan Parsons to become their pastor; and he was installed
on the 19th of March in the same year. The form of installation was certainly original and unique. The services having
been commenced by the singing of a hymn, Mr. Parsons having
mentioned the reasons against his settlement, made a final propo-
sition to the assembled church, to see if they still wished him to
remain as their pastor. The vote was taken by the clerk, and
passed unanimously in the affirmative. The pastor elect then said,
"In the presence of God and these witnesses, I take this people
to be my people;" and the clerk replied, speaking in the name of
the rest, "In the presence of God and these witnesses, we take
this man to be our minister." Mr. Parsons then went on and
preached the sermon he had prepared, no other ceremonies whatever (except prayer) being observed. On the 7th of April succeeding the installation of Mr. Parsons, they completed the organization of the church by the choice of six ruling elders, and in the
following September voted to unite with the Presbytery of Boston.

The "Fourth Religious Society" in Newbury was set off as
a separate parish in 1761, afterwards known as the "Bellville
Congregational Society" (incorporated in 1808),—the fifth in
Newbury. Incipient measures were taken to raise a meetinghouse as early as November, 1761, the parish occupying the
deserted building called Queen Ann's Chapel, until this was
accomplished (1763). The Rev. Oliver Noble accepted (August,
1762) a call of the parish to settle with them as their minister.

The Second Congregational Church was formed in 1768.
The society was incorporated as the "Third Religious Society
of Newburyport." Its origin was altogether a pleasant episode
in the ecclesiastical history of the town; the persons purposing
to form it having withdrawn from the First Society, in consequence of a difference of opinion as to some of the important

doctrines of Christianity which the two candidates in view of the First Society entertained. The disagreement was unattended with any of that excitement which had marked the separation of some of the earlier churches; and as evidence of the amicable feeling which prevailed, we may note a vote of the First Church (January 18, 1768) whereby they agreed to divide the church plate and stock between the seceding and remaining brethren.

The First Church settled the candidate of their choice, Rev. Thomas Cary, and the Second Church (Oct. 19, 1768) theirs, the Rev. Christopher Bridges Marsh; the latter recognizing the orthodox platform, so called, and the society concurring unanimously in the choice of the church. Mr. Marsh died December 3, 1773, and the church was for the next four years without a settled pastor, when the Rev. Samuel Spring was invited to preach to them as a candidate. His answer to the first request of the church is dated Ticonderoga, August 12th, in which he declines the invitation of the church, as incompatible with his engagements as chaplain in the army. On the conclusion of this engagement he accepted the renewed request of the church, and was ordained its pastor in August, 1777, which relation he sustained until his death, which occurred March 4, 1819,—a period of nearly forty-two years. Dr. Spring was a man of fine talents, devoted piety, and untiring activity.

The Fourth Religious Society was incorporated in 1794. The church was formed principally by dissentients from the ministry of Rev. John Murray, then pastor of the First Presbyterian Society. The first pastor of the church was the Rev. Charles W. Milton, who was installed into that office March 20, 1794, and continued with them until his death,—a period of forty-three years.

The Second Presbyterian Church was organized by the Presbytery of Londonderry, Oct. 29, 1795, with thirty-three members, who had withdrawn from the First Presbyterian Church, not being satisfied with the settlement over that body of Rev. Daniel Dana, D.D. The society was incorporated Nov. 24, 1796. The first pastor was the Rev. John Boddily, of Bristol, England, and a graduate of Lady Huntingdon's College. He was installed June 28, 1797. This church was based on the strictest Calvinistic platform of faith.

The Baptist Church of Christ, in Newbury and Newbury-port, was formed under many difficulties, and in the face of obstacles that would have disheartened less persevering or less conscientious persons. They had "not the same kind" of difficulties to encounter as had obstructed the growth and prosperity of some of the earlier churches of this vicinity; they had no legal hindrances, such as beset the Congregational and Presbyterian interests; but a more formidable opposition was to be met in the prejudices of the times and place. The denomination was new to this vicinity; there was no Baptist church in this or the neighboring township of Newbury. Some attempt was made by a few individuals as early as 1681 to form a church on these peculiar principles in Newbury, and they even went so far as to apply for assistance to the First Church in Boston, who assented to their organization, but they were too few in numbers to maintain a separate existence. The peculiarities of this denomination forced themselves, therefore, with all the intensity of novelty, on the settled habits and opinions of the community in which they were now to be first broached in a practical form. The young licentiate preacher, Joshua Chase, preached the first sermon to a Baptist society in this vicinity on the Sabbath of July 22, 1804, and later, having received ordination, continued with the church as their minister until the engagement of the Rev. John Peake, in the fall of 1805. The first persons baptized there were Stephen Goodwin, David Burbank, Benjamin Goodwin, Bart. Hurd, John Flood, Nathaniel Pettingill, and Mrs. Rebecca Dorman, on Sunday, Oct. 14, 1804. The church was not regularly organized until the 2d of May, 1805.

First Methodist Episcopal Church. The Methodist interest was commenced in Newbury (now Newburyport) in the year 1819, under the preaching and labors of the Rev. John Adams, a member of the New England Annual Conference of the Methodist Episcopal Church. The church was regularly organized by the Rev. B. Othman, June 20, 1827.

The First Universalist Society was organized on the 26th of December, 1834. The meetinghouse was dedicated in 1840, but the recognition of the church did not take place until Nov. 16, 1842. The recognition services were performed by Rev. Sylvanus Cobb.

The Christian Church was organized May 7, 1840, by a mutual covenant of ten persons, who met at a private residence, " and after prayer and solemn dedication to God, covenanted to take the Holy Scriptures, especially the last will and testament of Jesus Christ, as the rule of their faith and practice," and were then acknowledged by Elder Daniel P. Pike, their first minister, as a properly constituted church. The church requires the adoption of strict temperance principles by all its members.

Roman Catholic. The first church organization of this denomination in Newburyport was in May, 1843, and in May, 1848, the Rev. John O'Brien was appointed resident pastor of the church. On the 27th of April, 1852, the corner stone of a new church edifice was laid, in the presence of the bishop, some twenty priests, and an immense concourse of people ; the ensuing 17th of March the building was dedicated, under the title of the Church of the Immaculate Conception. The style of architecture is decorated Gothic, and the interior is finished in an appropriate and pleasing correspondence with the exterior plan of the house. The fee simple of the church property is vested in the bishop of the diocese for the Catholics of Newburyport and vicinity.

NEWBURYPORT PUBLIC LIBRARY.

" Soon after the Public Library went into operation, it was found (so great was the demand for its books, and so apparent the prospects of its future increase) that the room it then occupied would prove entirely inadequate for its purposes, and that larger and better accommodations would shortly be needed. The subject, therefore, began at that time to interest some of the more zealous friends of the Library ; and inquiries were instituted relative to the best means for obtaining a building that should be suited to its growing wants. An appeal to the city authorities to supply the requisite funds was considered impolitic, inasmuch as it was felt that the ordinary demands upon the city treasury were already onerous. The general desire, therefore, seemed to be that some feasible mode of raising the money without resort to public taxation should be adopted. As no organized body existed for the purpose, it was necessarily incumbent upon individual efforts to commence the undertaking."* It was dedicated Jan. 1, 1866. The house was built by

*A statement of the proceedings resulting in the purchase of the Newburyport Public Library Building, with a sketch of the History of the Library. Prepared by order of the Directors, for private distribution, 1866.

Patrick Tracy, an opulent merchant of his day, for his son, Nathaniel, who occupied it, and through whose great wealth and unbounded hospitality it acquired a wide celebrity. It was at this house, during his visit to Newburyport in 1789, that General Washington was entertained, and other distinguished persons have partaken, at different times, of its hospitalities.

The following odes were contributed as a poetic tribute for the occasion :—

ODE.

BY REV. GEORGE D. WILDES.

Gather them here around,—
    The guests of thought, the friendships of the mind;
Kinglier than kings, nobler than conqueror crowned;
    Sovereign o'er human kind.

With glad hearts greet them here,
    Noiseless and voiceless though they enter in;
Yet shall the quickening throb, the lightsome hour,
    Reward the welcoming.

What though no high acclaim
    Lifts its full thunders round these ancient walls;
What though no pæan sounds the patriot's fame,
    Or valor's deed recalls;

What though from court and throne,
    Hither the wandering exile comes no more,
Freedom's warm heart and Freedom's home his own,
    All that it gave of yore;

Relentless though the years
    To dim the glories of thy storied day,*
Wealth's generous heart, the household joys and fears,
    Forever passed away.

Still, through each brightening age,
    Hither, with cheer, the *living thought* shall come;
Bard, patriot, chronicler, the wit, the sage,
    Find, as of old, a home.

Gather them here around,—
    The guests of thought, the friendships of the mind;
Kinglier than kings, nobler than conqueror crowned;
    Sovereign o'er human kind.

---

*In allusion to the fact that the Tracy mansion was the temporary home of Washington, Lafayette, Talleyrand, Louis Philippe, the Marquis Chastellux, Brissot de Warville, and Chateaubriand, during their visits to Newburyport.

THE LIBRARY.

BY MISS HARRIET E. PRESCOTT.

We consecrate the storied place
Their hallowed feet have trod,
Who smoothed the way where Liberty
Leads up the arts to God.

They sowed; we reap and garner in
Such lettered treasure here,
That sweet enchantments of the pen
Rule all the atmosphere.

Here silently the poet's song
Perpetual music makes;
The former, long since overgrown,
Its silver thunder wakes.

The dramas' splendid phantoms here
Move real to the sense,
As heroes that once shook the world,
And, battling, vanished hence.

Turn but aside, and overhead
Ægian skies burn blue,
And to his crowd of eager Greeks
Homer recites anew.

A step, and Science to the search
Her awful gate unbars;
The riddle of the earth is read,
The secret of the stars.

Kind Heaven, upon the finished work
Thy blessing we implore;
To fair and holy purposes
Serenely guide its lore.

Here may no tumult of the day
Its troubled shadow fling!
Within these cloistered walls may Peace
Forever fold her wing!

TONNAGE TABLE.

Date.	Permanent Registered Vessels.	Enrolled in the Coasting and Fisheries	Employed in Coasting Trade.	Employed in the Fisheries.	Employed in the Whale Fisheries.	Total Tonnage.
	Tons. 95ths.	Tons. 95ths.	Tons. 95ths.	Tons. 95ths.		Tons. 95ths.
1794	14,819.54	2,461.39	2,005.60	455.79		17,280.93
1795	*					
1796	16,179.48	3,959.56	3,328.49	631.7		20,139.04
1797	16,290.18	4,614.1	4,256.48	357.62		20,904.19
1798	13,747.44	5,107.40	4,521.73	585.67		18,854.84
1799	15,414.16	2,761.73	2,447.47	314.26		18,175.89
1800	15,412.67	3,504.55	3,244.28	260.27		18,917.22
1801	13,348.23	3,717.92	3,072.41	645.51		17,066.15
1802	14,614.06	3,784.64	2,516.61	1,268.3		18,399.24
1803	16,351.42	4,367.19	2,765.34	1,601.85		20,718.61
1804	19,834.94	3,806.46	2,000.2	1,806.44		23,641.40
1805	24,019.47	4,314.06	1,603.69	2,710.37		28,333.53
1806	25,291.32	4,422.17	1,641.75	2,780.42		29,713.49
1807	26,799.16	4,998.1	1,162.91	3,835.10		31,797.17
1808	22,191.15	7,963.61	4,847.35	3,116.26		30,154.76
1809	29,571.54	4,820.	2,733.68	2,086.32		34,391.54
1810	29,897.6	5,398.47	3,889.77	1,508.70		35,296.07

* The Customhouse records for this period are missing, which accounts for the deficiency.

NOTES.

New London Gazette.

Nov. 6, 1767.—Boston, Nov. 2. At a meeting of the Freeholders and other inhabitants of the town of Boston, legally assembled at Faneuil Hall on Wednesday, Oct. 28, 1767, the Hon. James Otis, Esq., Moderator: voted, that this town will take all prudent and legal measures to encourage the produce and manufactures of this province, to lessen the use of superfluities, and particularly the following enumerated articles imported from abroad; viz., loaf sugar, cordage, anchors, coaches, chaises, and carriages of all sorts, etc., and that a subscription for this end be, and hereby is, recommended to the several inhabitants and householders of the town; and that John Rowe, Esq., Mr. *William Greenleaf*, Melarich Bourne, Esq., Mr. Samuel Austin, Mr. Edward Payne, Mr. Edmund Quincy (test), John Ruddock, Esq., Jonathan Williams, Esq., Mr. Henderson Inches, Mr. Sol. Davis, Joshua Winslow, Esq., and Thomas Cushing, Esq., be a committee to prepare a form for subscription, to report the same as soon as possible, and also to procure subscriptions to the same.

July 15, 1768.—Boston, July 11. One of "the honest ninety-two members who voted not to recind" (a vote of the last house to send circulars to the other colonies that they would unite in a petition for "redress of grievances"), *Benjamin Greenleaf*, Esq., of Newburyport.

Nov. 25, 1768.—New York, Nov. 17. On Monday last a report prevailed that the effigies of Governor Barnard and Sheriff *Stephen Greenleaf*, of Boston, were to be exhibited that evening. At four o'clock in the afternoon the troops in this city appeared under arms at the lower barracks, where they remained till after 10 o'clock at night, during which time parties of them were continually patrolling the streets, in order, it is supposed, to intimidate the inhabitants and prevent their exposing the effigies. Notwithstanding which, they made their appearance in the streets, hanging on a gallows, between eight and nine o'clock, attended by a vast number of spectators, who saluted them with loud huzzas at the corner of every street they passed; and after having been exposed some time at the coffee house, they were there publickly burnt amidst the acclamations of the populace, who testified their approbation by repeated huzzas, and immediately dispersed and returned to their respective homes. The affair was conducted with such regularity and good order that no person sustained the least damage either in his person or property. —*Journal*.

Nov. 25, 1768.—Boston, Oct. 24. The following complaint was this day regularly made, viz.:—

Suffolk, ss. To the worshipful Richard Dana, John Ruddock, and Joseph Williams, Esqs., Justices of the Peace in and for said county. Humbly shows: John Brown of Boston, in said county, weaver, that *Stephen Greenleaf*, of Boston, aforesaid Esq., and Joseph Otis of said Boston, gentleman, together with divers other malefactors and disturbers of the peace of our said Lord the King, whose names to the complainant are yet unknown, on the 20th day of Oct. inst. with force and arms, and with strong hand, at Boston, aforesaid, unlawfully and injuriously did break and enter into the dwelling house of the said John Brown; and that the said S. G. and J. O., together with the other said malefactors, then and there with force and arms, and with strong hand, unlawfully did expel, remove, and put the said J. B. from the possession of the said dwelling house; and with strong hand unlawfully and injuriously did keep out and still do keep out, to the great damage of him, the said J. B., and against the peace of our said Lord the King, etc.

Dec. 23, 1768.—Boston, Nov. 21. Journal of Occurrences. We have advice from New York that on the 14th inst. there was exposed and burnt in that city the effigies of Governor Barnard and *Sheriff Greenleaf* in resentment at the parts they acted in endeavoring to get the troops quartered in this town, contrary to the letter and spirit of the Act of Parliament relative to billetting troops in America, as also to the advice of His Majesty's Council.

(63)

Feb. 3, 1769.— Boston, Dec. 26. Journal of Occurrences. The Council met this day, and the Governor received his request that they would, agreeable to the petition of *Sheriff Greenleaf*, indemnify said Sheriff as to his conduct at the Manufactory House, in the action brought against him by Mr. William Brown; and in order to show the reasonableness of this requirement, he was pleased to tell the Council that in this business Mr. Greenleaf pursued their vote, and did not act as sheriff but as their bailiff, they having commissioned him so to do. The conduct of the Sheriff cannot be excused in his forcible entry, or in that aggravating circumstance of it, his calling the soldiery to his assistance, when some reputable inhabitants declared to him they stood ready to aid him in all legal steps upon this occasion, and that he could not but know that this was the disposition of the inhabitants.

June 9, 1769.— Boston, June 1. Election of " Gentlemen Councillors " for the ensuing year, by General Assembly. Eleven declined to be confirmed by Governor Barnard. Among names registered, *Benjamin Greenleaf*, Esq., James Otis, Esq.

June 8, 1770.— Boston, June 4. *Benjamin Greenleaf* chosen Councillor for ensuing year.

Friday, May 17, 1771.— Tuesday last was married, Mr. Samuel Eliot, Jr., to Miss *Elizabeth Greenleaf*, daughter of Mr. *William Greenleaf*, of this town, merchant.

June 3, Boston.— Benjamin Greenleaf, Esq., Councillor for ensuing year.

Jan. 17, 1772.—" To the Printers of the *Boston Gazette*. Dec. 27, 1771. Sirs: The enclosed I received some time since, and as it is explanatory of the conduct of the author, and may be of some importance to the public, I desire you to publish it in your next paper. I have not asked leave of the writer for this freedom, but hope he will excuse it.

I am sirs, your humble servant, A. Z.

Boston, Dec. 12, 1771.

" Dear Sir: As you are desirous of having an account of the late transactions of the Governor and Council relating to me, and of my conduct respecting the same, I shall gratify you by giving you a short detail, that you may be able to judge not of their unpoliteness, but of their cruelty towards me. I now consider myself as a magistrate or public person, and as such I had a right to be treated, but was disappointed. It may not be amiss to give you an account of the whole proceedings. On the 15th of November last, I received a polite message from the Governor and Council, by Mr. Baker, desiring my attendance at the council chamber. This I have no fault to find with. The distress of my family on account of a sick child, who died that day, was such that I could not attend, and as such I had a right to be treated, but was disappointed, in the most polite manner I was capable of. A few days after came a citation conceived in the terms following, viz.: —

" Province of Massachusetts Bay. To *Joseph Greenleaf* of Boston, in said Province, Esquire: You are required to appear before the Governor and Council at the council chamber in Boston on Tuesday the 10th of December next, at ten of the clock in the forenoon, then and there to be examined touching a certain paper called the *Massachusetts Spy*, published the 14th day of November, 1771. Whereoff, fail not at your peril. Dated at Boston, the 16th day of November, 1771. By order of the Governor with the advice of Council. Thomas Flucker, Secretary. This proceeding alarmed me, as I judged it wholly illegal. My duty to my country therefore forbade any obedience to it, especially as it might hereafter be used as a precedent (considers at length the legal points of the question and ends). This affair as it concerns myself gives me no uneasiness, for by leaving the county where I had jurisdiction I voluntarily relinquished it, yet according to Dalton I still have jurisdiction when I please to take my seat on the bench at the Court of Sessions in the County of Plymouth.

I am, Sir, your most humble Servant, *Joseph Greenleaf.*

" P. S. A secret has leaked out: it is said it was my duty, as a Magistrate, to have prevented the publication of a piece signed Mucius Scævola! But I have no such connections with Mr. Thomas or any other printer as give me a right to restrain him or them in any publication; though I must confess that if I had power to restrain the press, I should have no inclination to hinder Mucius or any other writer from laying their sentiments before the public."

June 1, 1772.—Boston. *Benjamin Greenleaf* chosen councillor for ensuing year.

March 26, 1773. To be sold at public vendue by the subscriber. At the dwelling house of Mr. Jesse Williams, in Norwich, the dwelling house now improved by said Williams, with a large and excellent garden. Said house is large, with two stacks of chimneys two stories high on the front which faceth the Town Street, and three stories on the rear, etc. Signed, *David Greenleaf.*

June 6, 1773.—Boston, May 31. *Benjamin Greenleaf* chosen Councillor.

May 27, 1773.—In House of Representatives. Passage of resolutions looking to a union of the colonies to preserve their rights and liberties. On committee chosen by the House for Correspondence and Communication with the other colonies, Captain *Jonathan Greenleaf.*

December 10.—Meeting in Faneuil Hall, November 29, relative to landing of tea. *Sheriff Greenleaf* reads proclamation from the Governor commanding the assembly to disperse.

May 30, 1774.—*Benjamin Greenleaf* chosen Councillor for late colony of Massachusetts Bay.

August 5.—Married at Boston, July 26, Mr. Duncan Ingraham, Jr., merchant, to Miss *Susannah Greenleaf,* third daughter of Mr. *William Gerenleaf.*

December 16. On committee of fifty-three persons appointed at a meeting of freeholders at Faneuil Hall to carry into execution, in the Town of Boston, the agreement and association of the late respectable Continental Congress: Mr. *William Greenleaf, Joseph Greenleaf,* Esq., on committee of seven to draught a vote of thanks of Boston for the assistance of the other colonies. *Joseph Greenleaf,* Esq.

Feb. 17, 1775.—Cash given by *Stephen Greenleaf* at his shop in Windham for good hair — where he still continues his business, and where all gentlemen may be supplied with wigs of any kind, very cheap for the ready cash, and all favors shall be thankfully received.

July 28.—Boston. *Benjamin Greenleaf* Councillor for current year.

Nov. 3, 1775.—*Stephen Greenleaf,* Boston, one of the signers to an address complimentary to Governor Gage on his departure for Great Britain.

Jan. 23, 1786.—An account of an experiment for raising Indian corn in poor land, by *Joseph Greenleaf,* Esq., of Boston. From the memoirs of the American Academy of Arts and Sciences.

Aug. 20, 1795.—From the New York *Journal.* A letter addressed *Citizen Greenleaf,* giving the objections of several towns of Long Island to "Jay's Treaty" with Great Britain.

April 27, 1797.—*Mr. Greenleaf,* of New York, printer of the *Argus,* has been tried before the Circuit Court of the United States for a libel, of which he was pronounced guilty, and fined by the Court, in which Judge Ellsworth sat as Supreme, seven hundred dollars. Mr. Greenleaf in his statement said the piece was averse from his own political principles, and in answer to one which had previously appeared in his paper, and published to support his character as an impartial printer. Mr. Greenleaf consoles himself under the reflection that the author of the piece will not suffer him to pay the penalty which he has incurred. The prosecutor, we understand, was Sir William Temple, the British Consul.

American Mercury, Hartford, Conn.

Sept. 20, 1798.—Died at New York, of the prevailing fever, *Mr. Thomas Greenleaf,* editor of the *Argus and Patriotic Register.*

Thursday, Sept. 8, 1803.—Married, on Sunday evening last, Mr. *William Greenleaf* Goldsmith to Miss Polly Williams, of this city, daughter of Mr. Elisha Williams.

Feb. 9, 1804.—Advertisement, watches. *William Greenleaf.* Shop at the head of Ferry Street.

Middlesex Gazette, Middletown, Conn.

Aug. 4, 1788.—Notice of an article in Mr. *Greenleaf's* paper, the New York *Journal*, describing the processions of citizens the day before, celebrating New York's adoption of the Constitution. The article gave great offence to the Federalists.

Mr. Greenleaf's printing office was broken into, and his types and other printing material turned out of the windows into the streets.

Connecticut Courant.

Sept. 15, 1774.—From *Connecticut Courant Extraordinary.* Among news from Boston, the following is an authentic copy of a letter which was thrown into both camps on Monday night last, directed " To the Officers and Soldiers of His Majesty's Troops at Boston " : "It being more than probable that the King's standard will soon be erected from rebellion breaking out in this province, it is proper that you soldiers should be acquainted with the authors thereof, and of all the misfortunes brought upon this province. The following is a list of them; viz., Messrs. Samuel Adams, James Bowdoin, Dr. Thomas Young, Dr. Benjamin Church, Capt. John Bradford, Josiah Quincy, Major Nathaniel Barber, William Mollineux, John Hancock, William Cooper, Dr. Cheney, Dr. Cooper, Thomas Cushing, Joseph Greenleaf, and William Deming. The friends of your King and country, and of America, hope and expect it from you soldiers the instant rebellion happens, that you will put the above persons immediately to the sword, destroy their homes, and plunder their effects; it is just that they should be the first victims to the mischief they have brought upon us.

A friend to Great Britain and America.

N. B. Don't forget those trumpeters of sedition, the printers, Edes, and Gill, and Thomas."

Sept. 26, 1774.—Boston, September 22. Last Monday, Capt. *Jonathan Greenleaf* was unanimously chosen to represent the town of Newburyport in General Court.

June 2, 1777.—Among Councillors for ensuing year for the late Colony of Massachusetts Bay, Benjamin Greenleaf, Esq., re-elected.

Aug. 3, 1779.—Deposition of Joseph Partrick before *Joseph Greenleaf*, Justice of the Peace, at Boston.

June 12, 1786.—Among Governor's Councillors, *Jonathan Greenleaf*, for Essex, senator, Boston, June 8.

Feb. 11, 1788.—Massachusetts General Assembly. Ratification of Federal Constitution. Among the yeas, Hon. *Benjamin Greenleaf.*

Nov. 2, 1789.—Married in Boston, October 26th, Noah Webster, Jr., Esq., of this city, to Miss *Rebecca Greenleaf*, daughter of *William Greenleaf*, Esq., of Boston.

March 14, 1791.—Marine list, Sloop Sukey *Greenleaf*, Portland.

April 30, 1792, *David Greenleaf* pays cash for old gold, silver, brass and copper. He has for sale gold beads, silver spoons, etc. Said *Greenleaf* continues the watch making and repairing business, as usual, etc. Wants two or three active lads as apprentices to the business, thirteen or fourteen years old, and a good journeyman who understands the business.

Feb. 10, 1794.—A letter signed " A Republican " speaks of an attempt (unsuccessful) to suppress the Republican paper of *T. Greenleaf*, New York. *Mr. Greenleaf* was enabled by the friends of liberty to enlarge his paper immediately after.

Oct. 15, 1798.—Report of Health Committee. New London deaths, *Joseph Greenleaf*, twenty. (Fever epidemic.)

Dec. 29, 1800.—Died at Coventry, the 11th inst., Mr. *David Greenleaf*, in the sixty-fourth year of his age.

Dec. 11, 1805.—Died, last Friday, Miss Sally Greenleaf, daughter of Mr. *David Greenleaf*, aged fifteen years. The young lady, about three weeks ago, set her gown on fire, which, communicating to her other clothing, burnt her in such a manner as to cause her death. Died December 6.

Jan. 17, 1810.—Died in Newbury, Mr. *Abner Greenleaf*, aged ninety-one, March 21. New Haven, March 15.—News of death of Captain Elisha Atwater, brought by Brig "Juno," *Greenleaf*, of Newburyport, bound to Alexandria.

May 3, 1814.—Died, in this city on the 1st inst., Mrs. *Mary Greenleaf*, aged seventy-eight.

April 1, 1828.—Married at New Haven, Mr. *Daniel Greenleaf* to Miss Aura Carrington, both of Hartford.

Jan. 6, 1829.—Married at Vernon, Mr. *David Greenleaf*, Jr., of this city, to Miss Clarissa Cooley, daughter of the late Simeon Cooley.

Sept. 27, 1831.—*Charles Greenleaf*, Dentist. Removed to Exchange Building, West Front.

October 25.—*David Greenleaf*, Jr. Advertised for sale.—The late residence of Mr. Edward Danforth, about one mile from the city. Two or three good mill seats in Vernon. An excellent farm in Vernon. Owner about to remove from the State. Enquire of Seth Terry, in Hartford, or of subscriber, living on the Danforth Place.

Jan. 20, 1834.—Married, in this city, by the Rev. Mr. Bushnell, Mr. H. L. Clark, of the firm of D. & H. L. Clark, to Miss Juliette, daughter of Dr. David Greenleaf, of this city.

New England Historical and Genealogical Register.

Volume VII. page 36.—Will of John Lowle (Lowell) proved August 27, 1647. *Edmund Greenleaf*, witness. Page 44.—Auction sale real estate. Samuel Adams' dwelling, malt house, etc., by *Stephen Greenleaf*. Page 195.—Hon. *Thomas Greenleaf*, Quincy, Mass., *obit:* Rev. Wm. P. Lunt, discourse on the "Christian Standard of Honor," Jan. 8, 1854, following the death, on Jan. 4, 1854, of Hon. Thomas Greenleaf, age eighty-six years seven months. Page 206.—Aug. 25, 1675. *Stephen Greealeaf* wounded by Indians. Page 250.—Cranch-Greenleaf. Page 292.—Daniel Greenleaf, Quincy, Mass., *obit*.

Volume IX. page 218, July 15, 1650.—Edmund Greenleaf certifies to claim of David Thompson to Thompson's Island, Boston Harbor.

Volume X., page 56, Nov. 9, 1726.—Benjamin Bradstreet married Mrs. Sarah Greenleaf. Probably a son of Dr. Humphrey Bradstreet, who died May 11, 1717, in Newbury, aged forty-nine. His widow, Sarah, married Captain Edwin Sargent, June 9, 1719. Anne Bradstreet, probably daughter of Dr. Bradstreet, married Benjamin Moody, Nov. 7, 1728.

Volume XIV. page 262.—A list of subscribers towards paying Mr. Samuel Adams' Land Bank Debts (without date), Mr. William Greenleaf, £13-6-8.

Volume XI. page 54.—Rev. Joseph Adams, born March 8, 1719, married 1746, widow *Mary Greenleaf*.

Volume XV. page 360.—Constitution of Maine formed 1819, Hon. Nicholas Emery, of Portland, Asa Clapp, and Hon. *Simon Greenleaf*, Colleagues in the House; Judge Potter Committee in the Senate. The members held their office from May, 1820, when the new government went into operation, to January, 1822. In this time the whole body of the Statute Laws was revised, modified and adapted to the constitution of the new State.

Volume XVIII. page 77, September, 1776.—Hon. Benjamin Greenleaf on Governor's Council. With majority of the Court grant commission of Captain to David Henshaw.

S. Greenleaf and others, memorial to the Town of Boston, 1746, for paving streets.

Volume XVIII. page 75.—A Journal of Proceedings. Martha's Vineyard from Oct. 2, 1712 to October 15, "Sabbath Day." October 12, Mr. Greenleaf of Yarmouth preached. Pages 119-121.—Ground plan of church at Quincy. Pew No. 2, Daniel Greenleaf; pew No. 18, Judge Thomas Greenleaf; pew No. 70, Dr. John Greenleaf. Page 123.—List of pews in Quincy Church and their owners. Page 153.—Abstract from the earliest wills on record and on files of Suffolk County, Mass. Nathaniel Robinson March 2, 1667. " I give to Goodman Greenleaf and Goodman Shaw, and each of their wives, a pair of gloves." Witness, John Greenleaf and others. Page 154.—Prefixed to this will is: " I owe as followeth (among others) Goodman Greenleaf, four shillings." Page 157.—Will of Elizabeth Robinson, August 21, 1666. "I give to my kinsman, John Greenleaf, my orchard . . . . . provided he pay to his sister, Mary Greenleaf, twenty pounds within six months after my decease, the which I do hereby give and bequeath to my said kinswoman. To my said kinman, John Greenleaf, one bedstead in the chamber with the furniture to it. I give to Mary Greenleaf, one feather bed and bedstead with furniture belonging to it, now standing in the parlor, together with one table, four stools and a few cushions." Page 160.—April, 1778, from Boston *Gazette.* Statement of an attempt to liberate slaves without the consent of their masters. Before Samuel Pemberton and Joseph Greenleaf, Justices. Spear Family Record.

Volume XIX.—November 2, 1772. Boston Committee of Correspondence appointed by the citizens of Boston. This committee was the basis of a subsequent union of the colonies. Their report presented a statement of the rights of the colonies, in which they pointed out the infringements and violation of them by the parliamentary assumption of the power of legislating for the colonies by the appointment of a large number of new officers to superintend the revenues; and by granting of the salaries out of the American Revenue to the Governor, the Judges of the Courts, the King's Attorney and Solicitor General. Signed, James Otis, Samuel Adams, Joseph Warren, Benjamin Church, William Dennie, *William Greenleaf,* and fourteen others.

Volume XXII. page 108.—In 1769 ten members, chosen to the House of Representatives, were rejected by Gov. Barnard, on account of their well-known opposition to the measures pursued by the Government toward the Colony; and this significant testimony to their love of country and devotion to principle gave them a still stronger hold upon the hearts of the people. These ten were: William Brattle, James Bowdoin, James Otis, Jerathmeel Bowers, Joseph Gerrish, Thomas Saunders, John Hancock, Artemus Ward, Walter Spooner, and *Benjamin Greenleaf.*

Same, page 278, November 17, 1735, is recorded the drawing of the lots of the 1st Division Narragansett Grantees, which were afterwards called the " Home Lots." Range of lots known by the letter " C," Capt. John Greenleaf, Jr., for Moses Durrell, 22. Page 437.—Bibliography of Massachusetts: A Statistical View of the District of Maine, by Moses Greenleaf, 1816.

Volume XXIII. page 54.—Bibliography of Massachusetts. Medfield. *Boston Magazine.* Greenleaf & Freeman, Boston, 1785. Page 56, same.—Milton, Medway and Needham. Page 59.—Massachusetts Historic Collections, by John W. Barber, Worcester, 1848. Page 338.—Memoirs and Notices of Prince's Subscribers. Andrew Eliot, Jr., minister of New North Church, Boston, married Elizabeth Langdon, parents of Mr. Samuel Eliot, born June 17, 1748, who married May 7, 1771, Elizabeth, daughter of Hon. William Greenleaf. Page 468.—Bibliography of Massachusetts. A Discourse on the death of Hon. Thomas Greenleaf, Jan. 8, 1848, by William P. Lunt.

Volume XXVI. page 134.—The New Hampshire *Gazette.* The oldest newspaper in America. Communicated by Frank W. Miller, of Portsmouth, N. H., with *fac simile,* Oct. 7, 1756, and picture of first printing office in the State, corner of Howard and Washington Streets, Portsmouth. 1834.—Albert Greenleaf admitted partner with Gideon Beck, A. Greenleaf & Son; Abner Greenleaf, Sr., editor.

Volume XXXI. page 69.—Rev. Thomas Smith succeeds Rev. Daniel Greenleaf as pastor of the church at Yarmouth, Mass.

Page 333, October 24, 1670.—Edmund Greenleaf, witness to a bill of sale of an Indian.

Volume XLI. page 345.—In memoriam. Rev. Wm. G. Eliot, D.D. Notice of publication by John H. Hayward and others. Page 415.—New England Historical and Genealogical Meeting. Remarks on efforts being made to have a full Index of documents relating to the War of the Revolution, now preserved in the various archives of Europe, which index has been nearly compiled by Mr. B. F. Stevens, of London, printed and published at the expense of the United States. The historiographer, Rev. Increase N. Tarbox, D.D., presented memorial sketch of Rev. William Greenleaf Eliot, D.D., of St. Louis, Mo.

Volume XLIV. page 207, July 21, 1760.—Petition of inhabitants of the Kennebec River for protection. Signed by Stephen Greenleaf, Richard Greenleaf, Samuel Greenleaf Joseph Greenleaf, and four hundred others.

Volume XLV. page 197.—The Craigie House, known of late years as the residence of the poet Henry W. Longfellow, Brattle Street, Cambridge. "Title and History of the Henry Vassall Estate. June 12, 1782.—Consideration of £850, the Vassall Estate was conveyed to Nathaniel Tracy, of Newburyport, Mass. Oct. 30, 1786, he conveyed to Thomas Russell. Jan. 1, 1792, to Andrew Craigie (see Book 110, page 406). Craigie owned it till his death. Mary, his sister, married ——— Foster, and Craigie having no children, the children of Foster would. be the legal heirs. Mr. Foster moved from Boston and resided there some years, until his death about 1820. Then, by agreement, the property was divided into four parts, and that part denominated No. 1 fell by lot to Elizabeth Haven, and this was the Henry Vassall estate, now so called. The present proprietor purchased the estate of Messrs. Greenleaf and Hilliard (Hon. Simon G.) representing the several parties in interest in December, 1841, just one hundred years after it was conveyed to Henry Vassall, in 1741."

Colonial Records.

1649, May.—On a committee of the deputies " to consider of a way, and draw up a law, for dividing the shires, and the treasury in each shire, bringing all courts to an equality for power and numbers,"—the law for division into counties, viz.; Essex, Middlesex, Suffolk, and Norfolk, the latter containing Salisbury, Hampton, Haverhill, Exeter, Dover, and Strawberry Bank (Portsmouth).

An Historic Rock.

An interesting memorial of the survey of 1652 is a large rock, exposed to view in consequence of a dam having been thrown across the head of the wears at the point where Lake Winnipiseogee discharges its water into the upper Merrimac. For more than a century afterwards, the whole country on the western shores of Lake Winnipiseogee remained an unbroken wilderness, covered with dense forests penetrated only by the native Indian, or by the scouting parties of the English which were sent out from time to time to secure the frontier settlements from the murderous attack of the savage foe. During all this period the existence of this memorial seems to have been unknown. On the very spot which the commissioners established as the most northerly line of the patent, or certainly very near to that spot, the rock was discovered about the year 1838 when building the dam :—it was " deeply imbedded in the gravel, with its surface but little above the water, and about twenty feet in circumference."

On this rock there is the following inscription, viz. :—

E I   S W

W P   IOHN

ENDICVT

GOV

This points unerringly to the time of the survey, and to the spot which the commissioners, in their return to the General Court, designate and establish as the north line of the patent; while the sculpture on the rock confirms the great fact, and marks the presence of the commissioners at that place, for that object, two hundred and forty-three years ago. Endicott was then the governor of the Colony of Massachusetts Bay, and the commissioners have very properly inscribed his name at full length, with the abbreviation

WP. for "worshipful." It would have been equally proper for them to carve out their own names in full, but want of time and the hardness of the stone may have prevented. E. I. is intended for Edward Johnson,* and S. W. for Simon Willard,† the joint commissioners, associated in public, and friends in private life. Besides their expenses the court allowed them "twenty markes a peece for their pajnes."‡ ["Willard Memoir," by Joseph Willard, 1858, pp. 168–170.]

* Captain Edward Johnson was brother of William Johnson, who married Elizabeth Storey, of Charlestown, Mass. They were sons of Abraham Johnson and his second wife, Cicely Chadderton. Abraham was born 1567, and married first Annie Meadows, in 1597. Their son Isaac married, 1623, Lady Arbella Clinton, daughter of Thomas, third Earl of Lincoln, Eng. She died at Salem, Aug. 30, 1630. Abraham with his family removed from Melton, Bryan to Canterbury, County Kent, Eng. William and Edward, sons of Abraham and Cicely, emigrated to America from Canterbury in 1630. William, from whom descended Eleazar Johnson and his family referred to in Newbury Notes and Greenleaf Genealogy, settled in Charlestown, Mass. Edward settled in Woburn, Mass. A descendant of his has prepared a history of the Johnson family.

† Major-General Simon Willard is referred to as the ancestor of the wife of the compiler of this book. See personal history of James E. Greenleaf, and Genealogy Calendar number 549.

‡ A mark was a money of account equal to two thirds of a pound sterling.

PERSONAL HISTORY.

1. EDMUND GREENLEAF,

The Common Ancestor of this Family, came to America and Settled in Newbury, Mass., in 1635.

Of the origin of the family, from all that can be gathered, it is believed that the ancestors of Edmund were Huguenots, the name being a translation of the French "Feuillevert." As the name has not been found among the English parishes, other than at Ipswich, County of Suffolk, England, it is believed that the family (Feuillevert) came as French refugees to England with many other Huguenots, who fled from their homes on account of their religious principles, and settled in England some time in the sixteenth century. Edmund Greenleaf was a silk-dyer by trade; a trade that does not appear among the English industries until about the time of the coming of the French refugees.

On the parish records of St. Mary's la Tour in Ipswich, County Suffolk, England, is recorded: "*Edmund Greenleaf*, son of John and Margaret, was baptized Jan. 2, 1574."

Among the family relics still preserved is the cane brought to this country by Edmund Greenleaf; it bears the initials "J. G." on a silver band near the handle.

Edmund Greenleaf married Sarah Dole, and by her had nine children, whose names appear on the records of the parish of St. Mary's la Tour above mentioned. It is supposed there were two others,—John, born about 1632, and who died in Boston, Dec. 16, 1712; and Mary,— referred to in "Savage's Dictionary," Vol. IV. p. 476: "John Wells, of Newbury, took the oath of allegiance, May, 1669, and was made a freeman the same month, a carpenter, married March 5, 1669, Mary, probably daughter of Edmund Greenleaf, and had, December 16th, Mary, who died the year following. Mary, again, born Feb. 16, 1673. William, born Jan. 15, 1675."

All of the nine children named in the chart, and whose baptismal records and deaths appear on the parish records of St. Mary's before mentioned, were born in England. Mr. Greenleaf lived near the old town bridge in Newbury, where for some years he kept a tavern. He was admitted a freeman on March 13, 1639,* and on May 22d of the same year was "permitted to keep a house of entertainment."

---

* A freeman in the early days of the colonies was one who held the right of franchise. No one was allowed that right without first becoming a member of the church. The laws were made by a quorum of the "assistants" or "magistrates" sent out and commissioned by the company in London, which held the charter. The law compelling church membership was passed by the "assistants" in 1631. In 1676 five sixths of the people of Boston were non-voters, because they were not church members, and were thus shut out from any participation in the local government.

The name of *Edmund Greenleaf* appears :—

June 1, 1642.—" On a commission of Newbury."

Sept. 8, 1642.—" Ordered to send home an Indian woman."

Sept. 27, 1642.—" On a committee to take charge of certain orders by the council."

Nov. 11, 1647.—Requests his " discharge from military service."

May 2, 1649.—On appraisement of real estate. (" Massachusetts Bay Records," Vol. I. page 258; Vol. II. pages 16, 23, 30, 215, and 276).

Capt. Edmund Greenleaf moved to Boston with his wife Sarah about 1650 (New England Historical and Genealogical Register, Vol. VI. page 102), where he buried his wife, and afterwards married Mrs. Sarah Hill, widow of —— Wilson, 2d, of William Hill, of Fairfield, Conn., who had several children by her former marriage. This marriage was rather an unhappy one. In the early part of 1671 Mr. Greenleaf died. His will, a very curious document, written, as is supposed, by himself, was proved Feb. 12, 1671, and is recorded in the " Probate Records " in Boston, in the volume for 1669 to 1674, page 112.

The following is a copy, the orthography being corrected :—

" In the name of God, Amen. The two and twentieth day of December, sixteen hundred and sixty-eight, I, Edmund Greenleaf, being mindful of my own mortality and certainty of death, and uncertainty of the same, and being desirous to settle things in order, being now in good health and perfect memory, do make, appoint and ordain this to be my last will and testament in manner and form following : that is to say— first and principally, I give and bequeath my soul into the hands of my blessed Redeemer, the Lord Jesus, who hath died and gave himself for me, and his blood cleanseth from all sin, and through his righteousness I do only look for justification and salvation ; and do commit my mortal body, after this life is ended, into the dust from whence it was taken, there to be preserved by the power and faithfulness of my Redeemer, Jesus Christ, until the resurrection of the just, and then to be raised up by the same power to immortality and life, where I shall see him as he is, and shall ever be with him ; and in this faith and hope I desire, through his grace nd assistance, to live and die, and at last to be found of him in peace.

" Nextly, my will is, being according to God's will revealed in his word, that we must pay what we owe and live of the rest, unto whose rule the sons of men ought to frame their wills and actions ; therefore, my mind and will is, that my debts shall be truly and justly paid to every man to whom I shall be indebted, by my executors hereafter named.

" And first I do revoke, renounce, frustrate and make void all wills by me formerly made ; and I declare and appoint this to be my last will and testament.

" *Imprimis*—I give unto my son Stephen Greenleaf, and to my daughter Browne, widow, and to my daughter Coffin, to each of them twenty shillings apiece. Item—I give unto my grandchild Elizabeth Hilton, ten pounds. Item—I give unto my grandchild Enoch Greenleaf, five pounds. Item—I give unto my grandchild Sarah Winslow, five pounds, if her father pay me the four pounds he oweth me. Item—I give unto my eldest son's son, James Greenleaf, twenty shillings; and after my funeral expenses, debts and legacies are discharged, I give and bequeath the rest of my estate unto my son Stephen Greenleaf, and to my daughter Elizabeth Browne, and to my daughter Judith Coffin, equally to be divided amongst them and their children. And, further, I desire and appoint my son, Stephen Greenleaf, and Tristram Coffin the executors of this my will, to see it executed and affirmed as near as they can; and I further entreat my cousin, Thomas Moon, mariner, to see to the performance of this my will.

"In witness whereof I have hereunto set my hand and seal, this twenty-fifth day of December, 1668.

(Signed) EDMUND GREENLEAF.   L. S.

"Signed, sealed, published, and declared to be my last will in the presence of us,

"GEORGE RUGGELL,
"JOHN FURNISIDE."

The inventory of Mr. Greenleaf's estate, which was appended to the will, amounted to £131-5-9.

The following paper is also recorded in the "Probate Records," appended to the will, as, probably, assigning the reason why the name of his second wife, who appears to have outlived him, was not mentioned:—

"When I married my wife, I kept her grandchild, as I best remember, three years to schooling, diet and apparel; and William Hill, her son, had a bond of six pounds a year, whereof I received no more than a barrel of pork of £3-0-0 of that £6-0-0 a year he was to pay me, and sent to her son Ignatius Hill, to the Barbadoes, in mackerel, cider, and bread and pease, as much as come to twenty pounds, and never received one penny of it. His aunt gave to the three brothers £50 apiece. I know not whether they received it or no; but I have not received any part of it.

"Witness my hand. (Signed) Edmund Greenleaf."

"Besides, when I married my wife, she brought me a silver bowl, a silver porringer, and a silver spoon. She lent or gave them to her son, James Hill, without my consent."

NOTE.—In reading the personal sketches of some of our early ancestors it will be observed that little is said of individual characteristics, personal appearance, etc. Search has been made in vain for such accounts concerning Edmund Greenleaf and some others. Could we have found in these early days some such biographical material and correspond. ence as appears in our time it would have been more satisfying. We want to know more in detail, more of the life of those who so earnestly wrought out our early history, and gave form to our destinies,—an insight to their chief characteristics,—and to follow them, with the mind's eye, through all the vicissitudes of their life; to be with them in their storm and sunshine; that we may the better realize their trials, adversities, and joys, and catch at least a glimpse of the experiences of their sympathies and affections.

The Dole Family. There seems to be good evidence that Dole, as a family name, is of French origin, introduced like many others into England by the Norman Conquest. It is supposed to have been derived from the ancient city of Dole, and it is found early written in some instances with the particle *de* before it.

Richard Dole, the first American ancestor, was baptized in Ring-worthy, near Bristol, Eng., Dec. 31, 1622. It was the residence of his grandfather, Richard, and his father, William. He came to Newbury in 1639. He married Hannah Rolfe, May 3, 1647, who died Nov. 16, 1678. His second wife was Hannah, widow of Capt. Samuel Brocklebank, of Rowley, Mass., whom he married March 4, 1679. His third wife was Patience Walker, of Haverhill, Mass.

Richard Dole (Richard[1]), b. Sept. 6, 1650, lived near his father, in Newbury, Mass., on the north bank of the river Parker, just below the Oldtown bridge. He married Sarah, daughter of Capt. Stephen Greenleaf.

1. **Elizabeth Greenleaf**, daughter of Edmund, b. about 1622, m. in 1642, Giles Badger, of Newbury, Mass., and had one son, John, b. June 30, 1643. This John was twice married. By his second wife, Hannah Swett, he had a son, Nathaniel, who removed to Norwich, Conn., and was the ancestor of Rev. Milton Badger, D.D., Corresponding Secretary of the American Home Missionary Society. Giles Badger d. July 10, 1647, and on Feb. 16, 1648, his widow married Richard Browne, by whom she had five children, and was again left a widow in 1661, and as such is mentioned in her father's will as his daughter Browne, widow. She resided in Newbury.

1. **Judith Greenleaf**, daughter of Edmund, b. Sept. 2, 1625, was married first to Henry Somerby, a merchant tailor of Newbury, by whom she had four children. Mr. Somerby was descended from Henry Somer-by, of Little Bytham, County Lincoln, England, who d. in 1609, leaving two daughters and one son Richard, who inherited his father's estate. Richard died March, 1639, leaving two sons, Anthony and Henry, who in that year, 1639, sailed from England in ship "Jonathan," landed at Boston, thence went to Newbury, where they purchased dwellings, and soon after erected some more commodious.

Of the children of Judith Greenleaf and Henry Somerby, Elizabeth, born November, 1646, married Nathaniel Clarke, of Newbury. Their son Henry Clarke married, Nov. 7, 1695, first Elizabeth, born Jan. 12, 1679 [daughter of Stephen Greenleaf, born Aug. 15, 1652, and Elizabeth (Gerrish) son of Stephen Greenleaf, Sr., and Elizabeth (Coffin)], and second Mary Pierce. Mercy Clarke, born Dec. 26, 1714, and daughter of Henry Clarke and Mary Pierce, married Jonathan Longfellow, Oct. 28, 1731. Their daughter, Sarah Longfellow, born Nov. 16, 1737, married Gen. Joseph Cilley, of Nottingham, N. H. Their daughter, Sarah Cilley, married Thomas Bartlett, of Nottingham, and their son Greenleaf married Jennie Nealley. Of the children of Sarah (Cilley) and Thomas Bartlett, was David, the father of Greenleaf Cilley Bartlett, who was the oldest practicing member of the Rockingham, N. H., Bar, and had long been its Secretary. Thomas Bartlett was the son of Samuel, who was son of Richard, who was son of Richard, who settled in Newbury, 1635. He died May 25, 1647.

Mr. Somerby died in 1652, and on March 2d, the next year, Mrs. Somerby married Tristram Coffin, Jr., who had been an apprentice to her first husband. By this marriage she had ten children, who are the ancestors of the Coffins in New England. Mrs. Coffin died in Newbury, Dec. 15, 1705. Tristram Coffin, Jr., was born in 1632, lived in Newbury, and was a merchant tailor. Further reference to the Coffin family will be found in the personal history of Stephen Greenleaf.

A gravestone in the burial ground at Oldtown, Newbury, has this inscription. It will be noticed that the date is at variance with other records : —

"To the memory of Mrs. Judith, late virtuous wife of Deacon Tristram Coffin, Esq., who having lived to see one hundred and seventy-seven of her children and children's children to the third generation, died Dec. 13, 1705, æ. 80."

"Grave, sober, faithful, fruitful vine was she,
A rare example of true piety;
Widowed awhile she waited, wished for rest,
With her dear husband in her Saviour's breast."

2. Enoch Greenleaf, son of Edmund, was b. about 1617 in Ipswich, Eng., and afterwards lived in the city of York, Eng. He was a silk dyer, and was a lieutenant under Oliver Cromwell. It appears by the Town Records that " Among the original settlers of Salisbury, Conn : No. 58 was Enoch Greenleaf. The whole number of settlers was 68, 3d day 12mo 1650 (Signed) Thomas Bradbury Recorder;" by which it would appear that he may have left the army of Cromwell after the battle of Dunbar (Sept. 4, 1650), going first to Salisbury, Conn., and afterwards to Boston, Mass., where his father and family were settled.

His father gave him a farm in Malden, in 1663, and he probably resided there many years, at least until the death of his father, in Boston, in 1671, when he probably succeeded him in business as hosier and dyer in that town.

The deed of the farm above referred to is recorded with Middlesex Deeds, Vol. VIII. p. 2, and reads as follows :—

"To all Christian people to whom these presents shall call to me, *Edmund Greenleafe* of Boston, in the County of Suffolk in New England, Dyer, sends greeting : Know ye that the said *Edmund Greenleafe*, for diverse good reasons and considerations him hereunto moveing, as the secureing the payment of twenty-five pounds in current New England silver, once within ten days by Enoch Greenleafe his Sonne. As also and more especially for and in consideration of the natural affection and love that he beareth unto the said Enock Greenleafe, and for his, and his wife and children better and more comfortably to maintain and support for the present and in after times, Hath absolutely given, granted, bargained, sold, aliened, enfeffed and confirmed, and by these presents doth absolutely give, grant, bargain, sell, alien, enfeff and confirm unto his Sonne Enock Greenleafe, for and during his natural life, and to Mary his now wife for and during her natural life, and to the heirs of their two bodies forever, the oldest sonne only to have a double portion; in all that his house and lands lying and being in Malden, in the county of Middlesex, which was lately the house and land of William Luddington, containing by estimation forty six acres in uplands, swamps and meadow ground, together with the new house erected thereupon, with all the out-houses,

orchards, garden, back side, fence and trees, with all the liberties and
privileges and appurtenances thereunto belonging, or in any wise apper-
taining,—

[The habendum is here omitted]

"And lastly the said Edmund Greenleafe for his said sonnes present
subsistence doth give, and hereby absolutely grant and deliver freely unto
his said sonnes possession and disseise, his two oxen, and mare, and one
sow going on the above granted premises to and for his the said Enock's
own proper use and benefit forever.

"In witness whereof the said Edmund Greenleafe hath hereunto set
his hand and seal this tenth day of July 1663, being the fiveteenth year of
the Reign of our Sovereign Lord Charles the Second, by the grace of
God of England, Scotland, France and Ireland, defender of the faith, etc.

"Signed *Edmund Greenleafe.*   L. S.

"Signed, sealed and delivered in the presence of us.
"Edward Rawson.
"Returne ———.

"Mr. Edmund Greenleafe appeared before me this 13th day of July
1663, and acknowledged this deed to be his act and deed.

"Jno. Endicott, Govr."

An interesting incident connected with the name of a daughter of
Enoch Greenleaf may be mentioned. A particular friend and companion
in arms with Lieutenant Greenleaf was Major Rooksby. At the battle of
Dunbar, in Scotland, Sept. 4, 1650, Cromwell routed the Royalists, and
in his letter to Parliament, says, "Not one commissioned officer was slain
save one Cornet and Major Rooksby, since dead of his wounds."

May we not very reasonably suppose that after the death of his
friend, he should name his daughter for him?

A mortgage deed of the Malden farm which his father gave him is
recorded with Middlesex Deeds, Vol. VIII. p. 425, dated 1683. He therein
styles himself "Silk-dyer of Boston." His wife, Mary, signs the deed, and
four of their children are mentioned in it; viz., Enoch, Jr., Joseph, Ruth,
and Rooksby.

4. Enoch[3] Greenleat, b. 1647, in England, son of Enoch[2] and
Mary, came with his father when he was quite young to America, and
settled in Malden. He married first Bethiah Woodman, who died in
1678, age 28, and Aug. 29, 1679, married Catherine Truesdale.

Enoch Greenleaf, Jr., is mentioned as saddler, 1693, in N. E. Hist.
and Geneal. Register, Vol. I. p. 38.

His son Joseph[4], b. April 4, 1687, by Catherine, was a distiller in
Boston, and is thus referred to in Mass. Bay Records, Vol. XVIII. p. 487:
"Joseph Greenleaf petitions with Jonathan Prescott, distillers, Boston,
Nov. 3, 1748, for license to retail at their stillhouse."

Enoch[4] Greenleaf, b. Sept. 2, 1686, son of Joseph[3] and Sarah, was
probably the Enoch referred to in Mass. Bay Records, Vol. IX. p. 18:

" 1709 Enoch Greenleaf, saddler, granted £40–17–8, for store sup-
plies;" and in same records, Vol. X. p. 442: "Petition granted Enoch
Greenleaf, Nov. 19, 1719, to open his case in court, vs. Seth Sweetzer,
for recovery of damages by detention of a horse. Suit had been defaulted."

Elizabeth Greenleaf, born 1716, daughter of Enoch, married Thomas
Gerry, an Englishman, shipmaster, who came to Marblehead, Mass., in
early life. Their son, Elbridge Gerry, born at Marblehead, July, 1744,
died Nov. 23, 1814, was Governor of Massachusetts, and Vice President of
the United States. He was named for his mother's great uncle John
Elbridge, Esq., Collector of the Customs at Bristol, England, who is said
to have left an estate of one million pounds sterling, a generous share of
which was bequeathed to some of his New England relatives. He was
educated at Harvard University, the usual honors of which he received in
1762 and 1765, and was a member of the American Academy of Arts and
Sciences. He was one of the envoys extraordinary to the Republic of
France, and was called in the course of his life to fill various other offices
of honor and trust, and was one of the signers of the Declaration of Independence. His remains were interred at Washington, where he closed
his days with the respect due to the high station he held.

Thomas Gerry was commander of a merchant ship for some years,
but finally devoted himself to merchandise in Marblehead, where he
settled when a young man. The children of Thomas and Elizabeth
(Greenleaf) Gerry were [1] Thomas, a merchant, [2] John, [3] Elbridge, [4] Elizabeth, the first wife of Burrill Devereaux, [5] Samuel Russell, who was
collector of the port of Marblehead.

6. Joseph[5] Greenleaf (Chart XXXIX.), b. Nov. 10, 1720, son of
William[4] and Mary (Shattuck), m. Abigail Payne, the daughter of Rev.
Thomas Payne, of Weymouth, Mass., and who afterwards became a
merchant in Boston. The wife of Mr. Payne was Eunice Treat, the
daughter of Rev. Samuel Treat, of Cape Cod. He was the son of
Governor Treat, of Connecticut. This Samuel Treat married Abigail
Willard, the daughter of Rev. Samuel Willard of Groton, Mass., and
afterwards pastor of the Old South Church in Boston. Rev. Samuel
Willard was son of Major Simon Willard, and was born at Concord,
Mass., Jan. 31, 1639–40. Hon. Robert Treat Payne was the son of Rev.
Thomas Payne. He was graduated at Harvard College, 1749; was one
of the signers of the Declaration of Independence, a distinguished lawyer,
Attorney General of the Commonwealth of Massachusetts, a Judge of the
Supreme Court, and a member of the Executive Council. The mother of
the Rev. Thomas Payne was the daughter of Mr. Thatcher, from whose
sister Judith, "Point Judith," a noted point on the south coast of Rhode
Island, takes its name. The tradition is that in former times she with her
father were on board a small vessel which got aground on that point and
came near being wrecked. She rendered great service and the vessel was
saved; in remembrance of this the crew called the point after her name.
The Rev. Thomas Payne was graduated from Harvard College, in 1717. The
children of Rev. Thomas and Eunice (Treat) Payne were [1] Richard,

[2] Robert, [3] Samuel, [4] Emma, [5] Abigail, born March 6, 1725, in Weymouth, Mass.; d. Jan. 15, 1809.

Mr. Joseph Greenleaf was a popular writer and an ardent patriot, and was the author of the "Noble Resolves" passed at a town meeting at Abington, March 10, 1770, which reflected great credit on him. (See Hobart's History of Abington.) He resided at Abington many years, near where the present Townhouse stands. In 1771 he moved to Boston, and frequently wrote for the Massachusetts *Spy*, printed by Isaiah Thomas. Nov. 14, 1771 he wrote an article under the signature of Mucius Scævola, which caused much excitement among the authorities. As they could obtain no satisfaction from Thomas, they summoned Greenleaf, Nov. 16, 1771, to appear before the Governor and Council. He refused to obey the summons, and was deprived of his commission of Justice of the Peace, Dec. 10, 1771. In 1773 he opened a printing office in Hanover Street, where he printed several pamphlets and books. In August, 1774, he published the *Royal American Magazine*. Nov. 22, 1772, he was on "a committee of twenty-one of correspondence, to state the rights of the Colonists, and of this Province in particular." March 9, 1773, one of a committee of five "to consider what is proper to be done to vindicate the town (Boston) from the gross misrepresentations and groundless charges in His Excellency's messages to both houses." May 5, 1773, Sept. 25, 1774, and May 23, 1776, one of a committee of five "to prepare instructions for our representatives in General Assembly." A draught of the latter instruction read on May 30, 1773, at a town meeting, contain these expressions: "The whole United Colonies are upon the verge of a glorious revolution." "Loyalty to him (the King) is now treason to our country." (See Boston Town Records.) It appears that on Aug. 3, 1779, and as late as 1796, he was again a Justice of the Peace at Boston, Mass. By a resolve of the General Court, Feb. 13, 1776, a "Committee of Correspondence, Inspection, and Safety was chosen, of which Joseph Greenleaf was chairman." (New England Geneal. Hist. Reg., Vol. XXX. p. 382.) His will is dated Sept. 15, 1809.

8. Thomas[6] Greenleaf (Chart XL.), b. 1755, son of Joseph[5] and Abigail, was a printer. In 1787 he purchased the *New York Journal* and published it weekly. He also published *The Argus*, or *Greenleaf's New Daily Advertiser*, as a daily. The Washington administration was violently opposed in his paper.

9. Rev. Joseph[8] Greenleaf, b. Nov. 9, 1838, son of Joseph and Emeline Matilda (Riley). Was graduated from Columbia College, 1860; Princeton Theological Seminary, 1863. Settled over Presbyterian Church, Palisades, N. Y., 1863–1866. Pastor Presbyterian Church, Bordentown, N. J., 1866–1871. Pastor Congregational Church, New Canaan, Conn., 1871–1886. Pastor Presbyterian Church, Washingtonville, N. Y., 1886.

3. Stephen[2] Greenleaf, son of Edmund and Sarah, b. about 1628, came to America with his father and resided in Newbury, Mass., until his death, Dec. 1, 1690. In 1651, he married Elizabeth Coffin, the daughter of Tristram and Dionis (Stephens) Coffin, Sr., of Newbury, Mass., by of whom he had ten children. The first of the name in America was Tristram Coffin, who was born in Brixham Parish, town of Plymouth, Devonshire, England, in 1609. He was the son of Peter and Joanna Coffin, and died 1681, æ. 72. Tristram m. Dionis Stevens, and came to New England in 1642, after the death of his father, bringing with him his mother, who died May, 1661, æ. 77, his two sisters, Eunice and Mary, his wife, and also five children, whose names were Peter, Tristram, Elizabeth, James and John. Stephen was born in Newbury, May 11, 1652, and Mary in Haverhill, Feb. 20, 1645. Two children were born in this country. He came first to Salisbury, thence to Haverhill, the same year, thence to Newbury about the year 1648, and in 1654 or '55 he removed to Salisbury, Mass., where he signs his name Tristram Coffin, Commissioner of Salisbury. In the year 1659, Thomas Macy, a name which had been noted in our Colonial annals on account of his persecution for entertaining Quakers in violation of the law of 1657, then a resident of Salisbury, desiring a greater freedom of conscience than he had hitherto been permitted to enjoy among his own people, formed a company for the purchase of the Island of Nantucket,— then inhabited solely by a tribe of Indians. Nantucket had previously been purchased by Thomas Mayhew, Oct. 13, 1641 of James Forrett, agent of Lord Sterling, in New York, who claimed for his principal all the islands lying between Cape Cod and the Hudson River, under the patent granted to him and Sir Ferdinando Gorges, but it had not yet been occupied. Richard Vines, of Saco, also claimed it, but he had bought out his rights. Though the purchase had been made in the winter preceding, the deed was not executed till the 2d of July, 1659.

Thomas Mayhew was a merchant of Watertown. The company formed by Macy consisted of Tristram Coffin, Thomas Macy, Christopher Hussey, Richard Swayne, Thomas Barnard, Peter Coffin, *Stephen Greenleaf*, John Swayne, and William Pike or Pile. To these were afterwards added others, among whom were Tristram, Jr., and James, sons of Tristram Coffin, Sr. There were twenty persons who became the proprietors in equal parts of the Island. The price paid was £30 and two beaver hats. The Island is fourteen miles long, east and west, and three and one-half miles wide.

Tristram Coffin was appointed as the first chief magistrate at Nantucket in 1671. One of the first votes of the town was that there "be a harrow for the use of the inhabitants, and that Mr. Tristram Coffin provide the harrow, and that he and Mr. Thomas Macy be empowered to see that every man sowed seed according to order."

Mr. Coffin's name appears as witness to the Indian deed of Haverhill, Mass., and he is said to have been the first to use the plough in Haverhill.

Mr. Greenleaf was admitted a freeman at Newbury, May 23, 1677. He was a religious man, a member of the First Congregational Church in Newbury, to which he was admitted Dec. 6, 1674. For several years

was Representative of Newbury to the General Court, 1676–86. Was
a member of Council of Safety, 1689. Mr. Greenleaf's will was dated Dec.
25, 1668; will was proved Feb. 12, 1691. (N. E. Geneal. Reg., Vol. X. p.
153.)

June 9, 1677, *Stephen Greenleaf*, in full communion with the church
of Christ at Newbury, Mass.:   " The 22, 3, '77. These may certify the
much honored General Court sitting in Boston the 23d of the 3, '77, that
the p'sons wohse names are underwritten, being in full communion with the
church of Christ in ————, and otherwise qualified according to Law, desire that they may be admitted to the freedom of this Commonwealth."

Stephen Greenleaf, appraiser to will of Benjamin Swett.   His
widow, Hester, administrator.

Stephen Greenleaf, married by Commissioner Dalton, March 31,
1678.—9? (Widow Swett 1678–9.)

12. Capt. Stephen[3] Greenleaf, Jr. (Chart I.), b. August 15, 1652,
son of Stephen,[2] Sr., and Elizabeth (Coffin). Was a prominent man in
public affairs, and famed for his services in the Indian wars. He was
known as the "great Indian fighter"; and while the public records of the
Indian troubles of those days are meagre in their accounts, family tradition has handed down through the generations, and the records bear
evidence of, some of that service, reference to which will be found in the
section of this book relating to military service.

In the town records he was distinguished as Captain Stephen.
Robert Pike thus writes in 1690: " Capt. Pierce, Capt. Noyes, *Capt.
Greenleaf*, and Lieut. Moores, with the rest of the gentlemen of Newbury:—whose assistance, next under God, was the means of the preservation of our towns of Salisbury and Amesbury, in the day of our distress,
by the assaults of the enemy."   In 1675–76 he was one of the selectmen of
Newbury. Aug. 25, 1675, he was wounded by the Indians. In 1689 he
was appointed agent of the State to treat with the Indians at Penacook.

May 18, 1695.—He files a petition for relief, and presents the bill
for professional services of Dr. Humphrey Bradstreet, which reads,
"Bill for curing Capt. Stephen Greenleaf, who was wounded while
moving a family who had been taken from Newbury by the Indians,
£12–6–9."

March 1, 1696.—The town granted to Stephen Greenleaf four or
five rods on the flats, from Watt's cellar spring to Ensign Greenleaf's and
Mr. Davidson's grant, from high-water mark to low-water mark, to build
a wharf and a place to build vessels upon on certain conditions; one was
that it come not within ten or twelve feet of the spring. On the 5th of
March, 1696, Captain Greenleaf addressed the following petition to the
General Court: " The petition of Capt. Greenleaf, of Newbury, Humbly
Showeth: That upon the Seventh of October last, about three o'clock in
the afternoon, a party of Indians surprised a family at Turkey Hill in
said town, captured nine persons, women and children, rifled the house,
carrying away bedding and dry goods. Only one person escaped, and
gave notice to the next family, and they the town; upon the alarm

Captain Stephen[3] Greenleaf.

Born August 15, 1652. From portrait taken 1722.

your petitioner with a party of men pursued after the enemy, endeavoring to line the river Merrimac to prevent their passage, by which means the captives were recovered and brought back. The enemy lay in a gully hard by the roadway, and about nine at night made a shot at your petitioner, and shot him through the wrist, between the bones, and also made a large wound in his side, which would have been very painful and costly to your petitioner in the cure of them, and have in a great measure utterly taken away the use of his left hand, and wholly taken off from his employment this winter. Your petitioner therefore honorably prays this honorable court that they would make him such compensation as shall seem fit; which he shall thankfully acknowledge, and doubts not but will be an encouragement to others, and possibly to relieve their neighbors when assaulted by so barbarous an enemy. And your petitioner shall ever pray. (Signed) Stephen Greenleaf."

March 6.—Read and voted that there be paid out of the province treasury to the petitioner the sum of forty pounds.

The first grandchild of Tristam Coffin was Stephen Greenleaf, who was born Aug. 15, 1652. He well remembered his great-grandmother, and lived to see his great-grandchildren, and transmitted the following account of the increase of the family at two different periods, from August, 1652, to August, 1722, and from August, 1722, to May, 1728; a period of five years and nine months, reckoning only children by blood.

The first column shows the number who were born before August, 1722, the second the number then living; the third the number which had been added between August, 1722, and May, 1728; the fourth, the number living in May, 1728. The whole number of his descendants which were born between 1652 and 1728 was 1582, of which 1128 were living in May, 1728:—

	1722		1728	
Peter	118	83	50	102
Tristam	319	225	127	336
Elizabeth Greenleaf	251	206	89	259
James	187	162	106	241
Mary Starbuck	119	90	36	117
John	64	52	17	69
Stephen	19	53	19	64
	1138	871	444	1128
	444			
	1582			

3. **Elizabeth Greenleaf,** daughter of Stephen and Elizabeth (Coffin), b. April 5, 1660, m. Col. Thomas Noyes. She was his second wife, the first being Martha, daughter of Daniel and Sarah Pierce.

Daniel Pierce, blacksmith, founder of the Pierce family of Newbury, Mass., and Portsmouth, N. H., came from Ipswich, England, 1634, in ship "Elizabeth." He was aged 25, and was made freeman May 2, 1638. He removed from Watertown to Newbury in the same year. Dan-

iel and Sarah Pierce had ¹Daniel, ²Joshua, ⁸Martha, born in Newbury,
Mass., Feb. 14, 1648-9, married Col. Thomas Noyes, of Newbury, Dec.
28, 1669. She died Sept. 3, 1674. Her husband married Elizabeth Greenleaf, Sept. 24, 1677, and they had eight children.

The Newbury town records show Sarah Pierce was there married
Aug. 24, 1659, to Caleb Moody, son of William, the first of that family in
Newbury.

There cannot be much doubt that Sarah, the wife of Caleb Moody,
was a daughter of Daniel and Sarah Pierce, and that she was born in
Watertown, Mass.

December 1, 1686. Capt. Daniel Pierce and Stephen Greenleaf, Sr.,
were added to the deacons, as Overseers of the Poor.

13. John³ Greenleaf, son of Stephen and Elizabeth (Coffin), b.
June 21, 1662, resided in Newbury until his death. He was admitted to
the First Congregational Church in Newbury, with his first wife, Elizabeth Hills, on Jan. 31, 1696. He was buried near the north corner of the
" Oldtown " meetinghouse. The house of worship occupying that site
in 1854, probably covers the grave.

NOTE. There were three John Greenleafs living in Newbury at the same time, viz.:
John, Senior, the son of Stephen; John, Junior, the son of Samuel, and nephew of John,
Senior; John, third, the son of John, Senior; and they are thus distinguished in the New-
bury records. John, Senior, is sometimes called " Quartermaster John."

14. Samuel³ Greenleaf (Chart II.), son of Stephen and Elizabeth
(Coffin), b. Oct. 30, 1665, resided in Newbury, Mass., and married Sarah
Kent, the daughter of John Kent, Jr., and Sarah (Woodman), and grand-
daughter of James Kent, who with his brother Richard owned Kent's
Island and much land in Oldtown, and were men of great local impor-
tance. Their father was Richard.

26. Stephen⁴ Greenleaf (Chart II.), son of John, Senior, and
Elizabeth (Hills), b. Oct. 6, 1704. Resided in Boston on what is now
Washington Street (then Newbury Street), a little south of the Lamb
Tavern, where he died Dec. 22, 1765. His remains lie in the tomb of
Mr. Wallis, near the north corner of Park Street Church. He had eleven
children. Of the five children who married, Thomas married the Widow
Harris, whose son by her first marriage was the Rev. Dr. Harris, of
Dorchester. John, another son, run the first stage from Boston to Ports-
mouth. Eunice married Samuel Franklin, of Boston. She left a daugh-
ter Hannah, and she married Samuel Emmons, of Boston. They resided
in Elliot Street.

17. Rev. Daniel⁴ Greenleaf, son of Captain Stephen³ and Elizabeth (Gerrish), was born in Newbury, Mass., Feb. 10, 1679-80. He was
graduated at Harvard College in 1699, and for about six years practiced
medicine in Cambridge, Mass., where he married Elizabeth, the daughter
of Samuel and Mary Gooking. About the year 1706 he commenced

Rev. Daniel[4] Greenleaf.

From portrait by Copley.

preaching, and in 1708 was ordained pastor of the Congregational Church in Yarmouth, Mass., succeeding the Rev. John Cotton* as minister, where he remained nearly twenty years. Some difficulties arising, he resigned his charge in 1727, and removed to Boston. His wife had taken her family of twelve children long before to Boston, an interesting account of which appears in a letter from his great-grandchild, Mrs. Elizabeth L. Sewall, wife of General Sewall, of Augusta, Me., written April 12, 1847, to Hon. Simon Greenleaf, of Harvard College, Cambridge, which is as follows :—

" My mother has often told me his wife, with 12 children, went to Boston, where, having some knowledge of medicine, from her father's being a physician, she opened an apothecary and grocer's shop, and thus supported her family and educated her eldest son at college. Mr. Greenleaf remained for a time with a remnant of his charge who were strongly attached to him, but finally, I believe, the majority quarrelled him away. I well recalled hearing my mother often say that at this juncture they brought an accusation against him 'that he talked of worldly matters on the Sabbath'; the worldly matters were that in the course of one Sabbath he received a letter from his wife, saying their eldest son appeared at the point of death with small-pox, and that unless he came on immediately he would not probably find him living. The good pastor was too poor to own a horse, and after the second service requested the loan of one from one of his deacons, that he might set off soon after midnight for Boston. He found the boy living, and he lived to be upwards of ninety (90) years old. I well recollect, when a child, hearing this case narrated by my mother, and thinking her grandfather must have been a very good man. He afterwards removed to Boston, and joined his family, many of whom married very young. My grandmother married a gentleman just established in the mercantile line, and he afterwards became very prosperous and very benevolent. She was but fifteen when she became mistress of a family.

" The good man (whose portrait † awaits your acceptance) was in the habit of going around once a week to see all his married children who were settled in Boston, and not very remote from his own mansion. On one of these occasions when coming out of the last house he fell, and so injured his back that he never rose from his bed after being put into it, but was confined two years, only being moved by his sons and sons-in-law from one bed to another on a sheet. This duty was performed when they assembled in the evening, after the business of the day was over. I have often heard my mother say how many pleasant hours she passed in her grandfather's sick chamber; he was always so cheerful and so in-

---

* Rev. John Cotton was brother of Rev. Roland, of Sandwich, and son of the Rev. John of Plymouth, who was son of Rev. John of Boston, who had been the minister in Boston, England, and came over in 1633.

† The portrait referred to in the letter above quoted descended to Rev. Patrick Henry Greenleaf, D.D., son of the Hon. Simon Greenleaf, and was by him presented to Mary Elizabeth, wife of his son, James Edward Greenleaf, and is now in her possession at the family home in Charlestown, Mass.

structive, it was a privilege to be near him; and she would likewise mention he read the Scriptures, and his devotional exercises in the family. At this time his wife had become totally blind, therefore the care and expenses of the family devolved on the children."

In the proceedings of the Massachusetts Historical Society, as reported in Vol. X., appears the following :—

List of principal manuscripts belonging to the Society, "Commendium Physical," by Charles Morton, of which there are four copies (manuscript) transcribed respectively by John Webb in 1677, *Daniel Greenleaf*, 1697.

By the Records of Massachusetts Bay, Vol. VIII. p. 124, it appears that on Friday, June 8, 1705, the Legislature passed an order allowing Rev. Daniel Greenleaf £6 for support to the present year, " and as the greater part of the Isles of Shoals belonged to the Province of New Hampshire, they were expected to supply the balance of his salary as minister, £14, to be paid from the public treasury." The allowance of £6 to be paid probably by the people of the Isle of Shoals, he being settled there as minister.

In the same records, Vol. XIII., we find he petitions to get his salary paid from October, 1723 to October, 1726, at the rate of £80 silver money 15 pennyweight, or £120 in Province Bills. Before the Legislature, Monday, Aug. 21, 1727.

The Shop was in what is now Washington Street, between Court and Cornhill, Boston, very near the old bookstore of Crocker & Brewster, which was near the corner of Court and Washington, where now stands the Ames Building. Here Mr. Greenleaf resided until his death, which took place suddenly on Aug. 26, 1763, at the age of eighty-three years. He was buried near the stone chapel on Tremont Street.

Elizabeth Gooking, wife of Rev. Daniel Greenleaf, came from distinguished stock in New England, an extended notice of which will be interesting to her descendants and others.

As has frequently occurred with modern surnames, the name Gooking appears to have undergone a number of transformations. In Harris' " History of the County of Kent, London, 1729," the following various spellings appear indexed as Gooking; viz., Cockayne, Cockoyn, Cokain, Cokin, Calkin, Gockin, Gokin, Gookin, and Gooking. Capt. John Smith, who evidently knew General Gooking's father, calls him Gockin and Gookin General Gooking's great grandfather spelled it Gokin. Burke, " Burke's Commoners," writes it Gookin to this day, while General Gooking's descendants write it Gooking, and General Gooking wrote it Gookin. It would seem that the name tallied originally with the coat of arms or device of the family, and coat armor is quite certain.

By the family record in the College of Heralds in the British Museum, being as far back as Arnoldus, great-great-grandfather of General Gooking, it is well settled that the family came originally, as far as known, from the city of Canterbury. They were proprietors of Worthgate in that city. William Gooking lived there in King John's reign

(1199-1206). He founded a hospital there, and was a prominent benefactor to other hospitals.

A William Gooking was ballivi (chief magistrate) of Canterbury in 1250 and in 1267, and Edmundus Gooking was also in 1358. On removing from Canterbury they built the country seat of Fredville, or Froidville, in the tenth year of King Edward III. Camden, in "Britannia, London, 1695," mentions Ashburn, in Derbyshire, as a town where the Gookings have long flourished.

Arnoldus, the great-great-grandfather of General Gooking, was of Kent County, England, and the heraldic genealogies give neither the name of his wife nor of any of their children but Thomas, the eldest son and heir.

Thomas Gooking was of Brakesbourne, Kent County, England, and married Elizabeth, only child and heiress of —— Durant. Salisbury's Charts, large quarto Volumes, say : "Thomas Goolkyn (or Goolken), Co. Kent, d. 1599, m. Amy Durant, 1st w." I have been unable to get information of any of their children but the eldest son and heir, John.

John Gooking was of Ripple Court, Kent County, England. He married Katharine Denne, daughter of G. and Agnes (Tufton) Denne, his wife. G. Denne was of the eleventh generation from Sir Allured Denne, Kt., Seneschal of the Priory of Christ Church. Sir Allured was son of William Denne, of East Kent, who was living in the time of King John. William Denne was son of Ralph de Denne, 20th from William the Conqueror, Lord of Buckhurst, Sussex, Kent, and Normandy, in the time of Edward the Confessor (V. Berry's "Kent Genealogies").

Agnes Tufton was daughter of Nicholas Tufton, and she died in 1588 at Brakesbourne, where John Gooking lived at that time. The children of John and Katharine Gooking were four; viz., Anna, John, Daniel, and Vincent, and of the first two I have been able to learn nothing but their names. The two younger sons (the younger of whom became Sir Vincent Gooking) married in England and emigrated to Carygoline, Ireland, from whence Daniel with his family returned to England, and in 1621 emigrated to Virginia, where he arrived November 22 (V. Capt. John Smith's " General Historie ") (Lord i. " Lempriere," 145). He brought with him, at his own expense, fifty men, with many or all of whom he had made a contract to provide for them. (Capt. John Smith calls them "his own men.") He settled at Newport News, Va., and I have been unable to learn of any of his family save his son, Daniel, who subsequently became General Gooking.

When the Indian troubles arose in Virginia, and the planters with their people were warned to fly for protection, Daniel Gookin remained at his plantation, or " Lordship," as it was called, and successfully withstood them. In Virginia he was styled Daniel Gookin, Gent.

Dec. 29, 1637, a grant of 2,500 acres in the upper country of Norfolk was made to Daniel Gookin, Esq., and in 1642 he was made Commander of the Military Commission of Upper Norfolk at about the time when a grant of 1,400 acres was made (Nov. 4, 1642) to his son, Daniel, the captain of a "trained band." This grant was on the Rappahannock River, "about thirty-five miles upon the north side."

The name Daniel Gooking is prominently identified with the early history of Virginia and New England, and it appears indubitable that there were two of them—father and son. Many references to a Daniel Gooking, by people of veracity and authority, who seem to have knowledge of the matters spoken of, are incompatible with the idea of a single person. History often repeated and irreproachable is in perfect harmony with the idea of two Daniels, of whom the elder was the prominent and wealthy immigrant and civilian who had been in the Kentish Militia, and the other the captain, magistrate, and general who died in Cambridge.

Certainly General Gooking could not have been in the Kentish Militia, as has so often erroneously been stated of him, for he was but nine years of age when he came to this country with his father; nor could he have been the Virginia immigrant of that time who brought fifty men at his own expense.

The Gookings, father and son, would appear to have considered England their home for quite a long period after emigration, as General Gooking, in 1639, styled himself Daniel Gookin, Gent., of St. Sepulchre Parish, London.

The earliest mention of the age of General Gookin which I have been able to find, is that given at his marriage license in November, 1639, as twenty-seven years, which would fix his birth in 1612, and this agrees with the record of his tombstone, which tells us that he was seventy-five years old in 1687. He died March 19, 1687. Though a mere child when he accompanied his father to this country in 1621, he went to England for his wife, and Nov. 11, 1639 he was granted a marriage license by the Bishop of London, to marry Mary Dolling, aged twenty-one, orphan spinster, of St. Dunstan in the west. He evidently returned immediately to this country, for in 1642 the grant of land to him was made, as already stated.

As a result of the preaching of the missionaries who had been sent from New England to Virginia in 1642 and 1643, he became converted, and was induced to come to New England, perhaps the more easily because of the troubles in Virginia which arose in consequence of the civil wars in England. Cotton Mather's " Magnolia," a prolific source of historic and genealogical errors, speaks of him as one of the constellations of converts made by the labors of Rev. William Tompson, who went from New England to Virginia in 1643 :—

> " Gookins was one of these: by Tompson's pains,
> Christ and New England a dear Gookins gains."

He purchased a ship from the Governor of Virginia, and with his family (wife and daughter Mary) and some others, he arrived at Boston May 10, 1644. He was admitted to membership in the Boston church May 16, 1644, and on May 19th was honored with the freedom of the colony. Such favors were rarely granted to persons of so short a residence, and this was probably intended as an acknowledgment of his kindness to the New England missionaries in Virginia. He was admitted a freeman in 1644, and in the same year was made captain in the Middlesex regiment. "At the General Court of Election held at Boston, the 3d of May, 1676, Capt. Daniel Gookin was by the whole Court chosen and appointed to be Sargant-Major of the Regiment of Middlesex." From his arrival he was prominently identified with the history of the colony, and enjoyed many of its honors. He appears to have settled at first in Roxbury, where two of his children, Elizabeth and Hannah, were born. He became a member of the Artillery Company in 1645. He removed to Cambridge in 1648, and on September 3d of that year was dismissed from the Boston church to the church in Cambridge. In 1649 he was chosen Representative from Cambridge, and again in 1651, in which latter year he was Speaker of the House. In 1652 he was a Magistrate and assistant to the Governor of Massachusetts Colony, and is said to have retained these positions until 1686,—a term of thirty-five years. He was of the High Republican party in politics, and stood firm to the old charter,—unwilling to yield the rights and liberties of the people when they were required to do this by the arbitrary measures of Charles II. Sewalls' Diary* thus speaks of him :—

"Daniel Gookin was a man of noble soul, of many virtues, especially those which are hardest to acquire and to practice, and his life was devoted to ends of public service." He was as conspicuous for his piety as for his morals. He was friendly to Cromwell, whom he went to visit in 1656. Cromwell employed him to persuade the inhabitants of Massachusetts to remove and settle the Island of Jamaica, which had lately been taken from the Spaniards; but in this he met with no success. He was in sympathy with the party of the Regicides, and because of his secreting, sheltering, and protecting two of the judges who had condemned Charles I., viz., Gen. Edward Whalley and Col. William Goffe, complaint was made against the Colony by the Royal Commissioners.† In 1662 he was appointed one of the licensers of the printing press in Cambridge, and in 1663 he was appointed a Public Censor of printing. Prior to 1675 he had been the Superintendent of all the Indians who had submitted to the Provincial Government, and knew more about them than all the other magistrates. He was Eliot's most trusted friend and helper in his work. What he wrote about the efforts in behalf of the Indians is of the highest value. May 11, 1681, he was elected Major General of all the military forces of the Colony. He was the last Major General under the old charter. This post of honor was continued under the charter of William and Mary.

The previous Major Generals had been Dudley, Endicott, Gibbons, Sedgwick, Atherton, Dennison and Leverett. He appears very respectably as an author. His work entitled "Historical Collections of the Indians of New England," by Daniel Gookin, Gentleman, is published in the first volume of the collections of the Massachusetts Historical Society. He died poor,—an old man whose days had been filled with usefulness. He died about five or six o'clock A. M., March 19, 1687. Of his wife, Mary Dolling, I have been able to learn but little. I find in my notes a

*Page 170, footnote; editorial comments.

† Drake, "History of Boston."

statement, the authority for which is not given, that she died after Oct. 4, 1681. Nor have I been able to learn the date of his marriage to his second wife, Mrs. Hannah (Tyng) Savage, widow of Habijah Savage, whose will was made in 1675, as he was going with his command to King Philip's war. She, Hannah Tyng, was born March 7, 1640, first child of Edward Tyng and his wife. She was married to Habijah Savage, May 8, 1661, and she died Oct. 28, 1689.

The children of General Gooking and his first wife Mary were: [1] Mary, born in Virginia, married June 8, 1670, Edmund Batter. [2] Elizabeth, born in Roxbury, March 14, 1645, baptized March 30, 1645, married May 23, 1666, Rev. John Elliot, Jr., died Nov. 30, 1700. [3] Hannah, born in Roxbury, baptized May 9, 1647, died July 31, 1647. [4] Daniel, born in Cambridge, April 8, 1649, died Sept. 3, 1649. [5] Daniel, born in Cambridge, July 12, 1650; Harvard, 1669; married Mary ———; remarried Sept. 28, 1708, Mrs. Hannah Biscoe, died Jan. 8, 1718. [6] Samuel, born in Cambridge, April 22, 1652, died Sept. 16, 1730. [7] Solomon, born in Cambridge, June 20, 1654, died July 16, 1754. [8] Nathaniel, born in Cambridge, Oct. 22, 1656; Harvard, 1675; married Hannah Savage, stepmother's daughter; died Aug. 7, 1692.

By his second wife, Hannah (Tyng) Savage, he is said to have had a daughter Hannah; but I am compelled to doubt this, as Mrs. Savage had a daughter Hannah when he married her, and as this Hannah afterwards became the wife of Rev. Nathaniel Gooking.

Samuel Gooking, third son of General Daniel, and father of Elizabeth, wife of Rev. Daniel Greenleaf, was born as stated, April 22, 1652. He inherited his father's military spirit, and was a captain as early as 1692. He was active in raising troops for the expedition to Canada in 1711. He was Sheriff in 1689, and Marshal General March 5, 1691. He held this office for a time in Suffolk, and was appointed to the same office in Middlesex, which he held until July 27, 1729, except for the period from December, 1715, to July, 1717. His first wife was Mary ———. They had five children: [1] Mary, born Aug. 26, 1679, thrice married: (1) married Dr. Samuel Gedney; (2) married Rev. Theophilus Cotton, July 16, 1711; (3) married ——— Newmarch. Children, [2] Elizabeth, born Nov. 11, 1681, married Rev. Daniel Greenleaf, Nov. 18, 1701. [3] Samuel, born Aug. 14, 1683. [4] Nathaniel, born Feb. 16, 1685, died young. [5] Daniel.

His wife Mary died subsequent to April 29, 1707, and Sept. 28, 1708, he was remarried to Mrs. Hannah Biscoe, widow of Thomas Biscoe. He died Sept. 16, 1730.

19. Stephen[4] Greenleaf (Chart II.), son of Captain Stephen[3] and Elizabeth (Gerrish). Was born in Newbury, Mass., Oct. 21, 1690, and resided there until after his marriage and the birth of four sons; viz., Enoch, Richard, Samuel, and Ebenezer. The records of the town of York, Me. (incorporated 1639), give the following: " Stephen Greenleaf, his children, born in York, of his wife Mary. Lydia, born May 3, 1722; Stephen, born Feb. 27, 1724-25; Joseph, born July 2, 1727; Mary, born Feb. 17, 1730-31."

It has been supposed that Stephen removed to Woolwich from Newbury about the year 1720, but it now appears he had intermediate residence between Newbury and Woolwich. In 1720 but slight beginnings
had been made in the settlement of the district; the Indian War soon
began and drove out, it is said, every one who had entered. It would
appear that he removed first to York, Me., from Massachusetts, probably
about 1720-21, then farther east to Falmouth, about 1731, as by the
records there we find :—

"Stephen Greenleaf, Mariner, York," bought lot and house in
present Portland in 1731. "Stephen Greenleaf, Pound Keeper," Back
Cove, Falmouth, March 26, 1734. "Stephen Greenleaf, of Falmouth, and
Mary, wife, sells title in Mill Stream and Mills in Falmouth," in 1736.
Stephen Greenleaf had conveyance of his land in June, 1738, in Woolwich. "Stephen Greenleaf paid for killing a Wild-cat," May 1, 1743.
Richard Greenleaf, his son, sells part of the same, "improved and possessed twenty-nine years last past," in 1767. It also appears upon the
records that "Stephen Greenleaf, York, Coaster," *et al.*, bought a right
in land in Monsweag Bay, in 1729, including the tract in which he afterwards lived. Land conveyances being accepted, under conditions, as evidence of residence, it would appear that 1738 was the time of his taking
up his residence in Monsweag (Woolwich).

25. **Benjamin⁴ Greenleaf** (Chart II.), b. Nov. 21, 1701, son of
John,³ Sr., and Elizabeth (Hills), died in Newburyport in 1783, at the age
of eighty-two, having been a Representative in the Legislature, and otherwise repeatedly honored with marks of the public confidence. July 8,
1741—May 31, 1749, Representative from Newbury, Mass.

37. **Dr. Daniel⁵ Greenleaf**, b. Nov. 7, 1702, son of Rev. Daniel⁴
and Elizabeth (Gooking). Was for a number of years a practicing physician at Hingham, Mass., and removed with his family to Boston in 1732.

38. **Hon. Stephen⁵ Greenleaf** (Chart IV.), b. Oct. 4, 1704, son
of Rev. Daniel⁴ and Elizabeth (Gooking). Was graduated at Harvard College in 1723, and received the degree of A.M. from that college, and in
1750 he received the honorary degree of A.M. from Yale College. On
leaving Harvard he went into a store in Boston as a clerk. At an early
age he commenced business on his own account, which he followed successfully for about forty years, and was then largely engaged as an
underwriter, there being no public insurance offices in the country at that
time. His house was in what is now Tremont Street, fronting the common, near where the Masonic Temple stood for many years at the corner
of Tremont Street and Temple Place, and his garden extended to West
Street. At the time of the American Revolution he was holding the
office of Sheriff of the County of Suffolk, under the King. The county
then comprehended what is now Suffolk and Norfolk Counties, together
with Hingham and Hull in the present county of Plymouth.

After Lexington battle, Boston was closely shut up, and Mr. Sheriff Greenleaf, being a Tory, remained there with the British troops, exercising his office only within the lines. The British evacuated Boston in March, 1776, and a new Legislature was chosen in May following.

Stephen Greenleaf was a protester against the Whigs in 1774, and one of the ninety-seven gentlemen and principal inhabitants of the capital who addressed General Gage on his departure, in 1775. He was reported by the Committee of Correspondence as "inimical to the Rights and Privileges of the United States of America," and a request was made for his arrest. His arrest was ordered by the Council of Massachusetts, April, 1776.

After the Declaration of Independence was declared he resigned his office, and keeping himself quiet, lived unmolested in Boston till his death, which took place in January, 1795, at the age of 91.

38. Abigail Greenleaf (Chart V.), b. Sept. 18, 1743. Daughter of Hon. Stephen and Mary (Gould), married Judge Howard, of the Supreme Court of South Carolina. During the war they went to England, where he died. Mrs. Howard returned to Boston, and lived with her father until his death. She had no children, and when she died she bequeathed a valuable collection of books to the "Boston Library," and a considerable amount of property to Trinity Church, making Bishop Parker her executor and trustee.

39. Dr. John[5] Greenleaf (Chart IV.), b. Nov. 8, 1717, son of Rev. Daniel[4] and Elizabeth (Gooking). Was bred a druggist, and bore the title usually of "Doctor," though he was not a practicing physician. He resided in Boston, where he died Aug. 27, 1778, and was buried, as is supposed, in a vault under Brattle Street Church. His name was cut in the stone on the south side of the church, fronting on Brattle Street.

April 15, 1756. Petitions for a share in the furnishing of medicines for the army. (Military Rec., Vol. LXXV. p. 499.)

40. Hon. William[5] Greenleaf (Chart IV.), b. Jan. 10, 1725, son of Rev. Daniel[4] and Elizabeth (Gooking). Was bred a merchant, and for many years resided on Hanover Street in Boston. He was a stanch Whig and active in the Revolution, and was one of the commission of seven chosen secretly at town meeting held in Boston, Nov. 2, 1772, to correspond with men in the other colonies in regard to measures to be pursued. That committee often met at his house. One of the number was Benjamin Greenleaf, of Newbury; another of that committee was Dr. Nathaniel Appleton. This committee undertook what was decidedly the most hazardous part of the Revolution : their lives were not only in each others' hands, but at the mercy and discretion of utter strangers throughout the colonies. They signed a bond in the most emphatic language, never in any emergency, even unto death, to betray each other or the cause.

Hon. William[5] Greenleaf.

From portrait by Blackburn.

Mary Brown.
Wife of Hon. William⁵ Greenleaf.

From portrait by Blackburn.

The prize brig "Medway," taken by the ship "Oliver Cromwell," was sold by *William Greenleaf*, for £3501-13, May, 1777. Sale of the prize brig "Anna," and her cargo, for the State of Connecticut, taken by Captain Smedley. The account rendered June 3, 1777, by *William Greenleaf*, £2635-9-7. "John Bradford's account against Connecticut for sale of four sixteenths of the proceeds of property sold by him of prizes taken by the 'Defense.' . . . . . By proportion of sundries sold by *William Greenleaf* paid to said Bradford, £82-1-4, £1,287-6-1¾."

He was appointed Sheriff of Suffolk by the Governor and Council Oct. 31, 1775, which office he held until the appointment of his successor, Joseph Henderson, Dec. 14, 1780, his elder brother, Stephen, holding the same office under the King. The Congress was then sitting in Watertown, and as Boston was closely shut up at the time, he exercised his office in the other parts of the county out of Boston.

Monday, July 15, 1776.—A committee of the council, consisting of John Winthrop, William Phillips, and Francis Dana, was appointed to take into consideration in "what way, manner, and form the declaration of the honorable Continental Congress should be made public." This committee reported on Wednesday, the 17th, and the council then ordered that "the said declaration be proclaimed by the Sheriff of the County of Suffolk, from the balcony of the Statehouse in Boston, on Thursday next at one o'clock P. M., in presence of, and under direction of, a committee of the council to be appointed for that purpose."

In July, 1776, when Independence was declared, the Sheriff, Mr. William Greenleaf, proclaimed it from the balcony of the Old State House, in State Street, at one o'clock in the afternoon, as appears by the *Continental Journal and Weekly Advertizer*, printed in Boston, July 25, 1776, in the following : "At one o'clock the declaration was proclaimed by the Sheriff of Suffolk, which was received with great joy, expressed by three huzzas from a great concourse of people assembled on the occasion."

Two boys, John Quincy Adams and William Cranch, about eight and ten years of age, wished to hear and see Mr. Greenleaf read the "Declaration of Independence;" much to their delight, two gentlemen raised them on their shoulders. One of the boys afterwards became President of the United States, and the other became Chief Justice of the Circuit Court of the District of Columbia. He married a daughter of Mr. Greenleaf. His son was Christopher Pearse Cranch, the Cambridge poet and painter. After the war, Mr. Greenleaf gave up business in Boston, and removed to New Bedford, Mass., where he died, July 21, 1803. Mr. Greenleaf was a tall, slim man, walking very erect. He dressed usually in a brown, single-breasted coat and cocked hat, after the fashion of those times. He usually carried a gold-headed cane, and wore ruffles in his bosom and on his wrists.

41. Dr. Daniel[6] Greenleaf, Jr. (Chart IV.), b. Sept. 2, 1732, son of Dr. Daniel[5] and Silence (Marsh). Studied medicine, and afterwards went to England, whereon May 5, 1763, he married Anna Burrell. Returning to America he practiced medicine in some part of Worcester County,

Mass., until his death, which took place Jan. 18, 1777. See "Military Service."

Copy of will of *Daniel Greenleaf, Jr.* Probate Records at Worcester, Mass., Vol. XIII. p. 390. "I, Daniel Greenleaf, Jr., of Bolton, in County of Worcester, etc., Physician, being engaged to go into the Continental Service as chief Surgeon in the Regiment, whom Jonathan Smith, Colonel (commanded), considering the vicissitude and danger these persons are exposed to who are engaged in war, especially as the present war is, being of health of body, and sound and perfect mind and memory, etc. To loving wife, Ann Greenleaf, one half real and personal estate except legacies hereinafter mentioned, as long as she remain my widow. And if she marries, use of one third of the real, and one third of the personal, estate forever. To son Daniel £13-6-8, to purchase a Silver Tankard, also my watch and stone ring. To daughter Silence £6-13-4, to purchase a silver Kan. To daughter Eleanor £6-13-4, to purchase a silver Kan. The Real Estate may be sold, if thought best, and the money put out on good security, said money to be equally divided among my three children. Wife to be their guardian so long as she remains my widow. If she marries, Samuel Baker to be guardian. Live stock, husbandry utensils, physical books, medicines, surgery instruments, and chaise may be sold and divided. To Ann Burrell, my wife's daughter, £6-13-4, to purchase for her a piece of plate as she shall choose. Other books to be divided between my wife and children, etc.

Witnessed.   Signed July 22, 1776.
JONATHAN LORING.   Probated March 4, 1777.
ELIZABETH LORING.
THOMAS LORING.

Amount of inventory taken at Bolton, March 1, 1777, £720-5-5."

42. Israel[6] Greenleaf (Chart IV.), b. March 29, 1734, son of Dr. Daniel[5] and Silence (Marsh). Was a farmer, and resided in Bolton for many years. About the year 1791, he removed to New Marlborough, in Berkshire County, Mass., and thence in a few years to Whitestown, in the State of New York; and thence, about the year 1800, he removed to Brookfield in the State of New York, now the town of Columbus, in Chenango County, where he resided until his death, which took place March 4, 1824, at the advanced age of 90 years. He was a very active and business-like man, and accumulated a considerable property. He owned several farms in and about Bolton, while he resided there, and was very successful in some land speculations in the State of New York. He purchased a large tract of land where the City of Utica is built, which he sold at a large advance. He then purchased largely in the town of Rome, which he turned to advantage, and then purchased at Chenango.

In person, Mr. Greenleaf was about six feet in height, very slim, and upright; he had keen blue eyes, rather small. He was rather prematurely bald, and wore a skullcap. In his later life he was a religious man, and was in communion with the Methodist church. When 84 years of age he would mount a spirited horse with as much agility as a boy of sixteen. He delighted much in riding, and generally kept spirited horses.

43. Stephen[6] **Greenleaf** (Chart IV.), b. Oct. 15, 1735, son of Dr. Daniel[5] and Silence (Marsh). Was the fifth child of Dr. Daniel Greenleaf, of Bolton. He married Eunice Fairbanks, of Boston, where he resided until the autumn of 1771, when he removed to Brattleboro, Vt., having purchased a tract of land of about eight hundred acres, then known as "The Governor's Farm," comprehending what is now the whole of the East Village of Brattleboro. Here he built mills, and opened, as is supposed, the first store in Vermont. His dwelling house occupied the present site of the "Phœnix House." The sawmill stood upon land afterwards occupied by the paper mill, and the gristmill was erected upon the spot afterwards used for the machine shop of Hines, Newman, Hunt & Co. That part of the village where the railroad depot is situated was used by Mr. Greenleaf as a goat pasture, Flat Street for a garden, and the rest of the land in the village not covered with forest as a cow pasture. For some time after Mr. Greenleaf moved into the place his was the only family residing within the limits of the village, and there were not more than twenty families in the town. He built the first dwelling house, the first sawmill, and the first gristmill erected in the village.

An old bill of lading found among the papers of his son Stephen, shows how intimately religious feeling mingled with the business transactions of life. Mr. Greenleaf, when living in Boston, was a shipping merchant, and received the following bill of lading, dated Aug. 26, 1767 : "Shipped by the grace of God, in good order, by Stephen Greenleaf, Jr., in the good ship 'Betsey,' whereof is now master, under God, for this voyage, Thomas Robson, now at anchor in the harbor of Boston, and by God's grace bound for London, two bags containing Spanish mills and dollars, etc., etc. And so God send the good ship to her desired port in safety, Amen."

44. David[6] **Greenleaf** (Chart IV.), b. July 13, 1737, in Bolton, Mass., son of Dr. Daniel[5] and Silence (Marsh). Was bred a goldsmith, which business he followed for the most of his life. He married Mary Johnson, of Norwich, Conn., June 2, 1763, daughter of Ebenezer and Deborah (Champion), and it appears their first child, Mary, was born there, and probably the second (David), also. We find he purchased land and dwelling of John Moore, in Lancaster, Mass., Nov. 1, 1769 (Worcester Records), and that he and his wife Mary were in Lancaster, or Bolton, 1769-1770-1771-1772. Jan. 1, 1772, he sells land in Lancaster, with buildings, to Calvin Greenleaf (Worcester Records). Nov. 11, 1772, "David Greenleaf and Mary, his wife, of Bolton, Mass., conveyed to Daniel Greenleaf, Physician, of Bolton, Mass., a parcel of land, with dwelling, situated in Norwich" (Norwich Records). From this, it appears that David and Mary returned to Bolton.

The first record of David's owning land in Coventry, Conn., is in 1778, when he purchased of Daniel Robertson, Jr., land, house, and blacksmith shop. Feb. 28, 1791, he sells this land to his son David, of Hartford, who sells it Jan. 15, 1805, to William and Susanna Lyman, of Coventry (Coventry Records). (See Military Service.)

45. Gen. William⁶ Greenleaf (Chart IV.), b. Aug. 23, 1738, son of Dr. Daniel⁵ and Silence (Marsh). Was bred to the business of a druggist in Boston, where he married Sally, the seventh child of Edmund Quincy. Dorothy, the fifth child, married John Hancock, Governor of Massachusetts. Some years after his marriage he removed to Lancaster, Worcester Co., where he resided until his death. Mr. Greenleaf was much in public life, being Sheriff of the County of Worcester for many years, and a Brigadier General in the militia of the State.

Sept. 8, 1777.—As one of the Selectmen of Lancaster, he makes returns,—under an order for a census of the male citizens of military age (sixteen years old and upward).

Lancaster, Nov. 19, 1781.—On Thursday morning last, a considerable number of the most respectable inhabitants of this place assembled at the Sun Tavern to celebrate the capture of Cornwallis, when, after mutual congratulations on this happy event, the company, conducted by *William Greenleaf*, Esq., formed and marched in procession through the principal streets of the town, preceded by an advance guard, fieldpiece, and band of music, with American colors displayed. Having fired sundry salutes, followed with three huzzas, the company returned to the " Sun," where an elegant dinner was provided for them and such gentlemen from the neighboring towns as were pleased to favor them with their company. After dinner the following toasts were drank, each being followed by a discharge of a fieldpiece with three cheers.—*Massachusetts Spy*, Nov. 22, 1781.

During the exciting times of the Shay Insurrection Col. *William Greenleaf* was sheriff of the county. On Wednesday, the 22d of November, 1786, he had, from the courthouse steps in Worcester, read the riot act and harangued the crowd, an armed mob, there congregated to prevent the sitting of the Court of General Sessions. One of the orators of the insurgents, in reply, took the occasion to state that among many grievances which they found too oppressive for human endurance, and from which they were resolved to have speedy relief, were the sheriff himself and his exhorbitant fees. Colonel Greenleaf coolly rejoined: " If you deem my fees for execution oppressive, gentlemen, you need not wait longer for redress; I will hang you all for nothing, with the greatest pleasure."

An interesting list of official prices current at the close of the second year of the war is found in the Lancaster town records, beautifully engrossed; it is entitled, " Regulating Act, 1777."

The Selectmen and committee for the town of Lancaster having met, agreeable to the order of the General Court, proceeded to set the price of the necessary and convenient articles of life as follows, viz. :—

Here follows a long list, commencing,

	s.	d.
Farming Labor in the Summer Season, June, July, and August, per day		3
September	2–	2
October and November	1–	10

	s. d.
December, January, and February	1– 6
March and April	1–10
May	2– 2

FOOD.

Cheese, good new milk, per pound	6
Butter by the single pound	9
Peas, good and clean, per bushel	6– 8
Beans, per bushel	5– 4
Potatoes, per bushel	1– 6
Mutton and veal, per pound	3
Wheat, flour, manufactured in this State, per hundred .	20
Milk in the winter, per quart	2
Flip made of New England rum, half a pint of rum in a mugg	9
Flip made of West India rum, a mugg	1
Dinner, roast or boiled	1
All other meals in proportion.	

CLOTHING.

Good stockings, men's, yarn, a pair	6
Shoes for women ware, cloth or leather, a pair . .	5– 8
To cutting out a man's coat	10
To ditto jackett and briches	5
Making a man's coat, lined and full trimmed . . .	8
Making a man's jacket with sleeves	3– 6
Making ditto cloth breeches	4
Making ditto buck skin ditto	6

And many other things specified.

Examined and entered by me, *William Greenleaf*, Town Clerk.

Lancaster, Feb. 28, 1777.

47. Hon. Thomas[6] **Greenleaf** (Chart V.), b. in Boston, May 15, 1767, son of Dr. John[5] and Ann (Wroe). Was graduated at Harvard College in 1784, and in 1806 was appointed a Special Justice of the Court of Common Pleas. He was admitted to the Bar in Suffolk County, 1809, and was Representative to the General Court from 1808 to 1820; a member of the Executive (Governor Brooks) Council, 1820 to 1822; and was for twenty-five years or more chosen moderator of town meetings at Quincy. During the progress of rioting known as " Shay's Rebellion," 1786–87, he served in the ranks, and went in pursuit of the rebels. On arrival at Groton the troops were told their services were not needed, as the rebels had already dispersed. (" New England Genealogical Register," Vol. VIII.). His name appears also as serving in the War of 1812. Mr. Greenleaf married Mary D., daughter of Hon. Ezekiel and Ruth (Avery) Price, of Boston. Mr. Price was for many years clerk of the court in Boston.

In Vol. XVIII. pp. 119–123 of the " New England Genealogical Register" may be found a map showing the " Ground Plan " of the old

church at Quincy, Mass., and the pew No. 18 which he occupied. Also
the pew No. 2 of his cousin Daniel, and pew No. 70 of his cousin John
Greenleaf (sons of Hon. William). Daniel bought and occupied the pew
(2), and the large and beautiful estate of Moses Black, the original estate
of Edmund, ancestor of the Quincy family.

On the death of the Hon. Thomas Greenleaf, Jan. 4, 1854, a funeral
discourse on "The Christian Standard of Honor," was delivered by the
Rev. W. P. Lunt, a copy of which may be found at the library in the
State House, also in the "New England Historical and Genealogical
Register," Vol. VIII. pp. 196, 197.

His daughter, Mary Ann Wroe (Chart V.), married Dr. Ebenezer
Woodward, of Quincy, Mass. Her husband, after providing liberally for
her, his sister, and other relatives, bequeathed the larger part of his great
wealth to the town of Quincy, to establish and maintain forever an institute for the education of females from the ages of ten to twenty, who are
born in Quincy, and none others; the property to be managed by the
Selectmen, together with the clerk and treasurer, and the school by the
ministers of Quincy. All ornamental as well as useful branches the donor
wished to have taught in the institute, which is to be located on the
Greenleaf farm. In case the town declines the bequest on these terms, or
fails to comply with the conditions of the will, the property is to go to
Dartmouth College without restrictions.

47. Ezekiel Price[7] Greenleaf (Chart V.), b. May 22, 1790, son of
Hon. Thomas[6] and Mary Deming (Price). For fifty years was a resident
of the picturesque town of Quincy, Mass. He lived the life of an ancho-
rite, and was brimful of eccentricities. Parsimony was his most salient
characteristic. With hundreds of thousands of dollars behind the stout
granite walls of the Safe Deposit Company, he would deny himself
nearly all the privileges and most of the necessaries of life. His neighbors in Quincy regarded him as inordinately irrational as regards his
habits and dress. But when he died he owed nobody. His latter years
were spent chiefly during the summer in the pretty little country village of
Nunda, in New York State. There, also, he pursued his hermit-like
methods. He lived in a little wooden house; what company he had was
confined to an old and trusted servant. What Mr. Greenleaf ate he raised
himself in the little garden hard by. He positively refused to be companionable to his neighbors. Since 1872 he spent his winters at 72 Waltham
Street in Boston. This uncommon personage was ninety-six years and
six months old when he died. He had nearly all his life been hale and
hearty, strong and muscular; for the past two years of his life, however,
he failed rapidly, and he died of old age. It was simply the going out of
the lamp of life. He died as easily as a child would go to sleep.

He was the last remnant of a union between the Greenleaf and Price
families, and with him the family in his line became extinct. He was
born on Beacon Street in Boston, where the Athenæum now stands, and
in which his picture hangs on its walls. He was a student of physiologi-
cal literature. There is a little nook in one corner of the library where it

was his wont to sit for hours at a time, apparently engaged in deep study. Mr. Greenleaf was educated in the Latin School in Boston. His education was made as thorough as was practicable in the early days of tuition in Boston. He was prepared for a business career, but subsequent events proved that he was not suited to it.

At an early age he engaged in mercantile pursuits in South Carolina. It is not known whether or no he was successful in the venture; however, he returned to Boston shortly afterwards and entered the flour trade, under the firm name of Apthorp & Greenleaf. About 1830 the firm failed. In the meantime his father had taken up his residence in Quincy, and the young man went there to live. He never entered business again,—that is, to any extent. During the half century that he lived in Quincy, Mr. Greenleaf passed his time in profound study and working in the garden attached to the house. He seldom went anywhere, and was rarely seen on the street. People called him a misanthrope. The first two decades of his residence in Quincy he was poor. When he went to live at his father's house Dame Rumor says he hadn't a farthing, but his father had money, and so had his aunt, Mrs. Daniel Greenleaf. He and two sisters were the only heirs to their personal effects. Their deaths brought Mr. Greenleaf, as nearly as can be learned, into the possession of property worth in the neighborhood of $40,000. When his sisters died he naturally came into possession of their property, and this rapidly accumulated wealth in his hands. Mrs. Appleton, the last of his two sisters, died in August, 1885. She was his sole companion in the winter residence on Waltham Street. It was principally through his saving habits that at the time of his death Mr. Greenleaf was worth about $500,000. This sum has since then increased in volume, and has been turned over to Harvard College, to aid that institution in preparing young men to fight the battle of the world with credit to themselves. The amount named by the Treasurer of Harvard College as having been received from his estate, was seven hundred and eleven thousand dollars ($711,000). So it will be seen that Mr. Greenleaf's idiosyncrasies were not without a method, after all. This noble gift is the sequel. Whether or no he has cherished this effort at benevolence, and denied himself even the privileges of life to accomplish it, is not known. But there can be no doubt of the ultimate purpose of his life.

Despite his peculiarities he bore an excellent character. He displayed sterling qualities while laboring under adversity. He was a firm believer in industry and perseverance. Concerning poverty, his theory was, the more you help poverty the more poverty there would be. He never forgot the division his Uncle Daniel made of the poor. His uncle said there were three classes,—the Lord's poor, the Devil's poor, and the poor devils. The Lord's poor were victims of extenuating circumstances. The Devil's poor became poor through their devilment; and the poor devils were made so by their indolence.

His will is dated Feb. 19, 1870, George T. Bigelow, Richard Cranch Greenleaf, and Stephen H. Williams being the executors. There are a few private bequests, which are mostly revoked in the codicil. The testator gives "all the rest, residue and remainder of his estate, real, personal and mixed, to the president and fellows of Harvard College, to have and to hold the same to their successors and assigns forever, absolutely, and in fee, in trust, nevertheless, for the uses and purposes herein set forth : The said president and fellows are to take and to receive said property and estates, and to hold, manage, and invest the same according to their best judgment and discretion, taking care, however, to keep said property and estates as a distinct and separate investment, apart from all other investments made, so that the same may at all times clearly appear on their books of account. The said trust fund thus held and invested is to be called and known as the 'Price-Greenleaf Fund'; the net income derived from said fund to be used and appropriated by said president and fellows as follows : viz., A sum equal to but not exceeding $3,000 a year shall be divided in 300 shares each, to be paid each year to an undergraduate of insufficient means to pursue his studies in the academic department of the college, preference being given to those who by industry and good conduct, and zealous effort, shall be deemed by the president and dean of the college entitled to encouragement, etc. The rest of the income is to be appropriated for the maintenance and support of the library of the college, etc.; but no part of the income is to be applied in the erection of any building."

The testator describes himself as formerly of Quincy, but now of Boston.

40. Susanna Greenleaf (Chart VI.), b. Feb. 6, 1754, daughter of Hon. William[5] and Mary (Brown); m. Capt. Duncan Ingraham, of Greenville Farm, near Poughkeepsie, N. Y. They had twelve children, one of whom, Susan Coburn, married Dr. Samuel Perry; another, Sophia May, married the Rt. Rev. Philander Chase; another, Maria, married Leonard Kip; and of their children, one was Leonard Kip, the author, and another the Rt. Rev. William Ingraham Kip, Bishop of California.

Com. Duncan Nathaniel Ingraham, who distinguished himself in rescuing Martin Koszta, the Hungarian refugee, at Smyrna, April 4, 1854, was a nephew of Capt. Duncan Ingraham, who was fifth generation from William Ingraham, who came to Boston, Mass., in 1653. He was born at Charleston, S. C., on Dec. 2, 1802, and was the son of Nathaniel Ingraham of the same place. He belonged to a family emipently naval in its character. His father, when but twenty years of age, took part as a volunteer with his intimate friend, John Paul Jones, in the engagement of the "Bon Homme Richard" with the "Serapis," off the British coast. His uncle, Capt. Joseph Ingraham, United States Navy, was lost in the old ship "Pickering," which foundered at sea in 1800, and was never heard of. His cousin, William Ingraham, a lieutenant in the navy about 1784, was killed at the age of 24 by the Indians at Nootka Sound, on the west coast of Vancouvers Island. The officers and entire crew, except Jewett and Thompson, of the ship "Boston," from Boston and bound to Pacific Coast, were massacred on Christmas Day, 1802. Having been invited on shore to a feast, they were betrayed and murdered.

Duncan N. Ingraham was sent at an early age to Boston to be educated in the family of his grandfather, and entered the navy as midshipman in 1812. He served continuously in the navy of his country from that time until the secession of his native State, South Carolina, in 1860. In 1825 he was promoted to a lieutenancy. In 1838 he was promoted to commander, and served two years on the Brig " Somers," blockading the Mexican ports. At the capture of Tampico, Captain Ingraham was sent ashore, and receiving the letters of capitulation himself, was sent by Commodore O'Connor with dispatches to Washington.

In 1852 he was ordered to command the Sloop of War " St. Louis," in the Mediterranean Squadron. While at Smyrna he with great promptness and decision rescued Martin Koszta, a Hungarian refugee, who had become a citizen of the United States, from the Austrians, threatening the Austrian vessels, although greatly outnumbered by them in guns and men. For this brave action the United States Government presented him with a medal. The working classes in England, in token of their admiration, presented him with a magnificent chronometer. The citizens of New York, at a monster mass meeting, presented him with a gold medal.

At the breaking out of the Civil War he returned to the United States, and resigned his commission Jan. 1, 1861. He entered the service of the Confederate States in March, 1861, and was in action several times in and around Charleston Harbor. In 1863 he, with two Confederate ironclads, the " Palmetto State" and " Chicora," broke the blockade of the harbor. In 1865, when the Confederates evacuated Charleston, Commodore Ingraham blew up his fleet and retired with General Johnston, who surrendered his command at Goldsboro, N. C.

Commodore Ingraham married Harriott Horry Laurens, granddaughter on the paternal side of the patriot, Henry Laurens, President of the Continental Congress. The issue of this marriage was eleven children, a number of whom are living in Charleston, S. C. He died at Charleston, Nov. 16, 1891.*

William Ingraham, second son of Sir Arthur (whose eldest son was created a Peer of Scotland, Viscount Irwin Lord Ingram), married March 14, 1656, Mary Barstow; issue, six children. (1) William, born Feb. 9, 1657; died soon. (2) William, born Jan. 27, 1658. (3) Timothy, born July 2, 1660; died 1748. (4) Jeremiah, born Jan. 20, 1664. (5) Mary, born June 26, 1666. (6) Elizabeth, born Feb. 1, 1669.

Timothy, son of William, born July 2, 1660; died, 1748. Married Sarah Cowell, daughter of Sarah (Wilson) and Edward Cowell (Sarah Wilson was daughter of Joseph Wilson); issue, eight children. (1) Joseph, born May 5, 1689; married Sept. 3, 1713, in Boston, 1, Mary McFarland, 2, Hannah Young. (2) Timothy, born June 7, 1691, in Bristol, R. I. (3) Jeremiah, born Jan. 18, 1697. (4) Edward, born Nov. 2, 1699. (5) John, born Dec. 8, 1701. (6) Joshua, born Feb. 1, 1705. (7) Isaac, born May 17, 1706. (8) Sarah, born Sept. 23, 1708.

Joseph, first son of Timothy, born May 5, 1689; married, Sept. 3, 1713, Mary McFarland, in Boston, Mass.; issue, nine children. (1) Mary, born 1714; died May, 1800. (2) Francis, born May 13, 1716; died, 1763.

* Part of above from the Baltimore *Sun*, June 23, 1885.

(3) Elizabeth, born Oct. 5, 1718. (4) Hannah, born Oct. 23, 1720. (5) Duncan, born Nov. 29, 1726; died Aug. 9, 1811. (6) Sarah, born Oct. 18, 1730; died, 1817. (7) Rebecca, born Oct. 15, 1732. (8) Martha, born Aug. 31, 1735; died, 1819. (9) Joseph, born Sept. 10, 1737; died, 1811.

Duncan, fifth child of Joseph, born Nov. 29, 1726; died Aug. 11, 1811; married, 1, Susanna Blake, Dec. 7, 1748; died, 1770; issue, six children. (1) Susanna, born 1750. (2) Duncan, born April 2, 1752; married, July 26, 1774, Susanna Greenleaf; had twelve children. (3) Polly, born 1754. (4) Henry, born 1757. (5) Nathaniel, born 1759; married Aug. 14, 1783; 1, Mary Cochran, of Boston, 2, Louisa Hall, of Charleston, S. C. (6) Joseph, born 1762; died 1800; lost in U. S. Ship "Pickering"; was captain in United States Navy. Duncan married, 2, Mrs. Elizabeth Tufts; died, 1830. Issue (7) Francis B., born Aug. 26, 1798.

(6) Rt. Rev. Bishop Philander Chase, D.D., was fifth generation from Aquilla Chase, who came from Cornish, Eng., and settled in New Hampshire, in 1630. His brother Dudley was Chief Justice of Vermont, and also Senator. Bishop Chase founded Kenyon College, in Ohio, and Jubilee College in Illinois. His residence in Peoria County was called the Robin's Nest. (7) Rt. Rev. William Ingraham Kip, D.D., Bishop of California, and author of a large number of books of Church History, was ordained deacon July 1, 1835, and priest the following November; Bishop of California, Oct. 23, 1853.

The Kip, or De Kype family, was originally settled for a long period near Alençon, in Bretagne, France. The first of whom there is any notice of in history is Ruloff De Kype, 16th century. He fled in 1562, and returned in 1569. (2) Ruloff; (3) Hendrick, born 1576; (4) Isaac; (5) Jacob, born 1666; (6) Isaac, born Jan. 8, 1696; (7) Leonard, born 1725, Loyalist during the Revolution, and his property was confiscated by the Continental Congress. He married April 11, 1763, Elizabeth, daughter of Francis Marschalk, Esq., of New York. She was born 1732; died, 1818. (8) Leonard, born 1774; died July 2, 1846.

Rev. Dr. Sparrow, who married Frances Greenleaf, youngest daughter of Susanna (Greenleaf) and Duncan Ingraham, Jr., and his three sons, served in the Virginia State troops in the Civil War.

40. William⁶ Greenleaf (Chart VI.), son of Hon. William⁵ and Mary (Brown). Was born in Boston, Feb. 5, 1760; graduated at Harvard College in 1777, and pursued the study of medicine and surgery. He died Nov. 24, 1778, of a malignant fever contracted on board a prison ship; he being the only student who would venture on board to separate the sick and dying from the dead.

49. John⁶ Greenleaf (Chart VI.), b. Sept. 10, 1763, son of Hon. William⁵ and Mary (Brown), was blind at ten years of age. He resided in Quincy, Mass. Of his long and beautiful life, which closed on earth in his eighty-fifth year, on March 29, 1848, the Rev. Dr. Lunt writes: " This venerable man had been blind from his youth, but the care which his

John[6] Greenleaf.
Of Quincy, Mass.

James[6] Greenleaf.

From portrait by Stuart.

condition required was an office of love, and never a burden, through his uniform cheerfulness and Christian goodness. Mr. and Mrs. Greenleaf were among the excellent of the earth; and the memory of their quiet worth is cherished in many hearts."

Mr. Greenleaf was quite proficient in music, as an organist and performer on other musical instruments. He was a constant attendant at church.

50. James[6] Greenleaf (Chart VI.), b. in Boston, June 9, 1765, son of Hon. William[5] and Mary (Brown). He was appointed very early in life Consul of the United States to Amsterdam, where he amassed a large fortune. Returning to his country in 1795, he embarked in speculation with Robert Morris and John Nicholson, and became with them one of the founders of the celebrated "North American Land Company," which resulted in the ruination of its originators; afterwards he took up his residence in the District of Columbia. When the Federal Capital had been located on the Potomac, Morris and James Greenleaf purchased from the commissioners six thousand lots in the prospective city of Washington at the price of $480,000, and it is said they purchased as many more from other persons. He was the owner of the ground upon which was built years ago an Arsenal and the District Penitentiary, and upon which is now located the military post known as Washington (D. C.) Barracks. It was in the Penitentiary grounds that the persons charged with the conspiracy to kill President Lincoln, Secretary Seward, and others,—viz., Booth, Atzerodt, Harold, Payne, and Mrs. Surratt,—were executed, and subsequently buried. The last four were executed by hanging; Booth was shot. The name given to this point of land is Greenleaf's Point.

Mr. Greenleaf's second wife was Ann Penn Allen, daughter of James Allen, founder of Allentown, Penn., and son of William Allen, Chief Justice of the Province before the Revolution. Her mother was Elizabeth Lawrence, a granddaughter of the distinguished Tench Francis, the uncle of Sir Philip Francis, the accredited author of "Junius."

40. Rebecca[6] Greenleaf (Chart VI.), b. May 27, 1766, daughter of Hon. William[5] and Mary (Brown), m. Noah Webster, the Lexicographer, who was a son of Noah and Nancy (Steele) Webster, born Oct. 16, 1758, in Hartford (the part now forming the separate town of West Hartford), and who died in New Haven, Conn., May 28, 1843. His house is still standing in West Hartford on the direct road, about one mile south of the church, which stands in the center of the town.

He came of substantial stock. His great-grandfather was one of the first settlers in Hartford, and Governor of Connecticut. His mother was a descendant of William Bradford, the Plymouth Governor. Mr. Webster entered Yale College in 1774. He had been but a few months in college when the thrilling story of Lexington and Concord came, followed soon by Bunker Hill.

General Washington and his staff passed through New Haven on his way to take command of the revolutionary force gathered in Cambridge.

They lodged there, and in the morning were invited to see the drill of a company of the students, who finally escorted General Washington as far on his way as Neck Bridge.   Webster had the honor of leading the way, blowing a fife.   In the third year of his course, on account of the war, college life in New Haven was broken up, and the classes were dispersed in various towns.   Webster's class went to Glastonbury, and on the alarm by the approach toward Connecticut of Burgoyne, accompanied by a large band of savage Indians, a company went from West Hartford, commanded by Deacon Webster, and in that company went his three sons, Noah among them.   This company took part in the brilliant victories which ended in Burgoyne's surrender.   The following year Noah finished his college course.

Mr. Webster produced a great number and variety of educational books before he was twenty-six years old.   His famous old Spelling Book has kept its place, and between forty and fifty millions of copies have been printed.   But it is on his more famous Dictionary that his real fame rests.

Of the children of Noah Webster and Rebecca, Emily S. married William Wolcott Ellsworth, LL.D., the third son of Oliver Ellsworth, second Chief Justice of the United States.   He received his early education at Windsor, Conn., where he was born.   In 1806 he entered Yale, and was graduated in 1810.   He began his legal studies at the Law School at Litchfield, under the guidance of Judges Reeve and Gould, and continued them in Hartford, in the office of his brother-in-law, the late Chief Justice Williams.   He was admitted to the bar in 1813, and established himself in Hartford in the practice of his profession.   In 1827 he was sent to Congress by the Whigs of his district, and continued there for five years. In 1838 he was elected Governor of the State by a large popular majority. He was continued in this office four years, being each time re-elected by the people.   While Governor he was twice offered an election to the Senate of the United States, but declined to be a candidate.   In 1847 he was elected by the Legislature a Judge of the Superior Court and Supreme Court of Errors.   He remained on the bench as an associate Judge of the Supreme Court until his office expired, by limitation of law, upon reaching the age of seventy.   In Judge Ellsworth were hereditary qualities of great mental and moral worth.   Like his father, the Chief Justice, he was remarkable for the simplicity of his taste and habits.   In manner he was dignified, and he had as fine a personal presence and bearing as any man of his time.   He loved his country unselfishly; he loved his state as a patriot should; he loved his profession; he loved his church; and his love for home and the enjoyments of social life was never weakened by his public callings.

Of the children of Judge Ellsworth, Elizabeth, born June 8, 1824, married Hon. Waldo Hutchins, a prominent lawyer of New York City, and who was graduated from Amherst College in 1842.   He became a law student in the office of Schell & Slossen, composed of Augustus Schell, the famous Tammany lawyer and politician, and John Slosson, who afterwards was a Judge of the Superior Court of New York.   After Mr. Hutchins' admission to the bar he was taken into partnership, and the

Rebecca.[6]

Daughter of Hon. William[5] Greenleaf, and wife of Dr. Noah Webster, the Lexicographer.

From silhouette photograph by Rebecca L. Webster.

firm name was changed to Schell, Slossen & Hutchins. In 1850 he was elected to the New York Legislature; in 1855 a member of the First Park Commission; in 1879 he was elected to Congress, and remained there until the day on which Grover Cleveland was inaugurated President of the United States.

40. Anna (Nancy) Greenleaf (Chart VI.), b. June 3, 1772, the youngest daughter of Hon. William[6] and Mary (Brown) Greenleaf, m. Hon. William Cranch, the eminent jurist, who for fifty years was Chief Justice of the Circuit Court of the District of Columbia, and of whose decisions in all that time only two were overruled by the United States Supreme Court. He was appointed to the Circuit Court by President John Adams, and Chief Justice by President Thomas Jefferson. He was first cousin to John Quincy Adams. His daughter, Abigail Adams Cranch, was wife of Rev. William G. Eliot, D.D., of St. Louis, Mo. The family belonged distinctively to Massachusetts, with the early history of which colony and state it was identified. They are both buried in the Congressional Burying Grounds.

53. Richard Cranch[7] Greenleaf (Chart VI.), b. Nov. 9, 1808, in Cambridge, Mass.; son of John[6] and Lucy (Cranch). Entered the dry-goods business as a boy when thirteen years old, with Penniman & Cutler. His next employers were Mayo & Hill; then Geo. Hill & Co., Mr. Greenleaf being a partner in the last-named firm from 1829 to 1834. Their place of business was on Washington Street, Boston. He withdrew from Hill & Co., and re-entered trade with Mr. John Chandler, as Chandler & Greenleaf, occupying the armory building, 337 Washington Street. Mr. Chandler finally withdrew in 1845, going to Europe, leaving Mr. Greenleaf to carry on the business alone, which he did successfully until 1846. Then he associated himself as an active partner in the newly formed house of Hovey, Williams & Co., afterwards C. F. Hovey & Co., in which he continued until his death. Mr. Greenleaf had been the longest in business of any retailer in Boston. He had long been interested in the study of natural history, which he made his pastime. He was president of the Boston Microscopic Society, a vice president of the Boston Natural History Society, a vice president of the Franklin Savings Bank, and succeeded Hon. Otis Norcross as president of the Home for Aged Men, in which he took an active interest from its foundation. In every relation Mr. Greenleaf won the esteem of those with whom he associated or had dealings, and his memory will long be cherished as that of a just, able, generous, and agreeable gentleman. His love of well-doing was inherent. It was not a studied effort for him to become interested in good works. It was a part of his nature and the outcome of his faith to seek to alleviate misery and to carry comfort to the suffering.

The last rites were performed and words of tender eulogy pronounced over the remains in the Arlington Street Church (Unitarian), Rev. Brooke Herford, minister of the church, officiating.

40. Christopher Pearse Cranch (Chart VI.), b. at Alexandria, Va., March 8, 1813, son of Anna [Nancy] (Greenleaf) and Hon. William Cranch. He was educated at Harvard College, and prepared for the ministry at the Divinity School at Cambridge, where he was graduated in 1835. Seven years later, however, he retired from the ministry, and determined to follow an artist's career. He studied art in Italy in 1846–48, and from 1853 to 1863 lived and painted in Italy and France. Then returning to America, was elected in 1864 a member of the National Academy, and made his permanent home in Cambridge, Mass. Among the best known of his paintings are: " October Afternoon," 1867; " Washington Oak, opposite Newburg, N. Y.," 1868; "Val de Moline Amalfi," 1869; " A Roman Citizen," " Venice," " Neapolitan Fisherman," and " Venetian Fishing Boats," 1871. His daughter, Caroline A. Cranch, who studied under him and under William Hunt, has attained success as an artist; and his brother, John Cranch, was a well-known portrait painter, and an associate of the National Academy.

It is, however, as an author that Christopher P. Cranch is best known, his graceful writings in prose and verse having multitudes of admiring readers throughout the English-speaking world. Perhaps his greatest work was his translation of Virgil's "Æneid " into English blank verse, which appeared in 1872. His first book was a volume of " Poems," in 1844. Others were: "The Last of the Huggermuggers," 1856, and " Kobboltozo," 1857; volumes of children's stories, illustrated by himself; " Satan," a Libretto, 1873; "The Bird and the Bell, and Other Poems," 1875, and "Ariel and Caliban, and Other Poems," 1886. His attractive personality, the purity of his aims, and the spirituality of his nature, won him a confidence and regard which his devotion to his art deepened into admiration.

57. Hon. David[7] Greenleaf (Chart VII.), son of Israel[6] and Prudence (Whitcomb), b. March 9, 1763, in Bolton, Mass. Left home when about twelve years of age, joining his brother John, who was in the Revolutionary army. Leaving Massachusetts in 1779, he went to South Carolina. Procuring a horse there, he started across the country to the Ohio River, meeting with many adventures from wild beasts and Indians. Frequently in traveling over the mountains night would overtake him, and finding no sign of a habitation, he would dismount, select a tree with low branches, tie his horse to a swinging limb, climb the tree, taking his saddle with him for a seat, and would then buckle himself to the tree with his surcingle, to prevent falling if he should drop asleep. Frequently the wolves made doleful howling around the tree, frightening the horse; and the cold would be so intense that he would often have to descend from his perch and run around the tree, clapping his hands, until thoroughly warmed. He traveled in that way until he reached the Ohio River, where he took a flatboat and landed in Natchez, Territory of Mississippi, a Province of Spain, about the year 1780. He served six months under the Spanish Government against the Indians, remaining in this Province; and after it was acknowledged, by treaty with Spain, to be within the limits of the United States, and the formation of a Territorial Government, he became one of the first members of the Legislature of the State.

He was by nature a man of great inventive genius and a natural machinist. He built the first cotton gin in Mississippi, about the year 1785, inventing a turning lathe to file out the teeth of the gin rags; also invented the square screw cotton press for cotton bales: before that the cotton was pressed in large bags.

In those early days the women had to pick the seed from the cotton with their fingers; he invented a little roller machine, which by feeding with one hand and turning with the other, a few pounds a day could be ground out. In 1799 he built a gin for himself, and did the public ginning for the neighborhood for several years. In 1816 he invented a cotton planter and scraper. It was worked by one man and one horse, would open the furrows, drop the seed, and cover with a small harrow attached. He also invented a screw propeller for flatboats and skiffs to cross the river at Natchez. At the time of his death, by yellow fever, in Warren County, Miss., Oct. 13, 1819, he was preparing models for patents. His invention of the cotton press, together with others mentioned, were greatly calculated to improve the culture and development of cotton, which was becoming a most important article of trade.

It was not an easy matter to get a patent in those days, so he passed away without having accomplished his wishes; and it is hardly known now that he was the inventor of some of the useful machines which have since been so greatly improved upon that the originals have been lost sight of and forgotten entirely. He was Assessor and Tax Collector at different times in Adams County, Miss., and was highly respected by all who knew him. He was generous to a fault, and full of fun and anecdote. He was a member of the Baptist Church for over fifteen years before his death, was very temperate in his living, and considered the use of ardent spirits as a beverage a great evil, and was never known to use them as such.

There is one other incident in the life of this man that is interesting and romantic: it relates to his first marriage, which occurred during the Spanish Provincial Government of what was then known as the Natchez District. A few years before, several families, mostly relatives, had emigrated to this district from South Carolina. The most prominent among them were members of the Baptist church, who were always regular in their family devotions and worship of God from their first settlement in the country; but the government, which was Roman Catholic, soon forbade them these privileges, and greatly persecuted them besides, so that they were compelled to worship and administer the rites of their religion in secret. The Rev. John Greenleaf Jones, a nephew of the first Mrs. David Greenleaf, in a series of letters descriptive of the introduction of Protestantism into Mississippi, and published in a religious paper of New Orleans, thus relates the incident: "Thus things were managed successfully for a few months; but an additional circumstance had transpired characteristic of the times, which, when known, greatly enraged the priesthood and Spanish officers. *David Greenleaf*, an accomplished young gentleman from the North, had gained the heart and hand of Miss Phebe Jones, daughter of John Jones; but such was their sense of the wrongs inflicted by the Catholic hierarchy that they resolved not to be married by priest or Spanish officer. They, moreover, believed that the uncle of Miss Jones, Rev. Richard Curtis, being a preacher of the gospel, was as duly authorized in the sight of God to solemnize the rites of matrimony as any one else, and made application to him accordingly. But no one, not even the parents of Miss Jones, were willing to risk the consequences of having the marriage performed in their house. Arrangements were therefore made for Mr. Greenleaf to go, on the 24th of May, 1795, with a few select young gentlemen, to the village of Gayoso, which was situated on the bluff about eighteen miles above Natchez, and there procure the license from the proper officer. Then, considerably after nightfall, they were to be found on the road two or three miles south of Greenville, and going in the direction of Natchez.

In the meantime the bridal party, including Mr. Curtis, were to be taking an evening ride in the opposite direction, and, lest some traitorous person might accidentally fall in with either party, they agreed upon a sign and countersign in case all was well; but if any suspicious person had fallen in with either company during the darkness of the night, they were to pass each other in silence. At the appointed time and place the parties met. Young folks, however, must have their fun—something to laugh about afterwards. On meeting, the bridal party announced the mysterious word, but there was no response, and they passed without recognition. " Who on earth can they be?" inquired one, in a suppressed tone. "It's them," said another, "and something has happened." A settled gloom was coming down on that lovely bride and her company, when the young men suddenly wheeled about and gave the countersign. The parties then alighted near the residence of William Stampley, on what is still known as " Stampley's Hill "; and by torchlight, under the widespread boughs of an ancient oak, the marriage ceremony was duly performed, and Mr. Curtis concluded by a most impressive prayer, long talked of by those who were present. The parties remounted, the light was extinguished, and each sought concealment in the privacy of home. " A numerous, intelligent, and pious posterity is the result of that remarkable wedding."

In person, Mr. Greenleaf was about five feet eight inches in height, thickset, and somewhat stoop-shouldered, with black eyes and black, curly hair, but quite bald in the latter part of his life. He was a man of great strength and energy. (See Military Service.)

73. Daniel[8] Greenleaf (Chart VIII.), b. Nov. 11, 1797, son of David[7] and Phebe (Jones). He was much like his father in appearance and disposition; was a good scholar, and a man of more than ordinary abilities. He was engaged in mercantile life, but at the age of twenty-seven turned his attention to the law, for which he found himself better adapted, and was for several years District Attorney. Later in life he was interested in several banking institutions; was president of a bank at Jackson, Miss., at the time of his death,—a position which he filled with great credit to himself. He was a professing Christian for many years before his death,—a member of the Episcopal Church.

73. Phebe Greenleaf (Chart VIII.), b. Aug. 15, 1806, youngest child of David. Married Franklin Beaumont, a druggist of Natchez. Phebe inherited very much of her father's happy disposition, and, besides, possessed in a great degree those virtues which make the Christian humble, yet so eminent and lovely. She was for many years a suffering invalid; but during it all she was ever the same cheerful, contented, and happy Christian. She was a member of the Presbyterian Church (O. S.), in which her husband had been a ruling elder for many years. The family emigrated to Texas in 1848, and settled on the San Antonio River, near Goliad, where she died Oct. 20, 1851.

58. Israel[7] Greenleaf (Chart VII.), b. Jan. 25, 1765, son of Israel[6] and Prudence (Whitcomb). Served in the United States Army, after which he purchased 750 acres of land near the Unadilla River, in Chenango County, N. Y., which he afterwards sold to his father, and removed to Pennsylvania and purchased land near Wellsburg, where he went into the millwright business. He was a powerful man, six feet two inches high, broad shoulders, full chest, high forehead, large blue eyes, full, plump, handsome face, commanding appearance and lofty bearing. In powers of endurance he yielded to none, save "Old General Putnam." As an example of his great strength, it was said of him he would go into the Laurel Mountain alone, carry all his tools and provisions, and in fourteen or fifteen days raise the stones out of the quarry, and complete them for the mill or grinding. (See Military Service.)

59. Levi[7] Greenleaf (Chart VII.), b. Feb. 19, 1767, son of Israel[6] and Prudence (Whitcomb). Was the first settler within the limits of Industry, Maine, as the town was afterwards incorporated. Removing from Bolton, Mass., he, with a considerable colony from Dunstable, N. H., and other places in that vicinity, took up land in 1787, his lot being numbered sixty-one. The farm, cleared by him, was in that part of the town set off to New Sharon in 1852, and is now known as the "Daniel Collins" farm. In 1803 he sold his farm, and removed to the south part of Industry. Here he continued to reside until his death, with the exception of about two years, when he resided in New Portland, Me.

Mr. Greenleaf was a man of character, energy, and of more than ordinary ability. He was a deacon of the Congregational Church in New Sharon, and was a member of the Board of Selectmen in Industry, in 1804. In person he was about the medium height, rather spare, and a little stooping, light complexion, and rather sandy hair. He was a very strong man for one of his size, and in his younger days an expert wrestler, frequently throwing opponents much heavier that himself. (See Military Service.)

60. Tilly[7] **Greenleaf,** born March 25, 1770, son of Israel[6] (Chart VII.) and Prudence (Whitcomb), was a pioneer, and many of his children have been also. He bought a tract of land in Augusta, Oneida County, N. Y., in 1790, and made himself a home. In 1831 he moved to the Western Reserve, Ohio, and many of his children followed him there, some of whom now live in Charlestown, Edinburgh, and Ravenna, Ohio. (See Military Service.)

62. Daniel[7] **Greenleaf** (Chart VII.), b. Jan. 1, 1786, son of Israel[6] and Ursula (Woods). Was employed as a teacher near Natchez, in Mississippi. He was in height six feet two inches, broad shoulders, rather spare, walked slightly stooping; very long arms, his fingers when extended touching the kneejoint; head medium size, high forehead, large blue eyes, Roman nose, small mouth.

64. Stephen[7] **Greenleaf** (Chart VII.), b. Sept. 12, 1790, son of Israel[6] and Ursula Woods. Was a merchant, and in person was about five feet eight inches in height, fair complexion, gray eyes, light hair originally, high forehead, somewhat bald.

Among the papers of the Rev. Jonathan Greenleaf, D.D., are many interesting letters from Mr. Greenleaf, who gave him much valuable information for his "Genealogy of the Greenleaf Family." Several manuscript copies of a genealogy which he compiled in 1838, and which bore this quaint inscription, "A record of Stephen Greenleaf, the first Greenleaf of the male line born in North America, together with a record of his posterity by families to the present time, Dec. 20, 1838, by Stephen Greenleaf, son of Israel," had been given by him to various members of the family. Rev. Jonathan Greenleaf was favored among others. A pleasant feature of these manuscript copies were occasional jottings from his pen, written on the back of a page of family record, a few of which are as follows :—

What will be said of this old coon when he is gone? I have every confidence that my children will do ample justice, but I wish to be a little in advance, so here it comes without alloy :—

> The tree has decayed, the leaf is now dry,
> But the spirit has fled to regions on high.
> And now, loving friends, why sorrow and sigh?
> Dry up all your tears, for you, by and by,
> Will meet with your friends in the regions of light;
> Take the straight, narrow way, and strive to do right.

> I am one of twenty-two;
>   My name grows on a tree.
> I walk erect like you;
>   Please tell my name to me.

Answer: My father has 22 children. Name, Greenleaf.

> Of twenty-two I am   1
> Likewise the third of   8
> The third of eight combined with 1
> Most strange to tell produces   8.

Explanation: My father had 22 children, my mother 8, and I was the third of my mother; then self and wife also had 8 children.

Like the Israelite, " he pitched his tents in many places." From New York he moved to Cincinnati, from there to Indiana, thence to St. Louis, and finally to Bloomfield, Davis County, Iowa.

84. Gardner[9] Greenleaf (Chart VIII.), b. Oct. 27, 1823, son of Joshua[8] and Betsey (Marsh). He attended the academy at Farmington, Me., as opportunity offered, and labored zealously to acquire an education. After his marriage he lived in Vassalboro and Anson, Me., and in 1855 moved to Stark, where he lived until his death. He was a successful farmer, and much respected by his townsmen. He was a member of the Board of Selectmen in 1871.

97. Orick Herman[9] Greenleaf (Chart IX.), b. July 18, 1823, son of William[8] and Almira (Sanford). The early days of Mr. Greenleaf were characterized by the usual hardships attending the growth of young men of that period.

The chances for education were very meager and yet while educational advantages in the form of schools were not at all to be compared with those of the present days, he contrived to pick up a fund of general information by the methods adopted by all men in those days, namely by what reading he could get hold of and by keeping his eyes open to what was going on in the world.

The times were such that every young man had to begin the carving of his fortune at a very early age and this was eminently true of him.

He went from his home in Nunda, N. Y., early in life to Seneca Falls, N. Y., to learn the trade of tanner and currier and it was because of his efficiency in the latter branch of business that he was induced in 1845 to make his home at Springfield, Mass.

It would seem like an exaggeration for any one to-day to think of starting in life and accumulating money out of the moderate earnings of those days; nevertheless, such was the case with Mr. Greenleaf.

No matter how small the compensation, he contrived to save something out of the same and in 1847 he left the business of tanner and currier and with what he could save out of a salary as superintendent, (that would not pay house rent in these days), he began business in the buying and selling of paper stock, organizing the firm of Greenleaf & Taylor, soon after adding the buying and selling of paper to the business.

The firm of Greenleaf & Taylor soon became very well known among paper manufacturers but Mr. Greenleaf did not dream of becoming a manufacturer until one day David Carson, of Dalton, said to him, " Some day you will be making paper." It was not long before, acting upon the above suggestion and studying into the processes of manufacturing, he found a large, pure spring of water in Huntington, Mass., and there decided to build a mill.

The firm of Greenleaf & Taylor then became changed and an incorporated company, under the name of Greenleaf & Taylor Manfg. Co., was organized and the mill built in Huntington commenced in 1853, the manufacture of news and book papers, while the paper and stock business was continued in the warehouse in Springfield.

Shortly after this, however, the mill at Huntington was changed to a fine writing paper mill and in 1865, Mr. Greenleaf bought out a controlling interest of Mr. Stephen Holman in the Holyoke Paper Co., and in 1868, the name of the Greenleaf & Taylor Manufacturing Co. was changed to the name of the Massasoit Manufacturing. Co.

The Holyoke Paper Company has been managed with great success from that time to this by Mr. Greenleaf. Some of the papers which he commenced manufacturing were of such merit as to receive a gold medal at the Paris Exposition in 1878.

In 1884, the nucleus of Forest Park in Springfield was established by Mr. Greenleaf, who gave seventy acres to the city and it is one of the greatest pleasures of his life at the present time to see the thousands of people enjoying themselves among the delightful ravines and shady nooks and retreats of that exceedingly lovely location. Many people wanted him to name it "Greenleaf Park" but he steadfastly refused. His idea was that his name would be properly preserved in calling it Forest Park.

Mr. Greenleaf, when he first came to Springfield, at once presented his letter and joined the First Baptist Church of that city and has been a member of the same for fifty years.

It has always been his idea that the best method for prosperous men to adopt in the disposal of their property by way of benevolence was to carefully study the direction in which the same was to be used and then to give it in such sums as would do the most good. This has always been his method. He has never been a sentimental giver, but has been exceedingly generous in giving along the lines that his judgment indicated was the wisest.

He has been a very earnest supporter of educational institutions, notably the Boys' School at Mt. Hermon, the Shaw University, of Raleigh, N. C. (in both of which he is a Trustee), the Worcester Academy and the Suffield, Conn. Institute; while the Springfield City Library, the Home for the Friendless, as well as the Home for Aged Women, have been generously helped by him.

Benevolence is a leading characteristic of the life of Mr. Greenleaf. He has been more than generous for good and worthy objects, and no one in suffering or need ever went to him in vain. His gifts to the Institutions of Springfield and that which laid the foundation of the most beautiful park, so far as natural resources are concerned, that there is in this country,—his honorable dealings with all men, his virtuous life and pleasing ways of modesty and unselfishness, have endeared him to the citizens of Springfield and given him a warm place in the hearts of all whose privilege it has been to meet him.

99.   Hon. William Henry[9] Greenleaf (Chart IX.), b. Dec. 7, 1834, son of William[8] and Almira (Sanford). Removed to Minnesota in 1858, and settled in Litchfield, Meeker County, where he now resides. He is engaged in the lumber business, and is President of the "Greenleaf Lumber Company," manufacturers of sashes, doors, blinds, laths, and shingles. Mr. Greenleaf filled the office of County Surveyor seven terms;

County Treasurer, one term; was a member of the Legislature three terms; State Senator, four years; Receiver of public money, and Disbursing Agent at Litchfield, Minn., five years. His son, Charles Albert Greenleaf, is associated with him in business, and is Secretary and Treasurer of the "Greenleaf Lumber Company."

60. Elizabeth Greenleaf (Chart IX.), b. March 3, 1802, daughter of Tilly and Polly (Spofford). Was crippled in her right hand when six months old by creeping into the fire after a "tin funnel." Her parents, believing she could never learn to do housework, spinning, etc., and certainly would never marry, gave her a fair common school education; and she, by her own efforts in assisting in paying the expense, attended several terms at the high school, and became a noted teacher. After the death of her mother, in 1827, she went to Western New York, teaching in Eden, Erie County, several years, continuing to teach after her marriage in her own house until 1850, when she moved onto a large dairy farm, —supposing her teaching days were over; but the district directors desired her services, and she taught a term, afterwards taking a few select pupils at home.

In 1857 she removed to Wisconsin, with her husband, Mr. George Wilcox, and they were among the first settlers of Dead Lake Prairie, in the town of Waterville, Pepin County. The marriage of their daughter, Mary E., was the third that took place in that town, Oct. 13, 1859. Here she received and taught a few pupils in her own home, and then taught in the district school where she lived, and later in several different towns, until the death of her husband, in 1869. She had a rare faculty of interesting her pupils. Ministers, doctors, and lawyers had been her pupils. She was a woman of great industry, and became a model housekeeper and an accomplished woman in all things necessary to a useful and valuable life.

Her daughter, Mary E., married Henry M. Miles. The young couple set up housekeeping in the village of Arkansaw in the town of Waterville, formerly known as Frankfort, a small manufacturing village. Mrs. Miles taught the first school in Arkansaw, Wis.; established the first Sunday school, and aided in building the first church in that section of the country. Although beginning as pioneers in an unbroken wilderness, they courageously persevered until the present time; and it has become one of the richest farming communities in the county.

60. Lucinda Greenleaf (Chart IX.), b. June 12, 1803, at Augusta, Oneida County, N. Y., daughter of Tilly and Polly (Spofford). She married Hiram Hitchcock, of the same county and state, the son of Amos, who was born in Oxford, New Haven County, Conn., Aug. 29, 1771, and descended from Matthias and Elizabeth Hitchcock, of Hull, England, who was born in 1610, and emigrated to New Haven, Conn., in 1635. Amos Hitchcock, the father of Hiram, was the son of Samuel born in West Haven, in 1722, the son of Samuel born in East Haven,

Conn., March 7, 1678, the son of Eliakim, born in England, in 1632, son of Matthias.

Of the seven children of Lucinda and Hiram, James L., born at Oriskany Falls, N. Y., is a hardware merchant in Cass City, Mich., where he settled Sept. 6, 1872. He is an enterprising and prominent man, much interested in public affairs, and influential among his fellow-citizens. He was the pioneer in the hardware business of Tuscola County, his shop being located in a dense forest abounding in bears, deer, wolves, and other wild animals. In 1859 he purchased his first bill of merchandise, and conveyed it to his log cabin, which he had built upon a 120-acre lot of land that he purchased of the Government in 1858. This primative mansion and store was temporarily covered with sheet iron, afterwards made into camp kettles, and sold to the Indians. He built the first frame house and barn for miles around, and manufactured tinware and other goods such as Indians and the first white settlers required. His wife taught school, walking daily two miles to and from school. On March 1, 1864, Mr. Hitchcock removed with his family to Wajamega, Mich., erected a store and residence, and while he worked at his trade his wife acted as his clerk. After a residence there of nearly eight years he removed to Cass City, where he is engaged in building, farming, and merchandise. He has held the office of Justice of the Peace, Road Commissioner, School Inspector, and Postmaster in Dayton's township; also Treasurer of Cass City and Councilman for many years.

60. Emily Greenleaf (Chart IX.), b. Oct. 12, 1811, daughter of Tilly Greenleaf. Married Saxton A. Curtiss. He was from Massachusetts. She was living in Charlestown, Ohio, whither her father and mother had removed from Oneida County, N. Y. They settled on a farm in Charlestown, which after his death, Feb. 18, 1868, remained in the hands of his widow until her death, in 1892, when it passed to her youngest daughter, Artelissa, who not long after removed to Southeastern Kansas, returning later to Ohio. Mrs. Emily Curtiss spent the last seven years of her life with her daughter Eliza. Her old age was a vigorous and healthy one. She celebrated her eightieth birthday by riding horseback. She was extremely youthful in manner and appearance. Her life was marked by benevolence, and was active in social and church work.

116. Robert Stephen[9] Greenleaf (Chart X.), b. Sept. 3, 1848, son of Eugene La Baum[8] and Martha Louise (Barr). Was born in St. Louis, Mo., and received his education in the schools of that city. Feb. 26, 1864, when but little over fifteen years of age, he enlisted in Company D, Tenth Illinois Volunteer Infantry, and served until the close of the war; was with Sherman in Tennessee, Alabama, and Georgia, on "the March to the Sea," and the campaigns in Carolina. At the close of the war he completed his education at Blackburn University, Carlinville, Ill.; took up the profession of civil engineering, which he has followed successfully. In the fall of 1882 he moved to Portland, Ore., and is now County Surveyor of Multnomah County. He is much interested in military matters, and is Captain of Battery A, Light Artillery, Oregon National Guards. He has accumulated considerable property, and has a comfortable home, which has been his residence for eleven years. (See Military Service.)

129.   Major Stephen[7] Greenleaf (Chart XII.), b. Jan. 31, 1759, son of Stephen[5] and Eunice (Fairbanks). Was by trade a carpenter and wheelwright. When he was twelve years of age his father removed to Brattleboro, Vt., where he continued to reside until his death, which took place March 5, 1850, at the advanced age of ninety-one years.

As a workman and a citizen, no fairer name is on the list of Brattleboro's residents. As a carpenter and wheelwright, much has been said in commendation. Many of the first buildings in Brattleboro were erected by his hands. In the study of mathematics, grammar, etc., he was obliged to search for knowledge from such books as he could obtain, having no other educational advantages, and few books worth mentioning. It is said of him by his daughter, Mrs. Ellis, that her "father educated himself, long winter evenings, by light from the kitchen fireplace. To get full advantage of the light he extended himself horizontally upon the floor," where he worked upon mathematical problems, practiced penmanship, and thus laid the foundation of such a character for ability and virtue as won the well-deserved respect, love, and confidence of three generations. His superior native resources were concealed under a modest, unassuming exterior, so faithfully shown in a painting which, to the honor of Brattleboro, now hangs in the Townhall.

In the year 1799 he was elected Town Clerk of Brattleboro, and was re-elected to the office for forty-five years in succession, declining it but a few years previous to his death. His penmanship in the old town books, for its uniformity and perfection, is the admiration of every one who has examined it. Each letter and word is made in full, giving so perfect exactness no one can mistake it. In 1834 he wrote several long, highly interesting letters to his friends, that were published in the *Phœnix*, respecting the past and present of Brattleboro, and he also furnished that brief though able sketch of this town in " Thompson's Historical Gazetteer of Vermont," published in 1846.

Mr. Greenleaf was a man of mild, benevolent, and charitable disposition; he was amiable and bland in his manners; courteous and accommodating to all; gentle and agreeable in his family; a pleasant neighbor, and an honest and upright man. In the social circle and the public gathering he was always ready with pleasantry and wit to contribute his full share of innocent amusement and pleasure. He was a true Christian, showing the strength and purity of his faith by his good works. (See Military Service.)

132.   James[7] Greenleaf (Chart XII.), b. Dec. 9, 1770, son of Stephen[6] and Eunice (Fairbanks). Resided in Guilford for about eight years after he was married, and then removed to Derby, Vt., the frontier town next to Canada, where he built mills, and was engaged in them for

the remainder of his life. He was a religious man, and a deacon in the
Congregational Church. In person he was six feet four inches tall, and
weighed one hundred and ninety-five pounds.

139. Miller Thaddeus[9] **Greenleaf** (Chart XII.), b. March 21,
1821, son of Major Thomas S.[8] and Lydia (Miller). Lived in Brattleboro, Vt., until September, 1840, and then removed to Columbus, Adams
County, Illinois, and was engaged in the manufacture of carriages and
wagons; remaining there until 1850, when he moved to Quincy, Ill., and
started in the machine business, manufacturing steam engines, mill
machinery, house castings, general repairing, etc. He continued in this
business over thirty years, doing a thriving and prosperous business, and
gained an honorable reputation. He had most of the steamboat repairing to do, also a large amount of railroad work; rebuilt several locomo-
tives for different roads running into Quincy, and furnished the greater
portion of the engines and machinery for the Flouring Mills; also other
manufacturing work in the city and through the growing Western country. He has worked some as an inventor, making tools and machinery
of different kinds that have proved more or less valuable. From 1873 the
business was conducted under the name of "Greenleaf Manufacturing
Company," manufacturing various patented articles for outside parties.
In 1880 he sold out and retired from the business; but the shop was run
under the same name for a number of years. He is still making models,
and assisting others getting out new inventions.

143. Jeremiah[8] **Greenleaf** (Chart XIII.), b. Dec. 7, 1791, son of
Daniel[7] and Huldah (Hopkins). Was the author of "Greenleaf's Grammar," and devoted a large part of his life to study, authorship, and
instruction in this special branch of education. He was also the author
of "Greenleaf's Gazetteer" and "Greenleaf's Atlas," both excellent works
of their kind, and highly esteemed at the time they appeared. He married
Elvira E., daughter of Simon Stevens, M.D., of Guilford, Vt. "A true
and noble woman, of no small degree of culture."

In his letter to Rev. Jonathan Greenleaf, dated Guilford, Vt., Oct. 18,
1847, in referring to the Greenleaf family as tall, and that they must have
sprung from a "race of giants," he says: "My grandfather was an Ajax
in strength, and my father and several of his brothers were the same,
being from six feet to six feet four inches in height. I am only six feet
high, and weigh only about two hundred and twenty-five pounds.

> "Could I in stature reach the pole,
>   Or grasp the ocean in my span,
> I must be measured by my soul;
>   The mind's the standard of the man."

(See Military Service.)

146. Hon. Halbert S.[9] **Greenleaf** (Chart XIII.), son of Jeremiah[8]
and Elvira Eunice (Stevens), was born in Guilford, Vt., April 12, 1827.
He spent his boyhood and youth in farm life, but from his nineteenth to
his twenty-third year he taught district and grammar schools in the winter

Jeremiah[8] Greenleaf.

Author of Greenleaf's Grammar, etc.

months, and during one season, so as to add as much as possible to his funds, worked in a country brickyard. At the age of twenty-three he made a six months' sea voyage in the whaling vessel " Lewis Bruce,'" serving before the mast as a common sailor.

On the 24th of June, 1852, shortly after his return from sea, he married, and in the month of September following removed to Shelburne Falls, Mass., where he obtained employment as a day laborer at the bench in a large cutlery establishment. A few months after engaging in this work he found a position in the office of a neighboring manufactory, and in a short time became manager of its growing business, and subsequently a member of the firm of Miller & Greenleaf. On the 11th of March, 1856, he was commissioned by the Governor of Massachusetts a Justice of the Peace, and was one of the youngest magistrates in the State not a member of the legal profession.

In 1859 he became member of the firm of Linus Yale, Jr., & Co., in Philadelphia, and went to that city to live, remaining in business there until 1861, when he returned to Shelburne Falls and organized the Yale & Greenleaf Lock Co., of which he became business manager.

His service in the State militia and that in the Civil War, in which he distinguished himself, will be found in its appropriate place among the "Records of Military Service." Soon after the close of the war he took charge of the extensive salt works on Petite Anse Isle, St. Mary's Parish, Louisiana. In June, 1867, he removed to Rochester, N. Y., and the 1st of July following the firm of Sargent & Greenleaf, of which he is the junior member, was organized. The firm of Sargent & Greenleaf manufacture, under patents held by them, magnetic, automatic, chronometer, and other burglar locks, combination safe locks, padlocks, drawer, trunk, house, chest, store, door, and other locks, night latches, etc.; and so successful has the firm been, that to-day their locks of every description have made their way to every part of the civilized world.

Although he did not seek the honor, in the fall of 1882 the Democratic Congressional Convention for the Thirtieth District, at Rochester, nominated Colonel Greenleaf for Congress by acclamation, and he was elected to the Forty-eighth Congress as a Democrat, receiving 18,042 votes against 12,038; and in 1890 was re-elected to the Fifty-second Congress. He is at present a member of the Board of Trustees of the Rochester Savings Bank, of the Rochester Park Commission, of the St. Lawrence University at Canton, N. Y., and of the Soldiers' and Sailors' Home at Bath, N. Y.

151. Samuel Knight[8] Greenleaf (Chart XIII.), b. March 19, 1803, son of Samuel[7] and Rhoda Louise (Knight). Settled in North Royalton, Cuyahoga County, Ohio, about 1832. He lived there a few years, and removed to Circleville, Pickaway County, Ohio, where he died. He served several years in the State (Vermont) militia, also in the War of 1812, and was captain from 1825 to 1827 (see Military Service). He married in January, 1825, Olive Osyor. Mrs. Greenleaf lived to the ripe old age of ninety, and, notwithstanding her advanced years, her faculties were well preserved, and she evinced a lively interest in all current events up to the time of her death (Jan. 9, 1894). She was born in Leister, Addison County, Vt., Sept. 22, 1804. She was a familiar figure in the community where she had resided for the past forty years,—in and near Paris, Ill., with her children,—being generally known by the affectionate name of "Grandma Greenleaf." Mrs. Greenleaf was a stanch member of the Baptist Church, and active in its duties until deterred by the feebleness of age. She was a useful member of society, charitable, kind-hearted, and just, exemplifying the highest type of Christian womanhood.

157. Rev. George Dixon[8] Greenleaf (Chart XIV.), b. Sept. 12, 1808, son of James[7] and Sarah (Bullock). Mr. Greenleaf devoted a large portion of his life to the pastorate: first in connection with the Methodist Episcopal Church in Canada, and for the last eighteen or twenty years of his life in the Black River and Northern New York Conference. In consequence of impaired health he received a superannuated relation, but continued to preach occasionally, and furnished articles for the press until near the close of life. He was an original thinker, an able minister, and an interesting writer. In person he was about five feet ten inches in height, with dark brown hair sprinkled with gray, dark-gray eyes, bald at top of his head, full, round face, and very stout and fleshy, weighing over two hundred pounds. He died at the residence of his son George in Moira, St. Lawrence County, N. Y., May 4, 1876.

164. Orlando C.[9] Greenleaf (Chart XIV.), b. July 21, 1829, son of Rev. George D.[8] and Sally (Stickney). Learned the trade of cabinet making, at which he worked for six years, residing temporarily at Napanee, Newburgh, and Sterling, Canada, when, in 1861, he removed to Belleville, Ont., to take the position of foreman in the large machine shop of J. M. Walker & Co., where he worked until the dissolution of the firm in 1889. He then started business for himself on a small scale, and has, with his son, worked up the largest bicycle agency and repair shop between Toronto and Montreal, being still engaged in this business.

168. Edward Everett[9] Greenleaf (Chart XIV.), b. Aug. 13, 1837, son of William Fairbanks[8] and Abigail (Ward). Was educated in the district schools of Vermont, and in early life was engaged in building mills in Wisconsin and Iowa. Returning to Vermont in 1861, he enlisted as private in the First Vermont Battery of Light Artillery. After mustering out he returned to Vermont, and engaged in building and manufacturing. Removed to Alabama in 1887, and engaged in manufacturing at Decatur, Morgan Co., and was afterwards appointed Chief Deputy to United States Marshal for the northern district of Alabama. In 1890 was appointed Deputy Clerk of the United States Courts for the northern district of Alabama, and in 1892 was appointed United States Commissioner. Resides at Huntsville, Ala. (See Military Service.)

169. William Luther[9] Greenleaf (Chart XIV.), son of William Fairbanks[8] and Abigail (Ward), was born at Derby, Vt., September 1, 1842.

He removed with his parents to Winooski, Vt., in 1848, and was educated in the common schools and at the Williston Academy.

He enlisted as private in Co. L of the First Vermont Cavalry, on August 11, 1862, and served with distinction throughout the Civil War. Having a fondness for the military, he joined the Vermont militia, and served successively as captain, major, lieutenant colonel, and colonel of his regiment. He was elected by the Legislature to the office of Brigadier General, December 1, 1886. On his return to Vermont from the war he engaged in business as a pharmacist, and followed it successfully for nearly twenty years. In 1882 he was appointed Deputy Collector of Customs for the district of Vermont, which position he still occupies.

General Greenleaf joined the Masonic fraternity in 1865, and a few years later was made Master of Webster Lodge, No. 61, which position he held for nine years by successive elections. He was also a member of the Grand Lodge of Vermont for a period of twelve years. (See Military Service.)

161. **Luther Leland[8] Greenleaf** (Chart XIV.), b. Feb. 7, 1821, son of James[7] and Sarah (Bullock). Was for several years in business at Boston, as one of the firm of Fairbanks, Brown & Co., the selling agents of the Fairbanks Scales. In 1859 Mr. Greenleaf removed to Chicago, Ill., in the interests of the Fairbanks Scale Co., residing at Evanston, a suburb of Chicago, noted as a charming residential place. Mr. Greenleaf's literary tastes led him to gather, in a long series of years, a library of choice and valuable books. At the time of his taking up his abode in Evanston the Northwestern University was making its first beginnings in the collection of a library. In 1865 Mr. Lunt established the Orrington Lunt Library Fund; in 1869 Mr. Greenleaf gave from his collection a large number of books, which are known as the "Greenleaf Library"; in 1872 the library of the late Prof. Henry S. Noyes was purchased and added to the library; in 1878 Messrs. Deering and Gage presented a portion of the library of the late Oliver A. Willard. Books have been added every year by purchase, minor gifts have been made, the library has become a depository of Government publications, and it now contains some 40,000 volumes and over 10,000 pamphlets, which constitute it one of the finest, if not the finest, college library in the West. The Greenleaf Library comprises some 11,000 volumes and 9,000 pamphlets, which he purchased from the heirs of the late Hon. Johann Schulze, member of the Prussian Ministry of Public Instruction, and a specialist in classical philology. It is rich in the department of classical philology. There are numerous editions of the more prominent writers (of Horace, for example, there are over thirty), and the best editions of the later and less-known writers. Some incunabula are found here, and the modern languages are also well represented. As a citizen of Evanston and Chicago, Mr. Greenleaf was prominent in business and philanthropic enterprises. He was a man of large heart and of a noble nature, and did much for the best interests of the communities in which he lived. In the days of his prosperity he lived for the good of his fellow-man; but the days of adversity came, and in the

great Chicago fire and other mishaps his entire fortune was swept away, and ill health followed. In 1875 he retired from business; broken in estate and health he removed to Beloit, Wisconsin, where he died November 23, 1884.

171.   **John Dickinson[8] Greenleaf** (Chart XIV.), b. Dec. 8, 1803, son of Dr. Christopher[7] and Tabitha (Dickinson). When five years of age his father removed to the town of Ellisburgh, N. Y., a short distance south of the village of Smithville, where he remained ten years of his early life, attending the village school, and acquiring the foundation of an education and business acquaintance that influenced and successfully directed his after life. When only fifteen years of age he purchased of an uncle, Stephen Woodard, five acres of cleared land, which was located three miles south of Log Mills, now La Fargeville. Here he built a small but comfortable log house, and to it he removed his father's family. Here they remained for two years, when they took up their residence in the little settlement of Log Mills.

In the early part of the year 1823 Mr. Greenleaf removed to Clayton (then French Creek), and for a short time was a clerk in the store of Wm. H. Angel, who also had but recently removed from Smithville. Angel soon after formed a partnership with one Stephen Wetherby, which was in time changed to Smith & Angel, and then to Smith & Merrick, who for many years conducted vast business interests in the rafting of staves, pine, and oak timber down the river St. Lawrence to Quebec. Mr. Greenleaf continued in the employ of the firm for many years, in several capacities. In the year 1833 he was placed in command of the steamboat "Black Hawk," running from Ogdensburg to Kingston. This was the first steamboat built on the St. Lawrence River. She made her trips in two days, going up one day and coming back the next. For nine summers Mr. Greenleaf had the entire management of Messrs. Smith & Merrick's immense lumber interests at Quebec, and possessed their fullest confidence and regard, which was never misplaced or changed for the twenty years that he was in their employ. He then returned to his home in La Fargeville, where he remained till the spring of 1857, when he removed to Seneca, Ontario County, N. Y., and engaged in the occupation of farming.

Mr. Greenleaf, now in his ninety-fourth year, is hale and vigorous, and resides with his youngest daughter at Hall's Corner, Ontario County, New York.

173.   **Louis Christopher[9] Greenleaf** (Chart XV.), b. Nov. 23, 1840, in La Fargeville, N. Y., son of John Dickinson[8] and Julia (Truesdell). Removed to Ontario County, and in 1860 located in Watertown, N. Y., where he was engaged in the county clerk's office for one year, when he enlisted, and was with the first company that left Watertown for the war. He was mustered out on expiration of his term of service, and entered the provost-marshal's office in the city of Watertown, where he remained until the close of the war, after which he found employment in the Jefferson

County National Bank as discount clerk for two years, when he entered the Merchants Bank as teller and assistant cashier, which position he ably filled for four years. In March, 1872, in company with Charles W. Sloat, under the firm name of Sloat & Greenleaf, he engaged in the lumber business, which he continued for twenty-one years.

The business of the firm became so extensive that in 1893 the co-partnership became incorporated under the name of "The Sloat & Greenleaf Lumber Company," of which Mr. Greenleaf is its secretary and treasurer. He has always been prominently identified with the interests of the city of Watertown. He was the first City Treasurer, which office he held two years; was County Treasurer six years, Supervisor of the Second Ward several years, and is now a member of the Board of Education. For many years he was an active member of the Fire Department. He is an enthusiastic member of the Masonic Order, and has held the honors of his Lodge, Chapter, and Commandery, besides receiving for three successive years the appointment of District Deputy Grand Master. He is a thirty-second degree Mason of the Scottish Rite Bodies, and at the present time is commander of Joe Spratt Post, No. 323, Grand Army of the Republic.

Mr. Greenleaf is a member of the State Street Methodist Episcopal Church and its large Sunday school, of which he is the superintendent. He has been active in the work of the Young Men's Christian Association, and for many years its president, and is now one of the trustees. (See Military Service.)

186. Dr. David[7] Greenleaf (Chart XVI.), b. June 19, 1765, son of David[6] and Mary (Johnson). Resided in Hartford, where he carried on the business of gold and silver smith for many years, and accumulated a large property, owning many pieces of real estate in that city, as appears from the property which he offered for sale between 1799 and 1828. He built some of the finest buildings in the city of that time, one of which is now standing on the corner of Main and Kingsley Streets (then Lee Street), in the very center of the city; here he had his store.

In 1806 he was a member of the Common Council. Retiring from the business of jewelry about 1811, he became a dentist. In the *Connecticut Courant*, Oct. 29, 1827, he advertises himself as having practiced dentistry sixteen years. (See Military Service.)

190. Dr. Charles[8] Greenleaf (Chart XVI.), b. June 2, 1788, son of Dr. David[7] and Nancy (Jones). Was a well-known dentist, and practiced his profession in Hartford, Conn. His office was on Exchange Corner. He had a reputation second to none, for good work, in all parts of the State. We find in the Hartford *Courant* of Nov. 28, 1820, an advertisement appointing H. Seymour & Co. his agents for disposing of gold leaf manufactured by him. Also, Sept. 27, 1831, notice of removal from Catlin's Corner (cor. Main and Asylum Streets) to Exchange Building. This building, or office, was used by his son, Dr. James M. Greenleaf, as a place of business until his death, in 1877. Dr. David

Greenleaf, who died in Alameda, Cal., Sept. 6, 1893, and his brother, Dr. James M., were at one time in company, under the firm name of J. M. & D. Greenleaf.

193. Dr. Charles⁹ Greenleaf, Jr. (Chart XVI), b. Sept. 1, 1809, son of Dr. Charles⁸ and Electa (Toocker). Was for many years a dentist in Hartford and in Essex, Conn. In 1847 he removed to Farmington, Ill.; afterwards he removed to Peoria, Ill., having a large practice. He was United States Inspector during and after the war. Removing back to Farmington, he spent his last years retired from active business. He was well and favorably known in Farmington and Peoria, Ill., as a quiet, pleasant, and companionable gentleman.

195. Dr. James Monroe⁹ Greenleaf (Chart XVI.), b. April 26, 1819, son of Dr. Charles⁸ and Electa (Toocker). Was a leading dentist in Hartford for many years, and as a gentleman was universally respected. At an early age he engaged in business with his father, who was a noted and successful dentist in his day. Dr. Greenleaf's office had been one of the heirlooms of the city. His life was full of generosity and kindness, and his presence always assured one of help and sympathy. Few men were more kindly disposed toward people generally. He was a model of courtesy and manliness. (See Military Service.)

196. Dr. David⁹ Greenleaf (Chart XVI.), b. Jan. 16, 1827, son of Dr. Charles⁸ and Electa (Toocker). Removed West about 1853, and settled in Peoria, Ill., where he practiced his profession, a dentist, for some years. He removed from there to Galesburg, and engaged in the drug trade. He was elected Mayor of that city by the Democrats. In 1889–90 he removed with his family to Alameda, near San Francisco, Cal.

191. Judge David⁸ Greenleaf (Chart XVI.), b. May 6, 1803, son of Dr. David⁷ and Nancy (Jones). Received a fair education in early youth, and at the age of seventeen engaged in mercantile employment at Boston, in which he remained for three years. He then removed to Hartford, Conn., living there until April 6, 1835, when he moved West, arriving in Quincy, Ill., May, 1836. In June following he entered land in St. Mary's township, Hancock County, and followed farming until April, 1843, when he moved to Chili township. At Chili he bought a piece of land at the first land sale held there.

The tavern at Carthage, Ill., where he "put up," was a primitive "log house." It was then kept by a man named Williams. A plank in the floor of the old hotel has been taken up from the exact spot in the room where the body of Joseph Smith, the Mormon apostle, lay the night after he was killed, and was manufactured into canes, and sent to Salt Lake City to be sold to the Mormons.

In April, 1847, he removed to Carthage, Ill., where he resided until his death, in 1890, with the exception of about three years in Adams County. His first employment in Carthage was in the dry goods business for some years, ultimately engaging in the drug trade, which business he followed until about 1880, when he retired from business. During his long residence in this county, Judge Greenleaf's official ability and integrity have been recognized in his election to numerous township and county offices of trust and responsibility. He held the office of Justice of the Peace in St. Mary's and Chili townships while living there, and in 1843 was elected Probate County Judge, holding the office for two terms. It was during this period that he saw much of the peculiarities of Mormon life and character, and of which he has given many interesting incidents. He was postmaster of this city (Carthage, Ill.), six years in the administration of Van Buren, Harrison, and Tyler. In his church relations he was an Episcopalian, to which church he was strongly attached.—From *Carthage Republican*, Carthage, Ill., April 9, 1890.

The predominating characteristic of Judge Greenleaf was the quietness of his manners. He was a man who strictly attended to his own business, and left his neighbors to attend to theirs; hence he made but few enemies, and the friends he won he retained. No citizen in his county was more honored and respected than the Judge.

203. Daniel Judson[10] Greenleaf (Chart XVII.), b. Feb. 13, 1848, son of John Harrison[9] and Elimira D. (Mondone) Greenleaf. Is a dealer in musical instruments at Port Jervis, N. Y. He married Hannah Mary, daughter of Benjamin S. and Martha M. Healy. Mrs. Healy was born in the town of Cohocton, Steuben County, New York, Dec. 18, 1832. Her mother, Mary Bronson Hess, was born in Cohocton, Oct. 21, 1813, being the first white child born in the town. Her maternal grandfather, John Hess, was born in Mohawk, Herkimer County, Jan. 7, 1801. His grandmother was killed, while feeding the pigs, by an Indian, who had hidden in the pen. Mr. Hess was a lineal descendant of the Hesses of Hesse Castle.

Benjamin Spaulding Healy, Mrs. Greenleaf's father, was born in the town of Dansville, Steuben County, N. Y., April 18, 1825. Her paternal grandfather, Joshua Healy, was born in Shoreham, Vermont, June 16, 1791. Both he and his wife, Lucy (Wilson), who was born in Shoreham, Nov. 11, 1793, were noted for their Puritan ancestry of good New England stock. Their wedding trip consisted of a ride in an ox cart, containing all their earthly effects, household utensils, etc., from their Vermont home to Steuben County, where, with the help of the Indians, a log cabin was erected and land cleared for a nucleus to the present farm. One of the best orchards in that section is that of the old homestead, the seeds of which were carried by Mr. Healy in his vest pocket from Vermont; and the first apples eaten by him or his family in their new home grew upon the trees raised from those seeds.

205. Daniel Toocker[8] Greenleaf (Chart XVII.), b. Feb. 11, 1809, near Mt. Hope, Orange County, N. Y., son of John[7] and Martha (Toocker). Removed to Seneca County in 1831, and settled at Canoga. He owned one of the finest farms on the shores of Cayuga Lake. Here he married Rebecca, daughter of Rulif Peterson, one of the earlier settlers of Canoga. Two years after their marriage they both united with the Presbyterian Church; to the close of their life they remained earnest supporters of its cause, and he was for many years a ruling elder in the church. In Mrs. Greenleaf's death, on Sept. 1, 1887, was severed a wedded life which had extended nearly fifty-six years. She was the only one of the numerous family who remained and resided on any portion of her father's land in the State. This farm was at the Canoga Ferry landing, and was Government land taken up by her father in 1805. Here she was born and spent the greater part of her life. She had a very retentive memory, and was good authority for local history of the village and surroundings. She died about a mile from where she was born, south end of Canoga Village, where her father built when he retired from farming, and occupied until he died, in 1850. Her son, Albert R. Greenleaf, is the third generation (maternal) who has occupied these premises, he moving there in 1856. The farm with village residence all connect; the residence is a half mile back from the lake.

For more than thirty years Mr. Greenleaf was engaged in the fire insurance business, having been a pioneer agent. Few rural families between Ovid and Wayne County line but had at some time business associations with him, and admired him for his promptness, uprightness, and integrity. He combined a courtly manner with perfect frankness. He had the hardy virtues of his Huguenot and New England ancestors, and was earnest and industrious. His ability and enterprise enabled him to accumulate a competency, while his public spirit and kindness of heart won him the respect and confidence of all who knew him. His memory will be pleasant to the many who, by his active life, were permitted to know him and call him friend and counsellor. During a long life of more than fourscore the good man kept his faith, and went to his reward trusting and ready.

207. Dr. William Alva[8] Greenleaf (Chart XVII.), b. Jan. 5, 1825, son of John[7] and Martha (Toocker). Was graduated February, 1847, at the Botanical Medical College in Ohio, and practiced in his profession at South Middletown, Orange Co., N. Y. At the breaking out of the War of the Rebellion he entered the service as acting assistant surgeon, United States Army, during which he was so injured as to partially cripple him for life. Although he had been at times a great sufferer and a chronic invalid, he courageously attended to the duties of his profession and the conducting of a drug store at Jersey City Heights, N. J., until his death, on June 11, 1894. (See Military Service.)

215. Harry Torrey[9] Greenleaf, C. E. (Chart XVII.), b. Oct. 1, 1852, son of Dr. William Alva[8] and Catherine W. G. (Wisnor). Resides at Elizabeth City, N. C. Has been engaged in the construction of railroads South, and was also the engineer for the State of North Carolina in settling the boundary line between North Carolina and Virginia in the years 1887-88. A large granite monument is placed on the east end of this line, where the State lines begin at the Atlantic Ocean, and his name is there engraved as the engineer of the work.

219. John Hancock[7] Greenleaf (Chart XVIII.), b. April 30, 1775, son of Gen. William[6] and Sally (Quincy). Learned the trade of a cabinet maker and house joiner in Boston, and then settled himself in Granville, Washington Co., N. Y. In March, 1817, he removed to Tioga Co., N. Y., where he died. He was a man of medium size, fair complexion, dark-brown hair, dark eyes, and high forehead. He walked very erect. He was a sedate man, of very uniform life, and for nearly fifty years was a consistent member of the Baptist church.

232. John Matthew[8] Greenleaf (Chart XIX.), b. May 19, 1806, son of John Hancock[7] and Polly (Norton), removed in 1813 with his father and mother to Owego County in New York State, and resided in the township of Richford till 1826; then removed to Owego, and in a few years formed a partnership with a Mr. Truman in what was then called a " general store," thus becoming one of the pioneers in that line of business. He continued as a merchant till 1849, when the great fire demolished the business part of the town, and then he retired. He was identified with all the early enterprises of the little hamlet, and spent fifty-six years of his life in Owego.

He was a man of fine organization, clean and honest in every way, a little too shy to be well known, but a man who had many stanch friends, and enjoyed the confidence of everybody. His judgment of men and things was true to a remarkable degree, and he clearly read human nature. In his dealings with men he was just to all and charitable to the foibles of those whom he knew.

235. Dr. John Talcott[9] Greenleaf (Chart XIX.), b. Jan. 26, 1847, son of John Matthew[8] and Emeline (Wilbur). Was graduated from the New York Homeopathic Medical College, March 2, 1867. Began practice in Candor, N. Y. Moved to Owego, November, 1867; has lived and practiced there ever since. Is now physician in charge and one of the proprietors of " Glenmary," a private asylum for the insane. He is a member of the American Institute of Homeopathy, New York State Homeopathic Medical Society, the American Association for the Advancement of Science, and other small local societies, and holds the degree of M.D. from the Board of Regents of University of New York State.

384. Sarah Greenleaf (Chart XXIII.), b. Oct. 1, 1779, daughter of Ebenezer[6] and Elizabeth (Chapman) Greenleaf. Married Lemuel Collins. He settled on Lot 49, adjoining his father's on the south, in the town of Industry, Maine, in 1801. This was set off to New Sharon in 1852, and is embraced in the well-known William Henry Manter farm. He felled the first trees on his lot, burned his " cut down," cleared the land and erected a log cabin, in which his oldest daughter, Eliza, was born.

After living ten years in a log house Mr. Collins built a larger and more convenient frame house, it being one of the first in that section of the town. He died on the homestead in New Sharon, July 31, 1851.

385. John[6] Greenleaf (Chart XXIII.), b. Nov. 6, 1755, son of Joseph[5] and Dorcas (Gray). Was born in Wiscasset, Maine. After his service in the Revolutionary War he returned to Wiscasset, and married Anna Pierce Roberts, of that town. Early in the spring of 1782 he and his brother Ebenezer, with their wives, together with Joshua, another brother, started for the Sandy River, in Starks. Here they each took up a farm of productive and valuable land. Joshua located immediately opposite, on the same river, in the town of Mercer. A few years later a younger brother, William, also four sisters, Martha, Sally, Rachel, and Lydia, came, married, and settled in the vicinity.

He was about five feet nine inches in height, light complexion, blue eyes, light hair, sandy beard, and slightly freckled. He was straight built, and retained his erect carriage till he was ninety years of age. He was possessed of a comfortable property at the time of his death. He had great caution, was very prudent and exact in all his dealings, but gave liberally to the poor. His remains lie in the old family burying ground, beneath the soil he used to till. (See Military Service.)

445. William[7] Greenleaf (Chart XXIII.), b. March 17, 1792, son of John[6] and Anna Pierce (Roberts). A remarkable feature of the beautiful and picturesque coast of Maine, is its many islands and great variety of scenery. Nestling among others near the mouth of the Kennebec, lies one of beauty, known as " Squirrel Island ": the rocks rough and wild in their grandeur; the calm and peaceful dunes suggest repose; living springs abound. The charms which it presented for a pastoral life, an ideal agricultural and sea-bound home, so possessed the mind and fancy of " Squire " William Greenleaf, that in 1825 he bought the island, and moved onto it the same year with his wife and two children; one daughter and two sons were born subsequently on the island. He was an eccentric and somewhat peculiar man in many ways, but he was always hospitable, and received everybody with a cordial greeting. His sons were cool and brave, and were excellent fishermen, while his daughters possessed the accomplishments of being familiar with literature, poetry, and song; and they were excellent cooks withal, and could handle an oar, read Horace, mow a field or catch a lamb on the cliffs, butcher the creature,—hanging it to a spruce—taking of the pelt in a jiffy; they were worthy offspring of a remarkable man. The Squire was highly cultivated, and a gentleman of the " Old School;" very proud, and especially so of his own personal appearance. He generally appeared in public clad in a tall beaver and a blue broadcloth coat with brass buttons, the tail of which was slightly clipped after the fashion of Henry Clay. Of Mr. Clay he was a great admirer. He liked to dress as Henry Clay did. And he loved his long-stemmed " T. D." pipe, and his cup and flask which often stood beside it. As a true disciple of the great statesman, from a sublime sense of duty he, too, regaled his classic throat with an occasional glass of brandy, the measurement whereof was suited to the traditions and inspirations of the Whigs, who were in the eyes of the Squire the most respectable portion of the then existing society. He kept a large flock of sheep and herds of cattle, and it was known to many that the Princess Roselinda, as his good wife was called, was skilled in the making of cheese. He was, in fact, the King of Squirrel Island, and the famous old farmhouse, long known as the King's Palace, was a happy resort for numerous friends and relatives for nearly forty years. The nautical fore room; the forecastle yarns; the chowders; the clambakes; the fish dinners; its merry tenantry,—all bear testimony to those now living who as guests were partakers of the royal entertainments of "King William of Squirrel Island." Nor was he unmindful of the needs of the intellect, for he supplied his guests with a collection of rare old books and papers; collections from nearly every point of the globe. He was a great reader, a fluent talker, and well informed in politics. Religiously, the Squire was somewhat like his house,—*at sea*. He believed in giving sixteen ounces for a pound, and in a yardstick thirty-six inches in length, but as between Calvinism and Arminianism, or as between any *issues*, however venerable, he did not care to choose. His eccentricity has brought to life many bright and breezy anecdotes, several of which have been published by the *Squirrel Island Squid*, an enterprising summer weekly issued by Park G. Dingley, of the *Lewiston Journal*, from 1875 to 1893, concerning his long and happy life on the Islands. Among his eccentricities was his method of emphasis. Of a strong mind, and only human, there were times when strong expletives, like strong brandy, were thought to be needed; but if he ever uttered oaths, which no conscientious historian would ever affirm, he discharged them in Latin, "By Jupiter," "By Venus," or "By Tam O'Shanter."

The Squire was bristling with little oddities and quiddities, for he was an inveterate consumer of the weed, and invariably had a tobacco field west of the royal palace,—square rods of precious loam now devoted to such commonplace crops as potatoes. The island was heavily wooded, and contained many large and very beautiful trees. Here he would often wander, and raise his musical voice in sonorous tones in the old hymns,

> "O for a thousand tongues to sing
> My dear Redeemer's praise."

Or, perhaps, seated at the cooling spring near the center of the island, a spring celebrated for many years, perusing Homer, or Virgil, or Horace, he could be heard reciting "Our Squirrel:"—

> "There are islands in the ocean,
> Where the wild and restless motion
> Of the heart that beats and surges,
> With its passion and its pain,
> May best be stilled to quiet dreaming,
> Till all pain is but a seeming,
> Of a land long left behind us,
> That we ne'er shall see again."

Or, when on the high cliffs at the south banks, he might be heard, saying :—

> "Again I linger by Squirrel's shore,
> And listen to the music of the sea
> For some familiar voice to speak to me
> Out of the deep, sad, harmonious roar,
> Whose murmuring cadences sound like a store
> Of loving words,—treasures of memory,
> Once breathed into the ambient air, to be
> Vibrated through the ages evermore.
> The infinite tides environ us; no strain
> That e'er awakened human smiles or tears
> Is lost; nor shall we call it back in vain.
> Beside the shore, amid the eternal spheres,
> Hark,—the beloved Voices once again
> Rise from the waves and winds to sooth mine ears! "

His peculiarities displayed themselves at their most grotesque point not long before his death. He was as much a believer in dreams and visions of the night as the most orthodox Hebrew patriarch. He had an abiding faith in the supernatural. One night he had a dream. The time and manner of his death were clearly revealed to him, and that he should die at Boothbay, and not at the Squirrel. He arose on the morning after this vision, and put on his Henry Clay coat, the cloth of which had been woven on a hand loom in the old foreroom at the Island farmhouse, brushed his hair with great precision, and deliberately set about making preparations to die. He went over to Captain Mac's, at Boothbay, and asked permission to die in his house. Captain Mac, in a tremulous voice, declined, and re-called his guest to sublunary things by this remark, "Mr. Greenleaf, take a little something to drink; it will steady your nerves." He invariably drank his brandy in three-fingered drinks; and so, steadying his nerves, he made arrangements to die at another house in Boothbay. He then went to a Boothbay coffin maker and asked him to take his measure for a coffin. To another man he went and engaged him to take charge of his burial. He went to the gravedigger, and begged that functionary to dig his grave at once. The Squire paid the gravedigger on the spot. The appointed time came, but not the time and place of the vision, though not far distant, and his friends came and went to his bedside in the old farmhouse on the Island he loved so well, where he died on May 4, 1868. His funer-al services were at the Congregational Church, Boothbay Harbor, and his mortal remains were taken to their last resting place at Boothbay Centre, where he had previously bought a lot, and buried by the side of the re-mains of his wife; and to-day, around the classic board of the royal palace, one may always see a vacant seat, and the shade of Squire Greenleaf is the shade with which fancy peoples that disused chair.

The Island was purchased of the Greenleaf heirs in 1870 by a party of Lewiston gentlemen, viz., Messrs. Ex-Mayor J. B. Ham, Gov. Nelson Dingley, Rev. Dr. Cheney, and others, for the small sum of twenty-one hundred and fifty dollars. It contains one hundred and twenty-five acres of land, and is well wooded. It is one of the most delightful and popular summer resorts on the Atlantic coast.

446. Stephen[7] Greenleaf (Chart XXIII.), b. Aug. 26, 1794, son of John[6] and Anna (Roberts). After completing his studies at the district school, he and his brothers, William and George, went to Wiscasset Academy, where they received thorough instruction for three years, from 1811 to 1814. While pursuing his studies, August, 1814, news came that the British were threatening to enter the mouth of the Kennebec River. He at once started on foot for home to join the militia and his brother's—Captain John—company. Contracting a severe cold, he was confined several weeks to his bed with fever. After recovering, he " scoured up " his father's old fusee, and started for the scene of action with the company as its clerk or orderly sergeant. Before the end of his service of sixty days the British abandoned their project, and the militia were dismissed.

For twenty years or more after the war he was a successful schoolmaster. He and his brother William purchased the two farms just north of Starks Village, in 1817, one of which he owned and occupied to the time of his death (a period of sixty-four years). He was a Justice of the Peace for nearly fifty years, and being a fine penman, he was sought by his townsmen, to a considerable extent, to draft deeds and other legal documents. He was a man of extensive reading, and kept in touch with events and current topics to the time of his death. In politics he was (as were his seven sons) a stanch and prominent Democrat, and did not fail to vote the straight ticket for more than sixty annual elections. He held the several town offices, viz., Town Clerk, Treasurer, School Committee, Selectmen, etc., for many years, and was a member of the House of Representatives in the State Legislature in 1837. He was familiarly known by his townsmen and friends as the " Squire," and addressed as Esquire Greenleaf. In person he was five feet and nine inches in height, and very straight built; weight about one hundred and sixty pounds; had blue eyes, high, full forehead, and fine, silky, dark hair, which held its luster to the time of his death.

He was exceedingly agile, and when past seventy-five years of age he was as spry as most boys. As an instructor, husband, and father he was greatly beloved. As a townsman he was highly and universally esteemed, and enjoyed the full confidence of his neighbors and acquaintances, who sincerely mourned his loss as that of an honest and good man. (See Military Service.)

His widow, " Aunt Fanny," as she was lovingly called, survived him until Feb. 12, 1895, living with her faithful and devoted daughter, Mrs. Lydia Greaton, when she peacefully entered her eternal home.

> Blest is his life, who to himself is true,—
>   And blest his death; for memory, when he dies,
> Comes with a lover's eloquence to renew
>   Our faith in manhood's upward tendencies.

> Serene with conscious peace, she strewed her way
>   With sweet humanities, the growth of love;
> Shaping to right her actions day by day—
>   Faithful to this world and to that above.

To her children she was a beacon light, always shining brightly to point out the way of life and those paths of peace which she so serenely trod. Blest with a voice of rare quality, purity, and volume of tone, the worshipers of the sanctuary had many years been led in their devotions by the sweet influence of her heart-felt songs; and it was remarkable that in her later years the voice of song was retained to her in a great degree. Many of the older residents can remember her as she appeared in early life,—possessing unusual beauty and a tall, graceful carriage, both of which she preserved in her later days,—her sunset of life,—which was so calm and beautiful, and in peaceful harmony with that long line of years in which her children will always fondly love to dwell. Their storehouse of memory is well filled with "precept upon precept" of her teachings of wisdom, and "line upon line" of love and devotion. Fortunate, indeed, are they in such possessions; and the loftiness of her pure and noble character, the gentleness and loveliness of her ways, will be to those she has left behind to follow her as a benediction of a life of a noble and generous woman.

456. Stephen Decatur[8] Greenleaf (Chart XXIII.), b. Oct. 26, 1817, son of Anthony[7] and Nancy (Brown). Left home at the early age of seventeen and at once engaged to be a sailor. He followed the sea for eight years, when he returned to his old home and entered at once vigorously into farming, and has ever since owned and occupied the same premises on Sandy River. In addition to his large farming interests he found time to give attention to other pursuits. During the war he was engaged largely in recruiting soldiers and filling quotas for various towns. He has dealt and operated to quite an extent in patents and patent rights. He was ever foremost in all matters of reform and improvements in his town and county. His hospitality was unlimited. His quick and energetic generosity to the unfortunate is worthy of special mention. Before and during the war he was an ardent Republican, but having the Greenback policy of finance and the free coinage of silver firmly established in his mind, he was one of the first to organize and form the Greenback party in Maine. He was elected County Commissioner of Somerset County in 1878, and served three years, declining a renomination. He was nominated as the candidate for governor by that party in 1879, but declined the honor and refused to have his name used. Although his early advantages for an education were limited, he acquired, by long study and application, much information and practical knowledge, and at various times contributed to farmers' papers and agricultural journals articles on garden vegetation and general farming.

462. Luke Sawyer[8] Greenleaf (Chart XXIII.), b. Jan. 6, 1814, son of Levi[7] and Amy (Greenleaf). Lived on a farm with his parents until he was over twenty-one years of age, when he went to Easton, Mass., and found employment with E. J. W. Morse & Co., thread manufacturers. He was in their employ for nearly fifty years when he resigned. He was first postmaster in South Easton, where he now resides, serving through Harrison's administration (1841).

478. Capt. Cyrus Metcalf[8] Greenleaf (Chart XXIII.), b. May 10, 1821, son of Stephen[7] and Rhoda (Metcalf). Was born in Starks, Maine, and was educated in the common town and high schools of that place. He remained on the farm until he was twenty years old, and in June, 1841, went to Gardiner and shipped with Capt. Charles Snow, of Schooner " Providence "; followed the sea two years, then returned to his native farm, married, and went into trade with Colonel Chapman under the firm name of Chapman & Greenleaf, which continued four years, and during which time he entered the Starch Company of that town, and helped build and become owner of one-sixth part of the large Starch Factory of V. Felker & Co. He was Town Clerk of Starks some ten years, besides holding other places of trust. In 1860 Captain Greenleaf was appointed United States Deputy Marshal for the State of Maine, and in the same year was census enumerator in the district composed of Starks and Mercer. In 1862 he removed to Anson and engaged in farming and mill business. In May, 1878, he removed to New Vineyard and lived there until November, 1882, and then returned to Starks where he now lives. (See Military Service.)

486. John Brown[9] Greenleaf, b. Oct. 23, 1850, son of Capt. Cyrus Metcalf[8] and Myra J. (Chapman). Went to California in 1876, and now resides in East Oakland. His business is that of contractor of earth and stone work. He is an energetic, thrifty, and successful man.

479. Enoch Lincoln[8] Greenleaf (Chart XXIII.), b. July 28, 1827, son of Stephen and Fanny (Taylor). Attended the village district school until he was eighteen years old, when he began work for himself. Being ambitious and in vigorous health he accumulated sufficient means to buy a good farm, and settled upon it at the age of twenty-four years. He was prosperous as a farmer and, having the assistance of an exceptionally charming and thrifty wife, he soon purchased the two adjoining farms, and later a fourth was added. He was a member of the Board of Selectmen of his town, and collector of taxes for several years. He sold his farm to his brother-in-law, George W. Greaton, in 1887, and moved to Farmington, where he now resides.

490. Enoch Owen[9] Greenleaf (Chart XXIII.), b. Dec. 17, 1853, son of Enoch L.[8] and Rebekah (Greaton). Was educated at the common and high schools, graduating at Westbrook in class of 1875. He read law in the office of Judge Bonney of Portland, Maine, and with G. C. Vose, Esq., of Augusta, being admitted to the bar at Augusta in 1879. Moved to Farmington in 1880 where he has since continued the practice of his profession. He has one of the best offices in the state, and a lucrative practice. He is active in politics, having served on the Democratic state committee for five years, and he is also active in all social and educational reforms. He has held as a citizen and business man many positions of trust and honor. Is prominent in masonic circles, having been master of

his lodge two years; H. P. of his chapter two years, and is now D. D. G.
M. of his district; holds the position of D. M. in the council, and J. W.
in the commandery of K. T.

480. Wakefield[8] **Greenleaf** (Chart XXIII.), b. March 4, 1829,
son of Stephen[7] and Fanny (Taylor). After finishing his studies at the
village school he entered the store of Col. Asa Chapman at Starks, and
remained with him for several years. He learned the trade of making and
finishing ladies' boots, and worked at it for several years in Starks, New
Sharon and Norridgewock. He has continuously held the office of Town
Clerk and Postmaster in Starks for many years. He is a Justice of the
Peace, and being a fine penman he has done considerable clerical work for
his townsmen. He has not enjoyed good health since a young man, being
afflicted with asthma.

482. George[8] **Greenleaf** (Chart XXIII.), b. Nov. 26, 1841, son of
Stephen[7] and Fanny (Taylor). Obtained a good business education at the
village, district and high schools. He was Deputy Sheriff for nine years
and in Somerset County—was a member of the Board of Selectmen of his
native town (Starks) for several years. He resided on the old homestead,
taking charge of the farm on which he was born. In 1885 he was appointed Postal Clerk, and held the position during the first administration
of President Cleveland. He moved from Starks to North Anson in 1886,
where he continued to reside until October, 1889, and then removed to
Portland, where he now resides. He is engaged in the retail business of
wall paper, curtains, and curtain fixtures. In November, 1893, he was re-
instated to the postal service with duties as Transfer Clerk at the Union
Station in Portland. He is a Freemason. (See Military Service). His
son, Dr. George Walter[9] Greenleaf, born Aug. 9, 1870, was brought up by
his grandmother, Mrs. Betsey Huntress, at Effingham, N. H., his mother
having died when he was three months old. After attending the common
schools in Effingham, he began to teach at the early age of sixteen in the
same town. He attended Anson Academy in 1887–88. He began to study
medicine with Dr. George Lougee at Freedom, N. H., in 1889, attended
Bowdoin College Medical Department, completing his course and graduating in the class of 1894, and is now a practicing physician in Somerville, Mass.

484. Levi[8] **Greenleaf** (Chart XXIII.), b. Dec. 30, 1849, son of
Stephen[7] and Fanny (Taylor). Received his early education at the public
schools. Attended Bloomfield and Anson Academies one year each,
then fitted for college at Nichols Latin School, Lewiston. After teaching two years he entered the Junior class at Westbrook Seminary in
1872, and graduated with his class in 1873. He was a successful and competent teacher in the public schools. In March, 1874, Mr. Greenleaf
began the study of law in the office of Hon. S. S. Brown, then at Fairfield, and was admitted to the bar in Somerset County in April, 1876.
He at once opened an office at Solon, Me. Moved to Pittsfield in 1878,

and in 1884 to Lewiston, remaining there until May, 1895, when he removed to Portland, where he now resides. In 1879 Mr. Greenleaf was
elected County Attorney for the County of Somerset, which office he
held one term, then of three years. While a resident of Pittsfield, Mr.
Greenleaf also held the offices of Chairman of the Board of Selectmen,
Assessors, etc., and was a member of the Superintending School Committee of that town for several years, resigning when he removed there-
from. He is a member of the Androscoggin and Cumberland Bar and
of the State Bar Association of Maine. In politics Mr. Greenleaf is a
Democrat of unswerving fidelity and is active and well known throughout the state in political circles. He was Chairman of the Democratic County Committee of Androscoggin County for several years. He
is a prominent Odd Fellow, and has held the offices of Senior Warden,
Chief Patriarch, and High Priest, of Worumbus Encampment No. 13, and
is a member of the Grand Encampment of Maine. In person he is
described as being five feet eleven and a half inches in height, straight
and well built; he has dark hazel eyes and auburn mustache; his hair is
dark brown, almost black, and his weight is one hundred and seventy-
eight pounds.

472. Capt. Edward Mellville[9] Greenleaf (Chart XXIII.), b.
Nov. 23, 1857, in Boothbay, Me., son of Edward Kent[8] and Mary Ann
(Wyatt). His early life up to nine years of age was spent at home, after
which, and for seventeen years, he followed the sea, mostly on the Atlantic
and Pacific Oceans, in which he easily won promotion, and in 1879 became
master of a West India and South American trader. In 1883 he left the
Eastern Coast and went to California, and from there went as Officer on
the Pacific Coast Steamship Co.'s steamer for two years. Since 1885 he
has been in the Goverment employ to Feb. 1, 1893, having had charge of
one of the Secret Service Detective Departments; his field of operation
being China, Japan, Sandwich Islands, Mexico, and Canada, with headquarters at Victoria, B. C. The first three winters he was stationed there
he taught navigation, school, and nautical astronomy, preparing candidates for officers and masters, for the British Board of Trade examinations,
etc. In February, 1893, he resigned that position with the Government
to accept the management of an Oil and Fishing Company, in British
Columbia, and having charge of one of the steamers belonging to the
Company up to Oct. 1, 1893, he took charge of the ship Dominion, which
position he now holds. She is owned by the Oil and Fishing Company
in San Francisco, Cal., and is a ship that carries two thousand five hundred tons.

386. Joshua[6] Greenleaf (Chart XXIII.), b. June 14, 1765, son of
Joseph[5] and Dorcas (Gray). Removed to Mercer, Maine, when eighteen
years of age. In 1790 he married Hannah Williamson, who was said
to be the first white woman who crossed the mill stream at Mercer. Their
first home was in a log house built on the intervale; for window glass they
took the pelt of a sheep, the wool being removed and the skin being

stretched on a frame to admit light. Letters were a luxury in those days, and the nearest post office (in 1804) was Farmington Falls, whither a journey would be made, an event of the day, to procure news of the outer world. As the children learnt to read, they would sit by the open fire, keeping it bright with birch bark, and with this light would pursue their studies, and in time, being qualified, became teachers.

Mr. Greenleaf was Deputy Sheriff for some years, and his son Seth was Coroner twelve years. Mrs. Hannah G. Ford, the daughter of Seth, and now living on the old farm of her grandfather, Joshua Greenleaf, at Mercer, writes, "I have before me three papers from three different Governors of Maine, where my father (Seth) was appointed Coroner, one from Gov. John Fairfield, another from Gov. H. D. Anderson, and one from Gov. John W. Dana, in their handwriting."

511. David⁵ Greenleaf (Chart XXIV.), b. July 25, 1721, son of Daniel⁴ and Sarah (Moody). Resided for some years in Boston; was a man of considerable property, and at one time held the office of Town Treasurer. He afterwards removed to Newburyport, where he died at the age of sixty-four, at Newbury. He is spoken of as a "little old man with a brown bob wig, and abounded in wit and waggery." (See Military Service.)

512. Daniel⁶ Greenleaf (Chart XXIV.), b. 1753, son of David⁵ and Sarah (Lamson). Was at sea some little time during the War of the Revolution, and was once a prisoner. About the year 1800 he removed from Newburyport to the town of Rumford, in Maine, where he died in 1839 at the age of eighty-six. His children resided in Oxford County, Maine, in or near Rumford. (See Military Service.)

513. Hon. Jonathan⁵ Greenleaf (Chart XXV.), b. July, 1723. Was the sixth child and second son of Daniel⁴ and Sarah (Moody) of Newbury. His father was drowned when he was but little over five years of age, and his mother was left in very destitute circumstances, with a large family of children. At seven years of age he was apprenticed to Mr. Edward Presbury, and learned the trade of ship carpenter. At the age of twenty-one he married Mary Presbury, the daughter of his master, with whom he lived more than sixty years. He carried on the business of shipbuilding in person for about twenty years, and after this carried it on more extensively, and accumulated a large estate. From about the year 1768 to 1792 he was much in public life, and the stirring scenes of the Revolution engaged his energies. For the whole of that time he sustained some public office. Sept. 26, 1774, he was unanimously chosen to represent the town of Newburyport in the General Court. He was a member of the Continental Congress at the commencement of the war. June 12, 1786, he was made one of the Governor's Council for Essex. Senator, Feb. 11, 1788. In the Massachusetts Assembly for the ratification of the Federal Constitution, he and Hon. Benjamin Greenleaf were among the "Yeas." Mr. Greenleaf was a well-built man, about five feet and four or six inches high, of spare habit, not inclining to corpulency. He had a high forehead, a large aquiline nose, full, dark, hazel eyes, and rather prominent front teeth, which he retained to the last. In his later years his dress was always of one color, being deep blue, London brown, or light drab. He generally wore shoes with oval silver buckles, and in cold weather a drab broadcloth great coat, or a blue cloak, a full white wig, after the fashion of his day, and a cocked hat. He walked very upright to the last, his gait being a measured and moderate step; he seldom walked fast. His manners were plain, unassuming, but very polite, such as one would expect from a gentleman who had drawn them from the teachings of St. Paul, and not from Chesterfield. His early advantages for education were limited, but he was a man of considerable reading, and had a large share of good common sense, joined with a knowledge of human nature; and in addition to this he possessed a remarkably kind disposition. He was a religious man from early life, becoming a member of the church about the time of his marriage in 1744. For many years he was an elder in the First Presbyterian church in Newburyport. In doctrine he was a strict Calvinist and in practice a consistent Christian. Nothing but absolute necessity kept him from public worship on the Sabbath, and he was scarce ever known to omit regular morning and evening family worship. He died of old age, May 24, 1807. His wife died but a few days previous. They lie buried near the eastern gate on "Burying Hill." (See Military Service.)

524. Simon[5] Greenleaf (Chart XXV.), b. 1752, son of Hon. Jonathan[5] and Mary (Presbury). In very early life was afflicted with rheumatism, insomuch that he became somewhat deformed in body, being hunchbacked, and was always a pet in the family, probably from his physical disability. He is said to have been a young man of some genius and wit, having a handsome face and agreeable manners. He was extravagantly fond of dress, in which he greatly indulged, probably to conceal his personal defects, and was rather a gay young man. He had learned the trade of goldsmith, but was never able to engage in much active business, and soon declined, dying of consumption in 1776, at the age of twenty-four years. His widow afterwards married Capt. John Lee, of Andover, Mass. Mr. Greenleaf left one son, named Jonathan, after his father. He was never married, and died suddenly in the year 1798 of yellow fever, on board of the United States Frigate "Essex," where he was a midshipman. The family name is extinct in this branch. (See Naval Service.)

525. Capt. Moses[6] Greenleaf (Chart XXV.), b. May 19, 1755, son of Hon. Jonathan[5] and Mary (Presbury). Was bred a ship carpenter, but at the age of nineteen entered the American Army as a Lieutenant. In 1776 he was commissioned as Captain. In 1781 he commenced the business of shipbuilding in Newburyport in connection with his father, and from that time till the year 1790 they built twenty-two sail of ships and brigs. Their shipyard was a little south of the lower Long Wharf, about where Johnson's Wharf is now built, and directly opposite the house occupied by George Greenleaf, which was the dwelling house of Hon. Jonathan Greenleaf. Moses Greenleaf and his brother Enoch both occupied the large old house "up the yard." In November, 1790, he removed with his family to New Gloucester, in the State of Maine, where he followed farming until his death.

In September, 1776, Captain Greenleaf married Lydia Parsons, born 1755, the daughter of Rev. Jonathan Parsons, of Newburyport, who married, Dec. 14, 1731, Phœbe Griswold, born April 22, 1716, the daughter of Judge John Griswold, who was the grandson of Matthew Griswold, born 1620, died 1698, who emigrated to New England in 1639 and settled in Windsor, Conn., and afterwards at Saybrook and Lyme, Conn. Matthew Griswold married, Oct. 16, 1646, Anna Wolcott, daughter of Henry Wolcott, of Windsor. He was one of three brothers, Edward and Thomas being the other two sons of George Griswold. All three brothers emigrated from Kenilworth County, Warwick, England. Of this remarkable family it appears that twelve were Governors of States, thirty-six high Judges (most of them distinct persons from any of the governors), and many other eminent men. Most of these governors and judges held, also, other high offices. Among them a few may properly be mentioned here, viz.: Matthew Griswold, Sr., Governor of Connecticut; Roger Griswold, Governor of Connecticut, also was offered by the elder President Adams, but declined, the post of Secretary of War; Roger Wolcott was Judge of the Superior Court, Connecticut; Roger Wolcott, Jr., was Judge of the Superior Court, Connecticut; Oliver Wolcott was Judge of the United States Circuit Court; Matthew Griswold, Sr., was Chief Justice of Connecticut; Matthew Griswold, Jr., was Judge of the Supreme Court, Connecticut; Roger Griswold was Judge of the Supreme Court, Connecticut.

Morrison Remick Waite, Chief Justice of the Supreme Court, descended from the first Matthew Griswold. Christopher P. Wolcott, of Ohio, was Attorney General of Ohio, afterwards Judge Advocate General, and died when Assistant Secretary of War. Samuel Holden Parsons was appointed by Washington the first Chief Justice of the Northwest Territory. Judge Parsons was Major General in the Revolution, and was a member of the court martial selected by Washington for the trial of Major Andre. He studied law with his uncle, Gov. Matthew Griswold, was made King's Attorney in 1774, and removed to New London; but at the commencement of the Revolution and went actively into military service, was at the Battle of Bunker Hill, was made a Brigadier General in 1776. Under an appointment as Commissioner of Connecticut, he obtained from the Indians a cession of their title to the "Western Reserve" of Ohio. He was a son of Rev. Jonathan and Phœbe (Griswold) Parsons. Of Mrs. Parsons (Phœbe Griswold) it is said in a funeral sermon preached on her death: "The God of nature was pleased to furnish her with mental endowments to an uncommon degree. In the solidity of her judgment and penetration of mind she shone superior to most of her sex. For readiness, liveliness, and keenness of wit she appeared to me unrivaled. Such was her courage and firmness of resolution as you can seldom find in the delicate sex. Her indefatigable industry in the affairs of her family was remarkable. She was a person of much Christian simplicity and integrity. Knowledge in divinity enters deeply into her character, and her acquaintance with church history was truly rare."

Captain Greenleaf was a well-proportioned man, about five feet eleven inches in height, with broad and square shoulders, fair complexion, high forehead, dark hazel eyes, and a nose somewhat aquiline. His hair was very dark, nearly black, which he wore queued, with the ear locks and foretop braided, turned back and tied in with the queue. He always wore a military cocked hat till he went to Maine, and dressed in a suit of reddish brown mixed broadcloth with boots and square silver knee buckles, but sometimes wore a blue coat. His overcoat was a close surtout. Becoming a military man in early life he acquired a military air, which he maintained through life, walking very erect with a firm step. Mrs. Greenleaf, his wife, was a small woman, below the middle size, of dark complexion, piercing black eyes and a prominent chin. She was remarkably quick in her movements, walking very upright to the last with a rapid and elastic step. She had a remarkably self-denying and benevolent spirit. She survived her husband more than twenty years, dying suddenly, and was buried in Williamsburg, Me., where she then resided with her eldest son. Captain Greenleaf was a member in high standing of the order of Masonry, and was instrumental in establishing Cumberland Lodge, Me. He received his masonic degrees in St. Peter's Lodge, Newburyport, Mass. The record, under date of Feb. 23, 1778, says, "Balited for Moses Greenleaf to become a member of this Society, and was accepted" (same date). "Maid Moses Greenleaf an Entered Apprentice. Rec'd for his making £4-0-0; for Tyler, 31s." The same evening he was passed to Fellow Craft. Dec. 27, 1780, he became Worthy Master of St. Peter's Lodge. The last record of his presence in St. Peter's Lodge is Aug. 30, 1790, which was about the time of his removal from Newburyport. Washington Lodge No. 10, a traveling lodge in the Revolutionary Army, was chartered Oct. 6, 1779. He was Worshipful Master of Washington Lodge "in the field, July 6, 1780. Older brethren have often heard him remark that he had many a time commanded the commanding general of the armies in the lodge meetings, for General Washington frequently attended, and always came as a private member without ceremony." (See Military Service).

526. Capt. Enoch[6] Greenleaf (Chart XXV.), b. Oct. 11, 1757, son of Hon. Jonathan[5] and Mary (Presbury). Resided in Newburyport, where he kept a store. In person he was taller than his father, say about five feet ten; and his walk rather more firm and military, but not so much so as his brother Moses. His face very much resembled his father's, the eyes, forehead, and nose being like his, but the mouth not quite so benevolent in expression. His hair was thick, light auburn, and he wore it clubbed, after the fashion of that day, and dressed on Sundays and trainings, etc., with powder. His person was well made, but not corpulent. He was much interested in military, and commanded a company of artillery for several years. (See Military Service.)

527. Richard[6] Greenleaf (Chart XXV.), b. July 3, 1762, son of Hon. Jonathan[5] and Mary (Presbury). Followed the sea for several years, and retained through life somewhat of the gait and air of a sailor. His speech and manner were rapid and vivacious; he was naturally witty, a man of fine genius and taste, a great lover of fun, very social, and the life of company where he went. He had a good taste for painting, and there is still in the family a very striking likeness of his mother from his hand. In person he was about five feet ten inches in height, had a high forehead, and hair nearly black, which he wore queued. He wore dressed ear locks, as was then the fashion. His mouth had a peculiar expression of humor, resulting partly from the curvature of his lips, and the peak in the center of the upper lip. (See Naval Service.)

556. Richard[7] Greenleaf, Jr., b. July 11, 1787, son of Richard[6] and Marcia (Tappan). Removed to Brunswick, Me., from Hampton, N. H. He was a prominent man in town affairs,—was Selectman from 1842 till 1855, most of the period Chairman; also in 1859 was several times the Democratic candidate for Representative to the Legislature; was Secretary and Treasurer of United Lodge, and a prominent Mason.

528. Judge Moses[7] Greenleaf, Jr. (Chart XXV.), b. Oct. 17, 1777, son of Capt. Moses[6] and Lydia (Parsons). At the age of thirteen his father removed to New Gloucester, in the state of Maine, where he was brought up. Although he had no special advantages for education, he was a very thorough English scholar, and particularly as a mathematician, in which he was excelled by few. In his early life he was engaged in trade, first at New Gloucester, and then at Bangor. He afterwards entered into some land speculations, and finally settled himself on a farm in Williamsburg, Me., in the then county of Penobscot, now Piscataquis, where he was one of the first settlers. He was engaged for many years in the work of land surveying, during which time he constructed and published a map of Maine, with a "statistical view" of about 150 pages, 8vo. In 1829 he published a new map, on a scale much enlarged and improved, accompanied by a "Survey of Maine," in an octavo volume of nearly 500 pages, and an atlas exhibiting various features of the state, titles of land, etc. For many years he was one of the principal acting magistrates in the county where he lived, and for several years was an Associate Justice of the Court of Sessions. In person Mr. Greenleaf was about five feet ten inches high, of a very open, fair countenance, rather large features, high cheek bones, brown hair, and dark hazel eyes. He stooped a little when walking.

525. Clarina Parsons Greenleaf (Chart XXV.), b. Nov. 12, 1779, daughter of Moses[6] and Lydia (Parsons). Married Eleazer Alley Jenks, of Portland, Me. He was a printer, editing and publishing the *Gazette* of Maine, at Portland, for several years. Mr. Jenks was drowned, in company with sixteen others, by the wrecking of a packet on Richmonds Island, near Portland Harbor, on July 12, 1807. In person Mrs. Jenks

Simon[7] Greenleaf, LL.D.

Royall and Dane Professor, Harvard Law School,
Cambridge, Mass.

was tall and slim; she was of very light complexion, with light hair and light eyes. She was a woman of much reading, and a well cultivated mind, excelled as a letter writer, and had a good poetical talent. She became interested in religion in the winter preceding the death of her husband, and united with the Congregational Church in New Gloucester, in the following year.

529. Capt. Ebenezer[7] Greenleaf (Chart XXV.), b. Nov. 23, 1781, son of Moses[6] and Lydia (Parsons). Was brought up in New Gloucester. At the age of nineteen he commenced going to sea, which he followed for his principal business for about seven years, passing through the several grades, until for some years he was master, and commanded one of the packet ships from Portland to Liverpool. After leaving the sea, he re. sided at Andover, Me., then at New Gloucester, and then removed to Williamsburg, Me., where he continued to reside till his death, employed as a farmer and land surveyor. Captain Greenleaf was a stout built man, about five feet eleven inches in height, of a light complexion, light gray eyes, and light brown hair. He generally walked very quick and upright. He was considered a very good navigator, a skillful shipmaster, and a man of much personal daring.

530. Hon. Simon[7] Greenleaf (Chart XXVI.), b. Dec. 5, 1783, in Newburyport, Mass., son of Moses[6] and Lydia (Parsons). Received an academic education at the Latin School in Newburyport, under the tuition of Mr. Michael Walsh, who was well known in his day, and for many years of the early part of the present century, as the author of the "Mercantile Arithmetic," which was not only a popular text-book, but a counting-house companion. At the age of eighteen he entered on the study of the law with Ezekiel Whitman, Esq., then of New Gloucester, Me., but afterwards of Portland, and a Judge of Common Pleas. He was admitted to the bar in Cumberland County, Me., in 1805, opened an office first in Standish, then in Gray, and in 1817 at Portland, Me. He received the honorary degree of Master of Arts in 1817 at Bowdoin College, and was also in that year an overseer of the College.

At Gray, being the first and only lawyer in the place, he soon acquired a very considerable practice, which he retained and enlarged by his fidelity and skill. As his family increased he desired to extend the range of his business and increase its emoluments, and in 1818 he removed to Portland. At that time the two leading members of the bar had been drawn aside from their profession into public life. Judge Mellen was in the United States Senate, and Judge Whitman in the House of Representatives; and Mr. Orr, who had a large practice in Cumberland, was also in Congress. This encouraged the accession of other prominent men to Portland: of these were Mr. Greenleaf and the late Judge Preble, who came the same year. Mr. Greenleaf was not disappointed; his business and his fame increased, and the larger and more cultivated society, and its superior advantages in other respects, stimulated his susceptible powers to higher efforts. He now took rank among the foremost men at the bar, and by his winning manners and persuasive style of speaking and address, accompanied by the skill and ingenuity of his arguments, established his reputation and his practice on a firm basis.

In the act of the new state, establishing the Supreme Judicial Court, passed June 24, 1820, the Governor and Council were required "to appoint some suitable person learned in the law to be a reporter of the decisions of the Supreme Judicial Court," and publish them whenever they would compose a suitable volume. His compensation was fixed at six hundred dollars a year salary and the profits arising from the publication. Mr. Greenleaf was immediately appointed reporter under this act, and entered on his duties at York, August term, 1820. He continued faithfully, promptly, and very ably to discharge the duties of this arduous and responsible office for twelve years, closing with the July term at Waldo in 1832. The cases determined during this period are contained in nine volumes, the last embracing a table of cases and a digest of the whole. The judges were: Mellen, chief justice, and Weston, judge, through the whole period; Judge Preble to 1828, and Judge Parris the remainder of the time. The reports are distinguished for the clear and concise manner in which the points of law are stated, and the arguments of counsel given. They took high rank in this class of legal productions, and were received as standards of authority throughout the Union. They were deservedly considered among the most valuable of American reports, and so highly were they esteemed that a new edition was demanded by the profession,— a very rare thing in this class of works,—which was published with annotations by Mr. Abbot, of Cambridge, a short time previous to Mr. Greenleaf's death. So conspicuous had Mr. Greenleaf become about the time that he closed his duties as reporter, that the attention of Judge Story, then at the head of the Law School at Cambridge, was turned to him as the most suitable person to supply the vacancy in that department of the University rendered vacant by the death of the lamented Professor Ashmun, and he immediately determined to bring Mr. Greenleaf to Cambridge if he could. At that time Judge Story, holding his court in Portland, had an interesting case in admiralty. This branch of the law was known only in our largest commercial cities, and not to many of the profession there. And Judge Story was surprised when he found that Mr. Greenleaf brought to this case a thorough acquaintance with this very peculiar system of law, which he himself deemed of great importance, and which, foreseeing its constantly increasing value, he wished to make prominent in the instruction of the school.

The case referred to was similar perhaps to one of which the following anecdote is related. Mr. Greenleaf's father was not only a ship carpenter, but an accurate draughtsman, and he took much pains in teaching his boys the art of constructing a vessel. Simon, in this, was his most apt scholar. It was his habit in his school days to spend his leisure hours in the shipyard, and the habit of observation, conspicuous through life, appeared very early, the benefit of which was shown in his legal practice. On one occasion he was engaged in an insurance cause; the vessel insured had been injured by pounding upon the bottom or side

while lying at a wharf. The defense was that the injury was occasioned
by carelessness in the insured in not securing her to the wharf, alleging
the damage to have been in her side, and not her bottom. One of the
witnesses for the plaintiff was a master builder who had repaired the ship,
and who, having testified that the injury was on the bottom, was thus cross-
examined by Mr. Greenleaf: "You are a ship carpenter, and master of your
trade?" "Yes." "In building a vessel, after laying your keel, you place
a row of crooked timbers crosswise, securing them to the keel with iron
bolts?" "Yes." "These you call floor timbers?" "Yes." "Between
these floor timbers the end of another crooked timber is inserted, as you
would insert the fingers of one hand between those of another, and these
you call foothook (futtuck) timbers?" "Yes." "And so you proceed,
filling in rows of crooked timbers, until you reach the top, calling the
third the rising timber, then the naval timber, and then the top timber?"
"Yes." "Now," said Mr. Greenleaf, "state to the jury, on your oath,
what kind of a timber you furnished for the repairing of that vessel.
Was it a floor timber, a foothook, a rising, or a naval timber?" "It was
a naval timber," said the witness. The case was clear; the jury saw it at
a glance. The injury was on the side of the vessel, and not on the
bottom; it was from carelessness and not accident; and the defense was
sustained.

In 1833 he was appointed Royal Professor of Law at Harvard College
as associate to Professor Ashmun. He received at Harvard, the year of
his removal to Cambridge, 1833, the degree of Doctor of Laws, and the
same degree at Amherst the next year. He was appointed Royal Professor
of Law at Harvard University as successor to Professor Ashmun, in 1833,
which office he held two years, when he was appointed to the chair of the
Dane Professorship, a worthy successor to that chair made vacant by the
death of Judge Story. In consequence of ill health he resigned this chair
in 1848, when he was honored with the title of Emeritus Professor of
Law in the University. His connection with the Law School marked a
season in its history of great prosperity. He became a mason in Cumberland Lodge, Maine, which his father was instrumental in establishing, and
was the second Grand Master of the Grand Lodge A. F. & A. M., of Maine.

In 1820 and 1821 he, with Asa Clapp and Nicholas Emery, represented Portland in the Legislature of Maine. As these were sessions
when the new government was put in operation the duty was responsible,
and, to a lawyer who was expected to pass upon the code of laws to be
adopted on careful revision, arduous. Mr. Greenleaf was faithful to his
trust, and beneficial to the country. With this experience he retired at
once and forever from political office. Mr. Greenleaf was a grave, sedate-
looking man, and very quiet in his movements. He was about five feet
ten inches in height, rather stout built, full face, with a small, sharp eye,
nearly black. His original hair was very dark brown; his posture a little
stooping, with his head projecting forward; his countenance was ex-
pressive of benignity and intelligence.

The following are some of the works which have proceeded from his
pen: "A Brief Inquiry into the Origin and Principles of Free Masonry;"

published at Portland in 1820. An anonymous pamphlet entitled, "Remarks on the Exclusion of Atheists as Witnesses," 8vo; published in Boston in 1839. "Catalogue of a Select Law Library," also a "Course of Legal Studies," etc. "A Letter to a Person Engaged in a Lawsuit by a Lawyer; by a Member of the Profession;" published as a tract by the American Tract Society. "An Examination of the Testimony of the Four Evangelists by the Rules of Evidence Administered in Courts of Justice; with an Account of the Trial of Jesus;" published in Boston in 1846, and reprinted in London in 1847. "A Discourse, Pronounced at His Inauguration as Royal Professor of Law, in Harvard University." "A Discourse Commemorative of the Life and Character of Joseph Story," pronounced Sept. 18, 1845. "Testamentary Counsels and Hints to Christians on the Right Distribution of their Property by Will, by a Retired Solicitor," carefully revised by a member of the American Bar; published at Troy, N. Y., in 1845. "A Treatise on the Law of Evidence," 3 vols. An edition of "Cruise's Digest of the Law of Real Property, with Notes, 1849-50."

531. Rev. Jonathan[7] Greenleaf, D.D. (Chart XXV.), b. Sept. 4, 1785, son of Capt. Moses[6] and Lydia (Parsons). Was brought up on the farm in New Gloucester, Maine. He united with the Congregational Church at that place in October, 1807. His early education was limited to the simple rudiments taught in the common country school of his day. Availing himself of such helps as he could command, he made sufficient advance in his studies as to prepare him for taking up a course of theology under the direction of Rev. Francis Brown, D.D., of North Yarmouth, and was licensed to preach by the Cumberland Association at Saco, Me., in September, 1814. He was ordained at Wells, Me., March 8, 1815, by York County Association, as pastor of First Congregational Church. Dismissed and settled as pastor of the Mariner's Church in Boston, in September, 1828; removed to New York as Corresponding Secretary of the American Seamen's Friend Society, December, 1833. Here he labored with untiring diligence and energy until November, 1841, when his connection with the Society terminated. He was then residing in Brooklyn, N. Y., and after supplying a few months the vacant Congregational Church, at Lyndon, Vt., but not accepting the call they gave him, and finding a fresh field for his usefulness on unoccupied ground within the city of Brooklyn, in the eastern section, he set himself to work to gather and organize and sustain a Presbyterian Church. Here a congregation was soon gathered on Franklin Avenue, and he was installed as its pastor on the 8th of March, 1843, remaining with them for twenty-two years, laying down his work only with his life. The Rev. Drs. Prime, who were both his intimate friends, thus speak of him in the *New York Observer*: "Always lively, genial, quaint, and often humorous, overflowing with pleasing anecdotes of men and old times, he was a pleasant companion and a warm-hearted friend. In the church he was a man of peace and a peacemaker, with decided opinions and ability to enforce them; he was so gentle in his persuasions, so kind in his self-assertions, so moderate in his language, that he conciliated all by his manner, for no one could doubt his sincerity and piety, and few questioned his judgment." He won not only the hearts of his own people, but of all others with whom he came in contact. While the poor and afflicted lost in him a friend ever ready to listen and help, they lamented him as such; equally attentive to the young and old, he was regarded with the utmost love. In his family circle no pleasure was complete unless shared with them. In his study it was a delight to him to have his children come and go with freedom, sharing with him, as though of the same age, in all the events of the day. He was exceedingly particular and methodical with all his papers and business affairs. He was honored by Bowdoin College bestowing her degrees upon him, and later in life, Princeton, also, giving him the degree of Doctor of Divinity. Among the books of which he was the author and publisher are the following : " Sketches of the Ecclesiastical History of the State of Maine," from the earliest settlement to the time of the author; "History of the Churches of New York"; "Thoughts on Prayer"; "Genealogy of the Greenleaf family," 1854; "A Sketch of Wells, Maine," published in the Maine Historical Collections, 1831; "A Sketch of Lyndon, Vt.," 1852; "A Memoir of Rev. Jonathan Parsons," in the *American Quarterly Register*, 1841; "A Doctrinal Catechism," and five tracts, entitled, "The Missing Disciple," "Experimental Religion," " Sudden Death," " Shall I come to the Lord's Supper," "Misery of Dying in Sin"; several religious tracts issued by tract societies of the Presbyterian and Methodist denominations; he edited the *Sailor's Magazine* nine years; published fourteen sermons, one of which was reprinted in London, England, in 1837. To the close of life he wrote more or less for the religious papers, especially for the *Christian Mirror*, of Portland, Me., and the *New York Observer*. He became a corresponding member of the New England Historic Genealogical Society in 1847.

546. Rev. Patrick Henry[8] Greenleaf, D.D. (Chart XXVI.), b. July 11, 1807, in Portland, Me., son of Hon. Simon[7] and Hannah (Kingman), and graduated at Bowdoin College in 1825, having as classmates Dr. George B. Cheever, Henry W. Longfellow, Nathaniel Hawthorne, and others subsequently distinguished in life. He was admitted to the Portland Bar in 1829, and was soon engaged in good practice, but, concluding to study for the ministry, he made his final argument before Judge Story in 1835. In the same year he became a student of Bishop Doane of New Jersey, and afterwards, proceeding to Cambridge, continued his studies with Bishop Griswold, then of the Eastern Diocese. He was ordained Deacon at Grace Church, Boston, in June, 1836, and Priest at Newport, in May, 1837. His first position was as Rector of the Church of the Ascension, Fall River, Mass., but in August, 1837, he became Rector of St. John's Church, Carlisle, Penn., where he remained four years. In September, 1841, he undertook the charge of St. John's Church, Charlestown, Mass., and continued as its Rector for ten years. In May, 1851, he founded St. Mark's Church, Boston. In September, 1853, he became Rector of Christ Church, Madison, Ind., and in May, 1855, Rector of St. Paul's Church, Cincinnati, O. At Easter, 1861, he became Rector of

Emmanuel Church, Carrol Park, Brooklyn, N. Y. Dr. Greenleaf has also temporarily officiated at St. Ann's and Grace Churches, Brooklyn. He received the degree of A.B. from Bowdoin College in 1825; M.A. from the same institution in 1828; M.A. from Trinity College, Hartford, Conn., in 1827*, and D.D. from the University of Indiana in 1854. A few of his sermons and addresses have been printed. He also contributed much to the reviews and newspapers.

In person, he was slightly under medium height, well proportioned for his size, and of easy, composed manners. He had a round head, quite bald and gray haired, and altogether appeared like one of those intelligent, good-natured old gentlemen whose companionship is always cheering and advantageous. His distinguishing traits were steadfast devotion to duty as a parish priest; a forwardness in encouraging and sustaining works of mercy and charity in the Master's name; singularly impressive in pulpit ministrations, possessing talent in this respect above the average of his contemporaries in the ministry, and yet his sermons, ever characterized by spirituality of tone and manly earnestness, and eminently profitable to the hearers, were calm intelligible statement, fair logical argument, and possessed a tone of sincerity and gentleness throughout. He had a happy tact in placing before the listener every fact which could completely and freely reveal the merits of his whole subject, and he never shrank from discussing the weak as well as the strong points. The language used was of a very simple character, at the same time the best forms of English composition, and the manner of delivery equally without the slightest pretension. Within his own denomination he proved himself a ready and willing co-operator in every good work, and with a large liberality of opinion and a disinterested Christian benevolence he joined heartily with others in measures of public utility.

The last Sunday that he officiated was the fourth Sunday after Trinity (June 20, 1869), when his favorite collect was for that day. It was one which he was especially fond of repeating in Latin: "O God, the protector of all that trust in Thee, without whom nothing is strong, nothing is holy; increase and multiply upon us thy mercy; that thou being our ruler and guide, we may so pass through things temporal, that we finally lose not the things eternal. Grant this, O heavenly Father, for Jesus Christ's sake, our Lord. Amen." He went the following evening to the vestry-room of his church, where he was wont to spend his leisure hours in preparing for the duties of his parish, and as he did not return at the usual time, search was made, and they found the venerable servant of the Lord sitting by his table, leaning back in his chair. On the table was found his open diary, and his pen near by. He had written a part of the word "house," the first three letters, then sank back in his chair. The spirit had returned to Him who gave it. His funeral was solemnized from his church in the presence of a very large number of relations and friends. There were present, besides the Bishop of the Diocese, above twenty of the clergy in surplices. The church was draped, except the altar, which, at his own wish, was clothed in white. It was a touching sight to see the

* Bowdoin College Catalogue.

Sunday and Industrial School children as they passed the coffin look upon their Rector and kind friend's features for the last time, each one to drop into the casket a little bud or flower. Many a tear fell from the moistened eyes with the flower, as a dearer tribute to his memory, showing how much he had endeared himself to their tender hearts.

530. Charlotte Kingman Greenleaf, b. Dec. 25, 1809, daughter of Hon. Simon[7] and Hannah (Kingman), m. July 15, 1830, Rev. Samuel Fuller, of Providence, R. I. He was born in Rensselaerville, New York, April 25, 1802. His father, Rev. Samuel Fuller, founded Trinity Church, Rensselaerville, and St. Paul's Church, Greenville, N. Y. He (the son) graduated from Union College, Schenectady, N. Y., in 1822, and in 1823 was principal of Hudson Academy. He then became private tutor in the family of Mrs. Carter, of Halifax, Va., where he became intimately acquainted with Bishop Mead, who persuaded him to become a candidate for orders. He graduated from the General Theological Seminary, New York City, in 1827, and was ordained by Bishop Hobart as Deacon, and preached his first sermon at St. Paul's Church, New York City. While at Union College he became personally attached to Bishop Alonzo Potter, then a Tutor in Union College, afterwards Bishop of Pennsylvania, father of Bishop Potter of New York. Bishop Potter appointed him in 1853-4 lecturer on Christian life at Philadelphia, where he was associated with Bishop Littlejohn, Rev. Dr. Edwin Harwood of New Haven, Rev. Dr. Charles Mason of Boston, Bishop Howe of Central Pennsylvania, Bishop Atkinson, Bishop Kerfoot, and others.

In 1827 he officiated at St. Paul's Church in Woodbury, Conn. In 1828 he became Rector of a church in Saco, Me., and in the fall was made Tutor in Trinity College, the first in the College. In 1830 he was appointed Rector of Grace Church in Providence, R. I. In 1831 he was editor of the *Episcopal Watchman.* In 1832 he was made Rector of St. Michael's Church, Litchfield, Conn., and remained with that church until 1837, when he became Rector of Christ Church, Andover, Mass. In 1843 he was made Milnor Professor at the Theological Seminary of Ohio, of which Kenyon College was a branch. In 1844 he was President *pro tem* of Kenyon, afterwards declining election to the Presidency. The next five years were spent in second Rectorship at Litchfield and Andover. In 1859 he was made Professor of Literature and Interpretation of the Holy Scripture at Berkeley Divinity School of Middletown, Conn., and retained his chair until 1883, when he became Professor Emeritus.

Dr. Fuller wrote several books. His first was "Loutron." Others were treatises on baptism, confirmation, creed, liturgy, and regeneration. He was also the author of a "Commentary on the Revelation of St. John the Divine." Among his pupils were Bishops Niles, Thomas Wells, Barker, Vincent, Leonard, Nichols and White, Dean Hodges, Professors Binney and Barbour, Dr. Vibbert of Trinity, New York, Dr. Brewster of Brooklyn, and Dr. Maxon of Pittsburg.

Their son, Rev. Simon Greenleaf Fuller, became rector of St. Paul's Church, Syracuse, N. Y., in February, 1870. He was unanimously called

from Yonkers, where he took leave of a parish to which he was deeply
devoted, and by which he was beloved. His ministrations won the love of
.his parishioners, to whom he became warmly attached; and as a citizen he
was highly respected by all denominations. He was at one time Rector of
Trinity Church in Hartford, Conn. He was a graduate of Harvard and
Middletown Theological Seminary. His first parish was at Wilton, Conn.,
and he subsequently became Rector of a prosperous parish at Pittsburg,
Penn., and at a later period responded to a call from Yonkers on the
Hudson.

547. James[8] Greenleaf, b. June 15, 1814, son of Hon. Simon[7] and
Hannah (Kingman). Graduated at Dartmouth College in 1834. He
immediately made a voyage to Calcutta in company with some old friends.
That long and pleasant voyage was never forgotten, and his interest in the
climate and customs of Calcutta had always a charm for him in remembrance. On his return he took up his residence in New Orleans, La.,
in the interests of the large and growing cotton manufactories of Lowell.
During the Civil War, being a strong Union man, his property in New
Orleans was entirely confiscated by the Confederate Government, but at
the close of the war it was restored to him. While residing at New Orleans
he built a house in Cambridge, on land adjoining that upon which formerly
stood the dwelling house owned and occupied by the late Hon. Simon
Greenleaf, and near the old Craigie House where his wife's brother,
Professor Longfellow, lived for many years. Here he spent his summers,
and suddenly died here Aug. 22, 1865.

He married Mary, daughter of Hon. Stephen and Zilpha (Wadsworth)
Longfellow. She is descended from John Alden and Priscilla Mullins
through her mother's family, and also from Elder Brewster and Henry
Sampson of the "Mayflower" Pilgrims. Mrs. Greenleaf still resides in
the house at Cambridge, and continues a warm and active interest in St.
James' Church, of which mention is made in the notice of Caroline A.
Greenleaf. Among the characteristics of Mr. Greenleaf were absolute
integrity and strict honesty in all business matters; unselfishness and
loyalty to his friends; a keen sense of philanthropy, often generously
exercised in his own quiet and unostentatious way; of a deeply religious
nature, exemplifying in his daily life the teachings of the Master.

530. Caroline Augusta Greenleaf (Chart XXVI.), b. Sept. 16,
1826, daughter of Hon. Simon[7] and Hannah (Kingman), m. Rev.
Andrew Croswell. He prepared for college mainly at the academy in
Falmouth, Mass. (his native town), and graduated at Brown University
in Providence, R. I., in 1843. Upon graduating, Mr. Croswell was
honored with a season's service as principal of the Providence High
School. His preparatory studies for the ministry were then formally
begun at the Alexandria Theological Seminary, Virginia, and were completed privately with the Rev. Samuel Fuller, then of Litchfield, Conn.

In 1846 Mr. Croswell's name appears as a candidate for Holy Orders
in the Diocese of Rhode Island, as reported by Bishop Henshaw in the

Journal of the Convention of that year. On Dec. 20, 1846, he was made deacon at Grace Church, Providence. His first charge was a mission at Johnston, near Providence. On Feb. 2, 1848, he was ordained priest in Trinity Church, Boston, by Bishop Eastburn, the Rev. Patrick H. Greenleaf preaching the sermon. He labored for a short time in Cabotsville, Mass., now Chicopee, and in October, 1849, became Rector of St. Paul's Church, Brunswick, Me.

In April, 1853, Mr. Croswell was made Rector of St. Mary's, Newton Lower Falls, Mass., and remained there until April, 1856. In 1860 he became a resident of Cambridge, Mass. Here, in the northern part of the present city, then known as North Cambridge, was opened a new field of labor in the vineyard of the Lord, and the present prosperous St. James' Church is the result of a small beginning in which both Mr. and Mrs. Croswell were most sympathetic and active. Mrs. Croswell is remembered as an exquisitely lovely and charming woman, of great gentleness, and sweetness, and strength of character; having a highly intelligent and cultivated mind, a grace and beauty of conversation, with a fascinating attractiveness which won the hearts of all.

The interest of Mr. and Mrs. Croswell in the parish of St. James' Church seems to call for more than a passing notice on these pages; a brief account of its early days, therefore, will be of interest. At the very end of 1864 an active beginning was made, and on the evening of Christmas Day, in a hall known as Atwill's Hall, fitted up for a chapel, the opening service was held, Bishop Huntington preaching the sermon. In June, 1866, a parish was legally organized and the Rev. Andrew Croswell was elected Rector, remaining until his resignation, by reason of ill health, in December, 1870. The Rev. Edward Abbott, D.D., its present Rector, in a discourse delivered at the Commemorative Service which marked the erection of the tablet to the memory of Mr. and Mrs. Croswell in St. James' Church, Nov. 9, 1879, gives an interesting account of the history of the parish down to that time, and a touching tribute to their memory, from which I quote in part: "If he (Mr. Croswell) was the father of the parish, she was the parish mother; she was the beloved Persis 'who labored much in the Lord,' the Phebe who was a succourer of many." "As he planted, she watered. They walked and worked together." Referring to the location of the church, the valuation of property in its vicinity in 1864 "was only about one third" of what it became in 1879. "The main features of the landscape show no great change; the difference is in matters of detail. The railroad was here, and the station, and the horse cars, and Porter's Tavern, and the old Davenport House on our adjacent corner, and a few other ancient buildings which still preserve their identity; but this now stately North Avenue, with its bricked sidewalks, lined with handsome dwellings and commodious shops, was then more of a rambling country road leading away to what was West Cambridge and the towns beyond." The history of the parish to the present time would show a remarkable record of vitality, growth, and usefulness.

549. James Edward[9] Greenleaf (Chart XXVI.), b. Aug. 2, 1832, in Portland, Me., son of Rev. Patrick Henry[8] and Margaret L. (Johnson).

At thirteen years of age entered the employ of the shipping house of Messrs. A. & C. Cunningham, ship owners in Mediterranean and North of Europe trade, and upon their retirement served with the house of Zipcy & Wyman, a shipping house in the trade with Turkey, etc. At nineteen years of age he went to Chicago, Ill., and engaged in forwarding and commission business under the firm name of D' Wolf & Greenleaf, occupying the first brick warehouse built in that city for shipping business. Two years later, removing to the East in the interest of new railroads then being built in the West, he located for a time in New York City and afterwards in Boston, where, in November, 1853, he married Mary Elizabeth, daughter of Hon. Paul Willard, a prominent lawyer of Charlestown, Mass., and Judge of the local court. Mr. Greenleaf retained his interests in the West for many years, at one time sending many Eastern people as colonists into Kansas, Minnesota, Nebraska, and Iowa, at which time he was appointed by Gov. Henry J. Gardner, Justice of the Peace, which office he held for the full term of seven years, and later became a commission merchant located at Boston, and having a business connection with his brother, Henry L. Greenleaf, at New Orleans, La. The effect of the war of 1861–65 changing his relations in business matters, he relinquished the commission business and engaged in other pursuits until about 1884, when, his health failing, he was for a short period practically retired from active life, but subsequently engaged in insurance. Having inherited strong literary tastes, he was from an early age a constant reader of history, etc., which in his later life, as a result of enforced inactivity by reason of ill health, it was his privilege to indulge; a large portion of his time being devoted to researches in the archives of our libraries, courts of record, etc., a never-failing source of learning and a fount of rich and varied knowledge. In the fifties he enlisted as a private in the Boston Light Infantry, with which he remained in active service many years, doing garrison duty at Fort Warren in 1861, and was afterwards commissioned as Captain of the 69th unattached Inf. M. V. M., which became Co. G, 7th Regt.; this position he held for three years, when the regiment was disbanded. Mr. Greenleaf has also been active in musical life, having been organist and director of music for twenty-seven years in prominent churches of Boston and vicinity. (See Military Service.)

The "Willard Memoir," by the late Joseph Willard, Esq., gives a history of the Willard family in England; also the life of Major Simon Willard, who was baptized April 7, 1605, at Horsmonden, County Kent, England, and came to New England in the year 1634.

Judge Paul Willard was a direct lineal descendant of Major Simon Willard, as follows: Henry Willard, fourth son of Major Simon and Mary Dunster, born June 4, 1655, at Concord, Mass., married (1) Mary Dakin, of Groton, July 18, 1674; married (2) Dorcas Cutler, 1689. Henry Willard, first son of Henry and Mary (Dakin), born in Groton, April 11, 1675; married (1) Abigail Temple, July 21, 1698; married (2) Sarah Nutting. William Willard, son of Henry, born in Lancaster, Mass., baptized there, May 24, 1713; married Grace Gates of Lancaster.

William Willard, son of the aforesaid William, born in Harvard, Mass., November, 1737; married Mary Whittemore, of Concord, Mass. He died, 1786, in Lancaster. Paul Willard, son of the last named William and Mary, born in Lancaster, Mass., Dec. 29, 1764; married (1), Dec. 18, 1792, Martha Haskell (daughter of Col. Henry Haskell, of Revolutionary Army); married (2) Polly Damon; died in Lancaster, Aug. 2, 1817. Children : Paul, and four others.

Paul Willard, son of Paul and Martha Haskell, born in Lancaster, Aug. 4, 1795. Was graduate of Harvard College, 1817; admitted to the bar, March, 1821; appointed Postmaster of Charlestown, Mass., Sept. 15, 1822, and continued to July, 1829; elected Clerk Massachusetts Senate, May, 1823, and continued to 1830; "filled many important offices of honor and trust under the Town and City Governments with great fidelity and ability;" married, Oct. 10, 1821, Harriet Whiting (daughter of Capt. Timothy Whiting, of Revolutionary Army), of Lancaster, Mass. (For historical and genealogical account of the Whitings, see "Drake's History of Boston," pp. 362, 363; also "Thompson's History of Boston, England;" "Memoir of Rev. Samuel Whiting, D.D., and of his wife Elizabeth St. John," by William Whiting, formerly President New England Historic Genealogical Society, published 1873.) Judge Willard died March 18, 1856, and his wife died Dec. 25, 1879.

Mrs. Harriet Whiting Willard was a direct lineal descendant of Rev. Samuel Whiting, her first ancestor of the Whiting name in America. He was a son of Hon. John Whiting, who was Mayor of Boston, Eng., 1600–1608. Rev. Samuel Whiting was born Nov. 20, 1597; died Dec. 11, 1679, age eighty-two years. His first wife with her issue, except her daughter Dorothy, died in England. Dorothy came with her father to America, May 26, 1636, and married Thomas Weld, son of Rev. Thomas Weld, of Roxbury, Mass. Rev. Samuel married (2) Elizabeth St. John, Aug. 6, 1629. The genealogy of Elizabeth St. John is clearly traced from William de St. John, who was one of the barons who accompanied the Norman Duke in his invasion of England, as on record "New England Historic and Genealogical Register," Volume XIV., January, 1860, also same journal, Volume XV., 1861. She was the daughter of the Rt. Hon. Sir Oliver St. John, Knight of Cayshoe, Bedfordshire, Eng., a sister of Lord Chief Justice Oliver St. John. The ancestry of this family, the St. John's, includes a list of kings from William I., Henry I., Henry II., Henry III., Edward I., and Henry VII. The pedigree of Elizabeth St. John may be found in the "Whiting Memoir."

Samuel Whiting, son of Rev. Samuel and Elizabeth (St. John), born in England, 1633. Graduate of Harvard, 1653; ordained minister at Billerica, Mass., Nov. 11, 1663; married Dorcas Chester, Nov. 12, 1656; died Feb. 28, 1713, age 79 years. Issue, eleven children. Oliver Whiting, of Lancaster, Mass., third son of last named Rev. Samuel, born Nov. 8, 1665; married Anna Danforth, Jan. 22, 1690; died Dec. 22, 1736, age seventy-one years. Nine children. Deacon Samuel Whiting, fourth son of Oliver above named, of Billerica, Mass., born 1702; married Deborah Hill; died 1772. Issue, Samuel and Timothy. Timothy Whiting, of

Lancaster, Mass., son of Deacon Samuel, born Feb. 24, 1732, in Billerica, Mass.; married Sarah Osgood; died July 12, 1799, age sixty-seven. Issue, five children. Timothy Whiting, third son of Timothy Whiting last named, born in Lancaster, June 17, 1758; married (1) Abigail Kidder, Aug. 21, 1781; married (2) Lydia Phelps, Oct. 14, 1799; died Jan. 12, 1826, age sixty-seven. Issue, first marriage, eight children; second, four children. Harriet Whiting, daughter of Timothy and Lydia, born in Lancaster, Mass., Dec. 13, 1800; married Paul Willard, of Charlestown, Mass., Counsellor-at-law, Oct. 16, 1821. Issue, five children: [1]Sidney A., [2]Paul, [3]Timothy, [4]Ellen Maria, [5]Mary Elizabeth.

549. Robert Willard[10] Greenleaf (Chart XXVI.), b. Jan. 24, 1855, in Charlestown, Mass., son of James Edward[9] and Mary Elizabeth (Willard). After attending private schools in his early life, entered the High School in Charlestown, then under the charge of Master Caleb Emery as the Principal. Military training being a part of the exercises, the school was organized as a battalion, the officers of which being elective, by the pupils, upon nomination by a competent committee he was advanced in succession through the various grades from that of private to the position of major commanding. Entered Harvard College, and was graduated there in 1877 with honors in Natural History. He was assistant in Botany in Harvard College, 1877–81. Received the degrees of A.M. and M.D. from Harvard College, 1885. Was House Officer and assistant to the Superintendent at the Boston City Hospital, 1884–1886, also House Officer at the Boston Lying-in Hospital, 1886, after which for three years he was assistant in Histology and Embryology at the Harvard Medical School, Instructor Materia Medica and Botany, Massachusetts College of Pharmacy, 1891–92. Professor of the same, 1892 to the present time at this college; also Lecturer at Boston Teachers' School of Science since 1891;—and has written the following, among other papers: "The Diet of Harvard Students," "The Recent Epidemic of Cholera," "The Charles River in Relation to Intermittent Fever," "Foods," "The Relation of Modern Therapeutics to the Practice of Dentistry." He is a practicing physician in Boston and Physician to Boston Dispensary.

551. Lieut. Col. Charles R.[9] Greenleaf, U. S. A. (Chart XXVI.), b. Jan. 2, 1838, in Carlisle, Penn., son of Rev. Patrick Henry[8] and Margaret L. (Johnson). In 1842 his father removed with his family to Charlestown, Mass., where he attended the public schools in his early youth; later on removing to Madison, Ind., and Cincinnati, O.

In 1860 he was graduated from the Medical College of Ohio, at Cincinnati, and in March of that year he was appointed Resident Physician to the Good Samaritan Hospital in that city.

In 1861, at the breaking out of the War of the Rebellion, he was, on April 19th, commissioned Assistant Surgeon, Fifth Ohio Infantry; his being the first war commission to a medical officer issued by the Governor of that State. He served with his regiment in the field until July 19, 1861, when he was appointed an assistant surgeon in the regular army,

his long and honorable career in which will be found recorded with the
" Military and Naval Service " of the Greenleafs. He married Georgiana
Henri Franck, daughter of George Henry Frederick Franck and Jane
Jacob (Belt) de la Roche, who was son of Baron Frederick Franck and
Elzina Marie Lespinasse (Merkus), daughter of Henry and Elzina (Vaster)
Merkus. Baron Frederick Franck was son of Baron George Antoine
Michael Franck and Sophie Marie (Von Gutterman-Von Guttershoven)
de la Roche. She was a celebrated German authoress. Baron George A.
M. Franck was son of Baron and the Princess (Von Lichtenstein) de la
Roche, son of Count de la Roche, of Provence, France (Huguenot).
Surgeon Greenleaf is stationed at present in San Francisco, Cal., in
charge of the medical supply department of the Pacific.

Of their children, their son Patrick Henry, now known as Harry S.,
graduated at the medical department of the University of Pennsylvania,
June 13, 1895.

542. Simon[8] Greenleaf (Chart XXVI.), b. May 3, 1822, in Williamsburg, Maine, son of Ebenezer[7] and Hannah D. (Haskell). At the
age of seventeen he began life on his own account, remaining in the East
until 1851, when he started west; the route then was rather indirect,
going by rail to Buffalo, through the lakes to Chicago; he went from
Chicago, across country to Galena, and up the Mississippi River to Stillwater, thence to Shakopee, Minnesota, in 1853, and became identified with
that place as one of its principal citizens until 1863. He then moved to
Davenport, Iowa, and was employed in the Quartermaster's office until
the close of the war, when he went to Racine, and entered the employ of
the Racine & Mississippi Railroad (later the Western Union) as contractor for wood and ties. In 1867 he removed his family to Savanna,
Ill., and Mr. Greenleaf continued in the employ of the railroad until
1871, when the wood business began to be greatly reduced on account of
the increased use of coal.

About this time he established himself in the insurance business, and
carried on collecting and conveyancing during the remainder of his active
life. He was exceptionally well read in law, and his sound judgment won
for him the entire confidence of lawyers whenever they came before him
in law cases. He enjoyed the reputation of being an expert in conveyancing, and the correctness of his legal papers has been always favorably
remarked upon by county officials. Though not the pioneer in Savanna
newspaperdom, he established the Savanna *Times* in 1875, which was the
first paper in the town since 1856, when the *Register* was suspended.
Though the predictions of failure were many, Mr. Greenleaf made a success of the newspaper business, and sold out in 1884. The following year,
in company with his son Frank, the *Journal* was established, although his
connection with that paper was merely nominal, and in 1886 it was placed
entirely in the hands of the young man. Mr. Greenleaf took a prominent
part in the politics of the county and district, and was always fair and
liberal in his views. In 1884 he was elected to the State legislature, and
served one term. In local affairs he was foremost in all enterprises for

the public good, and aided in every way any worthy enterprise that presented itself. Perhaps no greater evidence of his persistent effort in a worthy cause can be found than in his church work. An Episcopalian of ardent faith, he found himself the only one in Savanna. About the year 1870 he began his efforts toward building up a church, and although it took eighteen years, he finally succeeded, with the aid of others, of course, and it was a happy day for him when, in 1888, St. Paul's church was consecrated. In 1871 he was elected Justice of the Peace of Savanna Township and held that office continuously until his death.

543.   Lieut. Frederick W.[9] Greenleaf (Chart XXVI.), b. April 28, 1847, in Williamsburg, Me., son of Simon[8] and Frances Jane (Foss). Appointed to the United States Naval Academy from Minnesota by the Hon. William Windom in 1863.   Graduated in 1867.   (See Naval Service.)

542.   Ada Elizabeth Greenleaf (Chart XXV.), b. Nov. 13, 1852, daughter of Simon[8] and Frances J. (Foss), m. Rev. Francis Henry Potts, who graduated at Trinity College, Hartford, in 1868, and at the General Theological Seminary, New York, 1870. Was ordained that year by the Rt. Rev. Bishop Whitehouse, of Chicago. He has been engaged in ministerial work in Illinois and Minnesota ever since, and at present is in charge of St. Peter's P. E. Church, Shakopee, Minn.

22.   Hon. John[4] Greenleaf (Chart XXVIII.), b. Jan. 3, 1692, son of John[3] and Elizabeth (Hills). Is referred to frequently in the Massachusetts Archives Court Records as performing various and important public duties. He was a member of the Great and General Court, also a member of the Governor's Council. These records commence with his being sworn into service on Wednesday, July 8, 1741, and he served up to 1757. (See Vol. XVII, Part 3, p. 4; Part 5, p. 1.)

559.   Hon. Benjamin[5] Greenleaf, b. March 19, 1732, son of Hon. John[4] and Sarah (Smith). Was graduated at Harvard College in 1751, and for many years was Judge of Probate in Essex County, Mass. He resided some time in Kittery, also in Newburyport, Mass., where he died suddenly of disease of the heart. He was one of the councillors of the Colony of Massachusetts Bay in 1770, 1771, 1772, 1774, and was a member of the Executive Council of Massachusetts during the Revolutionary War, and signed in approval the resolve of the General Court under which the "Committee of Correspondence, Inspection, and Safety" was chosen on Feb. 13, 1776, and of which committee Joseph Greenleaf was chairman. He was a member, together with Hon. William Greenleaf, High Sheriff of the County of Suffolk, and Hon. Nathan Appleton, of a committee of seven, chosen secretly, to correspond with men in the other colonies in regard to measures to be pursued. He was also a member of the Senate after the adoption of the Constitution, and his name appears among the

"Yeas" on Feb. 11, 1788, in the Massachusetts Assembly upon the ratification of the Federal Constitution. He was also Chief Justice of the Court of Common Pleas. (See Military Service.)

565. Ebenezer[6] Greenleaf (Chart XXIX.), b. Oct. 4, 1763, son of Ebenezer[5] and Hannah (Titcomb), m. Jane, daughter of Capt. William Coombs. Memoirs of her life published by her daughter show that she was a woman of remarkable piety, widely known in the religious world, and having superior natural gifts. She outlived her husband nearly twenty years, dying at the age of eighty-five, May 15, 1851. (See Military Service.)

576. Abner[7] Greenleaf (Chart XXX.), b. March 12, 1785, son of Abner[6] and Elizabeth (Milk). Was twice married and has had twelve children, all by the second wife, Miriam Bell, daughter of Matthew Bell, of Newcastle, N. H. She was a great-granddaughter of Sir William Pepperell's sister Dorothy. At the age of twenty-one he removed to Portsmouth, N. H., where he carried on the business of coppersmith, plumber, and founder, for many years, and where he cast cannon for the Navy in the War of 1812. For that purpose he erected works on a small island in the Piscataqua, opposite the Navy Yard. For several years he was teacher of a public school in Portsmouth, and, in 1828, he was appointed Postmaster there by President Jackson, which office he held for ten years, 1829-39. He was also the first mayor of Portsmouth under the city charter. He was connected with the *New Hampshire Gazette* for many years, and the writer of the principal editorials. He was elected many times to the Legislature of New Hampshire, in terms ranging from 1816, when he defeated Daniel Webster, in Portsmouth, to 1864; and in 1829, as President of the Senate of that State, was at one time acting Governor, there being no Lieutenant Governor. His portrait now hangs in the State Department of that State among the Governors, by virtue of his Presidency of the Senate and acting Governor. He was a disciple of Jefferson in politics, but not a partisan; firm in his convictions, regardless of party policy. He died Sept. 28, 1868.

581. Albert[8] Greenleaf (Chart XXXI.), b. Sept. 17, 1810, son of Abner[7] and Miriam (Bell). Resided in Baltimore, Md. He lived in Portsmouth, N. H., until 1835, except one year spent in Boston, Mass. He was bred a printer, and was of the firm of Beck & Co., of Portsmouth, when they published the *New Hampshire Gazette*. Receiving an appointment in the Treasury Department, Washington, D. C., in 1835, he removed there, and resided there continuously until 1870, when he took up his residence in Baltimore. He held various offices there, and part of the time was engaged in reporting Congressional Proceedings, and in newspaper correspondence. He was commissioned several terms by the State Department as Justice of the Peace, and was, in 1856, Navy Agent, Navy and Army Pension Agent, under Presidents Pierce and Buchanan. Mr. Greenleaf's estimable qualities of character and mind at once secured him the confidence and esteem of the leading men of both parties in Washington. Mr. Webster, though differing from him politically, was a firm friend till his death, and many were the striking stories of that famous man which Mr. Greenleaf's retentive memory enabled him in after years to tell. Henry Clay was also his friend. But it was the great Calhoun whom Mr. Greenleaf especially delighted to honor. Mr. Calhoun's rare personal virtues, unbending devotion to principle, and profound logical mind, excited in young Greenleaf an admiration which, as time went on, ripened into reverence. Mr. Greenleaf used to say that he had heard all of Mr. Calhoun's great speeches, and that he was the only man of his day against whom no one dared, whatever his political opinions, to impute political insincerity or self-seeking. Since his residence in Baltimore, 1870, his life was that of a retired gentleman, availing himself of his leisure to study the political writings of the Democratic sages, with which he was familiar to an uncommon degree, and entertaining his friends with delightful anecdotes of the great men whom he met socially and otherwise in Washington. Mr. Greenleaf belonged to a political school which bossism has done much to banish from this country. He believed in political principles which were with him convictions, which it would be a crime to prostitute to personal ends, or to compromise for temporary political advantage. Mr. Greenleaf's sincerity of conviction and patriotic devotion to his country made him a severe critic of the political methods which have prevailed since the war; since when it appeared to him selfishness and ignorance had taken the place of patriotism and statesmanship, and party diverted from an instrumentality for the perpetuation of political principles, to the maintenance of personal power unworthily obtained and ignobly used. While first of all a political thinker and student of government, widely and accurately read in the history of government, Mr. Greenleaf also possessed great familiarity with the best literature of his day, which he applied with charming ease to the illustration of the topics of his conversation, which he never suffered to fall into the trivial or unworthy. He was a gentleman of dignified bearing, of scrupulous honesty, and exacting sense of the obligations of life. His death, which occurred on March 8, 1895, at the advanced age of eightyfour years, when most men have long lost touch with life, is keenly felt by those who had the privilege of personal intercourse with him, for he carried to the end an unimpaired intellect and the charm of manner and conversation which were peculiarly his.

Franklin, the second son, of Portsmouth, was a bookbinder, and resided in Brooklyn, N. Y. Abner, the third son, was bred a printer, and for several years was publisher of the *New Hampshire Gazette*, at Portsmouth, as were his brothers Albert and George at different times. He now resides in Brooklyn, N. Y. George, the fourth son, was also bred a printer.

594. Benjamin[7] Greenleaf (Chart XXXII.), b. Sept. 25, 1786, in Haverhill, Mass., son of Caleb[6] and Susanna (Emerson). Was Preceptor of Bradford Academy from Dec. 12, 1814, to April 6, 1836. The history of

Benjamin[7] Greenleaf.

Preceptor of Bradford (Mass.) Academy,
and Mathematician.

his early life,—one of struggle for knowledge,—remarkable for courageous and persistent perseverance, is a most interesting one, and is related in an extended form in "A Memorial of Bradford Academy," published by the Congregational Sunday School and Publishing Society in 1870. He lived on a farm, which meant in those days, for boys, hard manual labor, with but poor opportunities for an education; these opportunities he improved, and made such use of his hours for study and the few books at hand as to form a strong passion for knowledge. He once said to a friend, "If I ever offered up an earnest prayer it was for rainy days, that I might betake myself to my books." For these he early showed a strong desire, and, in their scarcity in those times, he would go miles to borrow them. His spare pennies he coined into books, and so was enabled to extend his borrowing by lending. It is said of this distinguished author and teacher that at fourteen years of age he did not know the multiplication table, but we find the striking indication of his scholarship in college that he sketched the transit of Venus while there, an event to take place Dec. 8, 1874.

In 1805, at the age of nineteen, he commenced a preparation for college under the instruction of the Hon. John Vose, of Atkinson, N. H. During the five years following he spent two of them in the academy, and the other three in teaching schools in Plaistow, Atkinson, Haverhill, Bradford, and Marblehead. Thus early in his scholar life he began what proved to be his professional life. On Sept. 29, 1810, he was entered as a Sophomore in Dartmouth in a class of sixty. After his graduation in 1813, Mr. Greenleaf renewed his work as a teacher, and took charge of the grammar school in Haverhill. On the 12th of Dec., 1814, he became the Preceptor of Bradford Academy. The Institution, during the eleven years of its existence, had already had thirteen Preceptors.

As a teacher Mr. Greenleaf was popular and successful. One of his pupils, Hon. Ira Perley, Chief Justice of the State of New Hampshire, in writing of him, says: "His personal appearance and manners were marked and somewhat peculiar. Everything in the man was frank, direct, and wholly unaffected. Though very plain and perhaps a little careless in his dress, he was always perfectly tidy and scrupulously neat. His manners were not much regulated by artificial rules of politeness, but he had what is much more important, great real kindness of heart and habitual regard for the feelings of others. He was devoted to his business of teaching, and justly regarded it as of the highest importance. It is quite clear that he chose the profession for which his natural endowments and all his training and habits had best qualified him."

He was a thoroughly sincere and honest man and was wholly incapable of disguise or false pretense. His moral and religious principles, firmly established, were made the guide of his life. His influence was all on the side of religion and virtue. A classmate of Mr. Perley, the Rev. William Clark, adds some important and bold lines to this striking picture. He says: "Mr. Greenleaf was an uncommon genius in the sense of having peculiarities entirely his own, in the structure of his mind, the contour of his head and face, the expression of countenance, his utterance, his manners, his motions, all his ways. His intellectual powers were great in the line of the higher mathematics, including all the natural sciences. A peculiarly nervous temperament was a marked element in Mr. Greenleaf. Sit or stand still he could not. In him experimenters for perpetual motion would have found a pretty good solution of their problem. So impatient were his thoughts of utterance, so crowded they one upon another, their struggle for development would set in motion his hands, arms, head,—his whole body." In his earlier manhood a head of heavy black hair threw a deep covering over his forehead and temples. It was braided behind in a queue of respectable length, which, in animated conversation, he was wont to seize with his right hand, tossing it over his shoulders, as if to help his impeded utterance.

Mr. Greenleaf was in the State Legislature 1837, 1838 and 1839, and while there he introduced an order for a geological survey of the State, and also one for a natural history survey; and the surveys were afterwards made. He was also a pioneer educator in the natural sciences by illustrated public lectures. Chemistry, astronomy, geology, and the various departments and labors in the life of a teacher were the most common themes.

In 1839 he founded and took the charge of the Bradford Teachers' Seminary, a school for both sexes, and continued as its head till its discontinuance in 1848. His professional labors as a teacher then closed. As an author Mr. Greenleaf was widely, eminently, and honorably known. The first of his mathematical series to the public was issued in 1835. As early as 1825 he published a duodecimo tract of eight pages, entitled, "Rules of Syntax"; of these there are forty-three. Mr. Greenleaf also worked off the mathematical calculations for a number of almanacs. For several years he did this for the Cherokee Mission, beginning with 1854, and continuing it for six or seven years. The labor was gratuitous, and he called the offering his "missionary money." He also made calculations for almanacs for the meridian of Boston, New Orleans, Vicksburg, Memphis, San Francisco, and Halifax, Nova Scotia. Of his common school arithmetic, alone, five hundred and sixty thousand were printed from the first set of plates, and considerable more than a million in all. He published text-books on arithmetic, mental and written, algebra, geometry, and trigonometry, plane and spherical, and left in manuscript a System of Practical Surveying. Their issue from the press began in 1835, and continued in new works and new editions almost to the time of his death. Some of his primary and elementary arithmetics have been translated into Burmese, and some of his works into modern Greek. Mr. Greenleaf was more than a local teacher, he was a public educator. Always active in whatever related to the advancement of his own academic charge, he was constantly adding to the native stimulus and enthusiasm that led him to adopt the profession of teaching, and so was always ready to co-operate with the friends of popular education in their efforts to raise the standard of instruction. Hence he was found among the pioneers in leading teachers to dispense with text-books in the recitation room, and before their classes. Hence, too, he was an early and efficient advocate of the Normal School system; and while he was

in the State Legislature, he urged statute foundations and regulations for
those schools now so indispensable to our educational system.

593. Anna Greenleaf (Chart XXXII.), b. March 2, 1793, daughter
of Caleb[6] and Susanna (Emerson), m. John Crowell, of Haverhill, Mass.
Dr. John Crowell, born Sept. 28, 1823, their son, at the age of twenty-one
took charge of the School Street Grammar School in Haverhill, Mass.,
and by his vigorous methods of instruction gained a high reputation as a
teacher, and many of his former pupils have acquired distinction in varied
spheres of life. Desiring to study the theory of medicine he came under
the instruction of Dr. George Cogswell, of Bradford, who had gained a
wide reputation as the leading physician and surgeon in the Essex North
Medical Society. He pursued his studies still further under the direction
of Prof. James McClintock, of Philadelphia, and afterwards in the
Pennsylvania Hospital in that city, and graduated with honor from the
Philadelphia College of Medicine in 1850. In 1856 he was admitted a
Fellow of the Massachusetts Medical Society, and in 1881-2 was President
of the Essex North Medical Society, which is a branch of the State Society.
In 1851 he commenced the practice of medicine in Haverhill, Mass., his
native town, identifying himself with its social and literary life, and always
taking a deep interest in whatever pertained to the welfare of his fellow-
citizens. He held many and important public offices, and in every position
of trust he has discharged his duties with rare zeal and tact. While on
the School Board, he was elected Chairman during very nearly the entire
term of his many years of service. In 1878 he was elected one of the
Trustees of the Haverhill Public Library. In 1880 he was appointed
member and Chairman of the Board of Health. Upon the establishment
of the Haverhill City Hospital, in 1882, he was appointed one of the
Trustees, and was chosen Secretary of the Board. In January, 1883, he
was appointed Trustee of Bradford Academy, and elected Secretary of the
Board. In March, 1883, he was elected Trustee of the Linwood Cemetery
Corporation. August, 1883, appointed one of the Consulting Board of
Physicians and Surgeons at Danvers Asylum. In his religious life he was
connected with the Centre Congregational Church since 1849, and filled
important official positions in the church and in the Sunday school. His
literary labors have been many and varied. He has written several papers
for the Massachusetts Medical Society. June, 1883, he delivered the
annual address before the Massachusetts Medical Society. Among the
numerous lectures, essays, reviews, etc., written by him for clubs, literary
societies, and periodicals, are those on John Ruskin, and Michael Angelo;
Architecture, Sources of the English Language, Thomas à Becket, Charles
Lamb, etc. He died April 28, 1890, at the age of sixty-six years seven
months.

605. William[7] Greenleaf (Chart XXXIII.), b. Oct. 7, 1788, son of
Jonathan[6] and Joanna (Manning). His mother died when he was eight
years old, and soon after this he was bound out and brought to Maine and
was almost lost to his relatives for a long time, and it was many years

before he saw any of them. He lived with Mr. Peter Holden, a shoe-maker (to whom he was bound to learn the trade). Mr. Holden moved to Otisfield, Me., taking William with him. He sometimes fared hard; was poorly fed and scantily clothed, but worked his time out and got his trade. He was ambitious, possessed an amiable disposition, was healthy, and grew to be a fine-looking young man, liked and respected by all who knew him. When he became of age, he bought a lot of land, cleared it, and built a house and barn, convenient for a home. He prospered in his business, working on his land, while his trade furnished him with work, more than he could do besides his farm work, so he was always busy, sitting late at night on his low bench, making shoes well suited to those good old times of home manufacture. A brook ran through his farm near his buildings, which, by the help of a dam, furnished water power sufficient for a mill. He bought machinery and built a mill, doing a successful business, sawing shingles. Later on he built a new house of modern architecture, and commodious for his family of seven healthy and happy children.

29. John Greenleaf Whittier, b. Dec. 17, 1807, at Haverhill, Mass. Descended from Thomas Whittier, born in England, 1622, who married Ruth Green, probably in Newbury, Mass., about 1646. Leaving Southampton, he sailed for Boston on the ship "Confidence," on April 24, 1638, and settled first in Salisbury, Mass., afterwards removed to Newbury, and in 1648 to Haverhill, at which place the town records say he "brought a hive of bees." Of the ten children of Thomas and Ruth, the youngest was Joseph, born May 8, 1669, at Haverhill, Mass. Joseph married Mary Peasley, daughter of Joseph and Ruth (Barnard), at Haver-hill, Mass., May 24, 1694. They had nine children; the youngest was Joseph, born March 31, 1716. He married July 12, 1739, Sarah, born March 5, 1721, daughter of Nathaniel[4] and Judith (Coffin) Greenleaf. They had eleven children; the youngest married son was John, born Nov. 22, 1760, at Haverhill, Mass. He married Abigail, daughter of Samuel and Mercy (Evans) Hussey, Oct. 3, 1804. They had four children, the second of whom was John Greenleaf Whittier. The members of this line of the Whittier family resided in Haverhill, Mass., occupying the ancestral home until about 1830, when John G. and his mother removed to Ames-bury.* The records of the Whittier family in this line may be found at Haverhill, and most of them are substantiated by the records in the Registry of Deeds and Probate at Salem, Mass. The childhood of the poet resembled that of most young people in the same walk of life in New England in the first decade of the century. As soon as he was old enough to be useful, the boy was set to work on the farm and to doing errands for his mother, who, besides attending to her household duties, busied herself in spinning and weaving the woolen cloth that was needed for the family. Like his brother poet Bryant, who was thirteen years older, he was fond of outdoor life, and, like him, was a diligent student of nature. When

* Whittier Genealogy, by C. C. Whittier, 40 Dartmouth Street, Boston.

he was fourteen, his first schoolmaster, Joshua Coffin, brought to the house a volume of Burns' poems, from which he read, greatly to the lad's delight. He begged him to leave the book with him, and set himself at once to the task of mastering the glossary of the Scottish dialect at its close. It was the first poetry that he had ever read, and it exercised so strong an influence over him that he began to rhyme and to imagine stories and adventures. When he was about nineteen, a young man named Garrison, a native of Newburyport, where he had served his apprenticeship as a compositor, started a paper on his own account, the *Free Press*, to which the family subscribed. It was in the poet's corner of this paper that his verse first saw the light. He was so overjoyed when he read himself in print that he was rooted to the ground (he was mending fences at the time), and had to be called several times before he was fully awake to this dull, work-a-day world. One summer day not long afterwards, a carriage drove up to the house and a young man, alighting, asked for Mr. John Greenleaf Whittier. He was sent for, and slipping in by the back door, barefooted, and without coat or waistcoat, he made himself presentable and appeared. The visitor was the editor of the *Free Press*, William Lloyd Garrison, to whom his elder sister had divulged the secret of authorship of his verses, and who, being a great lover of poetry, had come to pay his respects to the new poet. What passed between Whittier and Garrison that summer day, and between the pair and the parents of Whittier, can only be conjectured now. That they were made to see there was a future for their boy may be inferred from the fact that before the year was over he was sent to an academy in Haverhill. His first literary employment after quitting Haverhill was as the editor of the *American Manufacturer*, a paper published in Boston. His next employment was on the *Haverhill Gazette*, of which he was the editor for the first six months of 1830. He was now fairly well known through his poems in the *Yankee*, which was published in Portland, Me., and his contributions in prose and verse in the *New England Weekly Review*, which was published in Hartford, Conn. He was as proud of New England as Burns of Scotland, and what it was and had been was the chief source of his inspiration. His nationality was visible in all that he wrote. His first collection was "New England Legends in Prose and Verse" (1831), and his first poem of any length, "Moll Pitcher" (1832). He was strongly drawn to the past of his native land, now as it was recorded in history, and now as it was handed down by tradition. The Indians appealed to his sympathy, as they appealed to the sympathy of Bryant, but differently and less poetically; for while they were merely shadows against the background of Bryant's verse, they were prominent figures in the foreground of his verse,—dark, repellent, horrible. He published "Mogg Megone" in 1836. He figured among journalists in 1837, in the *Pennsylvania Freeman*, of which he soon became the editor, and in his thirty-third year he removed from Philadelphia and settled in Amesbury. From his contributions to the *Democratic Review*, which extended from the autumn of 1837 to the spring of 1846, and to two or three other periodicals and journals, he drew the materials for his next collection, "Lays of my Home, and Other Poems" (1843), which at once gave him a place among the poets of America. (See *Harper's Weekly*, Sept. 7, 1892.)

621. Samuel[6] Greenleaf (Chart XXXV.), b. March 14, 1766, son of Abner[5] and Mary (Whittier). Resided for about eight years at West Newbury after his marriage. Thence he removed to Bangor, Me., where he remained ten or twelve years; thence to Marietta and Cincinnati, O. At Cincinnati he established a carriage shop, which was destroyed by fire in 1821. After struggling with adversity several years, he, aided by his son Edward, succeeded in satisfying all claims against him. In 1832 Edward removed from Cincinnati. His father and mother and two sisters, Clarissa and Julia, followed him to Tennessee, near Bolivar. He (Samuel) was there but a few months when he died in July, 1835. His death was calm and peaceful to the last moment. He had no dread of death, and said it was "no more to him than passing through a doorway —from one room to another—where all was peace." He was tall and rather slender, with tender blue eyes and silvery hair; erect and dignified, though very quick in his movements; precise and careful in his dress and manners; a fine "old school" gentleman. In referring to the beauty and purity of his character, his granddaughter says, after an interval of sixty years: "I remember well how he would take me, a little girl, on his knee, and sing to me the old hymns, 'How firm a foundation,' 'The Lord will provide,' and the song of the Indian captive 'The Son of Alhnomac shall never complain.' How eagerly I awaited to hear grandpa's quick step, and the slight cough he always gave as he opened the gate, and shut it with a peculiar click." Samuel Greenleaf and his wife Miriam had twelve children, five of whom were born in West Newbury, six in Bangor, and one in Marietta.

635. Stephen[6] Greenleaf (Chart XXXVI.), b. April 11, 1766, son of Samuel[5] and Lois (Rowell). In the year 1789 removed with his mother to Salisbury, N. H., and engaged in farming. Mr. Greenleaf was a well built man, six feet in height, not much inclined to flesh, nor very slim. He had black eyes, auburn hair, and light complexion. He was of nervous temperament, very active, and quick in all his motions, walking very erect, even to the time of his death. His sons generally resemble him in person and height.

638. George H.[8] Greenleaf (Chart XXXVI.), b. Nov. 5, 1834, son of Thomas R.[7] and Mary (Hawley). Most of his life was spent in the States of Ohio and Missouri, his father removing from New England to Ohio, where he settled in the town of New Philadelphia. In 1885 he was President of the Laclede County Bank, at Lebanon, Missouri, established in 1869, which position he held for several years, and up to his death.

644. William[5] Greenleaf (Chart XXXVII.), b. Nov. 28, 1725, son of Edmund[4]. Settled in Haverhill, Mass. He was a religious man in early life, and a leading member of the Calvinist Baptist Church in that

town. He was in the Army of the Revolution, after which he kept the
"Sun Tavern," in Haverhill, until his death, when it was continued by
his son William.[6]

His name appears in the History of Haverhill as a member of the Fire
Society, Feb. 22, 1768, as does also that of his son William,[6] October, 1785.
(See Military Service.)

His son, Daniel[6] Greenleaf, born April 19, 1746, was also a member
of the Fire Department in 1769, at Haverhill, Mass.

645. Rebecca Greenleaf (Chart XXXVII.), daughter of Daniel[6]
and Ruth (Dalton), was born in Haverhill, Mass., March 28, 1778, and
married Ephraim Beaman, son of Joseph Beaman, of Lancaster, Mass.;
they resided in Boston, Mass., until 1836.

Ephraim Beaman was born in Lancaster, Mass., Nov. 17, 1770. His
father, Joseph Beaman, was born in Lancaster, in 1733. His earliest
American ancestor on his father's side was Gamaliel Beaman, who came
to Dorchester, New England, in 1635, a lad twelve years old, and after his
marriage in Dorchester he removed, in 1659, to Lancaster, Mass.

Rev. Charles Cotesworth Beaman, son of Ephraim and Rebecca,
received his early education at Boston in the public school on School
Street,—the building standing on the ground now occupied by the City
Hall. Afterwards, at the age of thirteen, he was placed in a private school
kept by Mr. Lawson Lyon, on Federal Street, where he remained four
years. Being then seventeen years of age, and looking forward to a life
of business, he was placed in the store of Blake & McLellan, on Long
Wharf. He afterwards served as clerk in other stores until 1829, when he
went into the auction and commission business for himself in the Faneuil
Hall building. In 1834 he gave up business, to prepare for the ministry.
He took a three-year course at Andover Theological Seminary, and
graduated in 1837. He was admitted at Houlton, Me., June 20, 1839,
and served as Congregational minister in Houlton, Me., North Falmouth,
Mass., Edgartown, Mass., Wellfleet, Mass., and elsewhere until 1874, at
which time he resided in Cambridge and Boston without a charge. He
married, July 10, 1839, Mary Ann Stacey, daughter of Nymphus and
Martha (Babson) Stacey, of Wiscasset, Me. His wife died in Cambridge,
Feb. 22, 1875. Mr. Beaman was a gentleman of fine personal appearance
and of exceedingly pleasant address. His voice and manner were especially attractive. His son, Hon. C. C. Beaman, was private secretary of
Hon. Charles Sumner, and is junior partner of the law firm of Evarts,
Choate & Beaman, of New York City.

661. Charles Beaman[9] Greenleaf (Chart XXXVIII.), b. Nov.
26, 1838, son of John[8] and Louisa (Poland). Entered the employ of Mr.
Dana, apothecary, in Portland, Me., in 1822, as clerk, and afterwards
held a similar position in the apothecary store of Mr. Gilson. In 1869 he
established himself in business, and was located for twenty years at the
corner of Spring and Brackett Streets, in Portland, as druggist and
apothecary.

He was one of the leading members of St. Luke's Cathedral, as vestryman, and was Treasurer of the Diocese, the Corporation, and Board of Bishops. In his will he bequeathed the sum of one thousand dollars to the Home for Aged Women.

663. Charles H.[9] **Greenleaf** (Chart XXXVIII.), b. Sept. 27, 1842, son of Charles T.[8] and Mary Jane (Wheeler). Resides in Bath, Me., and is the Treasurer of the Eastern Electric Company. He was a member of the city government, being in the Common Council two years, on the Board of Aldermen eleven years, and City Auditor two years. (See Military Service.)

600. Gardner[5] **Greenleaf** (Chart XXXIII.), b. Jan. 9, 1725–26, son of Stephen[4] and Mary (Gardner). Went during the Revolution with the British to Nova Scotia when they evacuated Boston, but returned to Medford after the war, and kept shop there many years. (See Military Service.)

615. Lawrence N.[8] **Greenleaf** (Chart XXXIII.), b. Oct. 4, 1838, son of Gardner[7] and Rebecca Jane (Caldwell). Was educated in the Boston public schools. Graduated at the English High School (Class of 1852) in 1855. Began his business career in a wholesale house in that city, where he remained four years. In the spring of 1860 started for the Pike's Peak gold region; was twenty-six days on the plains, reaching Denver, Colo., in May, where he engaged in mercantile business, and has since resided. He early displayed a literary taste, and has delivered poems on many public occasions in Colorado, besides contributing to the press. In 1868 he collected his poems, which were published by Hurd & Houghton, of New York, under the title of "King Sham and Other Atrocities in Verse." On Feb. 1, 1893, he became editor of the *Square and Compass*, a Masonic monthly published at Denver, and in July became its proprietor.

He has attained marked distinction in the Masonic Order, which he entered on March 19, 1863. Elected S. W., 1865, acting W. M. most of the term; W. M., 1866, 1868, 1869, 1877–78. Grand Lodge: J. G. W., 1866, 1878; S. G. W., 1879; G. M., 1880, Chairman Foreign Correspondence for past seven years. Chapter: received the degrees, 1863; H. P., 1868. Grand Chapter: G. H. P., 1885; High Priesthood, anointed June 9, 1868. President Grand Council of High Priesthood at Denver, 1886–94. Council: Boston, Select Master, Royal and Super Ex-Master, 1868. Commandery: Knighted in 1868; E. C., Colorado Commandery No. 1, 1890; Scottish Rite degrees up to thirty-second in 1868, etc. Was commissioned October, 1878, Deputy of the Supreme Council, southern jurisdiction of the United States, for Colorado. Oct. 20, 1880, invested with thirty-third degree at Washington, D. C. Deputy Inspector General since April 5, 1883.

MILITARY AND NAVAL SERVICE

BY THOSE BEARING THE NAME OF GREENLEAF.

IN presenting these records of service, the design in assigning numbers is to give a general direction which may lead to identify the names of those who have performed military or naval service. In many cases these numbers have been given from information by correspondents; in others, from historical or other records and family tradition. In doubtful cases the query mark (?) is placed against the calendar number, or more than one number is given.

A few brief notes relating to some of the various services, as " The Siege of Louisburg," " Crown Point Expedition," etc., are given here chiefly for the purpose of bringing before the reader the dates in the periods of their occurrence, and to call to mind some special point as may relate to a service; for example, that of Rutland, Mass., in which attention is called to the fact that old men and boys were placed on duty there, while the more able-bodied men were sent to the field, being better fitted for other and more hazardous duties.

Details of service for the War of 1812 are omitted, because of the absence of the muster rolls from our State archives. They may be found at Washington, but were inaccessible when looked for, because of the removal of the Library at Washington to its new quarters. In explanation of the removal of these muster rolls from the State archives,— and the course which led to their removal,—it may be mentioned that Governor Strong, when appealed to at a public meeting of the citizens of Boston about the first of September, 1814, to take active measures looking to the defense of the Commonwealth, at once ordered defenses made along the coasts of Massachusetts and Maine. This and similar acts on the part of the State led to a controversy which lasted nearly twenty years, between the Commonwealth of Massachusetts and the United States, which was finally terminated on the surrender by Massachusetts of the original muster rolls of her troops called into service in that war; which rosters the General Government insisted on holding as vouchers for the long-deferred reimbursement to the State of expenses of troops, and other costs involved in coast defense. In this discussion the old question of Federal *vs.* State rights was somewhat involved.

THE SIEGE OF LOUISBURG.

[*King George's War, 1744-49.*]

In the month of March, one hundred and fifty years ago, Governor Shirley was busily engaged in fitting out the famous expedition, under Gen. Sir William Pepperell, which was destined to capture that stronghold,—the Dunkirk, "the Gibraltar of America,"—Louisburg, on the easterly shore of Cape Breton.

On March 24, 1745, a fleet of some ninety transports set sail from Boston. April 5th some of the advanced vessels were at Canseau, where the most of them remained until the ice had melted, the 29th of April. On May 1st and 2d a landing was made on the shores of Cabarrus Bay; a sortie of French troops from the garrison was overcome; and the army under Pepperell, about four thousand two hundred men, settled down in rude quarters and began the famous Siege of Louisburg. These men were unused to war, undisciplined, and had never seen a siege in their lives. They had landed on a dangerous coast, in the face of the enemy. With Herculean labor they dragged siege guns over rocky hills and through morasses, and girt the fortifications about with batteries. For more than six weeks the work went on, aided by the British fleet under Commodore (late Admiral) Warren, and by sheer audacity they compelled the surrender on the 17th of June,—the day made yet more memorable thirty years later at Bunker Hill. The keys of the walled town, which had yielded to the "yeomanry of New England," were received by Sir William Pepperell from General Duchambon. The prizes of war exceeded in value a million pounds.

CROWN POINT EXPEDITION, 1755.

The French, alert and aggressive, not only claimed by right of discovery the Mississippi and its tributaries to their sources in the Alleghanies, but had gone far to make their claim good by encircling the English colonies with a cordon of blockhouses and forts, from the St. Lawrence to the Ohio. Against this French line of occupation, in 1755 four great expeditions were planned at widely separated points: Fort Duquesne, at the head of the Ohio River; Fort Niagara, on Lake Ontario; Crown Point, on Lake Champlain; and the Acadian forts at the head of the Bay of Fundy. The first expedition met with ignominious disaster, the second and third missed their aim, and the fourth won inglorious victory.—*Nourse's* "*Lancaster Annals*," *page 33.*

FORT WILLIAM HENRY ALARM, 1757.

Col. Joseph Frye marched from Fort Edward, Aug. 2, 1757, with his regiment of Massachusetts men and two hundred British troops to succor Fort William Henry, then besieged by Montcalm with an overwhelming force of French and Indians. On the surrender of that fort, August 9th, a massacre ensued, from which Colonel Frye and most of his men escaped with the loss of everything but life.—*Ibid., page 59.*

At the general alarm consequent upon the expectation that Montcalm, flushed with his victory at Fort William Henry, would make a bold push for Albany, the fourth part of the militia of Massachusetts were hurried toward that point with all possible speed. Captains Israel Taylor and Samuel Haskell of Harvard, Thomas Wilder of Leominster, John Carter and Nathaniel Sawyer of Lancaster, marched with from fifty to sixty men each as far as Springfield, whence Montcalm, having retreated to Canada with the rich spoils of easily bought success, they were recalled.—*Ibid., page 61.*

The following order relating to calling out the citizens on sudden emergency, is taken from the Council Records in the State Archives:—

PROVINCE OF MASSACHUSETTS BAY,
BY THE HONORABLE HIS MAJESTY'S COUNCIL.

To W. Brattle, Esq., greeting:—

It appearing to His Majesty's Council absolutely necessary that the militia of this Province be in such a Posture of Defence as to be ready to march at a moment's warning. These are, therefore, in His Majesty's name to require you in the most effectual manner to cause every Person, both upon the alarm and trained Band Lists in the Regiment of Militia

whereof you are Colonel, and the respective Town Stocks in said Regiment
to be immediately furnished with arms and ammunition according to Law,
if not already provided.

And you are alike required in case of an Invasion or near approach
of an enemy, before the notice thereof can reach the Captain General or
Commander in Chief to have direction or orders from him, to Assemble
in Martial Array the whole militia, or such Regiment or Section therein
as you shall judge needful upon any alarm, invasion or notice of the
approach of the Enemy by Sea or Land, and with them go arrayed to lead,
conduct and employ in any Place within this Province, for the assisting,
succoring and relieving any of His Majesty's subjects in it.

And for your so doing this shall be your sufficient warrant.

Dated at the Council Chamber in Boston the 10th day of May, 1757.

BY ORDER OF HIS MAJESTY'S COUNCIL.

Return of warrant and doings.

Cambg.: May 30, 1757.

THE WAR FOR INDEPENDENCE.

By a Resolve of the General Court, June 25, 1776, respon-
sive to a request from the Continental Congress for five thousand militia to co-operate with the armies at New York and in
the department of Canada, a bounty of three pounds was promised each volunteer, and eighteen shillings were allowed each
soldier for the use of arms and accouterments, if furnishing them
himself.

The term of service ended Dec. 1, 1776. Four battalions
were destined for Canada, and three, including all companies from
Worcester County, were to serve at New York in the Brigade of
Gen. John Fellows.

In 1891 the Legislature of Massachusetts directed the Secretary of State to prepare an indexed compilation of the records
of Massachusetts soldiers and sailors who served in the army or
navy during the Revolutionary War. For this purpose $10,000
was appropriated, and an additional sum of $5,500 was authorized
to be expended for the printing of one thousand copies of the
work, which will be distributed among public officials, libraries,
and historical and antiquarian societies, as well as one copy to
each state and territory in the Union. The work of compilation,
arduous and painstaking, has just been completed under the able
direction of J. J. Tracy, chief of the archives department of the
Secretary of State office. This history contains much data that
for years have been the secrets of documents rarely, if ever, looked

at. The names of soldiers are arranged in alphabetical order, and against each name everything that can be identified as belonging to the individual is noted.

The scope and extent of the work may be gathered from the fact that it will comprise from four to six volumes of one thousand pages each. It may be possible to confine the work within four volumes, and it may be necessary to print six. The publication is being carried on as rapidly as the State printers can perform the work.

Another work of great value and interest to the genealogical student is that recently compiled and published by Mr. B. F. Stevens, 4 Trafalgar Square, London, Eng. It is an index of documents relating to the War of the Revolution, and preserved in the various archives of Europe. Facsimiles of manuscripts in 1773–1783, with description, editorial notes, collations, references, and translations, strictly limited to two hundred copies foolscap folio. Issued only to subscribers, at twenty dollars a volume of five hundred pages. The issue will not exceed five volumes a year. To be completed in fifty volumes in book-looking cardboard boxes, with leather-covered wood backs, cloth sides, and jointed flaps. Twenty-two volumes are now in the Boston Public Library.

RHODE ISLAND SERVICE, 1778.

In 1778 an attempt was made to recover Newport by the combined efforts of the newly arrived French fleet, commanded by the Count d'Estaing, and an army of ten thousand men under Gen. John Sullivan, with Gen. Nathaniel Greene and Marquis de Lafayette as division commanders. A plan of combined attack was agreed upon, and on August 9th the advance began.

The American forces occupied Quaker and Butts' Hills, and the French troops, four thousand in number, were preparing to disembark, when suddenly the English fleet was reported in sight, and the Count d'Estaing, with favoring wind, went out to meet it. Everything seemed to promise triumph; but a tempest of unexampled severity set in, and on the night of the 10th drove both fleets to sea, damaging them seriously, and causing much suffering in the camps. When, on the 20th of August, d'Estaing again entered Newport Harbor, he deemed it necessary to pro-

ceed at once to Boston for repairs, and abandoned the enterprise
so favorably begun.   In view of the fact that reinforcements
might at any hour arrive from New York to the assistance of the
enemy, retreat was now unavoidable.   On the 28th, at night,
General Sullivan abandoned his siege works and marched to
the northern end of the island.   The British veterans were the
following morning led to an assault upon the American lines,
but were repelled by the combined force of militia and conti-
nentals after several hours of hard fighting.   In this action,
known as the Battle of Quaker's Hill, the Massachusetts detach-
ments won much praise.   The next day the retreat was skillfully
completed without molestation; and thus ended an expedition
that for a time gave fair promise of putting a glorious end to
the war.

The Second Worcester Regiment of militia, commanded by
Col. Josiah Whitney, of Harvard, was one of those detailed for
the Rhode Island campaign, and was engaged for one month
and fifteen days from Aug. 1, 1778.   Capt. Manasseh Sawyer's
company of this regiment numbered sixty-four, rank and file.
(Mass. Arch., XXII. page 207.)

RUTLAND BARRACKS, 1779.

Besides the frequent calls upon the militia for troops to go
beyond the State line upon sudden alarms, or during some
temporary emergency, there were constant details for guard duty
within the State.   The guards employed were many of them
boys, old men, and others unfit for field service.   Extensive
barracks were built at Rutland, and the English regiments of
General Burgoyne's troops, prisoners of war, were removed
thither from Cambridge, at which place they were thought too
easily accessible if the British forces, by sudden raid from
Newport, should attempt their release.   The transfer was made
during April, 1779.

SHAYS'S INSURRECTION, 1786-1787.

Daniel Shays, who had been a captain in the Continental
Army, at the head of a mob of a thousand armed men or more,
took possession of Worcester, and effectually prevented the session of the Supreme Court in that town.   At the head of another

smaller body he repeated the same operation at Springfield; but beyond preventing the session of the courts, these insurgents do not seem to have had any plan.

Governor Bowdoin called out at once four thousand militia, to serve for thirty days under the command of General Lincoln. Of these were the " Lancaster Volunteers," — " as fine a body of men as were ever assembled." " There were in this regiment fifty or sixty persons who have borne commissions, some of which to command regiments in the late Continental army and militia, who do duty in the ranks and submit to the hardships of a soldier's life in this inclement season with a spirit of patriotism and cheerfulness which nothing but the cause they are engaged in could inspire." *The Massachusetts Centinel* of January 27, 1787, in giving a list of some of the Volunteers, which list is headed by Col. *William Greenleaf*, says : "On Tuesday the 16th inst. (January, 1787), Col. Greenleaf waited on the two companies of militia in this town, assembled agreeably to his orders, when he communicated to them, with his usual propriety, the importance of showing their disapprobation to the illegal measures which have been adopted by the insurgents, and the necessity of evidencing their attachment to the Government. . . . . After some calm debates on the subject, the Colonel, in order to discover their minds, requested all who were friends to the Government to follow him ; when, with very few exceptions, the whole turned after him.   He then informed them that twenty-eight men were required of the two companies to support the Court to sit at Worcester the 23d inst., and gave them opportunity to engage voluntarily under these restrictions, viz. : whoever offers his services shall be held to march, or produce an able, effective man to the acceptance of the officer in lieu of himself ; when more than the required number promptly answered the requisition.   Col. *William Greenleaf* headed the list, followed by his son *William Greenleaf, Junior*," who served under the command of Col. Ephraim Stearns as Quartermaster Sergeant.

The march of this regiment from Hadley to Petersham, thirty miles through an almost mountainous country, and during the last part of the way facing a violent storm, was something to be remembered for life.   The drifting snow impeded their steps, and it grew so intensely cold that the majority of the force were frost-bitten.

Within twelve hours of the orders to move, the advance guard of the army had reached their destination, it being then Sunday morning.   Shays and his "regulators" were completely taken by surprise, and fled in hot haste, scattering in every direction.   The insurrection was practically at an end. No one was punished for sedition, and three years later the vigorous financial policy of Alexander Hamilton silenced the majority of the grumblers.

Colonel Greenleaf afterwards became Brigadier General in the militia of the State.

NAME AND SERVICE.

* 25. ⎫ Abel.[5] Son of Benjamin[4] and Ann (Hale) (Chart XXIX.),
294. ⎭ or, Abel.[6] Enlisted Jan. 1, 1778. Twelve months. Capt. Jonathan Evan's Co.   Col. Nathaniel Wade's Regt.   Rhode Island service, East Greenwich. Muster Roll for this duty, July–Sept., 1778. A pay abstract gives his home, Newbury. Mileage, Albany to Newbury, Mass., in Capt. Joshua French's Co. Col. Edw. Wigglesworth's Regt. Also service at North Kingston, Rhode Island, between July, 1778 and Jan. 1779. Same Co. and Regt. on East Greenwich duty. [Mass. Arch., Vol. ii. p. 6.]   On Capt. Richard Greenleaf's "Larrum List" for Newbury, 1757. [Mass. Arch., Muster Rolls, Vol. xcv. p. 424.]

572. Abner.[6] Sergeant, June 13, 1757, Capt. Stephen Emery's Co., of Newbury. [Mass. Arch., Muster Rolls, Vol. xcv. p. 403].

576. Abner.[7] War of 1812.

300. Abraham.[7] War of 1812.

* 400. Alpheus S.[9] Son of Levi[8] and —— (Chart XXIII.). Private Co. F., 3d Regt. Maine Vols., Civil War.

* 149. Amos.[9] Son of Flavel[8] and Eunice (Smith) (Chart XIII.). Private 96th Regt. Inf. Illinois Vols., Civil War.

452. Andrew Jackson.[8] Private Mexican War. Lost while in the United States service as gunner in sloop of war "Levant," 1859.

515. Andrew Peterson.[8] Private Co. G, Capt. Wm. W. Whittemore; Col. George L. Beal. Private Cos. H and A, 29th Regt. Maine Vols., Civil War. Fort McCleary, Kittery, Me., 60 days, April 27th to July 9, 1864. Killed at battle of Cedar Creek, Va., Oct. 19, 1864.

442. Anthony.[7] War of 1812.

308. Benjamin.[6] Sent home at Sheepscot River and Townsend on His Majesty's ship "Rainbow," Sept. 12, 1777. Town Woolwich: Capt. Walker's Co., May 28, 1778, Lincoln County; age (at enlistment) 18 years; height, 5 ft. 10 in.; complexion, dark. June 3, 1778, 9 months from time of arriving at Fishkill from Woolwich. Col. Cobb's (1st) Regt. Corporal, Capt. Benjamin Lamont's Co., Col. Samuel McCobbs' Regt.; enlisted July 9, 1779, disch. Sept. 24, 1779. Vol. xxxvii. p. 132.

559(?). Benjamin.[5] On Capt. Richard Greenleaf's "Larrum" List for Newbury, 1757. [Mass. Arch., Muster Rolls, Vol. xcv. p. 424]. Private: Jan. 22, 1761; Capt. Gideon Parker's Co., of Newbury. [Mass. Arch., Muster Rolls, Vol. xcix. p. 111]. Private: May 26, 1762; Capt. Henry Young Brown's Co. [Mass. Arch., Muster Rolls, Vol. xcix. p. 207.] On Alarm List, April 20, 1767, Maj. Richard Cutt's Co., Col. William Brattle. [Muster Rolls, Vol. xcv. p. 366.]

*272(?). Benjamin.[6] War of 1812.

495. Benjamin Lovell.[8] Private, 1861, Co. F, 3d Regt. Maine Vols. Civil War.

409. Benjamin W.[9] Private Co. C, 19th Regt. Maine Vols., Civil War.

593. Caleb.[6] Muster and Pay Roll, Nov. 10, 1777 to Feb. 3, 1778. Feb. 3, 1778 to April 4, 1778. Capt. Samuel Huse's Co., Col. Jacob Gerrish's Regt. Guards at Winter Hill. [Various Service, Vol. xx. pp. 21, 25.]

46. Calvin.[6] Private, Oct. 27, 1779 to April 27, 1780. Capt. Ephraim Hartwell's Co. Guards at Rutland, Mass. Autograph signature Books: Abstract of Rolls, Vol. xxxi. p. 57, Vol. lv. p. H 23. [Mass. Arch., Muster Rolls, Vol. xx. p. 25; Guard Rolls, Vol. xxv. p. 120.] April 4, 1759, on list to receive bayonet for his gun. (He and 14 others.) Col. Oliver Wilder's Regt. [Mass. Arch., Muster Rolls, Vol. xcvii. p. 248.]

251. Calvin Theophilus.[9] Private, 1862, Civil War.

253. Calvin Whitcomb.[8] Private, Co. K, 7th Regt. Vermont Vols., Civil War.

Charles. Private, April 9, 1756, Capt. Jabez Bradbury's Co., Boston. [Mass. Arch., Muster Rolls, Vol. xciv. p. 138.] Crown Point Expedition.

436. Charles Dexter.[8] Private, Civil War. Was killed in battle.

Charles F. Son of James S. and Jane T. (Whitney). Private Co. G, 10th Regt. Maine Vols., from Norway, Me. Discharged for disability Oct. 20, 1862, Civil War.

*194. Charles Henry.[10] Private, April 18, 1861. Rifle Co. A, 1st Regt. Conn. Vols., three mos., Capt. Hawley. Engaged in battle of Bull Run. Mustered out July 31, 1861. Private for three years' service. Cavalry, 5th N. Y. Regt.; served three years, and re-enlisted Private; was promoted to 1st Lieut. Was shot and killed at head of his Co., acting as Capt. in a battle near Charlestown, Va., Aug. 26, 1864. For full account of his services, see History 5th N. Y. Cavalry, Civil War, by the Chaplain.

663. Charles Henry.[9] Private; mustered June 4, 1861. Co. A, 3d Regt. Maine Vols., Civil War. Corporal, breveted to 2d Lieut. for gallantry in seven days' battles before Richmond, Va. Term of service, two years.

408. Charles L.[9] Private Co. C, 1st Regt. Maine Vols., Civil War.

551. Charles Ravenscroft.[9] Asst. Surgeon, 5th Ohio Inf., April 19, 1861. Served with his regiment on the field. Asst. Surgeon U. S. Army, July 19, 1861. Assigned to the staff of Gen. Mansfield, commanding

defenses of Washington. Collected the wounded after the battle of Bull
Run. In charge of Old Capital Prison Hospital. Served throughout
the Peninsula Campaign on the staff of Gen. McClellan. Received honorable mention from that general for services at Yorktown, and in the
battles of Fair Oaks, Hanover Court House, Gaines Mill, and Savage's
Station. Served at the battle of Antietam, and as Med. Director of the
base hospitals at Hagerstown and Harrisburg. In Oct., 1862, in charge
of construction and organization of the "Mower" General Hospital at
Philadelphia, the largest military hospital in the country, and remained
as its executive officer until the following year, when he was assigned as
Asst. Med. Director at Baltimore, during which time he participated in
the Gettysburg campaign. Brevet Capt. and Maj. at close of war for meri-
torious service, having served successively on staff of Gens. McClellan,
Schenck, Lew Wallace, H. G. Wright, and Hancock. After the war,
assigned to staff of Gen. Geo. H. Thomas. Served four years as his
Attending Surgeon; then assigned to duty with troops in Idaho, among
the Nez Perces Indians. After nearly five years frontier duty, served four
years in Alabama, Tennessee, and Louisiana. Again sent to frontier duty
in Montana. After four years' service there, served at Recruiting Depot
in Columbus, Ohio, and on the staff of Gen. Terry at Chicago, until
finally ordered to Washington as the Senior Asst. to the Surgeon Gen.,
where he remained six years. During this period he was intrusted with
many important duties, representing the Army Medical Department at
National Guard encampments in several of the States; as a delegate to the
American Medical Association; to the American Association for Physical
Education; to the Association Military Surgeons of the United States, of
which he was the Honorary President; to the International Medical Congress at Rome, Italy; investigating medico military methods in the
armies of Great Britain, France, Germany, and Switzerland; also, in the
selection of sites for new military posts. He also organized and administered the Hospital Corps, U. S. Army, which was authorized by Congress at the time of his arrival in Washington. In 1892 he was promoted
Deputy Surgeon Gen., with rank of Lieut. Col. Col. Greenleaf is the
author of a "Manual for Medical Officers of the Army;" "A System for the
Examination of Recruits," which is adopted by the Government as the
standard authority on the subject; "A Digest of Opinions;" "A System
of Personal Identity," which is also adopted by the Government, and in
use for the identification of deserters; and numerous articles on anthro-
pology, physical culture, and medico military matters in general.

    248. Charles Ward.[9]   Private, Co. K, 35th Regt. Mass. Vols.,
Aug. 1, 1861; served 3 years. Wounded twice in battle of Antietam,
Sept. 17, 1862, Civil War.

            Chester A. Capt. Co. D, 25th Regt. Maine Vols., Sept. 29,
1862. Enlisted, age then 37 years, from Brunswick, Me.

    478. Cyrus Metcalf.[8]   Private, State Militia, 1848 (5 years). 1st
Lieut. Capt. Waugh's Co., and on his retiring was made Captain. Raised
Company of Home Guards, 1861; was appointed its commander. Was
offered a commission in the service for the war, but declined.

127. Damon.[8] Private Co. I, 3d Minn. Vols., Nov. 1, 1861; Lieutenant, Jan. 1, 1862; discharged Aug. 16, 1864; Civil War.

Daniel. Private, Nov. 2, 1759 to February, 1761, Capt. Edward Mooers' Co., Boston. [Muster Rolls, Vol. xcviii. p. 368.]

37. Daniel,[5] **(Dr.)** Surgeon of Regt., siege of Louisburg, C. B. Sailed from Boston, March 24, 1745. He afterwards served in a Colony Ship at that same war.

41. Daniel,[6] **(Dr.)** Surgeon of Regt., Col. Jonathan Smith, Gen. John Fellows' Brigade for New York service. [Mass. Arch., Vol. lv. Folio I., p. 1]. See copy of his will, filed Probate Rec., Worcester, Mass., Vol. xiii. p. 390, and with his "Personal History."

512. Daniel.[6] Lieut. Col. David Henley's Regt., Boston, May, 25, 1778. Return for clothing. [Mass. Muster and Pay Rolls, Vol. lxxi. p. 96.]

407. Daniel.[9] Private, Co. G, 20th Regt., Co. K, 16th Regt., Maine Vols., Civil War.

57. David.[7] At the age of twelve years he served at the Battle of Bunker Hill, June 17, 1775, as a signal for the American Army, by being placed upon the embankments, and told to jump whenever the enemy were ready to fire. He served in Mississippi, his adopted State, as a soldier against the Indians.

David. Son of Bickford and Elizabeth (Middleton). Enlisted as Private, June, 1775, 3 mos.' service; enlisted as Private, Jan. 1, 1782 to Jan. 1, 1783, 10th Mass. Regt., Col. Benj. Tupper. Name appears as Private on a wage account [Mass. Arch., Vol. lx. p. 12]; also appears signed to a receipt for bounty paid him by Capt. Joshua Wood, chairman of Class I., for the town of Leominster to serve in the Continental Army for the term of three years. Receipt dated Worcester, May 30, 1782. [Vol. lxiv. p. 249.] It is said that he served at Lexington, Concord, Bunker Hill, was at the surrender of Burgoyne, and served through the war; that he was a scout most of the time, saw many battles, but was never wounded. He received a pension during his life of $144 per year. The gun which he carried is in the possession of Col. Charles. H. Greenleaf, of the Hotel "Vendome," Boston. David Greenleaf went to Lancaster, N. H., to live when a small boy, and after the war returned, living in Lancaster until his death.

511. David.[5] Private, 1757–58, Capt. Jeremiah Green's Co., Boston. [Mass. Arch., Muster Rolls, Vol. xcvi. p. 84.]

44. David.[6] Private, May 12, 1777. Five weeks, Capt. Jabez Hatch's Co., Boston Regt. Guarding stores at and about Boston, by order of Council, May 12, 1777, under Maj. Gen. Heath, commanded by Maj. Andrew Symmes. [Mass. Muster and Pay Rolls, Vol. xx. p. 3.] Enlisted July 30, 1778; discharged Sept. 13, 1778. Private, one month, fifteen days, Capt. Manasseh Sawyer's Co., 2d Worcester Regt., Col. Josiah Whitney. Rhode Island Campaign. [Mass. Arch., Muster Rolls, Vol. xxii. p. 207.] Enlisted Private, July 28 to Nov. 1, 1780. Capt. Thomas Brintnall's Co., Col. Cyprian Howes' Regt., Rhode Island Campaign. Raised for three months to reinforce Continental Army. [Mass. Arch., Muster Rolls, Vol.xvii. p. 83.]

186. David.[7] Private, Oct. 26, 1779, to April 23, 1780. Capt. Ephraim Hartwell's Co., Guards, at Rutland, Mass. [Mass. Arch.: Muster

Rolls, Vol. xx. p. 25; Vol. xxx. p. 120.] Autograph signature on Receipt [Vol. xxxi. p. 57.] He is referred to as "an officer of high rank." Guard Rolls, Vol. xxv. p. 120.

123. David Orlando.[8]   Enlisted July 21, 1862, Co. H, 29th Inf. Wisconsin Vols., Civil War. Died July 9, 1863, at Vicksburg, Miss., of contusion.

564. Ebenezer.[5]   Sergeant, 1757 (life), 5th Co. of Militia, Capt. Richard Greenleaf's list. [Mass. Arch., Muster Rolls, Vol. xcv. p. 418.] April 1, 1777 to May 26, 1777,—two mos.   Capt. John Bayley's Co., Col. M. Jackson's Regt.   From Woolwich.   Credited to Town Ipswich, County Essex. [Books: Enlisted Men and Officers, Vol. xxvii. p. 120. Various Services, Vol. lv. p. N 24.]

565. Ebenezer.[6]   War of 1812.

284. Edgar.[9]   Enlisted Sept. 10, 1862, for nine mos.   Served that term as Sergt. Co. G, 27th Regt. Maine Vols.   Honorably discharged, July 17, 1863.

1. Edmund.[1]   (Common ancestor).   In 1637 commanded a Company which marched against the Indians.   Nov. 5, 1639, ordered to be Ensign for the Company at Newbury, Mass.   1642, Lieut. Mass. Provincial Forces.   See Annual Reg. Society, Colonial Wars, for 1894, p. 106.   1644, "An ancient and experienced Lieut. under Capt. William Gerrish."   1648, Lieut.   May 14, 1645, Lieut.   1645, Capt.   1644, was head of the Militia under Gerrish. [Savage Dict., Vol. ii.]   1647, at his own request was discharged from Military office.

34. Edmund.[4]   Private, 1757, Capt. Richard Greenleaf's list of 5th Co. of Militia. [Mass. Arch., Muster Rolls, Vol. xcv. p. 418.]   Corp., June 13, 1757, Capt. Stephen Emery's Co. [Mass. Arch., Muster Rolls, Vol. xcv. p. 403.]

168. Edward Everett.[9]   1861, Private in First Vermont Battery of Light Artillery, which was attached to Gen. B. F. Butler's Division (of New England), and was stationed at Ship Island, Miss., until the capture of New Orleans.   After the capture was stationed at Camp Parapet, near New Orleans, until Gen. Banks took command of the 19th Army Corps. Was present and took an active part in the siege of Port Hudson, in the Sabine Pass Expedition, and in the Red River Campaign, and was present with the Battery during its entire term of service, and in all the engagements in which it took part, held the offices of 1st Sergt. and Sergt.-Major; was promoted to 2d Lieut. at the siege of Port Hudson, and to 1st Lieut. during the Red River Campaign, and was in command of the Battery at the time it was mustered out of service.   In the State Militia of Vermont, was Q. M. Sergt., Adjt., Inspector of Rifle Practice, Regt'l Commissary, and was senior Aid-de-Camp on Brigade Staff until resignation in 1887, after over twenty years of service.   Was Ass't Q. M. Gen. G. A. R. Dept. of Vermont for a number of years, resigning the position by reason of leaving the State; is still a member of that organization, and of the Loyal Legion 91, Commandery of Vermont.

*601. Elias Mason.[6]   April 9, 1781, credited to Reading, Middlesex Co.   April 10, 1781, enlisted for three years; age 16, height, 5 ft. 5 in., complexion dark, hair dark, eyes gray. Occupation, farmer. [Books: Enlisted Men, Vol. xxix. p. 5; Vol. liv. p. 29, file F.]

4. Enoch.[3] May 12, 1675, appointed by the Maj. and commissioned officers of Boston, Lieut. to the foot company under the command of Capt. Thomas Clark, in Boston. Sept. 3, 1675, Lieut. in Capt. Daniel Henchman's Co., in King Philip's Wars, and was wounded. June 11, 1680, the General Court, "in answer to the petition of Leiftent Enoch Greenleafe, the court refers the consideration of the petition to the Committee for Wounded Men."

19. Enoch.[5] Entered Private, Sept. 22, 1747, Capt. Samuel Brook's Co.; service 2 days, pay, £1-10-0 per mo.

6.ª Enoch.[5] Appears on the Alarm List 1773, Capt. John Haskins' Co. of Militia, Col. John Erving's Regt., Boston.

307. Enoch.[6] Private, June 1, 1775 to Aug. 1, Capt. McCobb's Co., Col. Thomas Nixon's Regt., Woolwich. Autograph signature, Vol. lxv. p. 203. Oct. 7, 1775, same Co. and Regt., Georgetown. Coat Rolls, eight months' service. [Vol. lvi. p. 30; Vol. xvi. p. 68.] Sept. to Nov., 1776, Capt. Winship's Co., 4th Regt. Receipt Dec. 24, 1776, for services Oct. and Nov., Col. Thomas Nixon's Regt.; age 25 years, height, 5 ft. 10 in., complexion, dark. March 2, 1777, Col. Nixon's Regt. May, 1778, Enoch Greenleaf's name appears on a resolution for gratuity due for services in Capt. Spurr's Co., 5th Regt., Col. Thomas Nixon. Feb. 16, 1779, Capt. Spurr's Co., Suffolk Co. Col. Thomas Nixon's 5th Regt. for gratuity due by Resolve of May, 1778. [Mass. Muster and Pay Rolls, Vol. liii. p. 195.] April, 1779, during the war, Capt. Pike's Co., Lieut. Col. Smith's Regt. (6th), Woolwich. July 14, 1780 to Dec. 3, 1782, Woolwich. 1782, Muster Rolls, Col. Thomas Nixon's Regt. (6th), enlisted during the war. An Enoch was wounded at Battle of Monmouth.

526. Enoch.[6] July 10, 1775 to Nov. 1, 1775. Nov. 1, 1775 to Jan. 1, 1776, Capt. Moses Nowells' Co., Newburyport, Mass. Commanded a Co. of Artillery at Newburyport, for several years. 1778, Maj. Thomas Thomas's Artillery. [Mass. Arch., Seacoast Defense Muster Rolls, Vol. xxxvi. p. 171, p. 148.] Service to Rhode Island. Pay warrant dated March 5, 1785. The Newburyport Artillery Co. formed in the winter of 1777-78, marched as volunteers in the expedition to Rhode Island in July, 1778, where they remained in service until the unsuccessful termination of that enterprise. In 1792 this corps was newly organized; William Cross was elected Captain, and *Enoch Greenleaf* and Samuel Brown, Lieutenants. Its first officers were Thomas Thomas, Capt.; David Coates, Capt. Lieut., then so called; and Michael Hodge, 1st, and Samuel Newhall, 2d Lieuts. The Company consisted of about eighty men, and were armed with muskets and two four pounders, one of brass and one of iron, which they received from the State, in Boston, on their march. These pieces were exchanged in 1793 for two beautiful six pounders. In 1785 Michael Hodge was elected Captain Lieutenant, and William Cross and *Enoch Greenleaf*, Lieutenants. [Cushing's Hist. Newburyport, p. 73.]

Enos. Private, 1776, Capt. Samuel Cobbs Co., Col. John Nixon's Regt., 5th Foot, Georgetown. "History of Bath, 1894."

543. Frederick William.[9] Appointed to United States Naval Academy from Minnesota by the Hon. William Windom in 1863. Graduated in 1867. Cruising with South Atlantic Squadron, 1867–70. Promoted to Ensign, 1868. Promoted to Master, 1870. Promoted to Lieutenant, 1871. Employed surveying for interoceanic canal, Isthmus of Darien, 1870–71. United States Naval Observatory, Washington, D. C., 1872. Cruising with China Squadron, 1873–76. Leave of absence, 1877. Cruising with Mediterranean Squadron, 1878–81. Cruising on northwestern lakes, 1882–83. Retired from active service for disability contracted in the line of duty, 1884. Took up residence in Augusta, Ga., in 1884. In 1886 elected to the chair of Natural Science in Academy of Richmond County, Ga., an institution endowed by the State of Georgia in 1783. He is now holding that position.

600. Gardner.[5] Corp., Aug. 16, 1757, Capt. Seth Blodget's Co., Col. William Brattal's Regt. Fort William Henry. Alarm Roll. [Mass. Arch., Muster Rolls, Vol. xcv., p. 247.]

555. George.[7] War of 1812.

482. George.[8] 1st Lieut., 1862, Maine Vols., of Starks, Me.

165. George Columbus.[9] Private, August 4, 1862, Co. —, 10th Regt. N. Y. Vols. Mustered in Sept. 11, 1862, U. S. Vols., for three years. Mustered out June 12, 1865, by Maj. E. E. Lord.

550. George Herbert.[9] Private, Co. A, Corporal Co. B, 2d Battalion Inf. Mass. Vol. Militia. Served at Fort Warren, 1861, Civil War.

*__392. George Howes.__[9] Private, Sept. 21, 1861, Co. G, 9th Regt. Maine Vols. Inf. Taken prisoner, 1862. Returned to Company, 1863. Private (re-enlisted), Jan. 1, 1864. Died at Point Lookout, Md., of wounds received before Petersburg, June 30, 1864, Civil War..

George Washington, b. Jan. 22, 1779. Son of Stephen and Mary (Savery), of Norway, Me. Enlisted at Portland. Private, Co. E, Cavalry, 1st Regt. Maine Vols., Civil War.

146. Halbert Stevens.[9] 1857, Capt. of Militia Co. at Shelburne Falls, Mass., August 29 to March 3, 1859. 1862, enlisted as Private, Co. E, 52d Mass., 9 mos. Commissioned Capt. Co. E, 52d Mass., Sept. 12. Unanimously elected Col. 52d Mass., Oct. 15th. Served under General Banks in the Department of the Gulf. Commandant of post at Barre's Landing, Louisiana, in General Bank's first Red River expedition: also in command of the 2d Brigade of Grover's Division for a short time. At the head of his regiment he participated in the Battle of Indian Ridge, and performed gallant service at Jackson Cross Roads; and in the grand assault on Port Hudson, June 14, 1863, and in the subsequent siege operations, resulting in the surrender of that important Confederate stronghold, he bore a conspicuous part, and distinguished himself by his coolness, judgment, and bravery. At the expiration of his military service Colonel Greenleaf was offered, and accepted, the command of the Government steamer, "Col. Benedict," on the lower Mississippi.

In February, 1882, he was elected commander of the First New York Veteran Brigade, with the rank of Brigadier General, and unanimously re-elected to that position in January, 1883. He is also president of the military organization in Rochester, N. Y., known as the Greenleaf Guards, which was named after him, and which is composed of an active corps of sixty-five young men of the highest respectability, and an honorary corps of one hundred of the leading business men of that city.

35. Henry.[4](?) Private, 1757, Haverhill, Capt. Richard Greenleaf's list of militia, 5th Co. [Mass. Arch., Muster Rolls, Vol. xcv. p. 418.] Private, enlisted April 8, 1757–58, discharged Nov. 4, 1758, Capt. Mooer's Co., Col. Jonathan Bagley's Regt. Reduction of Canada. [Mass. Arch., Muster Rolls, Vol. xcvi. p. 224; Vol. xcvii., p. 337.] Private, enlisted April 8, 1759, Capt. Edw. Moore's Co. Conquest of Canada, Hist. "Haverhill, Mass.," p. 355. Mar. 20, 1777 to June 16, 1777, Capt. Jonathan Drown's Co., Col. Gamaliel Bradford's Regt. Feb. 16, 1778, Capt. Brown's Co., Col. Lee's Regt. (2d), Newburyport.

126. Henry Clay.[8] Private, Co. K, 87th Regt. Indiana Vols.

433. Horatio Nelson.[8] Private, Co. F., 14th Regt. Maine Vols., Civil War.

602. Isaac.[5] Drafted in Medford Dec. 9, 1776, for duty at Noodle's Island. Private, 1778–82, Capt. John Walton's Co., Col. Marshall's Regt.

42. Israel.[6] Private, Sept. 15, 1755, Capt. Jeduthan Baldwin's Co., Col. Josiah Brown's Regt., for service Crown Point Expedition, commanded by Maj. Gen. Johnson. [Muster Rolls, Vol. xciv. p. 8.] Private, July 28 to Nov. 1, 1780, Capt. Thomas Brintnall's Co., Col. Cyprian Howe's Regt., from Middlesex Co. [Muster Rolls, Vol. xvii. p. 83.] Private, Jan. 1, 1781 to Jan. 1, 1782; Col. Benj. Tupper's 10th Regt., Mass.

58. Israel.[7] Private, March 22, 1781, for 3 years. Age, 16; height, 5 ft. 5 in.; complexion, dark; hair, light; eyes, blue. Occupation, farmer. Service credited to Marlboro, Mass.

573a. Jacob[7](?). War of 1812.

*****22. James.**[5] Private, Sept. 1, 1755, Capt. Roger Billing's Co. (the Billings resided in the vicinity of Norwich, Ct.); disch. Dec. 12, 1755; 14 weeks, 4 days; wages, £4–4s–2d. "Connecticut soldiers in French War."

549. James Edward.[9] Private Co. A, 2d Battalion Inf. M. V. M.; Captain 7th unattached M. V. M.; Captain Co. G, 7th Regt. Inf. M. V. M. Served at Fort Warren, 1861, Civil War.

*****54. James Leeds.**[8] Lieutenant of New Orleans Light Guard, 1861; Captain, and served on staff of Gen. Leonidas Polk (Bishop Polk, of Louisiana); Major: he distinguished himself as a brave and efficient officer in the Confederate service. He was a member of the famous White League; was on the staff of Gen. Ogden.

493. James Manter.[8] Private, Civil War. Wounded in the head; lost one eye.

195. James Monroe.[9] An officer in the famous Hartford Life Guard. An original member and officer of the Putnam Phalanx.

James Savery, b. Feb. 5, 1814, son of Stephen and Mary (Savery). Musician, Capt. Amos, F. Noyes' Co., 1839. Aroostook War, over the treaty between Maine and New Brunswick.

143.   Jeremiah.[8] Private, War of 1812, and won his commission as an officer.

John (of Hull), b. about 1741. Private, Lieut. H. Lincoln's Co., Col. Lovell's Regt.; two days from Jan. 14, 1776. Coast Defence, Vol. xxxvi. p. 112. Feb. 16, 1777. Return by Nathan Barker, Hingham, Mass. Capt. Wellington's Co., Col. Wigglesworth Regt., credited to Suffolk Co. Vol. xi. p. 65; Vol. xli. p. 39. March 1, 1777, Capt. Stower's Independent Co. Coast Defence of Hull; age thirty-six. July 2, 1778, enlisted. July 17, 1778, discharged. Coast Defence, Vol. xxxvii. p. 4. Guards at Winter Hill, Capt. Nathan Sargent's Co., Col. Jacob Gerrish's Regt.

John (of Boston) (?) b. Dec. 10, 1714, son of Samuel and Martha (Bull). Three months' service from Dec. 1, 1776 (for mileage money). Capt. Caleb Brooks's Co., Col. Nicholas Dike's Regt., credited to Waltham, Mass. [Mass. Arch., Vol. xvii. p. 155.]

John (?), b. June 6, 1775, d. Dec. 23, 1829, son of John and Mary (Gould). War of 1812.

John, b. about 1632, probably son of Edmund and Sarah (Dole). Nov. 29, 1675, pressed into service for the Indian Wars. The records show that he was impressed in Boston, and for a Boston Company. The list on which his name appears is with other lists from Cambridge Village, Braintree, etc. ("Records of the Colony of Mass. Bay," pp. 84 and 89.)

39 (?). John.[5] Colonel, 1755, Crown Point Expedition. [Mass. Arch., Muster Rolls, Vol. xciv. pp. 134–137.] Autograph [Mass. Bay Records, Vol. xci. p. 131].

385.   John[6] (of Pownalboro, Me.). A certificate of enlistment dated June, 1776, signed by himself and others, who promised to march to New York and continue in service till Dec. 1, 1776, unless sooner discharged. Muster and Pay Rolls, Vol. lv. and lvii. File H. Joined the American Army at New York in the early days of the Revolution, and served as a soldier at Valley Forge in the memorable winter of 1777-78. He was also in the engagements at Brandywine, Long Island, White Plains, and Fishkill. June 3, 1778, service 9 mos. from arrival at Fishkill. Capt. ——— Co., Col. McCobb's (1st) Regt., raised by resolve of April 20, 1778, from Pownalboro, Me. (Wiscasset). Return made by Brig. Gen. Charles Cushing. [Mass. Arch., Vol. xliii. p. 161.] Descriptive list of the men enlisted from Lincoln County for the term of 9 mos. from the time of their arrival at Fishkill. Age 22; stature 5 ft. 7 inches; complexion, light. From town of Pownalboro, Captain Decker's Co., (1st Regt.). Time of arrival at Fishkill, June 19. (Books: Militia Officers, etc., Vol. xxviii. p. 122.)

560.   John.[6] War of 1812.

573.   John[6](?). Colonel, April 19, 1775, Lexington Alarm. [Mass. Bay Records, Vol. xci. pp. 400, 432.] Return of Capt. Richard Kelley to Col. John Greenleaf. [Mass. Arch., Muster Rolls, Vol. xcv. p. 425.] Return of Capt. Richard Greenleaf to Col. John Greenleaf, Regimental Alarm List and trained band, and Col. John Greenleaf's return, also, as follows : Col. John Greenleaf's list trained men, 120; Alarm List, 31; total, 151. Capt. Richard Greenleaf's list trained men, 223, Alarm List, 64; total, 287. [Mass. Arch., Muster Rolls, Vol. xcv. p. 432.]

56. John[7] (of Bolton, Mass.) Enlisted June, 1776 to Dec. 1, 1776. Receipt for wages, Dec. 4, 1776, for October and November. Vol. lv. p. 25., File H. Appears on the Roll of Capt. Jonathan Houghton's Co. in the orderly book of Nathaniel Longley. [Mass. Arch., Worcester Rolls and Vols. lv. and lvi. pp. 20, 22, and 25, in 1776; Vol. lvi. p. 3.] Capt. Jonathan Houghton's Co., Col. Smith's Regt.

441. John.[7] War of 1812. Served ninety days at Wiscasset Point, Me.

509. John Eller.[8] Private, Co. L, 2d Cavalry, Me., Civil War.

John (?) of Hull, Mass., b. about 1717. List of "training soldiers" in company of militia, June 8, 1757. [Mass. Arch., Muster Rolls, Vol. xcv. p. 400.]

230. John Ruggles[9] (Dr.). Appointed Oct. 15, 1862. Hospital Steward, 46th Regt. Inf. Enlisted, Co. H. Same Regt., Oct. 30, 1862. Discharged July 29, 1863.

396. John W.[9] (?) Capt. Maine Vols., of Abbott, Me., 1862.

513. Jonathan.[5] Ensign, Feb., 1762, Capt. Joshua Coffin's Co., Newburyport, 1st Co. in the Regt. Col. Joseph Gerrish, 2d Regt. Militia. [Mass. Arch., Muster Rolls, Vol. xcix. p. 39.] Capt., commissioned March 25, 1767, Col. Jonathan Bagley's Regt., Lieut. Caleb Cushing. [Mass. Arch., Muster Rolls, Vol. xcix. p. 87.] Lexington Alarm Roll, Vol. xii. p. 114. Capt. Isaac Hull's Co. Col. Thomas Gardner's Regt., marched April 19, 1775, from Medford.

***524. Jonathan.**[7] Midshipman U. S. Navy. Served in U. S. Frigate "Essex." Died on board in 1798, of yellow fever.

268. ⎱ **Joseph.**[5] Commissioned June 3, 1745, 1st Co. of Artillery
298. ⎰ from York Co., Me. Capt. Peter Staples, afterwards commanded by Capt. Richard Mumford. 1st Mass. Regt., commanded by Sir William Pepperell. Capture of Louisburg. [Mass. Arch., N. E. Geneal. and Hist. Soc., Vol. xxiv. p. 377, Vol. xxv. p. 254.] Marshal of Court Martial, June 23, 1745.

268. Joseph.[5] Private, July 13, 1757, Maj. Joseph Coffin's list, Newbury. [Mass. Arch., Muster Rolls, Vol. xcv. p. 415.]

298. Joseph.[5] Entered, Sept. 24, 1750 to Nov. 1, 1750, Capt. James Thompson's Co., Boston Service, Ranging Woods, Muster Rolls Vol. xciii. p. 59. Private, April 30, 1757, Capt. Jonathan Williamson's Co., District of Wiscasset, Me. List of Militia men, Muster Rolls, Vol. xcv. p. 336. Ensign, Aug. 9, 1757, on a return of officers belonging to the Mass. forces, commanded by Col. Joseph Frye, that was in the capitulation of Fort William Henry. [Mass. Arch., Muster Rolls, Vol. xcv. p. 449]

271. Joseph.[6] Mustered April 22, 1756, Ensign, Capt. John Bartoll's Co., Marblehead. [Mass. Arch., Muster Rolls, Vol. xciv. p. 230.] Crown Point Expedition, Capt. Edward Mooer's Co., June 1, 1756. Crown Point Expedition. [Mass. Arch., Muster Rolls, Vol. xciv. p. 231.] Ensign, July 26, 1756, age, 20, Col. Plaisted's Regt. [Vol. xciv. p. 347.]

299. Joseph[6](?). Enlisted March 4, 1776; disch. May 31, 1776. Capt. Israel Davis Co. [Vol. xxxv. p. 276]. Col. Joseph Fry's Regt., Pownalboro, Me. (Wiscasset); also, June 1, 1776 to Sept. 1, 1776, service at Boothbay, Me., also, Sept. 1, 1776 to Dec. 5, 1776; also, Dec. 5, 1776 to Dec. 31, 1776, Lieut. Nathaniel Winslow's Co., Boothbay service. [Vol. xxxvii. p. 53.] Also Stony Point, under Gen. Wayne, March 10, 1777 to Dec. 31, 1779, Jan. 1, 1780 to March 10, 1780, Pownalboro, Me., Capt. Wiley's Co., Col. Michael Jackson's Regt. Residence, Woolwich. [Vol. viii. Part 2, p. 72.] April 22, 1780 to Dec. 16, 1780, Sergt. (promoted). Capt. Solomon Walker's Co., Col. Joseph Prime's Regt., under Brig. Gen. Wadsworth. March 11, 1777 to May 26, 1777. Capt. John Bayley's Co., Col. Michael Jackson's Regt. [Vol. lv. p. 24 N.]

*273.
388. } **Joseph.**[7]   War of 1812.

*274.
444. } **Joseph,**[8] or **Joseph.**[7] War of 1812.

*394. **Joseph Dearborn.**[9] Private, 19th Regt. Maine Vols.

Joseph W. 1st Lieut. 2d Battery, Boston.

569. Joshua.[5] April 13, 1755, Capt. Jonathan Pierce's Co.; Lieut., Oct. 11, 1756; camp at Fort William Henry. Service to Feb. 18, 1757. [Mass. Arch., Muster Rolls, Vol. xciv. p. 467.] Lieut. on Capt. Joseph Coffin's Alarm List; 1st Co. in Newbury, July 13, 1757. [Mass. Arch., Muster Rolls, Vol. xcv. p. 421.] Capt. 1st Co. Artillery in Newburyport, and 1st Co. in the Regt. Commissioned March 25, 1767. [Mass. Arch., Muster Rolls, Vol. xcix. p. 88.]

575. Joshua.[7] Major, about 1828–30, Newburyport, Mass.

59. Levi.[7] War of 1812.

173. Louis Christopher.[9] Enlisted in Co. A, 35th N. Y. Vols., May 9, 1861. After serving two years was promoted to rank of Sergt., then to Orderly Sergt. For ten or twelve years after the war he held a commission in the Militia of the State of New York, and resigned as Major in 1876.

Matthew N. Capt. 6th N. H. Vols.

*270. **Mayo.**[6] Age 22. Enlisted May 2, 1775, Capt. Lunt's Co., Col. Little's Regt. Service, Quebec, L. C. July 9, 1776 to Nov. 9, 1776, Lieut. Moses Pike's Co. Nov. 20, 1776 to Jan. 1, 1777, detached from Capt. Moses Nowell's Co. Service, Plum Island.

525. Moses.[6] Lieutenant, 1774; Captain, 1776; served until nearly the close of the war. Private; enlisted July 8, 1775; discharged Nov. 1, 1775. Lieut. Capt. Moses Nowell's Co., Nov. 1, 1775 to Jan. 1, 1776. [Vol. xxxvi. p. 171.] Residence, Newburyport. Lieut. by Legislative enactment, June 29, 1776. Second Lieut., Capt. Moses Nowell's Co., Jan. 29, 1776. First Lieut., Capt. John Peabody's Co., Col. Michael Farley's Regt.; also Col. Eben Francis' Regt. Marched to join Regt. Aug. 9, 1776, raised in defense of Boston. Capt. Feb. 3, 1777. [Militia officers, eight mos. men. Continental Balances. Vol. xxviii. p. 71] Retired Nov. 6, 1776. [Records at War Dept., Washington, D. C.]. Capt. Feb. 20, 1777. [Vol. xliii. p. 346.] Capt. June 1, 1777. Confirmed by Congress, Sept. 6, 1779. Eleventh Regt., Mass. [Vol. xxviii. p. 86.] Col. Tupper's Regt.,

Jan. 1, 1777 to Dec. 31, 1779. Capt. Col. Benj. Tupper's Regt., Jan. 25, 1778. [Vol. ii. p. 71.] Capt. Col. Benj. Tupper's Regt. (15th), April 5, 1779, West Point service. Capt. Col. Benj. Tupper's Regt., Jan. 1 to Oct. 15, 1780. Capt. Sept. 15, 1780; also October to December, 1780 (Huts near West Point). Col. Benj. Tupper's Regt. Retired, Capt. 11th Mass. Regt., January, 1781.

    535. Moses.[9] Private, Aug. 15, 1862, 9th Regt. Minn. Inf. Capt. when mustered out, Aug. 23, 1865. Never off duty or in the hospital.

    29. Nathaniel.[4] In "Second Company of Foot," Jan. 15, 1710–11. Capt. Hugh March.

    ***619. Nathaniel.**[6] Drafted from Essex Co. Militia to march to Howe's Neck, under Col. Coggswell, Capt. Ilsley's Co. Reported belonging to Newbury, Mass. [Vol. xxxii. p. 28-4.]

    Noah. War of 1812.

    Perry. 1st Lieut., Co. B, 1st Me. Regt.

    295. Richard.[5] Enlisted July 13, 1742, Capt. Arthur Noble's Co.; service, 4 weeks, 2 days; entered July 23, 1747 to Jan. 20, 1748, Capt. David Cargill's Co.; same, March 11 to July 20, 1748; same, July 29 to Dec. 18, 1748. [Muster Rolls, Vol. xcii. pp. 14, 76, 123, 188.] Corporal, April 30, 1757, Capt. Jonathan Williamson's Co., District of Wiscasset. [List of Militia Men, Muster Rolls, Vol. xcv. p. 336.] Captain, 5th Co. of Militia, 1757. [Mass. Arch., Muster Rolls, Vol. xcv. p. 418.] His Alarm List for Newbury, 1757. [Mass. Arch., Muster Rolls, Vol. xcv. p. 424.] His return to Col. John Greenleaf of list trained band, 223, Alarm List, 64; total, 287. [Mass. Arch., Muster Rolls, Vol. xcv. p. 432.] Capt. Nathaniel Alexander's Co., Col. —— Wigglesworth's Regt., service, on or before Aug. 15, 1777. [Vol. ii. p. 55.] Col. Calvin Smith's Regt. [Vol. xxxi. p. 187.] Feb. 6, 1777 to Nov. 12, 1777, reported left sick; Nov. 12, 1777, at Fishkill, Major's Co., Captain's name not given. Residence, Pownalboro (Wiscasset, Me.). [Continental Army Rolls, Vol. xiii., Part i. p. 148.] May, 1778, Camp Valley Forge; June 2, 1778, Fishkill (sick). [Vol. lxi. p. 28.]

    527. Richard.[6] Shipped at sixteen years of age on board Ship "Lion," Capt. Wingate Newman. His name appears in service to July 12, 1781. Complexion, dark. [Mass. Arch., Vol. xl. p. 62.]

    Richard O. Capt. 4th N. H.

    116. Robert Stephen.[9] Private, Feb. 26, 1864, Co. D, 10th Ill. Vol. Inf. for the war; with Sherman in Tenn., Ala., and Ga., on the march to the sea, and in the campaigns in Carolina.

    Rodney W. Son of Ozias W. Private, May 4, 1864. Nine months. Age 23. 7th Unattached. Mustered out Aug. 5, 1864.

    Samuel, b. May 8, 1758. Son of Paul.(?) Midshipman. Brought to Marblehead, Mass., in "Pacific," cartel sloop, to be exchanged for British prisoners. "Yankee Hero," Privateer, taken by British ship "Milford." [Vol. ix. p. 60.] Sept. 12, 1777, sent on shore at Sheep's Cot River from His Majesty's ship "Rainbow."

    Samuel, b. Oct. 28, 1740. Son of Jonathan and Mary (Cunningham). Private, May 29, 1778, Col. Hatch's Regt. Raised by town

of Boston for nine months, by Resolve April 20, 1778.   Arrived at Fishkill,
June 19, 1778.   Enlisted from Suffolk Co. for nine months.   Resided in
Boston; return dated Dorchester, June 29, 1778.   Age 38; five feet, 3
inches height; complexion, dark; hair, dark; eyes, gray.   [Mass. Arch.,
Vol. xl. pp. 131-159; Vol. xli.p. 30.]

    296. Samuel.[5]   Entered July 23, 1747 to Nov. 16, 1747.   [Muster
Rolls, Vol. xcii. p. 76.]   Capt. David Cargill's Co.   Same, March 11, 1748
to May 3, 1748.   [Vol. xcii, p. 123.]   Same, May 3, 1748 to July 12, 1748.
[Vol. xcii. p. 123.]   Same, July 29, 1748 to Dec. 18, 1748.   [Vol. xcii. p.
188.]   Lieut., Feb. 18, 1755 to Dec. 22, 1757.   Forty-one weeks, three
days, at £3-12-0 per month.   From Newbury, Mass., Col. Bagley's
Regt.   Crown Point Expedition.   [Mass. Arch., Muster Rolls, Vol. xcv.
p. 134.]   On Capt. Richard Greenleaf's " Larrum " List for Newbury,
1757.   [Mass. Arch., Muster Rolls, Vol. xcv. p. 424.]

    306. Samuel.[6]   Enlisted March 10, 1777; discharged May 26,
1777.   Capt. John Bagley's Co., Col. M. Jackson's Regt.   [Vol. lv. N,
p. 24.]   May 7, 1777, by order of Council, detached from Boston Regt. to
do duty under Maj. Gen. Heath for five weeks.   Rank, Private, Capt.
Thos. Bumstead's Co.   [Vol. xvii. p. 36.]   July 26, 1777 to Sept. 11, 1777,
drafted from Boston Regt. to Artillery Regt., stationed at Hull, Capt. Perez
Cushing's Co., Col. Thomas Craft's Regt.   [Vol. xxxviii. p. 63.]   Dec. 4,
1777, on roll sworn to that date, for Capt. Robert Davis Co., Col. Freeman's Regt.   Secret service to Rhode Island, one month seven days.   [Vol.
xviii. p. 21.]   Received from Maj. Badlam, and conducted by Capt. Robert
Davis to Brig. Gen. Warner at Fishkill.   [Vol. lxi. p. 310.]   Jan. 23, 1778,
enlisted; May 1, 1778, discharged.   Duty, Prison Ship " Kingston,"
Boston Harbor, as Guards, under Maj. Gen. Heath.   Lieut. Thomas
Holland's Co.   [Vol. xix. p. 174.]   Return from Essex Co. of 2d Regt.,
dated Essex, Feb. 16, 1778.   Town Woolwich; enlisted for Newburyport,
Capt. John Bayley's Co., Col. Michael Jackson's Regt.   [Vol. liii. p. 197.]
Enlisted Aug. 16, 1779.   Discharged Oct. 1, 1779.   Re-enlisted Oct. 1, 1779
to March 31, 1780.   Capt. Champney's Co.   [Vol. xviii. p. 132.]   Maj. Nathaniel Heath's Regt.   Detachment of Guards stationed at Boston.   [Vol.
xx. p. 35.]   Also same Regt. and duty, Feb. 1, 1780 to April 1, 1800.   [Vol.
xx. p. 31.]   Sergt. Sept. 7, 1782.   Capt. Caleb Champney's Co.

    646. Samuel.[6]   Drafted, 1775-76, 1st Co. Haverhill, Mass., Capt.
Eaton.   Served six weeks in Roxbury, Mass.   Hist. Haverhill, p.
593.

    151. Samuel Knight.[8]   War of 1812.   Served several years in
Vermont State Militia.   Capt. 1825-27.

    *152. Samuel Trant.[10]   Private 17th Illinois Cavalry.

    Samuel Wood.   Town Woolwich, County Essex.   Town en-
listed for, Newburyport.

    497. Seth.[7]   War of 1812.

    399. Simon.[9]   Private, Oct. 13, 1862.   Sergt. Co. K, 28th Regt.
Maine Vols.   Mustered out Aug. 31, 1863, Civil War.

    Solomon C., of Norway, Me.   Son of James S. and Jane F.
Private, Co. G, Aug. 6, 1862, 10th Regt. Maine Vols.   Transferred to Co.

B, Bat. 10, Maine Vols. Transferred again to Co. C, 29th Regt. Maine Vols. Discharged May 31, 1865.

367. Spencer.[7] War of 1812.

Stephen, b. Jan. 22, 1779, son of Stephen and Emma (Blowers). From Norway, Me. Private, Capt. Bailey Bodwel's Co., Col. Denny McCobb's Regt., 45th U. S. Inf. Service, War of 1812. Nov. to Jan., 1813. Again, Sept., 1814; Same Capt.

269. } **Stephen.** Private, July 10, 1780, Col. John Greaton's Regt.
129. } Service, three months, twenty-nine days. [Mass. Arch., Muster Rolls, Vol. xlviii. p. 395.]

3. Stephen.[2] Ensign, appointed May 31, 1670; Lieut., 1685; Capt., 1686. As Capt. of Militia he went with the disastrous expedition against Port Royal, Oct. 13, 1690, to Cape Breton, and was there wrecked in a vessel and drowned, in company with nine others, Dec. 1, 1690.

12. Stephen.[3] Served in the "King Philip's War," on the Connecticut River. Aug. 25, 1675, was wounded in the Battle of Hatfield, Mass. "The fight was of two hours, twelve miles from Hatfield." [Exliteris, S. Greenleaf, N. E. Geneal. and Hist. Reg., Vol. vii. p. 206.] "June 4, 1685, Ensign Greenleaf appointed Leftenant." [Rec. Mass. Bay, p. 483.] Aug. 2, 1689, in the Indian War. Sent to treat with Indians at Pennacook. Oct. 24, 1689, Lieut. Capt. Greenleaf was much distinguished in the Indian Wars, and is mentioned in "Mather's Magnalia" as commanding a company in the celebrated battle with the French and Indians at Wells, Me., in 1690, and in the King Philip War on the Connecticut River above Hatfield.

43. Stephen.[6] Private, 1757, Capt. John Carter's mounted Co., detached from Col. Oliver Wilder's Regt., and marched, in the Fort William Henry alarm, as far as Springfield. [Mass. Arch., Vol. xcvi. p. 181.] Sergt., March 1 to Dec. 16, 1758, Capt. Asa Whitcomb's Co., Bolton; Jonathan Bagley, Col. Regt. raised for the reduction of Canada. Served eight months, twelve days. [Mass. Arch., Vol. xcvi. p. 478-481.]

601. Stephen.[5] Served in the American Army during the Revolution under Governor John Brooks, of Massachusetts. Capt. Stowers' Independent Co., March 1, 1777. Service Hull, Coast Defense. Residence Hull. [Vol. xxxvii. p. 4.] Lieut. Col. Jabez Hatch's Regt., guarding stores at and about Boston. 1779, enlistment, nine mos., Middlesex Co., Continental Army. Age, 44; stature, 5 ft. 11 in. Capt. Fox's Co., Col. Foster's Regt. July 5, 1780, marched; Dec. 12, 1780, discharged. Reading. [Vol. iv. p. 130.] July 10, 1780, arrived at Springfield; July 11, 1780, in camp. [Vol. xxxv. p. 192.] Age 47; complexion, dark. Residence, Reading; occupation, farmer. May 10, 1781, enlisted for three years. Age 47; stature, 5 ft. 10½ in.; complexion, dark; eyes, dark; occupation, farmer. [Vol. liv. p. 29.] Account of Bounty paid him by town of Reading for three years' service, acct. dated Feb. 25, 1782. Receipt for Bounty for three years' service for town of Reading. Date of receipt, June 5, 1781. Enlisted May 10, 1781. [Vol. xxix. p. 5.] Lieut. Col. Fernald's Regt. List for six mos.; no dates. Reading. Warrant for pay, Michael Jackson's (8th) Regt. [Vol. xxx. p. 213.]

273. Stephen.[6](?) Private, 9th Co., 7th Regt., Col. Charles Webb, of Milford, Conn. Enlisted July 10; discharged Dec. 13, 1775. Drafted Aug. 21; discharged Nov. 10, 1777. Was of Windham, Conn. Clerk to Col. Jonathan Lattimer, Regt. of New London, Conn. Q. M., appointed Jan. 5, 1778, Col. Obadiah Johnson's Regt. Maj. Hezekiah Huntington, of Windham, Conn.; service, State of Rhode Island, two mos. after arrival in camp; Capt. Job Sumner's Co. [Mass. Arch., Vol. xxxviii. p. 395.]

129. Stephen.[7] The account of his service as a soldier in the conflict with Burgoyne, written by himself in his eightieth year, is still in the possession of a well-known local antiquarian, says the *Weekly Springfield Republican*, 1894. He explains how with his father he was at work in the Arms meadow, planting corn, the last of April, 1777, it being one of the earliest seasons ever known, when his father and himself were drafted, the papers being served by Sergt. Joseph Bates. " My father," he says, " being very infirm, I performed the service for us both. John Sargeant was my Captain, and Timothy Church and Israel Smith Lieutenants. Our first march was a short one, and our second terminated at Rutland. Its object was to intercept a division of Burgoyne's Army, said to be advancing toward Boston by crossing the Green Mountains in the direction from Rutland to Charlestown, N. H. Here we were joined by troops from New Hampshire, commanded by Col. Warner; but not being in sufficient force to withstand a formidable enemy, our officers held a council and ordered a countermarch. After a very short respite from our fatigue we returned home the second time, only to be again called out to join Gen. Stark at Bennington. We marched, and arrived there the day after the battle; from whence we, with a detachment from Massachusetts, were ordered to occupy as an outpost Van Ness buildings, near Renselaer's Mills and Little White Creek. After guarding this post a few weeks the militia were dismissed, but hardly returned home before an express came, and a new levy was ordered; and again I was on the march for Saratoga, where we arrived, and were annexed to Col. Schuyler's Regiment of Militia, of which Col. Rensalaer was one of the regimental officers. Here, I was, with several other Green Mountain boys,—the draft was made in Dummerston as well as in Brattleboro,—detached to make up a scout for observation and discovery. The party was a large one, and was commanded by Col. Morgan of the riflemen attached to Gates' Army. The line of march was upon the right of the enemy's encampment, and our route continued to the extreme rear of their position, when by countermarches we returned to headquarters and reported progress. In our course of march two of the enemy's scouting parties were driven in, which excited much alarm in their camp by the apparent bustle they exhibited on the occasion. Two days afterwards commenced the decisive battle near Stillwater, which terminated in the capture of Burgoyne and his army. Our company was selected and ordered to attempt the raising and floating several batteries scuttled and sunk, by the enemy, in the river during their retreat, which we successfully accomplished. Our way to the river led us by a redoubt newly erected by the British, where it was reported the remains of Gen. Fraser, of the British Army, were interred. Connected with this statement, there is a report in circulation that early in the day of the Battle of Stillwater, Col. Morgan, before mentioned, with a select party of his own regiment, was out reconnoitering on the right wing of the enemy's encampment, when he came suddenly to a halt. He had discovered by a glance through a glade between the trees opening upon said redoubt, an officer on horseback, whom by his perspective he discovered to be Gen. Fraser, of Burgoyne's Army. The question occurred to him, Can he be reached with effect by a rifle ball? and at once he put the question to a soldier standing by, who answered in doubt as to his own ability, but recommended another soldier, famed as the best shot with the best rifle in the regiment, who was immediately ordered to the stand, and the same question put to him. ' Can you with your rifle bring that man to the ground whom you see yonder on horseback?' The answer was, 'I believe I can.' Morgan remarked that he revolted at the thought, but it was indispensably necessary that it should be done, if possible. ' Try, soldier,' said he; ' do your best.' It was done, and Fraser fell. We were now ordered to pass the river and take a position on Bemis Heights, which post we occupied till after the capitulation of Burgoyne, and witnessed the surrender." Mr. Greenleaf's fellow-soldiers were Salathid Harris and Joseph Bemis, all of whom served more than six months in the army. In 1838 only two of the twenty Brattleboro soldiers were living,—Harris and Greenleaf. Mr. Greenleaf was subsequently commissioned a Major in the State Militia, and his picture hangs with others in the town hall.

    446. **Stephen.**[7] War of 1812. Served ninety days at Wiscasset Point, Me.

    566a. **Thomas.**[5] Enlisted April 1, 1755 to Feb. 30, 1756. Capt. Stephen Webster. [Muster Rolls, Vol. xciv. p. 127.] Crown Point. Entered, Oct. 20, 1755, Boston, Capt. Thomas Pike's Co. Crown Point. [Muster Rolls, Vol. xciv. p. 39.]

    8. **Thomas.**[6] Enlisted May 9, 1776; discharged Aug. 1, 1776. Capt. Daniel Lothrop's Co., Muster and Pay Roll. Col. Thomas Craft's Regt. [Vol. xxxviii. p. 93.] 1st Lieut. 7th Co. Lieut. Col. Craft's Regt. Artillery, Aug. 17, 1776 to Nov. 1, 1776; Nov. 1, 1776 to Feb. 1, 1777. Oct. 9, 1776, commissioned 1st Lieut. April 18, 1777, appointment concurred in by the Council. [Vol. lxvi. p. 353.] May 5, 1777, 1st Lieut. on Muster and Pay Roll, Capt. D. Lothrop's Co., Col. Thomas Craft's Regt. [Vol. xxxviii. p. 138.] Capt. 7th Co. Artillery Regt. Capt. Perez Cushing's Co., Muster and Pay Roll, Col. Thomas Craft's Regt., 7th Artillery. Service between Aug. 1, 1777 and Sept. 30, 1777, [Craft's Rolls. Vol. xxxviii. p. 58½.] Same, Nov. 1, 1777 and Dec. 31, 1777, [Craft's Rolls. Vol. xxxviii. p. 52.] Same, time of enlistment to Aug. 1, 1777. Oct. 18, 1777, petition to be removed from Hull, where he is Capt. Lieut., to be put into more active service. Enlisted July 5, 1780; discharged Oct. 10, 1780. Capt. Thomas Mighill's Co., Col. Nathaniel Wade's Regt., Essex Co. Three months' service. [Vol. xxi. p. 53.]

    47. **Thomas.**[6] Served in 1786-87 in the pursuit of Daniel Shays (Shays's Rebellion). War of 1812.

*268. Thomas.[6] Enlisted, 1757, Capt. Israel Davis's Co., Col.
Joseph Frye's Regt. Was captured at Fort William Henry, taken to St.
Francois, thence to Montreal, Quebec, Louisburg, Halifax, Boston. Peti-
tion for allowance for services, dated March 21, 1760. [Military Rec.,
Vol. lxxix. p. 53.]

136. Thomas Sargent.[8] Major.

590. Timothy.[6] Was "drawn" for a soldier to guard the British
and Hessian Troops after they were quartered at Charlestown. He hired
his brother Caleb to go in his stead.

15. Tristram.[8] Capt.

32. Tristram.[4] Capt. 1746, commissioned by Gov. Shirley.

Westover. 23d Maryland Vols. Died Aug. 11, 1862, from
effects of sunstroke at Newbern, N. C.

644. William.[5] Enrolled 1st Co. of Haverhill, 1757. [Hist. of
Haverhill.] Sergt., April 19, 1757, of Haverhill, Mass.; Lieut. John
Osgood's Co.; Lieut. Benjamin Gale's Co. [Mass. Arch., Muster Rolls,
Vol. xcv. p. 287.] Private, April 19, 1775; Capt., Lieut., John Brickett's
Co. Newbury to Cambridge. Marched April 19, 1775. [Mass. Arch.,
Muster Rolls, Vol. ii. p. 195.] Corp., Sept., 1776 to Feb. 1, 1777, Capt.
McFarland's Co. (7th), Col. Thomas Nixon's 4th Mass. Regt. [Mass.
Arch., Muster Rolls, Vol. li. part 34, p. 68.] His name also on a return
of service, Sept. to Nov., 1776. Also on a company receipt with list of
men who served in Capt. Jonathan Poor's Co., dated Newbury, March 18,
1777. Also a receipt for wages, Feb. 1, 1777, from Dec., 1776. [Mass.
Arch., Muster Rolls, Vol. lii. pp. 90, 106.] Private, Sept. 1, 1777. Ensign, Capt. Daniel Pillsbury's Co., Col. Edward Wigglesworth's Regt.,
4th Mass. Valley Forge, June 2, 1778. [Mass. Arch., Muster Rolls, Vol.
lxi. p. 29; Drake's Collection, p. 43.] Also name on a return for clothing
delivered Oct. 12, 1778. Also Col. Wigglesworth's Regt. [Mass. Arch.,
Muster Rolls, Vol. lxxi. p. 253.] 2d Lieut., 1762; Joseph Badger, 1st
Lieut., John Osgood, Col., 4th Regt., Mass. [Mass. Arch., Muster Rolls,
Vol. xcix. p. 59.] Lieut. Capt. Moses Greenleaf's Co., of Newburyport,
Mass. Capt. of same company. Capt., March 12, 1765, Col. Osgood's
Regt., Mass. 1st Foot Co., in Haverhill. [Mass. Arch., Muster Rolls, Vol.
xcix. p. 100.] Lieut., Jan. 2, 1759, Capt. Edward Mooer's Co., Haverhill,
Col. Bagley's Regt., Mass. [Mass. Arch., Muster Rolls, Vol. xcix.
p. 109.] Mass. Continental Inf., Jan. to Dec., 1776. Corp. Capt. Mat-
thew Fairchild's Co., Col. Edward Wigglesworth's (13th) Regt., Feb. 16,
1776, etc. [See Year Book, Soc. Sons of the Revolution, State of New
York, 1893.]

45. William.[6] Capt., March 20, 1776, 10th Co., 2d (Worcester
Co.) Regt. [Vol. xxviii. p. 104.] Commissioned March 20, 1776,
Lieut. Col., 2d (Worcester Co.), Regt. (Vol. xxviii. p. 5.) Commissioned Lieut. Col., chosen by the House of Representatives, and
appointment concurred in by the Council, Oct. 9, 1779. Capt. on Muster
and Pay Roll, Col. Whitney's Regt., Aug. 22 and Aug. 26, 1776,—four
days. [Vol. xix. p. 98.] 2d Maj. 5th (Worcester) Regt. Commissioned
Oct. 12, 1778. [Vol. viii. p. 52.] Lieut. Col. 2d (Worcester) Regt.

Commissioned Oct. 9, 1779. [Vol. xxviii. p. 54.] Col. Josiah Whitney.
Capt. on Pay Abstract of Officers in Col. Job Cushing's Regt. for services
in Northern Department from Aug. 12 to Oct. 12, 1777. [Vol. xxvi.
p. 9.] Capt. on Muster and Pay Roll, in Col. Job Cushing's Regt. Enlisted Sept. 1, 1777. Time of service, three months, ten days. Muster
Rolls dated Lancaster. [Vol. xix. p. 134.] Capt. on a Pay Abstract,
Col. Job Cushing's Regt. for rations from Oct. 13, 1777 to Dec. 9, 1777,
service in the Northern Department. [Vol. xx. p. 224.] A Roll made
up for service Sept. 3, 1777 to Nov. 29, 1777. [Vol. xix. p. 132.] Lieut.
Pay Account, service Sept. 1, 1777 to Dec. 31, 1779.

647. William.[6] Private, Continental Inf., Jan. to Dec., 1776;
Corp., 13th Mass. to Feb. 16, 1777. April 13, 1777, on Muster List, Capt.
Fairfield's Co., Col. Wigglesworth's Regt., Suffolk Co. Sergt., Sept. 1,
1777; Capt. Page's Co., Feb. 16, 1777 to Sept 1, 1777, Col. Smith's
Regt. (13th). Residence, Haverhill. Credited to Haverhill. [Mass.
Arch., Muster Rolls, pay account on or before Aug. 15, 1777, Vol. ii.
p. 56.] Name appears on a statement of Continental Balances, Col.
Calvin Smith's Regt., and for pay for service, three months in 1780 (late
Wigglesworth's Regt.). Ensign, Sept., 1777, Col. Edward Wigglesworth's
Regt., dated Boston (Soldiers' Orders), Oct. 5, 1778. [Vol. xi. p. 38.]
Return from Capt. Nathaniel Marsh's Co., Essex Co. Regt., dated Haver-
hill, Feb. 12, 1778. Date of enlistment expires Jan. 1, 1780, Capt. Fair-
field's Co., Capt. John McNallis' Co., Col. Wigglesworth's Regt. [Mass.
Arch., Muster Rolls, Vol. xli. p. 73; Vol. xi. p. 46.] Lieut., Feb. 13,
1778. Transferred to 6th Mass., Jan., 1781. Transferred to 3d Mass.,
Jan., 1783. Served to June 3, 1783. [Record of War Department, Wash-
ington.] Received Bounty, March 11, 1778. Lieut. in Gen. Glover's
Brigade, 13th Regt. In service Dec. 14, 1780, dated Boston. [Vol. xliii.
p. 283. Lieut. for last three months' service in 1780. [Mass. Line of the
Continental, Vol. lxxi. p. 66.] On a return for arrears of pay, Col.
Calvin Smith's Regt., June 1, 1778 to Dec. 31, 1780. [Mass. Arch.,
Muster Rolls, Vol. lxxv. p. 356.] On a return for clothing, Aug. 28,
1779, Maj. John Porter's Regt. (13th), Camp, Lower Salem, Lieut. Col.
Calvin Smith's Regt., Jan. 1 to Dec. 31, 1780. [Mass. Arch., Muster
Rolls, Vol. xix. Part 1, p. 106.]

650. William.[7] War of 1812.

153. William.[9] Enlisted 1862. Private, Co. D, 79th Regt., Illinois
Vols. Wounded at Battle of Stone River. Captured at Battle of Chicka-
mauga. Prisoner of War, eighteen months; Civil War.

303. William Allen.[8] Private, Co. A, 6th Regt., Maine Vols.,
1st Regt. Inf. : Civil War.

207. William Alva[8] (Dr.) Acting Asst. Surgeon, U. S. Army,
Aug. 12, 1863, General Hospital No. 8, Beaufort, S. C. Aug. 18, 1863, in
charge of same. May 17, 1864, in charge of U. S. Army General Hospital,
No. 1, Beaufort, S. C. Oct. 15, 1864, Quarantine Duty, Port Royal, S. C.
Nov. 23, 1864, U. S. General Hospital, Hilton Head, S. C. Dec. 26, 1864,
relieved from duty at his own request, receiving the thanks of Medical
Director Clymer for efficient and satisfactory service rendered. Jan. 16,

1865, again entered the U. S. Army (by contract). Jan. 24, 1865, in charge of Post Hospital at Camp Randall, Madison, Wis., to June 6, 1866, at which time the camp was broken up and discontinued, and he was relieved from further duty under the contract.

   651a. **William Arthur.**[9] Surgeon 17th N. H. Regt., Civil War.

   115. **William E.**[9] Lieut. U. S. Army.

   169. **William Luther.**[9] At the breaking out of the Civil War he joined a company that was being formed for the 2d Regt., Vermont Vols., but owing to the large number of men enlisting for that regiment, the company was not accepted. He afterwards enlisted as Private in Co. L, 1st Vermont Cavalry. Aug. 11, 1862, was made Sergt. at the organization of the company, and was mustered into U. S. Service as such, Sept. 29, 1862. At Hagerstown, Md., July 13, 1863, he was three times severely wounded, and had his horse shot under him. On his return to the regiment he was made 1st Sergt. of his company, and was commissioned 2d Lieut., Feb. 28, 1864. In June, 1864, while on "Wilson's Raid," he was again severely wounded, and fell into the hands of the enemy. After being exchanged he was commissioned 1st Lieut., Feb. 9, 1865, and was honorably discharged for disability from wounds received in action, June 15, 1865. He was commissioned Capt. of Co. E, 1st Regt., Vermont Vol. Militia, March 25, 1869, and was successively promoted Maj., Lieut. Col., and Col. of his regiment. He was elected by the Legislature to the office of Brig. Gen., Dec. 1, 1886, and as such commanded the entire State Militia until Dec. 1, 1892, when he was retired upon his own application. The order retiring him says: "The Commander-in-Chief takes this occasion to convey to Brig. Gen. Greenleaf his high appreciation of his long and faithful service of nearly twenty-seven years, and to extend the thanks of the State for the part taken by him in bringing the National Guard of Vermont to its present state of discipline and efficiency. In accordance with the provisions of the Act creating a retired list, he is the first officer to be placed thereon, and is entitled to wear the uniform of his rank on all occasions of ceremony." He became a member of the Grand Army of the Republic soon after its organization, and held at various times the positions of Post Commander, Assistant Quartermaster General, and Department Commander. He also joined the Military Order of the Loyal Legion at the organization of the Vermont Commandery, in 1891, and was elected its first Recorder, which position he still holds.

   *608. **Zebulon D.**[9] Co. C, 30th Regt. Inf., Maine Vols.

EXPLANATORY.

THE arrangement of numbering and indexing is as follows: The sons bearing the name of *Greenleaf* and who have married, are, with few exceptions, numbered in bold type consecutively from Edmund to Samuel, 1–666. These are called calendar numbers.

Numbers at the heads of lists of children are the parents' calendar numbers. For example: We desire to find the record of the parents of Abner[5] Greenleaf, whose calendar number is 619. We find at head of list of his brothers and sisters 29, which is the calendar number of Nathaniel[4] and Judith (Coffin) Greenleaf, the parents of Abner[5] 619. To trace the lineage to the common ancestor, continue thus: Turning to calendar 29 we find date of birth, marriage, and death of Nathaniel[4] and his wife Judith (Coffin). So likewise at head of this list of children we find the calendar number of Tristram[3] and Margaret (Piper) 15, parents of Nathaniel; and then turning to the calendar number 15, we find at the head of the list of children Stephen[2] 3; turning to calendar number 3, we find Stephen[2] as the son of *Edmund Greenleaf*, the common ancestor.

The records of the families of the daughters are all placed with their parents. In the index, they and unmarried sons bearing the name of Greenleaf take the calendar number of their parents. For example, Sarah Greenleaf, b. March 5, 1721, who m. Joseph Whittier, is found in the index as having her father's calendar number, 29; the records of her children and grandchildren form paragraphs with her parents, Nathaniel[4] and Judith (Coffin) Greenleaf.

The designation of families by "charts" in "Personal History," refers to the term used by Rev. Jonathan Greenleaf in his "Genealogy of the Greenleaf Family," published in 1854. This is retained for the convenience of those who have that book: it is omitted from this section for the reason that the method of indexing and numbering here used is better adapted to the larger number of names and families given.

The star (*) in Military and Naval Service refers to the unmarried men, and the calendar number is that of their parents.

A NAME.

The name the Gallic exile bore,
   St. Malo! from thy ancient mart,
Became upon our Western shore
   Greenleaf for Feuillevert.

A name to hear in soft accord
   Of leaves by light winds overrun,
Or read, upon the greening sward
   Of May, in shade and sun.

That name my infant ear first heard
   Breathed softly with a mother's kiss;
His mother's own, no tenderer word
   My father spake than this.

No child have I to bear it on;
   Be thou its keeper; let it take
From gifts well used and duty done
   New beauty for thy sake.

The fair ideals that outran
   My halting footsteps seek and find—
The flawless symmetry of man,
   The poise of heart and mind.

Stand firmly where I felt the sway
   Of every wing that fancy flew;
See clearly where I groped my way,
   Nor real from seeming knew.

And wisely choose, and bravely hold
   Thy faith unswerved by cross or crown,
Like the stout Huguenot of old
   Whose name to thee comes down.

As Marot's songs made glad the heart
   Of that lone exile, haply mine
May in life's heavy hours impart
   Some strength and hope to thine.

Yet when did Age transfer to Youth
   The hard-gained lessons of its day?
Each lip must learn the taste of truth,
   Each foot must feel its way.

We cannot hold the hands of choice
   That touch or shun life's fateful keys;
The whisper of the inward voice
   Is more than homilies.

Dear boy! for whom the flowers are born,
   Stars shine, and happy song-birds sing,
What can my evening give to morn,
   My winter to thy spring?

A life not void of pure intent,
   With small desert of praise or blame,
The love I felt, the good I meant,
   I leave thee with my name.

JOHN GREENLEAF WHITTIER.

This poem was addressed to Mr. Whittier's grandnephew, Greenleaf Whittier Pickard.*

To an inquiry about the legend of the Greenleaf family, in alluding to St. Malo, Mr. Whittier wrote: "I have for a long time heard the tradition of it;" and after quoting the passage in the Greenleaf genealogy, published in 1854, which refers to the Huguenot origin of the family, he says: "I am not sure that the old Greenleaf embarked from the port of St. Malo, but as that was the port from whence many of the persecuted exiles came, I took the liberty of using it in my verse. Marot was a somewhat celebrated French poet of the sixteenth century. He was inclined to the Protestant faith, and wrote the hymns of the Huguenots."†

* Poems by John Greenleaf Whittier, published 1892, by Houghton, Mifflin & Company, p. 176.

† Life and Letters of John Greenleaf Whittier, by Samuel T. Pickard, published 1894 by Houghton, Mifflin & Company, pp. 663, 664.

GENEALOGY.

1.

EDMUND[1] GREENLEAF, Common Ancestor,
b. 1573–74, baptized Jan. 2, 1574; m. 1, Sarah Dole,
perhaps sister to Richard Dole, b. ——; d. Jan. 18,
1663, in Boston; 2, Mrs. Sarah Hill, dau. of Ignatius Jurdaine, of Exeter, Eng., widow, first, of ——
Wilson; second, of William Hill, of Fairfield, Conn.;
b. ——; d. 1671, in Boston. He d. March 24,
1671, in Boston; children:—

   I. ENOCH, b. about 1613, baptized Dec. 1, 1613, at St.
Mary's; d. 1617; buried at St. Margaret's, Sept. 2,
1617.

  II. SAMUEL, b. ——; d. 1627; buried at St. Margaret's,
March 5, 1627.

2. III. ENOCH,[2] b. about 1617; m. Mary ——; was living
in 1683; six children.

 IV. SARAH, b. ——, baptized March 26, 1620, at St.
Mary's; m. William Hilton, of Newbury, Mass.
He d. Sept. 7, 1675, at Charlestown, Mass. He
came to Plymouth from London, Eng., in 1621;
thence to Dover, in 1623, with his brother Edward;
thence to Newbury, Mass. She d. 1655; five
children:—

    i. Sarah, b. June, 1641.
    ii. Charles, b. July, 1643.
    iii. Ann, b. Feb. 12, 1649.
    iv. Elizabeth, b. Nov. 6, 1650.
    v. William, b. June 28, 1653.

  V. ELIZABETH, b. ——; baptized Jan. 16, 1622, at St.
Mary's; m. 1642: 1, Giles Badger, of Newbury,
Mass., b. ——; d. July 10, 1647; 2, Feb. 16,
1648–49, Richard Browne, of Newbury, Mass. (his
second wife), b. ——; d. April 26, 1661; six children.

Children by 1st marriage:—
    i. John, b. June 30, 1643; m. about 1663: 1, Elizabeth Brown, of
Hampton, N. H.; 2, Hannah Swett; one child, Nathaniel.

EDMUND¹ GREENLEAF.
Common Ancestor,
page 190.

Enoch.   Samuel.   Enoch, page 194.   Sarah.   Elizabeth.   Nathaniel,   Judith,   Stephen, page 198.   Daniel.

Enoch, page 192.   Joseph,   Mary,   Rowksby,   Ruth,   James

Bethiah, Enoch, Mary, Nathaniel, Enoch, Martha, Catherine, Joseph, Rachel, William, page 196.

Mary, William, Joseph, Joseph, page 196, Mary, Catherine, Susanna, Abigail, Elizabeth, Hannah, Enoch, John, Richard, Oliver, page 196.

Abigail, Abigail, Joseph, Thomas, page 197, Mary, Catherine, Eunice Payne.

Joseph, page 197, Catherine, Abigail, Anna

A dau.   Thomas, page 198,   Anna,   Emeline Matilda,   Joseph,   Joseph,

A dau.   Katherine Nash,   Emeline Matilda,   James Leal,   Eleanor Leal.

Elizabeth, Rev. Daniel, Stephen, William, Joseph, Sarah, Stephen, page 204.   John, Benjamin, Moses.

Stephen, page 202.   Sarah,   Daniel.   Elizabeth.   John, page 202.   Samuel, page 202.   Tristram, page 202.   Edmund, page 204.   Mary,   Judith.

Elizabeth.   Jane   Judith.   Daniel.   Hon. John, Parker, Samuel, Martha, Benjamin, Stephen.

Daniel. John, page 412.   Stephen, page 442.   Sarah.

Nathaniel, Elizabeth, Stephen, Edmund, Sarah, Judith, Mary, Prudence, Tristram, page 448.   Enoch, page 460.   Samuel.

Judith, Abigail, Mary, Rebecca, Edmund, Henry, Rebecca, Richard, Rowksby.

Edmund (1) Greenleaf, Continued :—
V. Elizabeth.

Children by 2d marriage :—
ii. Elizabeth, b. March 29, 1649.
iii. Richard, b. Feb. 18, 1651; m. May 7, 1674, Mary Jacques.
iv. Edmund, b. July 17, 1654.
v. Sarah, b. Sept. 7, 1657.
vi. Mary, b. April 10, 1660.
VI. Nathaniel, b. ——; d. 1634; buried July 24, 1634; baptized June 27, 1624, at St. Mary's.
VII. Judith, b. Sept. 2, 1625; baptized Sept. 29, 1626, at St. Mary's; m. 1, Henry Somerby, of Newbury, Mass.; baptized March 17, 1612; d. Oct. 2, 1652; 2, March 2, 1653, Tristram Coffin, Jr., of Newbury, Mass.; b. about 1632; d. Feb. 4, 1704, at Nantucket, Mass. She d. Dec. 15, 1705 (gravestone 13th); fourteen children.

Children by 1st marriage :—
i. Sarah, b. Feb. 10, 1645; m. Dec. 8, 1663, John Hale, of Newbury, Mass. He first m. Rebecca, daughter of Richard Lowell, Dec. 5, 1660. Sarah, his second wife, d. June 19, 1672; he m. third, Sarah (Symonds), widow of —— Cottle, probably 1673.
ii. Elizabeth, b. Nov. 1, 1646; m. Nov. 23, 1663: 1, Nathaniel Clarke; b. 1644, a merchant at Newbury, Mass.; 2, Rev. John Hale, first minister of Beverly, Mass. She d. in Exeter, N. H. Eleven children by 1st marriage: 1. Nathaniel, b. Dec. 5, 1664; d. June 6, 1665. 2. Nathaniel, b. March 13, 1666; m. Dec. 15, 1685, Elizabeth Tappan. 3. Thomas, b. Feb. 9, 1668; m. 1689 or '90 Sarah ——. 4. John (Rev.), b. June 24, 1670. 5. Henry, b. July 5, 1673; m. 1, Nov. 7, 1695, Elizabeth, daughter of Stephen[3] and Elizabeth (Gerrish) Greenleaf, b. Jan. 12, 1678-79; he m. 2, Jan. 24, 1724, Mary Pierce. He moved from Newbury to Greenland, N. H. He had twelve children; by first marriage, ten. 6. Daniel, b. Dec. 16, 1675. 7. Sarah, b. Jan. 12, 1678; m. Nicholas Gilman. 8. Josiah, b. May, 1682. 9. Elizabeth, b. May 15, 1684. 10. Judith, b. Jan., 1687. 11. Mary, b. March 25, 1689.
iii. John, b. Dec. 24, 1648; d. Dec. 14, 1650.
iv. Daniel, b. Nov. 18, 1650. He was mortally wounded in a battle with the Indians, Dec. 19, 1675. The descendants of Henry Somerby in the male line then became extinct.

Children of Henry and Elizabeth (Greenleaf) Clarke. (1) Stephen, b. Feb. 21, 1697; d. about 1724. (2) Henry, b. Nov. 21, 1698; d. young. (3) Judith, b. Aug. 15, 1700. (4) Elizabeth, b. 1701 (?); m. Daniel Thing, of Exeter, N. H. (5) Sarah, b. Aug. 7, 1702. (6) Eunice, b. Oct. 15, 1704.

Edmund (1) Greenleaf, Continued :—

VII. Judith.

Children of Henry and Elizabeth Greenleaf Clarke :—

(7) John, b. July 20, 1706; d. July 25, 1706. (8) Mary, b. Aug. 5, 1707. (9) Enoch, b. Sept. 1, 1709; d. Feb. 16, 1759. (10) Anna, b. Feb. 20, 1711. By second marriage, two : (11) Mercy, b. Dec. 26, 1714; m. Oct. 28, 1731, Jonathan Longfellow,* residence, Deerfield, N. H. Ch. : Sarah, b. Nov. 16, 1737; m. Gen. Joseph Cilley, of Nottingham, N. H. They had twelve children, of whom Sarah, m. Thomas Bartlett, of Nottingham, N. H. Ch. : David, m. ——. Their child, Greenleaf Cilley, b. May 7, 1822; m. May 4, 1854, Charlotte Jane Kelley. He d. April 10, 1893. Their children were : Frederick David, b. March 16, 1855; d. March 2, 1877. Greenleaf Kelley, b. June 17, 1856, a lawyer, residence, Derry Depot, N. H. Charles, b. April 9, 1859, druggist and painter. William, b. Feb. 24, 1862, printer. Jennie Susan, b. March 25, 1864. (12) Henry, b. April 23, 1717.

Children by 2d marriage :—

v. Judith, b. Dec. 4, 1653, in Newbury; m. John Sanborn, of Hampton, N. H.

vi. Deborah, b. Nov. 10, 1655; m. Oct. 31, 1677, Joseph Knight.

vii. Mary, b. Nov. 12, 1657; m. Oct. 31, 1677, Joseph Little, b. Sept. 22, 1653. She d. Nov. 20, 1725. Nine children : 1. Judith, b. July 19, 1678; d. April 30, 1761. 2. Joseph, b. Feb. 23, 1680; d. Aug. 14, 1693. 3. George, b. Jan. 12, 1682; d. July 2, 1760. 4. Sarah, b. Oct. 23, 1683. 5. Enoch, b. Dec. 9, 1685; d. April 28, 1766. 6. Tristram, b. April 7, 1688; d. April, 1762. 7. Moses, b. May 5, 1690; d. Aug. 15, 1725. 8. Daniel, b. Jan. 13, 1692; d. Nov., 1777. 9. Benjamin, b. Oct. 13, 1696; d. Feb., 1737.

viii. James, b. April 22, 1659.

ix. John, b. Sept. 8, 1660; d. May 13, 1677.

x. Lydia, b. April 22, 1662; m. 1, Moses Little; b. March 11, 1657; six children; 2, March 18, 1695, John Pike, son of John and Mary. Children by 1st marriage : 1. John, b. Jan. 8, 1680; d. March 25, 1753. 2. Tristram, b. Dec. 9, 1681; d. Nov. 11, 1765. 3. Sarah, b. April 28, 1684; d. Dec. 10, 1710. 4. Mary, b. Jan. 13, 1686; d. Jan., 1761. 5. Elizabeth, b. May 25, 1688; m. Jan. 21, 1718, Anthony Morse. She d. March 25, 1719. 6. Moses, b. Feb. 26, 1691; d. Oct. 17, 1780.

xi. Enoch, b. Jan. 21, 1663; d. Nov. 12, 1675.

xii. Stephen, b. Aug. 18, 1664; d. Aug. 31, 1725.

xiii. Peter, b. July 27, 1667; d. Jan. 19, 1746.

xiv. Nathaniel (Hon.), b. March 22, 1669; d. Feb. 20, 1748–49.

* Of the Longfellow family William, b. 1651, in Hampshire, Eng., came to Newbury, m. Anne Sewall Nov. 10, 1676. He was drowned at Anticosta, 1690. Children : William, b. Nov. 25, 1679. Stephen, b. Jan. 10, 1681, and d. Nov. 13, 1683. Anne, b. Oct. 3, 1683. Elizabeth, b. July 3, 1688. Nathan, b. Feb. 5, 1690. [Coffin's History of Newburyport, p. 308.]

EDMUND (1) GREENLEAF, CONTINUED :—

3. VIII. STEPHEN,[2] b. about 1628; baptized Aug. 10, 1628,
at St. Mary's; m. Nov. 13, 1651: 1, Elizabeth,
daughter of Tristram and Dionis (Stevens) Coffin, of
Newbury, Mass., b. —; d. Nov. 19, 1678, ten
children, all by 1st marriage; 2, March 31, 1679,
Mrs. Esther Weare Swett, daughter of Nathaniel
Weare and widow of Benjamin Swett, of Hampton, N. H., b. —; d. Jan. 16, 1718, aged 89
years. He d. Dec. 1, 1690.

IX. DANIEL, b. —; baptized Aug. 14, 1631, at St.
Mary's; d. Dec. 5, 1654.

JOHN, b. about 1632; m. July 26, 1665, by Captain
Clapp, Hannah, daughter of William Veazie, of
Braintree. He died Dec. 16, 1712; nine children.

MARY, b. —; m. March 5, 1669, John Wells,
of Newbury, Mass.

Of John and Mary no record has been found by the compiler to
authenticate the tradition that they were children of *Edmund
Greenleaf*, but the names of the children of John and his
wife Hannah are nearly all found among the children and
grandchildren of the family; and bearing the name (John) of
the father of Edmund, the probabilities appear to justify
placing them with the children of Edmund, with this statement of uncertainty. In Vol. xxi. of the N. E. Hist. Geneal.
Register, page 250, is a letter from H. G. Somerby, dated
London, Sept. 10, 1866, giving a list of early settlers in New
England whose English ancestry he had either discovered or
verified. Among the one hundred or more names are Greenleaf and Dole.

2.

(Edmund 1.)

Children of **Enoch[2] Greenleaf** and Mary —.

4. I. ENOCH,[3] b. 1647, in England; m. Oct. 20, 1675: 1,
Bethiah Woodman, b. 1650; d. Dec. 28, 1678, age
28; buried in King's Chapel Burying Ground, Boston;
2, Aug. 29, 1679, Catherine Truesdale, b. 1653; d.
Aug., 1712, at Cambridge, Mass. He d. Sept. 8,
1705; ten children: by 1st marriage, two children;
by 2d marriage, eight children. He came to America
after the Restoration, and settled in Malden, Mass.

Enoch (2) Greenleaf, Continued :—

4a. II. Joseph,[3] b ——; m. Sarah S. ——, b. ——; d.
June 4, 1690; residence, Boston; children :—
    i. Sarah, b. Feb. 3, 1683.

4b.   ii. Enoch,[4] b. Sept. 2, 1686; m. Rebecca, daughter of
Samuel and Elizabeth (Elbridge) Russell. Of their
children, Elizabeth, b. about 1716, m. Thomas
Gerry, an Englishman, shipmaster, who came to
Marblehead, Mass., in 1730, in early life, from
Newton, Eng.; established himself as a merchant;
she d. Sept. 2, 1771; five children :—

    1. Thomas; 2. John; 3. Elbridge,* b. July 17, 1744; m. Ann,
daughter of James (or Charles) Thompson, of New York
City, Secretary of Congress. Elbridge Gerry graduated
at Harvard, A.M., 1762; LL.D., 1810; Fellow Am. Acad.;
Governor of Massachusetts; delegate to Continental Congress; delegate to Constitution Convention, U. S.; M. C.;
Vice President U. S.; U. S. Envoy to France; died Nov.
23, 1814; 4. Elizabeth, m. Burrill Devereaux, who after
her death married again; 5. Samuel Russell, late Collector of the Port of Marblehead, Mass.

    iii. Rachel, b. Feb. 17, 1688.

  III. Mary.

  IV. Rooksby, m. June 30, 1697, Thomas Cresse.

  V. Ruth, m. Dec. 16, 1689, John Cook.

  VI. James. (The son referred to in Edmund's will.)

4.

(Enoch 2, Edmund 1.)

Children of **Enoch**[3] **Greenleaf** and Bethiah (Woodman);
by 1st marriage :—

I. Bethiah, b. Aug. 11, 1676; d. 1678.

II. Enoch, b. 1678; d. 1679; buried in King's Chapel
Burying Ground.

Children by 2d marriage :—

III. Mary, b. June 17, 1680; d. 1693.

---

*Pedigree: John Aldworth, of Wantage, Berks Co., England; b. ——; m. ——;
d. 1525; their son Robert, b. ——; m. Alice Presey; d. ——; their son Richard (Sir
Knight), m. ——; their son John, m. —— Knight; their daughter Elizabeth, m. Giles
Elbridge; d. 1643-44; Giles Elbridge's son Thomas held Court as Lord Proprietor of
Penaquid Circ., 1647; m. Rebecca ——; their daughter Elizabeth, m. Samuel Russell; their
daughter Rebecca (Russell), m. Enoch Greenleaf; their daughter Elizabeth, m. Thomas
Gerry.

ENOCH (4) GREENLEAF, CONTINUED :—

    IV. NATHANIEL, b. Sept. 12, 1681; d. 1682; buried in King's Chapel Burying Ground.

    V. ENOCH, b. March 1, 1683; d. 1683.

    VI. MARTHA, b. May 22, 1684; d. 1684.

    VII. CATHERINE, b. Aug. 16, 1685; d. 1685.

    VIII. JOSEPH,[4] b. April 4, 1687; res. Boston, distiller.

    IX. RACHEL, b. Nov. 10, 1688; d. 1689; res. Boston.

5.   X. WILLIAM,[4] b. Feb. 5, 1693; m. June 10, 1714: 1, Mary Shattuck, b. ——; d. Aug. 18, 1732; eleven children; 2, March 2, or May 9, 1733 [Boston Records], Ruth Ruggles; three children. He died Sept. 20, 1756; res. Boston, a hatter.

5.

(Enoch 3, Enoch 2, Edmund 1.)

Children of **William[4] Greenleaf** and Mary (Shattuck); by 1st marriage :—

    I. MARY, b. ——; d. in infancy.

    II. WILLIAM, b. Sept. 1, 1716; d. Sept. 20, 1759.

    III. JOSEPH, b. Sept. 14, 1718; d. Sept. 24, 1718.

6.   IV. JOSEPH,[5] b. Nov. 10, 1720; m. Oct. 17, 1749, Abigail, daughter of Rev. Thomas,* and Eunice Payne, b. March 6, 1725, in Weymouth, Mass.; d. Jan. 15, 1809 (graduate of Harvard College). He d. Oct. 28, 1810, in Malden, buried in Granary Burying Ground, Boston. Residence, Abington, Mass.; seven children.

    V. MARY, b. May 9, 1722; m. Dec. 19, 1757, Col. John Leverett,† of Windsor, Vt., b. Jan. 28, 1726; d. 1777; had three sons and one daughter.

    VI. CATHERINE, b. Nov. 29, 1723.

    VII. SUSANNA, b. Sept. 1, 1725.

    VIII. ABIGAIL, b. Oct. 29, 1726.

*Children of Rev. Thomas and Eunice Payne. 1. Richard; 2. Robert; 3. Samuel; 4. Emma; 5. Abigail.

† Colonel Leverett had been a commissioned officer in Colonel Phillip's Regt., 1758. He was appointed Lieutenant Colonel, and subsequently Colonel of a Boston Regiment. He was son of Knight Leverett, who was son of Thomas, b. 1674, and Rebecca (Winsor), son of Hudson, b. 1640, and Sarah (Payton), son of Sir John, b. in England, 1616, and Hannah (Hudson), son of Thomas, b. about 1585, and Anne (Fisher). (See Memoir of Sir John Leverett.)

WILLIAM (5) GREENLEAF, CONTINUED :—

    IX. ELIZABETH, b. Oct. 17, 1727.

    X. HANNAH, b. Aug. 6, 1729.

6a. XI. ENOCH,[5] b. July 9, 1732; m. —— Gridley; no children.

    Children by 2d marriage :—

    XII. JOHN, b. March 17, 1734; d. 1735.

    XIII. RICHARD, b. April 26, 1735; d. 1735.

7. XIV. OLIVER,[5] b. about 1737; m. Dorcas Welch; five children :—

      i. George, b. ——; d. Feb. 7, 1818.

      ii. Oliver Cromwell, b. about 1790. (?) Lived in Boston and kept a bookstore on Washington Street, about 1795, under firm name of West & Greenleaf [N. E. Hist. Geneal. Register, Vol. XIV. p. 84]; d. about 1835.

      iii. Joseph, b. ——; d. 1816.

      iv. Ruth.

      v. Dorcas.

6.

(William 4, Enoch 3, Enoch 2, Edmund 1.)

Children of **Joseph**[5] **Greenleaf** and Abigail (Payne).

    I. ABIGAIL, b. 1750; d. in infancy.

    II. ABIGAIL, b. Feb. 28, 1753; m. Rev. Ezra Weld, of Braintree, Mass. (his third wife); she d. July 8, 1788; two children :—

      i. Joseph, b. July 14, 1784.

      ii. Thomas, b. Jan. 22, 1785.

    III. JOSEPH, b. May 28, 1754; d. November —— 1771, in Boston.

8. IV. THOMAS,[6] b. 1755; m. Oct. 13, 1791, Anna Quackenbos. A printer; res. New York; he d. 1798; four children.

    V. MARY, b. 1757; m. Aug. 14, 1791, Nathaniel Thwing, a merchant of Boston; she d. 1804; no children.

    VI. CATHERINE, b. June 11, 1760; m. Dr. Joseph W. Rhoades; six children: three sons and three daughters.

    VII. EUNICE PAYNE, b. Aug. 7, 1762; m. May 15, 1790, William Prentiss (his second wife), son of

Joseph (6) Greenleaf, Continued:—
  VII. Eunice Payne.
    Caleb and Lydia; she d. April 11, 1803. He was
    a merchant in London several years. He collected
    valuable MSS. Genealogy of the Prentiss family;
    of their children,—
  William Henry, b. Oct. 23, 1796, on Greenleaf's Point, Washing-
    ton, D. C.; m. July 1, 1818: 1, Sarah Stockwell; d. Jan. 8,
    1831; 2, Sept. 29, 1836, Sarah Ann Cooper, b. 1807; d. Nov.
    17, 1871. He d. Sept. 21, 1878; children, nine of whom died
    young, names unknown; the others, by first wife, were: 1.
    William Henry, b. Nov. 22, 1822. 2. Margaret Jane, b. Feb.
    2, 1824; by 2d wife: 3. Eunice Ann, b. Sept. 25, 1832. 4.
    Charles Appleton, b. Feb. 12, 1837. 5. Daniel Webster, b.
    May 21, 1843, M.D. of Washington, D. C. 6. Isaac Cooper,
    b. Oct. 21, 1846; d. young. 7. Juliet Virginia, b. Aug. 2,
    1849; d. young. Res., Washington, D. C.

8.
(Joseph 5, William 4, Enoch 3, Enoch 2, Edmund 1.)

Children of **Thomas**[6] **Greenleaf** and Anna (Quacken-
  bos).
9. I. Joseph,[7] b. Aug. 13, 1792; m. Emeline Matilda,
    daughter of Joseph Leal and Ann (Van Bergen)
    Riley, b. Jan. 15, 1796; d. June 2, 1846; he died
    June 6, 1871; res. in New York City; six children.
  II. Catharine, b. Oct. 19, 1794; d. Sept. 6, 1876.
  III. Abigail, b. April 4, 1796; m. Rev. Preserved
    Smith; she d. Oct. 6, 1882.
  IV. Anna, b. June 17, 1798; d. June 10, 1883.

9.
(Thomas 6, Joseph 5, William 4, Enoch 3, Enoch 2, Edmund 1.)

Children of **Joseph**[7] **Greenleaf** and Emeline Matilda
  (Riley).
  I. A daughter, b. July 30, 1821; d. in infancy.
10. II. Thomas,[8] b. July 30, 1826; m. Nov. 22, 1849,
    Eleanor Leal, of Delhi, Delaware Co., N. Y.; b.
    Feb. 9, 1819; five children.
  III. Anna, b. September, 1828; m. Jan. 5, 1853, George
    W. Thorp; d. 1872; children:—
    i. George W., b. ——; d. in infancy.
    ii. Emeline Greenleaf, b. 1859; unmarried.

JOSEPH (9) GREENLEAF, CONTINUED :—

   III. Anna.

      iii. Joseph Greenleaf, b. 1862; an architect in New York.
      iv. William W. Phillips, b. 1865; m. in 1888, Eleanor C. Papen-
         dick; child : 1. Gerald, b. 1892.
      v. Edward Yeomons, b. 1870.

   IV. EMELINE MATILDA, b. Oct. 4, 1830.

   V. JOSEPH, b. Jan. 11, 1836; d. Nov. 19, 1838.

10a. VI. JOSEPH,[8] b. Nov. 9, 1838; m. Nov. 9, 1863, Mary
      H. Ritch, of New York City; clergyman; child :
      Anna, b. 1865; d. 1883; res. Washingtonville, N. Y.

10.

(Joseph 7, Thomas 6, Joseph 5, William 4, Enoch 3, Enoch 2, Edmund 1.)

Children of **Thomas**[8] **Greenleaf** and Eleanor (Leal).

   I. A daughter, b. March 21, 1851 ; d. in infancy.

   II. KATHERINE NASH, b. July 21, 1852 ; m. April 9, 1854,
      Rev. George Howard Duffield, D.D., now pastor of
      First Presbyterian Church, New York City; chil-
      dren :—

      i. George Greenleaf, d. in infancy.
      ii. Howard Leal, b. 1879; d. 1884.
      iii. Eleanor Van Dyck, b. 1880.
      iv. Douglas Greenleaf, } twins, b. 1883; Douglas d. 1884.
      v. Stuart Kennedy,   }
      vi. Winifred, b. 1887.

   III. EMELINE MATILDA, b. Jan. 10, 1854; d. 1872.

11. IV. JAMES LEAL,[9] b. July 30, 1857; m. June 4, 1889,
      Bertha, daughter of George H. Potts; child : Donald
      Leal, b. June 5, 1890. Adj. Prof. Civil Engineering
      in Columbia College School of Mines; res. New
      York City.

   V. ELEANOR LEAL, b. Aug. 20, 1862 ; m. Oct. 4, 1881,
      Louis H. Blakeman, of New York City; children :—

      i. Frederick Tomlinson, b. 1883.
      ii. Thomas Greenleaf, b. 1887.

3.

(Edmund 1.)

Children of **Stephen**[2] **Greenleaf** and Elizabeth (Coffin).

12. I. STEPHEN,[3] b. Aug. 15, 1652, in Newbury, Mass. ; m.
      1, Oct. 23, 1676, Elizabeth, dau. of William and

Stephen (3) Greenleaf, Continued :—

I. Stephen.[3]

Mrs. Joanna (Goodale-Oliver) Gerrish, of Newbury, Mass., b. Sept. 10, 1654; d. Aug. 5, 1712; 2, 1713, Mrs. Hannah Jordan, of Kittery, Me. She d. Sept. 30, 1743. He d. Oct. 13, 1743, at Newbury, Mass.; ten children

II. Sarah, b. Oct. 29, 1655; m. June 7, 1677, Richard Dole, b. Sept. 6, 1650; d. Aug. 1, 1723; son of Richard, merchant, who was b. in Bristol, Eng., 1622. She d. Sept. 1, 1718; nine children :—

i. Richard, b. April 28, 1678.

ii. Elizabeth, b. ——, 1679; m. 1699, Joshua Plummer.

iii. Sarah, b. Feb. 14, 1681; m. Jan. 1, 1708, William Johnson, of Woburn, Mass.

iv. Hannah, b. Dec. 5, 1682; m. Nov. 16, 1702, Edmund Goodrich.

v. John, b. Feb. 2, 1685.

vi. Stephen, b. Dec. 2, 1686; d. in infancy.

vii. Stephen, b. ——, 1687.

viii. Joseph, b. Dec. 5, 1689.

ix. Mary, b. July 1, 1694; m. 1723, John Gerrish.

III. Daniel, b. Feb. 17, 1657–58, at Boston; d. Dec. 5, 1659.

IV. Elizabeth, b. April 5, 1660, in Newbury, Mass.; m. Sept. 24, 1677, Col. Thomas, son of Rev. James Noyes. He m. 1, Dec. 28, 1669, Martha Pierce. She d. Sept. 3, 1674. He d. 1730; eight children.

13. V. John,[3] b. June 21, 1662, in Newbury, Mass.; m. Oct. 12, 1685, 1, Elizabeth, dau. of Joseph Hills, of Newbury, b. ——; d. Aug. 5, 1712 (tombstone); ten children; 2, May 13, 1716, Lydia, widow of Benjamin Pierce, and dau. of Major Charles Frost, of Kittery, Me. She d. May 15, 1752, age 78. He d. May or June 24, 1734.

Joseph Hills, b. 1602, came from Malden, Eng., there a woolen draper, to Charlestown, Mass., 1638, where he remained until 1647, when he removed to Malden, Mass.; admitted church with wife Feb. 12, 1639–40; he afterwards removed to Newbury, Mass., where he d. Feb. 5, 1687–88. He m. 1, Rose Dunster, a sister of President Dunster, of Harvard College, who d. March 24, 1649–50; 2, Hannah Mellowes, June 24,

STEPHEN (3) GREENLEAF, CONTINUED :—

> V. John.³
>
>> 1651; 3, Helen Atkinson, Feb., 1655–56; 4, Ann Lunt, March 8, 1664–65, at Newbury. Children: (1) Joseph. (2) Rebecca. (3) Amy (?). (4) Mary. (5) A daughter, who m. George Blanchard. (6) Hannah, named in will, 1678. (7) Gershorm, b. July 27, 1639, of Malden. (8) Mehitable, b. Jan. 1, 1640–41; d. July, 1653. (9) John. (10) Samuel, b. July, 1652. (11) Nathaniel, b. Jan. 1, 1653; d. Feb. 26, 1653–4. (12) Deborah, b. March, 1656–57; d. Oct. 1, 1662. (13) Abigail, b. Oct. 6, 1658; d. Oct. 9, 1662.

14. VI. SAMUEL,³ b. Oct. 30, 1665, at Newbury, Mass.; m. March 1, 1686 (?), Sarah, dau. of John Kent, Jr., and Sarah (Woodman), b. Aug. 30, 1667; four children. He d. Aug. 6, 1694. She m. again, April 28, 1696, Peter, son of Dr. Peter Tappan or Toppan. Res., Newbury, Mass.

15. VII. TRISTRAM,³ b. Feb. 11, 1667–78, at Newbury, Mass.; m. Nov. 12, 1689, Margaret, dau. of Nathaniel and Sarah Piper, of Ipswich, Mass., b. June 16, 1668, at Ipswich, Mass.; ten children. He d. Sept. 13, 1740. Will probated Sept. 21, 1741. Res., Newbury, Mass.

16. VIII. EDMUND,³ b. May 10, 1670, at Newbury, Mass.; m. July 2, 1691, Abigail, dau. of Abiel Somberby, b. Jan. 25, 1670, at Newbury, Mass.; nine children. He d. about 1740; res. Newbury, Mass.

> IX. MARY, b. Dec. 6, 1671; m. 1696, Joshua, son of Caleb and Judith (Bradbury) Moody, b. Nov. 3, 1671; five children :—
>
>> i. Mary, b. June 26, 1697.
>> ii. Elizabeth, b. Dec. 4, 1698; m. Capt. James Smith, the first owner of the Crane-neck Hill Farm, Newbury, Mass.
>> iii. Joshua, b. Nov. 11, 1700.
>> iv. Abigail, b. Sept. 30, 1703.
>> v. Judith, b. Oct. 26, 1705.
>> Caleb Moody, m. 1 Sara Pierce, who d. Aug. 25, 1665. Ch.: ¹Daniel and ²Sarah; 2, Judith Bradbury. Ch.: ¹Caleb. ²Thomas. ³Judith, b. Sept. 23, 1669; d. Jan. 28, 1679. ⁴Joshua. ⁵William. ⁶Samuel. ⁷Mary. ⁸Judith. Caleb was son of William and Sarah Moody, who came from Ipswich, Eng., to Ipswich, America, in 1634, and to Newbury in 1635. Ch.: ¹Joshua. ²Caleb. ³William. ⁴Samuel.
>
> X. JUDITH, b. Oct. 23, 1673; d. Nov. 19, 1678.

12.

(Stephen 2, Edmund 1.)

Children of **Stephen**[3] **Greenleaf** and Elizabeth (Gerrish).

I. ELIZABETH, b. Jan. 12, 1678-79; m. Nov. 7, 1695, Henry Clarke, son of Nathaniel and Elizabeth (Somerby) Clarke. Henry Clarke m. 2, Jan. 24, 1714, Mary Pierce; lived in Newbury, Mass.; twelve children.

17. II. REV. DANIEL,[4] b. in Newbury, Feb. 10, 1679-80; baptized Feb. 22, 1679-80; m. Nov. 18, 1701, Elizabeth, dau. of Samuel and Mary Gooking, and gr. dau. of Major General Daniel Gooking, b. Nov. 11, 1681; d. November, 1762. He d. Aug. 26, 1763, in Boston; thirteen children.

III. STEPHEN, b. Aug. 31, 1682; d. Oct. 15, 1688.

IV. WILLIAM, b. April 1, 1684; d. April 15, 1684.

18. V. JOSEPH,[4] b. April 12, 1686; m. Nov. 18, 1707, Thomasine Mayo, b. June 10, 1689; lived in Newbury, Mass.; seven children.

VI. SARAH, b. July 19, 1688; m. March 30, 1710, Richard Kent; lived in Newbury, Mass.; first child, John, b. Nov. 6, 1710.

19. VII. STEPHEN,[4] b. Oct. 21, 1690; m. Oct. 7, 1712, Mary Mackcres, b. 1691; d. 1771, in Woolwich. He d. 1771; eight children.

20. VIII. JOHN,[4] b. Aug. 29, 1693; m. 1713, Abigail Moody; d. probably before 1725, as it is recorded that Abigail Moody (Greenleaf) married Benjamin, son of John and Elizabeth Hills, 1726.

IX. BENJAMIN, b. Dec. 14, 1695; d. ——.

X. MOSES, b. Feb. 24, 1697-98.

13.

(Stephen 2, Edmund 1.)

Children of **John**[3] **Greenleaf** and Elizabeth (Hills).

I. ELIZABETH, b. July 30, 1686; m. 1704, 1, Edmund Titcomb, of Newbury, Mass.; 2, Aug. 2, 1716, Thomas Oakes, of Medford, Mass. She d. Feb. 3, 1718; no children. Mr. Oakes m. Oct. 27, 1720, Abigail Brooks; five children.

JOHN (13) GREENLEAF, CONTINUED :—

 II. JANE, b. Nov. 10, 1687.

 III. JUDITH, b. July 15, 1689; d. Sept. 30, 1690.

21. IV. Daniel,[4] b. Dec. 24, 1690; m. Nov. 17, 1710, Sarah Moody; lived in Newbury. He d. January or February, 1729, drowned on Newbury bar; eight children.

22. V. JOHN[4] (HON.), b. Jan. 3, 1692; m. Sarah Smith, b. ——; d. May 11, 1774, aged 75. He d. Aug. 21, 1760; seven children.

23. VI. PARKER,[4] b. Feb. 23, 1694; m. Nov. 24, 1715, Mary Jacques; d. —— 20, 1720; res. Newbury.

  I. Deborah, b. Oct. 27, 1716.

  II. Elizabeth, b. Jan. 24, 1721.

  Family name extinct in this line.

24. VII. SAMUEL,[4] b. April, 1697; m. Elizabeth Kingsbury; resided in Newbury; tavern keeper; two children.

 VIII. MARTHA, b. April 23, 1699; m. —— Gage; lived in Joppa, Me.

25. IX. BENJAMIN,[4] b. Nov. 21, 1701; m. I, Ann Hale, b. ——; d. Sept. 7, 1725; 2, 1726, Abigail (Moody) Greenleaf, widow of John,[4] son of Stephen and Elizabeth (Gerrish) Greenleaf; b. ——; d. March 9, 1777. He d. July 4, 1783. Res., Newburyport; seven children.

26. X. STEPHEN,[4] b. Oct. 6, 1704; m. Nov. 2, 1727, Eunice Wallis, of Boston. He d. Dec. 22, 1765. Res., Boston; eleven children.

14.

(Stephen 2, Edmund 1.)

Children of **Samuel**[3] **Greenleaf** and Sarah (Kent).

 I. DANIEL, b. Feb. 28, 1687; d. ——.

27. II. JOHN,[4] b. Oct. 3, 1688; m. Abigail ——. He d. ——, 1778; resided in Newbury; ship blacksmith by trade; seven children.

28. III. STEPHEN,[4] b. Aug. 27, 1690; m. Mary Gardner, dau. of Thomas and Mary (Willis), the son of Andrew, b. ——; d. March 6, 1775. He d. Feb. 26, 1753; cordwainer. Will was probated at Middlesex County Probate Office. The estate appraised at over

SAMUEL (14) GREENLEAF, CONTINUED :—

    III. Stephen.[4]

        two thousand pounds, "currency of Massachusetts Bay." The town records from 1649, when the town of Medford was incorporated, to 1693, are missing. It is said they were burned in the Court House about the time of the Revolutionary War. The volume of records of births and deaths from 1693 to 1743 were discovered about Sept. 3, 1855, after having been lost about ten years. An intention of marriage between Stephen Greenleaf and Mary Cotton is found recorded May, 1715. She may have been his wife before he married Mary Gardner. Resided in Medford, Mass. ; seven children.

    IV. SARAH, b. Nov. 3, 1692 ; m. March 7, 1709, Ebenezer (?) perhaps Nathaniel Clarke (Newbury Town Records) ; children :—

        i. Samuel, b. April 13, 1710.
        ii. Elizabeth, b. Oct. 15, 1711.
        iii. Sarah, b. —— ; m. Benjamin Dole.
        iv. Ebenezer.
        v. Stephen, b. June 9, 1723 ; d. December, 1804.
        vi. Nathaniel, b. ——, 1728 ; d. Nov. 7, 1805.

15.

(Stephen 2, Edmund 1.)

Children of **Tristram**[3] **Greenleaf** and Margaret (Piper).

29. I. NATHANIEL,[4] b. Jan. 25, 1691 ; m. June 7, 1714, Judith, dau. of Stephen, son of Tristram, Jr., and Sarah (Atkinson) Coffin, b. Feb. 23, 1693 ; d. Dec. 17, 1769. He d. Dec. 19, 1775 ; six children.

    II. ELIZABETH, b. March 16, 1693 ; d. in infancy.

30. III. STEPHEN,[4] b. April 16, 1694 ; m. April 26, 1753, at Haverhill, Mass., Lydia (Soley), widow of John Stevens. She m. third, Caleb Call ; resided in Newbury and Haverhill, Mass. He d. about 1755. Child Stephen, b. March 23, 1754 ; admin. on Stephen, of Haverhill, to Widow Lydia, July 7, 1755.

31. IV. EDMUND,[4] b. June 24, 1695 ; m. March 12, 1718–19, Lydia Brown, of Newbury, Mass., b. —— ; d. Feb. 9, 1780, age 83 ; resided in Newbury, Mass. ; seven children (recorded at Newbury, 1720 to 1740) :—

TRISTRAM (15) GREENLEAF, CONTINUED :—

IV. Edmund.[4]

1. Francis,[5] b. March 16, 1720; m. Anna —— (?);
children :—

    1. Lydia, b. Sept., 1753. 2. Enoch, b. Jan. 2, 1759.

II. Lydia, b. Jan. 16, 1723; m. Sept. 16, 1742, William Moulton.

III. Edmund, b. April 29, 1726; m. April 18, 1754, Sarah Woodman (?); four children :—

    1. William, b. Feb. 4, 1755. 2. Lydia, b. June 18, 1758. 3. Catherine, b. Sept. 8, 1759. 4. Sarah, b. April 13, 1761.

IV. Enoch, b. Feb. 28, 1728.

V. Abigail, b. July 27, 1731.

VI. Eliphalet, b. Feb., 1734.

VII. Mary, b. March 9, 1740.

The will of Edmund Greenleaf is dated 1759, and mentions sons Francis and Edmund; daughters Lydia Moulton, Abigail and Mary. He gives his wife Lydia "the income of one half of all of my real estate . . . until such time as either of my daughters shall marry, who then shall have one third part thereof, and the other daughter on marriage shall have one third part thereof more, and my said wife shall enjoy but the remaining third part after the marriage of my said daughters which are Abigail and Mary."

V. SARAH, b. March 27, 1697; m. June 9, 1719, Tristram Knight.

VI. JUDITH, b. Sept. 28, 1698.

VII. MARY, b. Sept. 30, 1699; m. Nov. 30, 1721, Jonathan Clement.

VIII. PRUDENCE, b. June 10, 1702; m. April 28, 1725, Jonathan Dole, of Newbury.

32. IX. TRISTRAM,[4] b. Nov. 12, 1703; m. Nov. 5, 1728, by Rev. John Towle, Dorothy Rolfe; resided in Newbury, Mass.; eight children.

33. X. ENOCH,[4] b. about 1705; m. Feb. 17, 1726, Hannah Bradshaw; mentioned in will of Tristram as his son, to whom he bequeathes £100; six children.

XI. SAMUEL, b. Dec. 24, 1706; d. in infancy.

16.

(Stephen 2, Edmund 1.)

Children of **Edmund**[3] **Greenleaf** and Abigail (Somerby).

I. JUDITH, b. Dec. 15, 1692; m. April 22, 1713, John Coffin, eldest son of Nathaniel and Sarah (Brockle-

Edmund (16) Greenleaf, Continued :—

I. Judith.

bank), b. Jan. 1, 1694, in Newbury; d. Sept. 30, 1762. She d. Feb. 10, 1762 or 72 ; eleven children :—

i. Richard, b. Nov. 22, 1713; m. Nov. 30, 1738, Abigail, daughter of Joseph Hale, of Newbury, Mass., b. ——; d. Aug. 19, 1799. He d. Mar. 9, 1773; several children.

ii. Nathaniel, b. Sept. 7, 1716.

iii. Abigail, b. Nov. 8, 1718; m. Feb. 2, 1744, Rev. Aaron Whittemore, of Pembroke, N. H., b. ——; d. Nov. 16, 1767. She d. May 11, 1803.

iv. Mary, b. July 23, 1720; d. Nov. 25, 1737.

v. Peter, b. May 11, 1722; m. July 6, 1769, Rebecca Hazelton, of Chester, N. H., b. ——; d. Dec. 15, 1789.

vi. Apphia, b. April 13, 1724; m. May 8, 1746, Ichabod Jones, of Falmouth.

vii. William, b. July 3, 1726; m. Mar. 28, 1754, Sarah Hazelton, of N. H., b. ——; d. May 26, 1829. He d. Oct. 18, 1815.

viii. Samuel, b. Nov. 23, 1728; m. 1, May 27, 1752, Anna Pettengill; 2, June 17, 1777, Lydia Bartlett, b. ——; d. Aug. 29, 1821.

ix. A son, b. ——; d. infancy.

x. Judith, b. Sept. 3, 1732; d. Nov. 2, 1737.

xi. Sarah, b. Sept. 26, 1735; d. Nov. 1, 1737.

II. Abigail, b. Mar. 6, 1695 ; d. same day.

III. Mary, b. Sept. 10, 1697 ; m. Nov. 15, 1723, Rowland Bradbury, son of Wymond and Maria C. (Cotton), b. Dec. 15, 1699. He m. 2d, Elizabeth Oliver, of York.

IV. Rebecca, b. Feb. 23, 1699; d. Sept. 29, 1702.

34. V. Edmund,[4] b. Feb. 27, 1702 ; m. May 4, 1725, Mary, dau. of Joseph Hale and Mary (Moody). Joseph Hale was son of John Hale, who m. Sarah, dau. of Henry and Judith (Greenleaf) Somerby. Two children.

35. VI. Henry,[4] b. July 22, 1705 ; m. in Boston, June 26, 1726, Elizabeth Burnall.

VII. Rebecca, b. Nov. 5, 1707 ; d. Aug. 19, 1709.

36. VIII. Richard, b. May 11, 1710; m. (?).

IX. Rooksby, b. May 11, 1713; m. April 21, 1738, John Clark, of Kings Towne.

17.

(Stephen 3, Stephen 2, Edmund 1.)

Children of Rev. **Daniel**[4] **Greenleaf** and Elizabeth (Gooking).

37. I. Daniel[5] (Dr.), b. Nov. 7, 1702, at Cambridge, Mass. ; m. 1, July 18, 1726, Mrs. Silence (Nichols) Marsh,

Rev. Daniel (17) Greenleaf, Continued :—

   I. Daniel.[5]
      widow of David Marsh, dau. of Israel and Mary
      (Sumner) Nichols, b. July 4, 1702, in Hingham; d.
      May 13, 1762. He d. July 18, 1795. Removed from
      Hingham to Bolton, Mass., probably 1732; three
      children b. in Hingham. Physician; 2, Nov. 18,
      1762, by John Merrill, Mrs. Dorothy Richardson,
      widow of Josiah Richardson; intention of marriage
      declared Oct. 22, 1762; ten children.

38. II. Stephen[5] (Hon.), b. Oct. 4, 1704, at Newbury; m.
      Aug. 5, 1731, Mary Gould, b. Aug. 20, 1706; d.
      ——. He d. Jan. 26, 1795, in Boston, age 91;
      resided in Boston, Sheriff of the King for Suffolk
      Co., Jan. 3, 1757; seven children.

   III. Mary, b. Aug. 29, 1706, in Cambridge, Mass.; m. 1,
      Mar. 16, 1725, James Blinn; 2, Aug. 7, 1735, Josiah
      Thatcher. She d. April 2, 1774; sixteen children.

   IV. Elizabeth, b. Aug. 24, 1708, in Yarmouth, Mass.;
      m. 1, June 24, 1729, David Bacon; 2, Joseph Scott;
      3, Rev. Joseph Parsons, of Bradford, Mass.; 4, Rev.
      Jedediah Jewett, of Rowley, Mass. She d. May 15,
      1778; six children :—
   i. Hannah, b. July, 1732.
Children by 2d marriage :—
   ii. Joseph, b. Mar. 11, 1741-2.
   iii. William, b. May 17, 1743.
   iv. David, b. Aug. 23, 1744; d. May 11, 1780.
   v. Susanna, b. May 22, 1747.
   vi. Stephen, b. April 18, 1749.

   V. Sarah, b. April 16, 1710, in Yarmouth; single; d.
      Mar. 28, 1776.

   VI. Samuel, b. May 9, 1712; single; d. 1748.

   VII. Jane (Jenny), b. May 24, 1714, in Yarmouth,
      Mass.; m. Mar. 1, 1732-3, Hezekiah Usher, of
      Medford, Mass. and Newport, R. I. She d. Dec. 10,
      1764; twelve children. He m. 2d, Abigail, dau. of
      Aaron Cleveland, b. May 10, 1706, at Medford; three
      children.
   i. Hezekiah, b. June 2, 1734.
   ii. John, b. May 25, 1736.
   iii. Daniel, b. ——; d. young.

Rev. Daniel (17) Greenleaf, Continued :—

    VII. Jane.

      iv. Jane, b. ——; m. Dakin.

      v. Elizabeth, b.——; m. May 15, 1764, Joseph Francis.

      vi. Mary, b. ——; d. unmarried. And other children.

    VIII. HANNAH, b. Oct. 3, 1716, in Yarmouth, Mass. ; m. John Richards. She d. Jan. 3, 1799.

39.   IX. JOHN[5] (Dr.), b. Nov. 8, 1717, at Yarmouth, Mass. ; m. 1, Dec. 8, 1743, Priscilla Brown, b. ——; d. ——; six children; 2, May 1, 1759, Ruth Walker, b. ——; d. ——; two children; 3, July 15, 1764, Ann Wroe, b. ——; d. May 27, 1786; two children. He d. Aug. 27, 1778, in Boston.

    X. MERCY, b. Nov. 29, 1719, in Yarmouth, Mass. ; m. Mar. 10, 1735, John Scollay, b. ——; d. ——. She d. Oct. 7, 1793; thirteen children.

    XI. GOOKING, b. Sept. 18, 1721; d. Dec. 13, 1721.

    XII. SUSANNA, b. Nov. 12, 1722, in Yarmouth, Mass. ; m. John Coburn. She d. Feb. 26, 1782.

40.   XIII. WILLIAM[5] (Hon.), b. Jan. 10, 1725 ; m. June 3, 1747, Mary, dau. of Judge Robert Brown, of Plymouth, Mass., b. Mar. 15, 1728; d. Dec. 1, 1807. He d. July 21, 1803, at New Bedford ; fifteen children.

37.

(Rev. Daniel 4, Stephen 3, Stephen 2, Edmund 1.)

Children of Dr. **Daniel**[5] **Greenleaf** and Silence (Marsh).

    I. DAVID COFFIN, b. Jan. 29, 1728, at Hingham, Mass. ; d. Sept. 30, 1728, at Hingham, Mass.

    II. ELIZABETH, b. Oct. 30, 1729; marriage intention, Dec. 10, 1748; m. Jan. 6 or 16, 1750, Peter Joslyn, of Leominster or Lancaster, Mass., b. ——; d. ——; seven children :—

      i. Daniel.

      ii. Peter.

      iii. Samuel.

      iv. Calvin.

      v. Susan.

      vi. Percy.

      vii. Nabby.

41.   III. DANIEL[6] (Dr.), b. Sept. 2, 1732, at Hingham ; m. May 4 or 5, 1763, Anna Burrell, an English lady.

Dr. Daniel (37) Greenleaf, Continued :—

  III. Daniel.[6]

  He d. Jan. 18, 1777; three children, taken by the widow to England :—

   i. Daniel.
   ii. Silence.
   iii. Eleanor.

42. IV. Israel,[6] b. in Bolton, Mass., March 29, 1734; baptized March 31, 1734; m. Nov. 28, 1754, 1, Prudence Whitcomb, of Bolton, Mass., b. ——; d. Sept. 15, 1784; fourteen children; 2, March 10, 1785, Ursula Woods, b. Feb. 24, 1763; d. June 22, 1844; He was a farmer, and resided in Bolton for many years; eight children.

43. V. Stephen,[6] b. Oct. 15, 1735, in Boston; baptized Oct. 19, 1735; m. Jan. 11, 1758, Eunice Fairbanks, of Boston, b. ——; d. March 8, 1826; lived in Boston until 1771, when he removed to Brattleboro, Vt. He d. June 8, 1802; eleven children, six born in Boston, five in Brattleboro, Vt.

44. VI. David,[6] b. July 13, 1737, in Bolton, Mass.; m. June 2, 1763, Mary, dau. of Ebenezer and Deborah (Champion) Johnson, Ebenezer, b. Jan. 26, 1693, in Norwich, Ct.; m. Oct. 29, 1717; d. April 13, 1779. Deborah d. Aug. 22, 1778. Mary was b. April 7, 1738; d. May 1, 1814, in Hartford, Ct. David d. Dec. 11, 1800, in Coventry, Ct.; a goldsmith; resided in So. Coventry, Ct.; nine children.

45. VII. William[6] (Gen.), b. Aug. 23, 1738; baptized Aug. 27, 1738; m. Dec. 19, 1763, Sally, dau. of Edmund Quincy, of Boston, b. ——; d. March 12, 1790. He d. Jan. 13, 1793; resided in Boston first; moved to Lancaster, Mass., where he resided until his death; eight children.

46. VIII. Calvin,[6] b. March 31, 1740; m. Nov. 17, 1762, Rebecca Whitcomb, of Bolton, Mass., b. ——; d. Sept. 4, 1787. · He d. August, 1812; a farmer; resided in Bolton, Mass., on the homestead farm; eleven children.

Dr. Daniel (37) Greenleaf, Continued :—

IX. Mary, b. July 3, 1742 ; m. Jan. 8, 1760, Rev. Joseph Wheeler, of Harvard, Mass., b. ——— ; d. ———. She d. Aug. 28, 1783 ; resided in Worcester, Mass., 1781. A daughter m. Rev. Dr. Woods, of Andover, Mass.

X. John, b. June 13, 1744 ; d. Aug. 2, 1744.

38.

(Rev. Daniel 4, Stephen 3, Stephen 2, Edmund 1.)

Children of Hon. Stephen[5] Greenleaf and Mary (Gould).

I. Mary, b. Nov. 20, 1732 ; d. about 1820.

II. James Gould, b. Jan. 1, 1734 ; d. young.

III. Elizabeth, b. Dec. 10, 1738.

IV. Abigail, b. April 18, 1740 ; d. in infancy.

V. Anstice, b. Jan. 26, 1742 ; m. Benjamin Davis, a merchant in Boston and afterwards an officer in the Custom House ; d. 1775.

VI. Abigail, b. Sept. 18, 1743 ; m. ——— Howard,* a Judge of the Supreme Court of South Carolina, b. ——— ; d. ———, in England. She d. 1796 ; no children.

VII. Hannah, b. Aug. 28, 1744 ; m. John Apthorp, a merchant of Boston, b. Aug. 25, 1730 ; m. 1, Alicia, sister of Sir Horace Mann. He d ———, 1773 ; Hannah d. ———, 1773 ; lost with her husband in a storm at sea when going from New York to Charleston, S. C., on account of Mr. Apthorp's health. The family name is extinct in this line.

John Apthorp was son of Charles and Grizzell (Eastwicke). He (John) was brother to East Apthorp, who was the first Rector of Christ Church, Cambridge, Mass., in 1760, and died April 7, 1816, in Cambridge, England. One of the daughters married David Phipps, a Captain, and afterwards an Admiral in the British Navy. They resided in Bath, England, where she died. One of her sons was also an Admiral.

39.

(Rev. Daniel 4, Stephen 3, Stephen 2, Edmund 1.)

Children of Dr. John[5] Greenleaf and Priscilla (Brown). Children by first marriage.

I. A son, b. ———, 1745 ; d. in infancy. ⎫
II. A son, b. ———, 1745 ; d. in infancy. ⎬ Twins.

* Judge Howard left with the British troops in 1776, his wife dying a little previous.

Dr. John (39) Greenleaf, Continued :—

    III. Priscilla, b. Dec. 29, 1746; d. young. ⎫ Poisoned
    IV. Elizabeth, b. July 11, 1748; d. young. ⎬ by a slave
    V. John, b. Jan. 21, 1750; d. young. ⎭ nurse.
    VI. Daniel, b. July 24, 1757; d. young.

Children by second marriage :—

    VII. John, b. March 4, 1760; d. while a student of Harvard College.
    VIII. Isaac, b. July 25, 1761; d. young.

Children by third marriage :—

    IX. Elizabeth, b. Nov. 15, 1765; m. May, 1785, her cousin Daniel Greenleaf, son of Hon. William, b. Sept. 29, 1762; d. March 25, 1853, in Quincy, Mass. She d. Jan. 6, 1839; lived in Quincy; no children.

47.   X. Thomas [6] (Hon.), b. May 15, 1767; m. April 19, 1787, Mary Denning, dau. of Ezekiel and Ruth (Avery) Price, of Boston, b. ——; d. Feb. 21, 1855, aged 88 years. He d. Jan. 4, 1854; resided in Quincy, Mass. ; three children.

47.

(Dr. John 5, Rev. Daniel 4, Stephen 3, Stephen 2, Edmund 1.)

Children of Hon. **Thomas**[6] **Greenleaf** and Mary D. (Price).

    I. Ezekiel Price,[6] b. May 22, 1790, in Boston; single; d. Dec. 4, 1886, in Boston, Mass. ; residence, Quincy.
    II. Elizabeth, b. July 19, 1794; m. Feb. 19, 1835, William Greenleaf Appleton, of Quincy, Mass. She d. August, 1885 ; no children.
    III. Mary Ann Wroe, b. April 19, 1796; m. Dr. Ebenezer Woodward, of Quincy, Mass., b. March 12, 1798, in Cambridgeport; d. ——; no children. This branch of the family is extinct.

40.

(Rev. Daniel,[4] Stephen,[3] Stephen,[2] Edmund.[1])

Children of Hon. **William**[5] **Greenleaf** and Mary (Brown).

    I. Mary, b. March 15, 1748; d. infancy.
    II. Elizabeth, b. March 6, 1750; m. 1, May 7, 1771, Samuel Eliot,* a merchant of Boston, b. June 17,

---

*He was descended from Andrew Eliot, who came from Somersetshire, England, and settled at Beverly, Mass., about 1663.

HON. WILLIAM (40) GREENLEAF, CONTINUED :—
II. Elizabeth.

 1748, O. S.; d. March 2, 1784. 2. June 2, 1785, Judge Edward Pope,* of New Bedford, Mass., b. Feb. 25, 1740; d. June 10, 1818. She d. Dec. 4, 1841; children by 1st marriage, six :—

 i. Samuel, March 8, 1772; m. Oct. 28, 1806, Mary Johnson. He d. Oct. 17, 1822; eight children: 1. Catherine Mary, Oct. 24, 1807. 2. William Henry, b. April 3, 1809. 3. Henry Johnson, b. Dec. 2, 1810; d. July 18, 1814. 4. Charles, b. June 4, 1812; d. 1813. 5. Elizabeth Greenleaf, b. Jan. 19, 1814; d. July 18, 1814. 6. Johnson, b. Aug. 21, 1815. 7. George, b. May 3, 1817; d. 1818. 8. Wallace, b. Dec. 17, 1818.

 ii. Elizabeth, b. Jan. 2, 1774; m. March 30, 1798, John Ritchie She d. Dec. 17, 1847; six children: 1. Andrew, b. Dec. 31, 1798; d. Sept. 21, 1801. 2. Isabella, b. July 4, 1800; d. Sept. 13, 1801. 3. John Montgomery, b. April 8, 1802; d. June 8, 1805. 4. Mary, b. March 23, 1806; d. Oct. 3, 1817. 5. John, b. Nov. 22, 1809; d. Nov. 9, 1811. 6. Edward Samuel, b. Aug. 18, 1814; d. June 1, 1895, in Newton, Mass.

 iii. Mary, b. Sept. 19, 1775; m. March 29, 1801, James G. Almy. She d. Sept. 3, 1809; five children: 1. Edward Pope, b. April 8, 1802, at Nassau. 2. William Hield, b. Sept. 10, 1803, in Georgia; d. 1822. 3. Myra Matthews Johnston, b. March 1, 1805, in Georgia; m. David H. Robertson, Jan. 11, 1825. 4. Elizabeth Greenleaf, b. April 25, 1808, in New Bedford, Mass.; d. Jan. 18, 1854. 5. A son, b. and d. Sept. 2, 1809, in Savannah.

 iv. Andrew, b. Nov. 14, 1777; d. Aug. 4, 1783.

 v. Susanna, b. Dec. 19, 1779; m. April 25, 1802, John Rounseville Spooner, who d. March 17, 1844. She d. April 25, 1846; two children: 1. Edward Pope, b. March 22, 1803. 2. Walter, b. Oct. 17, 1814.

 vi. William Greenleaf, b. Dec. 25, 1781; m. July 14, 1807, Margaret Geenleaf Dawes, b. Dec. 6, 1789; d. June 15, 1875. He d. Dec. 16, 1853. . They were cousins; she was the daughter of Thomas Dawes, who married Margaret Greenleaf, daughter of Hon. William Greenleaf. Children: 1. Thomas Dawes, b. March 20, 1808; m. Nov. 3, 1834, Frances Lincoln Brock, of Nantucket, Mass., a descendant of Tristram Coffin, b. Oct. 1, 1815. He d. June 14, 1870; 2. Hannah Dawes, b. June 10, 1809; m. Oct. 27, 1828, Thomas Lamb. She d. Oct. 29, 1879. 3. Rev. William Greenleaf, b. Aug. 5, 1811; m June 29, 1837, Abigail Adams Cranch, of Alexandria, Va., his second cousin, and daughter of Hon. William and Nancy (Greenleaf)

* Edward Pope, m. 1st, Elizabeth Bullard. He was Judge of the Court of Common Pleas, and Collector of the Port of New Bedford, Mass.

Hon. William (40) Greenleaf, Continued :—
  II. Elizabeth.
      Cranch. She was b. Feb. 20, 1817. He d. Jan. 23, 1887. 4.
      Elizabeth Margaret, b. July 21, 1819; m. Oct. 25, 1838, James
      Thwing Furness, b. March 6, 1812. 5. Nancy Cranch, b. Dec.
      25, 1822; d. Sept. 4, 1823. 6. Francis Andrew, b. Aug. 8,
      1825; m. Mary Johnston Whipple; no children. He d. May
      3, 1862. 7. Horace, b. Feb. 12, 1828; d. Feb. 4, 1831. 8.
      Caroline, b. March 8, 1830; m. May 2, 1850, 1, John A Kas-
      son. Divorced; m. 2, Jan. 26, 1869, Rufus J. Lackland; no
      children. She d. Aug. 1, 1892.

  Children by 2d marriage, four :—
      vii. Edward, b. July 18, 1787 : m. Charlotte, daughter of Duncan,
      and Susanna (Greenleaf) Ingraham, his cousin.
      viii. Thomas, b. April 7, 1789.
      ix. Juliana, b. Oct. 10, 1791.
      x. A daughter, b. and d. April 2, 1795.
  Children of David H. and Myra M. J. (Almy) Robertson. (1)
      James David, b. November, 1825, in New York. (2) Marga-
      ret Elizabeth, b. Sept. 3, 1827. (3) Edward, b. July 30, 1829.
      (4) Myra Eliot, b. March 18, 1831. (5) Catherine Green-
      leaf, b. Aug. 21, 1832. (6) William Eliot, b. Nov. 14, 1834.
      (7) Charles S., b. February, 1837; d. October, 1838. Mrs.
      M. M. J. Robertson d. August, 1847.
  Children of Thomas Dawes and Frances L. (Brock) Eliot. (1)
      Caroline Dawes, b. Sept. 14, 1835; m. (2) Paul Mitchell,
      b. Sept. 13, 1837; d. 1859. (3) Eliza (Ida) Mitchell, b.
      Oct. 9, 1839. (4) Margaret Dawes, b. April 21, 1842; d.
      Aug. 2, 1843. (5) Frances, b. Sept. 3, 1844; m (6) Mary
      Rotch, b. Oct. 9, 1847; m. (7) Emily Lamb, b. March 25,
      1851. (8) Edith, b. Sept. 24, 1854.
  Children of Thomas and Hannah D. (Eliot) Lamb. (1) Emily
      Goddard, b. Sept. 19, 1829; m.; d. Feb. 5, 1894. (2)
      Margaret Eliot, b. Oct. 11, 1831; m. June 3, 1856, Wil-
      liam Ogilvie Comstock. He b. May 11, 1815, d. April 12, 1883;
      eight children : [1]Amelia W., [2]William O., [3]Thomas L., [4]Mar-
      garet E., [5]Samuel W., [6]Mabel, [7]Louisa W., [8]Susan W. She
      d. Jan. 27, 1878. (3) Thomas, b. June 10, 1834; d. Jan. 10,
      1838. (4) Hannah Eliot, b. Aug. 12, 1836; d. Jan. 29, 1838.
      (5) William Eliot, b. March 20, 1839. (6) Charles Duncan,
      b. May 13, 1841; d. Sept. 2, 1871. (7) Rosanna Dun-
      can, b. June 27, 1843. (8) Caroline, b. Jan. 6, 1846; d.
      Feb. 11, 1849. (9) Horatio Appleton, b. Jan. 11, 1850; m.
  Children of Rev. William G. and Abigail Adams (Cranch) Eliot.
      (1) Mary Rhodes, b. May 11, 1838; d. Jan. 6, 1855. (2)
      William Cranch, b. Nov. 26, 1839; d. Nov. 24, 1841.
      (3) Thomas Lamb, b. Oct. 13, 1841; m. Nov. 28, 1865,
      Henrietta Robbins Mack; eight children : [1]William Green-

Hon. William (40) Greenleaf, Continued :—
  II. Elizabeth.

leaf, b. Oct. 13, 1866; m. Clara Lessingham. [2]Mary
Ely, b. Sept. 22, 1868; d. April 21, 1878. [3]Dorothy.
Dix, b. Feb. 14, 1871. [4]Ellen Smith, b. Feb. 20, 1873.
[5]Grace Cranch, b. Sept. 13, 1875. [6]Henrietta Mack, b. Dec.
17, 1879. [7]Samuel Ely, b. May 22, 1882. [8]Thomas Dawes,
b. June 19, 1889. (4) Henry Ware, b. Nov. 25, 1843; m.
Oct. 27, 1868, Charlotte Champ Stearns; seven children:
[1]Abigail Adams, b. Sept. 30, 1869. [2]Margaret Dawes, b,
Dec. 2, 1871. [3]Charlotte Chauncey, b. Oct. 29, 1874.
[4]Marion Cushing, b. July 25, 1877. [5]Henry Ware, b. Dec. 7,
1879. [c]Theodore Sterling, b. July 25, 1885; d. Dec. 5, 1886.
[7]Thomas Stearns, b. April 26, 1888. (5) Elizabeth Cranch,
b. Dec. 7, 1845; d. Dec. 16, 1845. (6) Abby Adams, b. Dec.
17, 1847; d. Feb. 20, 1864. (7) Margaret Dawes, b. July 25,
1849; d. Oct. 9, 1858. (8) Frank Andrews, b. Feb. 28, 1851;
d. Jan. 18, 1857. (9) Sarah, b. and d. Feb. 8, 1853. (10)
Christopher Rhodes, b. Jan. 20, 1856; m. Mary Jackson May,
Sept. 7, 1888; three children: [1]Frederick May, b. Sept. 27,
1889. [2]Martha May, b. April ——. [3]Abigail Adams, b.
Oct. 9, 1892. (11) William Smith, b. Feb. 5, 1857; d. Aug.
6, 1857. (12) Edward Cranch, b. July 3, 1858; m. Mary
Augusta Monroe, Nov. 1, 1883; three children: [1]Edward
Monroe, b. Jan. 15, 1885. [2]Frank Monroe, b. Dec. 25, 1886.
[3]Alice Monroe, b. June 16, 1889. (13) John, b. Jan. 6, 1860;
d. Jan. 19, 1862. (14) Rose Greenleaf, b. Feb. 5, 1862.
Children of James Thwing and Elizabeth M. (Eliot) Furness.
(1) William Eliot, b. Aug. 20, 1839; m. Lucy Wadsworth;
had four children. (2) James Gill, b. Aug. 10, 1841; d.
April, 1845. (3) Charles Eliot, b. July 22, 1844; m. ——
Ramsey; had two children. (4) Dawes Eliot, b. Nov. 11,
1846. (5) George Eliot, b. March 4, 1849; d. July, 1850.
(6) Margaret Eliot, b. July 6, 1851; d. July 22, 1854. (7)
Rebekah Thwing, b. Oct. 13, 1854. (8) Laura, b. Sept. 9,
1857.

III. Mary, b. May 15, 1752; m. April 20, 1775, Daniel
  Bell, b. Dec. 28, 1752; d. Oct. 15, 1791. She d.
  Oct. 5, 1836; nine children :—

i. Daniel, b. April 20, 1776.
ii. William Greenleaf, b. March 28, 1778.
iii. Charlotte Williams, b. July 31, 1780.
iv. Mary Brown, b. Aug. 17, 1781.
v. George, b. Nov. 15, 1783.
vi. Henry, b. July 27, 1786.
vii. Rufus, b. April 14, 1788.
viii. Harriet, b. Aug. 8, 1790.
ix. Deziah Barker, b. Oct. 23, 1791.

Hon. William (40) Greenleaf, Continued :—

    IV. Susanna, b. Feb. 6, 1754; m. July 26, 1774, Capt.
Duncan Ingraham, Jr., b. Dec. 2, 1752, in Boston;
d. June 16, 1804, at Greenvale Farm, near Poughkeepsie, N. Y. She d. Feb. 24, 1832; twelve children :—

     i. Duncan, b. April 25, 1775; m. May 3, 1806, Mary E. De Costa,
daughter of the British Consul at Calcutta. Residence Calcutta, E. I. He d. June 16, 1835, at Calcutta; six children:
1. Louisa, b. June 22, 1807; d. May 11, 1826. 2. Edward, b.
Sept. 4, 1808; d. June 2, 1809. 3. James, b. Sept. 23, 1812;
d. May 28, 1819. 4. Walter, b. Jan. 6, 1814, attended Kenyon
College, Ohio. 5. Emily, b. Sept. 24, 1815. 6. Ellen, b.
Aug. 1, 1817. Mary E. De Costa's mother, the wife of the
British Consul, was a half-blood native of Calcutta.

    ii. Susan (Sukey), b. Oct. 27, 1776; d. Oct. 14, 1777.

   iii. William, b. Aug. 31, 1778; d. Dec. 25, 1802. Killed by Indians at Nootka Sound.

   iv. Susan Coburn, b. May 4, 1780; m. March 23, 1816, Dr.
Samuel Perry, b. Nov. 19, 1763; d. Oct. 26, 1820. She d.
Sept. 29, 1841, at New Bedford, Mass.; three children:
1. Leonard Kip, b. Feb. 23, 1817; d. Nov. 19, 1836. 2.
George Ingraham, b. Dec. 17, 1818; d. May 7, 1842. 3. Dun-
can Ingraham, b. Sept. 3, 1820.

    v. John, b. March 14, 1782; d. March 17, 1782.

   vi. Sophia May, b. Feb. 3, 1783, in Amsterdam, Holland: m. July
4, 1819, Rt. Rev. Philander Chase, D.D., b. Dec. 14, 1775,
in Cornish, N. H.; d. Sept. 20, 1852, at Robbin's Nest, Ill.
Last years of his life spent at Robbin's Nest, Ill., near Jubilee
College, which he founded in 1837. She d. Dec., 1864, at
Robbin's Nest; three children: 1. Henry Ingraham, b. Oct.
7, 1820; m. Susan Greenleaf, daughter of Henry E. Ingraham, Nov. 7, 1841 (his cousin). 2. Mary Chamberlain, b.
Feb. 15, 1822. 3. Philander Ingraham, b. June 8, 1824; m.
Anna Kip, May 14, 1843, daughter of Henry E. Ingraham
(his cousin). He d. April 24, 1872.

   vii. Maria, b. Nov. 17, 1784; m. Dec. 12, 1809, Leonard Kip, b.
Aug. 8, 1774; d. July 2, 1846. She d. May 26, 1877, at
Albany, N. Y.; six children: 1. William Ingraham, b. Oct.
3, 1811; m. July 1, 1835, Maria Elizabeth, daughter of Isaac
Lawrence, Esq., of New York; two children: (1) Lawrence.
(2) William Ingraham, b. Jan. 15, 1840. Secretary to United
States Legation to Japan, 1861–62. Resides San Francisco,
Cal. 2. Elizabeth, b. Aug. 7, 1814; m. Oct. 26, 1836, Rev.
Henry L. Storrs, Rector of St. John's Church, Yonkers,
N. Y.; three children: (1) Eliza. (2) Maria. (3) Leon-
ard Kip, Rector of St. Stephen's Church, Pittsfield, Mass.

HON. WILLIAM (40) GREENLEAF, CONTINUED:—

IV. Susanna.

3. Sophia, b. Oct. 24, 1816; m. Oct. 26, 1846, Rt. Rev. George Burgess, D.D., Bishop of Maine. 4. Anna Maria, b. Dec. 4, 1818. 5. Mary, b. Feb. 16, 1823; m. Jan. 27, 1848, John James Kane. 6. Leonard, b. Sept. 13, 1826; m. Oct. 26, 1852, Harriet Letitia, daughter of John S. Van Rensselaer, of Albany, N. Y. Leonard Kip is a lawyer and author. Residence, Albany, N. Y.

viii. George, b. Sept. 1, 1786; m. April 16, 1821, Clarissa Parsons, of Kingston, N. Y.; d. 1887. He d. May 17, 1830; five children : 1. Anna Maria, b. Feb. 12, 1822. 2. Duncan, b. Dec. 19, 1823; m. Julia L. Sudam; had three children : only one, Mary H., is now living at Kingston, N. Y. They lived in Memphis, Tenn. 3. Leonard Chester, b. July 25, 1826; d. Aug. 8, 1828. 4 and 5. George William and William Henry, twins, b. Aug. 1, 1829; both d. young.

ix. Charlotte, b. July 25, 1788; m. July 24, 1815, Col. Edward Pope, b. July 18, 1787; d. Feb. 15, 1842, son of Elizabeth (Greenleaf) and Edward Pope (her cousin). She d. April 4, 1865, at New Bedford, Mass.; three children : 1. Edward, b. Sept. 14, 1816. 2. Susan Greenleaf, b. Jan. 2, 1819; m. Walter Spooner. 3. Samuel Perry, b. March 4, 1852.

x. Henry E., b. Nov. 3, 1790, at Hudson, N. Y.; m. July 19, 1815, Content, daughter of William Wilson, New York City, b. Feb. 13, 1795; d. Sept. 14, 1840. He d. Dec. 20, 1852, at Jubilee, Ill. Residence, Kickapoo, Ill.; eleven children: 1. Henrietta, b. Jan. 17, 1817; m. April, 1842, Lewis C. Lighthipe, of Orange, N. J. She d. Feb. 7, 1858; six children. 2. Agnes Ann, b. July 5, 1818; d. July 9, 1820. 3. William, b. May 3, 1820; d. Feb. 3, 1821. 4 and 5. Susan Greenleaf and Janet Suffern, twins, b. April 14, 1822. Susan G. m. Nov. 7, 1841, Henry I., son of Rt. Rev. Philander Chase, D.D. (her cousin); eleven children. Janet S. m. Nov. 8, 1841, 1, Thomas L. Bennett; 2, Henry I. Chase; four children. 6. Anna Kip, b. June 10, 1824; m. May 14, 1843, Philander I., son of Rt. Rev. Philander Chase, D.D. (her cousin). She d. Nov. 26, 1893; ten children. 7. William Wilson, b. July 24, 1826; m. twice; d. June 9, 1888; ten children. 8. Agnes, b. Nov. 3, 1828; m. Henry H. Mayo, b. Nov. 3, 1828; five children. 9. Edward Henry, b. Jan. 25, 1832; d. July 15, 1894; no children. 10. Virginius, b. Jan. 30, 1834; unm.; d. Aug. 3, 1860; killed at sea by falling from aloft to the deck. 11. Duncan Greenleaf, b. April 10, 1838; m. Oct. 15, 1865, 1, Eliza A. Stickney; d. Aug. 19, 1866; one child; m. 2, Aug. 12, 1868, Marion Mason. Residence, Waitsburg, Washington; five children : (1) Anna May, b. 1869. (2) Janet Content, b. 1871. (3)

Hon. William (40) Greenleaf, Continued :—

   IV. Susanna.

   Sophia Marion, b. 1874. (4) Duncan Edward, b. 1883. (5)
   William Henry, b. 1884.

   xi. Eliza, b. June 13, 1793, at Poughkeepsie, N. Y.; m. Dec. 28,
   1824, J. H. Jansen, who d. July 3, 1847. She d. 1869; no children.

   xii. Frances Greenleaf, b. Aug. 26, 1796, at Poughkeepsie, N. Y.;
   m. Feb. 13, 1827, Rev. William Sparrow, D.D., of Alexandria,
   Va., who d. Jan 18, 1874. She d. Feb., 1873; ten children:
   1. Mary Roe, b. Sept. 17, 1827; m. Rev. J. A. Jerome. 2.
   Susan Ingraham, b. July 22, 1830; m. Rev. D. D. Smith.
   3. Frances Greenleaf, b. March 24, 1832. 4. Maria Kip, b.
   April 16, 1833; d. Dec. 17, 1834. 5. Elizabeth Ann, b. Aug.
   6, 1834; m. Rev. J. E. Grammer. 6. Wilhelmina, b. Nov.
   1, 1835; m. July 14, 1854, Rev. T. G. Dashiel; d. 1861. 7.
   William Edward, b. Feb. 18, 1838. 8. Thomas Wing, b.
   Aug. 28, 1839. 9. Leonard Kip, b. Oct. 30, 1841. 10. Catherine, b. July 30, 1843; m. Dec. 22, 1864, Rev. T. G. Dashiel.

   V. Priscilla, b. Oct. 25, 1755; m. March 18, 1794,
   John Appleton, of Salem, b. March 30, 1739, in
   Cambridge, Mass.; d. March 5, 1817. She d. June
   6, 1826. Mr. Appleton m. first, Oct. 6, 1767, Jane,
   dau. of Rev. John Sparhawk. She d. June 30, 1790;
   two children :—

   i. Alfred Greenleaf, b. Dec. 21, 1794, at Salem, Mass.; d. at Calcutta, July 6, 1865.
   ii. A daughter, b. Nov. 24, 1796.

   VI. Sarah, b. March 19, 1757; m. 1, June 29, 1780,
   Dr. Nathan W. Appleton, b. June 14, 1755; d.
   April 15, 1795; 2, Nov. 3, 1814, Joseph Haven, of
   Portsmouth, N. H., who d. 1838. She d. Jan. 2,
   1838; seven children by 1st marriage :—

   i. Sally, b. April 18, 1781; d. 1790.
   ii. Nathaniel Walker, b. Feb. 13, 1783.
   iii. Charles, b. Dec. 26, 1784.
   iv. George, b. Jan. 4, 1787; d. 1796.
   v. Mary, b. Nov. 21, 1789; m. Aug. 31, 1824, John Welch Foster,
   of Portland, Me.
   vi. William Greenleaf, b. Jan 7, 1791, in Boston.
   vii. Sarah, b. 1793, in Boston.

   VII. William, b. July 10, 1758; d. in infancy.

   VIII. William, b. Feb. 5, 1760, in Boston; d. Nov. 24,
   1778.

   IX. Margaret, b. May 22, 1761; m. Oct. 4, 1781, Hon.
   Thomas Dawes, b. July 8, 1757; d. July 21, 1825.

Hon. William (40) Greenleaf, Continued :—

IX. Margaret.

She d. March 21, 1836; buried in King's Chapel Burying Ground; sixteen children :—

    i. Margaret (Peggy), b. June 23, 1782; d. July 7, 1782.

    ii. Thomas, b. April 26, 1783; m. Aug. 29, 1815, Eliza Cunningham. He d. July 29, 1825.

    iii. Emily, b. May 29, 1785; m. 1804, Samuel B. Goddard. She d. 1840.

    iv. Hannah, b. Jan. 8, 1787; m. Nov. 5, 1807, Charles H. Appleton.

    v. Margaret Greenleaf, b. Dec. 6, 1789; m. William G. Eliot. She d. June 15, 1875.

    vi. James Greenleaf, b. July 10, 1792; d. July 18, 1815; drowned.

    vii. Harrison (Otis?), b. May 14, 1794; m. Aug. 15, 1820, Lucy Greenleaf (his cousin). He d. Jan. 27, 1835.

    viii. Elizabeth, b. July 3, 1795; m. 1, Francis A. Blake; no children; 2, Joseph Robert Cowdin; three children.

    ix. Anna, b. July 18, 1796; d. December, 1871; unmarried.

    x. Sarah Appleton, b. Nov. 28, 1797; m. Sept. 2, 1828, James T. Hayward.

    xi. Horatio, b. Dec. 7, 1798; d. Sept. 4, 1799.

    xii. Mary Greenleaf, b. Aug. 26, 1800; unmarried.

    xiii. George Minot, b. Jan. 25, 1802; m. April 4, 1827, Mary Elizabeth Greenleaf (his cousin). He d. Nov. 19, 1871.

    xiv. Rufus, b. Jan. 27, 1803; m. May 18, 1829, Elizabeth Eliot Cranch (his cousin), b. Feb. 8, 1805. He d. Nov. 29, 1859; no children.

    xv. Susan, b. Jan. 30, 1804; unmarried.

    xvi. Horatio, b. Aug. 20, 1805; m. Eliza (Cunningham), widow of his brother Thomas.

48. X. Daniel,[6] b. Sept. 29, 1762; m. May 25, 1785, Elizabeth, dau. of Dr. John Greenleaf, b. Nov. 15, 1765; d. Jan. 6, 1839. He d. March 25, 1853; res., Quincy, Mass.; no children.

49. XI. John,[6] b. Sept. 10, 1763; m. April 4, 1795, Lucy Cranch, b. Sept. 16, 1767; d. Feb. 18, 1846. He d. March 29, 1848; res., Quincy, Mass.; seven children.

50. XII. James,[6] b. June 9, 1765; m. 1, 1788, Antonia Cornelia Elbertine Scoten (or Schotten); divorced; m. 2, April 26, 1800, Ann Penn, dau. of James Allen, b. Feb. 19, 1772. He d. Sept. 17, 1843, in Washington, D. C.

Children by 1st marriage :—

    i. William Christian James, b. Sept. 6, 1790; unmarried.

HON. WILLIAM (40) GREENLEAF, CONTINUED :—

   XII. James.[6]

      II. Marie Josephine Wilhelmine Matilda, m. William
        Antoine Schwartz, Lieut. of Artillery; res. Flush-
        ing, in the Province of Zealand. The marriage is
        attested by the Mayor of Flushing and by a Com-
        mission at Middleburg, Zealand.

    Children by 2d marriage :—

      III. Mary, b. Jan. 31, 1802; m. Walter C. Livingston,
        of Philadelphia, Penn.; res. Philadelphia: two
        children, a son and a daughter.

      IV. Margaret, b. 1803 ; m. —— Dale, of Allentown,
        Penn. ; had one child. These two daughters, Mary
        and Margaret, were reputed the belles of Washing-
        ton society about the time of the administration of
        the second Adams.

    Ann Penn Allen was the daughter of James Allen, the founder of
    Allentown, Penn., and son of William Allen, Chief Justice of
    the Province before the Revolution. Her mother was Eliza-
    beth Laurence, a granddaughter of the distinguished Tench
    Francis, the accredited author of "Junius."

   XIII. REBECCA, b. May 27, 1766; m. Oct. 26, 1789 [see
     Hartford Courant, Nov. 2, 1789], Noah Webster,
     LL.D., of New Haven, Conn., the lexicographer, b.
     Oct. 16, 1758; d. May 28, 1843. She d. June 25,
     1847; eight children :—

    i. Emily Schotten, b. Aug. 4, 1790; m. Sept. 14, 1813, Gov. Wil-
      liam Wolcott Ellsworth, son of Chief Justice Oliver Ells-
      worth (William W. Ellsworth was governor of Connecticut
      several terms), b. Nov. 10, 1791; d. Jan. 15, 1868. She d.
      Aug. 23, 1861; six children: 1. Pinckney Webster, M.D., b.
      Dec. 5, 1814; m. 1, April 27, 1841, Julia M. Sterling, of
      Bridgeport, Conn., who d. March 18, 1854; 2, Dec. 9, 1856,
      Julia Townsend Dow, New Haven, Conn. 2. Emily, b.
      Sept. 27, 1816; m. April 27, 1841, Rev. Abner Jackson, D.D.,
      President of Trinity College, Hartford, Conn., b. Nov. 4,
      1811, of Scottish parentage, near Washington, Penn.; grad-
      uate of Trinity College; was tutor and professor there also;
      admitted to Priesthood of Protestant Episcopal Church, May
      30, 1847. After twenty-five years of life in Trinity College
      as student, tutor, and professor, he was called to the Presi-
      dency of Hobart College, in Geneva, N. Y., 1858, and con-
      tinued in it till 1867, when he returned to Trinity College as
      its President, and labored there till his death, April 19, 1874.

HON. WILLIAM (40) GREENLEAF, CONTINUED :—
XIII. Rebecca.

Trinity College conferred on him the degree of D.D., and Columbia College gave him the degree of LL.D. She d. July 1, 1853; their child, Emily Elizabeth, b. Nov. 12, 1845, m. April 8, 1869, Philip Norborne Nicholas, a lawyer; resided at Geneva, N. Y. He was Trustee of Hobart College, in Geneva; also a member of the State Board of Control of the Agricultural Experiment Station located at Geneva. He was b. March 26, 1845. The family is one of the earliest in Geneva, going there from Virginia, in 1803 or 4. One Nicholas was Governor of Virginia, while his brother was Governor of Kentucky. The Nicholas who came up from Virginia became the first Judge of Ontario County. 3. Harriet, b. July 4, 1818; m. Dec. 23, 1845, Rev. Russell S. Cook, Secretary American Tract Society; d. Feb. 24, 1848. 4. Oliver, b. Dec. 13, 1820; m. 1, June 14, 1854, Caroline C., only child of Roswell C. Smith, author of Smith's Grammar, Smith's Arithmetic, etc., b. Dec. 18, 1829; d. July 31, 1866, Hartford, Conn.; 2, Aug. 13, 1868, Mary W. Janvrin, Exeter, N. H., b. Sept. 7, 1830; d. Aug. 12, 1870; 3, Nov. 15, 1871, Orah A., a sister of Mary, b. July 1, 1836; d. Sept. 3, 1882. Oliver d. Nov. 10, 1878. 5. Elizabeth, b Nov. 17, 1822; d. Jan. 20, 1823. 6. Elizabeth, b. June 8, 1824; m. Dec. 14, 1853, Hon. Waldo Hutchins, New York, b. Sept. 30, 1822, in Brooklyn, Conn.

ii. Frances Julianna, b. Feb. 5, 1793; m. Oct. 1, 1816, Chauncey Allen Goodrich, Professor Pastoral Theology, Yale College; d. Aug. 17, 1869; res. New Haven, Conn; four children: 1. Chauncey (Rev.), b. July 20, 1817; m. Elizabeth E. Coe. He d. March 27, 1868; one child: Edward Elizur; 2. William Henry (Rev.), b. Jan. 19, 1823; m. Mary Pritchard. He d. July 11, 1874; five children: (1) Mary Pritchard. (2) Julia Webster. (3) Frances Louisa. (4) Ellen Chauncey. (5) Chauncey William. 3. Julia Webster, b. Sept. 20, 1828; m. Rev. George E. Hill. She d. Oct. 14, 1851. 4. Frances Louisa, b. March 6, 1832; m. H. K. W. Welsh. She d. Dec. 2, 1855.

iii. Harriet, b. April 6, 1797; m. 1, May 22, 1816, Edward H. Cobb, who d. 1818; 2, July 21, 1825, William Chauncey Fowler, Professor in Amherst College. She d. March 30, 1844; children by second marriage: 1. Emily Ellsworth, b. Aug. 26, 1826. 2. Charles Chauncey, b. Oct. 8, 1829; m. Oct. 19, 1864, Mary Camp; d. Oct. 30, 1876; children: (1) Harriet Webster, b. June 28, 1866. (2) Catherine Worthington, b. Aug. 31, 1869. (3) Charles Chauncey, b. April 9, 1873. 3. William Worthington, b. June 24, 1832. 4. Webster Winthrop, b. March 3, 1835.

iv. Mary, b. Jan. 7, 1799; m. May 10, 1818, Horatio Southgate, a widower, Portland, Me. He had several sons by his former marriage; one was Robert, the Bishop. She d. Feb. 28, 1819.

Hon. William (40) Greenleaf, Continued :—

XIII. Rebecca.

v. William Greenleaf, b. Sept. 15, 1801; m. May 5, 1830, Rosalie
Eugenia, dau. of Dr. David and Eleanor Calvert (Custis)
Stuart, of Faulkner County, Va.   She d. Oct. 19, 1886, in
Annapolis, Md. He d. Jan. 1, 1869; four children: 1. William
Eugene, b. Aug. 28, 1831, in New Haven, Conn.; m. Oct. 13,
1858, Fanny Lynn, b. May 27, 1834, in Cumberland, Md.
He d. June 27, 1862; two children: (1) Rosalia Eugenia
Stuart, b. Aug. 2, 1859; m. June 6, 1883, Judge Daniel Randall Magruder, of Annapolis, Md.; children: [1]Rosalie Stuart,
b. March 9, 1884. [2]Daniel Randall, b. Nov. 15, 1885. [3]Eugene
Webster, b. Jan. 27, 1888.   [4]Cecilus Calvert, b. Dec. 26, 1893.
(2) Rebecca Lynn, b. June 23, 1861, Annapolis, Md.   2. Calvert Stuart, b. Nov. 4, 1832, in New Haven, Conn.; d. Aug.
9, 1862, in New Haven, Conn.   He was a lieutenant in the
Union Army, Civil War.   3. Eleanor Rebecca, b. in Cincinnati, O.; d. in Winchester, Va., when about one year old.
4. Washington Calvert, b. in New Haven, Conn.; d. in
infancy.

At sixteen years of age Eleanor Calvert, of Maryland, a descendant
of Lord Baltimore, married John Park Custis, son of Mrs.
Washington.   He died at Yorktown during the siege.   His
widow and four children lived at Mt. Vernon; two of them,
George Washington Park Custis (father of Mrs. Robert E. Lee)
and Nellie Custis (who married Colonel Lewis, Washington's
nephew), appear with their mother in Rosciter's painting of
Mt. Vernon.   Mrs. Custis married again, Dr. David Stuart,
her first husband's executor and her children's guardian.   This
second marriage was approved by both General and Mrs.
Washington, as shown by letters and valuable gifts, now in
possession of Miss Rebecca L. Webster and her sister, Mrs.
Judge Magruder.   Doctor and Mrs. Stuart lived about two
miles from Mt. Vernon.

William Eugene Webster was educated at West Point, and was an
officer in the Confederate service.   He was drawn into the
Confederate cause by his attachment to General Lee, and Mrs.
Lee, who was his cousin.   He was in the seven-day fight
before Richmond, Va., and was killed in the battle of Cold
Harbor, and is buried in Richmond.   His name is inscribed
on a monument in Alexandria, Va., recently erected in memory of the officers who fell in the late war.   His daughter
Rebecca has a fine collection of Washington souvenirs,—a
collection quite celebrated: personal effects of General and
Mrs. Washington given after his death by Mrs. Washington
to the young Stuarts, her step-grandchildren, their mother
having been the widow of Washington Park Custis, her
grandson.   " She gave these miniatures, watch, flute, hair of
General Washington, dresses she had worn, of rich brocade,

Hon. William (40) Greenleaf, Continued:—

XIII. Rebecca.

gold snuffbox she had used," etc., says her niece, Mrs. E. E. Hutchins, "to my aunt's oldest sisters, who died unmarried, and gave them to my aunt, Mrs. William Greenleaf Webster, who was only two years old when Mrs. Washington died."

Fanny Lynn, wife of William Eugene Webster, was granddaughter of Capt. David Lynn, of the Revolutionary Army. He was son of Judge David Lynn, of Frederick, Maryland.

vi. Eliza Steele Greenleaf, b. Dec. 21, 1803; m. Sept. 5, 1825, Rev. Henry Jones, b. Sept. 5, 1803. She d. Nov. 16, 1888. She was the Belle of Bridgeport, Conn., to the time of her death; four children: 1. Frances Juliana, b. July 15, 1826; m. Jan. 21, 1857, Rev. Thomas K. Beecher, of Elmira, N. Y., a brother of Rev. Henry Ward Beecher. 2. Emily Ellsworth, b. Nov. 8, 1828; m. September, 1850, Daniel Jones Day, who belonged to the family of President Day, of Yale College, the famous mathematician. She d. July 28, 1869. Child: Robert W., b. Oct. 9, 1854; m. May 15, ——, Helen Leonard West; children: [1]Emily W. D., b. Feb. 21, 1879; [2]Rodney W. D., b. July 10, 1883. 3. Eliza Webster, b. 1833; d. in infancy. 4. Henry Webster, b. March 10, 1836; m. Annie Maria Ward. Child: Eliza Webster, b. February, 1859; d. in infancy.

vii. Bradford Greenleaf, b. Nov. 20, 1806; d. in ten weeks.

viii. Louisa Greenleaf, b. April 12, 1808; unmarried.

Children of Dr. Pinckney Webster and Julia T. (Dow) Ellsworth. (1) Julia Sterling, b. June 27, 1860; m. 1883, Augustus Julian, son of the late Bishop Lyman, of North Carolina; a lawyer; res. Asheville, N. C.; child: Ellsworth. (2) Emily Webster, b. May 21, 1864; res. Hartford, Conn. (3) Harriet, b. June 15, 1865; d. 1868. (4) Wolcott Webster, b. Oct. 25, 1867; m. Sept. 18, 1895, Leah Louise, dau. of Edward von Wettburg, of Hartford, Conn. Rev. W. W. Ellsworth is a clergyman Protestant Episcopal Church, graduate of Yale College; res. Unionville, a suburb of Hartford, Conn. (5) Ernest Bradford, b. April 27, 1870; law student, New Haven Law School: graduate of Yale College. (6) Edith Townsend, b. Feb. 4, 1872. (7) Alice Greenleaf, b. Oct. 6, 1877.

Child of Oliver and Caroline Cleveland (Smith) Ellsworth. William Webster, b. Oct. 30, 1855, m. June 4, 1878, Helen Yale, dau. of Morris W. and Julia P. Smith, of Hartford, Conn., b. June 5, 1855. Mr. William W. Ellsworth is secretary of the *Century Magazine;* their children: [1]Lucy Morris, b. April 27, 1879. [2]Bradford, b. Oct. 31, 1880. [3]Helen Adelaide, b. April 13, 1882. [4]Elizabeth, b. Jan. 27, 1892.

No children by second marriage. Children by third marriage: (1) Oliver, b. Aug. 22, 1873. (2) Emily, b. July 4, 1875.

Hon. William (40) Greenleaf, Continued :—

XIII. Rebecca.

Children of Hon. Waldo and Elizabeth (* Ellsworth) Hutchins.
(1) Julia Stirling, b. July 17, 1855; m. May 22, 1879, Henry
G. Wolcott, Fishkill on Hudson; their children : [1]Oliver, b.
March 11, 1880; d. Dec. 28, 1893. [2]Charles Mosley, b. Aug.
11, 1882. [3]Henry Goodrich, b. March 2, 1884; d. Aug. 10,
1885. [4]Elizabeth Ellsworth, b. Sept. 8, 1886. [5]Katharine
Rankin, b. Aug. 16, 1888. [6]Julia Hutchins, b. July 1, 1892.
(2) Augustus Schell, b. Nov. 11, 1856. (3) Waldo, b. Sept.
20, 1858; m. Oct. 18, 1894, Agnes Johnston Swan, Geneva,
N. Y.; one child : Waldo, b. Sept. 4, 1895. (4) William Ellsworth, b. Sept. 18, 1861; President of the North River Fire Insurance Company; the oldest fire insurance company in New
York City. Augustus Schell and Waldo Hutchins are lawyers.

Child of Horatio and Mary (Webster) Southgate : Mary Webster,
b. Feb. 5, 1819; m. July 24, 1838, Henry Trowbridge, of New
Haven, Conn. She d. May 2, 1860; children : (1) Mary
Webster, b. May 13, 1839; m. 1, May 13, 1857, Frederick
Hall, of Portland, Conn. m. 2, Feb. 21, 1860, Silas E. Bur-
rows. (2) Harriet Emily, b. April 8, 1841; m. Oct. 19, 1865,
William H. Allen. She d. Feb. 6, 1877. (3) Henrietta King, b.
July 19, 1845; m. June 15, 1871, Stephen Cambreling Powell.
(4) Jane L. F., b. Nov. 16, 1851; m. Feb. 25, 1875, Henry L.
Hotchkiss, of New Haven, Conn. (5) Henry Webster, b.
Aug. 9, 1852; d. April 18, 1857. (6) Ellen Eugenie, b. April
10, 1856; m. April 17, 1878, Huntington Denton.

51. XIV. Robert,[6] b. Dec. 16, 1768; m. Oct. 23, 1796,
Hannah Arnold, of East Greenwich, R. I., b. March
11, 1775. He d. June 28, 1816; res. East Greenwich, R. I.; two children.

XV. Anna (Nancy), b. June 3, 1772; m. April 6, 1795,
Hon. William Cranch, b. July 17, 1769; d. Sept. 1,
1855, in Washington, D. C. She d. Sept. 16, 1843,
in Washington, D. C.; thirteen children :—

i. William Greenleaf, b. Jan. 11, 1796; d. February, 1872; unmarried.

ii. Richard, b. June 26, 1797; d. August, 1824; unmarried.

iii. Anne Allen, b. April 28, 1799; d. April, 1822; unmarried.

iv. Mary, b. Sept. 26, 1801; m. 1820, Richard Cranch Norton.
She d. June, 1822.

v. John Quincy, b. Dec. 5, 1803; d. Jan. 14, 1804.

vi. Elizabeth Eliot, b. Feb. 3, 1805; m. June, 1829, Rufus Dawes.
She d. May, 1860.

vii. John, b. Feb. 2, 1807; m. April 15, 1845, Charlotte Dawes
Appleton.

---

* The Ellsworth family is quite fully treated in Stiles's Ancient Winsor, Vol. II. p. 223.

HON. WILLIAM (40) GREENLEAF, CONTINUED:—

XV. Anna (Nancy).

viii. Edward Pope, b. May 29, 1809; m. April 15, 1842, Bertha Wood. He d. Dec. 7, 1892.

ix. Christopher Pearse, b. May 15, 1811; d. July 21, 1811.

x. Christopher Pearse, b. March 8, 1813; m. October, 1843, Elizabeth De Windt. He d. Jan. 20, 1892.

xi. Virginia, b. January, 1815; d. Jan. 30, 1815.

xii. Abigail Adams, b. Feb. 20, 1817; m. June 29, 1837, Rev. William Greenleaf Eliot.

xiii. Margaret Dawes, b. April 15, 1819; m. Jan. 12, 1844, Hon. Erastus Brooks, b. Jan. 31, 1815; d. Nov. 25, 1886. She d. Jan. 30, 1895; res. Staten Island (West New Brighton), N. Y.; children: 1. Anna Greenleaf, b. Jan. 18, 1845; m. Eugene DuBois, who d. 1891. 2. Elizabeth Eliot, b. March 18, 1847; d. July, 1847. 3. Abigail Adams, b. July, 1849; d. November, 1849. 4. Bertha Greenleaf, b. July 6, 1851. 5. Arthur, b. July, 1855; d. July, 1856. 6. William Cranch, b. July, 1858; d. June, 1859. 7. Erastus Eliot, b. June 18, 1863; d. Aug. 18, 1890.

Hon. William Cranch graduated at Harvard College, 1787. President Adams appointed him Junior Assistant Judge, Circuit Court of the District of Columbia, in 1801. President Jefferson made him Chief Justice of the same court, in 1805,—an office that he held till 1855. Richard Cranch, father of Hon. William Cranch, was born at Kingsbridge, Devon, England, 1727; d. 1811. His wife, Mary Smith, of Weymouth, Mass., died the same day and year.

49.

(Hon. William 5, Rev. Daniel 4, Stephen 3, Stephen 2, Edmund 1.)

Children of **John**[6] **Greenleaf** and Lucy (Cranch).

I. LUCY, b. Sept. 14, 1797; m. Harrison Dawes (her cousin); six children:—

i. Lucy Cranch, b. Aug. 9, 1821; d. unmarried.

ii. Mary Greenleaf, b. Nov. 24, 1823; m. Frederick Stahlnecht, of N. Y.

iii. Harrison James, b. Aug. 17, 1826; m. 1, May 7, 1853, Marcia Jane Alger; 2, Dec. 31, 1856, Mary Ellen ——.

iv. John G., b. July 27, 1828; unmarried.

v. William G., b. July 12, 1831; m. 1855, Amanda Bigelow, of Quincy, Mass.

vi. Margaret Cranch, b. Jan. 24, 1834; m. Sept. 3, 1858, Lyman B. Ripley.

II. JOHN, b. July 2, 1799; d. June 3, 1826, in Baltimore, Md.; single.

JOHN (49) GREENLEAF, CONTINUED :—

52. III. WILLIAM CRANCH,[7] b. Sept. 4, 1801 ; m. Jan. 4,
1847, Mrs. Mary Brightwell, of Washington, D. C.,
b. ——; d. Feb. 27, 1858. He d. Aug. 19, 1868;
res. Washington, D. C ; three children :—

    I. Daniel, b. Oct. 23, 1847.

    II. William Cranch, b. March, 1850 ; d. January, 1852.

    III. George Rufus, b. Feb. 14, 1852. All born in
Washington, D. C.

  IV. DANIEL, b. Dec. 1, 1803 ; d. May, 1827, in Calcutta ; unmarried.

  V. MARY ELIZABETH, b. April 13, 1806; m. George
Minot Dawes (her cousin) ; res. Quincy, Mass. ; five
children :—

    i. Nancy Cranch, b. Feb. 23, 1828; d. May 29, 1828.

    ii. Mary E., b. May 9, 1829; m. Sept. 5, 1854, Henry Mitchell;
no children. She d. Jan. 25, 1870.

    iii. George Greenleaf, b. Feb. 13, 1832 ; unmarried.

    iv. Richard Cranch, b. July 16, 1838; m. Oct. 28, ——, Lottie Howe.

    v. Ambrose, b. Sept. 19, 1843; m. Sarah Shaw.

53. VI. RICHARD CRANCH,[7] b. Nov. 9, 1808; m. Feb. 10,
1841, Mary Parsons, b. Nov. 10, 1810; d. April
3, 1889; dau. of Rev. Peter Whitney, of Quincy,
Mass., b. Jan. 19, 1770; m. April 30, 1800. He
d. March 3, 1843, and Jane (Lincoln), b. 1775; d.
Nov. 11, 1832. Richard C. Greenleaf d. Aug. 3,
1887; merchant; res. Boston; two children :—

    I. A daughter, b. 1843; d. in infancy.

54.   II. Richard Cranch,[8] b. Feb. 12, 1845; m. June 21,
1870, Adeline Emma, b. July 14, 1849, dau. of
John Cameron and Adeline Emma (Bridge)
Stone, who were m. July 2, 1846 ; Richard Cranch[8]
Greenleaf, grad. Harvard College, 1866; grad.
Harvard Medical College, 1870; practiced medi-
cine ten years; res. Lenox, Mass. ; six children :
1. Marion Constance, b. June 17, 1871. 2. Lewis
Stone, b. July 26, 1872. 3. Richard Cranch, b.
Jan. 24, 1874; d. Aug. 15, 1874. 4. Alice Cam-
eron, b. July 15, 1875 ; m. January, 1894, William
Adams, of New York. 5. John Cameron, b. June
2, 1878. 6. Richard Cranch, b. Nov. 15, 1887.

  VII. JAMES HORATIO, b. Dec. 27, 1810 ; d. young.

51.

(Hon. William 5, Rev. Daniel 4, Stephen 3, Stephen 2, Edmund 1.)

Children of **Robert**[6] **Greenleaf** and Hannah (Arnold).

55. I. JAMES,[7] b. Sept. 9, 1797; m. —— Leeds, of Stonington, Conn.; d. August, 1840, in New Orleans; res. Stonington, Conn.; child:—

1. James Leeds,[8] b. about 1834; d. about July 1, 1894; res. New Orleans, La.

Known as Major Leeds Greenleaf; was a prominent resident of New Orleans. At the breaking out of the Civil War he was cashier of the Leeds Foundry, and went to the front a lieutenant of the Orleans Light Horse, taking with him from the Leeds Foundry three cannon on the 14th of September. A little while after the war he resumed his position at the foundry, and remained with that firm until his death. He was social, and a club man, belonging to the Pickwick and Chess, Checkers, and Whist Clubs. (Baltimore *Sun*, July 3, 1894.)

II. NANCY ALLEN, b. May 5, 1799.

42.

(Dr. Daniel 5, Rev. Daniel 4, Stephen 3, Stephen 2, Edmund 1.)

Children of **Israel**[6] **Greenleaf** and Prudence (Whitcomb).

I. DANIEL, b. May 6, 1756; d. July 22, 1774.

II. BETSEY, b. March 16, 1758, in Bolton; m. 1770, Daniel Lewis; seven children:—

i. Betsey.
ii. Sally.
iii. Israel.
iv. Rodney.
v. Eunice.
vi. Phebe.
vii. Louisa.

56. III. JOHN,[7] b. March 26, 1760, in Bolton; m. 1, Rebecca Lewis; 2, 1792, Anna Millington. He d. 1827; res. Volney, N. Y.; a farmer; seven children.

57. IV. DAVID,[7] b. March 9, 1763, in Bolton; m. 1, May 24, 1795, Phebe, third dau. of John and Anna (Brown) Jones, in the Wilderness, now Jefferson County, Miss.; b. Oct. 24, 1777; d. Dec. 29, 1808; 1780, removed to Natchez, Miss.; 2, Parmela Gove, b.

ISRAEL (42) GREENLEAF, CONTINUED :—

    IV. David.[7]

        ——; d. 1817; no children. He d. Oct. 13, 1819, near Warrenton, Miss.; seven children, all by first marriage.

58. V. ISRAEL,[7] b. Jan. 25 or 29, 1765, in Bolton; m. April, 1785, Sally Hoadly, b. ——; d. March, 8, 1839. He d. June 1, 1847, at Wellsboro, Penn.; six children.

59. VI. LEVI,[7] of Bolton, b. Feb. 19, 1767; intention of marriage, Feb. 10, 1787; m. 1, April 1, 1787, by Rev. Timothy Harrington, at Lancaster, Mass., Mary (Polly), dau. of Simon and Elizabeth Willard,[2] b. Dec. 4, 1762; d. August, 1811; seven children; 2, April 16, 1812, Mrs. Margaret (Smith) Daggett, of Industry, Me., widow of Elijah Daggett. Levi Greenleaf d. 1850.

    VII. SARAH, b. April 20, 1769; d. Dec. 2, 1800; unmarried.

60. VIII. TILLY,[7] b. March 25, 1770; m. 1, Dec. 31, 1795, in Northampton, Mass., Mary (Polly), dau. of Thomas Spofford, of Northampton, Mass., b. ——; d. Aug. 17, 1827; sixteen children by 1st marriage; 2, May 8, 1828, Widow Elizabeth (Dickinson) Wickwire, b. March 3, 1802, at Goshen, Litchfield Co., Conn.; d. August, 1863. He d. Aug. 24, 1850; res. Madison, N. Y.; two children by second marriage.

    IX. REBECCA, b. Aug. 10, 1771; d. in infancy.

    X. SILAS, b. Sept. 30, 1772; d. in infancy.

    XI. OLIVER, b. Oct. 18, 1773; d. in infancy.

    XII. OLIVER, b. March 31, 1775; d. in infancy.

61. XIII. JOSHUA,[7] b. Aug. 12, 1776; m. Sept. 8, 1799, Dency Hollister, of Columbus, N. Y., b. March 12, 1777; d. Aug. 30, 1858. He. d. Oct. 1, 1860; res. Columbus, Chenango Co., N. Y.; five children.

    XIV. PRUDENCE, b. Feb. 19, 1778, in Bolton; m. 1, Sept. 3, 1799, Alvin Lamb, b ——; d. Oct. 1, 1807; five children; 2, March 30, 1814, Sampson Spaulding, of Columbus, b. March 20, 1785; d. March 20, 1845; by trade a mason. She d. Oct. 6, 1851; four children.

ISRAEL (42) GREENLEAF, CONTINUED:—
XIV. Prudence.
Children by 1st marriage:—
    i. Reuben, b. 1800; d. 1802.
    ii. Minerva, b. Aug. 10, 1803; m. Andrew Walton, of Columbus, Penn.
    iii. Galen Greenleaf, b. Jan. 5, 1805.
    iv. Hannibal Alexander, b. August, 1806; m. —— Henderson.
    v. Alvin Milo, b. April 8, 1808; m. —— Tuttle.
Children by 2d marriage:—
    vi. Daniel, b. Dec. 25, 1814; m. Sybel Booth.
    vii. Israel, b. Oct. 29, 1815; d. Aug. 27, 1822.
    viii. Willis, b. Oct. 29, 1816.
    ix. Hannah, b. May 22, 1818; d. Sept. 6, 1822.

62. XV. DANIEL,[7] b. Jan, 1, 1786, at Bolton; m. Betsey
——. He d. Aug. 20, 1812, in Mississippi.

63. XVI. ISAIAH PARKER,[7] b. Nov. 25, 1788, in Bolton; m.
March 29, 1822, Patty Williams, of Columbus, Chenango Co., N. Y., b. Nov. 9, 1798; d. Dec. 6, 1861.
He d. May 6, 1853; a farmer; five children.

64. XVII. STEPHEN,[7] b. Sept. 12, 1790, in Bolton; m. 1,
Aug. 29, 1816, Pollina Anderson, of New Berlin,
N. Y., or Columbus, N. Y., b. ——; d. Aug. 12,
1855, at Bloomfield, Iowa; 2, Aug. 29, 1858, Amanda
A. Fountain, of Iowa. He d. Sept. 14, 1868; res.
Bloomfield, Davis Co., Iowa; eight children.

XVIII. POLLY, b. Aug. 22, 1792; d. March 9, 1877;
unmarried.

65. XIX. REV. WILLIAM,[7] b. Jan. 5, 1795, probably at
Whitestown, N. Y.; m. Jan. 30, or February, 1817,
Bethiah Cole, of Columbus, N. Y., b. March 28,
1798; d. April 1, 1879. He d. Nov. 11, 1850;
moved in 1846 from New York to Fox Lake,
Wis.; afterwards lived and died in Trenton, Dodge
Co., Wis.; eleven children.

XX. ESTHER, b. Dec. 1, 1796 or 1797, in New York
State; m. Oct. 11, 1819, Chauncy Baker, of Columbus, N. Y., b. April 17, 1793. She d. Aug. 8, 1878;
ten children:—
    i. Lorilla E., b. May 9 or Aug. 7, 1821; m. March 24, 1843, Hiram J. Sawyer; d. April 3, 1864. She died ——, 1856
    ii. David C., b. Dec. 22, 1822; enlisted Sept. 6, 1861, in United States Service at Helena, Ark.; d. July 22, 1863.

ISRAEL (42) GREENLEAF, CONTINUED :—

XX. Esther.

iii. Lucy Fidelia, b. Oct. 8, 1825; m. Oct. 9, 1844, Royal S. Williams, of Chillicothe, N. Y. She d. Aug. 12, 1855.

iv. Polly W., b. May 26, 1827; d. Oct. 11, 1827.

v. Sidney Devillo, b. Sept. 22, 1828; at the age of eighteen enlisted in the army and served in the Mexican War; was honorably discharged at its close; drowned while bathing, June 23, 1849.

vi. Harriet E., b. March 8 or 18, 1831; d. May 3 or 4, 1857.

vii. Sylvia Cornelia Jennie, b. Nov. 20, 1833; m. Jan. 25, 1868, W. G. Whitney, of Wiscoy, N. Y.

viii. Mary M., b. Feb. 1, 1836; d. Oct. 8, 1839.

ix. Rosilla B., b. and d. March 15, 1839.

x. Rose M., b. April 9, 1841; d. May 20, 1841.

66. XXI. JOSEPH,[7] b. Oct. 16, 1799, at Whitestown, N. Y.; m. Feb. 13, 1820, Electa Coates, of Otsego, N. Y., b. Feb. 5, 1802; d. May 17, 1882, at St. Paul, Minn. He d. April 20, 1855, at Brockport, N. Y.; jeweler; res. Brockport, N. Y.; ten children.

XXII. Lois C., b. Oct. 8, 1801, m. Feb. 13, 1820, Willard Alverson (not William), of Ellisburg, Jefferson County, N. Y., b. Jan. 26, 1796; d. Jan. 10, 1882. She d. Dec. 26, 1875; seven children :—

i. Israel Greenleaf, b. Nov. 5, 1821; d. November, 1825.

ii. Stephen Greenleaf, b. May 18, 1825; d. Oct. 29, 1826.

iii. Willard Nelson, b. March 11, 1828; m. Dec. 8, 1856, Elizabeth Ann Lea; had five sons and five daughters; res. Tomah, Monroe Co., Wis.

iv. William Wallace, b. June 12, 1831; m. Dec. 15, 1855, Melissa Elvira Fillmore, of Ellisburg, N. Y.; had two sons; res. Tomah, Monroe Co., Wis.

v. Knight Dexter, or Reed, b. April 13, 1833; m. September, 1851, Lucinda Fillmore. He d. Jan. 21, 1892; had four sons and three daughters.

vi. Lucy Ursula, b. Jan. 28, 1839; m. Dec. 15, 1855, Franklin McComber, of Clayton, N. Y. She d. July 16, 1870; four daughters.

vii. Eliza Louisa, twin sister to Lucy, b. Jan. 28, 1839; d. Jan. 29, 1839.

56.

(Israel 6, Dr. Daniel 5, Rev. Daniel 4, Stephen 3, Stephen 2, Edmund 1.)

Children of **John[7] Greenleaf** and Rebecca (Lewis). Children by 1st marriage :—

I. REBECCA, b. about 1788; m. James Newman.

John (56) Greenleaf, Continued :—

    II. Polly, b. about 1791 ; m. Roderick Wells.

Children by 2d marriage :—

67. III. John,[8] b. about 1793 ; m. Susan Averill.

    IV. Eunice, b. about 1795 ; m. Gamaliel Olmstead, Jr.
Gamaliel Olmstead, Sen., of New Hartford, Conn., b. June 14, 1759, was a soldier in the Revolution; m. Feb. 9, 1780, Esther Goodwin, b. Jan. 29, 1761. Soon after their marriage they moved to New Hartford, Oneida Co., N. Y. Esther d. April, 1793; Gamaliel d. July 3, 1832. Their children were: Sarah, b. April 1, 1789; m. Lawrence Seymour. Gamaliel, b. March 15, 1791; m. Eunice Greenleaf. His daughter Sarah was the first white female child born in that town.

    V. Phebe, b. ——, 1798 ; m. Justus Bristol.

68. VI. Abel,[8] b. Oct. 25, 1800; m. March 16, 1820, 1, Polly, dau. of Howe and Lucy (Lee) Nichols, of Paris, N. Y.; Polly d. May 9, 1852, at Sanquoit, Oneida Co., N. Y.; 2 ——. He died January, 1876, at Wilkesbarre, Penn.; Methodist minister, afterwards a machinist; res. at Kingston, Penn.; six children.

69. VII. Luke,[8] b. ——, 1803 ; m. Susan Warren ; farmer · res. Volney, N. Y.

68.

(John 7, Israel 6, Dr. Daniel 5, Rev. Daniel 4, Stephen 3, Stephen 2, Edmund 1.)

Children of **Abel**[8] **Greenleaf** and Polly (Nichols).

    I. Mary, b. Feb. 13, 1822 ; d. August, 1832.

    II. Lucy, b. Nov. 2, 1824, at Paris, N. Y.; m. March 16, 1849, Willard Church, of Columbus, N. Y. She d. May 12, 1858; no children.

70. III. George,[9] b. Jan. 14, 1827, at Hastings, N. Y.; m. March 16, 1849, Susan H. Brown, of New Hartford, N. Y. He d. Nov. 8, 1856, at Paris, N. Y.; three children :—

        i. Albert H.,[10] b. March, 1850; lives at Alleghany, N. Y.

        ii. J. Egbert,[10] b. September, 1851; d. 1872, at Owego, N. Y.

        iii. George W.,[10] b. September, 1854; d. January, 1876, at Florida.

ABEL (68) GREENLEAF, CONTINUED :—

71.   IV. JOSEPH HOWE,[9] b. Nov. 10, 1828, at Mexico, N. Y.;
          m. Nov. 29, 1849, Frances S. Jeandelle, of Flavigny,
          France; res. New Haven, Conn.; five children. He
          is a manufacturer of power looms for weaving chair
          cane, open, close, twilled, and plain. He has invented
          and patented several machines that are in use and of
          considerable utility.

      V. JANE LOUISE, b. May 28, 1831, at Paris, N. Y.; m.
          September, 1858, Isaac N. Dann, of New Haven,
          Conn. She d. Dec. 23, 1871; child: George Ed-
          ward, b. June 10, 1861, at New Haven, Conn.

     VI. MARY WELLS, b. Dec. 2, 1835, at Paris, N. Y.; m.
          May, 1856, William F. Dann, of New Haven, Conn.
          She d. Oct. 5, 1858, at New Haven, Conn.; no chil-
          dren.

71.

(Abel 8, John 7, Israel 6, Dr. Daniel 5, Rev. Daniel 4, Stephen 3, Stephen 2, Edmund 1.)

Children of **Joseph Howe**[9] **Greenleaf** and Frances S.
(Jeandelle).

      I. ADELIA LOUISE, b. Oct. 7, 1850, at Sanquoit, N. Y.;
          m. Dec. 28, 1876, Frederick H. Baldwin, of New
          Haven, Conn.; res. New Haven, Conn.; three chil-
          dren :—

          i. Charles Greenleaf, b. June 21, 1878, at New Haven.
          ii. Mattie Louise, b. July 30, 1882, at New Haven.
          iii. Edith Jeandelle, b. June 19, 1884.

     II. MARY LUCIE, b. Jan. 14, 1852; d. May 30, 1853.

    III. MARTHA MARIA, b. Sept. 6, 1853; d. Sept. 25,
          1881, at New Haven, Conn.

72.   IV. GEORGE EDWARD,[10] b. Dec. 25, 1858, at New Haven,
          Conn.; m. June 21, 1882, Addie S. Whipple, of
          Westville, Conn.; res. Plainfield, N. J.; one child:
          Harold, b. Nov. 17, 1885, at Westville, Conn.

      V. MARY LUCIE, b. March 19, 1861; m. Nov. 29, 1882,
          Harry C. Bush, at New Haven, Conn.; res. New
          Haven, Conn.; one child: Frances Louise, b. July
          12, 1886, at New Haven, Conn.

57.

(Israel 6, Dr. Daniel 5, Rev. Daniel 4, Stephen 3, Stephen 2, Edmund 1.)

Children of **David**[7] **Greenleaf** and Phebe (Jones).
I. ANN, b. Feb. 17, 1796, at Natchez, Miss.; m. 1, Jan.
18, 1813, Levi Hinckley Weeks, of Natchez, Miss., who
d. Sept. 20, 1819; a builder; four children; 2, about
1837, Ezekiel Harris, of Natchez, Miss.; a merchant.
He d. July 15, 1837; one child; res. Natchez.
Children by 1st marriage :—
  i. Caroline Hinckley, b. Jan. 17, 1814; d. Nov. 5, 1819.
  ii. Thomas Greenleaf, b. Sept. 15, 1815; massacred with Fannin's
  Army, Texas, 1836.
  iii. Sarah Catherine, b. June 8, 1817; m. 1835, Walter Irvine,
  Natchez, Miss.; ten children.
  iv. Levi Hinckley, b. Dec. 1, 1819; a druggist, Natchez, Miss.;
  d. 1885.
Child by 2d marriage :—
  v. Daniel Greenleaf, b. April 13, 1838; a carpenter, Natchez,
  Miss.
73. II. DANIEL,[8] b. Nov. 11, 1797; m. 1, Dec. 19, 1822,
Matilda, 1st dau. of William Henry and Mrs. Eliza-
beth (Duncan) Cooper Beaumont, of Natchez, Miss.
She d. 1827; 2, ——; no children; 3 ——; no chil-
dren. He d. Feb. 26, 1839, at Jackson, Miss.; a
lawyer; res. Natchez and Jackson.
Children by 1st marriage :—
  I. Virginia Beaumont, b. Sept. 19, 1823; m. March
  28, 1839, Horatio H. Lindsey, Jackson, Miss., b.
  ——; d. 1857; res. Edwards, Miss.; eight children.
  II. Rosanna Mary, b. Jan. 1, 1826, at Port Gibson,
  Miss.; d. Dec. 22, 1830.
III. EUNICE, b. Aug. 31, 1799; m. 1, July 14, 1816,
Joseph, son of Israel and L. Leonard, a planter of
Natchez, Miss., b. Dec. 2, 1791; d. Jan. 18, 1829;
2, Jan. 5, 1832, John Dixon, a Methodist preacher,
b. March 2, 1803; d. June 8, 1850, in California.
She d. Jan. 18, 1867; res. Natchez, Miss.
Children by 1st marriage :—
  i. Elizabeth, b. March 19, 1818; m. July 14, 1836, Loxley H.
  Thistle, a planter of Louisiana. She d. Jan. 7, 1882; ten chil-
  dren.

DAVID (57) GREENLEAF, CONTINUED :—
III. Eunice.
   ii. Israel Greenleaf, b. Jan. 6, 1820; m. Minerva Butler, of Nat-
      chez, Miss., June 30, 1842; d. in California, March 3, 1850;
      three children.
   iii. Mary Catherine, b. Nov. 22, 1821; d. Sept. 29, 1830.
   iv. Daniel Alexander, b. Feb. 14, 1823; d. March 6, 1824.
   v. Alexander, b. Jan. 25, 1825; d. Oct. 21, 1827.
   vi. David Cooper, b. Nov. 8, 1826; d. Aug. 2, 1830; a twin brother
      died at birth.
   vii. Joseph, b. Oct. 4, 1828; d. Dec. 3, 1872.
Children by 2d marriage :—
   viii. Phebe Ann Oliver, b. July 11, 1832; m. Feb. 24, 1857, James
      A. Noulen, a planter, of Louisiana. She d. Aug. 12, 1894;
      res. San Antonio, Tex.; five children.
   ix. John Somerfield, b. July 11, 1834; d. July 21, 1877.
   x. Eunice Victory, b. April 8, 1836; m. 1, Feb. 20, 1861, William
      A. Fowler; 2, April 10, 1878, at Natchez, Dr. Southworth.
      She d. March 9, 1879; no children.
   xi. William Henry, b. Oct. 4, 1838; d. June 26, 1869, in California.
IV. LEVI, b. April 26, 1801 ; d. in infancy.
V. ELIZABETH, b. April 1, 1803 ; m. Sept. 16, 1830, Richmond Bledsoe, a merchant of Natchez, Miss. He d.
   May 12, 1844. She d. Dec. 13, 1880 ; five children :—
   i. David Harris, b. Aug. 25, 1831, in Natchez; d. Jan. 19,
      1833, at Natchez, Miss.
   ii. Georgia Ann, b. March 20, 1833, in Natchez; m. Nov. 19,
      1851, 1, William H. Coleman, cotton planter, of Mississippi,
      b. ——; d. Sept. 18, 1853; res. Lee, Jefferson Co., Miss.; no
      children; 2, Nov. 1, 1859, Wiley S. McDonald, cotton
      planter of Mississippi, b. ——; d. October, 1865; 3, June 19,
      1867, R. M. T. Arnette, cotton planter, of Harriston, Miss.
      Children by 2d marriage: 1, Willis Richmond, b. Nov. 18,
      1861; m. July 28, 1886, Mattie Bieller Harper; children:
      (1) John Wiley. (2) Willis Richmond. (3) Julia Holtz.
      (4) Edith Ard. (5) Ronald Stuart; res. Jefferson Co.,
      Miss. 2. Marian, b. June 20, 1868; m. Jan. 26, 1887, Grant-
      ley Burkley Harper; children: (1) Grantley. (2) Burkley.
      (3) Hazel; railroad clerk; res. Vicksburg, Miss.
   iii. John Richmond, b. Jan 21, 1835, in Natchez, Miss.; d. March
      7, 1893, at the old home in Natchez; unmarried. He served
      through the entire Confederate War, and was in eighteen
      battles. He was successively Private Secretary to Maj.-
      Gen. Trimble, Maj.-Gen. Ed. Johnson, and to Maj.-Gen.
      Gordon, with whom he was when the war closed. He was
      a Mason and a Knight Templar in high standing, fond of
      scientific pursuits, and had an inherited, inventive genius.

DAVID (57) GREENLEAF, CONTINUED:—

V. Elizabeth.

iv. Sarah Elizabeth, b. Sept. 6, 1836, in Natchez; m. Jan. 14, 1858, Rev. Henry C. Harris, an Episcopal clergyman, of Mobile, Ala.; children: 1. Norman Bond, b. Nov. 17, 1858, at Natchez; an Episcopal clergyman; m. March, 1893, Margaret Van Beuthuysen; res. Augusta, Ga. 2. William Adams, b. Feb. 8, 1861, in Nashotah, Wis.; m. 1886, Sallie E. Paddock; res. Natchez, Miss. 3. John Augustus, b. Dec. 25, 1862, in De Kalb, Miss.; an Episcopal clergyman; m. 1886, Nellie Easter; res. Redlands, Cal. 4. Sarah Stannie, b. June 16, 1867, in Meridian, Miss.; m. February, 1887, B. S. Ellis; she d. November, 1887. 5. Henry Canover, b. May 24, 1869, in Dry Grove, Miss.; m. March 27, 1895, Katie Elizabeth Adams; pharmacist; res. New Orleans, La.

v. Augustus Greenleaf, b. Nov. 11, 1842; d. May 19, 1846.

VI. SARAH, b. Nov. 24, 1804; m. June 5, 1823, Jefferson Beaumont, b. March 12, 1801, 2d son of S. W. H. and E. D. Beaumont, a banker of Natchez, Miss., brother of Daniel's first wife. In 1848 the family moved to Texas, where he was soon elected Probate Judge of his county, which office he held several terms. He d. July 27, 1865, at Carrancahua, Calhoun Co., Texas. She d. 1875; res. Green Lake, near Indianola P. O., Texas; nine children:—

i. Henry, b. Sept. 2, 1824; lawyer; res. Indianola, Texas.

ii. Duncan, b. July 17, 1826; m. Mattie Willard, widow; civil engineer; res. Sacramento, Cal.

iii. Louisa, b. Oct. 5, 1828; m. December, 1849, William Deusen Goff, farmer; res. Lavaca, Texas; ten children.

iv. Rosanna Davis, b. Sept. 16, 1831; m. July 22, 1851, Judge Charles N. Creaner, of California; res. Stockton, Cal.; five children.

v. Edward, b. Oct. 21, 1833; farmer; Major in Confederate service; unmarried; res. Natchez, Miss.

vi. David Greenleaf, b. Dec. 18, 1835; m. Emma Lipscomb, Indianola, Texas. He d. ——, 1890; clerk; res. Indianola, Texas.

vii. Sarah Greenleaf, b. July 17, 1840; res. Natchez, Miss.

viii. Ann Elizabeth, b. Jan. 6, 1843; m. M. Cargile, of California; res. Natchez, Miss; one son.

ix. Mary Matilda, b. Feb. 20, 1845; d. ——, 1863, at Green Lake, Texas.

VII. PHEBE, b. Aug. 15, 1806; m. Jan. 8, 1824, Franklin Beaumont, of Natchez, Miss., b. May 12, 1799, at Maysville, Ky.; a druggist; he d. at Ludlowville,

DAVID (57) GREENLEAF, CONTINUED :—

VII. Phebe.

N. Y., Sept. 21, 1888; he was an elder brother of Matilda and Jefferson. She d. Oct. 20, 1851, at "Prairie Home," Victoria County, Tex.; nine children :—

i. Eckhart Lehman, b. Oct. 26, 1824; m. 1, July 11, 1849, Mary Adelaide, only dau. of Thomas and Mary (Travis) Fellows, of New Orleans, La., b. Feb. 18, ——; d. July 20, 1865; 2, Jan. 4, 1867, Caroline Mary, dau. of Edward and Ann L. Bellinger, San Antonio, Texas; physician; graduated at New Orleans, La., Medical College in 1848; res. Gonzales, Texas; children by 1st marriage: 1. Mary Travis, b. May 24, 1851; m. Rev. P. H. Hensley; four children. 2. Phœbe Greenleaf, b. July 10, 1852; unmarried. 3. Adelaide, b. Oct. 24, 1855; m. Eustice Bellinger; three children. 4. Franklin, b. Sept. 15, 1861. 5. ——, b.——; d. in infancy. Children by 2d marriage: 6. Eckhart Lucius, b. April 23, 1869; m. Sophia ——; one child. 7. Edmund Franklin, b. Feb., 1871; m. Maud Coates, one child.

ii. Eunice Matilda, b. Nov. 12, 1826; m. July 25, 1849, Alexander Thompson Hensley (her cousin), first son of William R. and Mary (Thompson) Hensley; merchant; she d. Aug. 17, 1882; res. San Antonio, Texas; children: 1, Philip Henry, b. June 16, 1850; m. Mary Travis (his cousin), dau. of Dr. Eckhart L. Beaumont. 2. Alice Euphemia, b. Dec. 31, 1851; m. William Goff, Jr.; she d. Nov. 17, 1880; three children. 3. Eva Greenleaf, b. June 5, 1854; unmarried. 4. Frank Alfred, b. Aug. 15, 1856; m. Ida Storey; three children. 5. Alex Duncan, b. Jan. 4, 1858; unmarried. 6. Olive Lee, b. Aug. 31, 1861. 7. Grace Greenleaf, b. May 3, 1865. 8. Merle Moore, b. Sept. 19, 1867.

iii. Gabriella, b. July 29, 1829; m. May 22, 1850, Henry W., son of Tilghman and Mary (Walker) Snodgrass, a farmer of Virginia, b. Aug. 7, 1819, at Amsterdam, Va.; d. Dec. 12, 1880, at Dallas, Texas; res. San Antonio, Texas; seven children: 1. Tilghman Edward, b. Jan. 10, 1852, at Green Lake; m. Nov. 25, 1874, Bessie D. Hutchinson; six children: (1) Zoe, b. Sept. 30, 1875, at Dallas, Texas. (2) Bessie, b. Nov. 27, 1880, at Dallas, Texas. (3) Edward T., b. April 7, 1883, at Dallas, Texas. (4) Henry Lehman, b. Oct. 21, 1885, at San Antonio, Texas. (5) L. Lindsley, b. Nov. 7, 1886, at San Antonio, Texas. (6) Vertnor McAlpine, b. June 13, 1894, at San Antonio, Texas. 2. Robert, b. July 25, 1854; d. Aug. 3, 1856. 3. Emma R., b. Aug. 16, 1858; m. Oct. 9, 1876, Charles O. Wood, of Richmond, Va.; children: (1) Caroline, b. Feb. 23, 1882, at Dallas, Texas. (2) Charles Oliver, Jr., b. April 16, 1885, at Dallas, Texas. (3) Edward

DAVID (57) GREENLEAF, CONTINUED:—

VII. Phebe.

Greenleaf, b. Jan. 27, 1888, at Dallas, Texas. (4) Henry Jackson, b. Oct. 11, 1892, at Dallas, Texas. 4. Isabella Quigley, b. Aug. 4, 1861; d. Dec. 26, 1887. 5. Phœbe Louisa, b. Jan. 25, 1865; res. Austin, Texas; bookkeeper Western Union Telegraph Office. 6. Franklin Beaumont, b. Nov. 16, 1867; res. Monterey, Mexico. 7. Henry Lehman, b. May 19, 1870; d. May 25, 1873.

iv. Franklin, Jr., b. June 26, 1831; m. 1, Jan. 26, 1859, Mary Jane Dicks, of Natchez, Miss., b. ——; d. April 8, 1876; 2, November, 1880, Jane Olivia Graves. He d. March 8, 1886; res. New Orleans, La.; children by 1st marriage: 1. Louisa Millard, b. Sept. 2, 1860; m. M. Black; one child. 2. Margaret Bartlett, b. June 25, 1866; m. J. E. Johnson; four children. 3. Ella, b. March 2, 1870; unmarried. 4. George, b. Jan. 5, 1876; d. in infancy. Child by 2d marriage: 5. Oliver, b. February, 1882.

v. Zadoc Cramer, b. July 29, 1833; d. 1834, at Natchez.

vi. Phœbe Elizabeth, b. June 6, 1835; m. Aug. 6, 1857, Ammon, son of Ammon and Clarissa Burr. She d. June 29, 1881, at Dallas, Texas; res. Lavaca, Texas; eight children: 1. Mary Elizabeth, b. May 3, 1858; unmarried. 2. Sarah Gabriella, b. Nov. 27, 1859; m. James Kirkland; eight children. 3. Clara Eliza, b. Sept. 13, 1861; unmarried. 4. William Winchester, b. Nov. 4, 1863; m. Lena ——; four children. 5. Phœbe Ruth, b. March 22, 1868; unmarried. 6. Cornelia, b. June 21, 1870; unmarried. 7. Franklin Clark, b. Dec. 15, 1873; unmarried. 8. Eckhart Alex, b. Oct. 28, 1875.

vii. Julia Finley, b. April 20, 1837; m. Oct. 5, 1858, Travis Hensley, a merchant (brother of A. T. Hensley), fourth son of William R. and Mary (Thompson) Hensley, b. March 17, 1836, at San Phillippe, Texas; d. Nov. 15, 1873, Dallas, Texas; res. Dallas, Texas; six children: 1. Sarah Millard, b. Oct. 20, 1859; d. 1873. 2. William Travis, b. Aug. 27, 1861; m. in San Antonio, Texas; no children. 3. Phœbe Winchester, b. Aug. 16, 1863; unmarried. 4. May, b. Dec. 9, 1865; d. in infancy. 5. Julia Mary, b. Oct. 19, 1868; unmarried. 6. Mary Travis, b. May 10, 1873; unmarried.

viii. Winchester, b. May 7, 1841; d. July 20, 1862, in hospital, Camp Priceville, near Tupelo, Miss.; a carpenter; res. Lavaca, Texas.

ix. William Henry, b. March 27, 1843; m. Aug. 17, 1871, Sarah Louisa, dau. of Jonas and Mary Randall, b. 1843, at Reutersville, Texas; County Clerk, Uvalde, Texas: six children: 1. Thomas Wilfred, b. Aug. 3, 1872; unmarried. 2. Annie Laurie, b. March 15, 1874. 3. Harry Winchester, b. April 6, 1876. 4. Augusta, b. 1878. 5. Edward Greenleaf, b. 1880. 6. Maidie Watkins, b. Feb. 18, 1885.

58.

Children of **Israel**[7] **Greenleaf** and Sally (Hoadly).

I. SARAH, b. Nov. 24, 1786; m. Jacob Radz, or Roads; moved to Ohio in 1810.

74. II. DAVID,[8] b. Dec. 31, 1788; m. 1, Jan. 7, 1810, Susanna Sligh; four children; in 1827, David was divorced and m. 2, July 4, 1828, Fanny Hildbolt, a Swiss; in 1854 lived in Wellsboro, Penn.; two children.

Children by 1st marriage :—
- i. A daughter; d. in infancy.
- ii. A daughter; d. in infancy.
- iii. A daughter; d. in infancy.
- iv. Israel Sligh, b. ——; m. Lucinda Lucas; three children.

Children by 2d marriage :—
- v. George Washington, b. Oct. 6, 1829; res. Wellsboro, Penn.
- vi. Sally Ann, b. March 13, 1831.

III. BETSEY, b. May 27, 1791; m. Henry Sligh, of Pennsylvania; blacksmith; five children :—
- i. Sophia, b. ——; m. Jacob Erva.
- ii. Mary Ann, b. ——; m. Edmund Wetherbee.
- iii. Henry, b. ——; m. Susan Richards.
- iv. David Greenleaf, b. ——; m. Susan Fuller.
- v. Sally, b. ——; m. Horace Broughton.

IV. POLLY, b. Nov. 15, 1794; d. in infancy.

V. SOPHIA, b. March 10, 1796; d. in infancy.

VI. William, b. Jan. 2, 1799; d. in infancy.

59.

Children of **Levi**[7] **Greenleaf** and Polly (Willard).

I. AMY, b. Aug. 12, 1789; m. Sept. 4, 1806, Samuel C., son of Jacob and Keziah (Chapman) Leeman, of Starks, Me. She d. June, 1811, and on May 14, 1812, he m. Love, dau. of Elijah and Margaret

LEVI (59) GREENLEAF, CONTINUED :—

I. Amy.

(Smith) Daggett; Samuel C. was a soldier in the War of 1812; three children :—

i. Joseph, b. ——; d. in infancy.
ii. ——, b. ——; d. in infancy.
iii. Levi Greenleaf, b. Nov. 18, 1809, in Mercer, Me.; lives at Home for Aged Men, 133 W. Springfield St., Boston.

75. II. ISRAEL,[8] b. May 14, 1792; m. Oct. 8, 1815, Sophia L. Trumbull; a carpenter; res. Nunda, N. Y., 1854; four children :—

I. Louis L., b. Aug. 12, 1816; d. in infancy.
II. Lucina L., b. Oct. 27, 1817; d. Dec. 13, 1835; unmarried.
III. Almira E., b. April 26, 1820; m. Jan. 16, 1835, John H. Lamb; res. Nunda, N. Y.
IV. Lucina Elvira, b. Sept. 21, 1835; m. Jan. 29, 1860, David Buck; res. Seymour, Jackson Co., Indiana, 1860.

III. MARY (Polly), b. June 24, 1794; m. 1, March, 1814, George Boynton, of Mercer, Me.; he started for Ohio in 1826; at Augusta, N. Y., he visited his brother-in-law, Israel; he was never heard from after he left Augusta; four children. She m. 2, 1829, John McKay, and moved to Embden, Me.; five children. He d., and she m. 3, James Hutchinson. She d. April 28, 1875.

Children by 1st marriage :—

i. Mary, b. 1814; m. William Gourly, in 1837.
ii. Betsey, b. 1816; d. 1837–8.
iii. James, b. 1818; m. 1, 1843, Mary Williamson; child: John, b. 1844; 2, Jerusha Carter; no children. He d. 1857.
iv. Livonia, b. 1823; m. John Redmond; twelve children; lived at Neilsville, Clark Co., Wis.

Children by 2d marriage :—

v. Caroline Elizabeth, b. 1830.
vi. Amy, b. 1832; m. 1, John Carl; five children; 2, Selden Benjamin; two children; live at North Anson, Me.
vii. Theodocia O., b. 1834; m. Elisha Townes; four children; live at Norridgewock, Me.
viii. Joshua, b. 1836; d. 1840.
ix. Susan Ann, b. 1840; m. William E. Getchell, in 1860; live in Chelsea, Me.; eight children.

Levi (59) Greenleaf, Continued :—

76.　IV. Levi,[8] b. May 11, 1797; m. Dec. 18, 1817, Sarah, dau. of Elijah and Margaret (Smith) Daggett, of New Vineyard, Me., b. Dec. 7, 1792. He d. 1882; he built a house in that part of Industry, Me., set off to New Sharon in 1852, afterwards owned by Bartlett H. Oliver; here he resided for some years; the house has since been destroyed by fire; in 1854 he lived in Illinois; nine children.

77.　V. John,[8] b. Sept. 21, 1799; m. Sept. 24, 1828, Clymene, dau. of Caleb and Dorothy A. (Gordon) Philbrick, of Mt. Vernon, Me. They lived in Lowell, Mass., in 1854; he was a carpenter and builder,—a superior workman; d. March 12, 1882, in Hancock, N. H. She d. June 6, 1879; five children.

78.　VI. Joshua,[8] b. Jan. 15, 1802; m. Feb. 22, 1821, Betsey, dau. of Nathan and Betsey (Hale) Marsh, of Anson, Me.; he was a mason by trade; res. Cross Hill, Vassalborough, Me., lived at Augusta, Me., in 1854. He d. Jan. 5, 1880, at Pleasant Ridge, Somerset Co., Me.; they are both buried at Bingham, Me.; eleven children.

　　　　VII. Sarah, b. ——; unmarried.

76.

(Levi 7, Israel 6, Dr. Daniel 5, Rev. Daniel 4, Stephen 3, Stephen 2, Edmund 1.)

Children of **Levi**[8] **Greenleaf** and Sarah (Daggett).

　　I. Anna Churchill, b. Sept. 15, 1818; d. Sept. 22, 1840.

79.　II. Isaac S.,[9] b. July 2, 1820, in New Portland, Me.; m. May 17, 1842, Mrs. Mary H. Willard. He d. Sept. 18, 1894; res. New Portland, Me., with his daughter, Mrs. Esther A. Knapp; two children :—

　　　　i. Esther A., b. May 8, 1843; m. Jan. 1, 1865, Capt. Charles Bingley Knapp, b. ——; d. May 25, 1893; res. New Portland, Me.; no children.

　　　　ii. Mary, b. Oct. 5, 1844; d. July 14, 1864, at Farmington, Me.; unmarried.

　　III. Esther D., b. Jan. 16, 1822; d. June 10, 1841.

Levi (76) Greenleaf, Continued :—

   IV. Emma, b. March 5, 1824, at New Portland, Me. ; m. 1846, Harrison Davis. She d. 1878.

80.   V. William C.,[9] b. May 31, 1826; m. 1850, at Lowell, Mass., Asaneth Pinkham. He d. 1889, in California.

81.   VI. John,[9] b. April 28, 1828, at Ottawa, Ill.; m. 1853, Jane Brown; res. Santa Rosa, Cal.

   VII. Sarah, b. Dec. 19, 1830, at Ottawa, Ill.; m. 1, Aug. 3, 1850, Ezra Drew, b. about 1825; d. October, 1863, in Libby Prison, Richmond, Va.; 2, 1872, Charles C. Cook; res. San Jose, Cal.

   VIII. Cordelia W., b. July 11, 1833, at Ottawa, Ill.; m. 1, Dec. 6, 1851, William Woods, b. about 1828; d. Nov. 15, 1854; 2, 1859, T. I. Terrell; res. Edwards, Colorado.

82.   IX. Levi Kelly,[9] b. June 23, 1835, m. at Ottawa, Ill., 1862, Sarah Jane Culver; res. Elk City, Kansas; went to Ottawa, in 1849; removed to Kansas, 1870; eight children :—

    i. Ida, b. April 18, 1864, at Ottawa, Ill.

    ii. Albert W., b. June 24, 1866, at Ottawa, Ill.

    iii. Flora, b. Jan. 20, 1869, at Ottawa, Ill.; m. Harvey Gastineau, d. Dec. 6, 1891.

    iv. Eva, b. Feb. 22, 1871, at Elk City, Kansas; m. Charles Swearingen.

    v. Cora, b. Jan. 5, 1874, at Elk City, Kansas.

    vi. Hayes, b. Sept. 13, 1876, at Elk City, Kansas.

    vii. Roy, b. May 7, 1883, at Elk City, Kansas.

    viii. Rockwell, b. Feb. 21, 1887, at Elk City, Kansas.

78.

(Levi 7, Israel 6, Dr. Daniel 5, Rev. Daniel 4, Stephen 3, Stephen 2, Edmund 1.)

Children of **Joshua**[8] **Greenleaf** and Betsey (Marsh).

83.   I. Gorham,[9] b. Jan. 10, 1822, in Industry, Me.; m. Melinda E. Bradley; lives in Santa Ana, Cal.; eight children.

84.   II. Gardner,[9] b. Oct. 27, 1823, in Industry, Me.; m. Nov. 17, 1847, in Vassalborough, Hannah Admath Pinkham, of Sidney, Me., b. March 14, 1824. He d. March 2, 1889, at Starks, Me.; res. Starks, Me.; eight children.

JOSHUA (78) GREENLEAF, CONTINUED :—

    III. ELIZABETH, b. April 21, 1826, in Anson, Me.; m. John Dinsmore. She d. Aug. 8, 1888, in Lowell, Mass.; no children.

    IV. CLYMENE PHILBRICK, b. March 25, 1828, in Anson, Me.; m. Charles B. Messer; d. ——; res. San Francisco, Cal.

    V. MARY WILLARD, b. July 29, 1830, in Norridgewock, Me.; m. 1, Horatio Andrews; four children; 2, —— Gordon; res. Pleasant Ridge, Me.

Children by 1st marriage :—
    i. Elizabeth, m. Joshua Rollins.
    ii. Emma, m. Altion Healy; res. Bingham, Me.
    iii. Chester, d. young.
    iv. Melvin Horatio, m. Mary Gould.

85. VI. GRANVILLE,[9] b. June 29, 1832, in Anson, Me.; m. May 27, 1855, in Providence, R. I., Georgiana, dau. of William and Phebe B. Belcher; res. East Holliston, Mass.; three children.

    VII. AMY LEEMAN, b. June 30, 1834, in Starks, Me.; m. Barzilla Coleman. She d. Nov. 2, 1862, in Augusta, Me.; three children :—
    i. Ellen Betsey, d. ——, age 24.
    ii. Anna M., m. Albert Merrill; res. Solon, Me.
    iii. George Edmund, m. ——; res. Readfield, Me.

86. VIII. GEORGE J.,[9] b. Oct. 31, 1836, in Mt. Vernon, Me.; m. in Providence, R. I., Ellen Arnold; lives in Malden, Mass.; one child :—
    1. Robie Elizabeth, b. June 12, 1874.

    IX. ESTHER M., b. Sept. 15, 1840, in Moscow, Me.; d. Dec. 27, 1840.

    X. SARAH A., b. March 19, 1842, at Pleasant Ridge, Me.; m. March 30, 1857, in Augusta, Me., Isaac P. Andrews; res. Pleasant Ridge, Me.; six children :—
    i. Gertrude, d. in childhood.
    ii. Clarence.
    iii. George, m. Nellie Turner.
    iv. Eugenie, m. Milford Healy. She d. November, 1893.
    v. Ernest, m. Nov. 27, 1894, Nellie Stevens.
    vi. Evanda.

    XI. NANCY P., b. July 28, 1844, at Pleasant Ridge, Me.; m. Jan. 1, 1865, in Charlestown, Mass.,

Joshua (78) Greenleaf, Continued:—

    XI. Nancy P.

        Samuel G. Colwell; res. Providence, R. I.; two children:—

        i. Ella Grace, b. June 3, 1868, in Providence, R. I.

        ii. Nellie Greenleaf, b. Dec. 12, 1874, in Providence, R. I.

83.

(Joshua 8, Levi 7, Israel 6, Dr. Daniel 5, Rev. Daniel 4, Stephen 3, Stephen 2, Edmund 1.)

    Children of **Gorham^9 Greenleaf** and Melinda E. (Bradley).

    I. Mary, b. April 14, 1842; m. F. C. Anderson.

    II. Preston, b. May 7, 1844; d. ——, in Iowa.

    III. Georgiana M., b. July 3, 1849, in Lowell, Mass.; m. 1, July 3, 1868, in Waverly, Iowa, George W. Davis, b. June 12, 1844, in Utica, N. Y.; divorced 1882; 2, Oct. 15, 1885, in Louisville, Ky., James M. L. Hughes, b. 1851, in Nashville, Tenn.

    Children by 1st marriage:—

        i. Laura May, b. Nov. 16, 1869.

        ii. Daisy, b. Aug. 1, 1871.

        iii. George James, b. Aug. 1, 1874.

    None living at this date (1894).

    IV. Edwin, b. May, 1854, d. in Iowa.

87.   V. George Henry,^{10} b. Aug. 13, 1859, in Tama Co., Iowa; m. Jan. 25, 1881, Carrie Emma Whipple, b. March 15, 1863, in Cumberland, R. I.; res. East Providence, R. I.; four children:—

        i. Minnie Emma, b. Nov. 3, 1881.

        ii. Frank Edwin, b. March 12, 1883.

        iii. Grafton Gardner, b. June 8, 1885.

        iv. Adelia Lorraine, b. Nov. 23, 1887.

    VI. Adelia, b. Dec. 8, 1862; m. Edwin S. Brown; two or three children.

88.   VII. Dr. William Ackley,^{10} b. May 2, 1867, in Waterloo, Iowa; m. Oct. 12, 1892, Hattie L., dau. of Edward A. and Annie A. Sanger; b. Dec. 3, 1868, in Providence, R. I.; res. Providence, R. I.

89.   VIII. Charles B.,^{10} b. July 9, 1869; m. Grace Wheildon or Whealden. He d. Aug. 20, 1893, in Santa Ana, Cal.; no children.

242 GENEALOGY.

84.

(Joshua 8, Levi 7, Israel 6, Dr. Daniel 5, Rev. Daniel 4, Stephen 3, Stephen 2, Edmund 1.)

Children of **Gardner**[9] **Greenleaf** and Hannah A. (Pinkham).

I. MARY ELIZABETH, b. Aug. 26, 1850, at Anson, Me.; m. Nov. 26, 1868, in Starks, Me., Brice H. Waugh, carpenter; res. Campello, Mass.; three children:—

  i. Cora Winona, b. Aug. 10, 1870; m. Sept. 28, 1890, Edward Kason Bartlett; address, Amherst Station, N. H.

  ii. Barnard Ellis, b. July 23, 1872.

  iii. Prince Edgar, b. July 25, 1875.

II. LUCINDA MELVINA, b. Jan. 31, 1853, in Anson, Me.; m. July 17, 1879, in Brockton, Mass., Reuben Francis Wright; res. North Jay, Me.; three children:—

  i. Arthur James, b. April 11, 1880, Boston.

  ii. Walter Stanley, b. Aug. 23, 1881, Boston.

  iii. Jennie Adelia, b. Feb. 15, 1883, Neponset, Mass.; d. July 27, 1883.

90. III. LEAVITT GRANVILLE,[10] b. Sept. 23, 1855, in Starks, Me.; m. July 12, 1887, Theresa Phinney, of Providence, R. I.; res. Providence, R. I.; one child:—
Adelia Eastman, b. July 19, 1889.

IV. ADELIA FRANCES, b. Oct. 18, 1857, in Starks, Me.; m. Feb. 5, 1880, in Boston, Charles W. Eastman. She d. July 17, 1882, in Boston.

V. JONAS SAWYER, b. Nov. 17, 1859, in Starks, Me.; res. Fargo, North Dakota; unmarried.

91. VI. GEORGE GARDNER,[10] b. Oct. 20, 1861, in Starks, Me.; m. Jan. 1, 1889, in Starks, Me., Sophia F. Waugh; res. Starks, Me.; no children.

VII. PRINCE EDWIN, b. Nov. 29, 1863; lives on the old homestead, Starks, Me.; unmarried.

VIII. FRANK ERNEST, b. Aug. 25, 1867, in Starks, Me.; unmarried.

85.

(Joshua 8, Levi 7, Israel 6, Dr. Daniel 5, Rev. Daniel 4, Stephen 3, Stephen 2, Edmund 1.)

Children of **Granville**[9] **Greenleaf** and Georgiana (Belcher).

92. I. EARLE GRANVILLE,[10] b. Nov. 7, 1859, in Providence, R. I.; m. ——, 1890, Julia Christine Taylor, of

GRANVILLE (85) GREENLEAF, CONTINUED :—

I. Earle Granville.[10] Mexico, N. Y., b. Sept. 10, 1869; principal and proprietor of the Wells Commercial School, 345 So. Warren St., Y. M. C. A. Building, Syracuse, N. Y.; res. Mexico, N. Y.; children :—
    I. Dorothy Isabelle, b. May 4, 1892, Syracuse, N. Y.
    II. Robert Earle, b. Aug. 24, 1894, Mexico, N. Y.

II. Emma Georgie, b. Nov. 21, 1861, in Providence, R. I.; m. March 21, 1886, in Boston, Frank Townsend Southwick. She d. May 15, 1886, in New York; no children.

III. CORA MABEL, b. Dec. 26, 1867, in Providence, R. I.; m. June 24, 1891, in East Holliston, Mass., William G. Rickard, of Jordan, N. Y.; children :—
    i. Lowell Greenleaf, b. April 17, 1893, at East Holliston, Mass.
    ii. Harold Egbert, b. Sept. 9, 1894, at East Holliston, Mass.

60.

(Israel 6, Dr. Daniel 5, Rev. Daniel 4, Stephen 3, Stephen 2, Edmund 1.)

Children of Tilly[7] Greenleaf and Polly (Spofford).

I. ANNA, b. Oct. 21. 1796; m. May 10, 1813, John Allen, b. Feb. 28, 1789; d. March 13, 1862, at Pipestone, Mich.; she d. Oct. 20, 1850; lived at Ypsilanti, Mich., about 1838, afterwards in Portage Co., Ohio; nine children :—
    i. Lucy Maria, b. Aug. 18, 1814; m. Oct. 1, 1835, W. H. McReay.
    ii. Artelissa, b. Aug. 3, 1816; d. Aug. 20, 1841.
    iii. Alonzo N., b. March 1, 1819; m. Widow Mary Dickens; he d. July 27, 1894, in Pueblo Insane Asylum; buried at Longmont, Col., at residence of his stepson, W. H. Dickens; five children: 1, a daughter, m. —— Washburn. 2. George. 3. Rodolphus. 4. Charles. 5. Alonzo.
    W. H. Dickens is son of Mrs. Allen. He is a farmer and stock grower at Longmont, Col.
    iv. Marcus Wellington, b. Aug. 7, 1821; m. Jan. 13, 1851, Elizabeth Barclay; he d. Aug. 22, 1888, in Oronoko Township, near Berrien Springs, Mich.; three children: 1. Hattie, b. June 6, 1855; m. Oct. 10, 1883, Henry Caldwell: children; (1) Allen Lee, b. March 13, 1886. (2) Vernie Greenleaf, b. Sept. 15, 1887. (3) Hazel Marian, b. Aug. 10, 1890. 2. Frank, b. June 15, 1858; m. Hattie Lemon, Nov. 5, 1880; children: (1) Lowell, b. May 10, 1882. (2) Bertie, b. Dec. 5, 1886. 3. Edward, b. April 14, 1861.
    v. John Milton, b. Feb. 28, 1823; d. March 23, 1823.

TILLY (60) GREENLEAF, CONTINUED :—

I. Anna.

vi. Randolph W., b. Jan. 10, 1828; d. Feb. 23, 1854; unmarried.

vii. Maria E., b. March 12, 1831; m. Orian Calvin; she d. ——.
1866, at Edinburg, Ohio; children : 1. Alice. 2. John.

viii. Israel M., b. March 25, 1834, in Oneida Co., N. Y.: m. 1,
May 19, 1862, Sarah J. Rector, d. Sept. 7, 1865; 2, Dec. 25,
1866, Emily S. Sharai. Child of 1st·marriage : 1. Anson A.,
b. March 11, 1863. Children by 2d marriage : 2, Chilli B., b.
Nov. 24, 1867. 3. Luke M., b. Aug. 2, 1869; m. July 12, 1893,
Helen S. Thomas. Mr. Allen went with his father from Ypsi-
lanti, Mich., to Portage Co., Ohio, and in 1854 returned to
Michigan. Commenced boating at fourteen years of age, con-
tinued in it eight years. Cleared forty acres of land near
Pipestone, Mich., and settled there. Enlisted in Co. I, 12th
Michigan, Sept. 1, 1861; discharged May 1, 1862; re-enlisted
Oct. 6, 1864; discharged at close of the war. Since then has
lived on a fruit farm near Sodus, Mich.

ix. Lucian, b. ——; m. ——, Allen Henry McCoy; children :
1. Freeborne. 2. Eliza. 3. Esther. 4. Liberty. 5. Henry.
6. Eva. 7. Randolph, and others.

93. II. WILLIAM,[8] b. Dec. 23, 1797; m. Oct. 19, 1820,
Almira Sanford, of Pawlet, Vermont; res. White
Water, Wis. ; nine children.

III. SOPHRONIA, b. Aug. 17, 1799; m. Jan. 20, 1820,
Christopher Stebbins, b. Jan. 24, 1797; d. Jan. 13,
1875. She d. Sept. 23, 1880; eight children :—

i. Amelia, b. Nov. 15, 1820; m. Henry Stillman; six children :
1. Franklin. 2. Eugene. 3. Alice. 4. Dwight. 5. Ella.
6. Charles.

ii. Joseph, b. Nov. 7, 1822; m. —— Farrington.

iii. William Alonzo, b. Aug. 28, 1824; m. Eliza Manchana Farrington, b. Sept. 27, 1826; children : 1. Orlando A., b. Jan.
26, 1845; m. Bell Carrol; children : (1) a daughter, b. ——;
(2) a son, b. ——. 2. Ada G., b. May 7, 1858; m. ——
Cogan; no children :—

iv. Mary Eliza, b. April 15, 1827; m. Nov. 3, 1846, James Keys.
She d. June 19, 1847.

v. Eugene, b. Aug. 24, 1829; m. 1846, ——. He d. 1850.

vi. Ruth S., b. Dec. 15, 1831; m. Dec. 3, 1853, James Keys; four
children : 1. Emery A., b. Aug. 6, 1855; m. Oct. 6, 1879; res.
Deansville, N. Y. 2. Jessie Eliza, b. June 27, 1858; m. Nov.
6, 1883, —— Jenks. 3. Mary Gertrude, b. 1865; d. March 26,
1866. 4. James De Laney, b. Aug. 6, 1867; res. Deansville,
Oneida County, N. Y.

vii. Lucy, b. Dec. 18, 1834; m. 1856, —— Wakely. She d. Sept.
30, 1861.

viii. Frank.

TILLY (60) GREENLEAF, CONTINUED :—

IV. ELIZABETH (Betsey), b. March 3, 1802, at Augusta, Oneida Co., N. Y.; m. Oct. 21, 1833, George, son of Julius and Elizabeth (Brown) Wilcox (dau. of Hugh and Olive [White] Brown, of Middleboro, Vt.), b. Oct. 30, 1804, at Middletown, Conn.; d. Feb. 3, 1869, at Arkansaw, Wis. Mrs. Elizabeth Wilcox d. Dec. 28, 1875, at Arkansaw, Wis.; two children:—

    i. Mary E., b. Nov. 15, 1837, at Shalersville, Portage Co.; Ohio; m. Oct. 13, 1859, Henry M., son of Jonas and Sally (Bellus) Miles, b. Jan. 4, 1834, in Chagrin Falls, Ohio; res. Arkansaw, Wis.; nine children: 1. Frank C., b. Jan. 22, 1861; d. Feb. 22, 1863, at Arkansaw, Pepin Co., Wis. 2. Geo. Melville, b. Dec. 11, 1862; m. Nov. 7, 1886, Minnie M., dau. of Silas and Lucinda L. (Wilcox) Ecker. 3. Eva, b. Oct. 13, 1864; m. Sept. 13, 1882, Henry C. Lobeck. 4. Albert Henry, b. June 3, 1867; m. Jan. 20, 1890, Minnie M., dau. of Frank and Mary (Caturic) Taylor. 5. Clark, b. and d. Sept. 28, 1869. 6. Marion Ernest, b. Dec. 21, 1870. 7. Nellie Mabel, b. Feb. 3, 1873; d. Feb. 6, 1873. 8. Harold M., b. Sept. 7, 1874; d. Nov. 20, 1874. 9. Calista Mary, b. Dec. 14, 1877. All born at Arkansaw, Wis.

    ii. George W., b. June 18, 1841, at Freedom, Portage Co., Ohio; d. Oct. 22, 1858, at Frankfort, Wis.

V. LUCINDA, b. June 12, 1803, at Augusta, N. Y.; m. Dec. 27, 1828, Hiram Hitchcock, b. Nov. 24, 1797, at Rome, N. Y.; d. Oct. 18, 1863, in Dayton, Mich.; lived at Cass City, Mich. She d. Oct. 2, 1876, in Millington, Mich.; seven children :—

    i. James L., b. June 10, 1830, at Oriskany Falls, N. Y.; m. Sept. 14, 1862, in Edinburgh, Ohio, Caroline Margaret, dau. of Robert and Margaret Turnbull, b. July 28, 1841, at North Jackson, Ohio; five children: 1. George L., b. Nov. 16, 1864, at Dayton, Mich. 2. Archibald Amos, b. Oct. 31, 1867, at Wahjamega, Mich. 3. Caroline Emmeline, b. July 6, 1870, at Wahjamega, Mich.; m. May 9, 1894, Dr. Homer Corbett Edwards, of Cass City, Mich. 4. Thomas, b. Sept. 15, 1873, at Cass City, Mich. 5. Iris, b. Oct. 1, 1880, at Cass City, Mich.; d. in infancy.

    ii. Luke E., b. Nov. 6, 1831; m. July 15, 1854, Sarah J. West.

    iii. Mark, b. Feb. 16, 1834; d. April 12, 1834.

    iv. John, b. Feb. 22, 1835; d. April 12, 1835.

    v. Mary E. R., b. Oct. 24, 1836; m. 1, Jan. 29, 1856, Curtis S. Hall; 2, March 28, 1878, Frank Wright. She d. October, 1890. Children by 1st marriage: 1. Charles Curtis, b. Feb. 28, 1859; m. 1, Mary Sherman; 2, Mary Wright; res. Millington,

Tilly (60) Greenleaf, Continued :—

 V. Lucinda.

   Tuscola Co., Mich.; children: (1) Ida May, b. Dec. 28, 1884.
   (2) Mary, b. 1886; d. in infancy. (3) Earl Curtis, b. 1887.
   2. Ella L., b. Sept. 3, 1860; d. July 11, 1863. 3. William
   Amos, b. May 23, 1866; lives in Alpena, Mich.; unmarried.
   4. Rosa May, b. Oct. 18, 1867; m. March 12, 1884, George
   Orlando Henderson; a farmer; children: (1) Mark E., b.
   Feb. 20, 1884. (2) Floyd C., b. Aug. 20, 1887. (3) Ray, b.
   May 2, 1892. 5. Frank Israel, b. May 17, 1869; unmarried.
   Child by 2d marriage: 6. Helen Frances, b. April 3, 1885.

   vi. Charles Hiram, b. Oct. 4, 1839; m. Jan. 3, 1863, Cornelia
   Brooks: enlisted and served in New York Regt. during the
   War of the Rebellion.

   vii. Amos D., b. July 19, 1843; 1862, enlisted and served as a
   bugler, Mich. 3d Cavalry, Co. M; d. November, 1865, at Dr.
   Carlos T. Greenleaf's house, in Syracuse, N. Y., from
   wounds received at the Battle of Atlanta, Civil War; unmarried.

 All the children of Lucinda were born at Oriskany Falls, N. Y.

 VI. Melinda, b. Oct. 10, 1804; m. May 16, 1831, Peleg
   Sanford. She d. 1893; eight children :—

   i. Tilly G., b. Jan. 3, 1834, in Clark Co., Ill.; m. Aug. 15, 1877, in
   South Dakota, Dora Millage; served in Co. D, 2d Cav., Iowa
   Vols., Civil War; res. Lincoln, P. O., Douglas Co., Wash.

   ii. Mary Eliza, b. Jan. 7, 1836, in Clark Co., Ill.; d. Aug. 16,
   1836.

   iii. John H., b. Dec. 16, 1837, in Clark Co., Ill.; m. March 6,
   1866, in Iowa, Mary Jane Nelson; served in Co. D, 10th
   Inf., Iowa Vols., Civil War; res. Moscow, Idaho.

   iv. Israel L., b. Sept. 20, 1840, in Vigo Co., Ind.; m. Jan. 3, 1882,
   in South Dakota, Nettie Mittage; served in Co. G, 23d Inf.,
   Iowa Vols., Civil War; res. Lincoln, Wash.

   v. Harriet, b. Sept. 20, 1840; d. Sept. 20, 1840. Twin.

   vi. Albert M., b. July 21, 1843; d. Nov. 21, 1844.

   vii. Alonzo L., b. Nov. 2, 1845; m. March 15, 1881, Alice Melinda
   McBride; served in Co. D, 10th Inf., Iowa Vols., Civil War;
   res. Covello, Columbia Co., Wash.

   viii. Christopher A., b. May 2, 1849; m. Sept. 20, 1873, in South
   Dakota, Agnes Mary Weitzell; res. Beresford, Union Co.,
   South Dakota.

 VII. Mary, b. Aug. 12, 1807; d. Sept. 14, 1807.

94. VIII. David,[8] b. July 2, 1808; m. Aug. 19, 1830, Lucretia Sanford. He d. Sept. 12, 1842; three children :—

   1. William, b. April, 1834, in Ohio; he was in Yuba
   City, Cal., Jan. 15, 1858.

Tilly (60) Greenleaf, Continued:—
  VIII. David.[8]
    ii. Janet, b ——; d. ——, in Clark Co., Ill.
    iii. David, b. ——, in Clark Co., Ill.
  IX. Abel Whitcomb, b. March 11, 1810; d. Sept. 30, 1834.
  X. Emily, b. Oct. 12, 1811; m. Jan. 22, 1836, Saxton A. Curtis, of Massachusetts, who d. Feb. 18, 1868. She d. Oct. 26, 1892; res. Northfield, Minn.; four children :—

  i. Mariette Fairchild, b. Oct. 1, 1838; m. April 15, 1856, in Adrian, Mich., George Carlton Canfield, of Freedom, Ohio; lives in Mankato, Minn.; twelve children: 1. Carlton Willie, b. Oct. 15, 1857, at Charlestown, Ohio. 2. Harland, b. June 13, 1859, at Louisville, Minn.; m. May 12, 1891, Minnie C. Keisling. 3. Lucien Augustus, b. Oct. 15, 1860, at Waterford, Minn.; m. Dec. 16, 1885, Maude D. Davis. 4. Lucy Bell, b. Jan. 11, 1863, at Waterford, Minn.; m. July 20, 1886, Fred J. Zitloe, Glencoe, Minn. 5. Frank H., b. Sept. 17, 1866, at Collins, McLeod Co., Minn.; d. Dec. 30, 1866. 6. May Delberta, b. Sept. 27, 1867, at Collins, McLeod Co., Minn. 7. Julia Eliza, b. April 28, 1869, at Collins, McLeod Co., Minn.; m. July 3, 1889, Damon D. Chapin, Brownton, Minn. 8. Alonzo E., b. July 26, 1870, at Collins, McLeod Co., Minn.; d. Aug. 20, 1871. 9. Achoa Blanche, b. May 23, 1872, at Collins, McLeod Co., Minn. 10. Clara Marie, b. July 10, 1873, at Collins, McLeod Co., Minn. 11. Elva Mariette, b. Dec. 11, 1874, at Collins, McLeod Co., Minn. 12. Augusta Rose, b. Aug. 25, 1876, at Collins, McLeod Co., Minn.
  ii. Eliza Harriet, b. April 7, 1840; m. July 15, 1871, B. R. Baker, of Northfield, Minn.; four children: 1, 2, and 3 d. in infancy. 4. Ethel Pearl, b. Dec. 16, 1878.
  iii. Calista Maria, b. April 16, 1844; d. April 2, 1868.
  iv. Artelissa, b. May 28, 1848; m. July 31, 1866, A. H. Botsford; six children: 1. Archie. 2. Herbert. 3. Arthur. 4. Albert. 5. Bell. 6. Sadie.

95. XI. Israel,[8] b. June 8, 1813; m. 1, Jan. 1, 1833, Emily Whitney, b. Oct. 24, 1810; d. Jan. 28, 1883; 2, December, 1883, Mrs. Philotha Morey, b. ——; d. Feb. 7, 1892; 3, Feb. 7, 1893, Wealthy Watrous; res. Norwalk, Huron Co., Ohio; four children.

  XII. Mary, b. Jan. 27, 1815; m. Feb. 27, 1836, Homer, son of Benona and Almena (Elmora) Peck, of Hartford, Conn. She d. April 7, 1884; four children:—

Tilly (60) Greenleaf, Continued :—

XII. Mary.

i. Adializia, b. Feb. 2, 1838; d. 1871; unmarried.

ii. George Elmore, b. Jan. 27, 1842; m. 1865, Mary Houston. He d. April, 1890; was an inventor and journalist. Prominent among his inventions were a grain binder and a printing press. The latter was exhibited at Chicago Exposition of 1873-4, and for which he received a diploma and the blue ribbon. Water meters and gas meters were among his inventions. As a journalist, he was editor of *The Southern Illinoisan*, a paper published at Du Quoin, Ill. Also special correspondent for some daily papers of prominence, essayist, etc. Child: Frank, d. at age of 17.

iii. Emma P. (Emily), b. Jan. 12, 1846; m. in 1871, William Hayden Naylor, b. ——; d. April 10, 1883; children: 1. Edith Lourie, b. Oct. 24, 1872, at Eaton, Ohio. 2. Winifred Belle, b. Sept. 2, 1880; d. February, 1881; res. Fresno, Cal.

iv. Harriet, b. Sept. 2, 1849; m. M. Bond, a wholesale merchant of Ogden, Utah.

XIII. Joseph, b. Oct. 4, 1816; d. May 26, 1839. It is supposed that he was blown up on the "Mozelle."

XIV. Harriet N., b. May 4, 1818; m. June 8, 1841, Anson S. Curtis, who d. March 2, 1893. She d. May 24, 1872; three children :—

i. Homer, m. ——; two children: both died; res. Charlestown, Ohio.

ii. Frank, m. ——; two children; res. Charlestown, Ohio.

iii. Mary.

XV. Maria, b. Aug. 27, 1820; m. Sept. 7, 1849, George Wilson Barclay, who d. May 15, 1891; res. Edinburg, Portage Co., Ohio; one child :—

i. Harriet E., b. July 15, 1851; m. Feb. 22, 1870, Thomas Owen, who d. Feb. 10, 1888; three children: 1. Mary. 2. Walter. 3. Lelan.

XVI. Louisa, b. Oct. 5, 1823; m. March 25, 1841, Melville, son of Jonas and Sally (Bellus) Miles. She d. Feb. 17, 1849; two children :—

i. Junius J., b. Jan. 4, 1842. He served in the late Civil War in Co. C, 8th Wisconsin Inf. Vol. (the "Eagle" Regiment). Having captured an eagle alive, the company carried it with them wherever they went; hence the name given to the regiment. He was wounded at the battle of Pittsburg Landing, and died in hospital in October, 1862, from a shot-wound when being carried off the field.

ii. Marion Josephine, b. May 5, 1844; m. 1, Aug. 3, ——, Manship Ingram, of Lincoln, Del., b. April 17, 1849; 2, T. J.

TILLY (60) GREENLEAF, CONTINUED :—

XVI. Louisa.

> Coker, of Los Angeles, Cal.; children by 1st marriage: 1. Harriet G., b. June 4, 1869; m. March 4, 1888, William C. Stith, of St. Paul, Minn., b. Feb. 2, 1860; now living at Chandler, Oklahoma; child: Minnie Adelphia, b. Nov. 3, 1890. 2. Junius Miles, b May 21, 1872; d. Oct. 30, 1890.

> Mr. Miles lives in Pepin, Pepin Co., Wis.

> Children of Tilly by 2d marriage :—

XVII. TILLY, b. July 11, 1829; d. Aug. 28, 1830.

96. XVIII. LEVI D.,[8] b. Aug. 3, 1832; m. 1, Oct. 10, 1853, Diantha Crandall, of Eaton, Madison Co., N. Y., b. Jan. 15, 1828; five children; 2, Feb. 27, 1867, Elizabeth L., dau. of Morris Davis, of Plymouth, N. Y., b. Nov. 30, 1847; druggist and M.D.; res. North Pharsalia, Chenango Co., N. Y.; two children.

93.

(Tilly 7, Israel 6, Dr. Daniel 5, Rev. Daniel 4, Stephen 3, Stephen 2, Edmund 1.)

Children of **William**[8] **Greenleaf** and Almira Sanford.

I. ORCELIA, b. Nov. 14, 1821; m. June 12, 1845, Ira C. Day, d. ——, 1864. She d. Dec. 25, 1888; four children :—

> i. Frederic Elton, b. Sept. 2, 1846; m. June, 1868, Josephine O'Connor; child: Virginia, b. March, 1872.

> ii. Mary Eliza, b. August, 1848; d. February, 1850.

> iii. Franklin Pierce.

> iv. George Leverett, b. Feb. 9, 1857; m. ——, 1881, Isabelle Barber; children: 1. Josephine. 2. Fred. 3. Marian.

97. II. ORICK HERMAN,[9] b. July 18, 1823, in Nunda, N. Y.; m. Jan. 31, 1846, Mary Ann Potwin, of South Windsor, Conn.; res. Springfield, Mass.; no children.

98. III. AUGUSTUS MITCHELL,[9] b. Aug. 8, 1825; m. March 4, 1852. Charlotte Elizabeth Stanford, b. April 15, 1831; d. Feb. 23, 1895; five children.

IV. MARY ANN, b. Aug. 3, 1827; m. 1, Jan. 3, 1846, Abram Brink; d. Nov. 1, 1849; 2, Feb. 12, 1852, Edward Sheldon Redington, b. ——; d. November, 1888. She d. June 10, 1895; res. Marietta, Ohio; child by first marriage :—

> i. A son, b. Jan. 19, 1848; d. Jan. 29, 1848.

WILLIAM (93) GREENLEAF, CONTINUED :—
  IV. Mary Ann.
  Children by 2d marriage :—
    ii. William Edward, b. Nov. 20, 1852; m. Oct. 2, 1879, Louise
        Davis Renwick, b. Sept. 13, 1852, in Connecticut; lives at
        Fairfield, Mass.; child: Florence Juliette, b. March 29, 1881.
    iii. Lilla Celia, b. Nov. 23, 1854; m. July 6, 1876, Prof. Joseph
        Hansen Chamberlin, Marietta, Ohio; children: 1. Mary
        Louise, b. May 6, 1877; 2. Juliette Redington, b. Aug. 12,
        1884.
    iv. Juliette Josephine, b. Feb. 2, 1855; m. November, 1885, John
        Braden Baird; children: 1. Edward Redington, b. Aug. 31,
        1886. 2. John Braden, b. Jan. 16, 1891; d. Sept. 28, 1891.
        3. Julian Braden, b. Nov. 15, 1892.
    v. Sarah Brink, b. March 19, 1860; m. Dec. 25, 1888, Edgar Le
        Claire; children: 1. Lawrence Greenleaf, b. ——, 1890; 2,
        Mary Jeanette, b. March, 1893.
  V. LEVERETT KETCHELL, b. Dec. 7, 1829; d. Nov. 20,
      1851; unmarried.
  VI. FRANCES MARIA, b. July 18, 1833; m. January,
      1856, Martin McGraw; d. ——, 1861; child :—
    i. Herman Greenleaf, b, July, 1861; m. 1892, ——.
99. VII. WILLIAM HENRY[9] (Hon.), b. Dec. 7, 1834; m. ——,
      1859, Cordelia, dau. of Hiram De Long, of Cold
      Spring, Wis., b. April 22, 1836; two children.
  VIII. HARRIET AMELIA, b. June 18, 1837; m. Henry
      J. Pierson; res. Boston.
100. IX. OSCAR SANFORD,[9] b. Jan. 16, 1845; m. May 28,
      1868, Mary O. Hitchcock; res. Holyoke, Mass.; two
      children :—
    i. Rose, b. March 3, 1869.
    ii. Arthur, b. Aug. 20, 1874; d. May 20, 1875.

98.

(William 8, Tilly 7, Israel 6, Dr. Daniel 5, Rev. Daniel 4, Stephen 3, Stephen 2, Edmund 1.)

Children of **Augustus M.**[9] **Greenleaf** and Charlotte E.
  (Stanford).
  I. MARY LOUISE, b. Dec. 1852.
  II. CARRIE FRANCES, b. Feb. 9, 1854; m. Sept. 25,
      1872, Edward F. Comstock, lawyer, of Comstock &
      Hess, Chicago, Ill., b. Dec. 20, 1842; res. Chicago,
      Ill.; five children :—

AUGUSTUS M. (98) GREENLEAF, CONTINUED :—

    II. Carrie Frances.

      i. Robert Greenleaf, b. June 22, 1873; d. Feb. 7, 1886.

      ii. Alice Marion, b. Oct. 15, 1877; d. Feb. 12, 1881.

      iii. Bessie Edith, b. May 20, 1882.

      iv. Stanford Edward, b. Aug. 13, 1884.

      v. Esther Lillian, b. March 21, 1893.

101. III. CHARLES HERMAN,[10] b. May, 1857; m. Ella Elizabeth Rohrer; two children :—

      i. Albert Edward.

      ii. Charles Leslie.

    IV. CHARLOTTE LILLIAN.

    V. EDITH STANFORD, b. November, 1868.

99.

(William 8, Tilly 7, Israel 6, Dr. Daniel 5, Rev. Daniel 4, Stephen 3, Stephen 2, Edmund 1.)

Children of **Hon. William H.**[9] **Greenleaf** and Cordelia (De Long).

102. I. CHARLES ALBERT,[10] b. Oct. 27, 1861; m. Jan. 18, 1887, Hattie Day Campbell, of Hartford, Conn., b. Nov. 20, 186–; child :—

      i. William Henry,[11] b. March 3, 1890.

    II. JESSIE, b. Aug. 18, 1863; m. Dec. 27, 1882, Hiram S. Branham, of Litchfield, Minn.; child :—

    Charles, b. 1884.

95.

(Tilly 7, Israel 6, Dr. Daniel 5, Rev. Daniel 4, Stephen 3, Stephen 2, Edmund 1.)

Children of **Israel**[8] **Greenleaf** and Emily (Whitney).

103. I. JOHN WHITNEY,[9] b. May 3, 1836; m. 1, Nov. 24, 1858, Martha O. Wadsworth, of Windham, Portage Co., Ohio; 2, Oct. 13, 1869, Mrs. Sarah E. (Mason) Strong. He d. Dec. 2, 1887; six children :—

      i. Clio.

      ii. Allaseba.

      iii. Ethel.

      iv. Manson.

      v. Mark, lives in California.

      vi. A daughter, d. age 22 months.

ISRAEL (95) GREENLEAF, CONTINUED :—

  II. SARAH, b. May 22, 1837; m. Aug. 23, 1857, C. L. Curtis. She d. June 29, 1871.

  III. ALLASEBA, b. Aug. 7, 1840; d. Oct. 16, 1866.

  IV. HATTIE A., b. July 5, 1848; m. March 6, 1867, D. R. King. She d. June 5, 1872.

96.

(Tilly 7, Israel 6, Dr. Daniel 5, Rev. Daniel 4, Stephen 3, Stephen 2, Edmund 1.)

Children of (Dr.) **Levi D.**[8] **Greenleaf** and Diantha (Crandall).

104. I. POMEROY J.,[9] b. Aug. 22, 1854; m. Hannah Breed; res. East Pharsalia, N. Y.; two children :—

    i. Ivan E., b. March 16, 1887.

    ii. Nellie Ethel, b. March 2, 1889.

  II. MARY, b. March 27, 1858.

  III. ELIZABETH, b. June 21, 1860; m. —— Curtis; two children :—

    i. Howard L., b. Jan. 5, 1877.

    ii. Cora Bell, b. Sept. 5, 1880.

  IV. LOTTIE, b. March 18, 1861.

  V. CLARA, b. Nov. 20, 1863.

Children by 2d marriage :—

  VI. MORRIS D., b. June 2, 1869.

  VII. LEVI D., b. Nov. 4, 1872.

61.

(Israel 6, Dr. Daniel 5, Rev. Daniel 4, Stephen 3, Stephen 2, Edmund 1.)

Children of **Joshua**[7] **Greenleaf** and Dency (Hollister).

  I. PRUDENCE WHITCOMB, b. May 28, 1800; m. April 18, 1825, James G. Ames, of Columbus, N. Y., b. Dec. 17, 1799; d. July 5, 1877. She d. July 22, 1869; eight children :—

    i. Pamelia, b. Jan. 15, 1826; m. Oct. 3, 1850, Amos Miller.

    ii. Polly, b. Jan. 15, 1827; m. Sept. 24, 1854, Lodowist Denezen.

    iii. David, b. Oct. 3, 1828.

    iv. Charles Greenleaf, b. Aug. 18, 1830; m. Dec. 25, 1864, Rhoda Rebecca Crandall, b. Dec. 24, 1838; lives at Tallette, N. Y.; six children : 1. Lincoln Jackson, b. March 15, 1866; d. Aug. 2, 1867. 2. Francis, b. June 29, 1867; d. March 12, 1869. 3. Julia C., b. April 17, 1871. 4. Pearl A., b. Sept. 20, 1875. 5. Lewis C., b. Feb. 8, 1878. 6. Lucia, b. Feb. 8, 1878, twin.

Joshua (61) Greenleaf, Continued :—

   I. Prudence Whitcomb.

     v. Laura Julia, b. July 28, 1833; m. March 26, 1856, Aaron Miller.
     vi. Sally Betsey, b. Oct. 9, 1835.
     vii. Edwin, b. Aug. 5, 1837.
     viii. Dency, b. April 21, 1841.

   II. Betsey Eliza, b. June 24, 1801; m. July, 1825, Hiram Risley, b. May 28, 1804; d. Feb. 1, 1861 or 1862. She d. Dec. 3, 1871, at Columbus, N. Y.; six children :—

     i. Mary Ann, b. Aug. 7, 1829; m. Daniel House.
     ii. Hiram Greenleaf, b. April 18, 1833; m. Feb. 2, 1854, Juliette Van Swoll, d. July 7, 1862.
     iii. Alvin, b. Jan. 24, 1834; d. Sept. 15, 1834.
     iv. Alvira Melinda, b. Jan. 24, 1834, twin; m. July 11, 1853, Theodore Ferrel.
     v. Caroline Betsey, b. July 4, 1836.
     vi. Alva A., b. March 12, 1838; d. Oct. 9, 1848.

105. III. Charles,[8] b. Oct. 6, 1807; m. July 12, 1828, Mary Ann Thorington, b. Oct. 6, 1812; d. ——, in Nevada. He d. ——, in Nevada; a farmer; six children.

   IV. Polly, b. July 1, 1811; m. Beckwith Rowland; d. ——, in Iowa; a farmer; no children.

   V. Harriet, b. Oct. 24, 1813; d. Feb. 24, 1814.

105.

(Joshua 7, Israel 6, Dr. Daniel 5, Rev. Daniel 4, Stephen 3, Stephen 2, Edmund 1.)

Children of **Charles**[8] **Greenleaf** and Mary Ann (Thorington).

   I. Maria, b. April 5, 1829; m. July 4, 1848, William Hardy, b ——; d. about 1873; six children.

106. II. Anson Leroy,[9] b. July 31, 1830; m. Sept. 11, 1853, Melizia Gould; res. Courtland, Republic Co., Kansas

   III. Marietta, b. Sept. 23, 1832; m. Sept. 11, 1853, Andrew Gould; one child :—

     i. Charles, m. Flora Louise, dau. of Manville T., son of Isaiah P. Greenleaf.

   IV. Charles Lewis, b. May 4, 1834.

   V. Levi A., b. Nov. 13, 1836.

   VI. Alice Adelaide, b. April 5, 1852; m. —— James in California.

63.

(Israel 6, Dr. Daniel 5, Rev. Daniel 4, Stephen 3, Stephen 2, Edmund 1.)

Children of **Isaiah P.**[7] **Greenleaf** and Patty (Williams).

107. I. CARLOS TRACY,[8] M.D., b. Jan. 17, 1823; m. May 9, 1847, Sarah C. Briggs, b. June 12, 1822; res. Brewerton, Onondaga Co., N. Y.; four children.

II. LUCY JERUSHA, b. April 3, 1826; d. Sept. 4, 1829.

108. III. MANVILLA TAUNT,[8] b. Aug. 12, 1827; m. March 30, 1856, Martha Maria Crum; res. New Berlin, Chenango Co., N. Y.; two children:—

    i. George T., b. Feb. 4, 1857; lives at Leonardsville, Madison Co., N. Y.

    ii. Flora Louise, b. Dec. 15, 1859; m. Dec. 24, 1879, Charles, son of Andrew Gould and Marietta, dau. of Charles[8] Greenleaf (105); res. Brisben, Chenango Co., N. Y.; one child:—

        1. Lelia Maud, b. Oct. 4, 1880.

IV. LOIS ALMIRA, b. May 3, 1830; m. April 29, 1855, Willis Spaulding, of Columbus, N. Y., b. ——; d. Feb. 5 or 16, 1892. She d. some years ago, probably Oct. 1, 1877, at ——, Michigan. Five children:—

    i. Ida Jane, b. Nov. 12, 1856.

    ii. Floyd, b. July 2, 1859.

    iii. Carrie, b. June 11, 1861.

    iv. Minnie, b. Aug. 26, 1864.

    v. Lucretia, b. Dec. 8, 1866.

V. MARTHA JANE, b. April 23, 1834; m. April 3, 1856, Alvin Malachi Lamb; res. Columbus, N. Y.; three children:—

    i. Mary Florence, b. Dec. 14, 1859; m. Nov. 4, 1878, Elmer Pultz; res. Rutland, Mass.; children: 1. Otto L., b. March 7, 1880. 2. Norman C., b. March 2, 1882. 3. Monroe W., b. June 3, 1888. 4. William A., b. May 5, 1890. 5. Mary A., b. June 29, 1892.

    ii. Elmer Lewis, b. Sept. 24, 1861; d. Sept. 21, 1887.

    iii. Clarence Otto, b. May 3, 1866; m. Nov. 3, 1885, Hattie R. Cheesebro; children: 1. Earl O., b. Feb. 19, 1888. 2. Alvin M., b. July 6, 1889. 3. Mable E., b. Nov. 23, 1891.

107.

(Isaiah Parker 7, Israel 6, Dr. Daniel 5, Rev. Daniel 4, Stephen 3, Stephen 2, Edmund 1.)

Children of **Dr. Carlos Tracy**[8] **Greenleaf** and Sarah C. (Briggs).

Dr. Carlos Tracy (107) Greenleaf, Continued :—

    I. Adelaide Genette, b. April 8, 1848; m. Jan. 30, 1873, Hector B. Johnson, of Brewerton, N. Y.; two children :—
      i. Herbert Briggs, b. Feb. 14, 1876.
      ii. Edith Jane, b. April 16, 1883.

109. II. Emmet Eugene,[9] b. Dec. 6, 1852; m. Oct. 13, 1877, Margaret H. Walkup, of Brewerton, N. Y.; two children :—
      i. Guy, b. May 16, 1881.
      ii. Jane, b. Nov. 26, 1890.

    III. La Verne Burnside, b. Aug. 25, 1860; d. Nov. 8, 1883.

    IV. Bertha L., b. Jan. 8, 1864; d. Aug. 7, 1864.

64.

(Israel 6, Dr. Daniel 5, Rev. Daniel 4, Stephen 3, Stephen 2, Edmund 1.)

Children of **Stephen**[7] **Greenleaf** and Pollina (Anderson).

110. I. Lawrence Morian (Dr.),[8] b. Oct. 5, 1817; m. March 17, 1851, Mary De Latree, of Mississippi. He d. February, 1891; res. New Orleans, La.; no children.

111. II. Eugene La Baum,[8] b. March 12, 1819; m. Nov. 26, 1840, Martha Louisa, dau. of Rev. Hugh Barr (Presbyterian), of Carrollton, Ill., b. June 20, 1823; d. April 24, 1880, at Kansas City, Mo. He d. April 13, 1881, at Kansas City, Mo.; architect; res. St. Louis, Mo.; eleven children.

112. III. Hannibal Alexander,[8] b. Jan. 10, 1821; m. Oct. 27, 1842, Ann Rogers, of Switzerland Co., Iowa. He d. Sept. 11, 1846, in Bluffdale, Ill.; two children.

113. IV. Daniel DeWitt Clinton[8] (Dr.), b. March 21, 1823; m. 1, July 29, 1852, Amanda Cecelia Young, b. Aug. 12, 1828; d. Dec. 11, 1857; three children; 2, Dec. 18, 1858, Augustine V. Young, sister of first wife; eight children; res. Bloomfield, Iowa.

    V. Armilla, b. Feb. 4, 1825; d. Nov. 6, 1836.

    VI. Pauline, b. March 21, 1827; m. Feb. 11, 1852, 1, Wilson T. Goble, b. ——; d. June, 1860; 2, Simeon J. Mitchell, b. ——; d. March 10, 1892; was lieu-

STEPHEN (64) GREENLEAF, CONTINUED :—
>VI. Pauline.
>>tenant in United States Service in late war, 1861–64. She d. April 12, 1892 ; res. Dallas, Texas ; five children.
>>Child by 1st marriage :—
>>>i. Alice; d. in infancy.
>>Children by second marriage :—
>>>ii. George F., b. Oct. 30, 1866; physician.
>>>iii. Cora Inez, b. ——; m. —— Burrows; d. Feb. 9, 1890, in Chicago, Ill.
>>The others died.
>VII. AURELIA, b. Aug. 12, 1829; m. July 27, 1847, Benjamin Fugit, of St. Louis, Mo. She d. April 7, 1849, at New Orleans, La. ; one child:—
>>i. A daughter; d. in infancy.
>VIII. MINERVA E., b. Nov. 24, 1832; m. Aug. 11, 1869, William G. Briggs; res. Indianapolis, Indiana; two children :—
>>i. Grace Greenleaf, b. May 18, 1871.
>>ii. Pauline C., b. Sept. 8, 1874.

111.

(Stephen 7, Israel 6, Dr. Daniel 5, Rev. Daniel 4, Stephen 3, Stephen 2, Edmund 1.)

Children of **Eugene La Baum**[8] **Greenleaf** and Martha Louisa (Barr).

114. I. LAWRENCE AUGUSTUS,[9] b. Nov. 14, 1841 ; m. Martine Logan Hardin ; res. Jacksonville, Ill. ; storekeeper at State Insane Institution ; two children :—
>i. Kate H., b. August, 1864; d. in infancy.
>ii. Loulie, b. Nov. 9, 1866; m. Fred Stevenson ; farmer ; res. Orleans, Ill.

115. II. WILLIAM EUGENE,[9] b. Jan. 19, 1844 ; m. 1, Kate A. Henry; b. Aug. 26, 1845; d. Jan. 4, 1875; 2, Mary Williamson; b. Jan. 29, 1854; architect and builder ; res. Kansas City, Mo.

Children by 1st marriage :—
>i. Henry Eugene, b. Oct. 31, 1869; res. St. Louis, Mo.
>ii. Alexina Louise, b. June 22, 1872; stenographer ; res. St. Louis, Mo.

Children by 2d marriage :—
>iii. Robert W., b. May 27, 1883.
>iv. Martha Eugenia, b. Sept. 15, 1890.

Eugene La Baum (111) Greenleaf, Continued :—

III. Kate Barr, b. July 24, 1846; m. Edward Sparhawk (536), son of Ebenezer Parsons Greenleaf (532); res. Jacksonville, Ill.; eight children.

116. IV. Robert Stephen,[9] b. Sept. 3, 1848, at St. Louis, Mo.; m. June 16, 1881, Agnes McConkin; res. Portland, Oregon; County Surveyor; no children.

V. Grace Eliza, b. Nov. 22, 1851; m. Sherman B. Pike; res. St. Louis, Mo.; Secretary and Manager Missouri Electric Light and Power Co., St. Louis, Mo.

VI. Hugh Barr, b. Dec. 16, 1852; d. Oct. 3, 1854.

VII. Effie Hodge, b. July 23, 1855; m. J. Howard Cavender; res. St. Louis, Mo.; real estate; two children :—

i. John.
ii. Lucile.

117. VIII. Frank Mosley,[9] b. March 25, 1858; m. Lottie Mount. He d. Nov. 10, 1882; res. Jacksonville, Ill.; no children.

IX. Prince, d. in infancy.

118. X. Malcolm Anderson,[9] b. Jan. 6, 1864; m. Sept. 26, 1885, at Carlinville, Ill., Georgiana Underkofler, b. Dec. 14, 1863. He d. March 24, 1894. He lived with his parents until their death; then entered the railroad business at Rich Hill, Mo.; was in the coal business from Sept. 1, 1883 until Oct. 1, 1890; was Superintendent of Mines (coal) for the Western Coal and Mining Company, at Foster, Mo.; again went into railroad business as local Freight Agent at St. Louis, in December, 1890, where he remained to the time of his death; res. St. Louis, Mo.; three children :—

i. Vera, b. July 26, 1886, at Rich Hill, Mo.
ii. Malcolm Fleming, b. Oct. 16, 1889, at Foster, Mo.
iii. Lawrence Batiste, b. May 21, 1894, at Carlinville, Ill.

XI. A son; d. in infancy.

112.

(Stephen 7, Israel 6, Dr. Daniel 5, Rev. Daniel 4, Stephen 3, Stephen 2, Edmund 1.)

Children of **Hannibal A.**[8] **Greenleaf** and Ann (Rogers).

HANNIBAL A. (112) GREENLEAF, CONTINUED :—

    I. ELVIRA GRACIA, b. May 15, 1844; d. June 1, 1845.

119.   II. HANNIBAL A.,[9] b. Jan. 26, 1846; m. Dec. 13, 1868; Mary A. Strain; physician; res. Markland, Switzerland Co., Ind.; six children :—

      I. Grace, b. Sept. 6, 1869; m. Nov. 23, 1891, William A. Pell, of Cave, Rock County, Ill.; one child :—
        Mary Ella, b. Nov. 20, 1892.

      II. Carroll Eugene, b. Aug. 4, 1872.

      III. Joseph, b. Feb. 16, 1874.

      IV. Augustus, b. July 31, 1875; d. July 8, 1876.

      V. Bennett Philip, b. July 2, 1877; d. July 15, 1878.

      VI. Paul Emmett, b. Nov. 12, 1885.

113.

(Stephen 7, Israel 6, Dr. Daniel 5, Rev. Daniel 4, Stephen 3, Stephen 2, Edmund 1.)

Children of **Dr. Daniel De Witt C.**[8] **Greenleaf** and Amanda Cecelia (Young).

Children by 1st marriage :—

120.   I. STEPHEN,[9] b. June 24, 1853; m. Sept. 28, 1876, Mary Lillian, dau. of Dr. S. H. Sawyer, b. Nov. 28, 1857. He d. Oct. 5, 1886; a physician; res. Unionville, Iowa; five children :—

      I. Thayne Lazelle, b. July 30, 1877.

      II. La Rue Lillian, b. May 28, 1879; d. Aug. 15, 1885.

      III. Harold Stephen, b. July 10, 1881.

      IV. Hale Carr, b. Dec. 2, 1883.

      V. Cecelia Mary, b. Dec. 13, 1885.

121.   II. EUGENE Y.,[9] b. Jan. 10, 1855; m. Aug. 5, 1883, Nettie Royce; a lawyer; lives at Rock Rapids, Iowa; two children :—

      I. Alma, b. Oct. 22, 1884.

      II. Infant, b. and d. July 26, 1891.

    III. A SON, b. Sept. 23, 1856; d. in infancy.

Children by 2d marriage :—

    IV. HORACE C., b. Oct. 18, 1859; painter.

    V. MARTHA, b. Nov. 10, 1861; clerk.

    VI. DELLA, b. Oct. 26, 1863; m. George T. Sowers, Bloomfield, Iowa; lawyer; one child :—
      De Witt Greenleaf, b. Dec. 12, 1892.

    VII. GERTRUDE, b. Aug. 16, 1866.

Dr. Daniel De Witt C. (113) Greenleaf, Continued:—
VIII. Ruth, b. May 13, 1869; music teacher.
IX. Edmund W., b. March 31, 1871; machinist.
X. Daniel De Witt,[9] b. Sept. 9, 1874; lawyer;
Rock Rapids, Iowa.
XI. Inez, b. March 8, 1876.

65.

(Israel 6, Dr. Daniel 5, Rev. Daniel 4, Stephen 3, Stephen 2, Edmund 1.)

Children of **Rev. William[7] Greenleaf** and Bethiah (Cole).

I. Minerva U., b. Sept. 2, 1817; m. Dec. 30, 1834,
Laban C. Cobb, of Gerry, Chautauqua Co., N. Y.
Both Mr. Greenleaf and his wife were preachers and
missionaries of the Freewill Baptist Church. She
d. March 6, 1890; res. Colman, South Dakota;
children:—
i. A son.
ii. Amelia, b. ——; m. Allen; res. Fox Lake, Wisconsin.

122. II. William Riley,[8] b. March 21, 1819; m. Jan. 9,
1842, Anne Eliza Higby, of Chautauqua, N. Y., b.
Sept. 15, 1820; d. April 8, 1865. He d. June 15,
1865; was proprietor of an iron foundry at Buffalo,
N. Y., and practical machinist; invented some important improvements in steam engines, veneering
machines, etc.; four children.

III. Mary M., b. Nov. 7, 1820; m. Jan. 9, 1842, Marvin
S. Higby, b. Jan. 31, 1819, in Manlius, N. Y.; d.
Oct. 6, 1885, in Orange City, Fla. She d. March 4,
1888, in Rochester, Minn.; four children:—
i. Flora F., b. Jan. 14, 1844, in New York; m. Dec. 24, 1861,
Marcus Wing.
ii. Alice M., b. Dec. 22, 1846, in New York; m. March 16, 1867,
Timothy H. Bliss; res. Rochester, Minn.
iii. Cassius M., b. May 4, 1854, in Westford, Wis.; m. June 4,
1878, Aurilla McFarlin.
iv. Clara B., b. April 22, 1859, in Westford, Wis.; res. Brownsdale, Mower Co., Minn.

123. IV. David Orlando,[8] b. Dec. 16, 1822; m. Aug. 3,
1848, Sarah Tuck. He d. July 9, 1863; one child, a
daughter.

V. Emily B., b. Aug. 28, 1824; m. 1, Oct. 3, 1841,
Monroe Carpenter, b. ——; d. Nov. 11, 1848; served

Rev. William (65) Greenleaf, Continued :—

V. Emily B.

in War of 1812 ; 2, July 8, 1849, Rev. John Calderwood, Methodist ; lives at Crary, North Dakota ; two
children, daughter and son.

VI. Julia Eliza, b. March 11, 1826; d. Nov. 11, 1842.

VII. Laura M., b. Jan. 25, 1828; m. Aug. 3, 1848,
Jeremiah Tuck. She d. about 1888, in Quincy, Ill.

VIII. Harriet A., b. Aug. 25, 1830; m. 1, Nov. 15, 1846,
Freeman Keith, b ——; d. May 28, 1851 ; 2, Dec. 12,
1852, Lyman J. Stafford. She d. Sept. 24, 1859.

IX. Delia H., b. April 24, 1833 ; d. Dec. 22, 1837.

X. Helen R., b. March 21, 1835 ; m. Nov. 26, 1854,
John Warren, b. March 28, 1829 ; res. Brownsdale,
Minn. ; five children :—

   i. Hattie Frances, b. Aug. 1, 1856; m. Sept. 14, 1875, Carlos O.
      Sleeper.

   ii. Clara Mabelle Amelia, b. Sept. 14, 1858; d May 3, 1865.

   iii. Louis Montgomery, b. Oct. 5, 1860; m. Dec. 3, 1888, Nettie
      H. Chase.

   iv. George Greenleaf, b. April 28, 1866.

   v. Arthur Edwin, b. Dec. 16, 1871.

XI. Delia Elvira, b. April 6, 1842, in Gerry, Chautauqua Co., N. Y. ; m. March 22, 1857, Richard
Maconnell, b. June 27, 1836, in New York Mills,
N. Y. He d. May 27, 1890; Minneapolis, Minn. ;
five children :—

   i. Carrie Amelia, b. Jan. 29, 1858; m. Nov. 11, 1877, Charles E.
      Cotton. She d. June 28, 1887; four children.

   ii. Nettie Harriet, b. March 31, 1862; m. 1, Nov. 9, 1876, George
      W. Chase, b. ——; d. May, 1882; 2, Dec. 3, 1887, Louis M.
      Warren; children by first marriage: 1. Grace D., b. Sept.
      14, 1878. 2. Ruth H., b. March 3, 1880. 3. G. Earle, b.
      Nov. 1, 1881. Child by second marriage: 4. Hazle E., b
      Feb. 6, 1890.

   iii. Walter Greenleaf, b. Sept. 25, 1867; m. Sept. 12, 1890, Nellie
      Roberts; child: a son, b. Sept. 12, 1893.

   iv. Charles Herbert, b. Jan. 24, 1870.

   v. George Edward, b. Oct. 24, 1873.

122.

(Rev. William 7, Israel 6, Dr. Daniel 5, Rev. Daniel 4, Stephen 3, Stephen 2, Edmund 1.)

Children of **William Riley**[8] **Greenleaf** and Anne Eliza
(Higby).

WILLIAM RILEY (122) GREENLEAF, CONTINUED:—

I. JULIA ELIZA, b. May 17, 1843, at Sinclairsville, N. Y.; m. May 11, 1865, in Buffalo, N. Y., George Peter, son of Geo. P. Horton, of Clavernack, N. Y., b. May 29, 1839, in Philmont, N. Y.; res. Buffalo, N. Y.; five children:—

  i. Henry Percy, b. March 15, 1866; m. March 24, 1887, Pauline Anna Hull.

  ii. Georgia Anna, b. Sept. 5, 1867; m. July 6, 1887, Alexander M. Barnum, She d. March 19, 1890; two children: 1. Laurance Findlay, b. July 21, 1888. 2. Harold Greenleaf, b. Feb. 19, 1890; d. Nov. 28, 1892.

  iii. Magdalena, b. Aug. 31, 1869; d. Oct. 29, 1869.

  iv. Julia Louise, b. Sept. 14, 1870; d. Dec. 25, 1874.

  v. Grace Clifford, b. Jan. 4, 1879.

124. II. GEORGE FRANKLIN,[9] b. May 3, 1848, at Silver Creek, N. Y.; m. Oct. 10, 1870, Agnes Dalgleish, dau. of Henry Boomby Staines and Janet (McIndoe), b. March 29, 1848; res. Chicago, Ill.; with Hibbard, Spencer, Bartlett & Co.; three children:—

  I. Janet Staines, b. Dec. 25, 1871.

  II. Frederick Staines, b. June 12, 1873.

  III. George Frank, b. Sept. 29, 1874.

III. WILLIAM HENRY, b. Aug. 3, 1853; d. Jan. 31, 1855.

IV. FRED STARR, b. Nov. 28, 1855; d. Nov. 14, 1888.

66.

(Israel 6, Dr. Daniel 5, Rev. Daniel 4, Stephen 3, Stephen 2, Edmund 1.)

Children of **Joseph**[7] **Greenleaf** and Electa (Coates).

I. MANVILLE, b. Oct. 16, 1821; d. April 20, 1823.

125. II. DE WITT CLINTON,[8] b. Dec. 16, 1823; m. 1847, Julia Ferree. He d. Sept. 12, 1876, at St. Paul, Minn.; child:—

Emma Louise, b. July, 1852; m. Maurice R. Todd, Banker, Preston, Minn.; children:—

  1. Maurice Clement, b. Feb. 12, 1884.

  2. Damon Greenleaf, b. May 22, 1893.

III. HELEN ELIZABETH, b. April 21, 1826; m. Charles Theophilus Morgan, of Green Bay, Wis. He d. 1861; res. Rutland, Vt.; two children:—

  i. Charles T., b. April 12, 1854; d. Dec. 13, 1884.

  ii. Harriet Elizabeth, b. May 15, 1856; m. Feb. 1, 1877, Edson P. Gilson; children: 1. Robert Morgan, b. Jan. 20, 1878. 2. John Lawrence, b. Oct. 26, 1881.

JOSEPH (66) GREENLEAF, CONTINUED:—

126. IV. HENRY CLAY,[8] b. March 20, 1828; m. May 13,
1855, Maria Edwards, of Mishawaka, Ind. He d.
Sept. 15, 1862; children:—

    I. Charles Damon, b. Aug. 16, 1859; m. Emma F.
Doolittle; no children.

    II. Joseph Henry, b. Oct. 7, 1861.

V. CAROLINE, b. June 10, 1830; d. May 10, 1831.

VI. CLARISSA, twin, b. June 10, 1830; d. July 24, 1832.

127. VII. DAMON,[8] b. Nov. 30, 1834; m. November, 1865,
Clementine Deuel, of Ballston, N. Y.; jeweler;
res. Jacksonville, Fla.; firm of Crosby & Greenleaf;
four children:—

    I. Deuel, b. ——; d. in infancy.

    II. Mary, b. ——; d. in infancy.

    III. Ruth Helen, b. Sept. 10, 1868; m. April 23, 1891,
Dr. John H. Douglass.

    IV. Julia Ferree, b. Aug. 15, 1878.

128. VIII. SYDNEY,[8] b. April 13, 1837; m. June 7, 1887, Mrs.
Carrie Teel; res. Monterey, Cal.; one child:—
Sidney S., b. Feb. 13, 1892.

IX. SARAH, b. Oct. 14, 1839; m. Jan. 1, 1876, David R.
Davis; res. St. Paul, Minn.; one child:—
Marie Louise, b. Sept. 25, 1878.

X. MARY, b. Jan. 25, 1843; res. St. Paul, Minn.; unmarried.

This family, after the father's death, in 1855, removed to St.
Paul, and some to Minneapolis, Minn.

43.

(Dr. Daniel 5, Rev. Daniel 4, Stephen 3, Stephen 2, Edmund 1.)

Children of **Stephen**[6] **Greenleaf** and Eunice (Fairbanks).

129. I. STEPHEN[7], b. Jan. 31, 1759, in Boston; m. 1, Anna
Sargent, b. ——; d. Oct. 11, 1813; 2, Mrs. Cynthia
Ryan, d. Sept. 7, 1859, aged 92. He d. March 5,
1850; res. Brattleboro, Vt.; three children.

II. EUNICE, b. Aug. 19, 1761; m. May 4, 1780, George
Dickson, a native of Smallholm, Scotland; d. Sept.
5, 1838. She d. Sept. 5. 1839; eleven children:—

i. George, b. May 4, 1781; m. 1810, Alice Hoxie. He d. 1855;
res. Bowdina, N. Y.

STEPHEN (43) GREENLEAF, CONTINUED :—

II. Eunice.

ii. Eunice, b. Aug. 14, 1783; m. Apollos A. Noble, of Colesville, N. Y. She d. 1853; res. Ohio.

iii. Susanna, b. Sept. 3, 1785; m. Isaac Humastun, of Colesville, N. Y.; res. Rochester, N. Y.

iv. John Martin, b. Feb. 6, 1788; m. Anna Brown, of Colesville, N. Y. He d. 1852.

v. Elizabeth, b. May 4, 1790; m. 1812, John Doolittle, of Colesville, N. Y.; res. Colesville, N. Y.

vi. Stephen Greenleaf, b. Aug. 13, 1792; m. 1826, Dulcy Sage, of Windsor, N. Y.; res. Binghamton, N. Y.

vii. William, b. April 8, 1795; d. 1795.

viii. Nancy, b. Aug. 4, 1796; d. 1803.

ix. Alexander, b. Oct. 14, 1798.

x. David, b. Feb. 27, 1801; m. 1824, Laura Watrous, of Colesville, N. Y.; res. Sanford, N. Y.

xi. Samuel, b. March 16, 1806; m. 1831, Eliza Shiffer; res. Norwich, N. Y.

130. III. DANIEL,[7] b. Jan. 16, 1764, in Boston; m. Huldah Hopkins. He d. Dec. 30, 1845, in Guilford, Vt.; res. Guilford, Vt.; seven children.

131. IV. SAMUEL,[7] b. April 25, 1765, in Boston; m. Rhoda Louise Knight. He d. at sea, while on a coasting voyage for his health. He sailed from Boston, 1803. The ship and none of the crew ever heard from. Res. New York State; four children.

V. SUSANNA, b. Nov. 19, 1767; m. Dr. Simon Stevens, of Guilford, Vt. She d. Jan. 15, 1847; three children :—

i. Eliza Almeda, b. Aug. 22, 1806; m. April, 1835, Edward Fish Henry. She d. July, 1882; children : 1. Edward Stevens, b. Feb. 10, 1836. 2. Abby Eliza, b. Dec. 5, 1837. 3. Esther, b. Jan. 8, 1840. 4. Katharine, b. Feb. 27, 1842. 5. Martha Frances, b. April 27, 1848.

ii. Elvira Eunice, b. Feb. 19, 1809; m. ——, 1826, Jeremiah Greenleaf (143), b. Dec. 7, 1791; d. April 4, 1864. She d. March 30, 1874.

iii. —— Greenleaf, d. young; unmarried.

132. VI. JAMES,[7] b. Dec. 9, 1770; m. April 15, 1791, Sarah Bullock, b. Dec. 1, 1776, at Guilford, Vt.; d. June 17, 1844. He d. Nov. 5, 1845; res. Derby, Vt.; fourteen children.

VII. ELIZABETH, b. June 18, 1774; m. James K. Goodenough, of Watertown, N. Y. She d. March 25, 1847, at Watertown, N. Y.

STEPHEN (43) GREENLEAF, CONTINUED :—

133. VIII. DR. CHRISTOPHER,[7] b. Nov. 26, 1776, in Boston;
m. Jan. 30, 1803, Tabitha Dickinson, of Hatfield, b.
Sept. 9, 1777. He d. May 18, 1837; res. Lafarge-
ville, N. Y.; five children.

134. IX. JOSEPH,[7] b. Feb. 28, 1779; m. 1, Lydia Warner; d.
about 1814; 2, ——, 1815, Mrs. Ruth (Perry)
Cooper. He d. February, 1842; res. New York
State; six children.

X. POLLY, b. March 1, 1781, m. Oliver Dean, of New
York. She d. Nov. 3, 1822.

135. XI. THOMAS LEE,[7] b. Sept. 4, 1783; m. March 30, 1806,
Sarah Marshall, d. Aug. 31, 1871. He d. Aug. 2,
1865; a baker for many years; res. Watertown,
N. Y.; afterwards removed to Sackett's Harbor,
N. Y., where he died; nine children.

129.

(Stephen 6, Dr. Daniel 5, Rev. Daniel 4, Stephen 3, Stephen 2, Edmund 1.)

Children of **Maj. Stephen**[7] **Greenleaf** and Anna (Sargent).

136. I. THOMAS SARGENT,[8] b. March 25, 1784; m. 1, Dimmis Nash; 2, Lydia Miller, of Brattleboro, Vt.;
res. Columbus, Ill.; ten children.

II. ANNE (NANCY), b. Sept. 24, 1788; m. Thomas Ellis,
of Brattleboro, Vt.

III. STEPHEN SCOLLY, b. Aug. 22, 1795; d. Sept. 20,
1813; unmarried.

136.

(Maj. Stephen 7, Stephen 6, Dr. Daniel 5, Rev. Daniel 4, Stephen 3, Stephen 2, Edmund 1.)

Children of **Maj. Thomas Sargent**[8] **Greenleaf** and
Dimmis (Nash).

137. I. WILLIAM CUNE,[9] b. Aug. 2, 1809, at Brattleboro,
Vt.; m. April 1, 1835, Sarah W. Morse, d. Dec. 25,
1875. He d. Jan. 28, 1892; res. Templeton, Mass.;
eight children.

II. MOSES, b. 1810; d. in infancy.

III. GRACE NASH, b. Oct. 20, 1811, in Brattleboro,
Vt.; m. ——, 1832, Alonzo Clark Hunt, of Northampton, Mass. He d. Feb. 19, 1887; res. Springfield, Mass.; no children.

MAJ. THOMAS SARGENT (136) GREENLEAF, CONTINUED :—
  Children by 2d marriage :—
138. IV. HENRY MILLER,[9] b. Aug. 22, 1815; m. Feb. 13,
   1845, Eliza Ann, of Paris, Bourbon Co., Ky., dau. of
   Samuel and Cynthia (McCann) Schwartzwelder, of
   Pennsylvania, b. May 13, 1818. Cynthia McCann's
   father, Admiral William Penn McCann, U. S. Navy,
   was from Scotland, and cousin of Eliza Ann Greenleaf. Her grandmother, on her mother's side, was
   a Miss Penn, and related to William Penn, the Quaker
   who bought Pennsylvania from the Indians. Mr.
   Greenleaf resided at Columbus, Ill., and d. July 2,
   1848. They had one child, Grace, b. March 26,
   1846; m. Oct. 2, 1879, Robert H. Sindle. They
   have one child, Robert Henry, b. March 12, 1882.
   Mrs. Sindle and her mother, Mrs. Eliza Ann Greenleaf, reside at Gallatin, Tenn.
  V. MARY SOPHIA, b. Aug. 6, 1818; m. March 3, 1842,
   Napoleon B. Lawrence; four children :—
  i. Caroline Grace, b. March 18, 1843; m. George Russell, of
   Woodhull, Ill.
  ii. William Thomas, b. May 6, 1845; d. April 6, 1864, in the U. S.
   service.
  iii. Annie Elizabeth, b. Dec. 18, 1849; m. B. Thompson; res.
   ——, Kansas; four children.
  iv. Mary Cylinda, b. Aug. 5, 1851; m. Edward Bickford.
139. VI. MILLER THADDEUS,[9] b. March 21, 1821, in Brattleboro, Vt.; m. Oct. 30, 1844, Mary Elizabeth, dau.
   of Dr. John I. Felix, formerly of Lexington, Ky., b.
   June 20, 1826. He is a machinist; res. Quincy, Ill.;
   seven children.
  VII. LYDIA ANN CLEMENTIA, b. April 20, 1825; m.
   Nov. 1, 1855, Nathaniel Herrick. She d. Feb. 27,
   1857; one child :—
  Lois.
  VIII. SARAH ELIZABETH, b. Nov. 13, 1829; d. in infancy.
140. IX. THOMAS SCOLLY,[9] b. Nov. 16, 1832; m. July 27,
   1865, Mattie Osborn; res. Quincy, Ill.; five children :—
141. i. Thomas William,[10] b. June 27, 1866; m. Feb. 2,
   1891, Eva Ware; res. Quincy, Ill; one child :—
  Florence Eva, b. Nov. 24, 1891.

Maj. Thomas Sargent (136) Greenleaf, Continued :—
  IX. Thomas Scolly.
    II. Isabel, b. Sept. 30, 1867.
    III. Harry Charles, b. Sept. 21, 1869; res. Quincy, Ill.
    IV. Annie Clementia, b. July 3, 1872.
    V. Edwin Edgar, b. March 1, 1878; res. Quincy, Ill.
  X. Sarah Elizabeth, b. Sept. 22, 1834; m. 1, Sept.
    21, 1853, Henry J. Hair, M.D.; he d. Aug. 21, 1859;
    2, Nov. 30, 1865, Josiah T. Davis; d. Jan. 3, 1892;
    res. Carthage, Ill.; child by 1st marriage :—
      i. Mary Lydia, b. Aug. 25, 1854; m. Feb. 7, 1875, John Bahr.
        She d. March 8, 1877; one child, Annabell, lives at Columbus,
        Ill. (?)
  Children by 2d marriage :—
      ii. Emmar Owen, b. Feb. 18, 1869; m. Dec. 28, 1892, Eliza Rand.
      iii. Anna Grace, b. Nov. 1, 1872.
      The widowed mother lives with her children on a farm near
        Carthage, Hancock Co., Ill.

137.

(Thomas S. 8, Major Stephen 7, Stephen 6, Dr. Daniel 5, Rev. Daniel 4, Stephen 3, Stephen
2, Edmund 1.)

Children of **William C.**[9] **Greenleaf** and Sarah W.
  (Morse).
  I. William H., b. April 6, 1836; d. Dec. 9, 1839.
142. II. James Scolly,[10] b. Feb. 13, 1838, in Templeton,
    Mass.; m. Jan. 19, 1860, Miranda Orcott, b. Feb.
    15, 1832, at Stafford, Conn.; res. West Springfield,
    Mass.; two children :—
      I. Edward Henry, b. Dec. 8, 1865; d. Aug. 30, 1866.
      II. Willie Henry, b. Dec. 26, 1867; d. July 28, 1868.
  III. George W., b. July 18, 1839; d. May 31, 1850.
  IV. Sarah G., b. Dec. 2, 1841; m. Rufus K. Crocker.
    She d. June 9, 1872; two children :—
      i. Rufus A., m.; has children; res. East Templeton, Mass.
      ii. Sarah G.
  V. Olive A., b. May 16, 1844; m. A. L. Stacy. She d.
    Dec. 25, 1868; res. Athol, Mass.; two children :—
      i. Minnie A.; res. Denver, Col.
      ii. William; res. Athol, Mass.
  VI. Abbie E., b. Feb. 16, 1847; m. A. L. Stacy; res.
    Sunshine, Col.

WILLIAM C. (137) GREENLEAF, CONTINUED:—
  VII. JANE D., b. July 10, 1849; m. G. Henry Hawkes;
    res. Templeton, Mass.; three children:—
    i. Elmer G.
    ii. Thomas T.
    iii. James H.
  VIII. LUCIE B., b. April 26, 1852; d. March 30, 1869.

139.

(Thomas S. 8, Major Stephen 7, Stephen 6, Dr. Daniel 5, Rev. Daniel 4, Stephen 3, Stephen 2, Edmund 1.)

Children of **Miller Thaddeus**[9] **Greenleaf** and Mary E. (Felix).
  I. JOSEPHINE GRACE, b. Dec. 4, 1845; m. Dec. 4, 1866, James S. Ingraham.
  II. CECILIA FRANCES, b. Oct. 28, 1848; m. Nov. 14, 1887, Ira H. Lucas; child:—
    Ann Mae, b. Nov. 9, 1888.
  III. SCOLLY LEROY, b. June 8, 1851; res. Quincy, Ill.
  IV. MARY FLORA BELL, b. Jan. 19, 1857.
  V. CLEMENTIA LILY, b. April 18, 1862; res. Quincy, Ill.
  VI. ELIZABETH ROSE, b. Jan. 3, 1865; res. Quincy, Ill.
  VII. CHARLES MILLER, b. Dec. 11, 1868; res. Quincy, Ill.

130.

(Stephen 6, Dr. Daniel 5, Rev. Daniel 4, Stephen 3, Stephen 2, Edmund 1.)

Children of **Daniel**[7] **Greenleaf** and Huldah (Hopkins).
143. I. JEREMIAH,[8] b. Dec. 7, 1791, in Brattleboro, Vt.; m.
    Elvira Eunice, dau. of Dr. Simon Stevens, of Guilford, Vt., and Susanna, dau. of Stephen Greenleaf (43), his cousin. He d. April 4, 1864, at Guilford, Vt.; six children; all born in Guilford, Vt.
144. II. EMORY,[8] b. Aug. 26, 1793, in Guilford, Vt.; m. Jan. 1, 1822, Gracia Houghton, of Guilford, Vt., b. Sept. 19, 1796; resided for many years at Charlemont, Mass.; then removed to Milwaukee, Wis. He d. 1849, in Milwaukee, Wis.; six children.
145. III. STEPHEN,[8] b. 1795, in Guilford, Vt.; m. Sarah Weatherhead; res. Brattleboro, Vt.; two daughters.

DANIEL (130) GREENLEAF, CONTINUED :—

IV. RHODA, m. Thaddeus Whitney, of Guilford, Vt.; three children :—
  i. A son.
  ii. A daughter.
  iii. Charles.

V. EUNICE, m. Alfred Arms, of Guilford, Vt.; one child :— Alfred.

VI. BETSEY, m. Timothy K. Horton, of Bernardston She d. about 1838; three children.

VII. CAROLINE, m. Timothy K. Horton (second wife); d. 1852; six children.

143.

Children of **Jeremiah**[8] **Greenleaf** and Elvira Eunice (Stevens).

146. I. HALBERT STEVENS[9] (Hon.), b. April 12, 1827; m. June 24, 1852, Jean F., dau. of John Brooks, M.D., of Bernardstown, Mass., b. Oct. 1, 1831, President Woman's Suffrage Association of the State of New York; res. Rochester, N. Y.; no children.

II. MARY HOPKINS, b. April 5, 1829; m. Norman Root, of Guilford, Vt. She d. March 16, 1862; no children.

147. III. MALCOLM CYPREAN,[9] b. Feb. 17, 1831; m. Martha (Stevens) Flint; res. Rochester, N. Y.; no children.

IV. SUSAN ANN, b. March 27, 1833; m. Horatio Selby, of Milwaukee, Wis. She d. February, 1870; two children :—
  i. Horatio.
  ii. Mary.

V. ELIZA MARIA, b. Feb. 23, 1835; d. March, 1889, at Rowe, Mass.; unmarried.

VI. THOMAS BENTON, b. Feb. 27, 1837; d. April 4, 1850, in Guilford, Vt.

144.

Children of **Emory**[8] **Greenleaf** and Gracia (Houghton).

I. GEORGE HOUGHTON, b. Aug. 6, 1823; d. May 6, 1832.

147a II. EMORY BRADFORD, b. July 2, 1825; m. 1, Sept. 9, 1847, Caroline Maria Chase; 2, ——; res. Milwaukee, Wis.; two children.

EMORY (144) GREENLEAF, CONTINUED:—
148. III. AUGUSTUS WARREN,[9] b. May 19, 1827, in Whitting-
ham, Vt.; m. Sept. 1, 1849, in New York, Sarah
Augusta, dau. of Thomas Lynde and Rectina Field
(Houghton), of Guilford, Vt.; b. Feb. 22, 1831. He
d. Feb. 28, 1878; a banker; res. New York. Four
children:—
  i. Warren Emory, b. June 5, 1850, in res. Milwaukee,
    Wis.; a banker; res. Pelouse, Wash.
  ii. Sarah Houghton, b. Aug. 5, 1852, in New York;
    d. April 20, 1892.
  iii. Alice Hazen, b. March 28, 1856, in New York;
    res. New York.
  iv. Ida, b. June 27, 1860, in New York.
IV. FRANCIS HENRY, b. Aug. 22, 1829; res. New York.
V. ELIZA MIRANDA, b. Nov. 2, 1832; d. Feb. 23, 1834.
VI. EMILY FIELD, b. June 8, 1835, Charlemont, Mass.

131

(Stephen 6, Dr. Daniel 5, Rev. Daniel 4, Stephen 3, Stephen 2, Edmund 1.)
Children of **Samuel**[7] **Greenleaf** and Rhoda Louisa
(Knight):—
149. I. FLAVEL,[8] b. Oct. 18, 1791; m. Eunice Smith, b. March
9, 1794, in Guilford, Vt.; d. Aug. 5, 1847. He
d. Oct. 30, 1850; res. Saratoga, N. Y., also Michigan, in 1831. Twelve children.
150. II. WILLIAM,[8] b. about 1792; m. 1 ——; d. 1839, in
Cincinnati, Ohio; 2 ——; res. Michigan. Had
three children; none living.
III. EUNICE FAIRBANKS, m. Abner Harvey Enos.
151. IV. SAMUEL KNIGHT,[8] b, March 19, 1803, in Brattleboro,
Vt.; m. Jan., 1825, Olive Osyor, b. Sept. 22,
1804; d. Jan. 9, 1894. He d. May 7, 1842, in
Circleville, Ohio; res. North Royalton, Cuyahoga
Co., Ohio, about 1832, and Circleville, Pickaway
Co., Ohio. Four children.

149.

(Samuel 7, Stephen 6, Dr. Daniel 5, Rev. Daniel 4, Stephen 3, Stephen 2, Edmund 1.)
Children of **Flavel**[8] **Greenleaf** and Eunice (Smith).
I. MARTHA MATOON, b. Aug. 27, 1816; m. Hiram
Harkins. She d. April 22, 1838; two daughters.

FLAVEL (149) GREENLEAF, CONTINUED :—

152. II. SAMUEL SMITH,[9] b. Jan. 23, 1818, in Guilford, Vt.;
m. Nov. 28, 1841, Elizabeth McOmber; shoe and
leather merchant; res. Waukegan, Ill., since 1837;
three children :—

    I. John Flavel, b. Oct. 20, 1845; teller in bank in
Chicago, Ill.

    II. Samuel Trant, b. Dec. 24, 1847.

    III. An Infant.

III. WILLIAM, b. Dec. 30, 1821; clerk in Circuit Court,
Chicago, Ill.

IV. GEORGE DICKINSON, b. Dec. 14, 1823; carpenter
and joiner; res. Wisconsin.

V. MARIA, b. Sept. 20, 1825; m. Warren Briggs; res.
Michigan.

VI. LUCIA ANN, b. Dec. 18, 1830; res. Michigan.

VII. AMOS, b. Dec. 19, 1836.

Five others born and died.

151.

(Samuel 7, Stephen 6, Dr. Daniel 5, Rev. Daniel 4, Stephen 3, Stephen 2, Edmund 1.)

Children of **Samuel Knight**[8] **Greenleaf** and Olive
(Osyor).

I. MARY KNIGHT, b. Aug. 28, 1825; m. 1, May 5, 1846,
Josephus Latham Woodbridge, who d. Nov. 10,
1859; 2, April 29, 1869, David A. Woodbridge, a
brother of Josephus L.; d. Nov. 28, 1881. She d.
March 1, 1894; res. Paris, Ill.; ten children.

Children by 1st marriage :—

    i. Latham G., b. Sept. 13, 1847; d. Sept. 3, 1848.

    ii. William A., b. July 8, 1849; m. April 14, 1875, Mina L. Hub-
bard, b. April 30, 1851.

    iii. Ella, b. April 11, 1851; m. March 24, 1874, Hugar H. Huston.

    iv. Henry Knight, b. June 2, 1853; d. in infancy.

    v. Samuel Addison, b. June 6, 1854; d. in infancy.

    vi. Mark Judson, b. Aug. 14, 1855; m. Nov. 14, 1876, Kate F.
Stinson.

    vii. Charles Carroll, b. Feb. 3, 1857; d. in infancy.

    viii. Louis C.; m. Dec. 8, 1881, Celia W. Curl.

    ix. Josephus L., b. Feb. 13, 1860; d. in infancy.

Child by 2d marriage :—

    x. A son, b. and d. Oct. 5, 1873.

Samuel Knight (151) Greenleaf, Continued :—

II. Rhoda Louisa, b. June 19, 1827 ; m. June 23, 1857, William Knox, b. July 9, 1823 ; d. Nov. 3, 1883, at Haywards, Cal. She d. Dec. 16, 1882 ; seven children :—

i. Milo, b. June 27, 1858; m. Oct. 5, 1879, Alice Warren; res. Haywards, Cal.; child : William, b. Sept. 19, 1881.

ii. William, b. Sept. 12, 1860; m. Dec. 28, 1885, Harriet Elizabeth Waterbury; res. Haywards, Cal.; children : 1. Nina Louise, b. June 13, 1887. 2. Ruby Corinne, b. May 25, 1889.

iii. John, b. Nov. 8, 1862; m. Nov. 22, 1887, Louise Taylor Holden, b. Jan. 3, 1868; res. Providence, R. I.; children : 1. Margaret, b. April 27, 1890. 2. Helen Louise, b. July 13, 1893.

iv. Lincoln, b. June 18, 1865 ; d. Dec. 16, 1865.

v. Alanson, b. Dec. 24, 1866; d. Jan. 28, 1882.

vi. George, } Twins, b. March, 1868; d. June, 1868.
vii. Charles, }

153. III. William,[9] b. Aug. 6, 1829, at Crown Point, N. Y.; m. Dec. 12, 1850, Sarah Ann McFerren, b. May 1, 1829; d. April 1, 1887. Moved to Vermont while he was a small boy ; thence to Ohio, where he married ; thence to Paris, Edgar Co., Ill, ; at close of War he moved to Terra Haute, Ind., where he now resides ; eight children.

IV. Esther Cook, b. Sept. 13, 1831 ; m. Henry Clark.

153.

(Samuel Knight 8, Samuel 7, Stephen 6, Dr. Daniel 5, Rev. Daniel 4, Stephen 3, Stephen 2, Edmund 1.)

Children of **William**[9] **Greenleaf** and Sarah Ann (McFerren).

I. Olive M., b. July 17, 1853 ; m. Aug. 22, 1871, George Couch, b. Feb. 2, 1850 ; res. Terre Haute, Ind. ; no children.

154. II. Latham Wiley,[10] b. Aug. 22, 1855 ; m. Dec. 6, 1881, Anna Conover, b. Aug. 23, 1860 ; res. Terre Haute Ind. ; five children :—

i. Guy William, b. Oct. 4, 1882.

ii. Wiley, b. July 6, 1885.

iii. George McFerren, b. July 20, 1889.

iv. John Whittier, b. July 4, 1891.

v. Catharine, b. Oct. 12, 1893.

III. Rachel, b. Dec. 7, 1856.

WILLIAM (153) GREENLEAF, CONTINUED:—

155. IV. SAMUEL KNOX,[10] b. Nov. 4, 1860; m. Sept. 7, 1881,
    at Terre Haute, Ind., Eva Snavely, b. Oct. 6, 1860;
    moved in 1888 to Omaha, Neb.; child:—
    William Stokely, b. June 15, 1882, at Terre Haute,
    Ind.

V. ANNA, b. Sept. 24, 1862; m. 1888, John A. Park-
    hurst, b. Sept. 24, 1861; res. Marengo, Ill.; no
    children.

VI. HENRIETTA, b. April 22, 1866; m. Nov. 13, 1884,
    Leander L. Swartz, b. May 7, 1864; res. Terre
    Haute, Ind.; two children:—
    i. Roy B., b. Sept. 4, 1885.
    ii. Orville A., b. Aug. 12, 1889.

VII. SUSAN BELL, b. Aug. 12, 1869; m. Nov. 26, 1889,
    Orville E. Batman, b. March 24, 1869; res. Terre
    Haute, Ind.; two children:—
    i. George Frederick, b. June 28, 1892.
    ii. Wesley Adelbert, b. Jan. 22, 1894.

VIII. GEORGE W., b. Oct. 22, 1870.

132.

(Stephen 6, Dr. Daniel 5, Rev. Daniel 4, Stephen 3, Stephen 2, Edmund 1.)

Children of **James**[7] **Greenleaf** and Sarah (Bullock).

I. CELYNDA, b. April 27, 1794; m. March 29, 1821,
    Henry Williams, b. June 18, 1799; d. April 3, 1867.
    She d. April 15, 1854; six children:—
    i. Mary Blake, b. Sept. 11, 1822; d. March 30, 1839.
    ii. Martha Spaulding, b. April 13, 1824; m. May 22, 1842, Wil-
        liam Rankin; about two or three years after his wife's death
        he married for third time. She d. Feb. 15, 1843; child: Sarah
        Martha, b. Feb. 9, 1843; m. Jan. 26, 1862, David Heath; lives
        at Waverly, Iowa.
    iii. Charles, b. Jan. 26, 1826; m. June 13, 1848, Maria Traversy,
        d. Oct. 21, 1892. He d. March 17, 1862; child: Emma Estella,
        b. March 4, 1850; m. March 4, 1874, Amos C. Sawyer.
    iv. Esther, b. Feb. 28, 1828; m. Jan. 25, 1882, Lorenzo Cummings;
        res. at Newport, Vt.
    v. Ellen Bruce, b. May 31, 1830; m. Oct. 14, 1851, Samuel Niles,
        d. May 12, 1891. She d. March 12, 1891; eight children: 1.
        Smith Henry, b. Aug. 16, 1852; m. 1, March 7, 1874, Effie A.
        Hill; 2, Oct. 3, 1881, Mary J. Fletcher. 2. Celynda Marion,
        b. Dec. 11, 1854; d. Dec. 19, 1868. 3. Avery Williams, b.
        March 1, 1857; m. Nov. 24, 1880, Ellen L. Wing; res. New-

JAMES (132) GREENLEAF, CONTINUED:—
I. Celynda.

port Centre, Vt. 4. Clarinda Mabel, b. Feb. 5, 1859; m. Nov. 23, 1879, William M. Rogers; res. Newport Centre, Vt. 5. Esther Millie, b. July 5, 1861; m. Aug. 26, 1886, William W. Griswold; res. Osage, Iowa. 6. Lydia Maria, b. May 9, 1864; m. Aug. 25, 1887, Edward Niles; she d. Nov. 14, 1888; res. Coventry, Vt. 7. Fannie Ellen, b. May 15, 1866; m. June 18, 1889, Charles G. Niles; she d. Feb. 17, 1891. 8. Gertrude Josephine, b. June 29, 1868; m. May 10, 1892, Charles G. Niles; res. Coventry, Vt.

vi. Sarah Milleson, b. June 13, 1834; m. 1, Dec. 5, 1855, Alden B. Lunt; 2, December, 1876, Joseph Whittemore, d. May 18, 1891. She d. Feb. 9, 1893; children by first marriage: 1. Alanson Eugene, b. March 20, 1857; m. June 20, 1880, Evaline Wilkins; res. Egan, Dakota. 2. Ellen Onata,* b. Oct. 3, 1858; m. June 13, 1876, Volney Strunk; res. Osage, Iowa. 3. Edward Ellis, b. Aug. 16, 1860; m. Feb. 22, 1888, Christina Raymond; res. Dill Rapids, Dakota. 4. Charles Schuyler, b. Nov. 14, 1862; d. March 10, 1865. 5. Millie Etta, b. Oct. 24, 1866; m. April 2, 1889, Charles B. Doty; res. Clarksville, Iowa. 6. Walter Howard, b. July 25, 1869; m. Sept. 15, 1890, Hattie Rosenfield; res. Sioux City, Iowa.

II. ALMIRA, b. May 18, 1796; m. Avery Williams. She d. March 20, 1866.

III. CLARISSA, b. May 26, 1798; m. John Dresser; left her husband. She d. April, 1855; res. Libby's Mills, Province Quebec; five children:—
i. Almira.
ii. Harriet, m. Sewall Clark.
iii. Emery.
iv. Albert.
v. Henry.

IV. ALANSON BULLOCK, b. April 5, 1800; d. Oct. 12, 1818; drowned.

156. V. SQUIRE STEPHEN,[8] b. June 29, 1802, at Derby, Vt.; m. Bethiah Church, who d. June 7, 1865. He d. March 22, 1871; ten children.

VI. POLLY, b. July 14, 1804; d. in infancy.

VII. CHARLES, b. Sept. 2, 1805; d. Dec. 14, 1848; unmarried.

157. VIII. GEORGE DIXON[8] (Rev.), b. Sept. 12, 1808; m. June 18, 1826, Sally Stickney, of Johnson, Vt., b. Dec. 15, 1807, in Mt. Vernon, N. H.; d. Nov. 3, 1894. He d. May 4, 1876; six children.

* An Indian name, i.e., forest leaf.

JAMES (132) GREENLEAF, CONTINUED :—

158. IX. ALBERT,[8] b. March 20, 1810, in Derby, Vt. ; m. 1, about July, 1833, Aurelia Mills, of Hounsville, N. Y., who d. about 1835 ; 2, Aug. 12, 1837, Mary E. Johnson, of Belleville, N. Y. He d. 1888 ; res. Marquette, Wis. ; four children :—
 i. George ; res. Portage, Wis.
 ii. Alonzo.
 iii. Albert.
 iv. Luther.

159. X. WILLIAM FAIRBANKS,[8] b. May 6, 1812, in Derby, Vt. ; m. Dec. 3, 1835, at Danville, Vt., Abigail Ward, b. July 24, 1812, at Abbottsford, C. E. ; d. Feb. 11, 1892, at Winooski, Vt. He d. Feb. 18, 1877 ; machinist ; res. Winooski Falls, Vt. ; four children.

  XI. SARAH, b. Sept. 12, 1814 ; m. May 22, 1836, William Rankin. She d. March 27, 1842 ; two children :—
 i. Ira Sweetland.
 ii. Henry Williams.
 Mr. Rankin afterwards married Martha S., daughter of Celynda (Greenleaf) and Henry Williams.

  XII. MARY, b. Oct. 15, 1816 ; m. Jan. 21, 1840, Rev. James Smith, a Methodist minister, b. Jan. 28, 1807, at Andover, N. H. He d. Nov. 20, 1875 ; res. Franklin, Vt. ; three children :—
 i. Mary Josephine, b. Oct. 4, 1841, at Groton, Vt. ; m. Dec. 2, 1868, Oliver F. Sisco ; res. Troy, Vt. ; three children : 1. Henry N., b. Sept. 22, 1870. 2. Smith James, b. Jan. 14, 1877. 3. Blanche May, b. Nov. 18, 1878.
 ii. James Greenleaf, b. Dec. 18, 1845, at Norwich, Vt. ; m. Feb. 23, 1869, Georgianna Widdifield ; one child : Kitty Josephine, b. Dec. 13, 1869 ; m. Nov. 2, 1892, James Sawyer Hedge, Buffalo, N. Y. James G. Smith ; res. Erie, Penn.
 iii. Almira Isabella, b. March 20, 1856, at West Newport, Vt. ; m. Oct. 27, 1879, James Hill ; res. Franklin, Vt. ; one child : Mary Leoline, b. Aug. 15, 1880.

160. XIII. JAMES (TABOR),[8] b. Jan. 25, 1819 ; m. 1, Sept. 27, 1840, Caroline Marsh, of Murray, Upper Canada, who d. July 1, 1846 ; 2, Aug. 7, 1848, at Winooski Falls, Vt., Mahala T. Beach, who d. March, 1854 ; 3, November, 1856, Mrs. Phebe A. Lasky ; res. Rockford, Iowa ; eight children.
 He dropped the name of Tabor.

JAMES (132) GREENLEAF, CONTINUED :—
161. XIV. LUTHER LELAND,[8] b. Feb. 7, 1821, in Derby, Vt.;
m. Elizabeth M. Kellum, of Irasburg, Vt.; he was
for many years a merchant in Boston, Mass.; d. Nov.
23, 1884, at Beloit, Wis.; children :—
   I. Mary Elizabeth, b. June 14, 1855; m. Sept. 10,
      1882, James C. Plant; res. Minneapolis, Minn.
   II. Helen Maria, b. Sept. 9, 1856; m. Aug. 11, 1892,
      James Simmons, Jr., Professor of Moral and Men-
      tal Philosophy, Grinnell (Iowa) College; res.
      Grinnell, Iowa.
   III. Leland, b. April, 1864; d. August, 1864.

156.

(James 7, Stephen 6, Dr. Daniel 5, Rev. Daniel 4, Stephen 3, Stephen 2, Edmund 1.)

Children of **Squire Stephen**[8] **Greenleaf** and Bethiah
(Church).
I. ALANSON, d. in infancy.
II. CELINA A., b. Dec. 1, 1830; m. Jan. 18, 1853, J.
E. W. Shonyo; they adopted Ella Jane, dau. of
Harriet A. and J. J. Babbitt; res. South Bend, Pa-
cific Co., Wash.
III. JOHN WESLEY, b. July 23, 1833.
IV. SARAH JANE, b. Feb. 22, 1835; m. Sept. 26, 1853,
Edson H. Laythe; she d. Aug. 22, 1891; they adopted
Fred S., son of Harriet A. and J. J. Babbitt; he
m. Dec. 25, 1883, Mary A. Holmes, adopted dau.
of Horace Holmes, of Derby Line, Vt.; her original name was Bailey; druggist, South Bend, Wash.
five children :—
   i. Lawrence Holmes, b. Sept. 27, 1884, at Farnham, Que.
   ii. Millicent Melinda, b. Sept. 10, 1885, at Rock Island, Que.
   iii. William Eugene, b. Sept. 9, 1888, at Derby Line, Vt.
   iv. Mary Kathaline, b. Sept. 13, 1892, at South Bend, Wash.
   v. Frederick Horace, b. Jan. 20, 1895, at South Bend, Wash.
162. V. STEPHEN A.,[9] b. June 7, 1837; m. Ann Robinson;
res. Derby Line, Vt.; one child :—
Edson, m. Georgia Harris.
VI. MARY C., b. Jan. 7, 1839.

SQUIRE STEPHEN (156) GREENLEAF, CONTINUED :—

    VII. HARRIET A., b. June 7, 1841; m. Oct. 1, 1859,
        J. J. Babbitt; res. South Bend, Pacific Co., Wash.;
        two children :—
        i. Ella Jane; m. E. W. Albee.
        ii. Fred S.; m. Mary A. (Bailey) Holmes.

163. VIII. LUTHER LEE,[9] b. Jan. 28, 1843; m. April 22,
        1866, Mary R. Adams; res. West Derby, Vt.; four
        children :—
        I. Mabel Bethiah, b. Nov. 15, 1874; d. Sept. 17, 1880.
        II. Etta Claire, b. April 9, 1880.
        III. Lucretia Maude, b. Dec. 7, 1884.
        IV. Celina May, b. Oct. 6, 1887.

    IX. SUSAN M., b. Feb. 2, 1845; m. Lewis F. Shonyo;
        res. Lyndonville, Vt.; one child :—
        Fred. C.; m. Annie Dickerson; stock farm, Valley View, Lyndon-
        ville, Vt.

    X. ELIZA E., b. Dec. 1, 1846; m. Gavin Shanks.

157.

(James 7, Stephen 6, Dr. Daniel 5, Rev. Daniel 4, Stephen 3, Stephen 2, Edmund 1.)

    Children of **Rev. George Dixon**[8] **Greenleaf** and Sally
    (Stickney).

164. I. ORLANDO CONSTANTINE,[9] b. July 21, 1829, in Eden,
        Vt.; m. 1, May 1, 1851, Margaret Dafoe, of Fred-
        ericksburg, Ont., who. d. Dec. 21, 1858, aged 29
        years, 6 months; 2, Nov. 19, 1859, Anna Cecelia,
        dau. of Benjamin Weller, of Carrying Place, Ont.;
        res. Belleville, Ont.; ten children.

    II. MARTHA ANN BUEL, b. May 13, 1833; m. Jan. 20,
        1852, Noah Herring, of Gouverneur, N. Y.; d.
        March 15, 1854; one daughter :—
        Mary Cynthia, b. Jan. 13, 1853, at Napanee, Ont.; m. June 19,
        1878, Asa Leroy Burke, b. Sept. 26, 1849, at Oshawa, Ont.;
        five children: 1. Lillian May, b. April 28, 1879, in Barrie,
        Ont. 2. Wilbert Emerson, b. Sept. 10, 1880, in Orangeville,
        Ont. 3. Eva Pearl, b. Aug. 8, 1882, in Stratford, Ont.
        4. Wellington Harold, b. May 23, 1884; d. July 3, 1886.
        5. Harlo Clayton, b. June 18, 1887; d. April 30, 1888.

    III. MARY JANE, b. Aug. 10, 1835; m. July 5, 1852, in
        Napanee, C. W., Charles Shepard Bonney, of Penn

Rev. George Dixon (157) Greenleaf, Continued :—

III. Mary Jane.

> Yan, N. Y., b. Nov. 3, 1828, in Milo, N. Y.; res. Marion, Ind.; five children :—

> > i. Albert Franklin, b. Aug. 5, 1853, in Napanee, C. W.; m. 1880, Frances Marie O'Neal, of Cascade, Iowa, b. June 12, ——. Physician and Postmaster; res. Buck Grove, Iowa; children : 1. Mary Margarette, b. March 5, 1881. 2. Thomas Chew, b. Feb. 15, 1882. 3. Henry Sidney, b. Dec. 12, 1883. 4. Bernece C., b. Aug. 6, 1887.

> > ii. Ella Nancy, b. July 12, 1855, in Gouverneur, N. Y.; m. April 16, 1873, Frank R. Rapp, of Irvington, N. J., b. Oct. 14, 1848, at Irvington, N. J. He was the son of Augustin Lafayette Rapp, b. Charleston, S. C., and his wife, Sarah (Elliott), b. in London, England, and dau. of Samuel M. Elliott, oculist of New York, b. in Inverness, Scotland, and Diana (Laylor), b. Northumberland, England. Augustin L. Rapp was son of Adam Rapp, b. in New York, and his wife Ann (Smith), b. in Charleston, S. C.; bus. Philadelphia, Penn.; res. Irvington, N. J.; children : 1. Ada Maud, b. Feb. 22, 1874, in Philadelphia, Penn. 2. Nellie Frances, b. April 21, 1876, in Germantown, Penn. 3. Sidney Charles, b. July 20, 1881, in Irvington, N. J.

> > iii. Henry Gardiner, b. March 30, 1857, at Penn Yan, N. Y.; m. in Philadelphia, Mary Clarke, b. April 22, 1857, in Philadelphia; res. Marion, Ind.; children : 1. Edith Madge, b. June 17, 1881, in Philadelphia. 2. Leslie Elizabeth, b. Jan. 27, 1887, in Philadelphia. 3. Kenneth Clarke, b. March 12, 1890, in Marion, Ind.

> > iv. Minnie Emmaretta, b. Dec. 28, 1862, at Wren Farm, Oil Creek, Penn.; m. 1883, Arch P. Goldsmith, of Lyons Farms, N. J.; child, Lela Bonney, b. Aug. 3, 1885.

> > v. George Dixon Greenleaf, b. Feb. 10, 1872, in Philadelphia; res. Philadelphia, Penn.; unmarried.

165. IV. George Columbus,[9] b. Sept. 14, 1839, in Belleville, C. W.; m. May 30, 1859, Anna Eliza Totman, of Moira, N. Y.; res. Brushton, Franklin Co., N. Y. He moved in 1859 to Massena, N. Y., where in 1860 he published *The Beacon*; three children.

V. Susanna Almina, b. Oct. 10, 1842, in Tyantinago, Province of Ontario; m. Aug. 3, 1860, in Massena, N. Y., Harris Wilbur, of Boston, Mass., b. Oct. 25, 1829, in Madrid, Me.; res. Norwood, N. Y.; six children :—

> i. Carrie Florence, b. July 3, 1861, in Charlestown, Mass.

> ii. Cora Eminojene, b. April 16, 1865, in Newport, R. I.; m. Dec. 28, 1881, in Norwood, N. Y., Fred. Cromer Hastings, b. June

Rev. George Dixon (157) Greenleaf, Continued :—

V. Susanna Almina.

> 29, 1859, in East Constable, N. Y.; he died April 19, 1894; children: 1. Cora Ethel, b. Sept. 22, 1882, in Constable, N. Y. 2. Alfred Arthur, b. May 13, 1886, in Constable, N. Y.

> iii. Gertrude S., b. May 11, 1870, in Lee Centre, N. Y.; m. Sept. 10, 1889, Walter Scott Austin, b. June, 15, 1866, in Plattsburg, N. Y.; children: 1. Walter Leon, b. June 20, 1891, in Norwood, N. Y. 2. Mabelle Pauline, b. Sept. 4, 1892, in Norwood, N. Y. 3 and 4. Twins, b. Sept. 8, 1894, in Norwood, N. Y.

> iv. George Harris, b. Dec. 23, 1872, in Lee Centre, N. Y.

> v. Ida May, twin, b. Dec. 23, 1872, in Lee Centre, N. Y.; m. Sept. 25, 1894, in Norwood, N. Y., Dr. Henry Dudley Wilbur, b. Aug. 10, 1870, in Constable, N. Y.

> vi. Mary Irene, b. March 4, 1880, in Brushton, N. Y.

VI. Albert Franklin, b. 1845; d. 1847.

164.

(Rev. George D. 8, James 7, Stephen 6, Dr. Daniel 5, Rev. Daniel 4, Stephen 3, Stephen 2, Edmund 1.)

Children of Orlando C.[9] Greenleaf and Margaret (Dafoe).

I. Frances Almira, b. Aug. 5, 1852; m. Erwin R. Waelde; res. Milton Station, N. Y.

II. Martha Ann Buell, b. July 21, 1854, at Newburg, Ont.; m. Dec. 24, 1877, W. H. Gordon, oldest son of Robert and Catherine Gordon, of Hungerford, Ont.; b. Aug. 27, 1856; member of the firm of George Ritchie & Co., Belleville, Ont. Was alderman two terms. Is now member of the City Board of Education. Mr. Gordon is a prominent member of the Tabernacle Methodist Church, of which he is treasurer, and superintendent of the Sunday school, president of the Epworth League, of Christian Endeavor, etc.; res. Belleville, Ont. Four children :—

> i. Erwin Raymond, b. April 19, 1880.
> ii. Merton Cloudsley, b. May 6, 1883.
> iii. Vera Katherine, b. Nov. 8, 1886.
> iv. Henry Challen, b. Oct. 3, 1888.

III. Cadelia Jane, b. Nov. 1, 1856; m. George Lovell, of Schenevus, N. Y.

IV. Margaret, b. May 24, 1859; d. in infancy.

ORLANDO C. (164) GREENLEAF, CONTINUED :—
Children by 2d marriage :—
V. GEORGE, b. Nov. 14, 1861 ; d. 1862.
VI. MARY CECELIA, b. Nov. 29, 1866.
166. VII. HENRY WILBER,[10] b. Feb. 10, 1871 ; m. Dec. 25,
1894, Minnie Pearl, dau. of Samuel James and Sarah
Demill, of Sterling, b. March 7, 1875 ; res. Belle-
ville, Ontario, Can. Mr. Greenleaf is in business
with his father on Front Street, Belleville, Ont.
VIII. EVA MERTLE, b. April 2, 1874.
IX. ADA ALBERTHA, b. July 3, 1876.
X. CHARLES ORLANDO, b. Nov. 17, 1878.

165.

(Rev. Geo. Dixon 8, James 7, Stephen 6, Dr. Daniel 5, Rev. Daniel 4, Stephen 3, Stephen 2,
Edmund 1.)

Children of **George Columbus**[9] **Greenleaf** and Ann
Eliza (Tolman).
167. I. FRANKLIN ALANSON,[10] b. June 2, 1860, in Massena,
N. Y.; m. July 4, 1882, Hattie Bell Davis, of
Fort Covington, N. Y.; b. June 26, 1862, in St.
Albans, Vt.; res. Brushton, N. Y. Four chil-
dren :—
I. Frank Willefred, b. July 26, 1883.
II. Hattie Bell, b. Aug. 27, 1885.
III. George Standish, b. Jan. 22, 1889.
IV. Winnefred Eliza, b. June 28, 1891.
II. GEORGIANNA MAY, b. Oct. 25, ——, in Moiva, N. Y.;
m. in Manchester, N. H., A. J. Fussell, in the
United States Post-office service.
III. FLORA AGNES, b. Dec. 6, 1867, in Depauville, N.
Y.; m. Jan. 12, 1888, Alvin Bates Baker, of
Delta, C. W. One child :—
Vernon Greenleaf, b. Oct. 30, 1889.

159.

(James 7, Stephen 6, Dr. Daniel 5, Rev. Daniel 4, Stephen 3, Stephen 2, Edmund 1.)

Children of **William Fairbanks**[8] **Greenleaf** and Abigail (Ward).
168. I. EDWARD EVERETT,[9] b. Aug. 13, 1837, at Derby,
Vt.; m. April 27, 1867, at Winooski, Vt., 1,

WILLIAM FAIRBANKS (159) GREENLEAF, CONTINUED :—

    I. Edward Everett.

        Carrie Van Vliet Knox, who d. April 13, 1883 ; 2, May 15, 1884, at Winooski, Vt., Lovilla White Forest ; res. Huntsville, Ala. ; three children by 1st marriage :—

           i. Enola, b. May 10, 1870, at Winooski, Vt.; m. Jan. 2, 1893, at Decatur, Morgan Co., Ala., William J. Polk.

           ii. Carrie, b. March 17, 1876, at Burlington, Vt. ; d. Jan. 24, 1878, at Winooski, Vt.

           iii. Edna, b. March 17, 1876, at Burlington, Vt. ; twin.

169.   II. WILLIAM LUTHER,[9] b. Sept. 1, 1842, at Derby, Vt. ; m. Dec. 25, 1865, at Winooski, Vt., Adelaide M., dau. of Horace W. Barrett, of Winooski, Vt. ; res. Burlington, Vt. ; no children.

    III. CHARLES HENRY, b. Jan. 29, 1845, at Derby, Vt. ; d. Aug. 23, 1847, at Winooski, Vt.

170.   IV. CHARLES ALPHONSO,[9] b. Dec. 11, 1849, at Winooski, Vt. ; m. April 19, 1876, Hattie Louise, dau. of Horace W. Barrett ; res. West Gardner, Mass. ; one child :—

        Horace William, b. May 8, 1879, in Ashburnham, Mass. ; res. West Gardner, Mass.

160.

(James 7, Stephen 6, Dr. Daniel 5, Rev. Daniel 4, Stephen 3, Stephen 2, Edmund 1.)

    Children of **James**[8] **Greenleaf** and Caroline (Marsh).

    I. ADELAIDE AMES, b. May 24, 1842, at Oswego, N. Y. ; m. Oct. 26, 1865, D. J. Purdy ; b. July 7, 1836, at Sidney, C. W. ; res. Mason City, Iowa.

    Children by 1st marriage :—

        i. George Hartley, b. Aug. 27, 1866 ; m. —— May 20, 1891.

        ii. Caroline Marsh, b. Feb. 18, 1868 ; d. Aug. 29, 1880, at Mason City, Iowa.

        iii. Margaret Louise, b. Sept. 23, 1872 ; d. April 23, 1880.

    II. MARY, b. Sept. 30, 1844, in Elyria, N. Y. ; m. Ralph Purdy ; she d. a year or two after marriage.

    Children by 2d marriage :—

    III. ELLA, b. May, 1849 ; d. young.

JAMES (160) GREENLEAF, CONTINUED:—
170a.IV. WINFIELD, b. March 25, 1852; m. Jan. 1, 1873,
Elvira, dau. of J. O. Seely; res. Kent, Wash.; four
children:—
    I. Charles O., d. in infancy.
    II. Ada P., b. April 2, 1876.
    III. Elmer E., b. 1879.
    IV. Sadie, b. 1882.
  V. ROSWELL W., b. about 1854, at Racine, Wis.; d. in
infancy.
Children by 3d marriage:—
  VI. A DAUGHTER, b. Jan. 3, 1858; d. 1868.
  VII. SARAH ELIZABETH, b. Oct. 12, 1860; m. O. J.
Hanson; res. Mason City, Iowa.
170b.VIII. LUTHER LELAND, m. Dec. 25, 1886, at Lime
Springs, Iowa, May Raymond, of Floyd, Iowa;
res. Rockford, Iowa; three children, daughters.

133.

(Stephen 6, Dr. Daniel 5, Rev. Daniel 4, Stephen 3, Stephen 2, Edmund 1.)

Children of **Dr. Christopher[7] Greenleaf** and Tabitha
(Dickinson).

171. I. JOHN DICKINSON,[8] b. Dec. 8, 1803, in Guilford, Vt.;
m. Aug. 14, 1838, in Quebec, L. C., Julia Trues-
dell, of Quebec, L. C.; res. Halls Corners, Ontario Co., N. Y.; eight children.
  II. LOIS BIGELOW, b. March 26, 1805; m. 1835, John
Wright, b. May 14, 1799. He d. Sept. 17, 1880.
She d. Dec. 29, 1887; one child:—
Edwin J., b. April 2, 1842; m. Jan. 2, 1862.
  III. DIMMIS DICKINSON, b. Sept. 22, 1806; m.——.
172. IV. ALFRED FAIRBANKS,[8] b. Aug. 18, 1809; m. Aug.
17 or 24, 1831, 1, Lucinda Waight, b. Feb. 18,
1811; d. May 21, 1837; 2, March 18, 1838,
Eliza Van Allen, b. Sept. 6, 1812; d. July 28,
1890, at Cumber, Sanilac Co., Mich. Mr. Green-
leaf went to Michigan in 1863. He was a mason
by trade. He d. May 28, 1880, at Cass City,
Mich.; twelve children.
  V. MARY WARING, b. Sept. 23, 1810; d. June 5, 1843;
unmarried.

171.

(Dr. Christopher 7, Stephen 6, Dr. Daniel 5, Rev. Daniel 4, Stephen 3, Stephen 2, Edmund 1.)

Children of **John D.**[8] **Greenleaf** and Julia (Truesdell).

I. JOHN EDWARD, b. June 21, 1839; d. Aug. 21, 1840.

173. II. LOUIS CHRISTOPHER,[9] b. Nov. 23, 1840; m. Sept. 8, 1868, Lorra Cornelia Shaffer, of Watertown, N. Y. Secretary of the Sloat & Greenleaf Lumber Co.; res. Watertown, N. Y.; three children :—

   i. Josephine Adele, b. May 22, 1870, is an art student in New York; m. June 4, 1891, Cornelius D. Shirley, who d. Dec. 12, 1891.

   ii. Lydia Cornelia, b. May 24, 1872; Syracuse Univ.

   iii. Alice Lunette, b. Feb. 27, 1874; d. Aug. 16, 1874.

III. JOSEPHINE PHILOMENE, b. Jan. 21, 1842; m. Nov. 28, 1865, Harvey Matthew Dixon; res. Seneca Castle, N. Y.; no children.

IV. MARY JULIA, b. Aug. 14, 1843; m. April 29, 1863, Lester Webster, of Seneca, N. Y. She died Aug. 19, 1895; six children; three now living.

174. V. HORACE DICKINSON,[9] b. May 11, 1845; m. Dec. 29, 1870, Frances Ella Dixon, of Seneca, Ontario Co., N. Y.; res. Hopewell, Ontario Co., N. Y.; two children :—

   i. John Dickinson, b. Nov. 4, 1876.

   ii. Lucy J., b. May 7, 1882.

VI. LUNETTE TABITHA, b. Dec. 22, 1846; m. Sept 4, 1877, Maitland Bascom Sloat, of Watertown, N. Y. (her cousin); res. Mt. Vernon, N. Y.; three children; two now living.

VII. HARRIET ALMEDA, b. July 3, 1850; m. Dec. 29, 1870, George Nelson Dixon; res. Hall's Corner, Ontario Co., N. Y.; four children.

VIII. A CHILD; d. in infancy.

172.

(Dr.Christopher 7, Stephen 6, Dr. Daniel 5, Rev. Daniel 4, Stephen 3, Stephen 2, Edmund 1.)

Children of **Alfred Fairbanks**[8] **Greenleaf** and Lucinda (Waight).

I. HORTENSIA DIANA, b. Oct. 15, 1832.

II. ——, b. and d. June 8, 1834.

III. LOIS AMELIA, b. Jan. 3, 1836.

ALFRED FAIRBANKS (172) GREENLEAF, CONTINUED :—
Children by 2d marriage :—
IV. LUCINDA ELIZA, b. July 19, 1840; m. 1858, Eph-
riam Farr, d. ——, 1874; seven children; four d.
in infancy.
V. GEORGE DICKINSON, b. Dec. 31, 1841; d. 1890.
VI. DIMMIS VIOLA, b. Sept. 6, 1843; d. May 21, 1854.
VII. ——, b. ——; d., May 23, 1846.
175. VIII. JAMES ALFRED,[9] b. Nov. 20, 1848, at Depauville,
Jefferson Co., N. Y.; m. Oct. 29, 1866, M.
Jane, dau. of Edward Belmer and Harriet Ann
(Stafford), of Almer, Tuscola Co., near the village
of Caro, Lower Canada. She was b. June 15,
1851; res. Cumber, Sanilac Co., Mich.; seven
children :—
i. Alverta H., b. Aug. 30, 1868; m. June 12, 1892,
Henry J. Knadler, of Cleveland, Ohio; one child :—
A son, b. Aug. 16, 1894.
ii. Henry Otis, b. July 5, 1870.
iii. Herbert Edward, b. Jan. 23, 1872.
iv. Wallace Clayton, b. Nov. 2, 1874.
v. Clarence Ozell, b. April 14, 1876.
vi. Zillah Pearl, b. April 22, 1877; m. April 14, 1895.
Charles Lang, of Holbrook, Greenleaf Township,
Sanilac Co., Mich.
vii. Alex Scott, b. Oct. 9, 1888.
IX. HENRY ABEL, b. Feb. 12, 1850, at Plessis, N. Y.;
d. May 7, 1864.
X. MARY JULIA, b. March 12, 1852, at Plessis, N. Y.;
m. E. R. Davis; she d. Dec. 13, 1875, at Detroit,
Mich.; seven children; five died.
176. XI. LLOYD BYRON,[9] b. Oct. 26, 1853, at Plessis, N. Y.;
m. 1, May 25, 1875, in Cass City, Mich., Emma A.
Carr; 2, July 2, 1887, in Cleveland, Ohio, Anna A.
Knadler; res. Cleveland, Ohio; three children by 1st
marriage :—
i. Meda, b. Dec. 11, 1876; d. Jan. 28, 1877.
ii. Norman L., b. Nov. 25, 1877.
iii. Herman C., b. Nov. 25, 1877; d. Dec. 16, 1877;
twin.

ALFRED FAIRBANKS (172) GREENLEAF, CONTINUED :—

> XII. CORA AURELIA, b. May 22, 1857; m. Oct. 13, 1880, King S. Work, of Pennsylvania; res. Cleveland, Ohio; four children :—
>
> i. Alfred Morison, b. Sept. 10, 1881.
> ii. Homer Greenleaf, b. June 20, 1883.
> iii. Laura Blanche, b. March 27, 1885.
> iv. Worth Howard, b. Jan. 6, 1888.
>
> They lived in Cass City, Mich., two years; thence Pittsburg, Penn., and lived there two years, and moved back to Cass City, where the children were all born except Laura, who was born at Pittsburg, Penn.; moved to Cleveland, Oct. 15, 1891.

134.

(Stephen 6, Dr. Daniel 5, Rev. Daniel 4, Stephen 3, Stephen 2, Edmund 1.)

Children of **Joseph**[7] **Greenleaf** and Lydia (Warner).

177. I. STEPHEN,[8] m. ———; he was a farmer; res. Battle Creek, Mich.; their daughter Mary m. Kingsworth.

178. II. LEE LEANDER,[8] b. June 1 or 3, 1810, in Brattleboro, Vt.; m. 1834, Marion, dau. of Henry Tiffany, a colonel in the War of 1812. She was b. Nov. 22, 1814; d. July 25, 1888. He was a Methodist Episcopal minister; d. May 14, 1882; five children.

Children by 2d marriage :—

> III. LYDIA, b. Oct. 24, 1817; m. Benjamin Bean. She d. 1888; ten children :—
>
> i. Charles.
> ii. William.
> iii. Nathaniel.
> iv. Julia, m. ——— Harris.
> v. Emma, m. ——— Barnes.
> vi. Warren, d. in infancy.
> vii. Egbert.
> viii. Harriet, m. ——— Spirling.
> ix. Henry.
> x. Mary, m. ——— Souls.
>
> IV. SOPHRONIA, b. May 24, 1819; m. George W. Downing; res. Apulia, N. Y.; five children :—
>
> i. Frances E., b. May 26, 1850; m. January, 1875, ——— Shaw.
> ii. Louis K., b. Nov. 12, 1851; d. Dec. 22, 1860.
> iii. Frank P., b. Sept. 17, 1853; m. Dec. 13, 1876; res. Apulia, N. Y.
> iv. George, b. Oct. 19, 1855; m. Nov. 15, 1875.
> v. Solomon A., b. Oct. 3, 1858.

JOSEPH (134) GREENLEAF, CONTINUED:—

V. ELIZABETH, b. April 18, 1821; m. April 2, 1863, Smith Gowing; res. Apulia, N. Y.

179. VI. JOSEPH,[8] b. July 7, 1823, at Apulia, Onondaga Co., N. Y.; m. 1850, Eda Ann Height, b. 1830, at Lafayette, Onondaga Co., N. Y.; d. 1873. He was a miller and farmer; d. June 2, 1891; res. Apulia, N. Y.; three children.

178.

(Joseph 7, Stephen 6, Dr. Daniel 5, Rev. Daniel 4, Stephen 3, Stephen 2, Edmund 1.)

Children of **Lee Leander**[8] **Greenleaf** and Marion (Tiffany).

I. WATSON, b. Dec. 4, 1836; d. April 5, 1850; unmarried.

II. MINERVA E., b. April 22, 1838; m. Oct. 30, 1855, Francis M. Nichols. She d. April 20, 1858; no children.

III. MARYETTE, b. Aug. 16, 1842; d. in infancy.

180. IV. EDWIN F.,[9] b. Jan. 24, 1844; m. May 5, 1866, Fanny A. Town; contractor and builder; res. Reese, Mich.; eleven children:—

i. Nettie C., b. Feb. 7, 1867; d. Sept. 2, 1868.

ii. Viola M., b. Nov. 14, 1868; m. James Nolan, of New York.

iii. Frederic L., b. Jan. 28, 1871.

iv. William E., b. May 10, 1873.

v. Bird C., b. Feb. 17, 1876.

vi. Edson B., b. March 1, 1878.

vii. Maud E., b. Oct. 22, 1880.

viii. Grover C., b. Aug. 25, 1884.

ix. Nolan W., b. Sept. 23, 1886.

x. Norton W., b. Sept. 23, 1886; d. same date; twin.

xi. Nellie, b. Dec. 1, 1889.

181. V. HENRY TIFFANY,[9] b. Aug. 16, 1847; m. Dec. 15, 1867, Amelia S. Draper; farmer; res. Reese, Mich.; three children:—

182. i. James F.,[10] b. Oct. 2, 1869; m. Oct. 3, 1890, Pressie J. Wills; one child: Ellis, b. Sept. 15, 1891.

LEE LEANDER (178) GREENLEAF, CONTINUED :—

  V. Henry Tiffany.

   II. Lillian M., b. May 10, 1873; m. April 9, 1892,
       John O. Newberry; one child :—
       Mabel, b. Dec. 15, 1892.

   III. Bessie D., b. Dec. 1, 1881.

179.

(Joseph 7, Stephen 6, Dr. Daniel 5, Rev. Daniel 4, Stephen 3, Stephen 2, Edmund 1.)

Children of **Joseph**[8] **Greenleaf** and Eda Ann (Height).

183. I. FRANK C.[9] b. Sept. 28, 1854, at Apulia, N. Y.; m.
          July 4, 1875, Rosanna Smith, of Blooming Valley,
          Crawford Co., Penn., b. Jan. 22, 1858; watchmaker;
          res. Syracuse, N. Y.; five children :—

       I. Nellie, b. July 1, 1876.

       II. Minnie, b. Jan. 26, 1878.

       III. Blanche, b. Aug. 8, 1885.

       IV. Lulu, b. Nov. 9, 1888.

       V. Charles H., b. May 2, 1891.

      II. FRANCES (twin), b. Sept. 28, 1854; m. 1870, Ed-
          ward Knapp, of Ashtabula, Ohio; res. Cherry
          Grove, Warren Co., Penn.; four children :—

       i. Estella, b. Sept. 21, 1872.

       ii. Delos, b. March, 1878.

       iii. Frank, b. 1880.

       iv. Loie, b. Feb. 21, 1886.

184. III. HIRAM W., b. Oct. 27, 1861, at Apulia, N. Y.; m.
          Dec. 5, 1889, Loie Alcorn, b. March 14, 1864, in
          Titusville, Penn.; teacher of music; res. Syracuse,
          N. Y.; one child :—
          Dale W., b. July 13, 1893.

135.

(Stephen 6, Dr. Daniel 5, Rev. Daniel 4, Stephen 3, Stephen 2, Edmund 1.)

Children of **Thomas Lee**[7] **Greenleaf** and Sarah (Marshall).

   I. EVELINA ANVILLA, b. Jan. 7, 1807; m. June 13, 1826,
      Jason Phelps, of Sackett's Harbor, N. Y. She d.
      Jan. 10, 1881. He d. Dec. 14, 1867; one child :—
      James Irwin, b. 1832; d. May 12, 1875.

   II. MARSHALL FAIRBANKS, b. June 19, 1809; d. March
       8, 1815.

Thomas Lee (135) Greenleaf, Continued:—

III. Eunice Augusta, b. Nov. 26, 1811; m. May 7, 1840, Benjamin Wood, of La Fargeville, N. Y., b. June 15, 1807; d. April 3, 1893; res. La Fargeville, N. Y.; eight children :—

    i. Evelina Louisa, b. Sept. 21, 1841; d. Dec. 9, 1877.

    ii. Mary Augusta, b. Jan. 11, 1843; d. Feb. 7, 1843.

    iii. Sarah Jane, b. April 28, 1844; d. March 10, 1850.

    iv. Marshall Williams, b. June 3, 1846; m. Dec. 7, 1870, Helen J. Hawes; Surgeon U. S. Army.

    v. Jason Phelps, b. Dec. 15, 1847; m. 1876, Lizzie Smith; he d. Nov. 24, 1892.

    vi. Sarah Jane, b. Feb. 7, 1850.

    vii. Anna Augusta, b. March 4, 1852.

    viii. Martha Lunette, b. Feb. 14, 1854; d. July 19, 1879.

IV. William H. Harrison, b. Jan. 14, 1814; d. Oct. 5, 1817.

V. Louisa Lunette, b. April 4, 1816, at Adams, N. Y.; m. Aug. 11, 1845, Benjamin F. Hunt, of Rutland, N. Y., b. May 20, 1810, at Rodman, N. Y. She d. April 21, 1893, at Bridgeport, Conn.; res. Bridgeport, Conn.; four children :—

    i. Frederick S., b. Nov. 26, 1849, at Rodman, N. Y.; m. Nov. 9, 1871, Mira A. Strickland, at Charlotte, N. Y.; res. Bridgeport, Conn.; one child: Mary S., b. May 6, 1874, at Charlotte, N. Y.

    ii. Henry G., b. May 8, 1851; d. October, 1851, at Rodman, N. Y.

    iii. Sarah L., b. Sept. 26, 1852, at Rodman, N. Y.; m. June 19, 1873, M. O. Stone, Rochester, N. Y.; she d. March 23, 1874, at Rochester, N. Y.

    iv. Mary E., b. Jan. 5, 1857, at Rodman, N. Y.; d. April 4, 1874, at Rochester, N. Y.

VI. Mary Jane Waring, b. May 13, 1819; d. Feb. 23, 1843; unmarried.

185. VII. Samuel Fairbanks,[8] b. Feb. 18, 1822; m. Sarah Elder, b. Jan. 27, 1823; d. July 3, 1890. He d. September, 1853; druggist; res. New York City; one child :—

Mary Augusta, b. Sept. 14, 1848; d. Nov. 13, 1874.

VIII. Nancy Ann Ingalls, b. Sept. 28, 1823; m. Feb. 7, 1865, Albertus L. Smith; res. Sacketts Harbor, N. Y.; no children.

IX. Charlotte Emma, b. July 17, 1827; d. Dec. 23, 1828.

44.

Children of **David**[6] **Greenleaf** and Mary (Johnson).

I. MARY, b. Jan. 7, 1764, at Norwich, Conn.; m. June 7, 1789, Don Carlos Brigham, of Coventry, Conn., b. Feb. 21, 1763; d. March 27, 1843. She d. Oct. 30, 1845, at Coventry, Conn.; res. Coventry, Conn.; res. of Mary is given as Mansfield, Conn., also; seven children :—

   i. Normand, M.D., b. March 7, 1790; m. Pamelia Dunham; a physician of professional eminence and extensive practice; res. Mansfield (?), Conn.; no children.

   ii. Gurdon, b. April 23, 1792; d. June 11, 1804.

   iii. Mary, b. Feb. 12, 1794; m. John Kingsbury; res. Tolland, Conn.

   iv. Charles, b. Jan. 29, 1797; m. Nov. 7, 1824, Betsey Royce, of Tolland, Conn. He d. Jan. 10, 1836; res. Woodstock, Vt.; one child : Charles Frederick.

   v. David, b. March 10, 1802; d. Jan. 19, 1804.

   vi. Eliza Ripley, b. April 3, 1805; m. Richmond Lovett; res. Tolland, Conn.

   vii. Susan Ann, b. Dec. 31, 1807; m. John Gager; res. Tolland.

186. II. DAVID[7] (Dr.), b. June 19, 1765, probably in Norwich, Conn.; m. Anna (Nancy), dau. of Rufus and Ann (Hartshorn) Jones, b. Nov. 7, 1765, in Norwich; d. Oct. 18?, 1828, in Hartford, Conn. He d. March 11, 1835; res. Hartford, Conn.; seven children.

Rufus Jones was b. Sept. 2, 1732; m. Ann Hartshorn, Nov. 2, 1757; she was b. March 9, 1734–5, both in Norwich, Conn. She d. March 26, 1816, aged 81. He was son of Sylvanus Jones and Kesia (Cleveland), his wife. Rufus and Ann (Hartshorn) Jones had nine children. Their fourth child was Anna (Nancy).

187. III. DANIEL,[7] b. Jan. 19, 1767, in Coventry, Conn.; m. Oct. 3, 1791, Abigail Forsyth. He d. Dec. 7, 1842, at Mount Hope, Orange Co., N. Y.; res. Mount Hope, N. Y.; four children.

IV. SARAH, b. Dec. 22, 1769; d. May 17, 1792.

Coventry, Conn., records have a Sarah (or Sally) Greenleaf; d. March, 1793; no age given.

V. NANCY (Annis), b. June 12, 1771; baptized in Lancaster, Mass., June 17, 1770 (?); m. Jan. 20, 1818, Jeduthan Kingsbury, son of Ephraim and

Davⁱᴅ (44) Greenleaf, Continued :—

    V. Nancy.

        Lydia, b. 1743 ; d. July 9, 1822, in Coventry, Conn.
        (his third wife). He lived in Plainfield, N. H.,
        for a time, and then settled in Coventry, Conn.

    VI. Susannah, b. Dec. 22, 1772 ; baptized in Lancaster,
        Mass., Jan. 5, 1772 (?) ; m. Major John Ripley,
        of New York. She d. Nov. 5, 1812, in New
        York.

188. VII. John,[7] b. Feb. 26, 1774; m. 1, March 8, 1798,
        Martha Tooker (or Tucker), b. Oct. 7, 1777 ; d.
        April 14, 1819 ; 2, May 10, 1820, Catherine (Du-
        bois), widow of John King, b. March 3, 1791 ;
        d. July 21, 1877. He d. Sept. 20, 1851 ; res.
        Mount Hope, Orange Co., N. Y.; fourteen chil-
        dren.

    A facsimile signature to a deed in Hartford, Conn., dated March
    31, 1802, Joseph Toocker, Jr., a brother of Electa, to William
    Ellery, gives this form of spelling the name. Mrs. Electa
    (Toocker) Greenleaf (190) said her name was so spelled.* It
    has also been spelled Tooker and Tucker.

    VIII. Eliza (Nabby), b. March 22, 1777 ; d. young.

189. IX. William,[7] b. Dec. 12, 1778; baptized December,
        1778, in Coventry, Conn.; m. in Hartford, Conn.,
        Mary Williams, of Hartford, Conn.; res. Stock-
        bridge, Mass.; six children.

186.

(David 6, Dr. Daniel 5, Rev. Daniel 4, Stephen 3, Stephen 2, Edmund 1.)

Children of **Dr. David**[7] **Greenleaf** and Anna (Nancy)
(Jones).

190. I. Charles[8] (Dr.), b. June 2, 1788, in Hartford, Conn.;
        m. 1808, Electa, dau. of Joseph and Hannah
        Toocker; Hannah d. Aug. 26, 1819, aged 72 years;
        Electa was b. Oct. 6, 1791 ; d. April 9, 1864, in
        Hartford, Conn. Dr. Charles d. Dec. 18, 1843 ;
        twelve children.

    II. Sarah, b. April 28, 1790 ; d. Dec. 6, 1805.

    " Her death was caused by her clothes taking fire. She lingered
    but three weeks and three days afterwards" (gravestone). See
    also *Hartford Courant*, December, 1805.

    *See W. F. J. Boardman's letter to the compiler, June 14, 1895, with facsimile sig-
    nature.

Dr. David (186) Greenleaf, Continued :—

    III. David, b. March 1, 1792; d. Jan. 18, 1795 (gravestone).

    IV. Daniel, b. March 24, 1794; d. Jan. 10, 1795 (gravestone).

    V. An Infant Son, d. Sept. 22, 1796, aged 10 days.

See tombstone in cemetery at Hartford, Conn.: "To the memory of four children of David Greenleaf: Daniel, David, An Infant Son, Sally."

191. VI. David[8] (Judge), b. May 6, 1803; m. Jan. 1, 1829, Clarissa, dau. of Simeon Cooley, of Vernon, Conn., b. Aug. 23, 1806. He d. April 7, 1890, at Carthage, Ill.; three children.

192. VII. Daniel,[8] b. Oct. 16, 1805; m. 1, ——; 2, March 24, 1828, Aura Carrington, b. 1805; d. March 11, 1884, aged 79. He d. Sept. 15, 1846, in Hartford, Conn.; a tailor; res. Hartford, Conn.

    Children by 1st marriage :—

      i. Henrietta, res. in New Haven, Conn., about 1863.

      ii. Isabel, res. in New Haven, Conn., about 1863.

    Child by 2d marriage :—

      iii. Jane, b. May 6, 1829; m. June, 1846, Edward Burr, of Hartford, Conn., merchant; one child :—

William Rollins, b. Jan. 12, 1847.

190.

(Dr. David 7, David 6, Dr. Daniel 5, Rev. Daniel 4, Stephen 3, Stephen 2, Edmund 1.)

Children of **Dr. Charles**[8] **Greenleaf** and Electa (Toocker).

193. I. Charles[9] (Dr.), b. Sept. 1, 1809, in Hartford; m. July 4, 1833, in Harwington, Conn., Caroline, dau. of Samuel and Annie Wilson, of Onondaga, N. Y.; d. Dec. 7, 1882. He d. Oct. 22, 1888, in Farmington, Ill.; res. Farmington, Ill.; three children.

194. II. William Henry,[9] b. Aug. 6, 1814; m. Oct. 19, 1839, Mary Ann, dau. of Ebenezer and Sarah (Brigden) Griffin, of Middletown, Conn., b. April 20, 1820. He d. Nov. 26, 1875; res. Hartford; a bookbinder; five children :—

    i. Charles Henry,[10] b. Feb. 21, 1841; d. Aug. 26, 1864.

Dr. Charles (190) Greenleaf, Continued :—

II. William Henry.

ii. Sarah Electa, b. July 10, 1842 ; res. Hartford, Conn.

iii. George Nelson, b. Feb. 12, 1845 ; d. Feb. 13, 1846.

iv. George Nelson, b. July 12, 1847 ; unmarried ; res. Hartford, Conn.

v. Caroline Wilson, b. July 6, 1850 ; m. Nov. 9, 1868, Charles Ferris Hubbard. He d. March 5, 1876 ; res. Hartford, Conn. ; one child :—

Carrie Greenleaf, b. Oct. 8, 1869.

Mr. Hubbard enlisted in Co. C, Capt. Edwin E. Rankin, Col. Frank Beach, 16th Regt. Conn. Vols., July 22, 1862. Was in the fight at Gettysburg. Captured April 20, 1864, at Plymouth, N. C. Paroled Feb. 28, 1865, and was mustered out of service June 24, 1865. He was a prisoner at Andersonville.

III. Harriet E., b. April 28, 1816 ; m. May 12, 1840, Spencer Lee Flower, merchant, of Hartford, Conn., b. Aug. 8, 1815. She d. April 13, 1882 ; res. Hartford, Conn. Mr. Flower m. Nov. 2, 1883, Mrs. Louisa (Terry) Price, of Enfield, Conn. ; three children :—

i. Charles Spencer, b. Jan. 23, d. March 19, 1841.

ii. Charles Spencer, b. Feb. 27, 1842 ; d. April 3, 1864.

iii. Hattie Rosamond, b. July 16, 1843 ; d. Feb. 19, 1865.

IV. Nancy, b. Feb. 2, 1818 ; m. Jan. 19, 1842, Leonard Butler, joiner and builder, of Hartford, Conn., b. July 17, 1811, in Wethersfield, Conn. ; d. Nov. 10, 1870, in Hartford, Conn. She d. Feb. 14, 1858 ; nine children, all born in Hartford, Conn. :—

i. Nancy Augusta, b. April 2, 1842 ; m. Sept. 7, 1865, Charles H. Rose, b. July 11, 1844, in New London, Conn. ; res. Dorchester, Mass. ; one child : Charles Frederick, b. July 29, 1872, Rochester, N. Y.

ii. Leonard, b. Aug. 22, 1844 ; d. July 25, 1848, in Hartford, Conn.

iii. A son, b. and d. April 5, 1846.

iv. A son, b. and d. May 25, 1847.

v. Mary Electa, b. July 17, 1848 ; d. Oct. 6, 1848.

vi. A son, b. and d. Sept. 15, 1849.

vii. Ida Roselle, b. Feb. 13, 1851 ; m. March 29, 1868, Benjamin Arthur Brown, of Mystic, Conn. She d. Feb. 24, 1886 ; one child : Frederick Arthur, b. March 11, 1869, in Hartford, Conn.

viii. Franklin Theodore, b. June 28, 1853 ; res. Hartford, Conn.

ix. Charles A., b. Nov. 21, 1855 ; d. March 22, 1856, in Hartford, Conn.

DR. CHARLES (190) GREENLEAF, CONTINUED :—

195. V. JAMES MONROE[9] (Dr.), b. April 26, 1819; m. Jan. 1, 1842, Jane E. Meyer, of Hartford, Conn., b. Nov. 11, 1820; d. Jan. 22, 1881. He d. Nov. 14, 1877; res. Hartford, Conn.; six children :—

I. James Monroe, b. Sept. 29, 1843; d. June 11, 1852.

II. Ellen Regina, b. Sept. 24, 1845; m. March 10, 1868, J. Donovan; eleven children :—
1. James Greenleaf, b. Oct. 24, 1869. 2. John M., b. July 7, 1871. 3. Daniel, and 4. Jeremiah, twins, b. July 6, 1873. 5. Walter Morgan, b. Aug. 13, 1875. 6. Arthur Curtis, b. Nov. 14, 1877. 7. Frederick Brown, b. Aug. 26, 1879. 8. Ellen Jane, b. Oct. 7, 1881. 9. Clarissa Electa, b. Jan. 29, 1883. 10. P. Sheedy, b. July 31, 1886. 11. Florence, b. June 12, 1888.

III. Alice Gallaudet, b. July 7, 1847; m. Feb. 25, 1868, Leroy Land; res. Richmond, Ind., and Hillsboro, Ohio; five children :—
1. Mabel, b. April 21, 1870; m. March 14, 1895, at Hillsboro, Ohio, Eugene Brubaker; res. Richmond, Ind. 2. Leroy, b. Dec. 12, 1877. 3. Mildred. 4. Milford. 5. Majorie.

IV. Emma Josephine, b. Jan. 11, 1852; m. Charles W. Camp.

V. Georgette, b. Jan. 2, 1858; d. Jan. 31, 1859.

VI. M. Jane, b. Jan. 13, 1859; unmarried.

VI. SARAH, b. Aug. 17, 1821, in Hartford; m. Jan. 1, 1846, Jacob Morgan, Jr., b. Oct. 21, 1823. She d. July 6, 1880, at Providence, R. I. Mr. Morgan is a cotton broker, also agent transportation company to New York; res. Providence, R. I.; nine children :—

i. Celia, b. Nov. 16, 1846; m. Aug. 12, 1868, Hon. Philip B. Durfee, of Providence, R. I.; seven children.

ii. Eliza Ann, b. Aug. 17, 1848; unmarried.

iii. Charles, b. Oct. 11, 1850; d. Nov. 23, 1876; unmarried.

iv. Harriet Electa, b. July 9, 1852; m. Nov. 1, 1893, Joseph R. Snow.

v. Lillie, b. July 11, 1854; d. July 18, 1854.

vi. Jacob, 3d, b. June 1, 1856; m. Dec. 23, 1886, Harriet E. Boynton; no children.

vii. Sarah Jane, b. July 4, 1860; m. Nov. 23, 1887, George D. McLane; no children.

viii. Nannie Strider, b. March 7, 1862; m. Oct. 11, 1888, Elmer E. Knowlton; no children.

Dr. Charles (190) Greenleaf, Continued:—

VI. Sarah.

ix. Joseph Henry, b. Nov. 9, 1864, now living with his third wife; res. Providence, R. I. (Union Horse Car Co.); had four children.

VII. MARY, b. March 24, 1823, in Hartford, Conn.; m. Jan. 7, 1844, Henry Lester, Jr., plater, of Hartford, Conn., b. Jan. 19, 1819. She d. June 28, 1872; three children:—

i. Charles Henry, m. Clara Hurlbut; had children and grandchildren. He enlisted Aug. 11, 1862, Co. D, Capt. Samuel Brown, 16th Regt. Conn. Vols., Col. Frank Beach. Was wounded at the Battle of Antietam, Maryland, Sept. 17, 1862; discharged for disability Dec. 19, 1862; res. East Hartford, Conn.

ii. James Greenleaf, b. Sept. 27, 1857, in Hartford, Conn.; m. June 7, 1879, Emma Josephine Baker, of Hartford, b. Sept. 28, 1860; two children: 1. Mary George. 2. Viola Lyle.

iii. A son.

VIII. JOHN, b. March 4, 1825; d. April 9, 1861, in Hartford, Conn. Was a sailor; m. Mary ——.

196. IX. DAVID[9] (Dr.), b. Jan. 16, 1827; m. Helen Johnston, of Peoria, Ill. He d. Sept. 6, 1893, at Alameda, Cal.; two children:—

i. Marianne, b. June 12, 1855, at Peoria, Ill.; m. Dec. 19, 1883, William James Martin, of Pittsburg, Penn., b. Jan. 15, 1857; res. South San Francisco, San Mateo Co., Cal.: three children:—

1. David Greenleaf, b. Aug. 22, 1886, at Galesburg, Ill. 2. John Johnston Miller, b. June 19, 1889, at San Jose, Cal. 3. Grace Marguerite, b. Sept. 20, 1892, at Alameda, Cal.

ii. David, b. November, 1873, at Galesburg, Ill.

X. ELECTA, b. Jan. 11, 1829; m. 1, June 27, 1860, Burton Hubbard, b. 1836, in East Hartford, Conn.; d. Sept. 7, 1864. Mr. Hubbard enlisted Aug. 6, 1862, in 16th Regt., Co. A., Capt. Henry A. Pasco, Col. Frank Beach, Conn. Vols.; was captured at Plymouth, N. C., April 20, 1864; he died in Andersonville Prison; the number of his grave is 8,148; 2, Nov. 26, 1867, Samuel Edwin Hurlbut, of Hartford, Conn., b. Aug. 2, 1845. She d. Aug. 30, 1877, in Chaplin, Conn.; buried at Hartford, Conn. He m. 2, Jan. 12, 1882, Mary

DR. CHARLES (190) GREENLEAF, CONTINUED :—

  X. Electa.

> Evelyn Hardy, of Poquonock, Conn.; res. Manchester, Conn. Mr. Hurlbut enlisted Dec. 7, 1863, from East Windsor, Conn., in Co. H., Capt. John B. Morehouse, Col. William S. Fish, 1st Regt. Conn. Vol. Cavalry; was made corporal Dec. 18, 1863; wounded March 29, 1864, at Grove Church, Va.; sergeant Oct. 28, 1864; mustered out of service Aug. 2, 1865.

  XI. GEORGE, b. Oct. 28, 1833; d. March 6, 1834.

  XII. JANE MARIA, b. Aug. 9, 1835, in Hartford, Conn.; m. Jan. 7, 1852, William F. J., son of the late William and Mary (Francis) Boardman, b. Dec. 12, 1828, in Wethersfield, Conn.; res. Hartford, Conn.

> Their only child, William Greenleaf, b. June 29, 1853, in Hartford, Conn.; m. Oct. 29, 1874, Eliza Fowler, dau. of Horatio and Abigail Whittier (Hussey) Root, b. May 11, 1853, in Hartford, Conn.; res. Hartford, Conn.; three children: 1. Francis Whittier, b. April 6, 1876; d. April 5, 1885. 2. Cedric Root, b. Jan. 23, 1886; 3. Dorothy Root, b. April 26, 1889.

193.

(Dr. Charles 8, Dr. David 7, David 6, Dr. Daniel 5, Rev. Daniel 4, Stephen 3, Stephen 2, Edmund 1.)

Children of **Dr. Charles**[9] **Greenleaf** and Caroline (Wilson).

197. I. CHARLES WILSON,[10] b. Sept. 18, 1834; m. Sept. 11, 1855, 1, Phebe, dau. of Caroline and Aaron Quimby, of Sing Sing, N. Y., b. May 12, 1832; res. Peoria, Ill.; dentist; 2, July 20, 1893, May, dau. of Dr. William H. Hamilton, capitalist, of Peoria, Ill. Three children by 1st marriage :—

  I. Adele, b. May 13, 1856; m. —— Shedayne; res. Chicago, Ill.

  II. Ellen, b. Feb. 13, 1858; m. —— Hotchkiss; res. Chicago, Ill.

Dr. Charles (193) Greenleaf, Continued :—
  I. Charles Wilson.
    III. Charles Henry, b. March 20, 1860; res. New York
      City.
198. II. Luther Birge,[10] b. Aug. 11, 1836; m. Dec. 25,
    1860, 1, Rachel Schurman; res. Farmington, Ill.;
    2, Feb. 25, 1877, Hester J. Balding, b. April 19,
    1849; six children by 2d marriage :—
    I. Florence May, b. May 29, 1878; res. Onarga, Ill.
    II. Clarence De Witt, b. July 2, 1880.
    III. Carrie Ellen, b. March 29, 1882.
    IV. Minnie Pearl, b. March 19, 1884.
    V. Hattie Alvine, b. March 1, 1887.
    VI. Clyde Raymond, b. May 21, 1891.
199. III. Henry Burnett,[10] b. Nov. 30, 1840; m. July 17,
    1867, Henrietta H. Thomas, b. July 21, 1843, at
    Farmington, Ill.; res. Farmington, Ill.; no
    children.

191.

(Dr. David 7, David 6, Dr. Daniel 5, Rev. Daniel 4, Stephen 3, Stephen 2, Edmund 1.)

Children of **Judge David**[8] **Greenleaf** and Clarissa
(Cooley).
199a. I. David Percival,[9] b. March 23, 1831, at Hartford,
    Conn.; m. Jan. 1, 1870, at Carthage, Ill., Mrs.
    Janet Warner. He removed from Carthage in
    1873, and settled in the town of Alma, Kan.,
    where he d. April 2, 1892; three children :—
    I. Clarissa Percival.
    II. William David.
    III. Anna Elizabeth.
  II. Mary Ann Ripley, b. Oct. 21, 1832, at Vernon,
    Conn.; m. May 1, 1850, Dr. John Mack. She d.
    March 17, 1867, in Lawrence Co., Ill.; three
    children :—
    i. David G.
    ii. John.
    iii. Mary, m. —— Keim; res. Carthage, Ill.
  III. Cornelia Clarissa, b. July 2, 1834, at Vernon,
    Conn.; lives with her mother in Carthage, Ill.

187.

(David 6, Dr. Daniel 5, Rev. Daniel 4, Stephen 3, Stephen 2, Edmund 1.)

Children of **Daniel**[7] **Greenleaf** and Abigail (Forsyth).

I. SARAH, b. July 13, 1794; m. Feb. 6, 1812, Joshua Mulock, b. Aug. 11, 1787; d. Dec. 23, 1862. She d. March 29, 1866; res. Minisink, Orange Co., N. Y.; sixteen children :—

i. Daniel, b. Feb. 28, 1813; m. Feb. 28, 1838, Cynthia Mulock, of Mt. Hope, N. Y., b. Aug. 31, 1818. He d. Dec. 26, 1887; nine children: 1. Abby Jane, b. Nov. 8, 1841; m. Feb. 13, 1862, Jacob Gumaer. 2. Sarah Frances, b. Feb. 2, 1845; res. Binghamton, N. Y. 3. D. Charles, b. Sept. 29, 1847; d. May 25, 1878; unmarried. 4. Justus H., b. July 23, 1850; m. Jan. 14, 1874, Frank Johnson. He d. Oct. 5, 1887. 5. Samuel Jesse, b. Dec. 3, 1852; m. Nov. 21, 1878, Mrs. Maggie Geers. 6. Mary Louise, b. Dec. 14, 1854; m. Feb. 25, 1880, George A. Wood. 7. David Greenleaf, b. Feb. 28, 1857; m. July 9, 1881, Susie Thompson. He d. April 27, 1893. 8. Emma Adelaide, b. Jan. 12, 1860; m. May 27, 1885, William Ellery Johnson. 9. Chauncey, b. April 28, 1862; m. Oct. 14, 1886, Laura Polley.

ii. Chauncey, b. Sept. 12, 1814; m. July 1, 1835, Thisby Andrews Forbes. He d. Nov. 2, 1879; seven children: 1. Emily. 2. Caroline, b. March 8, 1837; m. Nov. 16, 1864, George D. Sowers. 3. Harrison, d. young. 4. Emmavette. 5. John. 6. Jane, b. Jan. 29, 1848; m. Sept. 23, 1875, B. R. Beardsley. 7. Adelia Eveline, b. Dec. 21, 1849; m. June 19, 1870, C. W. Marvin. She d. Aug. 30, 1890.

iii. Jesse, b. Sept. 23, 1816; m. April 4, 1843, Josephine Doudale. He d. July 7, 1878; eight children: 1. Francis H. Nicholl, b. Feb. 4, 1844; d. May, 1845. 2. Ann Eliza, b. May 23, 1845; d. Sept. 10, 1855. 3. Fannie Johnson, b. Dec. 5, 1848; m. Jan. 8, 1868, Charles McNish. She d. Dec. 23, 1868. 4. Charles Frederick, b. Oct., 1850; d. June, 1852. 5. Mary Toomer, b. Sept. 1, 1851; d. Feb. 28, 1852. 6. Julia, b. Jan. 2, 1854; d. March 25, 1862. 7. Sarah Josephine, b. March 2, 1861. 8. Jessie Nolar, b. March 2, 1861, twin; d. Aug. 1, 1861.

iv. Eliza Jane, b. Aug. 13, 1818; d. Feb. 26, 1819.

v. Charles, b. May 4, 1820; m. Sept. 15, 1847, Maria Louisa Forbes Hotchkiss. He d. April 28, 1886; one child: Lucius Hotchkiss, b. July 12, 1848.

vi. Abigail, b. Feb. 28, 1822; d. Oct. 17, 1847.

vii. Phebe, b. Nov. 11, 1823; m. Oct. 8, 1846, Solomon W. Warren; four children: 1. Sarah Elizabeth, b. Oct. 25, 1847. 2. Martha Ann, b. Feb. 21, 1853. 3. David, b. Sept. 2, 1855. 4. Maria Louise, b. April 22, 1859; m. Oct. 4, 1882, Charles W. Sniffen.

GENEALOGY. 297

DANIEL (187) GREENLEAF, CONTINUED :—
I. Sarah.
viii. Mary Ann, b. Feb. 23, 1825; m. Nov. 21, 1850, George Mulock. She d. Nov. 9, 1894; one child: Ella L., b. March 2,
1853; m. May 6, 1874, Augustus R. Gumaer.
ix. John Greenleaf, b. Nov. 29, 1826; d. April 20, 1827.
x. Harriet Emeline, b. April 17, 1828; m. 1, Jan. 30, 1851, Henry
B. Swartwout; 2, Dec. 16, 1869, Watson Space; six children
by 1st marriage: 1. Maria Louisa, b. Dec. 22, 1851; d. Jan. 26,
1865. 2. Sarah Esther, b. Jan. 24, 1853; d. Feb. 12, 1860.
3. Mary Elizabeth, b. Dec. 25, 1859; d. April 7, 1860. 4.
Harriet Emeline, b. March 8, 1861; m. Jan. 20, 1883, Frank
Dunham. 5. Isabella, b. June 6, 1862; m. Oct. 16, 1883,
Emery S. Judd. 6. George Henry, b. Nov. 6, 1863; m. Dec. 16,
1891, Jemima Courtright Norris. Two children by 2d marriage: 1. Clarence W., b. May 1, 1871. 2. Irving Joshua, b.
Aug. 22, 1872.
xi. Isaac, b. Feb. 6, 1830; m. Dec. 24, 1856, Esther Gumaer. He
d. March 29, 1886; four children: 1. Peter, b. Sept. 20, 1858;
d. Jan. 2, 1860. 2. Sarah Esther, b. Oct. 21, 1860; m. Sept.
23, 1885, Alonzo P. Myer. 3. Louisa Jane, b. Oct. 11, 1862;
d. July 1, 1865. 4. Luella, b. Aug. 13, 1876.
xii. Ira, b. Jan. 7, 1832; m. Nov. 2, 1854, Helen H. Hallock. He
d. Feb. 2, 1893; five children: 1. Chauncey Edson, b. July
15, 1855; m. Dec. 23, 1882, S. Addie Binkley. 2. Ira Parker,
b. Nov. 18, 1858; m. May 29, 1882, Carrie Abrams. 3. Peter,
b. Aug. 3, 1861. 4. Sally Helen, b. April 22, 1863; m. Nov.
15, 1882, Charles McIntire. 5. Mary H., b. April 5, 1866; m.
Nov. 2, 1887, Charles W. Cross.
xiii. Elmira, b. June 18, 1833; d. Jan. 6, 1834.
xiv. Sarah Jane, b. Dec. 12, 1834; m. Dec. 29, 1853, Peter Low
Gumaer; res. Guymard, Orange Co., N. Y.; six children:
1. Georgiana Isabelle, b. Feb. 14, 1855; d. May 10, 1872. 2.
Laertes Webster, b. Nov. 22, 1857. 3. Chauncey Irving, b.
Feb. 20, 1860; m. Feb. 8, 1887, Belle Graham. 4. Franklin
Peter, b. Aug. 20, 1863; m. Nov. 25, 1887, Ida May Snell. 5.
Marie Louise, b. April 15, 1866. 6. George Seward, b. Aug.
12, 1874.
xv. Ely Perry, b. Oct. 18, 1836; m. June 27, 1861, Amanda Cuddeback, b. Aug. 9, 1839. He d. March 20, 1893; four children:
1. Adella, b. Jan. 10, 1864; m. Feb. 24, 1887, Seely Wintersmith
Mudd, b. Aug. 16, 1861; two children: (1) Harvey Seely, b.
Aug. 30, 1888; (2) Elizabeth Sarah, b. Jan. 20, 1891; d. Aug.
11, 1893. 2. Louisa, d. young. 3. Katheryn, b. Aug. 2, 1872;
unmarried. 4. William P., b. Aug. 4, 1874; unmarried.
xvi. Joshua, b. July 25, 1838; m. March 25, 1874, Clara Halstead.
200. II. JOHN,[8] b. Feb. 21, 1796; m. Feb. 19, 1820, Emeline
Forbes. He was drowned in Hudson River, N.

DANIEL (187) GREENLEAF, CONTINUED :—

II. John.
> Y., by the upsetting of Sloop "Neptune," Nov. 23, 1824. Two children.

III. DAVID, b. Sept. 2, 1800; d. Sept. 13, 1865, at residence of Daniel Mulock, Mt. Hope, Orange Co., N. Y.; unmarried.

201. IV. DANIEL RIPLEY,[8] b. Aug. 27, 1808; m. Oct. 30, 1841, Hannah Stoddard Arthur, who d. Feb. 3, 1892. He d. Feb. 4, 1868. He was a farmer, and lived on the old homestead near Howell's town, Mt. Hope, Orange Co., N. Y.; five children.

200.

(Daniel 7, David 6, Dr. Daniel 5, Rev. Daniel 4, Stephen 3, Stephen 2, Edmund 1.)

Children of **John**[8] **Greenleaf** and Emeline (Forbes).

202. I. JOHN HARRISON,[9] b. July 8, 1821, at Minisink, N. Y.; m. April 17, 1845, Elmira D. Mondone, of Port Jervis, N. Y., b. April 30, 1827, at Port Jervis; d. Nov. 20, 1883. He d. May 27, 1876; three children :—

203. i. Daniel Judson,[10] b. Feb. 13, 1848, at Minisink, N. Y.; m. Nov. 2, 1876, Hannah Mary, dau. of Benjamin S. and Martha M. Healy, of Cohocton, Steuben Co., N. Y., b. Oct. 4, 1854; dealer in music at Port Jervis, N. Y.; one child: Ada May, b. Jan. 7, 1880.

ii. Pamela Birdsall, b. April 19, 1854.

iii. Bertha Clark, b. March 31, 1867; m. Oct. 19, 1893, Christoph Graebner, of Port Jervis, N. Y.

II. SARAH JANE, b. July 10, 1823; m. Sept. 26, 1842, Ira S. Stoddard. She d. March 30, 1879; six children :—

i. Josephine, b. Dec. 23, 1845; m. John E. Iseman, a native of Germany. He established a bakery in 1861, at Middletown, N. Y., having now an extensive wholesale and retail trade. He has served four terms as Alderman, and was the first Mayor of that city; is now (1893) serving his second term as supervisor, is Director of Merchants and Manufacturers Bank and the Middletown Glass Works; also President Phœnix Engine Company, besides being prominent in various orders; one child: George H.

JOHN (200) GREENLEAF, CONTINUED :—
II. Sarah Jane.
  ii. Emmet Redfield, b. June 30, 1850; res. New York City.
  iii. Rosamond E., b. June 15, 1855; m. A. C. Harding, Council
       Bluffs, Iowa.
  iv. Charles Wesley, b. May 13, 1857; res. New Whatcom, Wash-
      ington.
  v. Washington Irving, b. Oct. 5, 1860; res. Hopewell, Washing-
     ton.
  vi. Florence N., b. Aug. 19, 1862; m. W. H. Bodine; res. Bellows
      Falls, Vt.

201.

(Daniel 7, David 6, Dr. Daniel 5, Rev. Daniel 4, Stephen 3, Stephen 2, Edmund 1.)

Children of **Daniel Ripley**[8] **Greenleaf** and Hannah
Stoddard (Arthur).

204. I. DANIEL,[9] b. April 2, 1842; m. Jan. 20, 1863, Jose-
       phine Cate, dau. of Dr. G. F. R. Baker, of Callicoon,
       Sullivan Co., N. Y. She d. Dec. 31, 1892; res.
       New York City; two children :—
    i. William Daniel, b. Oct. 20, 1863; unmarried.
    ii. Jesse Mulock, b. May 28, 1870; d. July 31, 1886.
  II. JOSEPHINE, b. Jan. 15, 1844; d. March 24, 1846.
  III. DAVID, b. Sept. 6, 1847; d. Sept. 19, 1847.
  IV. PHEBE JANE, b. Jan. 20, 1849; m. Jan. 18, 1871,
      Edward A. Fox, of Naugatuck, Conn. He d. Jan. 1,
      1893; res. South Riverside, Cal.; two children: —
    i. Albert William Edward, b. Dec. 2, 1874.
    ii. Grace Greenleaf, b. Aug. 12, 1876; d. July 9, 1877.
  V. SOPHRONIA, b. Nov. 14, d. Nov. 15, 1850.

188.

(David 6, Dr. Daniel 5, Rev. Daniel 4, Stephen 3, Stephen 2, Edmund 1.)

Children of **John**[7] **Greenleaf** and Martha (Tooker).
  I. KETURAH, b. March 8, 1799, at Mt. Hope, N. Y.; m.
     April, 1825, Dr. Aaron Davis; res. Livingston Co.,
     N. Y.
  II. MARY, b. Aug. 5, 1800; m. January, 1821, Ira Sey-
      bolt; res. South Middletown, Orange Co., New
      York.
  III. GABRIEL REEVES, b. June 22, 1802; d. Aug. 31,
       1837.

JOHN (188) GREENLEAF, CONTINUED:—

IV. EMELINE, b. Sept. 5, 1804; m. Feb. 5, 1825, Thomas Mitchell, b. May 27, 1800; d. Dec. 1, 1852. She d. April 18, 1887; res. Newcastle, Del.; eight children:—

   i. Martha Elizabeth, b. Oct. 15, 1826; m. March 18, 1852, William M. Wilson; two children: 1. Wilbur Thomas, b. May 4, 1853. 2. Annie Louisa, b. July 14, 1855, at Newark, Del.

   ii. Mary Eliza, b. Jan. 26, 1828; m. Oct. 19, 1853, Samuel D. Arthur; res. Jersey City, N. J.; four children: 1. Frank Thomas, b. June 6, 1855; res. New York City. 2. Mary Louisa, b. Aug. 6, 1857. 3. Emma Frances, b. March 13, 1862. 4. Harry E., b. June 10, 1869.

   iii. John Greenleaf, b. Feb. 28, 1831; m. June 22, 1858, Mary Elizabeth Finley; res. Colwyn, Delaware Co., Penn.; four children: 1. Frank A., b. Oct. 25, 1859; m. Oct. 25, 1887, Annie Hemphill. 2. Charles F., b. Nov. 15, 1861. 3. Mary Emma, b. July 6, 1863; m. Sept. 27, 1894, Henry W. Collings; res. Glen Olden, Delaware Co., Penn. 4. Samuel Finley, b. Oct. 12, 1865; d. Jan. 15, 1868.

   iv. Amanda M., b. Sept. 3, 1833; res. Newark, Del.

   v. Harriet Newell, b. June 4, 1836; m. April 27, 1870, James Riddle Maxwell, of Philadelphia, Penn.; one child: Jane Riddle, b. Dec. 22, 1874, in Peru, S. A.

   vi. Harvey Reeves, b. Feb. 12, 1839; m. Nov. 15, 1871, Malissia Stevens; res. New York City; three children: 1. Lillian May, b. Sept. 1, 1872; res. Jersey City, N. J. 2. George S., b. June 4, 1875. 3. Mary Emma, b. Jan. 26, 1878.

   vii. Sarah Louisa, b. Feb. 12, 1841; m. Feb. 21, 1867, George H. Corfield; res. Jersey City Heights, N. J.; one child: Edgar Tyler, b. May 3, 1868; res. New York City.

   viii. Emma Frances, b. July 7, 1843; m. July 7, 1862, William P. Patten; res. New York City; five children: 1. George Barker, b. June 10, 1863, New York City. 2. Laile Ida, b. April 7, 1865. 3. Alida D., b. March 20, 1867. 4. Eliza Drake, b. April 30, 1869. 5. William Brundage, b. March 21, 1872.

V. JOHN HARVEY, b. April 22, 1807; d. Aug. 24, 1831, in Whitehall, N. Y.; unmarried.

205. VI. DANIEL TOOKER (or Tucker),[8] b. Feb. 11, 1809, near Mt. Hope, Orange Co., N. Y.; m. Nov. 17, 1831, Rebecca, dau. of Rulif Peterson, of Canoga, N. Y., b. April 30, 1808; d. Sept. 1, 1887. He d. March 24, 1892; res. Canoga, N. Y.; four children.

John (188) Greenleaf, Continued:—

VII. Louisa, b. Aug. 20, 1811; m. Jan. 11, 1838, Harvey Hill. She d. July 11, 1865; res. Minisink, N. Y.

Children by 2d marriage:—

206. VIII. Charles Dubois,[8] b. Feb. 24, 1821, at Mt. Hope, Orange Co., N. Y.; m. Dec. 23, 1843, Julia Ann, dau. of Seth Mapes; res. New York City; nine children.

IX. Sarah Aramantha, b. Dec. 31, 1822; m. Jan. 20, 1843, Henry Penney, b. 1821; d. April 5, 1858, in Michigan; res. New York City; four children:—

i. Edgar, b. Feb. 13, 1845; m. Oct. 8, 1874, Marietta Sutherland; nine children: 1. Lillie Louise, b. Dec. 11, 1875. 2. Ralph Herbert, b. Dec. 11, 1877. 3. Eva Gertrude, b. Feb. 13, 1880. 4. Samuel Holmes, b. Aug. 13, 1882; d. Aug. 12, 1883. 5. Florence May, b. March 11, 1884. 6. Ruth Bowman, b. Feb. 3, 1886. 7. Charles Franklin, b. May 2, 1888. 8. Harold Eugene, b. March 31, 1890. 9. Edgar Lloyd, b. Jan. 26, d. July 28, 1892.

ii. Emma Amanda, b. Jan. 14, 1848; m. Jan. 26, 1875, Hiram M. Mapes; three children: 1. Leo A., b. June 17, 1877. 2. Daisy C., b. Aug. 18, 1878; 3. Edna G., b. March 2, 1881.

iii. Henry, Jr., b. Sept. 15, 1849; m. Aug. 22, 1887, Lena Wright.

iv. Tremont, b. June 25, 1856; d. April 15, 1874.

207. X. William Alva,[8] b. Jan. 5, 1825; m. May 18, 1848, Catherine Watkins Gould, widow of Thomas J. Wisner, of Canoga, N. Y., b. at Watertown, N. Y.; d. Dec. 27, 1883, at Jersey City, N. J. He d. June 11, 1894; a physician; res. Jersey City, N. J.; four children.

XI. Adeline, b. Oct. 5, 1827; m. at Pinckney, Mich., —— Colyer; res. Pinckney, Mich.

XII. Catherine Amanda, b. Oct. 15, 1830; d. Oct. 18, 1847.

XIII. Cordelia, b. Jan. 21, 1833; m. Oct. 9, 1856, Jonathan Everett, b. Nov. 24, 1824; res. Argentine, Genesee Co., Mich.; three children:—

i. Alma, b. April 9, 1860; m. April 8, 1880, Frank J. Welsh. She d. June 24, 1893; six children: 1. Julia Welsh, b. Jan. 29, 1881. 2. Alice, b. July 18, 1883. 3. Flora, b. July 18, 1883; twin. 4. Ezra, b. Jan. 21, 1886. 5. Cora, b. March 8, 1888. 6. Leroy, b. May 12, 1890.

ii. Ettie, b. July 3, 1863; m. Dec. 6, 1892, Frank Gaspie.

iii. Greely, b. April 7, 1874.

XIV. Charlotte, b. June 22, 1835; m. —— Cuddeback; res. Detroit, Mich.

205.

(John 7, David 6, Dr. Daniel 5, Rev. Daniel 4, Stephen 3, Stephen 2, Edmund 1.)

Children of **Daniel Tooker**[8] **Greenleaf** and Rebecca (Peterson).

208. I. JOHN HARVEY,[9] b. Sept. 12, 1832; m. Aug. 2, 1854, Ruth, dau. of Sebastian Chatham, a farmer, b. Dec. 25, 1834; d. May 16, 1864. He d. Sept. 8, 1864; a farmer and teacher; one child :—

Eva Justine, b. July 15, 1855; d. March 10, 1864.

II. HELEN ROXANNA, b. Sept. 21, 1834; d. June 11, 1854; unmarried.

209. III. ALBERT REAVES,[9] b. Jan. 19, 1846; m. April 3, 1871, Frances Elizabeth, dau. of Rev. E. H. Stratton, Presbyterian Minister, of Canoga, N. Y., b. Oct. 4, 1838, at Pavilion, Genesee Co., N. Y.; res. Canoga, N. Y.; one child :—

Clarence Albert, b. Sept. 17, 1872. He is studying medicine, and preparing to enter Columbia College, N. Y. (1894); graduated Minderse Academy, Seneca Falls, N. Y.

IV. RULIF PETERSON, b. May 12, 1849; d. Sept. 22, 1871; unmarried; he was a Cornell University student, at Ithaca, N. Y., 1869; was on his third year, from whence he went home sick, and died after a brief illness.

206.

(John 7, David 6, Dr. Daniel 5, Rev. Daniel 4, Stephen 3, Stephen 2, Edmund 1.)

Children of **Charles Dubois**[8] **Greenleaf** and Julia Ann (Mapes).

I. HARRIET EMMA, b. June 3, 1845; m. Oct. 8, 1884, James W. Acker; res. New York City; no children.

210. II. FREDERICK KINCH,[9] b. Dec. 21, 1846; m. Dec. 2, 1874, Sudia Jane Mapes; res. Mt. Hope, Orange Co., N. Y.; two children :—

i. Harriet Emma, b. Dec. 1, 1875.

ii. Martin Luther, b. May 4, 1879.

CHARLES DUBOIS (206) GREENLEAF, CONTINUED :—

    III. CHARLES AUGUSTUS, b. Sept. 20, 1848; d. June 11, 1867.

    IV. FRANCES DELPHINE, b. Aug. 19, 1850; m. Oct. 2, 1872, Charles E. Reeve, of Middletown, Orange Co., N. Y.; no children.

211.   V. JOHN EDWIN,[9] b. Sept. 17, 1852; m. Oct. 29, 1873, Jennie S. Shaw. He d. April 22, 1894; res. Otisville, Orange Co., N. Y.; seven children :—

    I. Charles D., b. Sept. 28, 1874.

    II. Oscar Shaw, b. July 16, 1876.

    III. Grace May, b. March 15, 1879.

    IV. Edwin H., b. July 22, 1880.

    V. Lillian, b. May 22, 1882.

    VI. Frank, b. Aug. 8, 1884.

    VII. James Acker, b. June 6, 1886.

212.   VI. FLOYD,[9] b. June 27, 1854; m. Dec. 9, 1875, Harriet Elmira Mapes; res. Mt. Hope, Orange Co., N. Y.; four children :—

    I. Anna Mary, b. Aug. 26, 1877.

    II. Harry Stewart, b. Aug. 17, 1880.

    III. Floyd Augustus, b. April 5, 1883.

    IV. Clara May, b. Dec. 3, 1885.

    VII. LUCINDA MAPES, b. July 1, 1856; m. Dec. 9, 1874, Merritt H. Parsons; res. New York City; one child :—

    Estella May, b. Nov. 25, 1875.

213.   VIII. HANFORD,[9] b. Sept. 28, 1858; m. Dec. 15, 1880, Alida B. Bright; res. New York City; two children :—

    I. Edna Bright, b. Aug. 10, 1881.

    II. Ethel May, b. April 9, 1887.

    IX. ANNIE MARY, b. May 10, 1862; d. Sept. 1, 1864.

207.

(John 7, David 6, Dr. Daniel 5, Rev. Daniel 4, Stephen 3, Stephen 2, Edmund 1.)

Children of **Dr. William Alva**[8] **Greenleaf** and Mrs. Catherine W. G. (Wisner).

214.   I. JOHN GOULD,[9] b. April 14, 1849, at Middletown, N. Y.; m. 1, Aug. 15, 1878, Hannah Alvina

Dr. William Alva (207) Greenleaf, Continued :—

    I. John Gould.

        Underwood, at Elizabeth City, N. C., b. 1850; d. Feb. 7, 1890, at Unionville, Centre Co., Penn.; res. Cleveland, Ohio; 2, June 27, 1891, at Cleveland, Ohio, Mary M. Smyth, of Bathurst, New Brunswick.

    Children by first marriage :—

        I. Robert Percival, b. July 21, 1879, at Jersey, City, N. J.

        II. Helen T., b. Dec. 14, 1881, at Jersey City, N. J.

        III. George S., b. Aug. 6, 1883, at Jersey City, N. J.

        IV. Charles, b. Feb. 26, 1886; d. in infancy.

        V. Walter, b. May 11, 1887; d. in infancy.

        VI. William, b. Dec. 10, 1888.

215. II. Harry Torrey,[9] b. Oct. 1, 1852, at St. Catherines, Dom. Canada; m. July 3, 1877, at Elizabeth City, N. C., Gertrude Pool, of Elizabeth City, Pasquotank Co., N. C., b. Oct. 28, 1853; land surveyor, etc.; res. Elizabeth City, N. C.; nine children, all b. at Elizabeth City.

        I. Catherine Ann, b. June 8, 1878.

        II. Harry Torrey, b. Feb. 26, 1880.

        III. Gertrude Beatrice, b. April 22, 1881.

        IV. Louise Gould, b. Jan. 1, 1884.

        V. William Alva, 2d, b. Jan. 22, 1885.

        VI. Joseph Pool, b. March 24, 1886.

        VII. Lillian Elizabeth, b. Oct. 28, 1888.

        VIII. Louis Edward, b. Feb. 7, 1891.

        IX. Jay Gould, b. May 29, 1893.

    III. Jennie Kate, b. Aug. 7, 1854, at St. Catherines, Dom. Canada; m. 1885, in Jersey City, N. J., Thos. De Witt Van Winkle; res. Jersey City, N. J.; three children :—

    i. Florence.

    ii. Thomas De Witt.

    iii. Leroy.

    IV. William Alva, b. Feb. 17, 1858, at Hamilton, Dom. Canada; d. Oct. 22, 1874, at Woodside, L. I., N. Y.

189.

(David 6, Dr. Daniel 5, Rev. Daniel 4, Stephen 3, Stephen 2, Edmund 1.)

Children of **William**[7] **Greenleaf** and Mary (Williams).

216. I. WILLIAM,[8] b. June 12, 1804; m. March 14, 1840, Hannah Howard. She d. Dec. 12, 1891. He d. April 18, 1874; res. Stockbridge, Mass.; two children.

II. SARAH, b. Sept. 23, 1806; m. Nov. 3, 1831, Benjamin, son of Benjamin Binney, of Boston, b. July 12, 1801; d. Jan. 3, 1877; tinman. She d. Jan. 23, 1888; five children:—

   i. Sarah E. Frances, b. Nov. 27, 1832; d. Sept. 25, 1833.
   ii. Harriet Jane, b. Sept. 3, 1834; d. Oct. 19, 1835.
   iii. Benjamin, 3d, b. July 15, 1836; d. May 27, 1857.
   iv. William Henry, b. Nov. 9, 1837; d. Dec. 16, 1841.
   v. Deodat Williams, b. Oct. 4, 1847; m. Josephine Morse. She was divorced from him.

III. JULIETTE, b. Oct. 25, 1808; m. Jan. 16, 1834, in Hartford, Conn., Henry L. Clark, of the firm of D. & H. L. Clark. She d. March 8, 1863; three children:—

   i. George L., b. Aug. 18, 1840.
   ii. Henry T., b. July 12, 1843.
   iii. Albert A., b. Oct. 9, 1845.

IV. MARY ANN, b. Sept. 1, 1812; m. Jan. 22, 1834, Daniel H. Bassett; six children.

V. HARRIET W., b. Feb. 27, 1815; d. Nov. 21, 1845.

VI. SUSAN E., b. April 18, 1821; m. June 29, 1865, Henry L. Clark, of Norwich, Conn. He d. Jan. 21, 1875; res. Norwich, Conn.; no children.

216.

(William 7, David 6, Dr. Daniel 5, Rev. Daniel 4, Stephen 3, Stephen 2, Edmund 1.)

Children of **William**[8] **Greenleaf** and Hannah (Howard).

I. HARRIET ELIZA, b. Aug. 29, 1841.

217. II. WILLIAM HOWARD,[9] b. March 14, 1844; m. Sept. 22, 1866, Maria L. Skimmings; business, Antique Bookstore, Old South Church, Boston; res. Melrose Highlands, Mass.; three children:—

   1. William Howard,[10] b. Dec. 4, 1867; d. Jan. 28, 1892; unmarried.

WILLIAM (216) GREENLEAF, CONTINUED :—

II. William Howard.

    II. Chester A., b. Sept. 16, 1869; m. Sept. 21, 1890, Bertha Ramsey; one child: Ruth Howard, b. March 29, 1893.

    III. Percy, b. Nov. 19, 1874; d. Sept. 20, 1875.

45.

(Dr. Daniel 5, Rev. Daniel 4, Stephen 3, Stephen 2, Edmund 1.)

Children of **General William**[6] **Greenleaf** and Sally (Quincy).

218. I. WILLIAM,[7] b. Jan. 26, 1766, in Boston; marriage intention filed Nov. 23, 1788; m. 1, Jan. 21, 1789, Maria Eayers, who d. Jan. 13, 1792; 2, Sarah Ruggles, of Newton, Mass. He d. June 27, 1849 or 1850 at Ware, Mass.; res. Ware, Mass.; seven children.

II. EDMUND, b. Dec. 10, 1767; d. Nov. 9, 1789.

III. ELIZABETH, b. Sept. 2, 1769; baptized Sept. 3, 1769; m. Oct. 21, 1795, John Gardiner, of Leominster, Mass., who d. July 4, 1818. She d. 1814; two children :—

    i. Sarah; m. William Greenough, of Boston.

    ii. Dorothy H.; m. Ferdinand E. White, of Boston.

IV. A SON, b. Aug. 8, 1771; d. in infancy.

V. SARAH, b. Feb. 21, 1773; baptized Feb. 28, 1773; marriage intention filed Aug. 12, 1791; m. Sept. 4, 1791, Thomas Chase, of Putney, Vt., and Boston, Mass.; res. Philadelphia, Penn.; two children :—

    i. Thomas.

    ii. William.

219. VI. JOHN HANCOCK,[7] b. April 30, 1775, in Lancaster, Mass.; m. Feb. 1, 1801, Polly Norton, of Granville, N. Y.; b. Oct. 23, 1780. He d. Jan. 28, 1852; six children.

VII. A SON, b. Nov. 15, 1776; d. in infancy.

220. VIII. DANIEL, b. Oct. 9, 1778, in Lancaster, Mass.; baptized Oct. 18, 1778; m. April 3, 1800, Mary, dau. of Deacon John Chamberlain, of Worcester, Mass. She d. March 25, 1867, at Worcester. He. d. Dec. 22, 1824, at Worcester. He was a printer; res. Worcester, Mass.; five children.

218.

(Gen. William 6, Dr. Daniel 5, Rev. Daniel 4, Stephen 3, Stephen 2, Edmund 1.)

Children of **William**[7] **Greenleaf** and Maria (Eayers).

221. I. EDMUND QUINCY,[8] b. Oct. 30, 1789, in Lancaster,
   Mass.; baptized June 13, 1790, in First Church;
   m. 1, about 1813, ——; had children; 2, Nov. 6,
   1831, widow Elizabeth W. Prouty, of Lancaster; res.
   Lancaster, Mass. Two children by 2d marriage:—

   I. George Ruggles, b. Sept. 3, 1832.

   II. Sarah Eliza, b. May 13, 1835.

222. II. WILLIAM JOSEPHUS,[8] b. July 8, 1791, in Lancaster,
   Mass.; baptized July 10, 1791; m. Jan. 8, 1817,
   Esther Calkins. He d. Feb. 22, 1842; res. Canton,
   Bradford Co., Penn.; seven children.

Children by 2d marriage:—

223. III. JOHN RUGGLES,[8] b. Aug. 27, 1797; m. Roxana
   Damon, who d. March 8, 1882. He d. Nov. 8, 1885,
   at Ware, Mass.; res. Ware, Mass.; three children.

   IV. ANN MARIA, b. March 1, 1800; d. Sept. 17, 1881,
   at Ware; res. Ware, Mass.

   V. ELIZA, b. April 1, 1802; d. Aug. 5, 1861, at Ware,
   Mass.

   VI. CAROLINE HULL, b. Aug. 8, 1805; m. Dr. Albert
   White. She d. Jan. 22, 1849, at Greenwich, Mass.;
   res. Greenwich, Mass.

224. VII. GEORGE SULLIVAN,[8] b. April 9, 1808; m. May 12,
   1831, Emeline Susan Chase, b. Nov. 18, 1810, at
   Belchertown, Mass.; d. Jan. 27, 1893. He d. Oct.
   9, 1880; res. Springfield, Mass.; five children.

222.

(William 7, Gen. William 6, Dr. Daniel 5, Rev. Daniel 4, Stephen 3, Stephen 2, Edmund 1.)

Children of **William Josephus**[8] **Greenleaf** and Esther
(Calkins).

225. I. IRA BROUGHTON,[9] b. June 27, 1818, at Smithboro,
   Tioga County, N. Y.; m. Hannah Robert, b. April
   22, 1822. He d. Aug. 10, 1864, in Hospital at
   Point Lookout, Virginia. He was in the employ of
   the United States Government as foreman of a gang
   of seventy carpenters; res. Canton, Penn.; five children.

WILLIAM JOSEPHUS (222) GREENLEAF, CONTINUED :—

226. II. DANIEL GARDINER,[9] b. June 20, 1820, at Smithboro, N. Y.; m. Almira P. ——; res. Canton, Penn.

III. RACHEL MARIA, b. July 23, 1822, at Smithboro, N. Y.; m. Albert S. Porter, who d. February, 1852. She d. June, 1850; two children :—

i. Anna M., res. Auburn, N. Y.

ii. W. H. (Rev.), b. March 19, 1850; m. Sept. 5, 1870, Isadore Kate, dau. of Rev. W. H. H. and Amanda D. (Whitcomb) Dwyer, b. Sept. 5, 1842. Rev. W. H. Porter is pastor of First Baptist Church, of Charleston, Tioga County, Penn. After the death of his parents he was adopted by Daniel G. Greenleaf (his uncle); three children: 1. Cora M., b. May 30, 1871. 2. L.'Belle, b. Aug. 14, 1873. 3. Grace Amanda, b. June 21, 1887.

IV. WILLIAM JOSEPHUS, b. Nov. 13, 1824, in Canton, Penn.

V. MARY JOSELYN, b. April 17, 1827, in Canton, Penn.; m. April 25, 1854, W. H. H. Dwyer ; seven children :—

i. Henry Vivian, b. Feb. 19, 1855.

ii. Charles Sumner, b. Oct. 9, 1856; m. Aug. 26, 1883, Edna W. Teeter; two children: 1. Margaret Joselyn, b. March 12, 1886. 2. Ermuld Delbert, b. Aug. 21, 1891.

iii. Vinton Harlow, b. March 16, 1858; m. November, 1879, Maggie E. Corman; five children: 1. Charles Matthews, b. March, 1882. 2. Carl, b. June, 1885. 3. Amy Eva, b. March, 1888. 4. Raymond Benison, b. May, 1890. 5. Frank, b. November, 1891.

iv. Eugene Kincard, b. Sept. 12, 1859; m. July 3, 1886, Elizabeth J. Ballou; two children: 1. Harold Winfield, b. April 5, 1887. 2. Eva Pearl, b. Oct. 27, 1888.

v. William Judson, b. June 28, 1861; d. Aug. 19, 1866.

vi. Samuel Albert, b. Jan. 20, 1863; d. Feb. 16, 1863.

vii. Edmund Benison, b. Oct. 11, 1865.

VI. EDMUND QUINCY, b. April 25, 1829, in Canton.

VII. AARON CALKINS, b. July 23, 1831, in Canton.

All of this family resided in Canton, Bradford County, Penn.

225.

(William J. 8, William 7, Gen. William 6, Dr. Daniel 5, Rev. Daniel 4, Stephen 3, Stephen 2, Edmund 1.)

Children of **Ira Broughton**[9] **Greenleaf** and Hannah (Robert).

227. I. MILTON PERRY,[10] b. Feb. 5, 1844; m. Aug. 11, 1864, at Troy, Bradford County, Penn., Rachel Williams,

Ira Broughton (225) Greenleaf, Continued :—

   I. Milton Perry.[10]

     of Canton, Penn., b. June 2, 1846; res. Minnequa,
     Penn.; eleven children.

   II. Esther Maria, b. June 5, 1846; unmarried; living
     with her mother, Mrs. Hannah Bothwell.

   III. Alice A., b. July 23, 1849; m. March 1, 1866,
     William Gregory, a farmer; res. Grinnell, Gove
     County, Kan.

228. IV. Jesse W.,[10] b. Jan. 22, 1852; m. Oct. 31, 1877,
     Lucy E. Freeman; res. Alba, Bradford County,
     Penn.; one child :—

     Mary, b. Nov. 20, 1879; d. Jan. 11, 1881.

   V. Ida, b. April 6, 1854; m. Dec. 8, 1875, Irwin
     Whitehead, of Canton, Bradford County, Penn., a
     farmer, b. Oct. 22, 1851 ; two children :—

     i. Frank C., b. Jan. 14, 1881; d. April 24, 1888.

     ii. Lynn, b. Feb. 22, 1886.

227.

(Ira Broughton 9, William J. 8, William 7, Gen. William 6, Dr. Daniel 5, Rev. Daniel 4,
Stephen 3, Stephen 2, Edmund 1.)

   Children of **Milton Perry**[10] **Greenleaf** and Rachel
(Williams).

229. I. Frederick Ira, b. June 12, 1867; m. Sept. 18, 1888,
     Georgia Walborn, of Leroy, Bradford Co., Penn.;
     two children :—

     i. Laura, b. July 24, 1889.

     ii. Hattie, b. Oct. 12, 1891 ; d. May 2, 1892.

   II. Cora May, b. May 7, 1869; d. Aug. 28, 1874;
     murdered by Albert Brown (a negro).

   III. Helen, b. June 1, 1871; m. Dec. 25, 1889, James
     Turner, of Grover, Bradford Co., Penn.

   IV. Emma, b. Aug. 26, 1872; m. Dec. 25, 1889, Philip
     A. Palmer, of Covert, Bradford Co., Penn.

   V. Myrtie, b. Jan. 31, 1875; m. Dec. 25, 1892, Carl
     Raisch, of Granville, Bradford Co., Penn.

   VI. Dora, b. Sept. 7, 1876; d. June 16, 1884.

   VII. Frank, b. March 5, 1879; d. Sept. 16, 1882.

   VIII. Charles Elmer, b. Dec. 9, 1881.

   IX. Lee, b. May 4, 1884.

MILTON PERRY (227) GREENLEAF, CONTINUED :—

    X. PERRY, b. May 19, 1886; d. Nov.5, 1888. Drowned
in a small stream running through his father's farm.

    XI. IDA BELL, b. March 24, 1888.

223.

(William 7, Gen. William 6, Dr. Daniel 5, Rev. Daniel 4, Stephen 3, Stephen 2, Edmund 1.)

Children of **John Ruggles**[8] **Greenleaf** and Roxana
(Damon).

    I. RHODA ELIZABETH, b. June 30, 1838.

230. II. JOHN RUGGLES,[9] (Dr.) b. July 31, 1840; m. June 10,
1873, Jennie S. Doake; res. Gardner, Mass.; two
children :—

    I. Edwin Hammond, b. Jan. 17, 1876; d. Aug. 10,
1876.

    II. Annie Eleanor, b. July 9, 1879.

    III. SARAH MELINDA, b. Sept. 27, 1842.

224.

(William 7, Gen. William 6, Dr. Daniel 5, Rev. Daniel 4, Stephen 3, Stephen 2, Edmund 1.)

Children of **George Sullivan**[8] **Greenleaf** and Emme-
line Susan (Chase).

    I. ANN MARIA, b. July 12, 1832, in Shutesbury, Mass.;
m. Sept. 7, 1852, Edwin P. Kellogg. She d. Jan. 23,
1863, at Hartford; res. Hartford, Conn.; one child :—

    ——, d. in infancy.

    II. ALFRED ELY, b. June 16, 1833; d. April 12, 1837;
drowned at Hartford, Conn.

    III. JULIA ANNA, b. Feb. 15, 1836; m. 1, Dec. 23, 1860,
Joseph Whitney, b. Jan. 17, 1824; d. Dec. 24,
1873; four children; 2, July 10, 1895, Joseph H.
Cooper, of Springfield, Mass.; res. Springfield, Mass.

Children by 1st marriage :—

    Three d. in infancy.

    iv. Bessie Ella, b. March 3, 1869; d. Sept. 19, 1876.

231. IV. JOHN QUINCY,[9] b. Jan. 31, 1838; m. March 26,
1860, Paulina, dau. of Arial Slater, of Crystal Lake,
Tolland Co., Conn., b. Nov. 26, 1839; res. Atlantic, Iowa; moved from Springfield, Mass., to the
West in 1862; three children :—

    I. Minnie Josephine, b. July 6, 1861; m. March 25,
1879, C. E. Hartshorn.

GEORGE SULLIVAN (224) GREENLEAF, CONTINUED:—
IV. John Quincy.
  II. Luella Maria, b. Oct. 17, 1866; m. Oct. 17, 1884, H.
    Ivanhoe Whitted; res. Lewis, Iowa.
  III. William Slater, b. Oct. 3, 1872. Physician; res.
    Atlantic, Iowa.
  V. GEORGE NOAH PORTER, b. Feb. 19, 1847, in Spring-
    field, Mass.; d. Oct. 8, 1890; res. New York City
    the last eight years of his life.

219.

(Gen. William 6, Dr. Daniel 5, Rev. Daniel 4, Stephen 3, Stephen 2, Edmund 1.)

Children of **John Hancock**[7] **Greenleaf** and Polly
(Norton).
  I. BETSEY GARDINER, b. about 1803; d. in infancy.
232. II. JOHN MATTHEW,[8] b. May 19, 1806; m. 1, June 20,
    1837, Lucy Talcott. She d. July 4, 1842; 2, Sept 27,
    1843, Emeline Wilbur. He d. Aug. 23, 1881; res.,
    Owego, N. Y.; three children.
  III. MARTHA NORTON, b. April 17, 1809; m. William
    Gordon. He d. about 1843. She d. Oct. 15, 1890.
  IV. BETSEY GARDINER, b. Sept. 25, 1811; m. George
    W. Allen. He d. about 1853.
233. V. WILLIAM JOSEPHUS,[8] b. Sept. 25, 1815; m. Oct. 13,
    1836, Mary L. Ford, b. Dec. 2, 1817. He d. March
    22, 1869; eight children.
234. VI. AMOS CANFIELD,[8] b. March 8, 1818, in Owego, N. Y.;
    m. Oct. 22, 1840, Mary Dougherty, b. July 8, 1819.
    He was associated with the firm of Bates, Reed &
    Cooley, Dry Goods, until about 1886, when he became
    interested with the firm of Dunham, Buckley & Co.
    He d. Aug. 1, 1894; resident of South Orange, N. J.,
    over twenty years; res. New York City; one child:—
    1. Sarah Amelia, b. Nov. 28, 1841; m. W. W. Miller,
      South Orange, N. J.

232.

(John Hancock 7, Gen. William 6, Dr. Daniel 5, Rev. Daniel 4, Stephen 3, Stephen 2,
Edmund 1.)

Children of **John Matthew**[8] **Greenleaf** and Lucy (Talcott).
  I. ANN ELIZABETH, b. July 28, 1841; d. June 28, 1843.

John Matthew (232) Greenleaf, Continued :—
Children by 2d marriage :—

235. II. John Talcott,[9] b. Jan. 26, 1847; m. 1, Sept. 4,
1867, Libbie C. Manning, d. Dec. 20, 1867; 2, Dec.
21, 1870, Martha S. McMaster, who d. March 11,
1872; 3, Oct. 22, 1873, Hattie Meeker; physician;
res. Owego, N. Y.; one child by 2d marriage :—
————, b. March 11, d. Sept. 28, 1872.

III. Frederic Hewitt, b. Oct. 11, 1855; d. Dec. 20,
1872.

233.

(John Hancock 7, Gen. William 6, Dr. Daniel 5, Rev. Daniel 4, Stephen 3, Stephen 2, Edmund 1.)

Children of **William Josephus**[8] **Greenleaf** and Mary
L. (Ford).

236. I. Albert B.,[9] b. Jan. 25, 1838; m. Dec. 25, 1867,
Addie Wood; res. Coldwater, Mich.; two children :—
    i. Grace M., b. July, 1871.
    ii. Arloa, b. September, 1880.

II. Martha E., b. May 1, 1839; d. June 23, 1860.

III. Lucy J., b. Dec. 4, 1840; m. April 18, 1866, James
Mosher; res. Idaho Springs, Col.

IV. John C., b. Jan. 18, 1842; d. Jan. 28, 1844.

V. Mary E., b. June 15, d. Sept. 21, 1844.

237. VI. William Carleton,[9] or C. J. (as he is called), b.
Aug. 9, 1846; m. in Dowagiac, Mich., Jan. 14, 1871,
Frankie Wares; res. St. Paul, Minn.; two children :—
    i. Ray, b. July, 1877.
    ii. Roy, b. September, 1878.

VII. Juliette E., b. Aug. 30, 1848; m. Oct. 23, 1867,
Elmer Gates. She d. Aug. 13, 1868.

238. VIII. Oscar F.,[9] b. Feb. 22, 1852; m. in Dowagiac,
Mich., June 15, 1884, Lizzie Watson; printer; res.
St. Paul, Minn.; two children :—
    i. Guy F., b. Sept. 24, 1890.
    ii. Pearl M., b. April 20, 1892.

220.

(Gen. William 6, Dr. Daniel 5, Rev. Daniel 4, Stephen 3, Stephen 2, Edmund 1.)

Children of **Daniel**[7] **Greenleaf** and Mary (Chamberlain).

239. I. William[8] Henry Scott, b. May 22, 1801, in Worcester, Mass.; m. Myra, dau. Luke and Sarah Joselyn,

Daniel (220) Greenleaf, Continued :—

I. William Henry Scott.

of Leominster, Mass., who d. July 26, 1874. He d.
May 4, 1869; res. Worcester, Mass. He dropped
the name of Henry Scott. One child :—
Sarah Lucretia, b. June 11, 1833; m. H. R. Hammond,
of Norwich, Conn. He d. Dec. 16, 1890. She d.
Jan. 2, 1892.

II. Mary Elizabeth, b. March 29, 1803; m. Tyler
Gibbs, of Norwich, Conn. He d. at Fitchburg,
Mass. She d. Aug. 17, 1893; res. Brookfield, Mass.
Six children, one son now living :—
John C. Gibbs, West Brookfield, Mass.

240. III. John Chamberlain,[8] b. Oct. 24, 1805, at Worcester,
Mass.; m. Julia, dau. of Israel and Lucy Whitney,
of Worcester. She d. Feb. 10, 1887. He d. March
9, 1885, at Rutland; three children :—
    i. John Whitney, b. Nov. 29, 1828; m. ——. He d.——.
    ii. Levi Chamberlain, b. March 2, 1835; m.——; res.
    Chicago, Ill.
    iii. Mary Chamberlain, b. Dec. 23, 1839; m. ——
    Fletcher. She is not living.

IV. Sarah Quincy, b. Feb. 2, 1808, at Worcester,
Mass.; m. Sept. 30, 1830, Matthew Bird, of Boston,
b. April 24, 1806; d. April 20, 1866. She d. March
19, 1865; res. Boston; eight children :—
    i. Charles Matthew, b. Sept. 4, 1831; d. July 6, 1834.
    ii. Rebecca Newton, b. June 23, 1833; m. Oct. 23, 1856, Charles
    B. Bedlington. She d. May 5, 1891.
    iii. Henry Chamberlain, b. June 17, 1835; m. 1, June 17, 1862,
    Sarah B. Lovell, who d. Sept. 3, 1872; 2, Aug. 26, 1873, Flora
    M. Chase; res. South Boston.
    iv. Lewis Jones, b. July 31, 1837; m. Oct. 14, 1862, Sarah E.
    Eaton; res. Roxbury, Mass.
    v. William Greenleaf, b. Nov. 10, 1839; m. Dec. 31, 1867, Louise
    Lorey; res. Boston.
    vi. Dolly Ann, b. Nov. 15, 1841; d. Aug. 31, 1847.
    vii. John Quincy, b. Dec. 11, 1843; m. Sept. 13, 1869, Mary H.
    T. Still; res. Newtonville, Mass.
    viii. Mary Ellen, b. Dec. 14, 1845; m. Nov. 24, 1864, A. W. Cole;
    res. Newtonville, Mass.

V. Dollÿ Ann, b. Sept. 2, 1812; m. James Harvey
Gerould, who d. June 14, 1871, at Worcester, Mass.;
res. Newtonville, Mass.

46.

(Dr. Daniel 5, Rev. Daniel 4, Stephen 3, Stephen 2, Edmund 1.)

Children of **Calvin[6] Greenleaf** and Rebecca (Whitcomb).

    I. CALVIN, JR., b. Nov. 1, 1763; d. 1785; unmarried.

    II. REBECCA, b. June 20, 1765; d. age 11 years.

241. III. JOHN,[7] b. March 20, 1767, in Bolton; m. April 3,
1788, Abigail Townsend. He d. about 1842; res.
Woodstock, Vt., and Templeton, Mass.; ten children.

    IV. DOROTHY, b. Sept. 2, 1769; d. age 7 years.

242. V. DANIEL,[7] b. in Bolton, Nov. 2, 1771; m. Sarah Townsend, b. about 1763; d. Sept. 12, 1849. He d. Nov.
16, 1858; res. Swanzey, N. H.   Six children.

    VI. SARAH, b. Jan. 11, 1774; d. in infancy.

    VII. BETSEY, b. April, 1776; m. Levi Moore, of Bolton,
Mass.; res. Bolton; one child :—
Lyman; d. March 21, 1892.

    VIII. ASA, b. Sept. 29, 1778; d. in infancy.

    IX. DOLLY, b. Feb. 11, 1780; m. Martin Houghton.

243. X. ELIAS,[7] b. Jan. 10, 1782; m. Nancy Townsend, b.
1784; d. March 13, 1860, at Bethel, Vt. He d.
April 28, 1876, at Bethel, Vt.; res. Chittenden, Vt.;
eleven children.

244. XI. MOSES,[7] b. Jan. 18, 1786; m. 1, Oct., 1814, Experience Sawyer, b. ——; d. 1830; seven children; 2,
1835, Lucy Sawyer, of Berlin. He d. Aug. 12, 1863;
res. Bolton, Mass., on the Old Farm.

Both Moses and his wife Experience (Sawyer) became insane.
Moses remained so about three months. In his second marriage he and his wife could not agree, so they parted in 1837.

241.

(Calvin 6, Dr. Daniel 5, Rev. Daniel 4, Stephen 3, Stephen 2, Edmund 1.)

Children of **John[7] Greenleaf** and Abigail (Townsend).

    I. ABIGAIL, b. April 11, 1789; m. Joshua Wheeler, b.
Dec. 22, 1788; d. 1877. She d. Aug. 12, 1859, at
Pittsfield, Vt.; nine children :—
i. Eliza Ann, b. Sept. 23, d. Oct. 8, 1813.
ii. Joshua Stedman, b. Nov. 3, 1814; m. ——; d. Dec. 13, 1886;
five children.

JOHN (241) GREENLEAF, CONTINUED:—

I. Abigail.

iii. Abigail G., b. April 12, 1817; m. William A. Hatch, of North Leverett, Mass.; d. Nov. 22, 1842; two children, d. in infancy.

iv. Harriet R., b. Sept. 12, 1819; m. Jan. 1, 1843, Almon Thompson, b. 1808; d. March 10, 1883; res. Pittsfield, Vt.; no children.

v. Samuel S., b. Oct. 25, 1821; d. April 16, 1822.

vi. Althea G., b. May 17, 1824; m. Lyndon Cleveland; res. Pittsfield, Vt.

vii. Charles G., b. Aug. 9, 1825; d. Nov. 23, 1828.

viii. Pamelia M. G., b. Dec. 17, 1828; m. Eli Chandler, of Stockbridge, Vt. She d. May 19, 1867; res. Sycamore, Ill.; three children: 1. E. C., res. Sycamore, Ill. 2. Mrs. E. C. Williams, Leominster, Mass. 3. Child, d. in infancy.

ix. Persis L., b. April 8, 1832; m. 1853, R. M. McIntosh, of Bethel, Vt.; res. Northfield, Vt.; two children: 1. Abbie L., b. Aug. 12, 1860; m. Oct. 26, 1887, George C. Sanborn, of Northfield, Vt., b. Jan. 5, 1860; two children: (1) George Max, b. Nov. 10, 1889. (2) Edward McIntosh, b. June 14, 1891. 2. Hattie B., b. Aug. 3, 1872; d. Aug. 24, 1872.

245. II. JOHN,[8] b. March 27, 1791; m. Abigail (his cousin), dau. of Daniel Greenleaf (242). He d. July 25, 1833, in Templeton, Mass.; four children:—

I. Nancy, d. in infancy.

II. Samuel, d. in infancy.

III. Sarah, m. —— Bridges.

IV. ——, d. in infancy.

III. REBECCA, b. April 22, 1793; m. Joshua Holman, brother of Jonathan, who m. Susan Townsend Greenleaf. They went into the western part of Iowa as missionaries and teachers to the Indians; they had eight or nine children; Rebecca and Joshua were the oldest son and daughter, living in 1849; they all died there.

IV. ELIZABETH W., b. April 14, 1795; m. Oct. 31, 1816, John Woodbury. She d. about 1845; six children, all born in Rutland, Vt.:—

i. Susan Woodbury, b. Oct. 13, 1817; m. 1, 1843, George Cheney, of Holden, Mass., b. Oct. 27, 1814; d. Sept. 16, 1849, in Holden, Mass.; res. Paxton, Mass.; 2, 1850, Luke Stratton, b. Aug. 16, 1811; d. March 28, 1890; children by 1st marriage, b. in Holden, Mass.: 1. Edward F., b. Sept. 12, 1843; d. 1843. 2. Herbert L., b. June 25, 1845; res. Leominster, Mass.

JOHN (241) GREENLEAF, CONTINUED :—

> IV. Elizabeth W.
>
>> 3. George F., b. June 28, 1849; res. Boston. One child by second marriage : Carlos Eugene, b. May 30, 1856; res. Paxton, Mass.
>
> ii. Abigail, b. March 30, 1819.
>
> iii. Mary E., b. Oct. 20, 1822 ; res. Pepperell, Mass.
>
> iv. John F., b. May 7, 1826; res. Manchester, N. H.
>
> v. Calvin, b. April 9, 1828; res. Spencer, Mass.
>
> vi. Lucy Ann, b. Nov. 22, 1830.
>
> V. SUSAN TOWNSEND, b. May 17, 1797, at Templeton, Mass.; m. Dec. 11, 1817, at Conneaut, Crawford County, Penn., Jonathan Holman, b. April 20, 1790, at Phillipston, Worcester County, Mass. ; d. June 26, 1855. She d. March 21, 1883, in Pennsylvania ; thirteen children :—
>
>> i. Leonard S., b. Feb. 14, 1819; m. 1, Feb. 29, 1852, Fannie C. Kimball, who d. July, 1856; no children; 2, 1858, Catherine Kimball, who d. Nov., 1863. He d. March 15, 1868; children by 2d marriage : 1. Fannie L. 2. Catherine, b. Dec. 31, 1860; both b. in Conneaut, Crawford Co., Penn.
>>
>> ii. Jonathan L., b. Sept. 15, 1820; m. April 4, 1847, Mary J. Bortles. He d. Feb. 21, 1890; five children : 1. Clara Jane, b. Feb. 24, 1850. 2. Tiffie A., b. Aug. 31, 1852. 3. Emma J., b. Nov. 26, 1855. 4. Nettie V., b. Feb. 8, 1857. 5. Sidney A., b. Dec. 12, 1860. All born in Conneaut, Penn.
>>
>> iii. John G., b. Feb. 28, 1822; m. Feb. 21, 1847, Abby Robbins; b. Sept. 6, 1831; d. Jan. 11, 1892; res. Conneautville, Penn.; nine children : 1. George A., b. Dec. 31, 1847. 2. William J., b. Feb. 3, 1852. 3. Sylvania J., b. Aug. 22, 1853. 4. Leonard S., b, Dec. 8, 1854. 5. John, Jr., b. Aug. 19, 1856. 6. Fred W., b. Dec. 26, 1863. 7. Minnie A., b. April 15, 1866. 8. Mabel L., b. Jan. 19, 1868. 9. Jessie E., b. July 17, 1870.
>>
>> iv. Susan, b. Oct. 12, 1823; m. Nov. 8, 1840, Elizur H. Tyler. He d. Jan. 20, 1885; res. Erie, Penn.; six children : 1. Jerome D., b. Dec. 1, 1841; d. Aug. 1, 1892. 2. Levi E., b. Dec. 11, 1843. 3. Jonathan M., b. Sept. 11, 1845. 4. William H., b. Aug. 18, 1848. 5. Charles H., b. Aug. 4, 1851. 6. Clara E., b. July 23, 1853. All born in Conneaut, Penn.
>>
>> v. Zilphia A., b. Aug. 3, 1825 ; m. 1, Nov. 1, 1848, Henry B. Palmiter, b. Aug. 23, 1819; d. Aug. 11, 1869; 2, May 3, 1881, Truman L. Andrews, b. Aug. 27, 1823; d. Aug. 26, 1890; res. South Bend, Wash.; three children by 1st marriage : 1. Mary Susan, b. Feb. 10, 1851; m. Dec. 10, 1869, Azro Hudson Petite. 2. Abbie Josephine, b. Dec. 14, 1860; m. Nov., 1879, Herman A. Eichelman. He d. Jan. 15, 1882. 3. Albert Jonathan, twin. All born in Conneaut, Penn.

JOHN (241) GREENLEAF, CONTINUED :—

V. Susan Townsend.

vi. Calvin J., b. Oct. 30, 1827; m. Sept. 4, 1852, Delia Oftensend; res. Chicago, Ill.; three children: 1. Emma Adell, b. Oct. 2, 1853; m. Hulbert F. White. He d. Aug. 23, 1892. 2. Delvin Frank, b. Sept. 22, 1855. 3. James Harlo, b. July 20, 1858.

vii. Charles T., b. Aug. 19, 1829; m. 1, Sept. 10, 1853, Pamelia Tyler, who d. Jan. 20, 1855; 2, April, 1857, Rebecca Strazer, who d. Dec. 23, 1881; 3, April 23, 1882, Elizabeth Dunlap; res. Atlantic, Crawford Co., Penn.; children by 2d marriage: 1. Charles J. 2. Susan A.; m. C. T. Hills. She d. Aug. 4, 1883. 3. Sheridan P. 4. Luela. Child by 3d marriage: Harry A., b. Aug. 23, 1883.

viii. Mary, b. Sept. 4, 1831; d. in infancy.

ix. Abigail C., b. Oct. 20, 1832; m. Sept. 10, 1853, Charles Bortles. She d. Nov. 1, 1856; one child: Charles, Jr., b. April, 1854.

x. Pamelia E., b. Nov. 6, 1834; m. 1, June 9, 1853, Augustus R. Fenner, who d. Aug. 4, 1872; 2, Dec. 23, 1885, George Gorton; res. Cold Brook, Herkimer Co., N. Y.; no children.

xi. Henry R., b. Jan. 29, 1837; m. Feb. 16, 1868, Hattie E. Adams; res. Jefferson, Ashtabula Co., Ohio; no children.

xii. David S., b. Feb. 24, 1839, at Conneautville, Penn.; m. Sept. 25, 1856, Jane Lawrence; res. Conneautville, Crawford Co., Penn.; four children: 1. Lettie A. 2. George J. 3. Jennie May. 4. Leda K.

xiii. Maria, b. April 6, 1841; m. Nov. 23, 1858, Stephen F. McLallin; res. Topeka, Kansas; four children: 1. Ella L., b. June 14, 1861. 2. Stephen A., b. July 17, 1868; d. Sept. 5, 1873. 3. Lena M., b. July 18, 1875. 4. Grace E., b. Dec. 14, 1878.

VI. PAMELIA M., b. Feb. 25, 1799; m. Daniel (her cousin), son of Daniel and Sarah (Townsend) Greenleaf (250); b. Aug. 7, 1800; d. July 3, 1874. She d. July 7, 1840; three children.

VII. ANN T., b. Oct. 26, 1801; d. July 17, 1803.

246. VIII. CALVIN,[8] b. May 13, 1803; m. Feb. 28, 1828, Clarissa Ames. He was ordained to the Baptist ministry Sept. 1, 1828; removed to Illinois, May 13, 1835; res. (1855) Griggsville, Ill. He d. in Colorado; four children.

247. IX. CHARLES WARD,[8] b. May 11, 1805, in Templeton, Mass.; m. 1, June 8, 1828, Louisa Greenwood, b. June 2, 1808; d. June 5, 1840; 2, Aug. 30, 1840, Eliza Gale Paige, of Woodstock, Vt.; res. Cleveland, Ohio; eight children.

JOHN (241) GREENLEAF, CONTINUED :—
    IX. Charles Ward.
    Children by 1st marriage :—
        I. A son; d. in infancy.
        II. A son; d. in infancy.
        III. Elizabeth P., b. 1835; m. 1855, Rev. William Cal-
derwood, missionary Presbyterian Board; went to
India. She d. Aug. 15, 1859, in Calcutta; no
children.
        IV. Almira L., b. Feb., 1838; m. Nov. 2, 1858, at
Orange, Mass., Thomas Howard White, of Cleveland, Ohio, of the White Sewing Machine Company, b. April 26, 1836, in Philadelphia, Penn.;
res. Cleveland, Ohio; eight children :—
        1. Alice Elizabeth, b. July 28, 1859, at Orange, Mass.; d. Sept. 3,
1861, at Templeton, Mass.   2. Mabel Almira, b. June 9, 1861,
at Templeton; m. Nov. 4, 1886, at Cleveland, Ohio, James
Armstrong Harris, of Citra, Fla., an orange grower.   She d.
July 19, 1888, at Pablo Beach, Fla.; one child: James A., Jr.,
b. Oct. 31, 1887.   3. Alice Maud, b. March 14, 1864, at Orange,
Mass.; m. Jan. 3, 1894, at Cleveland, Ohio, William Joseph
Hammer, of New York; electrical engineer; one child:
Mabel White, b. Oct. 24, 1894, in New Jersey.   4. Windsor
Thomas, b. Aug. 28, 1866, in Orange, Mass.; m. Sept. 14,
1892, Dellia Burkley Holden; Treasurer of Cleveland Screw
Co.; one child: Thomas Holden, b. Aug. 4, 1894, at Cleve-
land, Ohio.   5. Clarence Greenleaf, b. March 19, 1869, in
Cleveland, Ohio.   6. Rollin Henry, b. July 11, 1872, in Cleve-
land, Ohio.   Graduated June, 1894, Cornell University, Ithaca,
N. Y.   7. Walter Charles, b. Sept. 8, 1876, in Cleveland,
Ohio.   Entered Cornell University, Sept., 1894.   8. Ella
Almira, b. Jan. 9, 1883, in Cleveland, Ohio.
    Children by 2d marriage :—
248.   v. Charles W.,[9] b. July 3, 1841, in Barnard, Vt.; m.
Dec. 1, 1868, at Conneautville, Penn., Mary Stan-
ley, dau. of Hon. John Mason Eustis, of Dixfield,
Me.   Is member King Hiram Lodge F. and A. M.,
Dixfield, Me., St. Paul's Chapter R. A. M., Boston,
Roxbury Council of Royal and Select Masters, Joseph
Warren Commandery Knights Templar, Roxbury,
Mass.; res. Roxbury, Mass.; one child :—
    Mace Eustice, b. Dec. 8, 1872, at Dixfield, Me.
        VI. Emma M., b. March 28, 1843; m. 1, Nov. 21,
1861, Tappan S. Eaton, of Boston, b. Oct. 17,

JOHN (241) GREENLEAF, CONTINUED :—

  IX. Charles Ward.

     1838, in Augusta, Me.; d. Sept. 17, 1862. Enlisted at Lynn, Mass., June, 1862, and was killed at Antietam. 2, Dr. A. S. Bonsteel, of Elliottville, N. Y., b. July 17, 1838; d. Nov. 22, 1887; res. Corry, Penn.

     One child by 1st marriage: 1. Louis S., b. Jan. 5, 1863. Four children by 2d marriage: 2. Ray Livingstone, b. Jan. 1, 1870. 3. Lotta May, b. Feb. 11, 1872. 4. Morris C., b. Feb. 11, 1872, twin. 5. Mary E., b. March 25, 1877.

     Ray Livingstone, grad. High School; now Sec'y Y. M. C. A., Hamilton, Ohio. Morris Courtenay is Physical Director Y. M. C. A.

     Dr. Bonsteel was first at Chamberlain Inst., Randolph, N. Y., then graduated at University of Michigan, 1864; graduate Bellevue Hospital, N. Y. City, 1872; President Erie Medical Society several years; Sir Knight Clarence Commandery.

249.   VII. George S.,[9] b. Nov. 4, 1846, in Roxbury, Mass.; m. Dec. 26, 1882, Alice J. Baker, of Cleveland, Ohio; res. Cleveland, Ohio; one child :—

     Nettie May, b. Feb. 4, 1891.

  VIII. Jennie E., b. Aug. 30, 1848; m. April 10, 1875, John Greening; res. Cleveland, Ohio; three children :—

     1. Florence F., b. Jan. 16, 1876. 2. Rollin W. C., b. March 8, 1877. 3. Mab. C. J., b. Dec. 12, 1878.

  X. HARRIET, b. March 29, 1807, at Templeton, Mass.; m. Feb. 28, 1828, Nathan Allen. She d. May 3, 1882; res. Vermont; eight children :—

  i. Harriet, b. 1828; m. 1848, John Knight. She d. 1853; three children, two now living.

  ii. Nathan M., b. 1830; m. 1849, Louisa Babcock, of Bolton, Mass. He d. 1886; six children.

  iii. Charles G., b. 1832; d. Dec. 11, 1858; unmarried.

  iv. Lucinda, b. 1834; m. 1853, Augustus Willard; d. the next year after marriage.

  v. Permela, b. 1836; d. about two years of age.

  vi. John G., b. 1838; m. Oct. 8, 1862, at Rochester, Vt., Elizabeth Parker, of Hubbardston, Mass.; res. Sterling, Mass.; four children.

  vii. Susan, b. 1840; d. 1861.

  viii. Sumner D., b. Dec. 11, 1842; m. Oct. 27, 1869, at Pittsfield, Vt., Alice Segar, of Pittsfield, Vt.; res. Clinton, Mass., since 1868; five children: 1. John S., b. Jan. 5, 1871. 2. Bertie

JOHN (241) GREENLEAF, CONTINUED :—

   X. Harriet.

   Sumner, b. April 12, 1876; d. July 29, 1876. 3. Harris, b.
   Oct. 17, 1879. 4. Howard Damon, b. Oct. 14, 1884; d. Jan. 31,
   1885. 5. Ralph N., b. Nov. 14, 1886. All b. at Clinton, Mass.

242.

(Calvin 6, Dr. Daniel 5, Rev. Daniel 4, Stephen 3, Stephen 2, Edmund 1.)

Children of **Daniel**[7] **Greenleaf** and Sarah (Townsend).

   I. SARAH, b. May 22, 1792, at Bolton; m. Dec. 13, 1815,
      Timothy Switzer, of Warren, Mass.; d. Feb. 11,
      1872, at Madison, Wis.; twelve children :—

      i. Sarah T., b. Nov. 6, 1816; d. Feb. 25, 1818.
      ii. Charlotte Eaton, b. Feb. 4, 1818.
      iii. William Bently, b. June 23, 1819; d. ——.
      iv. Daniel Greenleaf, b. Feb. 2, 1821; res. Ypsilanti, Mich.
      v. Mary Townsend, b. July 1, 1822; m. Wm. Cross; res. Lansing,
         Mich.
      vi. Abbie Eliza, b. April 12, 1824; m. Chas. Howell; d. ——; res.
         Minneapolis, Minn.
      vii. Timothy Allen, b. Sept. 12, 1826; d. March 25, 1857.
      viii. Sarah Jane, b. July 21, 1829; m. Francis S. Cramer, June 7,
         1847. Mr. Cramer was private in Co. F, 33d Wis. Vols., Civil
         War; res. Walnut, Iowa.
      ix. Justin Parsons, b. June 16, 1831.
      x. Rial Lysander, b. April 12, 1833.
      xi. Catherine Cornelia, b. June 15, 1836; m. 1, June 28, 1855,
         Darwin D. Gibbs, b. June 14, 1833; three children: 1. Edla
         D., b. April 12, 1861; d. Aug. 29, 1864. 2. Percy A., b.
         April 25, 1864; d. Aug. 13, 1864. 3. Catherine L., b. Dec.
         30, 1866. 2, Sept. 11, 1882, Austin A. Bradford, who d.
         March 24, 1891; res. Smithville, N. H.
      xii. Rebecca Elizabeth, b. July 10, d. Sept. 10, 1838.

   II. A DAUGHTER, d. in infancy.

   III. A DAUGHTER, d. in infancy.

250. IV. DANIEL,[8] b. Aug. 7, 1800; m. 1, Pamelia, his cousin,
      dau. of John Greenleaf (241), b. Feb. 25, 1799; d.
      July 7, 1840; 2, Relief Wright, who lived less than
      one year after marriage; no children; 3, Miranda
      Carter, b. 1815. He d. July 3, 1874; eight children.

   V. MARY TOWNSEND, b. 1805; m. Levi Hill, b. March
      10, 1800; d. Nov. 26, ——. She d. Sept. 9, 1856;
      three children :—

      i. Sarah Ann, b. 1831; m. Samuel Kendall; res. Waterville,
         Mass.; two children: 1. Addie, b. Sept. 6, 1854. 2. Charles,
         b. July 22, 1865.

Daniel (242) Greenleaf, Continued :—
V. Mary Townsend.
ii. Adeline, b. Nov. 5, 1833; m. Heber Jackson. She d. at birth
of son, Clarence Alva, 1857.
iii. Charles P., b. July 6, 1842; m. Ellen Safford; two children:
1. Etta. 2. Leon.
VI. Abigail, m. John Greenleaf (245), b. March 27,
1791 ; res. Paxton, Mass. ; three children.

250.

(Daniel 7, Calvin 6, Dr. Daniel 5, Rev. Daniel 4, Stephen 3, Stephen 2, Edmund 1.)
Children of Daniel[8] Greenleaf and Pamelia.
I. Clarissa Maria, b. Jan. 5, 1825 ; m. April 12, 1843,
Norton E. Pratt, of Marlboro, Vt., b. Sept. 6, 1819;
res. Hinsdale, N. H. ; five children :—
i. Helen Maria, b. Dec. 18, 1845; m. March 7, 1866, Nathan
M. Worden; one child: a daughter, m. Clinton Bronson, of
Ashfield, Mass.
ii. Luana Jane, b. Oct. 17, 1847; m. April 22, 1868, Charles C.
Tolman, of Hinsdale, N. H.
iii. Charles N., b. Jan. 11, 1852.
iv. Henry P., b. Sept. 27, 1856.
v. Ida Gertrude, b. July 1, 1861.
251. II. Calvin Theophilus,[9] b. Nov. 25, 1832 ; m. July 3, 1853,
at Troy, N. H., Eliza Jane Wheeler, of West Swanzey,
N. H. ; res. Montreal, Canada ; four children :—
1. Frederick, b. 1855 ; d. 1862.
252. ii. Charles Amos,[10] b. about 1856 ; m.——; res. West
Swanzey, N. H. ; three children: 1. Hazel L., b.
Sept. 7, 1878. 2. Mellen E., b. March 20, 1880.
3. Leslie C., b. May 29, 1885.
iii. Clara, m. John Albert Lee; res. Springfield, Mass.
iv. Frank Chapin.
III. Estella, b. Dec. 15, 1833 ; d. July 7, 1840.
Children by 3d marriage :—
IV. Leaffie J., b. July 5, 1848; m. Oct. 4, 1870,
Lyman Stone, of Swanzey, N. H. ; three children :—
i. Lester L., b. May 13, 1875.
ii. Leon E., b. Nov. 10, 1879.
iii. Gena E., b. Jan. 17, 1883.
V. Amelia A., b. Sept. 4, 1850; m. Jan. 4, 1871,
Chauncey Wallace Healey, of Swanzey, N. H., b.
Dec. 4, 1848; res. New Britain, Conn. ; no children.

DANIEL (250) GREENLEAF, CONTINUED :—

VI. MARY T., b. Sept. 8, 1852 ; m. Feb. 23, 1871, Norris C. Carter, of Fitzwilliam, N. H. ; res. West Swanzey, N. H. ; two children :—

     i. Florence M., b. March 8, 1872; m. Oct. 22, 1890, Edgar C. Emery; one child : Clifford, b. Jan. 6, 1892.

     ii. Lillian M., b. Oct. 21, 1884.

VII. CHARLES D., b. July 20, 1854 ; unmarried ; res. West Swanzey, N. H.

VIII. WILLIAM H., b. July 4, 1856 ; d. June 23, 1865.

243.

(Calvin 6, Dr. Daniel 5, Rev. Daniel 4, Stephen 3, Stephen 2, Edmund 1.)

Children of **Elias**[7] **Greenleaf** and Nancy (Townsend).

I. NANCY, b. 1804 ; m. Luther Bullard, of Bethel, Vt. She d. 1883 ; eight children :—

     i. Pamelia, b. 1826; unmarried; res. Bethel, Vt.

     ii. Luther P., b. 1827; m. Emily Morse; four children : 1. Edson. 2. Alton. 3. Mattie. 4. Jessie.

     iii. Chastina L., b. 1830; m. Andis Twitchell. She d. 1870; two children; 1. Edgar. 2. Clara.

     iv. Oliver, b. 1832; m. Hattie Wellington. He d. 1877; four children : 1. Kate. 2. Luther. 3. John. 4. Ralph.

     v. Martha, b. 1835; m. Moses Dustin; she died April 3, 1895; no children.

     vi. Calvin, b. 1838; m. Mary Morse. He d. 1875; three children : 1. Charles; d. ——. 2. Fred. 3. Ernest.

     vii. Frank, b. 1843; m. Emma Dunbar; two children : 1. A daughter. 2. A daughter.

     viii. Nancy F., b. 1846; m. Christopher Noble; no children.

II. PAMELIA, b. 1806 ; m. William Whitaker. She d. 1825 ; res. Felchville, Vt.

III. POLLY ANNIS, b. Feb. 11, 1808 ; m. Oct. 27, 1831, Nathaniel Goodspeed, Franklin Falls, Franklin Co., N. Y. She d. May 30, 1865 ; twelve children :—

     i. Elias, b. July 10, 1832; m. April 19, 1868, Phebe Ling. Served in Civil War, 118th Reg. N. Y. Vols.

     ii. Augustus, b. Oct. 9, 1833; m. 1, Dec. 16, 1855, Rebecca Galuesha; 2. May 7, 1866, Louisa E. Colton. Served in Civil War, 17th Vt. Vols.

     iii. Roswell, b. Jan. 20, 1835.

     iv. Mellisa, b. Nov. 10, 1836; m. Feb. 22, 1873, Samuel S. Willcox.

     v. Wallace, b. Dec. 18, 1838; m. Aug. 10, 1864, Nancy Melinda Dix, b. Jan. 11, 1844; d. March 19, 1893; res. Stark, N. Y.;

ELIAS (243) GREENLEAF, CONTINUED :—

III. Polly Annis.

six children : 1. Lillian May, b. July 18, 1866; m. July 26, 1885, Hiram Flanders. 2. Edson Eugene, b. Oct. 18, 1868; m. Sept. 10, 1891, Mabel Barstow. 3. Charity Lodiska, b. May 22, 1870; m. March 26, 1892, Fred Watson. 4. Elida Vileta, b. July 21, 1871; m. Jan. 4, 1887, Arnold Covel. 5. Ida Anna, b. April 9, 1873; m. March 24, 1892, Arthur Passino. 6. Effie Lina, b. July 26, 1878.

vi. Martha, b. June 3, 1840; m. Dec. 5, 1856 (?), Sylvester Watson.
vii. William, b. Dec. 30, 1841; d. Aug. 17, 1864. Served in Civil War, 2d Vet. Cavalry, N. Y.
viii. Mary, b. April 10, 1844; d. April 15, 1871.
ix. Harriet, b. Aug. 8, 1845; m. Nov. 1, 1868, James E. Weston.
x. Ann, b. April 21, 1847; m. March 24, 1869, N. J. Arnold.
xi. Adelaide, b. Feb. 28, 1849; d. April 2, 1860.
xii. Herbert, b. Nov. 2, 1852; d. April 17, 1860.

253. IV. ELIAS K.,[8] b. 1810, in Putney, Vt. ; m. Frances Wentworth, of New York. He d. 1868; four children.

254. V. CALVIN WHITCOMB,[8] b. June 15, 1812, at Pittsford, Vt. ; m. Feb. 25, 1841, Sarah Crowl, of Petersham, Mass. He d. Oct. 8, 1864, at Fort Pickens, Fla. In 1868 she m. Ira Cook, of Athol, Mass., who d. 1879; res. Melrose, Mass. ; ten children.

VI. MARTHA, b. Nov. 27, 1816; m. Dec. 23, 1844, Jonathan Townsend, Stockbridge, Vt. She d. July 9, 1858.

VII. ARVILLA ; d. young.

VIII. FRANCES G. (Fanny), b. 1819; m. Phineas Curtis, Stockbridge, Vt. She d. 1885; six children :—
i. Elda.
ii. Phineas.
iii. Louis.
iv. Lavina.
v. Charles.
vi. Abraham Lincoln.

IX. REBECCA W., b. Feb. 23, 1822; m. May 3, 1860, Jonathan H. Townsend, of Stockbridge, Vt. She d. Jan. 15, 1872; res. Sherburne, Vt.

X. EUNICE ; d. young.

XI. SUSAN, b. 1826; m. Edmund Styles, Pittsford, Vt. She d. 1871; three children :—
i. Mary, m. George Savage; lives Pittsford, Vt.
ii. Fremont.
iii. Mattie.

253.

Children of **Elias K.**[8] **Greenleaf** and Frances (Wentworth).

255. I. CHARLES FRANKLIN,[9] b. Dec. 2, 1843, at Pittsford, Vt.;
m. Feb. 22, 1872, Zena Wilkins. He was engineer
Vt. Central R. R.; res. St. Albans, Vt.; one child:—
Ida May, b. Jan. 27, 1874.

II. WILLIAM H., b. Nov. 10, 1845.

III. MARY ELLEN, b. Jan. 28, 1848; m. July 29, 1871,
William Gifford, Sherburne, Vt.

IV. JERRY; d. in infancy.

254.

Children of **Calvin W.**[8] **Greenleaf** and Sarah (Crowl).

I. MARY L., b. Aug. 27, 1842; m. 1860, at Strafford, Vt.,
John T. Savery, of Rochester, Mass. She d. Feb.
26, 1884, at Boston.

256. II. WILLIAM CALVIN,[9] b. Aug. 27, 1844; m. 1, 1862,
Eleanor Howes, of White River Junction, Vt.; 2,
1883-4, Mrs. Matilda Howard, of Philadelphia,
Penn. Engineer on Reading R. R.; res. Sewaren,
N. J. Three children by 1st marriage:—

　　i. Edmund Styles, b. May 4, 1863; d. April 28, 1880,
　　　　at Hudson, Mass.

　　ii. Emma D., b. Feb. 16, 1865; m. Dec. 17, 1887,
　　　　William H. Wright, of Ashland, Mass., farmer,
　　　　b. Jan. 22, 1865, at Hopkinton, Mass.; no children.

　　iii. Calvin William, b. Aug. 1, 1871.

III. ADA S., b. March 25, 1847; m. Jan. 9, 1866, at
Chester, Penn., Warren O. Goodwin, of Grafton,
Mass.; res. Wilmington, Del.; two children:—

　i. Kate Florence, b. Dec. 24, 1867.

　ii. Alfred Bowers, b. June 10, 1875.

IV. ELIZABETH J., b. April 14, 1849; res. Melrose, Mass.

V. LUCY FRANCES, b. Sept. 7, 1851, in Stockbridge, Vt.;
m. 1, July 20, 1870, James Austin Tupper, of New
Salem, Mass.; painter; d. Nov. 2, 1876; 2, Sept. 21,
1879, Darius E. Nims; blacksmith; res. South
Gardner, Mass.; no children.

CALVIN W. (254) GREENLEAF, CONTINUED:—
257. VI. JOHN R.,[9] b. Oct. 31, 1853; m. Ida Horton, of Athol, Mass.; res. Boston; no children.

VII. JOSEPHINE A., b. May 3, 1856; m. Dec. 6, 1874, George A. Oakes, of Athol, Mass., b. March 16, 1850; d. July 19, 1888, at Boston; two children:—
i. Mary Lyon, b. June 27, 1879, Athol, Mass.
ii. Edith Greenleaf, b. Sept. 4, 1881, at Chicopee, Mass.

VIII. EMOGENE M., b. March 2, 1859; d. June 15, 1862, at White River Junction, Vt.

IX. GERTRUDE E., b. March 17, 1862; d. July 7, 1885, at Boston.

258. X. FREDERICK W.,[9] b. Sept. 23, 1864; m. May 11, 1887, Laura M. Cornwell, Gardner, Mass.; two children:—
I. Leon P., b. Oct. 16, 1890, at Gardner.
II. John Alton, b. Jan. 24, 1893, at Gardner.

244.

(Calvin 6, Dr. Daniel 5, Rev. Daniel 4, Stephen 3, Stephen 2, Edmund 1.)

Children of **Moses**[7] **Greenleaf** and Experience (Sawyer).
259. I. SILAS S.,[8] b. March 4, 1815, in Bolton, Mass.; m. May 28, 1838, at Lancaster, Mass., by Rev. John Davenport, Sarah F. Nowell, b. Jan. 21, 1819, at Brookfield, Mass.; d. March 10, 1892. He d. March 22, 1892; six children:—
I. Sarah E., b. April 27, 1839, at Greenwich, Mass.; d. Dec. 5, 1844.
II. Ellen A., b. Dec. 20, 1840, in Bolton, Mass.; m. June 4, 1862, in Bolton, Mass., by Rev. Wm. Houghton, Edward M. Lamson; four children:—
i. Rolla S., b. May 12, 1864, in Bolton, Mass.; m. 1, Lilla F. Brigham, Dec. 25, 1889, in Berlin, Mass.; d. May 10, 1891, at Hudson, Mass.; 2, Emma Taylor, June 22, 1892; one child: Chester T., b. June 4, 1893.
ii. Arthur C., b. Aug. 10, 1867, in Bethel, Vt.
iii. Walter E., b. Oct. 23, 1874.
iv. Albert W., b. June 13, 1877.
III. Mary L., b. Jan. 12, 1843, in Bolton, Mass.; d. Jan. 16, 1849, in Berlin, Mass.
IV. Alice E., b. Aug. 3, 1849, at Berlin, Mass.; d. Aug. 1, 1869, at Bolton, Mass.

Moses (244) Greenleaf, Continued :—
   I. Silas S.

     v. Sarah L., b. July 4, 1854, at Berlin, Mass.; m.
       March 4, 1875, Samuel M. Carter; res. Gardner,
       Mass.; six children :—
       i. Herbert E., b. Sept. 2, 1875.
       ii. Alice B., b. March 31, 1878.
       iii. Silas G., b. Oct. 16, 1880.
       iv. Ellen L., b. Sept. 21, 1882; d. May 7, 1885.
       v. Oliver, b. July 6, 1886.
       vi. Lucy S., b. May 14, 1890.
     vi. Silas N., b. Oct. 31, 1856, at West Randolph, Vt.;
       d. Sept. 1, 1861, at Bolton, Mass.
   II. Sarah H., b. Nov. 17, 1816; m. April 28, 1841, Syl-
     vanus Reed. He d. April 4, 1889; three children :—
     i. Olive M., b. Oct. 25, 1843; d. March 15, 1893.
     ii. Henry L., b. Jan. 25, 1846; m. April 28, 1870, Martha A. Hast-
      ings; res. Boylston, Mass.; two children: 1. Loring H., b.
      Dec. 11, 1870. 2. M. Esther, b. Nov. 22, 1876.
     iii. Sarah J., b. Feb. 4, 1849; m. Silas A. Wilder. He d. August,
      1893; res. Cambridgeport, Mass.; one child: Sylvanus W.,
      b. Aug. 11, 1882.
260. III. Calvin,[8] b. Dec. 11, 1818; m. March 22, 1846,
     Mrs. Mary Brown (Chase) Wheeler. He d. Sept.
     12, 1865; res. Hudson, Mass.; seven children.
261. IV. Laban,[8] b. Oct. 4, 1821; m. Elizabeth Roger, dau.
     of Gibson Gabriel and Ruth Bates, and widow of
     Joseph Andrews, b. May 22, 1833, in Brookline,
     Mass.; they were separated, and she m. 3, about
     1878, Franklin A. Pollard. Laban Greenleaf was a
     farmer. He d. July 9, 1874; res. Stowe, Mass.
   V. Loren, b. Jan. 23, 1824; d. Oct. 13, 1844; un-
     married.
   VI. Betsey S., b. May 12, 1826; m. Jan. 8, 1846, E.
     W. Brewer; res. Clinton, Mass.; two children :—
     i. Betsey E., b. Jan. 3, 1847; m. Dec. 20, 1868, J. C. Babcock;
      one child: Everett W., b. Nov. 14, 1869; d. June 4, 1881.
     ii. Julia E., b. July 28, 1851; m. Nov. 26, 1874, E. D. Maynard.
      She d. March 27, 1891; two children: 1. Gertrude E., b.
      Nov. 12, 1878. 2. Carl G. B., b. May 26, 1889.
262. VII. Thora,[8] b. April 15, 1829; m. Martha Osborn.
     He d. June 15, 1887; res. Shrewsbury, Mass.; two
     children.

GENEALOGY. 327

260.

(Moses 7, Calvin 6, Dr. Daniel 5, Rev. Daniel 4, Stephen 3, Stephen 2, Edmund 1.)

Children of **Calvin**[8] **Greenleaf** and Mary Brown (Wheeler).

263. I. GEORGE CALVIN,[9] b. May 12, 1847; m. Jan. 28, 1874, Etta Crowell. He. d. March 23, 1893; two children:—

    I. Grace Etta, b. Oct. 3, 1876.

    II. Maude Ellis, b. Aug. 16, 1879.

264. II. CHARLES HENRY,[9] b. Aug. 23, 1849; m. 1, June 1, 1872, Harriet Elizabeth Ellis, who d. Jan. 6, 1878; 2, Oct. 25, 1879, Nellie M. Collins; res. Boston; no children.

265. III. JOHN LORING,[9] b. Jan. 29, 1852; m. 1, July 22, 1871, Mary E. Hapgood; 2, Nov. 30, 1882, Mary E. Bond; detective, Boston; one child:—

    Clifton Gale, b. March 26, 1884.

    IV. LABAN SAWYER, b. July 29, 1854; d. Aug. 6, 1854.

    V. MARY ELIZABETH, b. Nov. 14, 1855; m. June 22, 1878, George Hapgood, Jr.; two children:—

    i. Ernest Herbert, b. Feb. 4, 1880; d. March 21, 1881.

    ii. George Irving, b. Sept. 18, 1881.

266. VI. LABAN HERBERT,[9] b. Oct. 19, 1857; m. Jan. 9, 1890, Emma E. Boyce; res. Waltham, Mass.; two children:—

    I. Delma May, b. June 29, 1892.

    II. Ernest Herbert, b. Aug. 23, 1894.

267. VII. WARREN GRANT,[9] b. May 18, 1864; m. July 10, 1889, Nellie Louise Russell; res. Arlington, Mass.; one child:—

    Ralph Russell, b. March 16, 1894.

18.

(Stephen 3, Stephen 2, Edmund 1.)

Children of **Joseph**[4] **Greenleaf** and Thomasine (Mayo).

I. SARAH, b. Dec. 6, 1708.

II. MARY, b. Oct. 1, 1712.

III. BENJAMIN, b. June 29, 1716.

268. IV. JOSEPH,[5] b. Sept. 25, 1717; m. Mary ——; res. Newbury, Mass.; five children.

It appears by the county records at Salem, Mass., that "the administration of the estate of Joseph Greenleaf, late of New-

JOSEPH (18) GREENLEAF, CONTINUED :—

IV. Joseph.

bury, innholder, deceased (was) granted to Mary Greenleaf, widow of the said Joseph, 30 March, 1751. The inventory of the estate was £315-6-8. Three persons were appointed by the Judge, July 1, 1754, to set off the right of dower in Joseph Greenleaf's estate to Mary Greenleaf, alias Peabody." [Essex Co. Probate Court, Vol. cccxxix., p. 530, Vol. cccxxx., p. 58.]

Nathan Peabody, born March 13, 1716, married for his second wife, Mary, widow of Joseph Greenleaf, of Newbury; child by Mary: Bradford, born May 25, 1755. [Peabody Genealogy, p. 12.]

Richard Kent was appointed guardian of Thomas Greenleaf (son of Joseph and Mercy), a minor upwards of fourteen years old, Aug. 25, 1752. [Vol. cccxxxii., pp. 369 and 529.]

The will of Mary Peabody, widow, of Newburyport, Mass., dated Jan. 16, 1769, was proved March 29, 1769.

269. V. STEPHEN,[5] b. March 9, 1725; m. Jan. 24, 1747, Mary Davis, of Gloucester, Mass.; five children :—

    I. Stephen,[6] b. June 1, 1750; res. Gloucester, Mass.

    II. Thomasine, b. Oct. 30, 1752.

    III. Elias Davis, b. Jan. 13, 1754.

    IV. Ephraim Morrow, b. March 26, 1755.

    V. William, b. about 1757.

    VI. HANNAH, b. March 9, 1725; twin.

270. VII. MAYO,[5] b. Nov. 17, 1729; m. Dec. 19, 1751, Sarah Merrill. He d. Aug. 25, 1765; res. Newbury, Mass.; three children.

268.

(Joseph 4, Stephen 3, Stephen 2, Edmund 1.)

Children of **Joseph[5] Greenleaf** and Mary.

271. I. JOSEPH,[6] b. June 7, 1736; m. Feb. 26, 1759, Mercy, dau. of Edmund and Anne Cottle, of Newbury, Mass., b. May 23, 1740; res. Newbury; seven children.

The name on the marriage record at Salem is Mary (the names Mercy and Mary were frequently used by the same person). On all the deeds, five in number, where she and her husband sold land, she is called and signs her name Mercy Greenleaf. Mr. Greenleaf was a ship carpenter by trade, and was in the employ of Edmund Cottle, a ship builder at Newbury, Mass., and after his death, the administration of the estate was granted to Joseph Greenleaf, Jr., April 13, 1761. Ezra Cottle, probably father of Edmund, commenced ship building at Newbury, in 1698.

JOSEPH (268) GREENLEAF, CONTINUED :—

    II. THOMAS, b. Aug. 18, 1738.

    III. MARY, b. June 3, 1743.

272. IV. BENJAMIN,[6] b. June 25, 1745; m. March 4, 1766, Thomasine Davis; res. Gloucester, Mass.; two children :—

      I. Benjamin, b. June 14, 1767.

      II. Mary, b. Feb. 27, 1770.

273. V. STEPHEN,[6] b. April 14, 1749; m. Ann Worthington; she afterwards m. William Butler; four children.

  A Stephen Greenleaf married, Sept. 19, 1772, Anna Redington. Wingate Newman, their son, is recorded in Windham, Conn., Town Records, born March 12, 1773; same records give also Ebenezer Greenleaf, of Hampton, Conn., married June 1, 1826, Lucy Webb. Dec. 27, 1782, Stephen Greenleaf, of Stonington, County of New London, Conn., and Timothy Larrabe, of Windham, quit claim right in shop to —— for £60. From this it appears that Stephen had removed to Stonington from Windham, December, 1782.

271.

(Joseph 5, Joseph 4, Stephen 3, Stephen 2, Edmund 1.)

Children of **Joseph**[6] **Greenleaf** and Mercy (Cottle).

    I. ANNE, b. March 22, 1761.

    II. JOSEPH COTTLE, b. May 31, 1762.

274. III. EDMUND COTTLE,[7] b. about 1764; m. Aug. 18, 1785, Abigail, dau. of David and Mary (Gaines) Peabody, of Ipswich, Mass., b. 1765; d. 1823; twelve children.

275. IV. WOODBRIDGE,[7] b. May 20, 1766; m. July 25, 1790, Mary Holman. He. d. Nov. 18, 1805; four children :—

      I. Mary, b. Nov. 15, 1790.

      II. Clark Cottle, b. Oct. 11, 1792.

      III. John, b. Sept. 3, 1796.

      IV. Anne, b. Aug. 4, 1804.

    V. LYDIA, b. Dec. 21, 1780; m. 1, 1800, Samuel Fowler, who d. January, 1808; 2, 1810, William Kent Wilson, who d. Aug. 23, 1820. She d. April 30, 1865; seven children. Children by first marriage :—

    i. Samuel, b. June 23, 1801; d. Aug. 27, 1821.

    ii. Lydia, b. Jan. 13, 1803; m. James Brown. She d. November, 1883; no children.

JOSEPH (271) GREENLEAF, CONTINUED :—
V. Lydia.
   iii. Mercy Cottle, b. Oct. 25, 1804; m. Jan. 19, 1861, George
      Dunn. She d. Dec. 16, 1887; no children.
  Children by 2d marriage :—
   iv. Louisa, b. Dec. 6, 1810; m. Peter Holt. She d. Feb. 20,
      1891; seven children: 1. Samuel Fowler, b. May 9, 1838; m.
      1864, Isabell N. Piper. 2. Susan Louisa, b. Jan. 16, 1840; m.
      Oct. 27, 1868, William A. Coggswell. 3. Stephen, b. Oct.
      25, 1841; m. Belinda Foster. 4. John Calvin, b. Dec. 11,
      1843; m. Susan A. Cochrane. 5. Joanna Bailey, b. Sept. 19,
      1845; m. March 29, 1865, William Gleason Goldsmith. 6.
      Peter, b. July 6, 1847; m. Susan P. Clarke. 7. Charles Ed-
      mund, b. Sept. 3, 1850.
   v. Joan, b. March 30, 1812; m. Dec. 25, 1834, Arad Bailey. She
      d. Aug. 24, 1890; nine children: 1. William Wilson, b. Oct.
      24, 1835; m. Dec. 18, 1865, Julia Vernon. He d. April 25,
      1873. 2. Lucy Derby, b. April 2, 1838; d. Dec. 23, 1862. 3.
      Joanna, b. March 11, 1840; m. Aug. 11, 1869, Abraham L.
      Richards. 4. George Arad, b. Aug. 3, 1842; d. Dec. 6, 1877.
      5. Clarissa Ann, b. Dec. 27, 1844; m. Sept. 11, 1871, John E.
      Sylvester. 6. Louisa Holt, b. Oct. 9, 1847. 7. Helen Jen-
      kins, b. June 11, 1850; d. Feb. 12, 1863. 8. Frank Martin, b.
      Jan. 20, 1853. 9. Charlotte Lydia, b. May 11, 1857.
   vi. William Kent, b. Oct. 3, 1814; m. Jan. 7, 1835, Sarah M.
      Stodder. He d. May 1, 1881; six children: 1. Louisa R.,
      b. 1835; m. 1, Samuel Bolton; 2, William Pentland. She
      d. Aug. 22, 1890. 2. Mary E., b. 1837; d. in infancy. 3.
      Mary E., b. 1840; d. in infancy. 4. William H., b. 1842; d.
      in infancy. 5. William H., b. 1843; d. in infancy. 6. An-
      drew Stodder, b. June 30, 1846; m. Achasa Tompkins.
   vii. Clarissa Ann, b. Dec. 19, 1818; m. May 1, 1849, Richard K.
      Powers; three children: 1. George K., b. Feb. 7, 1850; m.
      Dec. 26, 1888, Anna E. Wilder. 2. Ezra, b. July 30, 1851; d.
      Sept. 24, 1876. 3. Edmund, b. Sept. 18, 1855; m. April 4,
      1893, Helen Johnson.
  VI. LUCRETIA.
  VII. HARRIET.

274.

(Joseph 6, Joseph 5, Joseph 4, Stephen 3, Stephen 2, Edmund 1.)

Children of **Edmund Cottle**[7] **Greenleaf** and Abigail
  (Peabody).
  I. CATHERINE, b. Nov. 7, 1786; d. May 14, 1804.
  II. JOSEPH, b. Oct. 24, 1787.
  III. JOSHUA, b. Oct. 24, 1789.

EDMUND COTTLE (274) GREENLEAF, CONTINUED:—

276. IV. EDMUND COTTLE,[8] b. Feb. 7, 1793; married; two children:—

 I. Edmund.

 II. A son, d. 1816, at sea.

 V. WILLIAM, b. Aug. 23, 1794; d. 1853 (?).

277. VI. PEABODY,[8] b. Sept. 23, 1797; m. Dec. 30, 1819, Dorothy Lunt Jackman, d. Jan. 20, 1877. He d. Sept. 19, 1880; two children.

278. VII. JEREMIAH,[8] b. June 20, 1801; m. 1, Dec. 23, 1824, Mary Ann Lamson, who d. Feb. 4, 1849; 2, Nov. 29, 1850, Ann Currier Wood. He d. Feb. 19, 1868; nine children.

 VIII. MARY GAINES, b. April 18, 1803; d. 1825 (?).

 IX. CATHERINE, b. Jan. 28, 1805; m. Aug. 14, 1834, Capt. James Norton. She d. Feb. 14, 1894; res. Newburyport, Mass.; four children:—

 i. James Crosby, b. April 25, 1835; May 25, 1835.

 ii. James Henry, b. Oct. 29, 1837; d. June 15, 1845.

 iii. Greenleaf, b. Oct. 28, 1839.

 iv. Peabody, b. Sept. 23, 1842; d. June 12, 1845.

279. X. NATHANIEL SMITH,[8] b. Aug. 15, 1807; m. Emeline Philbrook. He d. 1847; res. Lowell, Mass.; three children.

 XI. A SON, d. in infancy.

 XII. A SON, d. in infancy.

277.

(Edmund Cottle 7, Joseph 6, Joseph 5, Joseph 4, Stephen 3, Stephen 2, Edmund 1.)

Children of **Peabody**[8] **Greenleaf** and Dorothy Lunt (Jackman).

280. I. DANIEL DAVIS,[9] b. Nov. 25, 1820; m. July 6, 1844, Lucy Goodwin (Pettingill), b. July 5, 1823. He d. Aug. 20, 1875; res. Newburyport, Mass.; two children:—

 I. Lucy Abby, b. April 11, 1845; m. Eben Little, Jr.; one child:—

 Henry Willard, b. July 17, 1865; m. Nov. 26, 1889, Caroline Emma Stone; res. Newburyport, Mass.; one child: Willard Stone, b. May 31, 1891.

281. II. George Peabody,[10] b. Dec. 25, 1851; m. Sept. 1, 1874, Mary Abbie Dyer, b. Nov. 2, 1855;

PEABODY (277) GREENLEAF, CONTINUED:—

 I. Daniel Davis.

   res. Newburyport, Mass.; two children: 1. Ella
   Graves, b. Nov. 9, 1877. 2. Daniel Davis, b.
   Sept. 27, 1886; d. Sept. 13, 1889.

 II. ABIGAIL A., b. Nov. 11, 1823; m. May 2, 1845,
   Moses Pettingill. She d. Dec. 23, 1866; res. Newburyport, Mass.; two children:—

   i. Peabody, b. Dec. 4, 1847; m. Carrie Goodwin; four children:
     1. Moses G., b. December, 1879. 2. Fred. W., b. February,
     1882; d. March, 1889. 3. Charles L., b. May, 1884; d. Sep-
     tember, 1886. 4. Harold E., b. May 2, 1890.
   ii. Caroline E., b. Dec. 11, 1852; d. March 2, 1869.

278.

(Edmund Cottle 7, Joseph 6, Joseph 5, Joseph 4, Stephen 3, Stephen 2, Edmund 1.)

Children of **Jeremiah**[8] **Greenleaf** and Mary Ann (Lamson).

 I. CATHERINE, b. Nov. 8, 1825 (Newbury Records,
   Jan. 8, 1826); m. Oct. 23, 1851, Alfred Hale.
   She d. Feb. 21, 1855.

 II. MARY ANN, b. Aug. 8, 1827; m. Dec. 19, 1861,
   Alfred Hale.

 III. HARRIET, b. Oct. 24, 1829; m. July 10, 1851, William W. Brown. She d. July 7, 1855.

 IV. ELIZABETH COFFIN, b. Jan. 8, 1833; m. Sept. 13,
   1855, William F. Chase. She d. April 9, 1873.

282. V. ALBERT WOOD,[9] b. July 12, 1836; m. Jan. 10, 1858,
   Abbie Mary, dau. of Joseph S. and Hannah (French)
   Pike, b. Aug. 30, 1838, at Salisbury, Mass.; res.
   Newburyport, Mass.; eleven children:—

   i. Alice, b. Nov. 7, 1858; m. Oct. 30, 1883, Charles
     W. Brown; five children:—

     1. Mary Agate, b. April 11, 1886. 2. Jacob Bartlett, b. July 14,
     1887. 3. Theodora Feuillevert, b. Sept. 15, 1889. 4. Alice
     Greenleaf, b. Nov. 22, 1891. 5. Charles W., b. April 4, 1895.
   ii. Albert Pike, b. Jan. 2, 1860; d. Aug. 21, 1864.
   iii. Katherine Hale, b. April 7, 1861.
   iv. Abbie Pike, b. May 27, 1863; d. Aug. 26, 1864.
   v. Jere Harvey, b. Aug. 31, 1865; d. Dec. 15, 1893,
     suddenly, in Colorado.

JEREMIAH (278) GREENLEAF, CONTINUED:—
  V. Albert Wood.
    VI. Hattie Wood, b. Oct. 17, 1867; d. Nov. 15, 1867.
    VII. Annie Edwards, b. Jan. 30, 1872.
    VIII. Edith Hoyt, b. July 2, 1874; m. Oct. 24, 1894,
      Edward Brackett Raymond.
    IX. Bertha, b. July 22, 1877.
    X. Margaret Stone, b. May 2, 1880.
    XI. Albert Wood, Jr., b. Feb. 17, 1882.
  VI. ABBY SANBORN, b. Oct. 11, 1839; d. April 23, 1860.
283. VII. RUFUS LAMSON,[9] b. Aug. 1, 1844; m. July 2,
    1865, Mary J. G. Emery, b. March 5, 1847, in South
    Berwick, Me. He d. June 21, 1880, in Newbury-
    port, Mass. His widow married William S. Coffin,
    March 30, 1882.
  Children of Rufus L. Greenleaf:—
    I. Laura Franklin, b. March 3, 1866.
    II. George S., b. Nov. 24, 1867; d. Dec. 3, 1870.
    III. Lillian Worster, b. July 13, 1871.
    IV. Mary Lamson, b. May 29, 1873; m. April 6, 1895,
      Herbert Storey, b. Nov. 19, 1874, in Newburyport,
      son of William Herbert Noyes, who was born
      in West Newbury, Mass., 1847.
  VIII. CHARLES H., b. Dec. 30, 1848; d. Jan. 1, 1849.
Child by 2d marriage:—
  IX. ADA MARIA, b. Jan. 8, 1855.

279.

(Edmund Cottle 7, Joseph 6, Joseph 5, Joseph 4, Stephen 3, Stephen 2, Edmund 1.)

Children of **Nathaniel Smith**[8] **Greenleaf** and Emeline
  (Philbrook).
  I. JULIA, m. William K. Stiles; res. Bath, Me.
284. II. EDGAR,[9] b. Feb. 17, 1838; m. Dec. 5, 1861, Georgie
    W. Haley; res. Malden, Mass.; three children:—
285.   I. George Edgar,[10] b. Nov. 24, 1862; m. Oct. 4, 1887,
      Mary E. Corbett; res. Malden, Mass.; no children.
286.   II. Stillman Allen,[10] b. Sept. 22, 1865; m. Oct. 7,
      1889, Anna A. Abrams; res. Wakefield, Mass.;
      one child: Allen Raymond, b. June 13, 1894.
    III. An Infant, b. April 18, 1868; d. 1869.
  III. A DAUGHTER, d. in infancy.

273.

Children of **Stephen**[6] **Greenleaf** and Ann (Worthington).

287. I. JOHN,[7] b. about 1780, in Connecticut; m. Ann Evans, of Lancaster, Penn.; of Welsh descent; res. Lancaster, Penn.; nine children.

> His son John writes to Dr. R. P. Greenleaf, of Wilmington, Del., Feb. 18, 1881: " My father was born in Connecticut, and both his parents died when he was quite young. He was taken to Chester, Penn., near the Gap. His grandmother's name was Butler."

II. SAMUEL WINGATE NEWMAN, b. about 1782.

III. JOSEPH,[7] b. about 1785.

IV. MARY, b. about 1787.

287.

Children of **John**[7] **Greenleaf** and Ann (Evans).

I. STEPHEN, b. Sept. 5, 1807.

II. SARAH ANN, b. March 11, 1809, in Western Pennsylvania; m. Alvin Hynes; two children :—

   i. A son; died.

   ii. A daughter; died.

288. III. JOHN,[8] b. Oct. 3, 1812; m. Jan. 10, 1837, Hannah Chamberlain. He was President of Franklin Insurance Company, Columbus, Ohio; res. Columbus, Ohio; four children :—

   i. A son, b. 1838.

   ii. A son, b. 1840.

   iii. Mary, b. 1842; m. Howard Bancroft; res. Columbus, Ohio.

   iv. Alice T.; res. Columbus, Ohio.

289. IV. WILLIAM,[8] b. April 2, 1814; m. Lucinda Stephens; res. Lancaster, Ky.; six children.

V. MARY, b. Feb. 1, 1817; m. Elis Moore; res. Belmont County, Ohio; one child: a son; d. in infancy.

290. VI. SAMUEL E.,[8] b. Aug. 31, 1819; m. 1, Rebecca Pennington; 2, —— Muzzy; one child: Osborn.

VII. JAMES, b. Oct. 26, 1821.

JOHN (287) GREENLEAF, CONTINUED:—

VIII. ELIZA P., b. Oct. 14, 1825; m. May 5, 1846, in Belmont County, Ohio, David Wilson. She d. April 28, 1873; res. Wenona, Ill.; eleven children:—

i. Mary A., b. Dec. 31, 1846; m. Howard McCarty; res. Seldon, Sheridan Co., Kan.; six children: three sons and three daughters.

ii. Hannah B., b. Oct. 8, 1848; m. Thomas Gants; res. Fairburg, Ill.; four children: daughters.

iii. Sarah E., b. Nov. 26, 1850; m. Levi Spargrove; res. Winona, Ill.; one child: a daughter.

iv. Ruth Ela, b. April 3, 1853; m. William Griffith; res. Geyserville, Sonoma Co., California; four children.

v. Alice, b. May 26, 1855.

vi. John Newman, b. March 5, 1857; m. Mary Givens; res. Putnam County, Ill.; three children: sons.

vii. David E., b. Jan. 12, 1859; d. 1873.

viii. C. Jeanette, b. Feb. 1, 1861; m. William McLaughlin; res. Ong, Clay Co., Neb.; five children: three sons and two daughters.

ix. Amos, b. Jan. 11, 1864; res. Wenona, Ill.

x. Bessie, b. Dec. 19, 1865; m. Robert Newburn; res. New Rutland, Ill.; three children: a son and two daughters.

xi. Laura E., b. Nov. 18, 1868; m. Alexander Carithers; res. near Toluca, Ill.

291. IX. DAVID NEWMAN,[8] b. April 14, 1829, in Lancaster, Penn.; m. Sarah Elizabeth, daughter of Thomas Miller, of Lexington, Ky., and Agillia (Helm), of Glasgow, Ky. He d. in Keokuk, Iowa; res. Jefferson City, Mo.; three children:—

I. Charles Warner, b. in St. Louis, Mo.; d. in infancy.

II. Mary Agillia, b. in Jefferson City; lives with her mother in St. Louis, Mo., and is teaching in one of the public schools.

III. A son.

289.

(John 7, Stephen 6, Joseph 5, Joseph 4, Stephen 3, Stephen 2, Edmund 1.)

Children of **William**[8] **Greenleaf** and Lucinda (Porter).

I. LEONIDAS, b. April 7, 1837; res. Marshall, Tex.

II. WILLIAM, b. March 5, 1842; d. in infancy.

III. GABRIEL, b. July 21, 1844; unmarried; res. Lancaster, Ky.

292. IV. JOHN EVANS,[9] b. Sept. 8, 1850; m. 1, Annie Busby, d. July 22, 1873; 2, April 19, 1879, Ida Van Jen-

WILLIAM (289) GREENLEAF, CONTINUED :—
    IV. John Evans.
            nings; cashier Richmond National Bank; res. Rich-
            mond, Ky.; four children; child by 1st marriage :—
        1. Hood, d. in infancy.
    Children by 2d marriage :—
        II. John Jennings, b. Nov. 2, 1880.
        III. Van, b. Sept. 30, 1882.
        IV. May, d. in infancy.
    V. Emma, b. Feb. 28, 1854; m. H. Clay Kauffman;
            res. Lancaster, Ky.; four children :—
        i. Louise, b. Sept. 30, 1880.
        ii. Alice, b. April 10, 1882; d. July 9, 1890.
        iii. Frankie, b. Dec. 25, 1883.
        iv. Clay, b. Oct. 21, 1886.
293. VI. WILLIAM H.,[9] b. April 8, 1856; m. W. Belle Ows-
            ley, of Lancaster, Ky.; res. Little Rock, Ark.; no
            children.

270.

(Joseph 4, Stephen 3, Stephen 2, Edmund 1.)

Children of **Capt. Mayo[5] Greenleaf** and Sarah (Merrill).
    I. MAYO,[6] b. Feb. 24, 1754.
294. II. ABEL,[6] b. May 6, 1756; m. Catharine ——; seven
            children :—
        I. Sarah, b. Jan. 22, 1780.
        II. Anna Merrill, b. Feb. 18, 1782; twin.
        III. Abigail Peverly, b. Feb. 18, 1782; twin.
        IV. Mayo, b. Nov. 6, 1786; twin.
        V. Mary, b. Nov. 6, 1786; twin.
        VI. Catharine, b. June 11, 1796; m. Joseph Rawlins, of
                Newbury, Mass.
        VII. Thomas, b. June 26, 1797.
    III. JOSEPH, b. May 31, 1762.

19.

(Stephen 3, Stephen 2, Edmund 1.)

Children of **Stephen[4] Greenleaf** and Mary (Mackcres).
    I. ENOCH, b. June 23, 1713.
295. II. RICHARD,[5] b. Nov. 2, 1715; m. May 19, 1747, Mary
            Boucher; res. Newbury; four or more children.

STEPHEN (19) GREENLEAF, CONTINUED:—

296. III. SAMUEL,[5] b. June 12, 1718; m. Hephzibah Preble, of York, Me., b. 1725; d. 1792, at Woolwich, Me. He d. 1792, in Westport, Me.; seven children.

297. IV. EBENEZER,[5] b. April 23, 1720, near Squam Island, Southport, Me.; marriage intention filed Jan. 20, 1767; m. Feb. 16, 1767, Mary Preble; eight children.

V. LYDIA, b. May 3, 1722, in York, Me.

VI. STEPHEN, b. Feb. 27, 1724–25, in York, Me.

298. VII. JOSEPH, b. July 2, 1727, in York, Me.; m. about 1752, Dorcas Gray, who d. 1812 or 13. He d. 1772. She m. 2 (by Thomas Moore) Lieut. Moses Hilton (intention filed March 22, 1781); eight children.

VIII. MARY, b. Feb. 17, 1730–31, in York, Me.

295.
(Stephen 4, Stephen 3, Stephen 2, Edmund 1.)

Children of **Richard**[5] **Greenleaf** and Mary (Boucher).

299. I. JOSEPH,[6] b. about 1748; marriage intention filed Nov. 5, 1782, m. by Thomas Moore, Margaret Nason, of Pownalboro, Me.; res. Norridgewock, Me. He moved to Starks from Wiscasset about 1780 to 1785, among his cousins, about the time they did; thirteen children.

II. ELIZABETH, b. 1756; m. Sampson Sherff. She d. 1835; res. Norridgewock, Me.; six or seven children.

III. —— m. —— Melton or Melvin.

IV. —— m. —— Groves.

299.
(Richard 5, Stephen 4, Stephen 3, Stephen 2, Edmund 1.)

Children of **Joseph**[6] **Greenleaf** and Margaret (Nason).

I. ABIGAIL (Nabby), b. April 12, 1783; m. Jonathan Lovell.

II. MERCY, b. Aug. 15, 1784.

III. SARAH, b. Jan. 12, 1786; m. James Duley, of Starks, Me.

300. IV. ABRAHAM,[7] b. Sept. 2, 1787; m. Emma ——, b. April 19, 1791; d. July 1, 1816. He d. Jan. 15, 1818; three children:—

1. Phebe, b. March 20, 1812.

JOSEPH (299) GREENLEAF, CONTINUED :—

  IV. Abraham.

    II. Luther, b. March 22, 1813.

    III. Emma, b. Jan. 21, 1815.

  V. LYDIA, b. Sept. 17, 1792.

301. VI. THOMAS,[7] b. Feb. 5, 1794; m. May 14, 1818, Mary Young, b. Sept. 11, 1793; d. Nov. 17, 1874. He d. April 30, 1874; res. Norridgewock, Me. ; seven children :—

    I. Harriet K., b. Feb. 25, 1819; m. Oct. 3, 1847, Robert D. Ela, who d. about 1872. Mrs. Ela lives with her niece, Mrs. E. T. Hescock, Monson, Me. ; no children.

301a. II. Abraham,[8] b. Sept. 22, 1820; m. ——; res. Crystal River, Fla. ; two children.

302. III. Joseph Warren,[8] b. Nov. 16, 1822; m. Sept. 15, 1850, Melissa E. Morton. He d. 1880; seven children.

302a. IV. Cyrus Stilson,[8] b. Sept. 28, 1825 or 29; m. ; heard from last in Spartanburg Court House, Spartanburg District, S. C. ; no children.

    V. Lydia Works, b. Aug. 9, 1826; unmarried.

303. VI. William Allen,[8] b. 1828–34 or 1836; m. ; one child.

    VII. Thomas, b. May 8, 1839.

Children of Thomas and Mary (Young), all born in Norridgewock, Me.

VII. BETSEY, b. Feb. 23, 1796; m. Rev. Stephen Williamson, a Free Baptist minister, of Starks, Me. ; two children :—

    i. Henry (Hon.), an extensive farmer on the Sandy River, in Starks; once a State Senator, Judge of Probate, member of Governor's Council, Trustee of Bates College for years; not now living.

    ii. Orrin, a prominent citizen and wealthy merchant, Augusta, Me.

VIII. JOSEPH, b. Oct. 1, 1797; unmarried.

IX. ANNA, b. May 3, 1799; m. John Bean.

X. NASON, b. Sept. 5, 1802; m.

XI. MARGARET, b. May 3, 1804.

XII. PATIENCE, b. June 16, 1806; unmarried.

XIII. EMELINE, m. —— Crawford.

302.

(Thomas 7, Joseph 6, Richard 5, Stephen 4, Stephen 3, Stephen 2, Edmund 1.)

Children of **Joseph W.**[8] **Greenleaf** and Melissa E. (Morton).

I. MARY E., b. July 30, 1851; m. E. T. Hescock; res. Monson, Me.

II. CHARLOTTE M., b. March 19, 1854.

304. III. JAMES BATCHELDER,[9] b. Sept. 6, 1856; m. Aug. 17, 1877; merchant; res. Abbot, Me.; two children:—
   i. Dellie F., b. Oct. 2, 1878.
   ii. Archie W., b. Nov. 2, 1891.

IV. ERNEST WARREN, b. June 8, 1858.

V. JOHN CYRUS, b. July 19, 1862; m.; res. Arkansas City, Kan.

304a.VI. LUTHER CARROLL,[9] b. Dec. 27, 1866; m.; res. Dorchester, Mass.

VII. CHARLES THOMAS, b. Jan. 3, 1869; res. Worcester, Mass.

296.

(Stephen 4, Stephen 3, Stephen 2, Edmund 1.)

Children of **Samuel**[5] **Greenleaf** and Hephzibah (Preble.)

305. I. STEPHEN,[6] b. 1747; m. Nov. 25, 1769, Mary Knight, of Scarboro, Me., b. May 2, 1749; d. May 11, 1832. He d. 1813; res. Westport, Me.; eleven children.

306. II. SAMUEL,[6] b. 1749; m. Abigail Sheldon. He d. at Westport, Me.; one child.

307. III. ENOCH,[6] b. 1751; m.; a blacksmith; res. Boothbay, Me.; two children.

IV. OLIVE, b. 1755.

308. V. BENJAMIN,[6] b. Sept. 8, 1759; m. Jan. 7, 1784, Rachel Arnold, b. Dec. 25, 1765; d. April 2, 1828. He d. Nov. 2, 1843; res. Wiscasset, Me.; ten children.

VI. HANNAH, b. 1760.

VII. DORCAS, b. 1763.

305.

(Samuel 5, Stephen 4, Stephen 3, Stephen 2, Edmund 1.)

Children of **Stephen**[6] **Greenleaf** and Mary (Knight).

309. I. NATHANIEL,[7] b. May, 1770; m. 1796, Patience Sheldon; six children.

STEPHEN (305) GREENLEAF, CONTINUED :—

II. SARAH, b. 1772 ; m. 1793, John Dunton.

III. MARY, b. 1774 ; m. Thomas Parsons, who d. about 1823.

310. IV. STEPHEN,[7] b. Nov. 14, 1775 ; m. 1819 or 1820, Mrs.
Mary (Calderwood) Knight, b. July 18, 1798, in
Lincolnville, Me. ; d. Jan. 22, 1887, in Westport,
Me. (see 340). He d. June 26, 1835 ; res. West-
port, Me. ; seven children.

311. V. WESTBROOK,[7] b. 1778 ; m. 1, 1800, Mary Dunton,
who d. Nov. 6, 1825 ; 2, intention filed March 8,
1828 ; m. March 23, 1828, Ruth B. Harriman, who
d. Nov. 29, 1881. He d. June 26, 1865 ; res. Edgecomb, Me. ; ten children.

VI. ABIGAIL, b. April, 1780 ; d. September, 1796.

VII. EBENEZER, b. April, 1782 ; d. November, 1790.

VIII. SAMUEL, b. June, 1784 ; d. June, 1801.

IX. OLIVE, b. June 11, 1786 ; m. Sept. 11, 1808, Capt.
Jotham Parsons, of Brooklyn, N. Y., b. April 2,
1783 ; d. Dec. 14, 1860. She d. Jan. 5, 1875 ; res.
Westport and Wiscasset, Me. ; eleven children :—

Capt. J. Parsons's mother was Sarah Sewall, the daughter of
Henry Sewall, of York, Me., son of Nicholas, son of John,
son of Henry, son of Henry, settled in Newbury, Mass., 1634,
son of Henry Sewall, Esq., who was sometime Mayor of the
city of Coventry, England.

Sarah Sewall was the sister of Rev. Jotham Sewall, of Chester-
ville, Me., and of Gen. Henry Sewall, of the Revolutionary
Army of Augusta, Me., and of Judge David Sewall, of Ken-
nebunk, Me. (See "Memoirs of Jotham Sewall," p. 10).

Capt. Jotham Parsons was much interested in Bates College,
Lewiston, Me., and during his life contributed sums of money
to the Divinity School,—now and for some years since connected with that college,—leaving the school at his death
$15,000 ; which sum, one of the professors declared, "con-
stituted him a founder of that School as really as Mr. Bates's
donations constituted him the founder of the College."

i. Samuel, b. May 29, 1809 ; d. June 3, 1809.

ii. Emeline, b. April 5, 1810 ; m. September, 1833, in Wiscasset,
Me., Romulus Haskins, merchant of Bangor, Me., who d.
Oct. 8, 1863. She d. June 11, 1871. Mr. Haskins graduated
in 1823 at Bowdoin College. His father was the surgeon of
the "Bon Homme Richard" in the famous battle with the
"Serapis," off Flamburgh Head, Sept. 23, 1779, under the
command of John Paul Jones ; res. Bangor, Me. ; three chil-

STEPHEN (305) GREENLEAF, CONTINUED:—
IX. Olive.

dren: 1. Mary Knight, b. June 7, 1837, at Bangor, Me.; d.
Oct. 3, 1867, at Hudson City, N. J. 2. Emeline Parsons, b.
Nov. 23, 1841, in Bangor, Me. 3. Charles Robert, b. Jan. 15,
1843; m. 1, March 27, 1884, in Asheville, N. C., Mrs.
Helen Livingston Weed, dau. of the late Judge Platt, of Plattsburg,
N. Y. She d. Oct. 7, 1884, at Atlanta, Ga.; 2, Nov. 2, 1892,
Clara, dau. of the late Samuel B. Dorlan, of Dorlan's Mills,
Penn. Mr. Charles R. Haskins is a lawyer; res. Atlanta, Ga.
iii. Sophia, b. Oct. 27, 1811, at Westport, Me.; m. Jan. 31, 1836,
at Bangor, Me., by Rev. S. L. Pomroy, Samuel P. Baker, of
Wiscasset, Me., cashier of Bank, b. March 3, 1805; d. May
12, 1875. She d. May 27, 1884; nine children: 1. Olive
Amy,.b. Jan. 13, 1837, at Wiscasset, Me.; d. April 10, 1872,
at Philadelphia, Penn. 2. Sophia Sewall, b. March 6, 1839,
at Wiscasset, Me.; m. Oct. 1, 1860, at Wiscasset, Me., by
Rev. Josiah Merrill, George Samson Marshall; five children:
(1) Mary Greenleaf, b. May 6, 1861, at Worcester, Mass.; d.
Dec. 16, 1868, at South Malden, Mass. (2) William Baker,
b. May 12, 1867; m. June 12, 1888, Inez Celia Rideout; three
children: [1] Olive Rideout, b. June 10, 1889. [2] Esther Celia, b.
Dec. 5, 1890. [3] Violet Baker, b. July 20, 1892. (3) Isabelle
Everett, b. Feb. 22, 1870, at South Malden, Mass. (4)
George Davidson, b. Aug. 16, 1873, at Wiscasset, Me. (5)
Eddie Parsons, b. Nov. 22, 1878, at Everett, Mass.; d. Sept. 21,
1880. 3. William Mather, b. June 28, 1840, at Wiscasset,
Me.; m. May 11, 1869, by Rev. Albert Bryant, Emma
Harding Blossom. 4. Caroline Parsons, b. Nov. 8, 1841, at
Wiscasset, Me.; m. July 16, 1863, by Rev. Josiah Merrill,
Noah Payson Smith, of Brooklyn, N. Y.; five children: (1)
Annie Frances, b. Oct. 21, 1864, at Nashua, N. H. (2)
Nellie Payson, b. Nov. 2, 1866, at Nashua, N. H.; m. Sept.
27, 1891, at Pepperell, by Rev. W. R. Stocking and Rev.
Tombleu, Bayard Ellmore Harrison: one child: Edward
Smith, b. July 13, 1892. (3) Walter Tenny, b. April 2, 1870,
at Pepperell, Mass. (4) Amy Baker, b. Jan. 31, 1872, at
Pepperell, Mass. (5) Edward Parsons, b. Nov. 25, 1875, at
Pepperell, Mass.; d. Dec. 1, 1877. 5. Henry Clark, b. May
21, 1843, at Wiscasset, Me.; m. Dec. 7, 1881, Laura Blagden,
of Wiscasset, Me. 6. Ann Johnston, b. May 8, 1845, at Wiscasset, Me.; m. Nov. 18, 1878, by Rev. W. R. Stocking, of
Persia, Charles Henry Woodman; one child: Sophie Parsons, b. Jan. 14, 1886, at New York City. 7. Emma Louise,
b. Dec. 4, 1846, at Wiscasset, Me; d. Dec. 20, 1846. 8. Isabella Coffin, b. July 1, 1848, at Wiscasset, Me.; m. Oct. 28,
1873, in Casa Guidi, Florence, Italy, by Rev. W. S. Alexander, Rev. Luther Gulick, M.D., and Rev. G. W. Heacock,

STEPHEN (305) GREENLEAF, CONTINUED:—

   IX. Olive.

      D.D., Rev. William Redfield Stocking. She d. Aug. 17,
1890, at Williamstown, Mass. Rev. Mr. Stocking and his
wife were missionaries of the American Board in Turkey;
nine children: (1) Sophia Cochran and (2) Emily Holmes,
twins, b. July 18, 1875, in Seir, near Oroomiah, Persia. (3)
Lyman Gilbert, b. Dec. 9, 1876, in Oroomiah; d. Dec 1,
1887, at Blackwells Island. (4) Ethel, b. Feb 7, 1878, in
Oroomiah. (5) Annie Woodman, b. Jan. 7, 1880, in Wiscasset. (6) William Redfield, b. May 17, 1881, in Wiscasset.
(7) Samuel Baker, b. Nov. 7, 1883, in Williamstown, Mass.
(8) Charles Parsons, b. Nov. 9, 1887, in Blackwells Island.
(9) Isabella Caroline, b. Jan. 21, 1889, in Blackwells Island;
d. March 11, 1890, at Harts Island. 9. Emeline Parsons
Haskins, b. March 7, 1850, at Wiscasset, Me.; d. April 23,
1866.

   iv. Ebenezer Greenleaf (Rev.), b. May 15, 1813; m. 1, July 19,
1840, Caroline Mellen Nye, of Freeport, Me., who d. Jan. 1,
1862; 2, July 11, 1865, Sarah Dana McMillan, of Danville,
Vt. Rev. E. G. Parsons graduated at Bowdoin College,
1833; graduated Bangor Theological Seminary, 1837; Mr.
Parsons was pastor of the Congregational Church in Freeport, Me., fourteen years, and at the church in Derry, N. H.,
eighteen years; and was after that Principal of Pinkerton
Academy, at Derry, and Dummer Academy, at Byfield, Mass.,
thirteen years, and is now residing in Derry, N. H.; three
children: 1. Francse Appleton, b. May 30, 1841; d. May 23, 1843.
2. Caroline Nye, b. March 20, 1844; m. April 29, 1868, Frank
G. How; five children: (1) Caroline Mellen, b. April 18, 1869.
(2) Philip Parsons, b. April 23, 1872. (3) Helen Louisa, b.
June 8, 1877. (4) Maria Sewall, b. Oct. 6, 1884. (5) Dana
Greenleaf, b. Aug. 31, 1887. 3. Maria Sewall, b. Dec. 18, 1847.

   v. Pamelia, b. Jan. 20, 1815, at Westport, Me.; m. April 25, 1839,
at Bangor, Me., Rev. Samuel Howard Shepley, b. March 5,
1810; Mr. Shepley graduated at Bowdoin College, 1833;
Andover Theological Seminary, 1838. He was pastor of the
Congregational Church at New Gloucester, Me. Mr. and
Mrs. Shepley were proprietors and conductors of the Female
Seminary many years in Blairsville, Penn., where Mrs. Shep-
ley still resides (1895), her husband having died there; four
children: 1. Howard Parsons, b. June 14, 1841, in New
Gloucester, Me.; m. June 11, 1872, Laura Purse, b. June 29,
1838; two children: (1) Mary Purse, b. Oct. 29, 1873, at
Blairsville, Penn. (2) Samuel Howard, b. Sept. 15, 1876, at
Blairsville, Penn. 2. Helen Pamelia, b. Aug. 13, 1845, in
New Gloucester, Me.; m. June 13, 1867, Thomas Davis Cun-
ningham, b. Aug. 17, 1839; six children: (1) Samuel Howard, .

STEPHEN (305) GREENLEAF, CONTINUED:—
IX. Olive.

b. June 24, 1868; m. Sept. 5, 1892, Julia Zimmers. (2) Helen
Shepley, b. July 20, 1871. (3) Rachel Wallace, b. Aug. 15,
1875; (4) Thomas Davis, b. July 15, 1879. (5) Mary Craig,
b. Aug. 22, 1881. (6) George Smith, b. July 21, 1883. 3.
Samuel Harris, b. Aug. 12, 1848, at Yarmouth, Me.; d. Sept.
12, 1849. 4. Charles Henry, b. July 17, 1853, in Blairsville,
Penn.; m. 1, Oct. 8, 1873, at Brady's Bend, Penn., Ida James,
b. July 18, 1854; d. March 14, 1879, in Baltimore, Md.; 2,
April 7, 1883, Mary E. Abrams, who d. May 30, 1884, at
Mt. Pleasant, Penn.; 3, Sept. 30, 1885, Elizabeth Adair, b.
March 26, 1865; three children by 1st marriage: (1) Margaret
J., b. Oct. 30, 1874. (2) Charles Henry, b. March 18, 1877,
at Brady's Bend, Penn.; d. Jan. 30, 1881. (3) James Colburn,
b. Feb. 22, 1879, in Baltimore, Md.; d. Nov. 11, 1879, in
Brady's Bend. Two children by 3d marriage: (4) John
Adair, b. Nov. 19, 1887, at Allegheny, Penn. (5) Charles
Henry, b. Feb. 1, 1891.

vi. Josiah, b. Jan. 27, 1817; d. Feb. 8, 1817.

vii. Jotham Sewall, b. May 28, 1818; m. Anna Wilkins. He d.
May 6, 1853, in Manilla, Ph. I.; was a shipmaster; had children; none of the family now living.

viii. Benjamin Franklin (Rev.), b. June 21, 1820, at Wiscasset,
Me.; m. 1, Aug. 11, 1846, Sarah Jane Erskine, who d. in
1851; 2, Nov. 8, 1853, Mary Ann Nesmith, of Derry, N. H.
Mr. Parsons graduated at Bowdoin College and at Bangor
Seminary; was pastor of the Congregational Church in
Dover and Nashua, N. H.; res. Derry, N. H.; two children
by 1st marriage: 1. Sarah Frances, b. May 28, 1848; she was
employed as a teacher in London, Eng., and for many years
in Chicago, Ill. 2. Maria McKown, b. Oct. 15, 1851. Eight
children by 2d marriage: 3. Frank Nesmith, b. Sept. 3, 1854;
m. Oct. 29, 1880, Helen F. Pike, of Franklin, N. H. He is a
lawyer; was a member of the Governor's Council in 1893.
He is the first mayor of the new city of Franklin, N. H., one
of the Governor's Council, and has recently been appointed
a Justice of the Supreme Court of New Hampshire. He
graduated at Dartmouth College in 1873. 4. Eliza Parker, b.
Jan. 31, 1856; m. Jan. 3, 1878, Ellis John Underhill, of Maroa,
Ill., who. d. Dec. 2, 1879; two children: (1) Ellis John, b.
March 6, 1879. (2) Dorothy, b. July 2, 1880. Mrs. Underhill
is principal of a young ladies' boarding and day school
at Lowell, Mass. She received the honorary degree of
A.M. from Smith College. 5. James Augustus, b. April 3,
1858; m. April, 15, 1884, Harriet E. Chittenden, of Greenville, Ill.; one child: Harriet Chittenden, b. Nov. 8, 1885.
He is a member of an insurance company in Illinois. 6.

STEPHEN (305) GREENLEAF, CONTINUED :—

 IX. Olive.

  Ebenezer Greenleaf, b. Oct. 11, 1860; m. June 15, 1888, Mary Josephine Perry, of Webster, Mass.; four children : (1) Grace Hobart, b. Sept. 19, 1889. (2) Josiah Perry, b. May 13, 1891. (3) Josephine Sewall, b. October, 1892. (4) Mary Nesmith, b. Oct. 1, 1894. Mr. E. G. Parsons was some years superintendent of a woolen mill at Franklin, N. H., and is now in a similar position at Webster, Mass. 7. Mary Nesmith, b. Jan. 1, 1863, is preceptress and instructor in Greek in Pinkerton Academy. 8. Olive Sewall, b. March 1, 1866. 9. Edward Erskine, b. July 7, 1868, is assistant superintendent of a woolen factory. 10. Archibald Livingstone, b. Sept. 20, 1875.

 ix. Samuel Miller, b. Sept. 28, 1822, at Wiscasset, Me.; m. March 2, 1848, in Washington, D. C., Virginia Whitwell, b. 1825, in Richmond, Va.; d. June 22, 1869, in Norwood, N. J.; Mr. S. M. Parsons is a lawyer; graduate of Yale College; resides in Brooklyn, N. Y. Two of his daughters are proprietors of a school in Los Angeles, Cal., and two sons are engaged. in business in the same State; seven children : 1. George Whitwell, b. Aug. 26, 1850, in Washington, D. C. 2. Emeline Haskins, b. Jan. 10, 1854, in Brooklyn, N. Y. 3. Alice Knight, b. Nov. 5, 1855. 4. Mary Wilson, b. May 3, 1858; d. July 2, 1865, at Elizabeth, N. J. 5. Samuel Sewall, b. March 3, 1862, in Brooklyn, N. Y. 6. Arthur Whittemore, b. April 3, 1865, in Brooklyn, N. Y.; d. Aug. 7, 1865, at Elizabeth, N. J. 7. Helen Shepley, b. Oct. 5, 1867, in Brooklyn, N. Y.; d. there Aug. 6, 1868.

 x. Charles Henry, b. June 18, 1826; m. July 30, 1850, Esther Rosetta Smith, b. Sept. 26, 1826; merchant; res. New York City; four children : 1. Charles Ashbel, b. July 14, 1857; m. Oct. 25, 1881, Antoinette De Forrest Ingersoll, d. Dec. 31, 1885. 2. Addie Elizabeth, b. Feb. 9, 1859; d. Jan. 3, 1860. 3. Frank Henry, b. Aug. 26, 1861; graduated at Amherst College and Columbia Law School; lawyer; res. New York City. 4. Edward Smith, b. Aug. 9, 1863; m. Dec. 4, 1889, Mary Augusta Ingersoll; two children : (1) Esther, b. Oct. 29, 1890. (2) Charles Edwards, b. Feb. 29, 1892. Mr. Edward S. Parsons graduated at Amherst College and Yale Theological Seminary. Is professor in Colorado College.

 xi. Silas Payson, b. July 2, 1829; d. September, 1851; res. Wiscasset, Me.

 X. THANKFUL, b. Oct. 5, 1788; m. Jan. 16, 1812, Thomas Hodgdon, b. Oct. 15, 1781; d. May 18, 1871. She d. Feb. 16, 1870; six children :—

  i. Wilmot, b. July 9, 1813; d. Aug. 18, 1819.

  ii. Mary, b. March 28, 1815; d. May 23, 1816.

Stephen (305) Greenleaf, Continued :—
X. Thankful.

iii. Olive P., b. April 19, 1817; m. April 2, 1837, Samuel Tarbox.
d. May 10, 1873. She d. Sept. 6, 1863.

iv. Stephen G., b. May 31, 1820; m. 1, Sept. 6, 1840, Ruth
Thomas; 2, Aug. 17, 1863, Emeline P. Jewett.

v. Emeline P., b. April 7, 1822; m. Jan. 5, 1842, Allen Lewis, d.
March 6, 1879.

vi. Eliza A., b. April 11, 1826; m. July 3, 1859, Joseph Sherlock,
d. July 29, 1875.

312. XI. Ebenezer,[7] b. June 29, 1791; m. April 18, 1816,
Abigail Hodgdon, b. April 12, 1798; d. Aug. 2,
1890. He d. July 9, 1870; res. Westport, Me. :
eleven children.

309.

(Stephen 6, Samuel 5, Stephen 4, Stephen 3, Stephen 2, Edmund 1.)

Children of **Nathaniel**[7] **Greenleaf** and Patience (Sheldon).

I. George, b. 1799; d. 1820.

II. Abigail, b. 1801; m. 1835, Frederick Hutchings.
She d. Dec. 18, 1859 or 1864; two children :—

i. Eliza, b. 1836; m. Charles Taber; res. Woolwich, Me.
ii. Stephen Darius, b. 1840.

III. Zilphia, b. 1803; m. —— Fields. She d. May 15,
1859.

313. IV. Nathan,[8] b. October, 1808; m. Oct. 10, 1833, Martha Giles, b. March 11, 1804. He d. June 24, 1887.
Mrs. Greenleaf is now living in her ninety-second
year with her daughter, Mrs. Martha A Rines, in
Somerville, Mass.; five children :—

i. Mary Eliza, b. Feb. 6, 1835; m. Nov. 20, 1853,
David W. Shaw, of Westport, Me. She d. Dec.
2, 1855; one child :—
George W.

314. ii. George F.,[9] b. April 16, 1837; m. Martha E., dau.
of Hartley Sherman, of Edgecomb, Me., b. June,
1840. He d. March 4, 1876.

315. iii. Eleazer G.,[9] b. Nov. 28, 1839, in Westport, Me.;
m. Dec. 20, 1879, Mrs. Martha E. (Sherman),
widow of his brother George F.; res. Edgecomb,
Me.; one child :—
Nellie G., b. Nov. 3, 1881.

NATHANIEL (309) GREENLEAF, CONTINUED :—
  IV. Nathan.
      iv. Martha Adelaide, b. Oct. 12, 1841 ; m. Nov. 12,
          1859, Samuel Rines; res. Somerville, Mass. ; three
          children :—
          1. Charles E., b. Aug. 21, 1864; d. April 1, 1883. 2. Aldus D., b.
             Dec. 16, 1870. 3. Harry W., b. Jan. 12, 1883; d. July 13, 1883.
      v. Abbie C., b. Aug. 23, 1847 ; d. July 9, 1848.
  V. STEPHEN, b. 1810.
  VI. DECATOR, b. 1812 ; d. at sea.

310.

(Stephen 6, Samuel 5, Stephen 4, Stephen 3, Stephen 2, Edmund 1.)

Children of **Stephen**[7] **Greenleaf** and Mary Calderwood
(Knight).

316. I. BENJAMIN K.,[8] b. Dec. 19, 1820; m. Feb. 10, 1851,
         Olive P. Dunton; res. Westport, Me. ; no children.
     II. MARY ANGELINA, b. March 30, 1823; m. Dec. 7,
         1843, Rufus Crawford. She d. Sept. 12, 1888.
     III. SUSAN CAROLINE, b. Feb. 9, 1826, at Westport,
          Me. ; m. Feb. 26, 1851, Cyrus Hodgdon, b. March
          4, 1819; farmer; res. Westport, Me. ; one child :—
          Cyrus Edward, b. Oct. 6, 1852; d. Nov. 29, 1871. Lost at sea.
     IV. WILLIAM L. C., b. Dec. 9, 1827 ; d. May 26, 1859.
     V. STEPHEN D., b. Dec. 16, 1829.
     VI. MARIA ANTOINETTE, b. Jan. 15, 1832; d. Aug. 14,
         1853.
     VII. FREEMAN, b. Jan. 24, 1834; d. May 13, 1838.

311.

(Stephen 6, Samuel 5, Stephen 4, Stephen 3, Stephen 2, Edmund 1.)

Children of **Westbrook**[7] **Greenleaf** and Mary (Dunton).

  I. ABIGAIL, b. Dec. 16, 1800, at Westport, Me. ; m. May
     17, 1821, Silas Lewis, of Boothbay, Me. ; seven chil-
     dren :—
     i. Westbrook, b. Aug. 29, 1822.
     ii. Eliza, b. July 27, 1826.
     iii. Abigail, b. Jan. 12, 1829.
     iv. Mary E., b. Nov. 11, 1831; m. May 28, 1854, Robert W. Page,
         of Bristol, Me. He d. April 7, 1878; res. Boston, Mass. ; six

Westbrook (311) Greenleaf, Continued:—

I. Abigail.

> children: 1. Isaac C., b. March 29, d. Oct. 7, 1856, in Boothbay, Me. 2. Elizabeth O., b. Aug. 1, 1858, in Boothbay, Me. 3. Lewis S., b. May 8, 1861, in Boothbay, Me.; d. Nov. 18, 1895. 4. Waldo J., b. March 18, 1863, in Boothbay, Me. 5. Josephine A., b. Oct. 23, 1867, in Northfield, Vt. 6. Edgar G., b April 3, 1872, in Northfield, Vt.; d. Oct. 7, 1891.
>
> v. Silas Nelson, b. Oct. 20, 1833.
> vi. Antoinette, b. Sept. 7, 1837.
> vii. Silas Stinson, b. Dec. 23, 1844.

II. Mary, b. Jan. 7, 1804; m. May, 1825, James McCarty, of Westport, Me. He d. Feb., 1868. She d. June, 1828; two children:—

> i. James, b. 1826; d. Feb. 16, 1894.
> ii. B. Frank, m. Nov. 19, 1854, Abigail H., dau. of Ebenezer and Abigail (Hodgdon) Greenleaf (312), his cousin; three children: 1. James Frank, b. Nov. 26, 1856. 2. Mary Abbie, b. Feb. 10, 1859; m. Oct. 29, 1878, Edward A. Newman, of Portland, Me.; Supt. Portland Street R.R.; res. Woodfords, Me., one child: Ethel M. Greenleaf, b. Dec. 15, 1879.

317. III. Westbrook,[8] b. Jan. 28, 1806; m. 1, 1830, Emeline, dau. of William Clifford, of Edgecomb, Me. She d. May 4, 1846; 2, Mrs. Diademia Cathran Gove. She d. April 3, 1893. He d. Jan. 18, 1883; ten children.

318. IV. Austin,[8] b. Oct. 17, 1809, at Westport, Me.; m. Dec. 29, 1836, Eliza A. Tibbets, b. March 14, 1816; d. April 29, 1878, at Edgecomb, Me. He d. Sept. 25, 1871, at Edgecomb, Me.; nine children.

> Mr. Greenleaf resided at Edgecomb, Me., and was in the Maine Legislature, House of Representatives, in 1870.

V. Mercy, b. Dec. 22, 1811; m. April 30, 1835, David Shattuck, of Newcastle, Me.; five children:—

> i. Wilmot G., b. April 24, 1836; m. Eliza A. Hatch; res. Newcastle, Me.
> ii. Ruth Ellen, b. Sept. 8, 1837; m. June 29, 1863, Capt. Warren Adams. He d. Oct. 12, 1889. She d. Nov. 25, 1887; res. Newcastle, Me.
> iii. David A., b. Sept. 24, 1842; m. Nov. 19, 1873, Jennie Burchstead; res. East Somerville, Mass.
> iv. Charles E., b. Feb. 28, 1845; m. Dec. 18, 1876, Julia Packard. She d. April 11, 1880. He d. Sept. 28, 1882; res. Newcastle, Me.
> v. Mary F., b. Aug. 20, 1846; m. Capt. Amos Jewett; res. Westport, Me.

WESTBROOK (311) GREENLEAF, CONTINUED:—

319. VI. DANIEL D.,[8] b. April 10, 1814; m. Nov. 4, 1845, Antoinette Clifford. She d. July 12, 1893. He d. April 23, 1890; one child:—

Emma D., b. June 22, 1847; m. Jan. 6, 1869, Charles H. Cunningham. They had one child:

Charles S., b. Nov. 26, 1875.

VII. ELIZA A., b. June 12, 1817; m. Nov., 1837, Nathaniel Nelson. She d. April, 1862.

320. VIII. WILMOT,[8] b. June 20, 1821; m. Jan. 30, 1852, Sarah P., dau. of Samuel Tarbox; res. Westport, Me.; two children.

Children by 2d marriage:—

IX. MARY MCCARTY, b. Jan. 9, 1829; d. Aug. 2, 1834.

321. X. SILAS H.,[8] b. April 4, 1831; m. Isabelle Farnham.

317.

(Westbrook 7, Stephen 6, Samuel 5, Stephen 4, Stephen 3, Stephen 2, Edmund 1.)

Children of **Westbrook**[8] **Greenleaf** and Emeline (Clifford.)

I. MERCY, b. Jan. 9, 1831; m. Nov. 1, 1869, Benjamin Frank Packard; three children:—

i. Ida.

ii. Emma, m. —— Bryant.

iii. Lillian, m. —— Spofford.

II. SARAH C., b. July 21, 1832; m. Elijah K. Hasack.

322. III. WILLIAM CLIFFORD,[9] b. Nov. 14, 1833, in Westport, Me.; m. May 19, 1861, in Boston, Mass., Louisa Tarbox, dau. of Joseph and Abigail (Knight) Greenleaf (340), b. July 24, 1835, in Westport, Me.; master mariner; res. Golden Gate, Cal.; three children:—

I. Abbie Louise, b. Oct. 10, 1863, in San Francisco, Cal.; d. Dec. 20, 1863.

II. Joseph Lincoln, b. Dec. 27, 1864, in San Francisco, Cal.

III. Willie Freeman, b. Oct. 8, 1867, at Westport, Me.; d. Nov. 3, 1876.

323. IV. DANIEL D.,[9] b. Dec. 5, 1835; m. Casselda Barter. He d. February, 1872; lost at sea,—vessel never heard from; four children:—

I. Levi Woodbury.

Westbrook (317) Greenleaf, Continued :—

IV. Daniel D.

  ii. Emeline.

  iii. Lida.

  iv. Mary.

324. V. Silas Nelson[9] (Capt.), b. Aug. 23, 1837; m. June 24, 1861, Annie A. Palmer; shipmaster. He commenced a seafaring life when twelve years of age, and followed it almost steadily up to 1889, and commanded American merchant ships, sailing all over the oceans to many ports of the world; res. Seattle, Wash.; three children :—

  i. Annie E., b. Oct. 8, 1865; m. June 28, 1887, Rev. C. H. Percival.

  ii. Joseph Tucker, b. Feb. 14, 1870; m. June 26, 1895, Ruth, dau. of ex-Mayor George Moulton, Jr., of Bath, Me.; he is a paying teller in People's Savings Bank, Seattle, Wash.

  iii. Herbert Nelson, b. April 8, 1874; d. Aug. 4, 1875.

VI. Levi Woodbury, b. March 12, 1839; d. Oct. 2, 1858; lost at sea on Prince Edward's Island.

VII. James D., b. Jan. 18, 1841; d. Feb. 21, 1850.

325. VIII. Richard M. J.,[9] b. March 21, 1843; m. 1865, Phebe Augusta Brooks; one child :—

Frank H.

326. IX. Granville C.,[9] b. Nov. 8, 1844; m. April 23, 1867, Clara E. Fowle, who d. May 11, 1890; res. Bath, Me.; two children :—

  i. Gertrude C., b. Nov. 1, 1868.

  ii. Earle G., b. Jan. 6, 1870.

327. X. Westbrook F.,[9] b. May 1, 1846; m. Minerva Pinkham; three children :—

  i. William.

  ii. Walter.

  iii. Sarah.

318.

(Westbrook 7, Stephen 6, Samuel 5, Stephen 4, Stephen 3, Stephen 2, Edmund 1.)

Children of **Austin[8] Greenleaf** and Eliza A. (Tibbets).

I. Gorham P., b. Oct. 25, d. Nov. 2, 1837.

II. Casilda, b. Oct. 7, 1838, in Boothbay, Me.; m. Sept. 15, 1867, Frank Gardiner, of Boston, Mass.;

Austin (318) Greenleaf, Continued :—
  II. Casilda.
        res. Atlantic, Mass.; five children, all born in Boston :—
        i. Frank Austin, b. March 17, 1869.
        ii. Atherton Greenleaf, b. July 11, 1871; d. June 11, 1872.
        iii. Algernon Sidney, b. March 13, 1873.
        iv. Carmi Percival, b. Jan. 10, 1875.
        v. Casilda Greenleaf, b. Jan. 16, 1879.
328. III. James T.,[9] b. Sept. 24, 1840; m. 1862, Mary
        McLain, who d. Aug. 27, 1891, aged 47; eight
        children.
    IV. Eliza E., b. April 15, 1844; m. Dec. 18, 1864,
        Francis Greenough; res. South Edgecomb, Me.;
        three children :—
        i. Frank G., b. Sept. 25, 1866; m. Sept. 30, 1890, Mary C. Davis,
           of North Edgecomb, Me.
        ii. Anna V., b. May 3, 1868; d. Oct. 22, 1882.
        iii. Granville E., b. Oct. 22, 1870.
329. V. Woodbridge C.,[9] b. March 25, 1846; m. March 1,
        1869, Jane E., eldest dau. of Dea. Eben Chase, of
        Edgecomb, Me.; res. South Edgecomb, Me.; five
        children :—
        I. Walter T., b. Jan. 23, 1870.
        II. Maud M., b. Dec. 16, 1872.
        III. Lina L., b. Sept. 25, 1877.
        IV. Eliza A., b. Dec. 20, 1881.
        v. Theodore W., b. Nov. 5, 1884.
    VI. Infant Son, b. Nov. 20, d. Nov. 21, 1848.
    VII. Mary Viola, b. Feb. 10, 1851; d. March 26,
        1853.
330. VIII. Atherton C.,[9] b. March 6, 1854; m. Sept. 7,
        1875, Susan P. Chase; res. South Edgecomb, Me.;
        seven children :—
        I. Grace A., b. May 3, 1876.
        II. Susan (Sunie) C., b. June 16, 1878.
        III. Chester E., b. Aug. 26, 1880.
        IV. Arthur P., b. June 5, 1883.
        v. Florence M., b. July 1, 1886.
        VI. Albert M., b. June 23, 1889.
        VII. Gladys I., b. Feb. 2, 1892.

AUSTIN (318) GREENLEAF, CONTINUED :—

331. IX. AUSTIN P.,[9] b. May 16, 1859; m. Jan. 25, 1889, Minnie E. Stone, of Edgecomb, Me. ; res. Southport, Me. ; two children :—

    I. Marion E., b. Feb. 10, 1890.

    II. A Daughter, b. Oct. 14, d. 1894.

328.

(Austin 8, Westbrook 7, Stephen 6, Samuel 5, Stephen 4, Stephen 3, Stephen 2, Edmund 1.)

Children of **James T.**[9] **Greenleaf** and Mary (McLain).

332. I. CHARLES A.,[10] b. Sept. 6, 1863; m. Nov. 11, 1886, Eva M., dau. of Roswell C. and Sarah F. Murch, of Boston; res. Everett, Mass. ; two children :—

    I. Cuthbert Tibbetts, b. April 28, 1888.

    II. Earl Austin, b. Sept. 21, 1894.

333. II. EDWARD S.,[10] b. Dec. 28, 1864; m. March 9, 1886, Lina C., dau. of Lewis and Julia Grant, of Ipswich, Mass. ; res. Ipswich, Mass. ; three children :—

    I. Edward T., b. Feb. 19, 1888.

    II. Irene C., b. Oct. 24, 1891.

    III. Roswell F., b. May 16, 1894.

  III. ARCHIBALD, b. Oct. 6, 1866; d. Oct. 27, 1885.

  IV. MINNIE E., b. Oct. 16, 1868; m. May 19, 1887, William E. Rose, of Ipswich, Mass. ; three children :—

    i. Grace, b. June 16, 1888.

    ii. Andrew, b. September, 1889.

    iii. James, b. February, 1891.

  V. LILLIAN E., b. May 11, 1870; m. July 16, 1889, Orlando L. Wylie, of Beverly, Mass. ; res. Beverly, Mass. ; two children :—

    i. Mabel, b. Feb. 2, 1890.

    ii. Kenneth G., b. June 28, 1895.

334. VI. RICHARD J.,[10] b. Oct. 11, 1871 ; m. 1892, Nellie Lord, of Ipswich, Mass. ; res. Ipswich, Mass. ; one child :— Sylvanus S., b. Aug. 7, 1893.

  VII. VIOLA M., b. Aug. 19, 1881 ; twin.

  VIII. IZORA M., b. Aug. 19, 1881 ; twin.

320.

(Westbrook 7, Stephen 6, Samuel 5, Stephen 4, Stephen 3, Stephen 2, Edmund 1.)

Children of **Wilmot**[8] **Greenleaf** and Sarah P. (Tarbox).

  I. SEWALL P., b. Jan. 30, 1854; d. December, 1854, in Westport, Me.

Wilmot (320) Greenleaf, Continued :—

335. II. Herman E.,[9] b. April 5, 1856, in Westport, Me. ; m. Nov. 2, 1882, in Allston, Mass., Sarah A. Galvin ; selectman ; res. Westport, Me. ; four children :—

    i. Wilmot L., b. Oct. 9, 1883, in Tekamah, Neb.

    ii. Edith H., b. Jan. 27, 1885, in Tekamah, Neb.

    iii. Claire A., b. Oct. 13, 1886, in Tekamah, Neb.

    iv. Norman S., b. Dec. 10, 1891, in Westport, Me.

312.

(Stephen 6, Samuel 5, Stephen 4, Stephen 3, Stephen 2, Edmund 1.)

Children of **Ebenezer**[7] **Greenleaf** and Abigail (Hodgdon).

  I. Susan B., b. June 24, 1817; m. Nov. 20, 1843, John McNear. She d. July 9, 1846; one child :—

    ———, m. Carleton Cheney (?)

  II. Sophia P., b. April 13, 1819; m. Oct. 17, 1844, George W. Shaw, of Montsweag, Me. She d. Sept. 5, 1854; three children :—

    i. Henrietta J., b. June 22, 1846; m. Dec. 12, 1881, James A. Reed; res. Boothbay, Me.; two children: 1. Harry A. 2. Nellie E., b. Aug. 8, 1882; twins.

    ii. Susan A., b. June 22, 1846; twin; d. April, 1847.

    iii. George W., b. Sept. 22, 1850; m. 1882, Mrs. Ella Butler, of Bath, Me.; res. Montsweag, Me.; two children: 1. Harold, b. March, 188–. 2. Robert.

  III. Mary Ann, b. Sept. 26, 1820; m. Feb. 19, 1846, Lewis E. Wright, b. July 4, 1820; res. Woolwich, Me. ; nine children :—

    i. Susan Abbie, b. Jan. 12, 1847; m. Jan. 17, 1869, George S. Dodge, b. Aug. 8, 1841; res. Woolwich, Me. ; nine children : 1. Anneliza, b. Nov. 12, 1869. 2. Wilmot Wood, b. May 20, 1872. 3. Mary Louise, b. July 20, 1874. 4. Sarah Webb, b. May 6, 1876. 5. Solomon, b. May 27, 1877. 6. Lewis Sylvester, b. May 5, 1879. 7. Pamelia Gertrude, b. April 24, 1881. 8. Eva Sophia, b. May 12, 1883. 9. George Ossian Adams, b. Dec. 19, 1885.

    ii. Pamelia G., b. Dec. 2, 1848; m. Nov. 21, 1869, Edward S. Dunton.

    iii. Louisa G., b. Nov. 2, 1850; d. July 4, 1872.

    iv. Frederick, b. Oct. 13, 1852; m. Nov. 19, 1879, Leoraine E. Stone, b. July 4, 1852; res. Bath, Me.; three children: 1. Mary Abbie, b. Dec. 7, 1881; 2. Arthur Percy, b. April 25, 1886. 3. Harrison, b. Oct. 24, 1888.

EBENEZER (312) GREENLEAF, CONTINUED :—

III. Mary Ann.

   v. Annie M., b. June 13, 1855; d. Oct. 21, 1866.

   vi. Sophia G., b. May 2, 1857.

   vii. Elwell L., b. Jan. 13, 1859; d. Nov. 10, 1882.

   viii. Winfield Scott, b. Feb. 13, 1861.

   ix. Wilson McNear, b. March 13, 1864.

336. IV. JACKSON,[8] b. Feb. 25, 1823; m. Dec. 28, 1854, Rachel Brooks. He d. Aug. 2, 1874; one child :—

336a. Henry F.,[9] b. May 21, 1858; m. Dec. 15, 1888, Ida F. Leavitt, of Bath, Me.; four children: 1. George Henry,[10] b. Oct. 20, 1889. 2. Mercy Ellen, b. Oct. 31, 1891. 3. George Luther,[10] b. 1893. 4. A son,[10] b. Feb. 12, 1895.

  V. EMELINE P., b. July 7, 1825; m. 1, Feb. 29, 1848, James R. Jewett; 2, Aug. 17, 1863, Stephen G. Hodgdon, b. 1820; res. Trevett, Me.

Child by 1st marriage :—

   Eva R., b. Nov. 18, 1852; m. Sept. 17, 1873, William E. Schweppe; res. St. Louis, Mo.

Child by 2d marriage :—

   Charles S., b. Oct. 17, 1864; m. Sept., 1887, Edith Adams; res. Trevett, Me.

  VI. HENRIETTA, b. Feb. 11, 1827; d. Sept. 30, 1845.

  VII. ABIGAIL H., b. Jan. 21, 1830; m. Nov. 19, 1854, B. F. McCarty, her cousin. He d. June 25, 1886. See Mary, dau. of Westbrook[7] Greenleaf and Mary (Dunton) (311). She d. Jan. 15, 1887; three children.

  VIII. LOUISA JOSEPHINE, b. April 3, 1832; d. March 19, 1833.

  IX. PAMELIA P., b. May 27, 1834; m. Jan. 23, 1859, Joshua R. Trevett; res. Trevett, Me.; six children :—

   i. James Robert, b. Nov. 14, 1859; d. Aug. 6, 1866.

   ii. John Henry, b. Aug. 3, 1864; m. June 5, 1892, Nellie Burgess; res. Bath, Me.

   iii. Wilmot Greenleaf, b. March 21, 1866; res. Medfield, Mass.

   iv. Emma Chase, b. Dec. 3, 1869; m. May 12, 1892, Charles E. Fuller; res. Medfield, Mass.

   v. Mary Spring, b. Sept. 10, 1872; res. Trevett, Me.

   vi. Abbie Louise, b. Sept. 11, 1875; res. Medfield, Mass.

337. X. EBENEZER M.,[8] b. Dec. 22, 1836; m. April 15, 1878, Emma F. Moore. He d. Jan. 19, 1894, at Westport, Me; eight children. :—

EBENEZER (312) GREENLEAF, CONTINUED :—
X. Ebenezer M.
    I. Abbie S., b. Aug. 16, 1879.
    II. Josephine, b. March 17, 1882; d. Jan. 19, 1886.
    III. Robert T., b. Oct. 12, 1883.
    IV. Irving M., b. Nov. 30, 1886; d. May 27, 1887.
    V. Fred J., b. March 3, 1887.
    VI. Avis H., b. Jan. 9, 1890; d. April 22, 1890.
    VII. Elmer T., b. Jan. 13, 1891.
    VIII. Matthew Hervey, b. Nov. 3, 1893.
    XI. SARAH LOUISA, b. Dec. 7, 1840; d. Aug. 6, 1859.

306.

(Samuel 5, Stephen 4, Stephen 3, Stephen 2, Edmund 1.)

Child of **Samuel**[6] **Greenleaf** and Abigail (Sheldon).

338. ZEBULON,[7] b. 1781; m. 1, Ruth Gray, of Wiscasset, Me.;
    2, Mrs. —— Decker, dau. of Isaac and Eunice
    Moore, d. Dec. 28, 1814. He d. 1823; res. West-
    port, Me. Seven children :—
Children by 1st marriage :—
    I. Samuel, b. 1802; d. about 1840, at sea; buried on
    St. Catherine's Island, South America; un-
    married.
339.   II. William Wigglesworth,[8] b. Dec. 28, 1804; m April,
    1836, Louisa M. Tarbox, b. May 23, 1811; d.
    Sept. 28, 1855; res. Squam Island, Westport, Me.;
    five children.
340.   III. Joseph,[8] b. Sept. 28, 1806; m. Dec. 28, 1834,
    Abigail, dau. of Capt. Benjamin and Mary (Calder-
    wood) Knight, b. March 23, 1816. He d. June 5,
    1859; res. Westport, Me.; nine children; all born
    at Westport.
    IV. Zebulon, b. 1808.
    V. Phinette, b. 1810.
Children by 2d marriage :—
    VI. George W., burned to death at two years of age.
341.   VII. George Washington,[8] b. Dec. 20, 1814; m. 1838,
    Betsey, dau. of Simon and Abigail Madden, b.
    March 17, 1822. At the death of his mother he
    was adopted and brought up by his mother's

SAMUEL (306) GREENLEAF, CONTINUED :—
Zebulon.

> parents. Simon Madden was drowned in 1823, and his wife Abigail died Nov. 29, 1880, aged 90 years, 1 month, 18 days; ten children.

339.

(Zebulon 7, Samuel 6, Samuel 5, Stephen 4, Stephen 3, Stephen 2, Edmund 1.)

Children of **William Wigglesworth**[8] **Greenleaf** and Louisa M. (Tarbox).

I. ANNIE M., b. Aug. 13, 1837; m. 1859, George W. Jewett, b. 1832; d. June 4, 1879. She d. Dec. 13, 1887; three children :—
   i. James R., b. March, 1862; res. Westport, Me.
   ii. M. Louisa, b. July, 1867, in Bath, Me.
   iii. Geo. F., b. Feb. 1870, in China, Me.

342. II. ANDREW P.,[9] b. April 1, 1839; m. 1873, Augusta Crawford; d. 1876. He d. Sept. 20, 1883; no children.

III. ZEBULON, b. July 21, 1843; d. Dec. 28, 1873; unmarried.

343. IV. W. SCOTT,[9] b. July, 1849; m. June 18, 1877, Nellie Ludd, b. June 4, 1850, Abbott, Me.; res. Westport, Me.; two children :—
   I. Dora L., b. April 30, 1883.
   II. George F., b. Aug. 30, 1889; both born in Brockton, Mass.

V. SEDGWICK P., b. April 22, 1851; res. Westport, Me.

340.

(Zebulon 7, Samuel 6, Samuel 5, Stephen 4, Stephen 3, Stephen 2, Edmund 1.)

Children of **Joseph**[8] **Greenleaf** and Abigail (Knight).

I. LOUISA TARBOX, b. July 24, 1835, in Westport, Me.; m. May 19, 1861, William C., son of Westbrook Greenleaf (322), of Westport, Me.; res. Golden Gate, Cal.

II. INFANT SON, b. May 14, d. Sept. 24, 1837.

344. III. FREEMAN,[9] b. Aug. 14, 1838; m. Oct. 21, 1866, Emily Adell, dau. of Zachariah Sherman, of Boothbay, Me.; res. Edgecomb, Me.; four children :—
   I. Roscoe Freeman, b. Dec. 26, 1868; res. Boston.
   II. William Everett, b. Jan. 13, 1872; res. Boston.

JOSEPH (340) GREENLEAF, CONTINUED :—
III. Freeman.
    III. Celia Lincoln, b. July 19, 1874; res. Boothbay, Me.
    IV. Melville Theron, b. Sept. 28, 1881; res. Boothbay, Me.
IV. MARY EMELINE, b. Aug. 2, 1840; d. Nov. 17, 1869.
V. HARRIET, b. Feb. 17, 1843; m. Nov. 16, 1865, Marcus L. Dunton, of Westport, Me.; res. Farmington, Cal.
VI. SUSAN, b. June 24, 1845; m. September, 1871, Cornelius I. Carpenter, of Stockton, Cal. She d. Jan. 16, 1884.
VII. RUTH, b. April 11, 1848; m. Dec. 25, 1865, George Bailey. She d. Sept. 17, 1876.
VIII. MARCIA, b. April 5, 1850; d. May 5, 1856.
IX. ANNETTE, b. Jan. 11, 1853; m. June 12, 1875, Marcus S. Chapman, of Stockton, Cal.; res. Fowler, Fresno Co., Cal.
    Children all born at Westport, Me.

341.

(Zebulon 7, Samuel 6, Samuel 5, Stephen 4, Stephen 3, Stephen 2, Edmund 1.)

Children of **George Washington**[8] **Greenleaf** and Betsey (Madden).

    I. EMILY A., b. April 9, 1840; m. 1860, Cornelius Rairdon.

345. II. GEORGE W.,[9] b. March 3, 1842, in Edgecomb, Me.; m. April, 1866, Orila, dau. of Alvah and Sarah Sherman, of Liberty, Me. She d. Dec. 25, 1893. He d. 1880. He was for a long time mate of the brig " Prairie Rose," Captain Griffin; and afterwards, Captain Griffin being in command of a new barque, he became captain, and was in command of the " Prairie Rose" when she was wrecked on the Cedar Keyes, near Key West, Fla., after which he went as mate of the schooner " Mary Cloud," which sailed from New York, Oct. 5, 1876, for Wilmington, N. C., and was never heard from; res. North Union, Me.; three children :—

346.   I. Henry L.,[10] b. Aug. 7, 1867, in Edgecomb, Me.; m. 1890, Carrie Jenesse, of New York; res. for-

GEORGE WASHINGTON (341) GREENLEAF, CONTINUED:—
II. George W.
merly North Union, Me., now New York City;
two children: 1. Mark Jenesse, b. June 4, 1891, in
Waterville, Me. 2. Sarah Lloyd, b. Sept. 14,
1893, in Union, Me.
  II. Alta, b. March 16, 1869, in Falmouth, Me.; m.
January, 1890, Charles A. G. Simmons, of Union,
Me.; one child: Vero Burdeen, b. May 21, 1891.
  III. Manton, b. Aug. 22, 1872, in Liberty, Me.; un-
married; res. Union, Me.
III. BETSEY H., b. Jan. 6, 1846; d. July 10, 1857.
IV. ABBIE L., b. Dec. 9, 1848; m. Joseph McDonald;
res. Medford, Mass.
347. V. BENNIAH,[9] b. July 6, 1850; m. Olivia Knight; res.
North Woburn, Mass.; four children:—
  I. Flora.
  II. Wallace.
  III. Lelia.
  IV. Jennie.
VI. ANNIE J., b. Sept. 16, 1852; d. August, 1863.
VII. HENRY M., b. Jan. 18, 1857; d. Aug. 21, 1863.
VIII. EDWARD J., b. 1860; d. Aug. 8, 1864.
IX. LIZZIE B., b. Jan. 11, 1862; m. Dec. 21, 1879,
George Gove.
X. JOHN P., b. Dec. 13, 1865; unmarried; res. North
Edgecomb, Me.

307.
(Samuel 5, Stephen 4, Stephen 3, Stephen 2, Edmund 1.)
Children of **Enoch[6] Greenleaf** and ——.
348. I. HENRY,[7] m. Paulina Dunton. He d. Oct. 14, 1850; res.
Barter's Island; P. O., Trevett, Me.; twelve children.
II. ABIGAIL, m. —— Harding.

348.
(Enoch 6, Samuel 5, Stephen 4, Stephen 3, Stephen 2, Edmund 1.)
Children of **Henry[7] Greenleaf** and Paulina (Dunton).
I. HARRIET, b. Sept. 10, 1811.
349. II. JOHN DUNTON,[8] b. July 29, 1812; m. Nov. 30, 1837,
Naomi Barter Abbot, of Boothbay, Me. He d.
January, 1881; six children.

Henry (348) Greenleaf, Continued :—

    III. Enoch, b. Nov. 4, 1814; d. Dec. 21, 1839.

    IV. Sarah, b. Feb. 10, 1816.

    V. Henry, b. Oct. 9, 1818; d. July 2, 1838.

350. VI. Silas Payson,[8] b. May 12, 1820; m. Mary ——;
res. Boothbay, Me; eight children.

351. VII. Rufus,[8] b. Aug. 29, 1822; m. Rebecca Stover, of
Sullivan, Me.; res. Westport, Me.; ten children.

    VIII. Abigail, b. Jan. 17, 1825; d. Jan. 20, 1837.

    IX. Paulina, b. Feb. 22, 1827.

352. X. William,[8] b. May 10, 1829; m. April 6, 1852, at
Boothbay, Me., Martha Jane Pinkham, b. March 24,
1834; res. Barter's Island, Trevett P. O., Me.; eleven
children.

    XI. May Elizabeth, b. Sept. 12, 1831.

    XII. Adaline, b. June 22, 1834.

349.

(Henry 7, Enoch 6, Samuel 5, Stephen 4, Stephen 3, Stephen 2, Edmund 1.)

Children of **John Dunton**[8] **Greenleaf** and Naomi B.
(Abbot).

    I. Angeline, b. Oct. 15, 1838; m. 1858, Alpheus
Campbell. She d. 1883.

    II. Naomi, b. Dec. 30, 1839; m. 1863, Alden Pinckham.
She d. 1876.

353. III. Orenthaell,[9] b. Aug. 21, 1841; m. 1866, Emma,
dau. of David and Sarah A. Lewis, b. April 22,
1845; res. Boothbay, Me.; four children :—

      i. Celia S., b. Jan. 9, 1867.

      ii. Howard Alden, b. Aug. 7, 1873.

      iii. Raymond O., b. March 27, 1876.

      iv. David Lewis, b. Sept. 4, 1879.

    IV. Sarah Elizabeth, b. July 15, 1843; m. 1867,
Theodore Roberts.

354. V. Sanford,[9] b. March 9, 1847; m. 1873, Ella McKown.
He d. 1882.

    VI. Alice B., b. March 23, 1856; m. 1880, Edgar J.
Norris.

350.

(Henry 7, Enoch 6, Samuel 5, Stephen 4, Stephen 3, Stephen 2, Edmund 1.)

Children of **Silas P.**[8] **Greenleaf** and Mary (——).

355. I. ENOCH,[9] b. Jan. 6, 1842; m. Margaret ——. She d.
June 3, 1878; two children :—
    I. Lena Bell, b. Sept. 5, 1868; d. Feb. 15, 1874.
    II. Annie, b. Aug. 4, 1872.

356. II. GEORGE FREEMAN,[9] b. Jan. 8, 1844; m. Mary J.
——; res. Boothbay, Me.; ten children :—
    I. James L., b. Aug. 27, 1869; res. Boothbay, Me.
    II. Florine, b. Feb. 26, 1871.
    III. Charles F., b. July 7, 1873.
    IV. Daniel M., b. Sept. 2, 1875.
    V. Mattie M., b. Jan. 10, 1878.
    VI. Edward T., b. Aug. 26, 1880.
    VII. Ina Susan, b. Oct. 23, 1882.
    VIII. Silas S., b. July 17, 1885.
    IX. Susie M., b. Aug. 13, 1888; d. May 14, 1890.
    X. Corridon G., b. July 20, 1891; d. April 8, 1892.

357. III. ELWELL,[9] b. Oct. 29, 1846; m. Aurelia ——; res.
Boothbay, Me.; six children :—
    I. Jesse, b. Jan. 21, 1871.
    II. Hollis, b. March 5, 1873.
    III. Charles, b. Oct. 23, 1874.
    IV. Hiram P., b. Aug. 13, 1876.
    V. Perley D., b. Aug. 30, 1878.
    VI. Merrill L., b. Aug. 31, 1882.

IV. JANE MAY, b. Aug. 7, 1849.

V. SARAH, b. Oct. 14, 1853; d. May 17, 1854.

358. VI. PAYSON S.,[9] b. Aug. 7, 1854; m. Susan ——; res.
Boothbay, Me.; two children :—
    I. Delia H., b. April 30, 1879.
    II. Edith L., b. Dec. 15, 1882.

VII. SUSAN, b. Jan. 12, 1862.

VIII. FLORA ETTA, b. Nov. 27, 1865.

351.

(Henry 7, Enoch 6, Samuel 5, Stephen 4, Stephen 3, Stephen 2, Edmund 1.)

Children of **Rufus**[8] **Greenleaf** and Rebecca (Stover).

359. I. WILLIAM HENRY,[9] b. Aug. 25, 1847, at Westport,
Me., m. April 8, 1869, Margaret Jane O'Connor, of

Rufus (351) Greenleaf, Continued :—

　　I. William Henry.
　　　　Gloucester, Mass., b. Dec. 16, 1848, in Canso, Canada ; res. Gloucester, Mass. ; eight children :—
　　　　　i. Margaret May, b. Dec. 19, 1870; d. in infancy.
　　　　　ii. Henrietta, b. April 2, 1873.
　　　　　iii. Harriet, b. March 2, 1875.
　　　　　iv. William H., b. Sept. 19, 1876.
　　　　　v. Clara, b. July 28, 1880.
　　　　　vi. George H., b. Sept. 15, 1882.
　　　　　vii. Charles H., b. Nov. 25, 1883.
　　　　　viii. Margaret, b. Nov. 28, 1886 ; d. in infancy.
360. II. Nathaniel,[9] b. June 15, 1849; m. Elizabeth Handlon; res. Gloucester, Mass. ; seven children :—
　　　　　i. Elizabeth J. ; res. Gloucester, Mass.
　　　　　ii. Charles Merrill.
　　　　　iii. Lucretia Adaline.
　　　　　iv. Nathaniel S.
　　　　　v. John Walter.
　　　　　vi. Dorothea.
　　　　　vii. Roger Raymond.
　　III. Harvey Francis, b. Aug. 19, 1851.
　　IV. Merrill H., b. March 20, 1853; d. about 1873; drowned at sea.
　　V. Julia Eveline, b. July 30, 1856; m. Warren Watson, of Michigan ; no children.
361. VI. Franklin, m. Drowned at sea ; res. Westport, Me. ; one child :—
　　　　Albertha F.
　　VII. Naomi, m. March Warren ; res. Wiscasset, Me. ; two children :—
　　　　　i. Albert.
　　　　　ii. Frank.
　　VIII. Henrietta, d. young.
362. IX. Lafayette,[9] m. Ellen Blackburn ; res. Wiscasset, Me. ; three children :—
　　　　　i. Hermon.
　　　　　ii. Alice.
　　　　　iii. Florence.
　　X. Chester ; res. Westport, Me. ; unmarried.

352.

(Henry 7, Enoch 6, Samuel 5, Stephen 4, Stephen 3, Stephen 2, Edmund 1.)

Children of **William**[8] **Greenleaf** and Martha Jane (Pinkham).

363. I. MENZIES B.,[9] b. Sept. 25, 1852; m. March 27, 1877, Lizzie Stuart; res. Boothbay, Me.; seven children:—

   i. Ina E., b. Sept. 1, 1878.

   ii. Leland, b. Aug. 6, 1880.

   iii. Martha J., b. Sept. 2, 1882.

   iv. Chester, b. Dec. 18, 1884.

   v. Clinton, b. Nov. 7, 1886.

   vi. Fynette, b. May 28, 1890.

   vii. Ursula, b. Feb. 1, 1891.

II. FYNETTE, b. Nov. 2, 1853; d. July 4, 1869; drowned.

364. III. IRVING,[9] b. July 29, 1855; m. Jan. 3, 1883, Annie Stuart. She d. June 20, 1892; res. Boothbay, Me.; two children:—

   i. Sarah J., b. May 18, 1884.

   ii. Laura, b. Aug. 2, 1886.

IV. GEORGIANA, b. Dec. 30, 1856; m. Sept. 25, 1877, Isambert Stuart; res. Milton Mills, N. H.

V. EMMA R., b. July 20, 1859; res. Barter's Island, Trevett P. O., Me.

VI. LINCOLN, b. Dec. 31, 1860; d. July 11, 1862.

VII. LIZZIE M., b. Aug. 31, 1863; m. Oct. 24, 1888, Allen Gove; res. Boothbay, Me.

VIII. ABBIE J., b. Nov. 28, 1865; m. June 20, 1888, Giles Day; res. Boothbay, Me.

IX. LOTTIE, b. May 28, 1868; d. June 16, 1869.

X. HAYDEN R., b. June 27, 1870; res. Boothbay, Me.

XI. HENRY B., b. July 17, 1874.

308.

(Samuel 5, Stephen 4, Stephen 3, Stephen 2, Edmund 1.)

Children of **Benjamin**[6] **Greenleaf** and Rachel (Arnold).

I. ELIZA (Betsey), b. Dec. 26, 1784; marriage intention filed Jan. 14, 1810, m. Henry Adams. He d. 1848. She d. Sept. 22, 1875.

365. II. BENJAMIN,[7] b. April 7, 1786; marriage intention Sept. 14, 1811; m. 1, Nancy Pressy, who d. Sept. 23, 1816,

Benjamin (308) Greenleaf, Continued :—
   II. Benjamin.
         age 28; 2, intention July 13, m. Aug. 24, 1823,
         Nancy Murphy. He d. April 8, 1849.
366. III. Samuel,[7] b. April 19, 1788; m. Nov. 25, 1817,
         Abigail G., dau. of John and Mary (Groves) Lowell,
         of Wiscasset, Me. She d. Dec. 12, 1847 (rec. 1846).
         He d. Feb. 20, 1857; six children.
367. IV. Spencer,[7] b. March 4, 1790; m. 1, Nov. 20, 1813,
         Pamela Adams, b. Oct. 24, 1789; d. Dec. 25, 1843;
         2, intention Nov. 16, m. Dec. 5, 1844, Frances Mc-
         Clintock (Wiscasset, Me., rec.). He d. April 18,
         1857; eleven children.
   Children by 1st marriage :—
         I. Polly, b. Sept. 20, 1814; d. in youth.
         II. Olive P., b. Jan. 19, 1817; m. Nov. 24, 1844, in Boston,
            James Baker. She d. Dec. 11, 1845; no children.
         III. Ann (Joanna), b. Nov. 3, 1818; m. Jan. 27, 1857,
            John Williams. She d. Dec. 31, 1893, at Jamaica
            Plain, Mass.; one child :—
            Wallace D., with Jordan, Marsh & Co., Boston.
         IV. Pamela, b. Feb. 6, 1820; d. Nov. 27, 1839; unmarried.
         V. Rachel, b. Jan. 8, 1822; m. James Baker. He d.
            1859; res. Boston, Mass.; one child :—
            Evelyn Greenleaf; m. 1879, Dr. John Preston Sutherland; no
            children.
         VI. Lydia, b. Sept. 16, 1823; m. Oct. 13, 1845, in
            Wiscasset, Me., William Carleton. She d. Oct.
            16, 1846; no children.
         VII. Harriet White, b. July 5, 1825, in Wiscasset, Me.;
            m. Jan. 2, 1848, at Boston, Sargent Calvin, son of
            Levi and Mary (Sanborn) Witcher (or Whittier),
            b. Jan. 30, 1824, in Danville, Vt. She d. May 15,
            1866, in Somerville, Mass. He m. 2, Dec. 5,
            1867, Julia, dau. of Caleb and Julia (Merriam)
            Stetson, Lexington, Mass., b. April 1, 1834, in
            Medford, Mass. Harriet White and S. C. Witcher
            had three children :—
            1. Harriet Louise, b. Nov. 13, 1848; m. Edward E. Batchelder.
            2. Henry Ellsworth, b. July 1, d. Aug. 8, 1861.   3. George
            Greenleaf, b. Aug. 9, 1862.

Benjamin (308) Greenleaf, Continued :—

IV. Spencer.

    viii. Sophia P., b. Feb. 6, 1827; intention, Oct. 18, m. 1, Dec. 28, 1845, Daniel Cate, of Dresden, Me.; 2, Horace Clark. She d. Feb. 27, 1889, at Lynn, Mass.; three children by 1st marriage :—

      1. Edward, d. in childhood. 2. Pamela, m. Dudley Johnson. She d. 1877; two children: (1) William, d. 1892. (2) Frederick. 3. Frederick, m. Carrie Batchelder; three children: (1) Florence. (2) Alice. (3) Walter. One child by 2d marriage : 4. Lillian, m. June 4, 1889, Francis E. Galloupe; res. Lynn, Mass.; one child : Chauncey, b. November, 1891.

    ix. Adeline, b. May 18, 1830; m. Peter Smith; three children :—

      1. Horace Greeley, d. in childhood. 2. Walter, m. 1883, Emma Leavitt. 3. Adeline, d. 1889; unmarried.

    x. Eliza, b. Jan. 16, 1832; m. April 13, 1850, John Woodbury Adams, of Dresden, Me. She d. 1874; no children.

  Child by 2d marriage :—

    xi. James B., b. Nov. 1, 1845; d. July 2, 1846.

V. Abigail, b. Dec. 4, 1791; d. May 14, 1828; unmarried.

VI. Polly, b. Nov. 23, 1793; unmarried.

VII. Joseph, b. Oct. 9, 1795; d. April 10, 1817 (rec. April 4) ; unmarried.

VIII. Rebecca, b. Aug. 29, 1797; d. Dec. 19, 1830; unmarried.

IX. Lydia, b. Aug. 6, 1799; d. Aug. 12, 1876; unmarried.

X. Ebenezer H., b. Aug. 9, 1801; d. April 16, 1831; unmarried.

366.

(Benjamin 6, Samuel 5, Stephen 4, Stephen 3, Stephen 2, Edmund 1.)

Children of **Samuel**[7] **Greenleaf** and Abigail G.(Lowell).

368. I. John Lowell,[8] b. Sept. 2, 1818; m. Abby (Decker) Groves, b. July 15, 1818; d. Sept. 22, 1873. He d. July 7, 1888; six children.

  II. Susan, m. Bradford Holbrook.

369. III. Arnold,[8] m. Aug. 21, 1867, Mrs. Helen (Ballard) Murphy; res. Wiscasset, Me.; no children.

SAMUEL (366) GREENLEAF, CONTINUED :—

370. IV. VALENTINE,[8] b. Oct. 18, 1825 ; m. Jan. 9, 1854, Julia, dau. of Charles Blagden, of Wiscasset, Me. ; b. May 4, 1833, in Wiscasset, Me. ; d. March 7, 1894 ; grocer ; res. Wiscasset, Me. He d. April 6, 1874. She afterwards resided and died in Jamaica Plain, Mass. ; six children :—

   I. Samuel Willis, b. July 18, 1855 ; d. June 25, 1878.
   II. Grace Lee, b. Jan. 22, 1861 ; m. June 30, 1883, Wilmot L. Lowell ; one child :—
Gertrude Greenleaf, b. May 22, 1885.
   III. James Baker, b. Oct. 30, 1865 ; d. Nov. 17, 1882.
   IV. Annie Valentine, b. Oct. 31, 1866 ; m. June 19, 1889, Alva W. Polk ; one child :—
Hadley Greenleaf, b. Jan. 12, 1892.
   V. Fred Stinson, b. Nov. 19, 1869 ; detective, Boston.
   VI. Edward Goodridge, b. March 19, 1871 ; d. Sept. 6, 1871.

371. V. HIRAM,[8] b. Nov. 26, 1829 ; m. Jan. 29, 1851, Mary Ann, dau. of John Jones, of Wiscasset, Me. ; b. May 1, 1833 ; d. about 1885 ; res. Wiscasset, Me. one child :—
Ellen R., b. Dec. 2, 1851 ; m. Sept. 1, 1875, William P. Foye ; two children :—
   i. Frank D., b. March 1, 1876.
   ii. Edith G., b. Jan. 1, 1881.

372. VI. WILLIAM,[8] m. Jane Savage ; res. Wiscasset, Me. ; two children :—
   I. Harriet.
   II. Henry.

368.

(Samuel 7, Benjamin 6, Samuel 5, Stephen 4, Stephen 3, Stephen 2, Edmund 1.)

Children of **John Lowell**[8] **Greenleaf** and Abby (Groves).

373. I. JOHN M.,[9] b. Dec. 4, 1847 ; m. Aug. 31, 1878, Emma Rittal, of Wiscasset, Me. ; res. Wiscasset, Me. ; one child :—
Joseph, b. July 16, 1890.

   II. SUSAN E., b. Sept. 22, 1849 ; d. April 2, 1877.

374. III. JOSEPH H.,[9] b. March 29, 1852 ; m. Jennie Pottle, of Wiscasset, Me. ; two children :—
   I. Jossie, b. June 12, 1891 ; d. in infancy.
   II. Jennie, b. June 12, 1891 ; twin.

JOHN LOWELL (368) GREENLEAF, CONTINUED :—
    IV. ALICE P., b. Nov. 6, 1854; d. Oct. 8, 1876.
375. V. ABIEL G.,[9] b. Feb. 2, 1857; m. June 2, 1881, Sarah
    L. Stinson, of Wiscasset, Me., b. Feb. 6, 1857; three
    children :—
      I. Ella M., b. March 27, 1882.
      II. Alice F., b. Oct. 17, 1888.
      III. Abbie P., b. April 22, 1891.
    VI. HATTIE W., b. Oct. 26, 1862.

297.

(Stephen 4, Stephen 3, Stephen 2, Edmund 1.)

Children of **Ebenezer**[5] **Greenleaf** and Mary (Preble).
    I. LOIS, b. Oct. 22, 1768; m. George Bolton; res. Sidney,
    Me.
376. II. JAMES,[6] b. April 9, 1770; m. Olive Bickford. He d.
    1827; res. near Whitefield, Me.; two children :—
      I. Louisa.
      II. Mitty.
377. III. STEPHEN,[6] b. Feb. 13, 1772, in Whitefield, Me.; m.
    Lydia Wheeler, of Bowdoinham, Me. He d. 1815;
    seven children :—
      I. Hepsebeth, b. 1801 ; m. Benjamin Heath, of Jeffer-
      son, Me. She d. 1870.
      II. Abraham, b. 1803; d. 1825; unmarried.
      III. Dolly, b. 1805; m. M. Sinclair; res. New York.
      IV. Olive, b. 1807; m. Josiah Peaslee, of Whitefield,
      Me.
378.   V. Stephen,[7] b. June 13, 1809; m. May 7, 1835, Sarah
    Turner, of Palermo, Me.; res. North Washington,
    Me.; now (Oct., 1895) at East Palermo, Me., with
    his son, Samuel T. Greenleaf; three children.
379.   VI. Eben,[7] b. 1811, in Whitefield, Me.; m. 1838, Mar-
    tha Dodge, Whitefield, Me.; d. June, 1880; six
    children: 1. Charles, b. 1840; d. 1867; killed in
    a railroad accident in Massachusetts. 2. A daugh-
    ter, b. 1842; m. Reuben ——; d. 1889 (?); and
    other children.
    VII. John, b. June, 1815; d. 1834; unmarried.
  IV. MARY, m. Eben Vose.

EBENEZER (297) GREENLEAF, CONTINUED:—
   V. HANNAH, m. Daniel Howard; res. Alna, Me.
   VI. OLIVE, m. Eliphet Blackman; res. Whitefield, Me.
   VII. SUSAN, m. Nehemiah Turner; res. Palermo, Me.
   VIII. SARAH, m. Timothy Weymouth; res. Appleton, Me.

378.

(Stephen 6, Ebenezer 5, Stephen 4, Stephen 3, Stephen 2, Edmund 1.)

Children of **Stephen**[7] **Greenleaf** and Sarah (Turner).
380. I. JOHN,[8] b. Aug. 14, 1835; m. July 12, 1858, Eliza A.
   Turner, of Palermo, Me. He d. July 15, 1876; res.
   Palermo, Me.; four children:—
      I. Sarah E., b. April 20, 1860; m. William Leigher,
      of Washington, Me.; eight children.
381.   II. Mark,[9] b. Oct. 12, 1861; m. September, 1883,
      Ellen Ladd, of Baltic, Conn.; res. New Bedford,
      Mass.; three children.
382.   III. Hollis T.,[9] b. March 5, 1863; m. June, 1881, in
      Central Falls, R. I., Ellen Fox; res. Attleboro
      Falls, Mass.; four children.
      IV. Susan A., b. July 29, 1866; m. June 4, 1892,
      Fred E. Fairfield, of Augusta, Me.; res. Eastport,
      Me.; two children:—
      1. Zetella Gertrude, b. March 24, 1893.
      2. Roy Greenleaf, b. Nov. 16, 1894.
383. II. SAMUEL T.,[8] b. Nov. 3, 1837; m. Dec. 14, 1870,
   Mary J. Boynton, of Palermo, Me.; res. Palermo,
   Me.; no children.
   III. LYDIA A., b. May 27, 1842; m. June, 1874, Milton
   M. Stone, of Augusta, Me. She d. April 9, 1886,
   in Augusta, Me.; res. Augusta, Me.; two children:—
   1. Ione Gertrude, b. Aug. 30, 1876.
   2. James Blaine, b. July 23, 1880.

298.

(Stephen 4, Stephen 3, Stephen 2, Edmund 1.)

Children of **Joseph**[5] **Greenleaf** and Dorcas (Gray).
384. I. EBENEZER,[6] b. 1753; marriage intention filed, July 6,
   1774; m. July 12, 1775, at Pownalboro (Wiscasset),
   Me., Elizabeth Chapman, of Pownalboro, Me. He
   d. Aug. 15, 1817; eleven children.

JOSEPH (298) GREENLEAF, CONTINUED :—

385. II. JOHN,[6] b. Nov. 6, 1755, on Gewnky Neck, in Woolwich, or Wiscasset, Me. ; marriage intention filed, Dec.
24, 1781 ; m. Dec. 29, 1781, Anna Pierce Roberts,
of Wiscasset, Me., b. 1761 ; d. April 27, 1853. He
d. June 5, 1846 ; twelve children.

III. MARTHA, b. 1757; marriage intention filed Jan. 1,
1778 ; m. Peter Holbrook, of Pownalboro, Me. She d.
December, 1832 ; eight children,—five sons and three
daughters.

IV. SALLY, b. 1760; m. Benjamin Arnold. She d. June
6, 1816 ; ten children,—seven sons and three daughters.

V. RACHEL, b. April 7, 1763 ; m. Aug. 24, 1784, Luke
Sawyer, b. June 20, 1760, in Templeton, Mass. ; d.
April 8, 1841, in Starks, Me. She d. Oct. 6, 1852.
He was one of the earliest settlers in Starks ; eight
children,—four sons and four daughters.

386. VI. JOSHUA,[6] b. June 14, 1765, in Wiscasset, Me. ; m.
1790, Hannah Williamson, b. Sept. 14, 1770; d.
Nov. 1, 1859. He d. Sept. 29, 1856; res. Mercer,
Me. ; nine children.

387. VII. WILLIAM,[6] b. 1767; m. Sally Lander. He d. Sept.
16, 1817; ten children.

VIII. LYDIA, b. Aug. 12, 1770; m. Samuel Hinkley.
She d. January, 1853; ten children,—three sons and
seven daughters.

All of the above children of Joseph Greenleaf settled within the
space of six miles in Starks or Mercer on the Sandy River, in
Maine, and all brought up their families and died within that
space; none of them were ever married the second time.
Ebenezer and John moved to Sandy River, Feb. 11, 1782 (then
a wilderness), and the other brothers and sisters about the
same time or soon after. Ebenezer, John, and Joshua lived
and died on the farms they first settled on.

384.

(Joseph 5, Stephen 4, Stephen 3, Stephen 2, Edmund 1.)

Children of **Ebenezer**[6] **Greenleaf** and Elizabeth (Chapman).

388. I. JOSEPH,[7] b. Dec. 29, 1775 ; m. Nov. 28, 1798, Tamson Stover, of New Sharon, Me. He d. about 1816 ;
res. Industry Plantation, Me. ; six children.

Ebenezer (384) Greenleaf, Continued :—

389. II. Daniel,[7] b. Oct. 25, 1777; m. 1, Anna Young, of
Starks, Me. ; 2, Sophia Delano, of Woolwich, Me.
He d. Dec. 30, 1852 ; nine children.

III. Sarah, b. Oct. 1, 1779; m. Dec. 4, 1779, Lemuel,
son of Lemuel and Mercy Collins, b. Aug. 21, 1781 ;
d. July 31, 1851. She d. Feb. 13, 1853 ; res. New
Sharon, Me. ; fourteen children :—

    i. Eliza, b. March 25, 1801 ; m. Isaiah Higgins ; res. Rochester, N. H.
    ii. George, b. Feb. 21, 1803; m. Mary Ann Norcross.
    iii. Abigail, b. Nov. 15, 1804; m. 1, Thomas Beckett; 2, Edward Page.
    iv. Mahala, b. July 6, 1806; m. John L. Williamson.
    v. Sarah Greenleaf, b. April 21, 1808; m. Granville T. Beedle.
    vi. John Greenleaf, b. Dec. 31, 1809; m. Betsey Yeaton.
    vii. Henry Leeman, b. July 18, 1811 ; d. young; unmarried.
    viii. Belinda, b. June 10, 1813; m. Bartlett Benson.
    ix. Betsey, b. Oct. 18, 1815; d. 1829.
    x. Lemuel, b. Nov. 17, 1817; m. Betsey K. Fish.
    xi. Ann, b. Nov. 17, 1817; twin; m. 1, John S. Tolman; 2, Ezekiel Tolman, brothers.
    xii. Eben Greenleaf, b. July 15, 1819; m. 1, Cordelia A. Howes; 2, Lois J. Hersey.
    xiii. Lucy S., b. April 11, 1821; m. John N. Dutton.
    xiv. Betsey, b. Sept. 2, 1825; m. David Joy.

390. IV. John,[7] b. Oct. 6, 1781 ; m. Martha (Patty) Willard.
He d. Nov. 28, 1808 ; one child :—

Salome, b. about 1805 ; m. Samuel Odlin, Orono, Me.

V. Betsey, b. Nov. 30, 1784; m. Daniel Young.

VI. Dorcas, b. March 9, 1787; m. Nov. 3, 1808, John,
son of Lemuel and Mercy Collins, b. May 14, 1789;
d. March 4, 1875. She d. June 5, 1880; res. Starks,
Me. ; nine children :—

    i. Katherine, b. April 2, 1810; m. Abbot Doyen.
    ii. John Sullivan, b. July 5, 1811; m. 1, Sylvia Williamson; 2, Susan Jane Millay.
    iii. Ebenezer Greenleaf, b. April 22, 1813; d. about 1844; a physician; unmarried.
    iv. Mercy Howes, b. Sept. 25, 1815; m. Levi Young. She d. Dec. 19, 1889.
    v. James, b. Jan. 27, 1820; m. Christina C. Wallace. He d. about 1850.
    vi. Amy, b. June 14, 1822; m. Stephen D., son of Anthony and Nancy (Brown) Greenleaf (456); res. Starks, Me.; eight children.

EBENEZER (384) GREENLEAF, CONTINUED :—

VI. Dorcas.

   vii. Apphia Higgins, b. Dec. 29, 1824; m. Benniah P. Bradford.

   viii. Lydia Williamson, b. April 20, 1827; m. John Piper.

   ix. Daniel Garrin, b. April 27, 1830; m. Mary Ann, dau. of Anthony and Sarah (Perkins) Greenleaf (442).

391. VII. EBENEZER,[7] b. April 19, 1789; m. 1, Mary Chapman, who d. May 16, 1834; 2, Hannah Pressey. He d. Aug. 10, 1849; seven children.

VIII. AMY, b. June 9, 1791 ; m. Levi,[7] son of John[6] and Anna Pierce (Roberts) Greenleaf (443). She d. Nov. 7, 1870; eight children.

IX. ELI, b. June 25, 1793 ; d. about 1814 ; unmarried.

X. ANNA, b. July 9, 1796 ; m. —— Young ; d. about 1817.

XI. ASA, b. April 6, 1800; d. April 23, 1801.

388.

(Ebenezer 6, Joseph 5, Stephen 4, Stephen 3, Stephen 2, Edmund 1.)

Children of **Joseph**[7] **Greenleaf** and Tamson (Stover).

  I. MARY (Polly), b. 1801 ; m. Jan. 22, 1819, James, son of Lemuel and Mercy Collins, b. March 20, 1795 ; d. Nov. 6, 1873. She d. Oct. 23, 1881 ; res. New Sharon, Me. ; ten children :—

   i. Mary, b. 1820; d. 1822.

   ii. Simon, b. July 30, 1821; m. Martha Jane Paine.

   iii. Daniel, b. Dec. 6, 1823; d. about 1873; unmarried.

   iv. William Greenleaf, b. June 13, 1825; d. Sept. 5, 1847; unmarried.

   v. John, b. April 29, 1829; d. Sept. 28, 1854; unmarried.

   vi. Lemuel, b. Jan. 23, 1831; m. Mary Ann Buker.

   vii. Mary Jane, b. Feb. 22, 1835; m. Granville B. Williamson.

   viii. Orlando, b. March 31, 1837; m. 1, Mary R. Bruce; 2, Hattie Gilmore.

   ix. Harriet Adaline, b. May 9, 1840; m. Joseph Stevens.

   x. Amanda, b. Jan. 9, 1843; d. Dec. 12, 1864.

392. II. SIMON,[8] b. May 9, 1802; m. June 9, 1825, Betsey, dau. of Alvin and Mercy (Collins) Howes, b. July 24, 1806. He d. Nov. 15, 1866; res. New Sharon, Me. ; ten children.

393. III. JOHN,[8] b. 1806; m. Roxy (or Rozy) Bassett.

  IV. ADELINE, b. Nov. 7, 1809; m. William C., son of Daniel and Anna (Young) Greenleaf (404). She d. Nov. 25, 1865; res. New Sharon, Me. ; seven children.

Joseph (388) Greenleaf, Continued :—

> V. Fanny, b. 1811; m. Jan. 5, 1831, Daniel Collins, b. March 31, 1801, of Industry, Me. He d. Nov. 15, 1885. She res. Skowhegan, Me.; seven children :—
>
> > i. Charles, b. Dec. 20, 1831; d. July 12, 1855.
> > ii. Mary Pease, b. Dec. 24, 1833; m. Thomas Houghton.
> > iii. John Nelson, b. Jan. 10, 1836; m. Nannie W. Luce.
> > iv. Daniel, b. July 25, 1838; m. 1, Lorinda A. Sawtelle; 2, Abbie M. Learned.
> > v. Clarinda Malcolm, b. Aug. 14, 1840; m. Frank L. Houghton.
> > vi. Fannie, b. Aug. 21, 1844; m. J. Henry Dane.
> > vii. Clarissa Ann, b. Aug. 20, 1852; m. Richard Emmonds.

394. VI. Eli,[8] b. Jan. 12, 1815, in New Sharon, Me.; m. 1, Elizabeth Shaw Blake, of Epping, N. H., b. July 1, 1808; d. Dec. 24, 1851, in Monmouth, Me.; 2, Catherine Keene, of Sidney. He d. Feb. 27, 1877, in Monmouth, Me.; res. New Sharon, Me.; eight children.

Children by 1st marriage :—

> i. Mary Frances, b. Feb. 15, 1837, in Monmouth, Me.; m. Jan. 8, 1881, John Heath; was member of Co. E., 16th Regt. Maine Vols.; res. Hallowell, Me.; one child :—
> Linnie Elizabeth, b. July 30, 1882; d. Jan. 16, 1887.
> ii. Julia Adaline, b. June 16, 1839; res. Hallowell, Me.
> iii. Joseph Dearborn,[9] b. April 30, 1842, in Litchfield, Me.; d. Jan. 3, 1888, Topsham, Me.
> iv. Ellen Sophronia, b. Feb. 27, 1845, in Litchfield, Me.; d. Nov. 19, 1882, in Monmouth, Me.
> v. Sarah E., b. 1847, in Topsham; d. in infancy.
> vi. Agnes Jane, b. Oct. 29, 1849, in Topsham, Me.; d. 1867, in Wales, Me.

Children by 2d marriage :—

395. vii. Frank W.,[9] b. Sept. 18, 1858, in Monmouth; m. May 10, 1883, Julia F. Boyd; res. Monmouth, Me.; one child: Frank Girard, b. Oct. 9, 1891.

> viii. Annie May, b. in Monmouth; m. —— Stedman; res. Boston.

392.

(Joseph 7, Ebenezer 6, Joseph 5, Stephen 4, Stephen 3, Stephen 2, Edmund 1.)

Children of **Simon**[8] **Greenleaf** and Betsey (Howes).

396. I. John Wesley,[9] b. Sept. 24, 1827, in New Sharon, Me.; m. Helen Howes; eight children.

Simon (392) Greenleaf, Continued:—

II. Tamson Jane, b. March 11, 1829, in New Sharon, Me.; m. 1857, Harvey Knight; res. Norwich, Vt.; four children.

397. III. Rufus Stover,[9] b. Dec. 3, 1830, in New Sharon, Me.; m. Nov. 18, 1854, Mary A. Jordan, of Ripley, Me. He was killed March 29, 1856, in a railroad accident at Cambridge, Mass., where his widow now resides; they had one child, not now living.

398. IV. Alvin Howes,[9] b. Aug. 14, 1832, in New Sharon, Me.; m. Rhoda, dau. of Jacob Chandler. He d. Sept. 23, 1881; one child, d. in infancy.

V. Sarah George, b. Aug. 28, 1834, in New Sharon, Me.; m. 1857, Charles C. Brown, of Boothbay, Me.; res. Brooklyn, N. Y.; seven children.

399. VI. Simon,[9] b. Aug. 29, 1836, in New Sharon, Me.; m. Oct. 7, 1854, Elizabeth B., dau. of Daniel and Lydia C. (Smith) Trask, of New Sharon, Me.; holds the office of deputy sheriff; res. New Sharon, Me.; three children:—

   i. Leona E., b. Dec. 7, 1855.

   ii. Ella T., b. Jan. 19, 1857; m. May 16, 1876, George H. Brown, of New Sharon, Me.

   iii. ———.

VII. George Howes, b. Sept. 4, 1838; d. Aug. 10, 1864.

VIII. Charles Smith, b. Oct. 24, 1843, in New Sharon, Me.; d. April 5, 1846.

IX. Emily Lydia, b. May 12, 1848, in New Sharon, Me; m. Jan. 6, 1869, James W., son of Benjamin and Abigail (Tuttle) Smith, of New Sharon, Me.; res. New Sharon, Me.; two children.

X. Mary Helen, b. Aug. 4, 1850, in New Sharon, Me.; m. Oct. 5, 1874, Alfred L., son of William and Sarah (Hodgdon) Bruce; res. Bath, Me.; four children.

389.

(Ebenezer 6, Joseph 5, Stephen 4, Stephen 3, Stephen 2, Edmund 1.)

Children of **Daniel**[7] **Greenleaf** and Anna (Young).

400. I. Levi,[8] b. July 29, 1799; m. Jane Pomeroy. He d. Dec. 28, 1832; one child:—

Alpheus S., b. Jan. 5, 1832; d. in Belgrade, Me.

DANIEL (389) GREENLEAF, CONTINUED :—

401. II. JONATHAN Y.,[8] b. April 16, 1802, in Starks, Me. ;
m. 1, March 9, 1825, Celestia Sears, who d. July 24,
1842 ; 2, Jan. 7, 1844, Hannah Bugbee, who d.
March, 1889. He removed from Starks to Amity,
Me., and settled there in 1826, being one of the first
three settlers there. He d. Sept. 16, 1869, in Amity,
Me. ; res. Amity, Me. ; fourteen children.

III. MELINDA Y., b. April 26, 1804 ; m. 1, Jeremiah
Goodwin, who d. in Augusta, Me. ; 2, John Safford.
She d. in Augusta, Me.

402. IV. THOMAS Y.,[8] b. June 3, 1806 ; m. March 4, 1829,
Eunice, dau. of Peleg Bradford, Esq., a prominent
citizen of Starks, Me., b. August, 1809 ; d. Aug. 20,
1894, at Kahoka, Mo. He moved to Clark County,
Mo., in 1848 ; res. Farmington, Iowa ; twelve children.

403. V. ASA,[8] b. May 19, 1808 ; m. Mary Stephens. He d.
about 1840, near Hallowell, Me. She afterwards m.
Isaac Snow, of Augusta, Me. ; two children :—

   I. Asa, d. in Winthrop, Me.

   II. Silas, killed in Salt Lake City, Utah, while sitting in
a courtroom.

404. VI. WILLIAM C.,[8] b. Feb. 20, 1811, m. 1, 1830, Adeline, dau. of Joseph[7] and Tamson (Stover) Greenleaf
(388), b. Nov. 7, 1809 ; d. Nov. 25, 1865 ; 2, Mary
Ann Taylor, of Augusta, Me. ; res. New Sharon,
Me. ; seven children.

VII. REUBEN H., b. 1813 ; d. Nov. 2, 1895, at Charlestown, Mass., aged 81 years 10 months.

405. VIII. ELI F.,[8] b. July 12, 1816 ; m. 1, Mary E. McIntire ; 2, Lucy A. Sweet. Physician. He d. April
28, 1883 ; sixteen children.

406. IX. CHARLES S.,[8] b. March 1, 1823 ; m. Nov. 5, 1846, in
Readfield, Me., Harriet H., dau. of John Williams, of
Woolwich, Me. He d. Feb. 20, 1895, in Augusta,
Me. ; merchant ; res. Augusta, Me. ; three children.

401.

(Daniel 7, Ebenezer 6, Joseph 5, Stephen 4, Stephen 3, Stephen 2, Edmund 1.)

Children of **Jonathan Y.**[8] **Greenleaf** and Celestia (Sears).

407. I. DANIEL,[9] b. May 26, 1826 ; m. 1, 1847, Martha J.
Betts, of Amity, Me. ; d. March 1, 1856 ; 2, Dec. 14,

JONATHAN Y. (401) GREENLEAF, CONTINUED:—
  I. Daniel.
      1858, Sylvia E., dau. of Theodore Wilder, of Pem-
      broke, Me. He d. Sept. 13, 1889; res. Washburn,
      Me.; eleven children.
  II. MALINDA, m. Alexander McDougall, of Kirkland,
      Carlton Co., N. B.; res. Washburn, Me.
  III. ASA, b. 1828; d. Jan. 17, 1848.
408. IV. CHARLES L.,[9] b. 1830; m. Jan. 17, 1857, Susanna
      A., dau. of Theodore Wilder, of Pembroke, Me. He
      d. Jan. 13, 1890; nine children.
  V. MARIA, m. William Knight.
  VI. SARAH, m. Charles Schofield.
409. VII. BENJAMIN W.,[9] b. July 4, 1840; m. Marcia A.
      Churchill, of Starks, Me.; res. Starks, Me.; removed
      from Aroostook Co. to Starks in 1860; five children:—
        I. Celestia S., b. June 12, 1865; d. Nov. 22, 1880.
        II. Eveline, b. Nov. 7, 1867; m. Nov. 2, 1889, Caleb Wade[9]
          (466), son of Cyrus and Susan Greenleaf (465).
        III. Thankful M., b. March 25, 1869.
        IV. Jonathan Sanford, b. June 24, 1871.
        V. Benjamin Charles, b. May 9, 1873.
  Children by 2d marriage:—
  VIII. HARRIET, b. March 1, 1845; m. George Daggett.
410. IX. THOMAS,[9] b. May 11, 1846; m. Annie Hall; d.
      1870; res. Amity, Me.; no children.
  X. CELESTIA, b. March 1, 1849; d. Dec. 1, 1853.
411. XI. JOHN B.,[9] b. Feb. 16, 1852; m. June 20, 1877,
      Amelia N. Gidney, of Amity, Me.; postmaster; res.
      Amity, Me.; seven children:—
        I. Clarence M., b. Sept. 10, 1878.
        II. Mattie M., b. July 5, 1880.
        III. Nettie S., b. Aug. 25, 1882.
        IV. Hannah B., b. Dec. 18, 1884.
        V. Mildred C., b. April 2, 1887.
        VI. Grace A., b. July 4, 1889.
        VII. Don A., b. March 17, 1892.
  XII. WILLIAM, b. Jan., 1854; d. young.
  XIII. GEORGE, b. Feb., 1858; d. July 25, 1859.
  XIV. ANNIE, b. 1861; d. young.

407.

(Jonathan Y. 8, Daniel 7, Ebenezer 6, Joseph 5, Stephen 4, Stephen 3, Stephen 2, Edmund 1.)

Children of **Daniel**[9] **Greenleaf** and Martha J. (Betts).

    I. CAROLINE A., b. May 8, 1849; m. Abner Harris, formerly of Houlton, Me., now of Ossipee, N. H.

    II. JUDITH A., b. Feb. 22, 1852; m. Feb. 21, 1879, William Bickford, of Caribou, Me.

412.   III. MELVIN A.,[10] b. Jan. 24, 1854; m. Aug. 11, 1878, Lunette Story, of Washburn, Me.; res. Washburn, Me.

Children by 2d marriage :—

413.   IV. WALTER V.,[10] b. April 19, 1860, in Washburn, Me.; m. March 5, 1881, Alice, dau. of James F. Thompson, of East Pittston, Me., b. Feb. 9, 1866. He d. May 19, 1894; res. Gardiner, Me.; three children :—

        I. Perley M., b. July 24, 1882.

        II. Ruby, b. Aug. 20, 1884.

        III. Ellie J., b. Aug. 6, 1886.

    V. MATTIE J., b. Oct. 4, 1861; m. Nov. 25, 1880, Wellington Blair, So. Gardiner, Me.; res. Gardiner, Me.; one child :—

    Winnefred May, b. March 6, 1884.

    VI. LUCY M., b. Dec. 9, 1863; m. Willis C. Ireland, Fairfield, Me.

414.   VII. LINCOLN E.,[10] b. June 6, 1866, in Washburn, Me.; m. Aug. 8, 1889, Flora, dau. of Elias Douglass, of Chelsea, Me. She d. April, 1894; one child :—

    Guy Lewis, b. Oct. 21, 1893.

    VIII. CELESTIA A., b. Dec. 29, 1871; m. Philip S. Durgin, Washburn, Me.

    IX. JOHN T., b. Feb. 1, 1877.

    X. LEON A., b. Sept. 20, 1879.

    XI. LINWOOD E., b. Sept. 10, 1882.

408.

(Jonathan Y. 8, Daniel 7, Ebenezer 6, Joseph 5, Stephen 4, Stephen 3, Stephen 2, Edmund 1.)

Children of **Charles L.**[9] **Greenleaf** and Susanna A. (Wilder).

    I. BENJAMIN A.,[10] b. June 23, 1858; m. June 4, 1890; res. Royalton, Minn.

    II. CHARLES S., b. July 6, 1860; d. Dec. 24, 1877.

Charles L. (408) Greenleaf, Continued:—

415. III. Clarence L.,[10] b. July 6, 1860; twin; m. in Washburn, Me., May 22, 1887, Huldah, dau. of William Raven, of Woodland, Me., b. 1868; d. May 14, 1894; res. Washburn, Me.; three children :—

  i. Lulu Blanche, b. Oct. 7, 1887; d. May 10, 1888.
  ii. Charles E., b. April 19, 1889; d. Nov. 20, 1891.
  iii. Fred. B., b. Nov. 14, 1892.

IV. Hattie C., b. Oct. 17, 1862; m. Jan. 1, 1880, George E. Easler, of Washburn, Me.

V. Etta M., b. Oct. 11, 1864; m. Dec. 25, 1882, Hanniford Carr, of Perham, Me.

VI. Ida F., b. Aug. 14, 1866; d. Dec. 8, 1877.

VII. Lillie A., b. Dec. 13, 1868; d. Dec. 11, 1877.

VIII. Sadie S., b. Feb. 13, 1870; d. Dec. 9, 1877.

IX. Mabel P., b. Nov. 10, 1874; d. Dec. 10, 1877.

402.

(Daniel 7, Ebenezer 6, Joseph 5, Stephen 4, Stephen 3, Stephen 2, Edmund 1.)

Children of **Thomas Y.**[8] **Greenleaf** and Eunice (Bradford).

416. I. Bradford Peleg,[9] b. Nov. 9, 1830, in Somerset County, Me.; m. Oct. 22, 1852, Caroline, dau. of Andrew and Nancy Meredith, of Indiana. He d. April 25, 1895. Mr. Greenleaf moved with his parents to Clark County, Mo., in 1848; removed later to Kahoka, Mo., where he died; six children.

II. Melinda, b. June 13, 1832; m. in Clark County, Mo., June, 1849, John Keyes Field, of Warren, Mass., who d. Aug. 15, 1850, aged 27 years. She d. Nov. 10, 1852; res. St. Louis, Mo.

III. Thomas Warren, b. June 14, 1834; res. Avert, Stoddard Co., Mo.

IV. Lucy Bradford, b. Dec. 23, 1836; m. 1, Aug. 10, 1856, Luther F. McNeal, of New York. He d. Dec. 19, 1863, from wounds received while serving in the Union Army, Civil War; 2, Sept. |4, 1867, C. A. Baldwin, of New York; res. Grand Island, Neb.

Children by 1st marriage :—
  i. Nora, b. May 30, 1857; d. June 12, 1862.
  ii. William W., b. Dec. 19, 1859; d. Aug. 30, 1863.
  iii. Almeda J., b. June 6, 1861; d. March 21, 1862.

THOMAS Y. (402) GREENLEAF, CONTINUED :—
IV. Lucy Bradford.
Children by 2d marriage :—
    iv. Frank L., b. Sept. 27, 1868.
    v. Fred G., b. March 25, 1873.
    vi. Myrtle M., b. May 1, 1880.

417. V. BENIAH BRADFORD,[9] b. Nov. 1, 1838; m. Aug. 25, 1860, Joanna Curts, of Alexandria, Mo.; res. Santa Ana, California; nine children :—
    I. Nellie Jane, b. Sept. 7, 1861; m. May 5, 1880, Charles Lambie.
    II. Allie May, b. June 27, 1863; m. Dec. 14, 1884, J. H. Cross.
    III. Laura Ann, b. Sept. 21, 1865; m. Oct. 13, 1886, Charles L. Norman.
    IV. Lutie Bell, b. Oct. 17, 1867; m. March 27, 1886, Gilbert T. Sewell.
    V. Lula Lee, b. Aug. 7, 1869; m. April 13, 1887, O. A. Upson.
    VI. Charles Thomas, b. June 8, 1871.
    VII. Lillie Eudora, b. March 16, 1873; d. Sept. 3, 1874.
    VIII. Marietta, b. March 19, 1875; m. April 28, 1892, W. H. Norman.
    IX. Hattie Mabel, b. March 19, 1877; d. Feb. 23, 1887.

VI. ARABELLA, b. Jan. 28, 1840; m. 1, March 8, 1858, Isaac Bunch. He was killed at the battle of Pittsburg, while serving in the Union Army, Civil War; 2, Dec. 3, 1863, Thomas B. Nelson; res. Farmington, Iowa.
Children by 1st marriage :—
    i. Eller N., b. Feb. 5, 1859; d. Aug. 23, 1886.
    ii. Frank, b. Dec. 6, 1860.
Children by 2d marriage :—
    iii. Mary E., b. Nov. 11, 1864.
    iv. Martha A., b. Aug. 27, 1866; d. April 22, 1886.
    v. William W., b. July 9, 1868.
    vi. Rosal, b. July 12, 1873.
    vii. Thomas Y., b. July 6, 1875.
    viii. Birdie E., b. Nov. 7, 1877.

418. VII. ALONZO M.,[9] b. March 24, 1844; m. 1, Nov., 1869, Martha Hires; 2, Dec. 27, 1876, Mary Hobson; res. Farmington, Iowa.

THOMAS Y. (402) GREENLEAF, CONTINUED :—
VII. Alonzo M.
Child by 1st marriage :—
    I. William, b. Aug. 12, 1872.
Children by 2d marriage :—
    II. Albert, b. Sept. 22, 1878.
    III. Carrie Ethel, b. May 2, 1880.
    IV. John O., b. Nov. 5, 1881.
    V. Walter F., b. Sept., 1885 ; d. April 20, 1889.
    VI. Grace M., b. Aug. 8, 1888 ; d. April 27, 1889.
VIII. HARRIET MELISSA, b. May 26, 1846.
IX. MARTHA ANN, b. Aug. 4, 1848; m. March 31,
    1867, Charles W. Sherrick ; res. Keosauqua, Iowa ;
    seven children :—
    i. Albert, b. March 8, 1869.
    ii. John, b. Sept. 23, 1874; d. April 23, 1875.
    iii. Otto, b. July 2, 1876.
    iv. Norah, b. Sept. 10, 1879.
    v. Guy, b. Oct. 27, 1881.
    vi. Charles, b. Dec. 28, 1885.
    vii. Lula D., b. Dec. 11, 1892.
X. JOSEPHINE, b. June 13, 1850.
XI. MARIETTA, b. March 31, 1853.
XII. ALBERT J., b. April 30, 1855 ; d. 1861.

416.

(Thomas Y. 8, Daniel 7, Ebenezer 6, Joseph 5, Stephen 4, Stephen 3, Stephen 2, Edmund 1.)

Children of **Bradford Peleg**[9] **Greenleaf** and Caroline
(Merideth).

419. I. FRANKLIN P.,[10] b. Sept. 10, 1853 ; m. Nov. 11, 1875,
    Mary McWorter; res. Clark Co., Mo. ; three chil-
    dren :—
    I. Bradford, b. Dec. 23, 1876.
    II. Dee, b. May 20, 1881.
    III. Stella, b. April 11, 1885 ; d. April 6, 1889.
420. II. THOMAS A.,[10] b. May 20, 1855 ; m. 1882, Eugenie
    Edwards, of New York; res. San Luis Obispo, Cal. ;
    no children.
    III. JOHN J., b. Sept. 2, 1857 ; d. Sept. 3, 1858.
421. IV. LEVI M.,[10] b. June 28, 1859; m. 1, Aug. 4, 1878,
    Rebecca J. Fine; d. June 15, 1890; 2, April 6, 1892,
    Laura Bell Hays; res. Kahoka, Clark Co., Mo.

BRADFORD PELEG (416) GREENLEAF, CONTINUED :—
  IV. Levi M.
    Children by 1st marriage :—
        I. Elmer, b. Sept. 5, 1882.
        II. Edson L., b. Oct. 20, 1885.
        III. Harry, b. Nov. 23, 1889.
  V. MARY SCOTT, b. Aug. 22, 1862; m. Dec. 3, 1884,
        Edward L. Weaver; d. March 20, 1892; one child :—
      Emma, b. Jan. 25, 1889.
422. VI. WILLIAM HENRY,[10] b. Oct. 26, 1866; m. May 22,
        1889, Nina Dinsmore, of Iowa; res. Trenton, Mo.;
        two children :—
        I. Nina Marguerite, b. Sept. 21, 1890; d. July 24,
            1894, at Trenton, Mo.; buried at Fort Madison,
            Iowa, July 26, 1894.
        II. Lucilla, b. Feb. 19, 1893.

404.

(Daniel 7, Ebenezer 6, Joseph 5, Stephen 4, Stephen 3, Stephen 2, Edmund 1.)
Children of **William C.**[8] **Greenleaf** and Adeline.
  I. CHARLES L., b. Nov. 2, 1831; d. 1833.
423. II. ELI W.,[9] b. Aug. 14, 1834; m. Nov. 19, 1857, Harriet
        L., dau. of Levi[7] and Amy (443) Greenleaf, b. Oct.
        25, 1830; res. New Sharon, Me.; five children :—
424.   I. William L.,[9] b. Jan. 11, 1859; m. 1, Nov. 19, 1889,
            Clara E. Dyer, who d. Nov. 15, 1890; 2, June 5,
            1892, Cora E. Paine, of Jay, Me.; res. Jay, Me.
425.   II. Daniel E.,[9] b. Feb. 16, 1861; m. Jan. 26, 1890,
            Florence Lillian, dau. of Wilbert White, of Hal-
            lowell, Me.; res. Gardiner, Me.
426.   III. Elmer E.,[9] b. Sept. 9, 1863; m. May 7, 1887, Izzie
            M. Whitehouse, of Belgrade, Me.; res. Roslin-
            dale, Mass.; two children: I. M. Lillian, b.
            March 23, 1888. 2. Carlos W., b. Sept. 18,
            1892.
427.   IV. Eli Seymour,[9] b. June 5, 1868; m. Feb. 3, 1892,
            Mary Agnes, dau. of Benj. Berry, of Litchfield,
            Me.; res. Gardiner, Me.
        V. Amy B., b. Aug. 18, 1871; res. New Sharon, Me.
  III. MERCY JENNIE, b. Sept. 28, 1837; m. John G.
        Powers, of Wilton, Me.; res. New Sharon, Me.

WILLIAM C. (404) GREENLEAF, CONTINUED :—

IV. ROSINA ANN YOUNG, b. Sept. 18, 1841 ; m. Eleazer S.[8] Greenleaf (507), son of Gason[7] and Nancy (Joy) Greenleaf (506), of Sharon, Mass. She d. August, 1863 ; res. Dedham, Mass.

V. SARAH E., b. Oct. 16, 1846; m. Cornelius Norton, of Industry, Me. She d. Aug. 22, 1871.

VI. CHARLES, b. Jan. 16, 1849; d. January 12, 1851.

VII. ALICE V., b. May 18, 1852 ; m. George W. Flood, of Monmouth, Me. ; res. Farmington, Me.

405.

(Daniel 7, Ebenezer 6, Joseph 5, Stephen 4, Stephen 3, Stephen 2, Edmund 1.)

Children of **Dr. Eli F.**[8] **Greenleaf** and Mary C. (McIntire).

I. VIRGINIA, b. Nov. 24, 1839; d. ——.

428. II. EDWARD FRANKLIN,[9] b. Nov. 22, 1841 ; m. at Hollister, San Benito Co., Cal., Fannie S. Moore; physician ; res. Santa Ana, Cal. ; four children :—

  I. Walter Frank, b. March 12, 1878.

  II. Mary, b. Aug. 18, 1879 ; d. in infancy.

  III. Elvin Johnston, b. Oct. 7, 1882.

  IV. Clifford Augustus, b. March 31, 1891.

III. ISABELLA C., b. Sept. 16, 1843.

IV. MARY H., b. May 20, 1846; m. J. E. Shurard.

V. VIRGINIA J., b. April 20, 1848.

VI. ANA, b. May 18, 1850; m. Jeff. Welsh, in Colorado.

Children by 2d marriage :—

429. VII. J. EDGAR,[9] b. Aug. 5, 1855; m. Lottie Brown. He d. May 3, 1883.

VIII. AUGUSTUS, b. Dec. 31, 1856; d. Aug. 3, 1880.

430. IX. MELVILLE,[9] b. Jan. 7, 1858; m. Clara Parton; four children :—

  I. Edna.

  II. Alice.

  III. Jone; twin.

  IV. Melville.

X. ROBERT LEE, b. Dec. 12, 1860.

431. XI. STERLING G.,[9] b. March 5, 1863 ; m. Amanda Daw; two children :—

  I. Mignon.

  II. Hazel.

Dr. Eli F. (405) Greenleaf, Continued :—

XII. Walter S., b. Sept. 25, 1865.
XIII. Sue M., b. Aug. 27, 1867.
XIV. Kate, b. Sept. 17, 1869.
XV. Charles B., b. April 22, 1875 ; d. Dec. 25, 1875.
XVI. Fannie Grace, b. May 30, 1878.

406.

(Daniel 7, Ebenezer 6, Joseph 5, Stephen 4, Stephen 3, Stephen 2, Edmund 1.)

Children of **Charles S.**[8] **Greenleaf** and Harriet H. (Williams).

432. I. Charles Hollis,[9] b. Sept. 4, 1847, in Augusta, Me. ; m. June 15, 1872, Etta Adelia, dau. of Jeremiah F. and Julia Ann Waugh, of Gardiner, Me., formerly of Starks, b. Aug. 20, 1853, in Starks, Me. ; d. Dec. 14, 1883, in Augusta, Me. Mr. Greenleaf was educated at Bowdoin Medical College, and graduated there in the class of 1870 ; res. Augusta, Me. ; two children :—

   i. Lottie M., b. March 20, 1873 ; unmarried.
   ii. William Everett,[10] b. July 15, 1876.

After the death of his mother he went to Madison, Me., and lived in the family of George W. Ladd until July, 1895, when he moved to Portland, and is now in the employ of the Maine Central R. R. Co. He is known as Willie Ladd.

II. Isadore Grace, b. Oct. 23, 1852 ; m. A. W. Kimball ; res. Gardiner, Me.

III. Minnie Maud, b. June 18, 1862.

391.

(Ebenezer 6, Joseph 5, Stephen 4, Stephen 3, Stephen 2, Edmund 1.)

Children of **Ebenezer**[7] **Greenleaf** and Mary (Chapman).

433. I. Horatio Nelson,[8] b. Aug. 12, 1820 ; m. March 14, 1843, Hannah S. Cook, of Starks, Me. He d. Jan. 14, 1896 ; res. Allens Mills, Me. ; six children :—

   i. Walter N., b. May 12, 1850.
   ii. Mary J., b. Aug. 13, 1852 ; m. December, 1867, Henry T. Allen.
   iii. Annie H., b. June 29, 1853 ; m. 1. Albert W. Scootz ; 2, William A. Purdy ; res. Boston, Mass.
   iv. A dau., b. Nov. 20, 1856 ; m. Nov. 14, 1878, Cyrus F. Wilson.

EBENEZER (391) GREENLEAF, CONTINUED :—
I. Horatio Nelson.
433a. v. Franklin J.,[9] b. May 25, 1858; m. March 13, 1896, Mrs. Mahalah Frederick, of Industry, Me.
    VI. Horatio N., b. Oct. 30, 1863; d. April 17, 1866.
II. JUSTIN, b. Aug. 27, 1822; d. May 19, 1859. He was blind.
434. III. THOMAS SELDEN,[8] b. April 22, 1825, at Starks, Me.; m. Nov. 9, 1848, Julia A., dau. of George and Mary Ann (Norcross) Collins, b. June 22, 1828. He d. Dec. 20, 1889, in New Hampshire; res. Stark, N. H.; eight children.
435. IV. JOHN NEWELL,[8] b. Oct. 14, 1827; m. Nov. 29, 1849, Rebecca Jane Pomeroy. He d. Dec. 21, 1871; res. New Sharon, Me.; five children :—
    I. Lisbon Eugene, b. Feb. 15, 1851; d. July 7, 1875.
    II. Sarah C., b. Oct. 12, 1853; m. Feb. 5, 1874, James F. Arnold. She d. June 18, 1879; res. Farmington Falls, Me.; one child :—
A son.
    III. Mary E., b. Oct. 13, 1855; d. Sept. 27, 1874.
    IV. Etta J., b. March 14, 1860; d. Oct. 12, 1879.
    v. Jennie H., b. Aug. 1, 1864; m. Sept. 15, 1881, Joseph Madrue.
V. MARY HANNAH, b. Dec. 23, 1836; m. Timothy Oliver, of Bath, Me.; res. Bath, Me.; two children :—
    i. Ebenezer, Jr., married.
    ii. Hannah Pressy.
VI. LOUISA JANE, b. Jan. 22, 1838; d. March 10, 1842.
436. VII. CHARLES DEXTER,[8] b. Sept. 24, 1840; m. 1861, Martha A., dau. of Asa and Patience Quimby, of Starks, Me.

434.

(Ebenezer 7, Ebenezer 6, Joseph 5, Stephen 4, Stephen 3, Stephen 2, Edmund 1.)

Children of **Thomas Selden**[8] **Greenleaf** and Julia A. (Collins).
I. GEORGE EBEN, b. Sept. 9, 1849, at Starks, Me.; d. Sept. 25, 1857.
437. II. THOMAS ADELBERT,[9] b. Dec. 4, 1854, at Georgetown, Me.; m. Oct. 24, 1888, Emma M. Hinds, of

THOMAS SELDEN (434) GREENLEAF, CONTINUED :—

  II. Thomas Adelbert.

    Townsend, Mass., b. Jan. 21, 1860; res. Brookline,
    N. H.; one child :—

    Elsie Mae, b. Sept. 22, 1889.

438. III. ALVAH JOSIAH,[9] b. Oct. 9, 1857, at Farmingdale,
    Me.; m. 1, Dec. 25, 1880, Elvira Miles, who died
    Sept. 18, 1885, aged 21 years, 5 months, 4 days; 2,
    Aug. 26 or 27, 1893, Ella F. Severance, b. 1859, in
    Townsend, Mass.; res. Townsend, Mass.; one child
    by 1st marriage :—

    Alvah, b. Dec., 1881; d. in infancy.

439. IV. CHARLES HENRY,[9] b. June 16, 1860, at New Sharon,
    Me.; m. July 28, 1881, Almira Farwell, of Stark,
    N. H., b. Sept. 27, 1864; two children :—

    I. Maud G., b. June 25, 1882, at Stark, N. H.

    II. Roland C., b. Dec. 31, 1885; d. Aug. 9, 1887.

440. V. EBEN SELDEN,[9] b. July 15, 1862, at New Sharon,
    Me.; m. 1888, Annie Grover, of Lynn, Mass., b.
    Aug. 18, 1860; one child :—

    William E., b. July 16, 1890.

  VI. MAUD DELLA J., b. Dec. 30, 1865, at New Sharon, Me.;
    m. June 22, 1884, Patrick Fitzgerald; one child :—

    Florence, b. Aug. 7, 1885.

  VII. GEORGE HORATIO, b. Dec. 31, 1871, at New
    Sharon, Me.

  VIII. ERNEST H. (or Elmer), b. Jan. 31, 1875; d.
    March, 1878.

385.

(Joseph 5, Stephen 4, Stephen 3, Stephen 2, Edmund 1.)

Children of **John**[6] **Greenleaf** and Anna Pierce (Roberts).

441. I. JOHN,[7] b. Oct. 12, 1782, in Starks, Me.; m. Martha
    (Patty), dau. of Luke Sawyer, of Starks, Me. (298),
    b. 1788; d. Feb. 2, 1868. He d. June 5, 1854, in
    Holliston, Mass. He was captain in militia of Maine
    from Starks; nine children.

  II. SARAH (Sally), b. July 10, 1784; m. 1806, Asa Brown;
    d. July 5, 1835. She d. Sept. 11, 1843; ten children :—

    i. Anna, b. December, 1807; m. 1822, Sewell Lovell. She d. 1845.

    ii. Martha, b. May, 1809; m. 1835, James Trask, of New Sharon,
     Me. She d. 1847.

JOHN (385) GREENLEAF, CONTINUED :—

    II. Sarah (Sally).

        iii. Ephraim, b. Aug. 24, 1811; m. 1831, Sylvia Fish. He d. Aug. 27, 1875.

        iv. Ann G., b. December, 1813; m. 1854, Rufus Weymouth, of New Sharon, Me. She d. 1875.

        v. Asa, b. Jan. 23, 1816; m. 1836, Harriet Trask, of New Sharon, Me. He d. 1874; res. Farmington, Me.; children: Theodore F., now a resident of California, and several daughters, one of whom is Mrs. John H. Grant, of Portland, Me.

        vi. John Greenleaf, b. June 23, 1818; m. May 30, 1843, Mary Boardman, dau. of Francis and Mary (Boardman) Remick, b. April 27, 1824, in Industry, Me. Mr. Brown was born and resided in Starks many years. He was a teacher in younger days, farmer, held town offices, Register of Probate of Franklin County, etc. He moved to Illinois in 1865, returned to Maine in 1866, settled on a farm in New Sharon in 1869, and moved to Farmington, Me. in 1875, and has since then resided there; four children: 1. Leonard Boardman, b. Feb. 25, 1844; m. Nettie A., dau. of Isaac and Nancy (Smith) Higgins, of Starks, Me.; one child: Harry B. (Capt.); m. May Gertrude Coombs, of Concord, N. H.; one child: Gladys A., b. June 22, 1890. L. B. Brown was a teacher, studied law with Hon. E. F. Pillsbury; was editor of Farmington, Me., *Franklin Patriot*, afterwards of *Maine Standard;* went to Concord, N. H., from Augusta, Me., in 1874; was editor of Concord *People and Patriot* several years; has been employed by Boston *Globe, Herald, New York Herald*, etc. He has held an office in Custom House, Naval Department, Boston; res. Dover, N. H. 2. Rose Ellen, b. Oct. 13, 1848; m. Aug. 25, 1864, Asa S., son of Earl and Lydia (Snell) Duley, of Starks, Me.; five children: two daughters and three sons. 3. Flora A., b. June 27, 1852; m. May 24, 1871, David Jordan, of New Sharon. 4. John Herbert, b. Feb. 15, 1858; d. Nov. 3, 1872.

        vii. Cyrus Greenleaf, b. August, 1820; m. May 11, 1848, Almira, dau. of Geo. and Olive (Winslow) Hobbs, of New Sharon, Me., b. Nov. 11, 1824, in Industry, Me.; d. April 1, 1859. He d. March, 1871; three children: 1. George H. 2. Asa. 3. Elmira.

        viii. Rosalind Greenleaf, b. September, 1822; m. 1849, William F. Brown. She d. 1873.

        ix. Levi Greenleaf, b. July 15, 1825; d. July 16, 1838.

        x. Sarah Greenleaf, b. December, 1829; d. June 1, 1851; unmarried.

442. III. ANTHONY,[7] b. June 3, 1786; m. 1810, 1, Nancy Brown, b. January, 1788; d. April 8, 1824; 2, Sept. 29, 1827, Sally Perkins. He d. Jan. 9, 1869; res. Starks, Me.; nine children.

JOHN (385) GREENLEAF, CONTINUED :—

443. IV. LEVI,[7] b. Aug. 22, 1788 ; m. about 1813, Amy, dau.
of Ebenezer[6] and Elizabeth (Chapman) Greenleaf
(384), b. June 9, 1791. He d. May 30, 1875 ; res.
Starks., Me. ; eight children.

444. V. JOSEPH,[7] b. March 10, 1790; m. Rhoda, dau. of Peter
and Martha (Greenleaf) Holbrook (298). She d. March
16, 1875. He d. Feb. 17, 1848 ; eleven children.

445. VI. WILLIAM,[7] b. March 17, 1792 ; m. Rosalind Bryant
Merrill, of Damariscotta, Me. He owned and lived
on Squirrel Island, near Boothbay, Me., where he d.
May 4, 1868 ; five children.

446. VII. STEPHEN,[7] b. Aug. 26, 1794 ; m. 1, 1819, Rhoda,
dau. of William Metcalf, of Anson, Me., who d.
July 27, 1823 ; 2, May 6, 1826, Fanny, dau. of Robert and Lydia (Williamson) Taylor, of Starks, Me.,
b. Feb. 16, 1805; d. Feb. 12, 1895. He d. Oct. 15,
1881 ; res. Starks, Me. ; ten children.

447. VIII. GEORGE,[7] b. Jan. 27, 1797 ; m. Helena Hinkley,
of Mercer, Me. He moved to Waterloo, Clark Co.,
Mo., in 1849, and d. there 1869 ; seven children :—

  I. Eric Hinkley, b. Jan. 13, 1827, in Starks, Me. ; d.
1863, in Holley Springs, Mo.

  II. Isaac Newton, b. May 20, 1831 ; d. March 23, 1849,
in Starks, Me.

  III. Ruby Jane, b. Nov. 20, 1832.

  IV. Samuel, b. April 5, 1836.

  V. Simon, b. Dec. 7, 1837; in Starks, Me.; res. in
Waterloo, Mo., also Paradise City, Cal., in 1864.

  VI. Baldwin, b. Nov. 27, 1839; d. Oct. 11, 1851, in
Waterloo, Clark Co., Mo.

  VII. Elihu, b. March 23, 1843 ; d. May 26, 1850, in
Waterloo, Mo. ; drowned.

  IX. CYRUS, b. Feb. 14, 1799 ; d. May 22, 1820 ; unmarried.

448. X. JOSHUA,[7] b. March 23, 1801 ; m. Asenath, dau. of Luke
and Rachel (Greenleaf) Sawyer (298). She first
married a Mr. Robinson. She d. Feb. 13, 1889. He
d. Jan. 18, 1866 ; res. Starks, Me. ; seven children.

  XI. RACHEL, b. Aug. 14, 1803 ; m. Imri, son of Luke
and Rachel (Greenleaf) Sawyer (298), b. Aug. 15,

JOHN (385) GREENLEAF, CONTINUED :—

XI. Rachel.

1799; d. Aug. 1, 1886. She d. Jan. 26, 1891; res. Starks, Me.; twelve children :—

i. Keturah, b. March 14, 1823; m. Dec. 28, 1847, Gideon A. Gilman, of Augusta, Me.; res. Augusta; five children : 1. Albert 2. Harriet. 3. Harry. 4. Eliza. 5. Emma.

ii. Rose A., b. Oct. 21, 1824; d. Sept. 8, 1847; unmarried.

iii. Elmira Varnum, b. July 4, 1826; d. Oct. 8, 1849; unmarried.

iv. Rachel, b. Sept. 28, 1828; m. Aug. 16, 1844, Warren Gray, of Starks, Me.

v. Luke G., b. Dec. 6, 1830; m. September, 1860, Alice McKenney; res. Madison, Me.; one child : a son.

vi. John Greenleaf, b. Jan. 31, 1833; d. Jan. 19, 1894; unmarried.

vii. Stephen Greenleaf, b. Feb. 14, 1835; m. May 15, 1867, Joan Furbish, of Anson, Me. He d. Feb. 5, 1894, at Starks, Me.

viii. Fanny Greenleaf, b. March 28, 1837; m. April 7, 1854, Almon Sawyer, of Madison, Me. She d. Aug. 20, 1893; res. Madison, Me.; children : Dr. W. G. Sawyer and others.

ix. Jophanus H., b. March 25, 1839; d. Jan. 22, 1862; unmarried.

x. Vesta A., b. April 27, 1842; m. 1, March 31, 1861, Josiah Bacon, of Madison, Me.; 2, Nov. 7, 1868, James Sawyer, of Madison, Me. She d. Aug. 4, 1895; res. Madison, Me.

xi. Anthony Greenleaf, b. March 21, 1844; m. Aug. 21, 1878, Ella M. Taylor; farmer and selectman; res. Starks, Me.

xii. Augustus Imri, b. Dec. 11, 1846; m. June 24, 1877, Rose Derrill; merchant; res. Skowhegan, Me.; two children.

XII. ELIAS, b. Sept. 5, 1805; d. March 22, 1856; unmarried.

441.

(John 6, Joseph 5, Stephen 4, Stephen 3, Stephen 2, Edmund 1.)

Children of **Capt. John[7] Greenleaf** and Martha (Sawyer).

I. SUSAN M., m. 1, Edmund Curtis, Mercer, Me.; 2, —— Webster. She d. 1861; two children by 1st marriage :—

i. Hartley K., m. Mary McLaughlin, of Starks.

ii. Perry G., m. Lizzie Corson, of Starks.

II. LOVINA W., b. 1814; m. David Robinson, of Ashland, Mass. She d. April 15, 1891; seven children :—

i. Curtis E., b. 1837; d. 1892, in Chicago, Ill.

ii. Thomas M.

iii. Nathan S.; res. South Framingham, Mass.

iv. David; res. Ashland, Mass.

v. Martha M.; res. South Hadley Falls, Mass.

vi. Bessie E.; res. South Framingham, Mass.

vii. Fred. N.

III. PERRY, d. in infancy.

CAPT. JOHN (441) GREENLEAF, CONTINUED :—

449. IV. PERRY,[8] b. 1818; m. Margaret Curtis, of Mercer,
Me. He d. 1840; one child :—
Perry, b. 1840.

450. V. THOMAS McDONOUGH,[8] b. 1820, in Starks, Me.; m.
1847, Harriet N. Kimball, of Mercer, Me. He d. July
4, 1894, in Boston; res. Boston; two children :—

451. I. Hartley K.,[9] b. 1850, in Mercer, Me.; m. Mary F.
Titcomb; one child: Abbie P., b. 1884.

II. John F., b. 1852, in Mercer, Me.; unmarried.

VI. BETSEY L., m. Elbridge H. Eames, of Holliston,
Mass.; four children :—
i. George Henry.
ii. Mary Ann.
iii. Ellen Maria.
iv. Edgar F.

VII. SARAH, m. James H. Lamb, of Ashland, Mass.;
res. Cleveland, Ohio; five children :—
i. Ella Sophronia.
ii. Janes R.
iii. Marion.
iv. Ellen Maria.
v. Charles B.

VIII. SOPHRONIA S., m. 1848, Joseph H. Chase, of Ashland,
Mass.; seven children, all res. of Leominster, Mass. :—
i. William Henry.
ii. Charles Leroy.
iii. Clarence Edmund.
iv. Edgar Francis.
v. Ela Lenora.
vi. Cora Eliza.
vii. Frank Melvin.

452. IX. ANDREW JACKSON,[8] b. June 9, 1828; m. Dec. 7, 1849,
Mahalah, dau. of Samuel and Betsey Chapman, of
Starks, Me.; four children :—
I. Anna, b. Feb. 5, 1851; d. Oct. 10, 1851.

453. II. Elbridge Eames,[9] b. March 22, 1852, in Holliston,
Mass.; m. Aug. 20, 1874, Lizzie F., adopted dau.
of Rev. Moses Brown, of Gardiner, Me.; five children: 1. Grace M., b. May 24, 1875. 2. Gertrude M., b. Jan. 5, 1877. 3. Ralph E., b. May
28, 1881; d. Jan. 5, 1889. 4. Rupert L., b.
Sept. 21, 1882. 5. Clara V., b. Oct. 27, 1889.

Capt. John (441) Greenleaf, Continued :—

454. iii. James H.,[9] b. Aug. 29, 1853; m. March 11, 1875, Hattie M., dau. of William H. and Cordelia Libby, of La Grange, Me., b. Feb. 6, 1856; three children: 1. William L., b. March 11, 1877; d. March 12, 1879. 2. Fay D., b. May 6, 1879. 3. Mattie L., b. Aug. 9, 1891.

iv. Clara, b. April 5, 1857; m. Oct. 10, 1881, in New York, Samuel Davis. She is a widow, and resides in La Grange, Me.

442.

(John 6, Joseph 5, Stephen 4, Stephen 3, Stephen 2, Edmund 1.)

Children of **Anthony**[7] **Greenleaf** and Nancy (Brown).

455. I. Anthony,[8] b. Dec. 24, 1811, in Starks, Me.; m. Oct. 31, 1832, Anna Snell; no children.

II. Sarah, b. June 16, 1813; m. James Trask, of New Sharon, Me.; res. Dixmont, Me.

III. Lydia, b. July 5, 1815; m. 1, John Warren Thompson; res. Starks, Me. He d. in Starks. 2. John,[8] son of Levi[7] and Amy Collins Greenleaf (463). She d. March 27, 1876; two children by 1st marriage :—
i. Stephen G., res. Australia; several chil dren.
ii. John Warren; res. formerly Starks, Me., now Ashland, Mass.; was a sergeant in Co. F, Third Regt. Maine Vols., Civil War.
Three children by 2d marriage.

456. IV. Stephen Decatur,[8] b. Oct. 26, 1817, in Starks, Me.; m. Dec. 22, 1842, Amy G., dau. of John and Dorcas (Greenleaf) Collins (384). He d. Jan. 22, 1895; res. Starks, Me.; eight children.

V. Rachel, b. May 2, 1819; m. Oct. 17, 1839, Joseph N., son of John and Huldah (Stover) George; res. New Sharon, Me.; four children :—
i. Flavilla, b. Oct. 26, 1840; d. Oct. 8, 1883; unmarried.
ii. Almon J., b. June 10, 1843; m. Lois E., dau. of James P. and Betsey Pressy George; no children.
iii. Silas C., b. Dec. 28, 1847; m. 1, Lisle, dau. of Louis and Mary Wentworth Gordon; one child: Sadie L., d. aged two years; 2, Nellie, dau. of Daniel Gilman; no children.
iv. Loretta J., b. Feb. 10, 1850; m. Abel, son of Jacob and Amy (Metcalf) Chandler; three children: 1. Dora R., b. March 26, 1870; m. George W., son of William and Lois Frizelle Smith. 2. George J., b. June 25, 1875. 3. Etta A., b. July 3, 1885.

ANTHONY (442) GREENLEAF, CONTINUED :—

457. VI. JOTHAM BALWIN,[8] b. Feb. 22, 1824; m. Oct. 9,
1845, Dorcas Chapman. He d. May 14, 1856; res.
Starks, Me.; four children :—

  I. Nancy, b. May 31, 1847; m. Samuel S. Taylor.
  She d. March 2, 1873; two children :—
    1. Walter S., b. March 3, 1868. 2. Lillian, b. 1871.
  II. Seraphina W., b. Feb. 23, 1849; m. Aug. 22, 1867,
  Oren A. Nickerson; res. Starks, Me.; one child :—
  Arthur H., b. Feb. 20, 1870.
  III. Rosanna S., b. Dec. 10, 1850; d. Jan. 22, 1864.
  IV. Lydia Elvira, b. Aug. 18, 1853; d. Oct. 17, 1867.

Children by 2d marriage :—

  VII. NANCY, b. Dec. 29, 1828; m. 1, Anthony,[8] son of
  Joseph[7] and Rhoda (Holbrook) Greenleaf (467); 2,
  Elias Churchill; res. New Sharon, Me.; two children.

  VIII. BEULAH AUGUSTA, b. Sept. 18, 1831; m. Oct. 12,
  1847, Moses Pressey; res. San Luis Obispo, Cal.;
  six children.

  IX. MARY ANN, b. Nov. 22, 1835; m. 1, Daniel Garrin
  Collins. He went to California and never returned;
  she obtained a bill of divorce, and m. 2, William
  Merrow, who d. Sept. 7, 1888. She resides in New
  Sharon, Me.; two children by 1st marriage :—
    i. Stephen G., b. March 23, 1856, in Starks, Me.; d. in San Luis
    Obispo, Cal.
    ii. Frederick Perkins, b. Sept. 13, 1861, in Starks, Me.; m. Louisa
    Ball; res. San Luis Obispo, Cal.

456.

(Anthony 7, John 6, Joseph 5, Stephen 4, Stephen 3, Stephen 2, Edmund 1.)

Children of **Hon. Stephen Decatur[8] Greenleaf** and
Amy (Collins).

  I. LOUISA ANN, b. March 30, 1844; m. May 10, 1863,
  John M. Pratt; res. Starks, Me.; four children :—
    i. Lozira, b. Feb. 7, 1864.
    ii. Annie S.
    iii. Isabella T.
    iv. Stephen D.

  II. ROSETTA LUVERNA, b. Aug. 11, 1846; m. July 4,
  1869, Albion Swift; three children.

458. III. AUSBURY C.,[9] b. Jan. 16, 1849; m. Aug. 26, 1894, Eliza
J. Smith, of Farmington, Me.; res. Farmington, Me.

Hon. Stephen Decatur (456) Greenleaf, Continued:—

459. IV. Commodore Decatur,[9] b. Feb. 18, 1851; m. June 13, 1885, Mary Hammons; res. New Sharon, Me.; no children.

V. Jane Elzora, b. June 21, 1853; m. March 21, 1886, Hiram M. Waugh; res. Starks, Me; no children.

460. VI. Lafayette S.,[9] b. May 3, 1857; m. May, 3, 1881, Ada E. Lovell; res. New Sharon, Me.; one child:— Addie R. H., b. Nov. 29, 1892.

461. VII. Zelber Eben,[9] b. Dec. 8, 1859; m. Oct. 7, 1882, Lena Elpha Flu, b. Aug. 1, 1863; five children:—
i. Stephen Decatur, b. Jan. 5, 1884.
ii. Everett Othello, b. Sept. 15, 1885.
iii. Marohn Torsey, b. Nov. 26, 1887.
iv. Ernest Leroy, b. Sept. 7, 1890.
v. Sherman Stanley, b. March 8, 1893.

VIII. Zuella, b. Dec. 8, 1859; twin; m. May 11, 1878, John L. Sterry; four children.

443.

(John 6, Joseph 5, Stephen 4, Stephen 3, Stephen 2, Edmund 1.)

Children of **Levi**[7] **Greenleaf** and Amy.

462. I. Luke Sawyer,[8] b. Jan. 6, 1814, in Starks, Me.; m. 1, April 23, 1843, Sally Wilbur, who d. Jan. 1, 1850; 2, 1857, Susan Patterson Howard; d. 1885; res. South Easton, Mass.; two children by 2d marriage:—
i. Fred H., b. Oct. 9, 1859; d. 1885.
ii. Harriet F., b. Oct. 9, 1864; m. Henry F. Frost; res. So. Easton, Mass.

463. II. John,[8] b. Nov. 19, 1815; m. Lydia (Greenleaf), widow of John Warren Thompson and dau. of Anthony and Nancy Greenleaf (455), b. July 5, 1815; d. March 27, 1876. Mr. Greenleaf died (Oct. 30, 1886) on the farm in Starks where he was born; three children:—

464. i. Levi,[9] b. May 2, 1846; m. Sept. 6, 1880, Eunice T. Jennings; res. East Madison, Me. He is an engineer; two children: 1. Flora L., b. Jan. 18, 1886. 2. Calsia W., b. Dec. 25, 1888.
Lost his left arm by the premature discharge of a cannon, while celebrating the Fourth of July at Starks, in 1869. He is quite skillful in playing the cornet with one hand.

LEVI (443) GREENLEAF, CONTINUED :—
II. John.

    II. Harriet Luverna, b. March 14, 1848; m. 1, John Churchill. He was killed by an accident on the railroad in Waynesville, Ohio, Sept. 9, 1888; three children, daughters, by 1st marriage; 2, 1890, Isaac T. Smith.

    III. Sally Dean, b. May 12, 1850; m. George N. Ward; res. Starks, Me.; no children.

III. ANN, b. April 27, 1818; m. William Frederick Wade. She d. Feb. 13, 1890. He served and died in the late Civil War. His widow went to North Dakota, and died there; res. Starks, Me.; three children :—

    i. Caleb, lost in war. Was in same Co. and Regt. with his father.

    ii. Cleveland B., m. Hattie, dau. of Cyrus Snell, of Starks, Me.; res. Fargo, N. D.

    iii. Amy G., m. Frank Athearne, formerly of Starks, Me.; res. Grafton, N. D.

465. IV. CYRUS,[8] b. Feb. 13, 1821; m. Feb. 16, 1853, Susan Waugh. He d. Jan. 20, 1892; farmer; he was born, lived, and died in Starks, Me.; nine children :—

    I. Luke S., b. Dec. 30, 1854; d. Sept. 17, 1857.

    II. John F., b. Oct. 11, 1856; d. Sept. 20, 1857.

    III. James B., b. March 4, 1857; res. in Starks, Me.; unmarried.

    IV. Carrie T., b. June 8, 1858; m. J. S. Moores; res. in New Sharon, Me.; two children.

466. v. Caleb Wade,[9] b. April 2, 1860; m. Nov. 2, 1889, Eveline, dau. of Benj. W. Greenleaf (409); res. in Starks, Me.; two children: 1. Junietta, b. May 12, 1891; d. Sept. 13, 1891. 2. Alton Caleb, b. May 9, 1893.

    vi. Cora Bell, b. Sept. 22, 1863; m. F. Spofford; res. New Sharon, Me.

    vii. Nellie, b. May 15, 1866; m. George Hammonds; res. New Sharon, Me.; one child :—

    A son, b. May, 1891; d. Sept. 10, 1895.

    viii. Charles Franklin, b. April 22, 1868; res. Starks, Me.; unmarried.

    ix. George P., b. Feb. 7, 1870; res. Starks, Me.; unmarried.

LEVI (443) GREENLEAF, CONTINUED :—

V. LIBBEY, b. March 2, 1825; res. Mercer, Me.; unmarried.

VI. ELIZABETH, b. Jan. 26, 1827; d. Aug. 17, 1894;
res. New Sharon, Me.; unmarried.

VII. HARRIET L., b. Oct. 25, 1830; m. Eli W. (423),
son of William C. Greenleaf (404), b. Aug. 14, 1834;
res. New Sharon, Me.; five children.

VIII. AMY, b. Oct. 22, 1835; m. Reuben F. Oliver, of
Starks, Me.; res. Starks, Me.; no children.

444.

(John 6, Joseph 5, Stephen 4, Stephen 3, Stephen 2, Edmund 1.)

Children of **Joseph**[7] **Greenleaf** and Rhoda (Holbrook).

I. ANNA, b. Nov. 23, 1815; m. James Wood, of Starks.
She d. Sept. 20, 1895; res. Skowhegan, Me., with
her dau., Mrs. Benjamin A. Sawyer (387); three
children :—

i. Antoinette, m. Smith Norton, of Starks, Me.

ii. Maora, m. Benjamin Allen, son of Levi Greenleaf Sawyer and
Elvira E., dau. of William[6] Greenleaf (387). Mr. B. A. Sawyer was formerly of Starks, now of Skowhegan, Me.

iii. Henry Alphonzo, d. young.

II. WILLIAM B., b. Nov. 25, 1817; d. March 7, 1844;
unmarried.

467. III. ANTHONY,[8] b. Sept. 17, 1819; m. April 17, 1845,
Nancy, dau. of Anthony[7] and Sally (Perkins) Greenleaf (442). He d. Aug. 30, 1856; two children :—

468. i. William Henry,[9] b. Nov. 16, 1848; m. 1, Aug. 16,
1870, Rhoda Ann Lane, of Starks, Me.; 2, Aug. 17,
1876, Emma Knox. He d. June 3, 1888. Three
children by 1st marriage : 1. Rose Lillian, b. May
4, 1871. 2. Calvin Lane, b. Sept. 4, 1872. 3.
Charles Mace, b. 1874. Four children by 2d
marriage : 4. Willie Leon, b. Oct. 15, 1878. 5.
Della May, b. Nov. 20, 1879; d. October, 1881.
6. Eva Blanche, b. March 16, 1881. 7. Hattie
M., b. Oct. 19, 1882.

ii. Lydia Jenette, b. June 19, 1851; m. Sept. 25, 1870,
Asa Chapman, of Starks, Me.

Joseph (444) Greenleaf, Continued:—
  IV. Angeline M., b. Sept. 7, 1821; m. Henry B.
      Thompson, of Lawrence, Mass. She d. June 14,
      1883; res. Lowell, Mass.
  V. Saul Holbrook, b. July 2, 1823; d. July 4, 1825.
  VI. Thomas Jefferson, b. May 12, 1825; d. May, 1855.
  VII. John Quincy Adams, b. Oct. 26, 1826; d. Nov.,
      1854, in California; unmarried.
469. VIII. Andrew Jackson,[8] b. Nov. 5, 1828; m. 1, Mar-
      tha M. Dickinson, of Mercer, Me., b. Oct. 22, 1821;
      d. March 2, 1872; 2, July 3, 1873, Martha Eliza-
      beth, dau. of Freeman Allen. Mr. Greenleaf d. Oct.
      26, 1874, in Mercer, Me., and his widow m. July 15,
      1880, Rev. Otis Andrews, of New Sharon, Me.
    Children by 1st marriage:—
470. I. Samuel W.,[9] b. June 26, 1852; m. Dec. 31, 1873,
        Susan L. Sawtelle; res. Mercer, Me.; no children.
      II. Cyrus J., b. Aug. 16, 1855; d. November, 1873.
      III. John C. F., b. Dec. 6, 1857; d. 1873, one week
        after Cyrus.
      IV. Abbie M., b. Aug. 26, 1859; m. April 10, 1885,
        Stephen Bagley, of Montville, Me.
  IX. Amy, b. Nov. 20, 1830; m. Asa Snell. She d. Nov.
      14, 1892; res. Woolwich, Me.
  X. Martha J., b. April 3, 1833; m. Daniel G. Harring-
      ton; res. Lowell, Mass.
  XI. Elmira C., b. Oct. 14, 1835; m. Joseph Follansby,
      of Haverhill, Mass. She d. Oct. 5, 1864.

445.

(John 6, Joseph 5, Stephen 4, Stephen 3, Stephen 2, Edmund 1.)

Children of **William[7] Greenleaf** and Rosalind B. (Merrill).
  I. Betsey, b. March 3, 1822, in Starks, Me.; res. Low-
      ell, Mass.; unmarried.
471. II. Nathaniel Bryant,[8] b. Jan. 4, 1824, in Starks,
      Me.; m. Oct. 11, 1849, Mary Frances, dau. of
      Jason and Jane Fuller, of Boothbay, Me.; res. Low-
      ell, Mass.; seven children.
  III. Rosalind, b. Feb. 11, 1826, on Squirrel Island, Me.;
      d. Dec. 22, 1888; res. Lowell, Mass.; unmarried.

WILLIAM (445) GREENLEAF, CONTINUED:—

    IV. WILLIAM BOYD, b. Feb. 1, 1828, on Squirrel Island, Me.; d. April 19, 1885, at Woodinville, King Co., Wash.

472. V. EDWARD KENT,[8] b. June 2, 1831, on Squirrel Island, Me.; m. May 24, 1854, Mary Anna, dau. of John and Anna Wyatt, of Bath, Eng.; res. Boothbay Harbor, Me.; seven children.

471.

(William 7, John 6, Joseph 5, Stephen 4, Stephen 3, Stephen 2, Edmund 1.)

Children of **Capt. Nathaniel B.**[8] **Greenleaf** and Mary F. (Fuller).

    I. EMMA JANE, b. June 23, 1851; m. James W. Mitchell; res. Lowell, Mass.; one child:—

Francis, b. 1886.

    II. CARRIE FRANCES, b. April 1, 1853; d. Oct. 6, 1870.

473 III. CHARLES MELVILLE,[9] b. Oct. 22, 1854; m. Sept. 22, 1877, Florence A. Smith; res. Lowell, Mass.; one child:—

Roy W., b. Feb. 24, 1879.

    IV. WILLIAM FREDERICK, b. Jan. 2, 1857; d. Feb. 27, 1858.

474. V. JASON FULLER,[9] b. Aug. 17, 1858; m. Dec. 12, 1883, Anna A. Young. He d. June 3, 1893; res. Lowell, Mass.; one child:—

Ethel Lena, b. July 4, 1884.

    VI. NELLIE MAY, b. July 1, 1860; m. July 26, 1879, Lindsey Ingalls, of Lowell, Mass.; res. Lowell, Mass.

475. VII. GEORGE HENRY,[9] b. Sept. 24, 1863; m. Aug. 16, 1888, Mary Beals; res. Lowell; three children:—

    i. Carrie Frances, b. Aug. 12, 1889.

    ii. Anna Augusta, b. Feb. 7, 1891.

    iii. Grace, b. Dec. 22, 1892.

472.

(William 7, John 6, Joseph 5, Stephen 4, Stephen 3, Stephen 2, Edmund 1.)

Children of **Edward Kent**[8] **Greenleaf** and Mary Anna (Wyatt).

    I. MARY ANNA, b. May 19, 1855; m. Jan. 27, 1878, John M. McFarland; res. Boothbay Harbor, Me.; six children:—

    i. Nathaniel Curtis, b. April 27, 1879.

    ii. John Winthrop, b. Aug., d. Oct., 1880.

EDWARD KENT (472) GREENLEAF, CONTINUED:—
   I. Mary Anna.
      iii. Richard Merritt, b. Oct., 1881.
      iv. Margery Jane, b. July 29, 1885.
      v. Frank Le Forrest, b. Dec., 1890; d. June, 1893.
      vi. Marian, b. May 30, 1894.
   II. EDWARD MELVILLE, b. Nov. 23, 1857; res. Victoria,
      British Columbia.
476. III. WILLIAM FRANKLIN,[9] b. Aug. 13, 1862; m. Jan.
      31, 1889, Mary McPartland, of New York; res. Low-
      ell, Mass.
   IV. LIZZIE JOSEPHINE, b. Dec. 8, 1868; m. Sept. 27, 1893,
      Frank H. Skillin; res. Portland, Me.; one child:—
         Gladys B., b. Aug. 8, 1894.
477. V. GEORGE WYATT,[9] b. March 8, 1871; m. Nov. 21,
      1892, Maggie M. Alley, of Southport, Me.; res.
      Boothbay Harbor, Me.; two children:—
         i. Gladys Wyatt, b. Oct. 2, 1893.
         ii. Lewis Sheldon, b. April 24, 1895.
477a. VI. CHARLES FREDERICK,[9] b. March 31, 1873; m. Nov.
      27, 1895, Laura E. Nickerson, of Southport, Me.;
      res. Boothbay, West Harbor, Me.
   VII. CARRIE EMMA, b. May 30, 1875; res. Boothbay, Me.

446.

(John 6; Joseph 5, Stephen 4, Stephen 3, Stephen 2, Edmund 1.)

Children of **Stephen**[7] **Greenleaf** and Rhoda (Metcalf).
Child by 1st marriage:—
478. I. CYRUS METCALF,[8] b. May 10, 1821; m. Sept. 1, 1843,
      Myra J., dau. of Col. Asa and Hannah (Williamson)
      Chapman, of Starks, Me.; res. Starks, Me.; ten
      children.
Children by 2d marriage:—
479. II. ENOCH LINCOLN,[8] b. July 28, 1827; m. 1, May 25,
      1851, Rebekah W., dau. of Major Leonard and Clar-
      issa Greaton, of Starks. She d. Nov. 17, 1870; 2,
      March 25, 1872, Mrs. Frances A., dau. of Hon. John
      H. and Eunice (Waugh) Smith, of Starks, Me.; res.
      formerly Starks, now Farmington, Me.; three children.
480. III. WAKEFIELD,[8] b. March 4, 1829; m. May 3, 1855,
      Ellen Gordon, dau. of Col. Asa and Hannah (Wil-
      liamson) Chapman. Mr. Greenleaf has been post-

STEPHEN (446) GREENLEAF, CONTINUED :—

III. Wakefield.

master, town clerk, and justice of the peace for many
years; res. Starks, Me.; five children :—

   I. Otis Herbert, b. Oct. 28, 1857; d. Feb. 18, 1884, at
     Boston, Mass.

   II. Henry Pearson, b. Sept. 20, 1859; d. Sept. 17, 1860.

   III. Floretta, b. June 27, 1867; d. Nov. 10, 1868.

   IV. Della, b. Dec. 7, 1871; m. March 10, 1894, Fred
     H. Brackett, of Starks, Me.; two children :—

     1. Harold G., b. Dec. 25, 1894. 2. A daughter, b. April 22, 1896.

   v. Addie Leone, b. March 29, 1873; d. May 13, 1891.

IV. RHODA, b. Nov. 20, 1830; m. March 17, 1858, Wil-
liam Henry Pearson, formerly of Skowhegan, Me.
She d. April 23, 1891, in Augusta, Me.; res. Augusta,
Me.; one child :—

   Fannie D., b. Dec. 29, 1858; m. June 12, 1895, Horatio W. Cushing, of Skowhegan, Me.; res. Skowhegan, Me.

V. LYDIA, b. June 9, 1832; m. 1, July 11, 1852, John
B. Maxfield, formerly of Skowhegan, Me. They lived
at Little River Mills, a village in New Brunswick oppo-
site Fort Fairfield, Aroostook Co., Me., where Mr.
Maxfield d. Nov. 17, 1873. She then came back to
Starks with her children, and m. 2, May 11, 1887,
George W. Greaton; res. Starks, Me.; four children :—

   i. Fannie M., b. Nov. 4, 1855; m. May 10, 1875, Warren M. Higgins, of Starks. He was a merchant and prominent man
   there. He d. Jan. 6, 1886. She d. Jan. 16, 1882; one child:
   John Warren, b. Aug. 23, 1877; lives with his grandmother,
   Lydia Greaton, and is a school-teacher in Starks.

   ii. William H., b. May 15, 1858; d. Nov. 20, 1884. He was a
   teacher in public schools in Louisiana in 1874; studied for the
   ministry, and was ordained and preached in that State till
   Nov., 1884, when he had a call to a parish in Montana, and
   died soon after reaching there. He was a young man of great
   promise, a close student, fine scholar, and an eloquent speaker.

   iii. Herbert W., b. Oct. 10, 1860; m. Jan. 1, 1890, Lydia, dau. of
   Samuel Remick, of Starks; res. Starks; a merchant, and
   chairman of the Board of Selectmen there.

   iv. Stephen Greenleaf, b. Aug. 26, 1862; m. 1882, in Lowell,
   Mass.; res. Chicago, Ill.

481. VI. GASON,[8] b. Dec. 31, 1833; m. Oct. 24, 1853, Margaret Ann, dau. of Capt. Timothy and Jane (Cook)

Stephen (446) Greenleaf, Continued:—
  VI. Gason.
      Wight, of Starks, Me., b. Jan. 18, 1837; d. Jan. 9,
      1859, at Casco, Me. He d. Jan. 18, 1859; res.
      Casco, Me.; one child:—
      Mary Marilla, b. March 16, 1855; d. Jan. 11, 1859.
  VII. Mary Mooers, b. Jan. 20, 1838; d. Oct. 22, 1853.
482. VIII. George,[8] b. Nov. 26, 1841; m. 1, Aug. 29, 1866,
      Jennie F., dau. of Robert and Betsey (Saywood)
      Huntress, of Effingham, N. H. She d. Oct. 30, 1870;
      2, Jan. 6, 1880, Almira L., dau. of Eben and Emma
      G. Williamson, of Starks. She d. Oct. 15, 1880; 3,
      March 11, 1886, Mrs. Annie E., widow of Capt.
      Charles H. Dyer, of New Sharon, Me., and dau. of
      Hon. James G. Waugh, of Starks. Mr. Greenleaf is
      a merchant; res. Portland, Me.; one child:—
      George Walter,[9] b. Aug. 9, 1870; physician; res. Som-
        erville, Mass.
483. IX. Charles,[8] b. Nov. 5, 1844, in Starks, Me.; m. 1,
      Dec. 13, 1865, Mary Adelaide, dau. of Elisha K.
      Fish, of Industry, Me.; 2, Sybil Smith, of Hancock,
      Me. He. d. Jan. 5, 1895, at Portland, Me.; res.
      Portland, Me.; one child by 1st marriage:—
      Frank Herbert,[9] b. July 29, 1869, in Starks, Me.; m.
        July 1, 1891, Carrie M., dau. of Freeman Boyn-
        ton; res. Augusta, Me.; two children: 1. Boyn-
        ton Locke, b. Oct. 13, 1892. 2. Beatrice Adelaide,
        b. Sept. 25, 1893.
484. X. Levi,[8] b. Dec. 30, 1849; m. Oct. 3, 1878, Adelaide,
      eldest dau. of Charles and Melissa (Russell) Mason, of
      Bethel, Me.; lawyer; res. Portland, Me.; no children.

478.

(Stephen 7, John 6, Joseph 5, Stephen 4, Stephen 3, Stephen 2, Edmund 1.)

Children of **Cyrus Metcalf[8] Greenleaf** and Myra J.
(Chapman).
  I. Hannah Frances, b. Feb. 23, 1845; m. 1867, David
      F. Tarr, of Anson, Me. He d. April 7, 1890; eight
      children:—
      i. Winnie F., b. March 27, 1869; m. J. H. Preston.
      ii. Bennie D., b. Aug. 7, 1871; d. Aug. 23, 1888.

CYRUS METCALF (478) GREENLEAF, CONTINUED :—
    I. Hannah Frances.
        iii. Fred C., b. May 25, 1874.
        iv. Ida May, b. April 4, 1877; d. July 16, 1880.
        v. Arthur C., b. Dec. 8, 1880.
        vi. Fannie M., b. Aug. 20, 1883; d. Feb. 20, 1884.
        vii. John L., b. May 8, 1885.
        viii. Clarence, b. March 15, 1890.
485. II. THOMAS H. BENTON,[9] b. May 9, 1847; m. 1, Oct. 20,
        1871, Lorana, dau. of Daniel Maguire, of New Port-
        land, Me. She d. Feb. 5, 1889, at Leeds, Me.; 2.
        March 31, 1892, Mrs. Minnie Cummings, of Auburn,
        Me.; a farmer; res. Turner, Me.; child by 1st mar-
        riage :—
        1. Frank Carroll, b. Sept. 1, 1876.
    Child by 2d marriage :—
        II. Carleton Quincy, b. Aug. 17, 1893.
486. III. JOHN BROWN,[9] b. Oct. 23, 1850; m. Nov. 9, 1878,
        Etta H., dau. of Warren N. and Catherine (Heald)
        Manter, formerly of Norridgewock, Me., now of
        East Oakland, Cal., b. April 5, 1854; res. East Oak-
        land, Cal.; four children :—
        I. Bertha May, b. Oct. 30, 1880.
        II. Kate Myra, b. March 18, 1884.
        III. Grace Etta, b. Jan. 6, 1890.
        IV. George Cyrus, b. Jan. 24, 1891; d. April 6, 1891.
487. IV. GASON G.,[9] b. June 6, 1853; m. Jan. 13, 1876, Lillian
        Joan, dau. of David D. Tarr, of Anson, Me. She d.
        March 3, 1888; res. Anson, Me.; five children :—
        I. Maud Florence, b. July 9, 1877; d. July 12, 1880.
        II. William A., b. Feb. 6, 1879; d. Aug. 14, 1880.
        III. Nellie M., b. Jan. 27, 1881.
        IV. Abbie A., b. June 9, 1883.
        v. Grover Cleveland, b. July 7, 1885.
488. V. JAMES BUCHANAN,[9] b. April 12, 1856; m. Lizzie R.
        Chandler, of Starks, Me.; res. Madison, Me; no
        children.
    VI. MARY ETTA, b. May 27, 1859; m. 1, Jan. 14, 1883,
        Charles Carroll Moore, of Anson, Me., b. May 6,
        1860; d. Aug. 28, 1883; 2, Oct. 2, 1886, John T.
        Bemis, of Turner, Me.; res. Keene's Mills, Turner, Me.

CYRUS METCALF (478) GREENLEAF, CONTINUED:—
VI. Mary Etta.
Children by 2d marriage :—
i. Annie Myra, b. July 11, 1890.
ii. Henrietta, b. Sept. 21, 1892.
VII. RHODA ELLEN, b. Jan. 16, 1862 ; d. March 2, 1883.
VIII. QUINCY WENTWORTH, b. Aug. 15, 1864; d. May 8, 1887.
489. IX. GEORGE F.,[9] b. July 27, 1868 ; m. March 28, 1892, Lizzie A. Booker; one child.
X. CYRUS ALBERT, b. Dec. 25, 1871 ; d. Dec. 17, 1894, at Starks, Me.

479.

(Stephen 7, John 6, Joseph 5, Stephen 4, Stephen 3, Stephen 2, Edmund 1.)
Children of **Enoch Lincoln**[8] **Greenleaf** and Rebekah W. (Greaton).
490. I. ENOCH OWEN,[9] b. Dec. 17, 1853; m. in Starks, Me., March 27, 1881, Cornelia, dau. of Moses S. and Harriet (Jose) Mayhew, of Mt. Vernon, Me. ; res. Farmington, Me. ; lawyer; no children.
491. II. ORRIN LINCOLN,[9] b. Dec. 6, 1859, in Starks, Me. ; m. April 15, 1888, Lizzie, dau. of James Wood, Jr., of Starks, Me. ; res. Haverhill, Mass. ; no children.
Child by 2d marriage :—
III. FORREST S., b. Sept. 21, 1873, in Starks, Me. ; d. Aug. 11, 1894, in Farmington, Me.

448.

(John 6, Joseph 5, Stephen 4, Stephen 3, Stephen 2, Edmund 1.)
Children of **Joshua**[7] **Greenleaf** and Asenath (Sawyer-Robinson).
492. I. COLUMBUS SAWYER,[8] b. May 12, 1828; m. ; a farmer; res. Seattle, Wash. ; no children.
493. II. JAMES MANTER,[8] b. Feb. 7, 1830; m. Mary E. Rackliff; res. Starks, Me. ; a farmer; seven children :—
i. Clarence H., b. Dec. 4, 1853 ; d. Oct. 14, 1861.
ii. Ernest S., b. June 25, 1858 ; d. Oct. 5, 1861.
iii. Fannie Isora, b. Jan. 29, 1862 ; m. William Spaulding, of Madison, Me.

Joshua (448) Greenleaf, Continued:—

    II. James Manter.

494.   iv. Sheldon M.,[9] b. Dec. 12, 1864; m. Jennie Messer.

        v. Ralph H., b. July 23, 1868; d. Dec. 12, 1871.

        vi. Alice G., b. Sept. 27, 1870; m. June 10, 1893, Charles C. Bartlett, of New Sharon, Me.

        vii. Clyde Irwin, b. Dec. 4, 1872.

    III. Susan Manter, b. Jan. 27, 1832; m. Edmund Snell, of Starks, Me., who went to Venezuela, and died there. She resides in Madison, Me.; two children:—

        i. Ida, unmarried; res. Madison, Me.

        ii. Roscoe, unmarried; res. Madison, Me.

495.   IV. Benjamin Lovell,[8] b. June 5, 1834; m. Nov. 7, 1868, Mrs. Emily M. Brann; res. Madison, Me.; four children:—

496.   i. Benjamin Franklin,[9] b. Sept. 27, 1869; m. ——.

        ii. Sarah B., b. July 24, 1871; d. April 7, 1878.

        iii. Joshua Lindsey, b. July 26, 1873.

        iv. Clarence H., b. Oct. 6, 1876.

    V. Maria N., b. Dec. 1, 1836; m. Sylvanus Chapman; res. Skowhegan, Me.; two children.

    VI. Betsey Steward, b. Oct. 30, 1841; d. Jan. 30, 1859.

    VII. Sarah Brown, b. April 24, 1844; d. March 6, 1866.

386.

(Joseph 5, Stephen 4, Stephen 3, Stephen 2, Edmund 1.)

Children of **Joshua**[6] **Greenleaf** and Hannah (Williamson).

    I. Amata, b. Sept. 1, 1791; m. John Laughton, of New Sharon, Me. She d. Aug. 31, 1840; six children:—

        i. Joshua, d. young.

        ii. Esther, m. —— Richardson.

        iii. Hannah, m. —— Willard, of New Sharon, Me.

        iv. Warren J., m. 1, —— Nutting, of Norridgewock, Me.; 2. —— Prince, of New Sharon, Me.

        v. Alburtus, m. Hitty Lake, of Farmington, Me.

        vi. Amata Emma, m. Frank McLaughlin, of Weeks Mills, New Sharon, Me.

497.   II. Seth,[7] b. Aug. 26, 1794; m. Sept. 11, 1817, Eliza Wiley. He d. Aug. 20, 1865; six children.

Joshua (386) Greenleaf, Continued :—

    III. Dorcas, b. Feb. 6, 1796; m. Jackson Folsom. She
        d. July 5, 1831; four children.

498. IV. James,[7] b. Feb. 15, 1798; marriage intention filed
        Jan. 25, 1824, Clarissa McKinney, of Wiscasset, Me.
        He d. March 20, 1846; two children.

    V. Betsey, b. April 14, 1800; m. Samuel Chapman, of
        Starks, Me. She d. Aug. 21, 1868; res. Starks,
        Me.; fourteen children.

    VI. Hannah, b. Nov. 17, 1803; m. Thaddeus H. Coburn.
        She d. Feb. 20, 1841; one child :—

        Mrs. Dr. Danforth, of Norridgewock, Me. She has two children.

499. VII. Joshua,[7] b. Oct. 22, 1807; m. Margaret Wil-
        liamson. He d. Oct. 3, 1838 or 1839; four chil-
        dren :—

        i. Albert.

        ii. A daughter.

        iii. A daughter.

        iv. ——.

    VIII. Seraphina, b. May 17, 1809; m. March 6, 1833,
        Charles Wiley. She d. Sept. 7, 1894; res. Freedom,
        Ill.; five children :—

        i. Samuel Charles, b. Nov. 11, 1833; res. Earlville, Ill.

        ii. Henry, b. March 12, 1835; res. on Homestead, at Freedom, Ill.

        iii. Martha W., b. Jan. 2, 1845; m. ——Davis; res. Earlville, Ill.

        iv. A daughter, d. in infancy.

        v. A daughter, d. in infancy.

    IX. Sarah (Sally), b. July 24, 1811; m. Andrew New-
        ell. She d. Oct. 26, 1859; five children.

497.

(Joshua 6, Joseph 5, Stephen 4, Stephen 3, Stephen 2, Edmund 1.)

Children of **Seth**[7] **Greenleaf** and Eliza (Wiley).

500. I. Alden B.,[8] b. Jan. 5, 1819; m. July 14, 1843, Harriet
        B. Benner, of Waldoboro, Me., b. 1823; d. Sept. 30,
        1867, at Washington, Me. He d. Nov. 30, 1848;
        res. Mercer, Me.; one child :—

        Adelaide B., b. Jan. 31, 1848; m. Jan. 15, 1868, Charles
        A. Brown, of Hallowell, Me.; two children :—

        i. Herbert L., b. May 26, 1869; res. Worcester, Mass.

        ii. Irving L., b. Nov. 26, 1872; res. Hallowell, Me.

Seth (497) Greenleaf, Continued:—

501. II. James,[8] b. July 18, 1820, at Brighton, Me.; m. Oct. 1, 1848, Charlotte P. Graves, of Lexington, Mass. He d. Jan. 10, 1893; res. Mercer, Me.; four children:—

502. i. George Augustus,[9] b. June 14, 1850; m. Aug. 23, 1876, Flora A., dau. of John Williamson of Mercer. He d. Jan. 6, 1888, in Sierra Madre, Cal. She m. 2, Oct. 10, 1893, Freeman H. Cook, of Farmington, Me.; res. Farmington, Me.; two children: 1. Ethel Florence, b. Nov. 27, 1877; m. Nov. 6, 1894, Timothy H. Ames, of Farmington, Me. 2. Elsie Louise, b. Feb. 20, 1882.

ii. Emily Frances, b. Dec. 22, 1857; m. June 18, 1885, S. R. G. Twycross, of Dresden, Me.; one child:—
1. Converse Lilly, b. March 14, 1886.

503. iii. Charles Philip,[9] b. July 7, 1863, in Mercer, Me.; m. Marion George, of Norridgewock, Me. Merchant; moved to Portland, Me., May, 1895; one child: Walter James, b. March 23, 1889.

iv. Nellie Hannah, b. Jan. 26, 1870; m. Sept. 1891, Leland S. Coffin; res. Portland, Me.

III. Charles W., b. June 15, 1828; d. June 2, 1854.

IV. Reuel, b. April 29, 1831; d. Aug. 20, 1859.

V. Hannah, b. May 17, 1834; m. Nov. 9, 1857, Isaac S. Ford, in Freedom, Ill.; res. Mercer, Me.; one child:—
Nellie A., b. Feb. 28, 1875.

VI. Sabra E., b. April 5, 1842; d. April 3, 1849.

498.

(Joshua 6, Joseph 5, Stephen 4, Stephen 3, Stephen 2, Edmund 1.)

Children of **James[7] Greenleaf** and Clarissa (McKinney).

I. Franklin, b. April 2, 1827, at Mercer, Me.; d. May 5, 1848.

504. II. Samuel Austin,[8] b. Nov. 2, 1832, at Mercer, Me.; m. Jan. 30, 1856, at Bath, Me., Christiana Fraser. He d. Sept. 1, 1857, at Bath, Me.; one child:—

505. Franklin A.,[9] b. Nov. 26, 1856; m. 1, Emma L. McBride. 2, Lottie L. McBride, sister of first wife; res. Boston, Mass.; three children by 1st marriage:

JAMES (498) GREENLEAF, CONTINUED :—
  II. Samuel Austin.
          1. Clara L., b. Feb. 23, 1879, at Boston.   2. Lot-
       tie I., b. March 20, 1881, at Boston.   3. Franklin
       A., b. March 16, 1883, at Boston; d. Jan. 30, 1884,
       at Boston.   Two children by 2d marriage : 4. Lizzie
       E., b. May 14, 1885, at Somerville, Mass.   5. Hazel
       Florence, b. Sept. 16, 1894, at Somerville, Mass.

387.

(Joseph 5, Stephen 4, Stephen 3, Stephen 2, Edmund 1.)

Children of **William**[6] **Greenleaf** and Sally (Lander).
  I. THIRZA, b. April 6, 1795 ; m. Eleazer Snell, of
     Starks, Me.; b. Sept. 8, 1789.   She d. Sept. 3, 1848 ;
     ten children :—

  i. Diana, b. Oct. 7, 1814; m. June 3, 1838, Caleb G. True, of In-
     dustry, Me.   She d. July 1, 1882; eleven children.
  ii. Jane F., b. Dec. 15, 1815; d. May 3, 1818.
  iii. James M., b. May 3, 1818; m. Dec. 10, 1845, Leonora True, of
     Industry; res. Madison, Me.; one child : Bethel Levant.
  iv. Mahalah B., b. Feb. 12, 1820; m. Feb. 8, 1846, Charles A. Hol-
     brook, of Boston, Mass.; one child : Elizabeth.
  v. Alfrida G., b. June 29, 1822; m. Dec. 19, 1844, Benjamin M.
     Allen, of Industry.   She d. Sept 2, 1849.
  vi. William G., b. Jan. 4, 1824; m. Nov. 5, 1859, Mary, dau. of
     David Norton, of Starks, Me.; res. Madison, Me.; four
     children.
  vii. Betsey A., b. July 19, 1826; m. 1, Nov. 24, 1851, Benjamin M.
     Allen.   He d. ——; 2, Dec., 1868, William D. Smith, of New
     Sharon.   She d. Jan. 27, 1884.
  viii. Turner W., b. Nov. 7, 1829; d. July 16, 1854, in Stillwater,
     Minn.
  ix. Jennie F., b. Oct. 20, 1832; d. July 22, 1859.
  x. Orintha M., b. Aug. 14, 1835; d. Feb. 17, 1889; unmarried.

506. II. GASON,[7] b. Oct. 24, 1796 ; m. Nancy Joy, of Starks.
     He d. in Starks Jan. 26, 1854.   He resided in Starks
     till a few years before his death.   Was a sheriff in Som-
     erset County, selectman, etc.   Moved in 1852 to
     Sharon, Mass.; seven children :—

     I. Sarah, b. March 3, 1823 ; d. July 31, 1846.
     II. Sabrina, b. March 18, 1825 ; m. Elam Richards, of
         Sharon, Mass.
     III. Jeremiah B., b. March 7, 1827 ; d. at Warwick,
         Mass.

WILLIAM (387) GREENLEAF, CONTINUED :—

II. Gason.

507. IV. Eleazer Snell,[8] b. March 5, 1829; m. Rozina Ann Young, dau. of William C. and Adeline Greenleaf (404). She d. Aug. 27, 1863; res. Dedham, Mass.

v. Mary, b. Dec. 28, 1831; m. George N. Richards, of Sharon, Mass.

VI. John, b. May 4, 1835; d. Feb. 11, 1839.

VII. Harriet, b. June 12, 1838; m. Amaziah Pickering, of Sharon, Mass.; moved to Iowa.

III. MAHALAH, b. Aug. 17, 1798; m. 1, Lemuel Bangs; 2, —— Putnam. She d. in Freeman, Me.

Children by 1st marriage :—
  i. Esther, m. Zenas Vaughan; res. Skowhegan, Me.
  ii. Fuller.
  iii. Putnam; res. Eustis, Me.
Four children by 2d marriage.

IV. ALFRIDA, b. Oct. 22, 1800; m. Aaron Stoyell, of Farmington, Me.; res. Farmington, Me.; eight children. One daughter, m. Joel Wright.

V. SABRINA, b. March 28, 1802; d. Sept., 1817.

VI. LYDIA, b. March 26, 1804; m. Joseph Mudgett, of Prospect, Me. She d. Feb. 4, 1889; four children.

VII. VAUGHAN, b. May 31, 1807; d. young.

VIII. JULIA A., b. Feb. 4, 1810; m. Cyrus Rogers, of Starks, Me. She d. Jan., 1895. Res. Norridgewock, Me.; seven children.

IX. ELVIRA E., b. Oct. 10, 1812; m. Levi G. Sawyer, of Starks, Me. She d. Nov. 14, 1889; three children :—
  i. Benjamin A., m. Maora, dau. of James Wood and Anna, dau. of Joseph[7] Greenleaf (444).
  ii. Ella, m. James V. Greaton, of Starks.
  iii. Etta E., m. Aug. 14, 1872, R. D. Trask, lawyer, formerly of New Sharon, Me.; res. Haverhill, Mass. She d. prior to 1879.

508. X. WILLIAM,[7] b. June 4, 1817; m. Dec. 20, 1840, Harriet H. Twitchell, b. Nov. 19, 1817, of New Portland, Me. He d. Nov. 9, 1880; res. New Vineyard, Me.; six children :—
  1. James Elmer, b. Jan. 3, 1843; d. March 11, 1862, at Lewinsville, Fairfax Co., Va.

WILLIAM (387) GREENLEAF, CONTINUED :—
X. William.

509. II. John Eller,[8] b. Sept. 9, 1844, at New Vineyard, Me.; m. Dec. 4, 1868, Hattie M., dau. of William and Eliza (Smith) Wade, of Farmington, Me.; res. Farmington; two children, 1. Flora L., b. June 4, 1871 ; m. Jan. 1, 1892, Edwin F. Stewart, of Farmington, Me. 2. Ellice Mae, b. June 29, 1875.

III. Anna Maria, b. May 22, 1847, at New Vineyard, Me.; m. Oct. 4, 1865, William Kempton, son of George K. Howes; res. Strong, Me.; three children :—

    1. Carrie A., b. March 9, 1867; d. Nov. 5, 1884. 2. C. May, b. May 30, 1869; m. Nov. 11, 1888, J. Henry Ramsdell, of New Vineyard, Me. 3. Daisy A., b. March 9, 1879.

510. IV. Melvin Gason,[8] b. Dec. 25, 1849 ; m. July 17, 1881, Emma P., dau. of S. D. Stewart ; one child : Nellie Anna, b. July 31, 1884 ; res. New Vineyard, Me.

V. Addie Ella, b. June 14, 1853 ; m. June 4, 1881, Z. Morton Vaughan, Jr. ; res. Strong, Me. ; one child :—
Alice Evelyn, b. Sept. 7, 1882.

VI. Henry Mitchell, b. Aug. 1, 1855; d. March 9, 1878, at New Vineyard, Me.

412.

(Daniel 9, Jonathan Y. 8, Daniel 7, Ebenezer 6, Joseph 5, Stephen 4, Stephen 3, Stephen 2, Edmund 1.)

Children of **Melvin A.**[10] **Greenleaf** and Lunette C. (Story).

I. MABEL R., b. Sept. 15, 1880.

II. ERNEST F., b. Jan. 13, 1883.

III. MONA M., b. Sept. 27, 1886.

IV. RAY E., b. Sept. 17, 1888.

21.

(John 3, Stephen 2, Edmund 1.)

Children of **Daniel**[4] **Greenleaf** and Sarah (Moody).

I. ELIZABETH, b. June 10, 1713.

II. MARTHA, b. March 18, 1715 ; m. May 10, 1733, Isaac, son of William and Martha (Pierce) Johnson, b. about 1709.

William Johnson was b. Nov. 27, 1671. He moved from Charlestown, Mass., to Newbury in 1698. He was son of Nathaniel,

DANIEL (21) GREENLEAF, CONTINUED :—

> II. Martha.
>
>> b. 1642, and Joanna (Long), son of William, b. 1606, and Elizabeth (Storey), of Charlestown, Mass., son of Abraham, b. 1567, who m. 1, Annie Meadows in 1597. They had one child, Isaac, who m. the Lady Arbella Clinton, dau. of Thomas Furness, the third Earl of Lincoln, England. She d. at Salem, Mass., Aug. 30, 1630. Isaac d. Sept. 30, 1630, either in Charlestown or Salem. Isaac arrived with Winthrop in the " Eagle," otherwise the " Arbella," 1630; continued residence in Salem.
>>
>> Abraham m. 2, Cicely Chadderton, in 1602. He was probably descended from Maurice Johnson, who in the reign of Henry VIII. was, in 1523, M. P. for Stamford, England. Abraham, with his family, removed from Melton-Bryan to Canterbury, County Kent, England. William and Edward, sons of Abraham and Cicely, emigrated to America in 1630. William settled in Charlestown, Mass. Edward settled in Woburn, Mass. A descendant of his has prepared a history of the Johnson family.
>
> III. JANE, b. July 16, 1717; d. in infancy.
>
> IV. SARAH, b. July 6, 1719; m. Jan. 1, 1738, Moses Pearson, of Byfield, Mass.

511. > V. DAVID,[5] b. July 24, 1721, in Newbury, Mass.; m. Sarah Lamson. He d. June, 1785; one child :—

512. >> Daniel,[6] b. Sept. 20, 1753, at Newbury, Mass.; m. Polly Bridges. He d. 1839; res. Rumford, Me.; six children.

513. > VI. JONATHAN[5] (Hon.), b. July, 1723, in Newbury, Mass.; m. 1744, Mary, dau. of Edward Presbury. She d. May, 1807. He d. May 24, 1807; res. Newbury, Mass.; nine children.

>> Edward Presbury m. Aug. 27, 1713, Catherine Pierce. She was sister of Col. Daniel Pierce, of the Stone House and farm, afterwards Tracy's. Of their other children, Abigail m. Edward Harris, Eunice m. Jonathan Knight; another dau. m. Obed (?) Pearson. Edward Presbury and his wife were admitted to the First Church in Newbury, March 31, 1728. " Mr. Presbury was a tall, grave old man, of a strong mind and will, and a pious Presbyterian or Independent. He was by trade a shipbuilder, and passingly well off among that class of men. He owned the land from Ship Street to the rear of the lots on Federal Street, and down to Water Street, and the Ship Yard in front, afterwards owned by Hon. Jonathan Greenleaf."*

* Hon. Simon Greenleaf in letter, dated Nov. 10, 1845, to Rev. Jonathan Greenleaf, and numbered six in his collection of papers now with the compiler.

DANIEL (21) GREENLEAF, CONTINUED:—
    VII. PARKER, b. Feb. 21, 1725; d. in infancy.
    VIII. MARY, b. Sept. 8, 1729; d. in infancy.

512.

(David 5, Daniel 4, John 3, Stephen 2, Edmund 1.)

Children of **Daniel**[6] **Greenleaf** and Polly (Bridges).
    I. WILLIAM, b. Aug. 27, 1786; d. in infancy.
    II. WILLIAM, b. June 21, 1789; a teacher.
513a. III. CHARLES,[7] b. June 9, 1792; m.; a teacher; was drowned in eastern part of Maine; no children.
    IV. SARAH, b. March 1, 1794; m. Joseph Berry; d. April 24, 1831. She d. Nov. 14, 1836; eight children:—

      i. Mary P., b. Aug. 28, 1812; m. Benjamin Blanchard; three children.
      ii. Joseph S., b. May, 1814; m.; three children.
      iii. Jonathan S., b. May, 1816.
      iv. William H., b. May, 1818.
      v. Eben. P., b. Nov., 1820.
      vi. Elizabeth, b. Oct., 1824.
      vii. Martha J., b. April, 1827.
      viii. Daniel G., b. Feb., 1830.
514. V. JAMES B.,[7] b. May 25, 1796; m. Sybil Goddard; d. Aug. 2, 1872. He d. July 8, 1870; res. Rumford, Me.; ten children.
    VI. MARY, b. July 26, 1801; m. July 7, 1835, Nathaniel Etheridge; one child:—
    Stephen L., b. Jan. 30, 1840.

514.

(Daniel 6, David 5, Daniel 4, John 3, Stephen 2, Edmund 1.)

Children of **James B.**[7] **Greenleaf** and Sybil (Goddard).
515. I. WILLIAM T.,[8] b. Oct. 10, 1822, in Rumford, Me.; m. Oct., 1847, Betsey E. Ackley; res. Auburn, Me.; moved there 1883; three children:—
      1. Ella V., b. March 31, 1848; m. John C. Swett; carriage maker; res. Merrimac, Mass.; five children:—
      1. Frank W. 2. Alice G. 3. Leo M. 4. Fannie B. 5. Robert, d. young.

James B. (514) Greenleaf, Continued:—
  I. William T.

516.   ii. John A.,[9] b. Aug. 6, 1849; m. Etta M. Knights, of
    Peru, Me.; res. Auburn, Me.; contractor and
    builder; four children: 1. Bertha May, b. Sept.
    22, 1877; d. Aug. 20, 1879. 2. William A., b.
    Oct. 22, 1880. 3. Fred. B., b. Aug. 15, 1883. 4.
    Frank F., b. Aug. 15, 1892.

  iii. Alice J., b. Oct. 10, 1852; d. Jan. 8, 1868.

517. II. Andrew Peterson,[8] b. April 16, 1825, in Rum-
    ford, Me.; m. 1, Betsey Wardwell, of Otisfield,
    Me.; 2, Betsey Washburn Faunce, b. Dec. 31, 1828,
    in Paris, Me. He had been Deputy Sheriff in Maine
    for many years, and was killed at Cedar Creek, Va.,
    Oct. 19, 1864; res. Norway, Me.

Child by 1st marriage:—
    1. Ella B., b. March 15, 1852; m. Clarence Holmes.
      She d. Dec. 1, 1889.

Children by 2d marriage:—

518.   ii. Elgin A.,[9] b. Oct. 18, 1853, at Hebron, Me.; m.
    1883, Hattie, dau. of James O. Jaques, b. 1858;
    res. Bangor, Me.; no children.

  iii. Alma W., b. Feb. 17, 1855, at Hebron, Me.; m.
    Clemence Bailey.

  iv. Frank F., b. Feb. 26, 1857, at Norway, Me.; d.
    Feb. 7, 1865.

  III. George B., b. March 9, 1826; d. July 2, 1828.

  IV. Eleanor D., b. Feb. 20, 1828; m. Cyrus Millett, of
    Woodstock, Me. She d. 1866.

  V. Caroline G., b. Feb. 11, 1830; m. 1850, Thomas F.
    Maddox.

519. VI. George Barton,[8] b. Feb. 3, 1833; m. April 24,
    1857, Eliza W. Faunce, of Hebron, Me. He d.
    March 18, 1876, in Bethel, Me.; house carpenter; two
    children:—

    1. George Herbert, b. July 20, 1860, in Woodstock,
      Me.; res. in the West.

520.   ii. Harry Faunce,[9] b. May 10, 1868, at Auburn, Me.;
    m. June 28, 1892, Edith L., dau. of Luther W.
    Abbott, of Albany, Me.; res. Norway, Me.; fruit

JAMES B. (514) GREENLEAF, CONTINUED :—

VI. George Barton.

    raising on a farm ; two children : 1. George Luther, b. Oct. 26, 1893. 2. Elgin Abbott, b. Feb. 12, 1895.

521. VII. ROBERT H.,[8] b. March 6, 1834 ; m. Olivia Gray, of Paris, Me. ; res. Albuquerque, N. M. ; two children :—

522.   I. Victor,[9] m. Susan Blake, of Oxford, Me. ; lawyer ; res. Albuquerque, N. M.

    II. John, res. ——, Mass.

VIII. JULIA ANN, b. Sept. 1, 1836 ; m. Llewellyn Goodwin ; res. Geneseo, Kansas.

523. IX. JAMES LEWIS,[8] b. Jan. 9, 1839 ; m. Nov., 1874, Mary E. Dudley. He d. March, 1876, at Milford, Mass.

X. MARIA P., b. Feb. 11, 1843 ; m. Henry Davis, of Milton Plantation, Me. She d. July, 1889 ; four children :—

  i. George Davis.
  ii. Cora.
  iii. Frank.
  iv. Lizzie.

513.

(Daniel 4, John 3, Stephen 2, Edmund 1.)

Children of **Hon. Jonathan**[5] **Greenleaf** and Mary (Presbury).

I. DAVID, b. 1747 ; d. 1756.

II. JONATHAN, b. June 27, 1749 ; d. 1756.

III. MARY, b. 1750 ; d. in infancy.

524. IV. SIMON,[6] b. 1752 ; m. Hannah Osgood, of Andover, Mass. He d. 1776 ; one child :—

  Jonathan,[7]* b. June 21, 1774 ; d. 1798 ; unmarried.

V. SARAH, b. May 31, 1753 ; m. Oct., 1770, Capt. William Pierce Johnson, of Newburyport, Mass., b. 1745 ; d. June 4, 1804. She d. Feb. 3, 1839 ; res. Newburyport, Mass. ; six children :—

  i. Mary, b. April 25, 1777 ; d. Jan. 19, 1860.
  ii. Catherine, b. Jan. 4, 1780 ; d. April 27, 1858.
  iii. William Pierce, b. May 13, 1785 ; m. 1, Jan. 18, 1807, Henrietta, dau. of John and Margaret (Laughton) Tracy, b. June 28, 1782 ; d. July 8, 1811–12. 2, Sarah Waite. He d. July 7,

---

*Newbury Records : d. June 30, 1800, probable date of record, as he died suddenly in the year 1798, of yellow fever, on board of the U. S. Frigate " Essex," where he was a midshipman. (Greenleaf Genealogy, 1854, p. 95, Note 83.)

Hon. Jonathan (513) Greenleaf, Continued :—
V. Sarah.

1832; res. Newburyport, Mass.; three children by 1st marriage: 1. William Pierce, b. Nov. 10, 1807; m. Mrs. Elizabeth A. (Johnson) Gerrish, b. July 10, 1813; d. March 2, 1883. He d. Aug. 18, 1876; res. Chelsea, Mass.; no children. 2. Margaret Laughton, b. Jan. 20, 1809; m. April, 1829, Patrick Henry, son of Hon. Simon and Hannah (Kingman) Greenleaf (546). She d. July 8, 1879; eight children. 3. Edward Augustus, b. Aug. 11, 1810; m. March 26, 1835, at St. Louis, Mo., Harriet Klein, of Kattskill, N. Y., b. Aug. 13, 1816; d. Dec. 4, 1893. He d. June 5, 1851; res. St. Louis, Mo.; six children, all born at St. Louis, Mo.: (1) Frederick A., b. Jan. 13, 1836; m. Dec. 25, 1858, Elizabeth Reilly. He d. Sept. 28, 1887, at New Orleans, La. (2) Henrietta, b. Dec. 3, 1837; m. Oct. 27, 1858, Henry N. Soria, of New Orleans, La., b. at New York; res. New Orleans; three children: [1] Henry Johnson. [2] Henrietta May. [3] Genevieve. (3) Helen, b. Sept. 4, 1841; d. Dec. 9, 1843. (4) Albert Henry, b. Aug. 20, 1844; m. Mary P. Mowry. He d. Sept. 15, 1872, at St. Louis. (5) Alice, b. July 8, 1846. (6) Eugenia, b. Aug. 18, 1849. Five children by 2d marriage: 4. George Frederick. 5. Lucretia, married. 6. Sarah Jane, m. 1, Mr. Stimpson, of Baltimore, Md. 2, Major Treyhern; no children. 7. Eliza. 8. Freeman, married.

iv. Sarah, b. 1788; d. 1791.

v. Eleazer, b. Nov. 12, 1790; m. Oct. 1, 1811, Fanny Toppan, b. Aug. 14, 1791; d. Aug. 11, 1870. He d. Feb. 27, 1870; city clerk for many years of Newburyport, Mass.; six children: 1. Eleazer, b. April 25, 1813; m. July 14, 1841, Eunice B. Fernald, d. 1869. He d. Nov. 26, 1881; nine children: (1) Sarah Frances, b. Aug. 26, 1842; d. July 4, 1843. (2) William P., b. Nov. 17, 1844. (3) Henrietta Gerrish, b. July 28, 1846. (4) Edward Toppan, b. May 5, 1848. (5) Fanny Toppan, b. March 10, 1850. (6) Clara Toppan, b. Dec. 7, 1851. (7) Marie Louise, b. Oct. 16, 1854. (8) Charles Toppan, b. Dec. 28, 1857. (9) Margaret Andrews, b. Sept. 9, 1862. 2. Nancy Toppan, b. Sept. 30, 1814; m. April 27, 1854, John Gray, b. Dec. 5, 1798; d. Nov. 22, 1859; res. Newburyport, Mass.; one child: Fanny, b. Aug. 31, 1855; m. Sept. 11, 1878, Henry Bailey Little, b. Jan. 3, 1851; res. Newburyport, Mass.; eight children: [1] Edward Henry, b. Oct. 8, 1879. [2] John Gray, b. June 1, 1883; d. Jan. 23, 1887. [3] Eleanor Johnson, b. May 26, 1886. [4] Leon Magaw, b. Dec. 30, 1887. [5] Marion, b. May 25, 1889; d. July 30, 1890. [6] Allan Dodge, b. Oct. 10, 1891; d. Aug. 14, 1892. [7] Josephine Pierce, b. Aug. 25, 1893. [8] Charles Gray, b. July 9, 1895. 3. Sarah, b. Aug. 25, 1816; res. Newburyport, Mass. 4. Charles Toppan, b. Nov.

Hon. Jonathan (513) Greenleaf, Continued :—
  V. Sarah.

   21, 1819; m. Nov. 24, 1865, Sarah A. Bedell, b. Nov. 28, 1839;
   no children. 5. Philip Henry, b. Aug. 2, 1822; d. June 15,
   1825. 6. Fanny, b. April 19, 1824; d. June 15, 1847.
  vi. Jonathan Greenleaf (Dr.), b. Nov. 12, 1790, twin; m. 1813,
   Elizabeth, dau. of Major Gilman White. Dr. Jonathan G.
   Johnson d. Sept. 9, 1868; res. Newburyport, Mass.; nine children: 1. Jacob Perkins, m. Mary Emily Knight; children:
   (1) Greenleaf Adams, b. June 2, 1866. (2) Jacob Perkins, b.
   March, 1874. 2. Hannah Greenleaf Perkins, married. 3. Sarah
   Elizabeth, married. 4. Gilman White, married. 5. Thomas
   Edward, d. young. 6. Mary Addie, d. young. 7. Francis
   William. 8. Lewis Henry, married. 9. Lydia Hodge White.
525. VI. Moses,[6] b. May 19, 1755; m. Sept. 17, 1776, Lydia,
   dau. of Rev. Jonathan and Phebe (Griswold) Parsons,
   of Newburyport, Mass., b. April 3, 1755; d. March
   21, 1834. He d. Dec. 18, 1812, at New Gloucester,
   Me.; five children.
526. VII. Enoch,[6] b. Oct. 11, 1757, at Newburyport, Mass.;
   m. 1, May 13, 1783, Mary Stone, who d. Feb. 2,
   1789, aged 28; 2, Dorothy (Dolly) Ingersoll, d. April
   17, 1816, aged 59. He d. Jan. 9, 1798; res. Newburyport, Mass.; four children.
   VIII. Catherine, b. Nov. 12, 1759; m. Nov. 25, 1788,
   Anthony Davenport, of Newburyport, Mass., his 3d
   wife. She d. Nov. 15, 1838. Their son, Anthony,
   Jr., b. Jan. 24, 1802, m. May 10, 1825, Sarah Jackson Little, b. Sept. 13, 1801; nine children :—
   i. Catherine De Ford, b. Nov. 25, 1825; m. April 15, 1850, Au-
    gustus Pearson; res. Newburyport.
   ii. Sarah, b. Oct. 16, 1827; m. March 23, 1852, Silas P. Leigh, of
    Newbury, Mass.
   iii. George, b. Dec. 10, 1829; m. Nov. 24, 1859, Caroline M.
    Surrey, of Castine, Me.
   iv. Ichabod Nichols, b. Feb. 1, 1832; d. Feb. 15, 1835.
   v. Augusta Smith, b. Feb. 3, 1834; d. July 26, 1857.
   vi. Edward Little, b. March 17, 1838; m. Sept. 3, 1863, Sophronia
    A. Cross, of Ipswich, Mass.
   vii. Henry Walton, b. Nov. 19, 1839; m. Dec. 5, 1877, Lucy Ellen
    Little.
   viii. Albert Wood, b. Jan. 7, 1842; d. Jan. 21, 1863.
   ix. Frederick, b. Oct. 22, 1844; d. Dec. 14, 1844.
527. IX. Richard,[6] b. July 3, 1762, in Newburyport; m. Oct.
   2, 1786, Marcia, dau. of Caleb and Mary (Greenleaf)

Hon. Jonathan (513) Greenleaf, Continued :—

IX. Richard.

Tappan, b. June 21, 1764; d. May 23, 1832. He d. Feb. 11, 1796; res. Newburyport, Mass.; three children.

525.

(Hon. Jonathan 5, Daniel 4, John 3, Stephen 2, Edmund 1.)

Children of Capt. **Moses**[6] **Greenleaf** and Lydia (Parsons).

528. I. Moses,[7] b. Oct. 17, 1777, in Newburyport, Mass.; m. Feb. 11, 1805, at East Andover, Me., Persis, dau. of Dea. Ebenezer Poor, b. Oct. 22, 1775, at Andover, Me.; d. Jan. 18, 1851. He d. March 20, 1834, at Williamsburg, Me.; four children.

II. Clarina Parsons, b. Nov. 12, 1779, in Newburyport, Mass.; m. Nov. 26, 1801, at the house of her father, in New Gloucester, Me., Eleazer Alley Jenks, of Portland, Me.; d. July 12, 1807; a printer; published *Gazette* of Maine, at Portland, for several years. She d. Dec. 12, 1841; res. Brownville, Me.; three children :—

   i. Elizabeth, d. Feb. 1, 1869, at her brother's in Brownville, Me.

   ii. Alexander Hamilton, unmarried.

   iii. Eleazer Alley, m. Eliza Brown, of Brownville, Me.; d. 1874-5, at Brownville. He d. 1873-4; six children.

529. III. Ebenezer,[7] b. Nov. 23, 1781, at Newburyport, Mass.; m. 1, Sept., 1808, Hannah Dennison Haskell, of New Gloucester, Me., who. d. at Williamsburg, Me., April 1, 1839, age 55; 2, Jan., 1846, Mrs. Elizabeth Morrell. He d. Nov. 29, 1851; sea captain, packet Portland to Liverpool, England, farmer and land surveyor; res. Williamsburg, Me.; eight children.

530. IV. Simon,[7] b. Dec. 5, 1783, in Newburyport, Mass.; m. Sept. 18, 1806, Hannah, dau. of Ezra and Susanna (Whitman) Kingman, b. Aug. 5, 1787; d. Jan. 13, 1857. He d. Oct. 6, 1853. Mr. Kingman res. Bridgewater, Mass. Mrs. Kingman was dau. of Peter Whitman. Mr. Greenleaf res. Cambridge, Mass.; fifteen children, eleven of whom died in infancy.

CAPT. MOSES (525) GREENLEAF, CONTINUED :—

531. V. JONATHAN,[7] b. Sept. 4, 1785; m. Nov. 2, 1814,
Sarah Johnson, of New Gloucester, Me., b. Sept.
15, 1815; d. Feb. 28, 1858. He. d. April 24, 1865;
buried in Greenwood Cemetery; Presbyterian clergyman; res. Brooklyn, N. Y.; six children.

528.

(Moses 6, Hon. Jonathan 5, Daniel 4, John 3, Stephen 2, Edmund 1.)

Children of **Moses**[7] **Greenleaf** and Persis (Poor).

532. I. EBENEZER PARSONS,[8] b. Nov. 27, 1805, at Bangor,
Me.; m. Oct. 7, 1831, at Milo, Me., Mary Abigail,
dau. of Col. Joseph and Priscilla (Sparhawk) Lee,
b. July 6, 1804; d. April, 1847. He d. July 13,
1853, at Alton, Ill.; res. first at Williamsburg, Me.,
then in Milo. He afterwards removed to Illinois;
five children.

John Lee, the ancestor of Mary Abigail and Martha Laurens, who
married Moses, brother of Ebenezer P. Greenleaf, was an
early settler of Ipswich, Mass. The " History of John Leigh
or Lee, of Ipswich, 1634–1671, published at Albany, N. Y.,
1888," contains accounts of transfers of property: Thomas
Lord to John Leigh, Aug. 20, 1666; John Perkins to John
Lee, Nov. 4, 1669. " It was by the calmness and resolution
of John Perkins," says the author, " that the little colony
(Ipswich) in its first spring plantation, 1633, was preserved
from extermination by the Indians, the Tarrantines, who
visited them in forty canoes."

II. CLARA PARSONS, b. Sept. 20, 1807, at East Andover,
Me.; m. Oct. 11, 1831, at Williamsburg, Me., Rev.
William C. Greenleaf (566). She d. Dec. 20, 1881,
at Jacksonville, Ill.; no children.

She lived with her nephew Moses, in Newton, Iowa, and adopted
Ebenezer P. Greenleaf's children, and brought them up as her
own; living first in Shakopee, Minn., and afterwards in
Galesburg, Iowa.

III. LYDIA GRISWOLD, b. Oct. 1, 1811, at Williamsburg,
Me.; m. Sept. 24, 1835, at Williamsburg, Me.,
Samuel John Wilder. She d. Sept. 23, 1879, at the
home of her son, at Shakopee, Minn.; one child :—

John Arthur, b. July 6, 1836, at Charlestown, Mass.; d. at Shakopee, Minn.

533. IV. MOSES,[8] b. Jan. 24, 1815, at Williamsburg, Me.; m.
Jan. 1, 1849, at Bucksport, Me.; Martha Laurens

Moses (528) Greenleaf, Continued :—
IV. Moses.

Lee, of Milo, Me., b. May 18, 1814; d. Aug. 6, 1855, at Bucksport, Me. He d. Jan. 15, 1868, at Galesburg, Iowa; no children.

532.

(Moses 7, Moses 6, Hon. Jonathan 5, Daniel 4, John 3, Stephen 2, Edmund 1.)

Children of **Ebenezer Parsons**[8] **Greenleaf** and Mary Abigail (Lee).

534. I. Henry Lee,[9] b. June 30, 1834; m. August, 1868, in Chicago, Ill., an English lady; res. Belle Plaine, Iowa.

535. II. Moses,[9] b. Aug. 7, 1836; m. Dec. 15, 1870, Anna B., dau. of Capt. George Morris, b. Jan. 26, 1845; furniture dealer and undertaker; res. Newton, Iowa; five children :—

    i. Helen M., b. Sept. 8, 1872.
    ii. William Lee, b. Dec. 13, 1875.
    iii. Julia M., b. May 6, 1878.
    iv. Anna B., b. Jan. 30, 1881.
    v. Edith W., b. Jan. 1, 1883.

536. III. Edward Sparhawk,[9] b. June 5, 1838; m. May 8, 1867, Kate Barr, dau. of Eugene La Baum Greenleaf (111); res. Jacksonville, Ill.; eight children :—

537.   i. Eugene Lee,[10] b. May 26, 1868; m. Ella Hawkins; res. Kingman, Kan.; one child: Frank, b. June 16, 1894.
    ii. Clara May, b. April 5, 1870; m. William L. Alexander; res. Jacksonville, Ill.; one child :—
James G., b. Oct. 12, 1889.
    iii. Martha Louise, b. March 1, 1872.
    iv. A son, b. Dec. 1, 1874; d. in infancy.
    v. Malcolm Edward, b. May 19, 1877.
    vi. Grace, b. Aug. 29, 1880.
    vii. Moses, b. March 24, 1883.
    viii. Kate Hodge, b. July 28, 1889.

IV. Clara Elizabeth, b. March 17, 1840; d. Oct. 19, 1878, at Galesburg, Iowa, buried at Jacksonville, Ill.; unmarried.

EBENEZER PARSONS (532) GREENLEAF, CONTINUED :—

V. MARY ABIGAIL, b. June 17, 1842 ; m. Dec. 10, 1868, Hamilton M. Staley, of Mokena, Ill. ; res. Kingman, Kan. ; five children :—

   i. Clara, b. Sept. 24, 1870.
   ii. Kate Hamilton, b. Jan. 6, 1873.
   iii. John Greenleaf, b. Jan. 5, 1875.
   iv. Mary Elizabeth, b. Oct. 19, 1876.
   v. Edward Lee, b. June 15, 1878.

529.

(Moses 6, Hon. Jonathan 5, Daniel 4, John 3, Stephen 2, Edmund 1.)

Children of **Ebenezer**[7] **Greenleaf** and Hannah D. (Haskell).

538. I. ELEAZER ALLEY,[8] b. May 17, 1809, at Andover, Me. ; m. June 17, 1836, Susan P. Greely. She d. Oct. 20, 1881. He d. July 17, 1878, at Stillwater, Minn. ; a clergyman Protestant Episcopal church ; no children.

II. PERSIS POOR, b. Aug. 18, 1810 ; m. Feb. 12, 1829, Adam Huse Merrill, of Belfast, Me., b. Sept. 3, 1805 ; d. Nov. 27, 1888, at Williamsburg, Me. She d. July 30, 1895 ; res. Williamsburg, Me. ; thirteen children :—

   i. Adolphus, b. Jan. 22, 1830, at Williamsburg, Me. ; m. at Corinth, Me., June 26, 1851, Susan B. Perkins ; thirteen children : 1. Adams Huse, b. Nov. 4, 1852. 2. Alice, b. March 5, 1854. 3. Alfred, b. Oct. 11, 1856. 4. Helen, b. Sept. 15, 1857. 5. Maud, b. Sept. 22, 1859. 6. Marion, b. Dec. 27, 1860. 7. Eugene, b. Nov. 20, 1862. 8. Clarence Adolphus, b. Oct. 4, 1864. 9. Greenleaf P., b. 1866. 10. Wiggin, b. 1868. 11. Susan, b. Feb. 22, 1870. 12. Persis, b. March 16, 1873. 13. ———.
   ii. Henry Adams, b. Feb. 29, 1832, at Barnard, Me. ; m. 1853, at Brewer, Me., Sarah W. Dexter ; one child : Margaret, b. 1857.
   iii. Julia A., b. Jan. 2, d. May 15, 1834, at Barnard, Me.
   iv. Helen, b. March 18, 1835, at Barnard, Me. ; m. June 8, 1857, Samuel Pearson Johnson, at Williamsburg, Me. ; two children : 1. Carrie Marie, b. April 1, 1858. 2. Hattie Merrill, b. Aug. 28, 1868.
   v. Harriet, b. April 23, 1837, at Charleston, Me. ; m. Sept. 26, 1855, Charles Lincoln Dunning, at Williamsburg, Me. ; three children : 1. Charles Herbert, b. July 23, 1859. 2. Helena S., b. June 21, 1865. 3. Kate E., b. Feb. 11, 1867.

E<small>BENEZER</small> (529) G<small>REENLEAF</small>, C<small>ONTINUED</small> :—

II. Persis Poor.

vi. Marie, b. May 28, 1840, at Barnard, Me.; m. 1, Jan. 1, 1861, at Williamsburg, Me., John Frederick Dunning. He served in the Civil War, and died, 1862, in the United States Army; 2, Nov., 1869, at Bangor, Me., Alexander Hamilton Jenks; one child by 1st marriage: Frederick, b. May, d. Oct., 1862; three children by second marriage: 2. Charlotte Elizabeth, b. July 7, 1871. 3. Margaret Hamilton, b. May, 1884. 4. Kate Greenleaf, b. May, 1884; twin.

vii. Ferdinand Wilsey, b. July 5, 1842, at Corinth, Me.; m. March 2, 1868, at Lee, Me., Annette Rich; two children: 1. Guy b. Nov. 28, 1868. 2. Edward Arthur, b. April, 1874.

viii. Frederick, b. April 24, 1844, at Corinth, Me.; m. 1885, at Brownville, Me., Sarah E. Smith; two children: 1. Mason, b. March 4, 1888. 2. Arthur Sherman, b. March 4, 1888; twin.

ix. Kate, b. July 22, 1846, at Corinth, Me.; m. Nov., 1869, at Bangor, Me., Rufus Littlefield Wilder. She d. March 31, 1874, at Bangor, Me.; two children: 1. Henry Merrill, b. Jan. 19, 1871. 2. Frederick Mason, b. March 18, 1874.

x. Elizabeth, b. Aug. 15, 1848, at Corinth, Me.

xi. Martha, b. March 30, 1850, at Corinth, Me.; m. April 13, 1873, at Williamsburg, Me., Charles Albert Whitney, b. Jan. 17, 1851; d. Jan. 2, 1891; res. Andover, Mass.; two children: 1. Richard Merrill, b. Nov. 10, 1874. 2. Philip Lawrence, b. Sept. 15, 1880.

xii. Arthur, b. April 15, 1852, at Corinth, Me.; m. Feb. 14, 1874, at Newburgh, Me., Olive Elizabeth Whitney; three children: 1. Kate, b. Dec. 31, 1874. 2. Josephine M., b. Dec. 31, 1876. 3. Barbara, b. 1879.

xiii. Jessie, b. Aug. 26, 1855, at Williamsburg, Me.; m. May 3, 1874, Horace B. Nason; four children: 1. James Hamilton, b. Nov. 21, 1876. 2. Robert B., b. July 15, 1878. 3. Frederick Arthur, b. Feb. 6, d. Aug., 1881. 4. Julian H., b. Feb. 6, 1892.

539. III. M<small>ARSHFIELD</small> P<small>ARSONS</small>,[8] b. Jan. 23, 1813; m. Lydia Haskell, of Danville, Me. He. d. at Sioux City, Minn.; res. Williamsburg, Me.; no children.

IV. H<small>ANNAH</small> D<small>ENNISON</small>, b. May 1, 1814; m. Albert Harris, of Brunswick, Me. She d. Oct., 1840; three children.

V. E<small>LIZABETH</small> J<small>ENKS</small>, b. Aug. 8, 1818; m. July 8, 1845, Albert Harris, who had m. Hannah D. G. She d. April 19, 1853; res. Stillwater, Minn.

E BENEZER (529) G REENLEAF, C ONTINUED :—
540. VI. F REDERICK W ILLIAM,[8] b. May 21, 1820; m. Caroline W. Otis, of Boston. He d. July 28, 1850. She d. 1872; res. Worcester, Mass.; one child :—
541.　　Edward Hale,[9] b. 1848; formerly resided in Boston, Mass., moved to Santa Barbara, Cal., in 1893.

Mr. Greenleaf was for many years actively connected with the Museum of Fine Arts in Boston, being appointed Secretary in 1878, and Curator of the famous Gray collection of engravings in 1886. Also in charge of the Library until his appointment in Jan., 1889, as Curator of the Museum of Fine Arts, which position he resigned in 1893. He was also Secretary of the Archæological Institute of America, at Boston, chosen May 21, 1881.

542. VII. S IMON,[8] b. May 3, 1822; m. Frances Jane, dau. of John Foss, of Dover, N. H., b. Aug. 13, 1824. He d. March 13, 1893, at Savanna, Ill.; res. Savanna, Ill.; six children :—
543.　　I. Frederick William,[9] b. April 28, 1847; m. Oct. 31, 1872, Mary Irvine Hostetter; Lieut. U. S. N. Retired list; res. Augusta, Ga.; two children: 1. John Hostetter, b. March 22, 1876; d. in infancy. 2. Frederick Raymond, b. Feb. 6, 1884; d. in infancy.

II. Henry Harrington, b. Nov. 9, 1848; connected with Mexican Central R. R. many years.

III. Ada Elizabeth, b. Nov. 13, 1852; m. Aug. 31, 1879, Rev. Francis H. Potts, of Shakopee, Minn., b. Jan. 27, 1848, Galena, Ill.
544.　　IV. Oliver Wyatt,[9] b. Aug. 5, 1854; m. Dec. 24, 1877, Jessie Hampton Jenks; connected with Northern Pacific R. R.; two children: 1. Wyatt Hampton, b. Oct. 8, 1878. 2. Paul Armstrong, b. Dec. 26, 1885; d. June 13, 1892.
545.　　v. Francis Simon,[9] b. Aug. 16, 1859; m. Feb. 4, 1885, Margaret Teresa Kenney; owns and publishes the *Savanna Journal;* two children: 1. Kenneth, b. Nov. 4, 1886. 2. Frederick Harold, b. April 25, 1888.

VI. Edward Powers, b. Aug. 18, 1864; Editor *Savanna Journal.*

EBENEZER (529) GREENLEAF, CONTINUED:—

VIII. PHEBE GRISWOLD, b. April 2, 1826; m. Edwin
A. Willard. She d. March 2, 1882; res. Brownville, Me.; three children:—

i. Abbie G., b. March 19, 1850; m. July 4, 1870, E. E. Wheeler;
no children.

ii. Fred C., b. Aug. 22, 1857.

iii. Edwin A. Willard, Jr., b. March 8, 1864.

530.

(Moses 6, Hon. Jonathan 5, Daniel 4, John 3, Stephen 2, Edmund 1.)

Children of **Hon. Simon**[7] **Greenleaf** and Hannah (Kingman).

546. I. PATRICK HENRY,[8] b. July 11, 1807; m. April, 1829,
Margaret Laughton, dau. of William Pierce Johnson,
of Newburyport, Mass., b. Jan. 20, 1809; d. July 8,
1879. He d. June 21, 1869; clergyman; res. Brooklyn, N. Y.; eight children.

II. CHARLOTTE KINGMAN, b. Dec. 25, 1809; m. July 15,
1830, Rev. Samuel Fuller, D.D., son of Rev. Samuel
and Ruth (Pond) Fuller, of Rensselaerville, N. Y.,
b. April 25, 1802; d. March 8, 1895; res. Middletown, Conn.; seven children:—

i. Samuel, b. Dec. 15, 1832; d. Feb. 6, 1838.

ii. Charlotte, b. Dec. 2, 1834; m. June 8, 1863, Ange Albert Pattou.
She d. July 24, 1865.

iii. Harriet Elizabeth, b. Oct. 13, 1836; d. April 25, 1863.

iv. Simon Greenleaf, b. Sept. 11, 1838; m. May 23, 1861, Celeste
Parmalee, dau. of Rev. William Bostwick. He d. Nov. 21,
1872; clergyman; three children: 1. Henry Riley, b. June
16, 1862; m. Genevieve Gardner; three children: (1) Louis
Gardner, b. Oct. 15, 1881. (2) Harold William, b. Jan. 18,
1886. (3) Charlotte Celeste, b. Dec. 13, 1893. 2. William
Bostwick, b. Jan. 30, 1864; m. Gertrude Dada; one child:
Chester Dada, b. Aug. 1, 1891. 3. Caroline Mary, b. April
20, 1871; d. Sept 20, 1879.

v. Caroline A., b. June 19, 1845; m. Oct. 23, 1873, W. J. de Mau-
riac. She d. Jan. 3, 1893; four children: 1. Philippe Octave,
b Nov. 10, 1880. 2. Henry de Wolf, b. Sept. 27, 1882. 3.
Pierre Greenleaf, b. Nov. 23, 1885. 4. Charlotte Greenleaf,
b. Nov. 19, 1887.

vi. James Robert, b. March 19, 1848; m. Oct. 16, 1872, Josephine
Brown Lester, b. Sept. 7, 1850; physician; res. Boston,
Mass.; two children: 1. Samuel Lester, b. June 12, 1875.
2. James Greenleaf, b. Nov. 14, 1885.

Hon. Simon (530) Greenleaf, Continued :—

II. Charlotte Kingman.

vii. Samuel Richard, b. Jan. 5, 1850; m. 1, June 27, 1872, Leora Campbell, dau. of Norman L. and Leora (Campbell) Brainerd, b. Jan. 24, 1850; divorced. 2. Aug. 22, 1895, Lucy, dau. of the late Elias Hasket Derby. Mr. Fuller is a clergyman; res. Malden, Mass.; two children by 1st marriage: 1. Samuel Richard, b. Feb. 19, 1879, at Corning, N. Y. 2. Robert, b. March 17, 1880, at Corning, N. Y.

547. III. James,[8] b. June 15, 1814; m. Oct. 22, 1839, Mary, dau. of Stephen and Zilpha (Wadsworth) Longfellow, b. June 28, 1816. He d. Aug. 22, 1865; res. Cambridge, Mass.; no children.

IV. Caroline Augusta, b. Sept. 16, 1826, at Portland, Me.; m. April 30, 1850, at Andover, Mass., Rev. Andrew, son of Samuel and Mary (Palmer) Croswell, b. July 9, 1822, at Falmouth, Mass.; d. June 30, 1879. She d. Nov. 8, 1878; res. Cambridge, Mass.; five children :—

i. James Greenleaf, b. Aug. 29, 1852; m. May 10, 1888, Letitia, dau. of Charles Loring Brace, of New York, and Letitia (Neill) of Belfast, Ire. Mr. Croswell was educated at Cambridge High School; graduated Harvard, A.B., 1873; studied in Europe, 1878–81; tutor and professor Greek at Harvard, 1874–78, 1881–87; head master of Brearley School, New York, 1887 to the present.

ii. Simon Greenleaf, b. Aug. 3, 1854; unmarried; educated at Cambridge High School; entered Harvard College, 1871; graduated A.B., 1875; graduated Harvard Law School, LL.B., 1878; admitted to Suffolk Bar, 1879. *Writings:* Edited "Greenleaf on Evidence," twice, 1883 and 1892; edited " Washburn on Easements," 1884, and (with Joseph Willard, Esq.) " Washburn on Real Property," 1887; lectured in Boston University Law School, 1887–89; wrote a book on the " Law of Executors and Administrators," 1889, and on the law relating to Electricity, 1895.

iii. Alice, b. Aug. 14, 1856; d. Aug. 12, 1858.

iv. Anna, b. Nov. 26, 1858.

v. Mary Caroline, b. April 28, 1862.

546.

(Hon. Simon 7, Moses 6, Hon. Jonathan 5, Daniel 4, John 3, Stephen 2, Edmund 1.)

Children of **Rev. Patrick Henry**[8] **Greenleaf, D.D.,** and Margaret L. (Johnson).

548. I. Henry Loring,[9] b. April 25, 1830; m. Nov. 24, 1854, Harriet Gregory, of Montreal, Can., b. Dec. 9, 1831;

Rev. Patrick Henry (546) Greenleaf, Continued :—
I. Henry Loring.
d. April 16, 1893, in Everett, Mass., at the residence
of her son, Rev. Arthur P. Greenleaf. Mr. Henry
L. Greenleaf d. July 23, 1860; res. New Orleans,
La.; three children.
She m. 2, Nelson W. Perry, of Mobile, Ala., b. Feb. 5, 1811; d.
Aug. 31, 1884. By her 2d marriage one child: Nelson Wil-
kinson, b. Jan. 25, 1872.
II. Henrietta Tracy, b. April 25, 1831; m. Nov. 25,
1851, Rev. Charles Whitfield Homer, D.D., b. Jan.
22, 1828; res. Brooklyn, N. Y.; five children :—
  i. Charles Patrick, b. Sept. 17, 1852, in Cambridge, Mass.; d.
  July 18, 1853, at New Bedford, Mass.
  ii. Henry Greenleaf, b. May 27, 1854; m. Nov. 5, 1885, Sarah
  Elizabeth Stoddard, b. Feb., 1856; res. Brooklyn, N. Y.;
  four children: 1. Margaret Greenwood, b. July 8, 1886. 2.
  Charles Whitfield, b. May 9, 1889. 3. Langley Stoddard, b.
  Sept. 2, 1890. 4. Sarah Elizabeth, b. Dec. 15, 1892.
  iii. Adeline, b. Oct. 10, 1855, in Newark, N. Y.; m. Oct. 8, 1885,
  Edward Fitzgerald de Selding, a widower, lawyer, of New
  York City; two children: 1. Helen, b. Oct. 2, 1886. 2. Henrietta Tracy, b. March 4, 1891.
  Mr. de Selding m. 1, Sept. 18, 1855, Elizabeth Monroe Shrews-
  bury; their children were: 1, Herman. 2. Joseph Shrews-
  bury.
  iv. Frances Prentiss, b. Oct. 23, 1856, in Newark, N. Y.; m. Jan.
  29, 1880, William de Forrest Curtis, b. Aug. 26, 1853, in Philadelphia, Penn.; res. Boston, Mass.; two children: 1.
  Frances de Forrest, b. Nov. 21, 1880. 2. Edward de Forrest,
  b. July 21, 1884.
  v. Margaret Greenleaf, b. June 26, 1862, in Lowell, Mass.; m.
  Dec. 31, 1889, John Stevens Melcher, b. Aug. 24, 1859; a
  lawyer; res. New York City; two children: 1. Margaret
  Sybil, b. Sept. 4, 1892. 2. John, b. March 28, 1895.
549. III. James Edward,[9] b. Aug. 2, 1832; m. Nov. 7,
1853, Mary Elizabeth, dau. of Hon. Paul and Harriet (Whiting) Willard, b. July 10, 1831; res. Charlestown, Mass.; three children :—
  i. Robert Willard,[10] b. Jan. 24, 1855; physician; res.
  Boston.
  ii. Ellen Willard, b. Dec. 22, 1857.
  iii. Mary Willard, b. July 29, 1861; artist.
IV. Charlotte Kingman, b. Dec. 10, 1833; d. Oct. 7,
1834.

REV. PATRICK HENRY (546) GREENLEAF, CONTINUED :—

550. V. GEORGE HERBERT,[9] b. Nov. 25, 1834; m. May 6, 1869, Elizabeth B. Chew, b. June 18, 1846. He d. Jan. 20, 1879; res. Philadelphia, Penn.; no children.

551. VI. CHARLES RAVENSCROFT,[9] b. Jan. 2, 1838; m. Sept. 10, 1862, Georgiana Henri Franck de la Roche, b. Nov. 12, 1839; lieutenant colonel and deputy surgeon general U. S. A., station, San Francisco, Cal.; four children :—

    I. Charles de la Roche,[10] b. July 30, 1863; d. Jan. 2, 1867.

    II. Edith, b. Oct. 23, 1867.

    III. Patrick Henry,[10] b. Sept. 15, 1870; has adopted Henry Simpson Greenleaf as his name. He is a physician; res. Philadelphia, Penn.

    IV. George Ravenscroft,[10] b. Jan. 28, 1873.

  VII. CHARLOTTE, b. May 1, 1839; m. June 6, 1865, Henry Martyn Congdon, b. May 10, 1834; architect; res. Brooklyn, N. Y.; five children :—

    i. Ernest Arnold, b. Aug. 9, 1866; Professor of Chemistry at Drexel Institute, Philadelphia, Penn.

    ii. Elizabeth Tracy, b. Oct. 28, 1868; d. Nov. 19, 1868.

    iii. Mary Louise, b. Dec. 4, 1871; d. July 12, 1872.

    iv. Harold Greenleaf, b. Feb. 21, 1875; d. July 25, 1875.

    v. Herbert Wheaton, b. May 9, 1876.

  VIII. MARGARET LAUGHTON, b. April 8, 1841; d. Feb. 20, 1847.

548.

(Rev. Patrick Henry 8, Hon. Simon 7, Moses 6, Hon. Jonathan 5, David 4, John 3, Stephen 2, Edmund 1.)

Children of **Henry Loring**[9] **Greenleaf** and Harriet (Gregory).

552. I. WALTER GREGORY,[10] b. Feb. 14, 1856; m. Ellen Louise De Golyer, b. Jan. 24, 1864; res. Riverside, Ill.; two children :—

    I. Harriet De Golyer, b. Oct. 19, 1892.

    II. Margaret De Golyer, b. March 30, 1894.

553. II. ARTHUR PERRY,[10] b. April 26, 1857; m. July 15, 1884, Harriet Louisa, dau. of Isaac Newton and Emily (Dunbar) Gregory, b. March 9, 1861. Protestant

HENRY LORING (548) GREENLEAF, CONTINUED:—

II. Arthur Perry.

Episcopal clergyman, rector of Grace Church; res. Everett, Mass.; two children:—

i. Helen, b. June 3, 1885.
ii. Newton Gregory, April 27, 1889; d. Sept. 29, 1890.

III. MARGARET LAUGHTON, b. May 13, 1859; m. Aug. 31, 1880, Harrison Hancock Bowes, b. Dec. 11, 1855; lawyer; res. Tekamah, Neb.; eight children:—

i. Kate Greenleaf, b. July 9, 1881; d. Oct. 14, 1881.
ii. William Rudolph, b. Oct. 22, 1882.
iii. Ruth Laughton, b. Jan. 1, 1884; d. Aug. 29, 1891.
iv. Harrison Hancock, b. Feb. 21, 1886; d. Oct. 4, 1886.
v. Frank Jewell, b. Oct. 1, 1887.
vi. Marion, b. Dec. 13, 1888.
vii. Mary Eliza, b. June 21, 1890; d. Nov. 16, 1890.
viii. Arthur Greenleaf, b. Sept. 22, 1891.

531.

(Moses 6, Hon. Jonathan 5, Daniel 4, John 3, Stephen 2, Edmund 1.)

Children of **Rev. Jonathan[7] Greenleaf, D.D.**, and Sarah (Johnson).

I. SARAH JOHNSON, b. Sept. 18, 1815; d. Aug. 6, 1816.
II. MARY PRESBURY, b. Feb. 9, 1817; m. Lucius Kimball, of Lyndon, Vt.; res. Garfield, N. J.; no children.
554. III. JONATHAN PARSONS,[8] b. Nov. 3, 1818; m. Mary L., dau. of Judge John Terhune, of New Brunswick, N. J. She d. June 22, 1889, at New Brunswick, N. J. He d. Feb. 22, 1843, at sea; graduate of Rutgers College; Presbyterian minister; no children.
IV. CATHERINE DAVENPORT, b. Dec. 20, 1819; m. John D. McKenzie, of Brooklyn, N. Y. She d. Nov. 3, 1871, at Dobbs Ferry, N. Y.; nine children.

i. George Sampson, b. Dec. 25, 1841; m. 1, Nov. 24, 1863, Charlotte Ida Swertcope, who d. Dec. 31, 1874. 2, March 15, 1876, Mary Amelia Bynner; res. Chicago, Ill.; five children by 1st marriage: 1. Louise, b. May 6, 1865, in Chicago, Ill. 2. Kate, b. April 1, 1867, in Brooklyn, N. Y. 3. Frederick Ives, b. Aug. 24, 1868, in Brooklyn, N. Y.; d. June 18, 1875. 4. Grace, b. Oct. 16, 1871, in Brooklyn, N. Y. 5. Kenneth, b. May 31, 1873, in Flatbush, N. Y.; d. Feb. 13, 1876. Child by 2d marriage: Rex, b. March 28, 1880.

Rev. Jonathan (531) Greenleaf, Continued :—

    IV. Catherine Davenport.

      ii. Sarah Parsons, b. Sept. 17, 1843; d. Aug. 18, 1864.

      iii. Parsons Greenleaf, b. Oct. 18, 1845; d. Aug. 21, 1846.

      iv. Jeromus Johnson, b. May 28, 1847; d. July 18, 1849.

      v. Donald, b. April 21, 1851; m. Oct. 21, 1874, Mary Jane Van
Horn, b. June 21, 1851, in Communipaw, Jersey City, N. J.;
res. Cleveland, Ohio; three children: 1. Catherine Greenleaf, b. Dec. 1, 1876, at Jersey City, N. J. 2. Mary, b. Dec.
25, 1878, at Grand Rapids, Mich. 3. Jean, b. July 22, 1891,
at Cleveland, Ohio.

      vi. John Caswell, b. Feb. 25, 1853; d. April 4, 1882.

      vii. Spencer Goodrich, b. Jan. 19, 1858; m. March, 1894, ——
Lorens; res. Brooklyn, N. Y.

      viii. Malcolm, b. March 18, 1861; m. Nov. 1, 1893, Josephine,
dau. of Israel C. Pierson, of Plainfield, N. J.; res. New York
City; no children.

      ix. Angus, b. March 18, 1861, twin; m. Oct. 10, 1893, May, dau.
of John A., and granddaughter of the late John J. Cisco,
Treasurer of the United States; res. New York City; one
child: Mildred May, b. Oct. 6, 1894.

    V. Ann Elizabeth, b. Jan. 23, 1822; m. Edward A.
Cahoon, of Lyndon, Vt.; res. Garfield, N. J.; no
children.

    VI. Sarah Joanna, b. June 6, 1832; m. Jan. 16, 1856,
Elisha Scott Young, of Brooklyn, N. Y.; res. Garfield,
N. J.; four children :—

      i. Anna Greenleaf, b. Oct. 28, 1856.

      ii. Charles Elisha, b. Aug. 27, 1858; m. Sept. 13, 1888, Caroline
T. Dennis, of New York; physician; res. White Plains, N. Y.;
one child: Florence Greenleaf, b. Sept., 1890.

      iii. Jonathan Greenleaf, b. March 14, 1861; m. July 6, 1887, Lau-
rette May Dutton, of Milford, N. H.
By an act of Assembly of New York State his name was changed
and is now Jonathan Greenleaf. He is a Presbyterian clergyman, and settled in Princetown, N. Y.; two children: 1. Jonathan Parsons, b. May 2, 1888. 2. Anna Elizabeth, b. Sept.
5, 1894.

      iv. James Scott, b. Jan. 19, 1864; Presbyterian clergyman; res.
Garfield, N. J.

526.

(Hon. Jonathan 5, Daniel 4, John 3, Stephen 2, Edmund 1.)

Children of **Enoch**[6] **Greenleaf** and Dorothy (Ingersoll).

555. I. George,[7] b. July 22, 1790; m. 1, Oct. 19, 1813, Elizabeth Coggswell, dau. of Capt. Abraham Wheel-
wright, of Newburyport, Mass., who d. May, 1844.

Enoch (526) Greenleaf, Continued :—

I. George.

2, Mrs. —— Huse ; res. Newburyport, Mass. ; eight children by 1st marriage :—

i. Mary Ann, b. Sept. 29, 1814; d. Dec. 30, 1844.

ii. George, b. Aug. 31, 1816; d. March 11, 1840, at sea, on board ship "Daniel Webster," on the coast of New Zealand.

iii. Elizabeth W., b. Aug. 26, 1818; d. Sept. 1, 1819.

iv. Abraham W., b. Dec. 6, 1820; d. April 20, 1842.

v. Caroline E., b. Feb. 8, 1823; m. March 3, 1870, William Thurston, of Newburyport, Mass. He first married Dorothea Pearson Coleman, who died Jan. 4, 1868.

vi. Laura W., b. Oct. 31, 1826; d. July, 1853.

vii. Rebecca K., b. Nov. 4, 1827; d. Aug. 7, 1830.

viii. Rebecca Wheelwright, b. Nov. 14, 1832; m. Sept., 1855, George F. Choate, of Salem, Mass. He was Judge of Probate Court. She d. Aug., 1858; one child : a son, d. in infancy.

II. Dorothy (Dolly), b. Jan. 18, 1792, in Newburyport, Mass. ; m. Aug. 29, 1814, Henry Sleeper Pearson, of Portland, Me., b. May 23, 1789, in Newburyport, Mass. She d. Oct. 5, 1842. He d. Aug. 30, 1878; res. Portland, Me. ; ten children :—

i. Caroline Greenleaf, b. May 29, 1815; d. June 4, 1834.

ii. Elizabeth P., b. Dec. 2, 1816; m. William Senter. He d. Dec. 22, 1888; res. Portland, Me. Mr. Senter was at one time mayor of Portland, Me.

iii. Clarina Jenks, b. Aug. 17, 1818; d. Aug. 2, 1819.

iv. Miranda, b. Oct. 8, 1820; m. William J. Robinson, of New York. She d. Nov. 6, 1876; six children.

v. Henrietta, b. Oct. 21, 1822.

vi. Harriet Jane, b. Nov. 30, 1824; d. July 29, 1828.

vii. Mary Greenleaf, b. Feb. 16, 1827; m. James Young, of Rock Hall, Maryland, who d. in 1890.

viii. Sarah Payson, b. Feb. 16, 1827; d. April 3, 1828, twin.

ix. George Henry, b. Feb. 27, 1829; m. Mary F. Hitchcock; three children : 1. Harry Greenleaf, b. Dec. 26, 1870; graduated Harvard College, 1892; teacher in Boston School of Technology 1894. 2. Arthur Manning, b. Oct. 7, 1875. 3. Bertha, b. Nov. 21, 1881.

x. Ann Louisa, b. Oct. 3, 1831; m. John Ballou, of Portland, Me., who d. in 1864; one child: Joseph Willard, of New Haven, Conn.

ENOCH (526) GREENLEAF, CONTINUED :—

   III. ENOCH, b. Oct. 20, 1793; d. Sept. 27, 1797.

   IV. CAROLINE, b. July 20, 1796; m. March 22, 1819, at
        Newburyport, Mass., Jonathan Call, of Charlestown,
        Mass., b. Feb. 2, 1786; d. July 26, 1853, at West
        Cambridge, Mass. She d. Feb. 17, 1830, at Charles-
        town, Mass.·

        Mr. Call m. 2, Sarah Payson, of Charlestown. Their dau. Emily
        Payson Call m. her cousin Henry Call. They had three chil-
        dren. He d. ———; she m. 2, Dr. E. A. Whiston, and res.
        Newtonville, Mass. They have two children.

    Caroline and Jonathan Call had four children :—

    i. Caroline Greenleaf, b. April 4, 1820, at Charlestown, Mass.;
       m. 1, Dec. 5, 1838, Nathaniel, son of Hon. Heman and Julia
       (Strong) Norton, of East Bloomfield, N. Y., b, July 16,
       1808; d. March 29, 1847, at Brooklyn, N. Y.; 2, April 6,
       1848, at Norwich, Conn., Walter Scott, son of Griffith Ap.*
       and Phœbe (Andrus-Scott) Griffith, b. July 22, 1808; d. Nov.,
       1872. She d. Aug. 29, 1864, at Litchfield, Conn. Four chil-
       dren by 1st marriage, born at Brooklyn, N. Y.: 1. Nathaniel,
       b. Oct. 7, 1839; m. Sept. 27, 1865, at Mt. Kisco, N. Y.,
       Emma Sylvia, dau. of Jehiel and Sylvia (Smith-Kendrick)
       Read, b. Nov. 24, 1842, at Scottsville, N. Y. Mr. Norton
       graduated at Yale College, 1860, and at Columbia Law
       School; a merchant at New York since 1864; four children :
       (1) Nathaniel. (2) Emma. (3) Stella. (4) William Strange.
       2. Caroline Philippa, b. July 15, 1841; m. Oct. 9, 1861, in
       Brooklyn, N. Y., Charles Augustus, son of George Corlis and
       Mary Ann (Hubbard) Sherman, b. May 26, 1838; d. April 25,
       1882; graduate Law School Albany University, May, 1859; a
       lawyer; res. Watertown, N. Y.; six children, all born at
       Watertown, N. Y.: (1) George Charles, b. July 25, 1862; m.
       Nov. 17, 1886, in Watertown, N. Y., Alice Lee, only dau. of
       William Watson and Susan Safford (Lee) Taggart, of Evans
       Mills, N. Y., b. Oct. 31, 1862; res. Watertown, N. Y.; two
       children : ¹Katharine Lee, b. Aug. 29, 1887. ²Carolyn Nor-
       ton, b. Sept. 11, 1889. (2) Caroline Greenleaf, b. Dec. 11,
       1863; m. June 5, 1889, in Watertown, N. Y., Henry, third
       son of William Tileston and Adriana (Lawrence) Whitte-
       more, of New York City; res. Englewood, N. J.; one child :
       Elizabeth Lawrence, b. June 9, 1890, in New York City.
       (3) Francis Augustus, b. Jan. 31, 1865; res. Watertown, N.
       Y. (4) Charles Norton, b. June 18, 1871; m. June 14, 1894,
       in Watertown, N. Y., Grace Adelaide, only dau. of Jean R.
       and Adelaide C. (Cooper) Stebbins, of Watertown, N. Y.
       (5) Nathaniel Norton, b. Jan. 26, 1873; d. Oct. 21, 1893.

   *For Biography see Johnson's New Universal Cyclopædia, Vol. II., Part 1.

Enoch (526) Greenleaf, Continued:—
IV. Caroline.

Cornell University, Ithaca, N. Y., class of 1895. (6) Margaret Alice, b. March 19, 1875. 3. William Augustus, b. Feb. 20, 1845; d. June 21, 1847. 4. Julia Elizabeth, b. July 5, 1847; d. June 28, 1848. Six children by 2d marriage: 5. Greenleaf, d. young. 6. Emily Call, teacher in Mrs. Piatt's School; res. Utica, N. Y. 7. Margaret Tillinghast, trained hospital nurse; res. Brooklyn, N. Y. 8. Charles Greenleaf, unmarried; a mining engineer and assayer; res. Helena, Montana. 9. Angeline, d. young. 10. George F. X.; a priest in the Roman Catholic Church; res. Italy and Germany for four years past. He has translated several books from the French. From Sept. 1896 Professor of *Belles-lettres* in Yonkers Seminary, New York.

ii. Philippa, b. July 16, 1822; m. Dec. 31, 1846, at Charlestown, Mass., Rev. Charles P. Bush, b. Nov. 11, 1813, at Rochester, N. Y. She d. Aug. 28, 1858, at Beloit, Wis. Four children: two died young, two daughters now living. 1. Caroline, missionary of the A. B. C. F. M. in Harpoot, Turkey. 2. Annie Everett.

iii. Sarah Payson, b. and d. Aug. 24, 1826.

iv. Sarah Payson, b. July 10, 1829; d. Jan. 10, 1830.

527.

(Hon. Jonathan 5, Daniel 4, John 3, Stephen 2, Edmund 1.)

Children of **Richard**[6] **Greenleaf** and Marcia (Tappan).

556. I. Richard,[7] b. July 11, 1787, in Newbury, Mass.; m. March 22, 1821, Sophia, dau. of Moses and Sarah (Towle) Leavitt, b. Sept. 28, 1800; d. May 18, 1859. He d. April 29, 1862; magistrate; res. Brunswick, Me.; five children:—

i. Marcia, b. Feb. 25, 1822, in Hampton, N. H.; m. Feb. 25, 1841, Capt. Richard Merriman, of Brunswick, Me.; four children: 1. Sophia G., b. Dec. 14, 1842; at school in Liverpool, Eng., 1860. 2. Maria Lincoln, b. Jan. 11, 1845; d. Sept. 5, 1845. 3. Richard G., b. March 14, 1846; at school, Farmington, Me., 1860; graduated Bowdoin College, 1867; teacher at Applegate, Cal., 1886. 4. Ella.

ii. Jonathan Leavitt, b. Jan. 30, 1825, in Hampton, N. H.; d. Nov. 7, 1842.

RICHARD (527) GREENLEAF, CONTINUED :—

   I. Richard.

557.   III. Charles W.,[8] b. Nov. 18, 1828, in Hampton, N.H. ;
            m. Arabella, dau. of Capt. Joseph Lunt, of Bruns-
            wick, Me. ; a carpenter. She d. about 1855.

558.   IV. John O'Brien,[8] b. March 2, 1832, in Brunswick,
            Me. ; married ; three children : 1. Charles, kept a
            clothing store. 2. A daughter. 3. A daughter.

He was mate of ship, and afterwards resided in Newburyport,
Mass., whence he removed to Brunswick, Me., in 1850, and
lived there about ten years. He was Secretary of United
Lodge. Soon after the death of Richard Greenleaf, Mrs.
Marcia Merriman and John O'Brien Greenleaf removed to
California, and resided in San Francisco.

         V. Mary, b. Nov. 27, 1837, in Brunswick, Me. ; m. about
            1866, Rev. Dr. Lapham, a Methodist clergyman.

He was a talented and energetic man; through his efforts the
Methodist Church on Pleasant Street was erected in 1866.

   II. MARY, b. June 27, 1789, in Newbury, Mass. ; m.
       June 20, 1819, Gen. Richard T. Dunlap, of
       Brunswick, Me. She d. July 9, 1834; four chil-
       dren :—

       i. John, b. June 22, 1820; d. unmarried.
       ii. Robert P., b. April 20, 1823; d. unmarried.
       iii. Mary, b. March 29, 1825; m. 1861, Dr. Holt, of Lowell, Mass.
       iv. George, b. June 10, 1830; d. Oct. 8, 1833.

   III. WILLIAM, b. June 11, 1792, in Newbury, Mass.; d.
        May 18, 1797, at Hampton, N. H.

22.

(John 3, Stephen 2, Edmund 1.)

Children of **Hon. John**[4] **Greenleaf** and Sarah (Smith).

   I. A SON, b. Nov. 4, 1719; d. in infancy.

558a II. RICHARD,[5] b. April 23, 1721 ; m. Mary ——, who d.
             Dec. 22, 1789, aged 65. He d. July 4, 1780; no
             children.

       III. JANE, b. Aug. 29, 1723.

       IV. SARAH, b. July 30, 1725.

       V. JAMES, b. Oct. 7, 1727.

       VI. HANNAH, b. Dec. 30, 1729.

559. VII. BENJAMIN[5] (Hon.), b. March 19, 1732 ; m. 1,
             Sept. 22, 1757, Elizabeth, dau. of Rev. Charles and

HON. JOHN (22) GREENLEAF, CONTINUED :—
VII. Benjamin.
Elizabeth (dau. of Judge Hirst) Chauncey, D.D., b.
Nov. 12, 1731; d. July 12, 1769; 2, Jan. 22, 1784,
Mrs. Lucy (?) Derby. She had been m. twice be-
fore, and survived the judge many years. He d. Jan.
11, 1799; res. Newburyport, Mass.; six children.

559.
(John 4, John 3, Stephen 2, Edmund 1.)

Children of **Hon. Benjamin[5] Greenleaf** and Elizabeth
(Chauncey).
I. ELIZABETH, b. July 13, 1758; m. Jan. 13, 1780,
Theophilus Parsons, b. Feb. 24, 1750, grad. Harvard College, 1769, A.M., LL.D., 1804; Dartmouth,
1807; Brown, 1809; chief justice Supreme Court
Massachusetts; d. 1813. She d. Feb. 13, 1829;
one child :—
Charles Chauncey, b. 1782; m. Judith Parsons. He d. 1851;
Grad. Harvard College, 1801; two children.
560. II. JOHN,[6] b. July 8, 1760; m. 1, Nov. 2, 1791, Elizabeth, only child of Capt. Coates, of Newburyport,
Mass. She d. about a year after, aged 27. 2, the
widow of Capt. Thomas Greenleaf.* John d. about
1830; res. Newburyport and Topsham, Me.; one
child by 1st marriage :—
1. David Coates, b. Oct. 18, 1792; d. Sept. 18, 1793.
Child by 2d marriage :—
561. 11. John,[7] b. June 22, 1796; m. Jan. 19, 1825, Fraisilette
Cutler, dau. of Capt. Francis Lane, of Newbury-
port, Mass.; res. Topsham, Me.; five children :—
562. 1. Charles Chauncey,[8] b. June 6, 1826; m. Sept.
31, 1849, Clara Robie, of Chester, N. H. 2.
Elizabeth Coates, b. Sept. 14, 1830. 3. Francis
William, b. March 7, 1833; d. Nov. 27, 1851.
4. Sarah Parks, b. Oct. 23, 1834. 5. John
Clement, b. Sept. 25, 1848.
III. SARAH, b. June 21, 1763; d. in old age; unmarried.

* A Thomas Greenleaf appears in the Newbury Records, who m. June 13, 1789, Elizabeth Coats. They had two children: 1, Mehitable Coats, b. March 20, 1790; m. Feb. 19,
1818, Capt. William Young. 2, Elizabeth, b. Aug. 8, 1792. "——, relict of Thomas
Greenleaf, d. March 29, 1825."

Hon. Benjamin (559) Greenleaf, Continued:—
  IV. Mary, b. Nov. 1, 1765; unmarried.
  V. Hannah, b. Nov. 1, 1765; twin; m. Sept. 22, 1807, Robert Boyd, of Portland, Me.
  VI. Jane, b. July 23, 1768; m. April 12, 1802, Ralph Cross, of Portland, Me.

24.

(John 3, Stephen 2, Edmund 1.)

Children of **Samuel**[4] **Greenleaf** and Elizabeth (Kingsbury).

  I. Margery, b. Sept. 6, 1725; m. Sept. 25, 1746, Daniel Lunt, of Portsmouth, N. H.

563. II. Samuel,[5] b. Sept. 8, 1727; m. May 17, 1749, Anna Bradbury, b. 1731; d. May 10, 1786. He d. April 23, 1793, at sea; res. Newbury, Mass.; nine children:—

    i. Anna, b. Sept. 11, 1750; m. Capt. Green Pearson; three children:—

      1. Isaac Green, m. ——; three daughters. 2. Mary, m. Henry Lunt. 3. Betsey.

    ii. Samuel, b. Sept. 26, 1752; d. at sea; unmarried. The family name is extinct in this line.

    iii. Sarah, b. Nov. 2, 1755; d. Dec. 26, 1824; unmarried. Deaf and dumb, but very intelligent.

    iv. Margery, b. June 28, 1758; m. 1, Capt. Roberts; 2, Peter Rousseau, of Newburyport; one child by 1st marriage:—

    Ann, m. James Carter; one child: Ann Parsons, m. James Sever.

    v. Elizabeth, b. Oct. 22, 1760; m. 1780, William Parsons, of Boston; no children.

    vi. Mary, b. March 2, 1763; m. —— Sigourney, of Boston; four children:—

    i. Eliza, m. Geo. Channing; one son, five daughters.
    ii. Jane, m. Dr. Farley; two sons, two daughters.
    iii. Ann, m. William Rollins.
    iv. Mary, m. —— Froding.

    vii. Jerusha, b. Aug. 28, 1765; m. Nov. 16, 1795, Rev. Pearson Thurston, of Somersworth, N. H., and St. Johnsbury, Vt.; four children:—

    i. William.
    ii. A daughter.
    iii. A daughter.
    iv. A daughter.

Samuel (24) Greenleaf, Continued:—
II. Samuel.

VIII. Judith, b. March 12, 1768; m. Enoch Sawyer, of Newbury (Bellville), Mass., b. 1767; d. March, 1808. She d. July 2, 1834; eight children:—
1. Elizabeth, b. June 27, 1791; m. 1815, John Rollins, b. about 1794; d. Feb. 23, 1833. She d. Oct 16, 1826; res. Newburyport, Mass.; six children: (1) John, b. Feb. 7, 1816; d. Feb. 21, 1816. (2) John R., b. Feb. 9, 1817; res. Lawrence, Mass.; d. ——. (3) Elizabeth, b. Feb. 13, 1819; d. March 14, 1819. (4) Elizabeth Sawyer, b. Feb. 27, 1820; m. Sewall Tappan (Wainwright & Tappan, Boston). (5) Marietta, b. May 17, 1822; m. Oct. 16, 1844, Jonathan Mann, M.D., Kittery, Me. She d. ——. (6) Eunice Greenleaf, b. Dec. 29, 1824; d. Nov. 3, 1850. 2. Anna, b. Oct. 27, 1795; m. Amos Atkinson, of Boston, Mass., b. May 11, 1792; d. June 26, 1864. She d. Sept. 29, 1871; six children: (1) William Parsons, b. Oct. 12, 1820; m. Sarah Cabot Parkman; d. March 11, 1890. (2) George, b. May 19, 1822; m. Elizabeth Staigg. (3) Elizabeth Parsons, b. April 21, 1824. (4) Edward,* b. Feb. 10, 1827; m. Oct. 4, 1855, Mary Caroline Heath, b. June 1, 1830. (5) Henry, b. March 4, 1831; d. Sept. 4, 1832. (6) Annie, b. April 16, 1837; m. 1872, R. M. Staigg; res. Boston, Mass. 3. Edmund, b. May 4, 1798; d. Dec., 1831, at Marseilles, France. 4. Micajah, b. Nov. 24, 1799; d. Aug. 30, 1801. 5. Judith, b. May 6, 1801; m. William, nephew of William, and nephew of Theophilus Parsons, Chief Justice Supreme Court of Massachusetts. She d. May 18, 1835; one child: Elizabeth, m. Dr. George Derby. 6. Eunice Greenleaf, b. Sept. 24, 1802; d. Dec. 27, 1822. 7. Hannah Moody, b. June 21, 1806; m. June 2, 1830, Silas, son of Henry and Abigail Titcomb. She d. Aug. 21, 1872. Mr. Silas Titcomb was for a long time cashier of the Ocean Bank, Newburyport, Mass.; res. Portland, Me., 1874; five children: (1) Anna Greenleaf, b. April 10, 1831; m. Dr. Joseph P. Fessenden, of Portland, Me. She d. July 27, 1872. (2) Caroline Harrod, b. Nov. 18, 1832; m. Rev. William Sewall, of Lunenburgh, Vt. She d. Dec., 1857. (3) Elizabeth R., b. Feb. 20, 1834; m. Hon. Thomas A. D. Fessenden. (4) Mary Sawyer, b. and d. June, 1836. (5) William Parsons, b. July 28, 1839; res. Washington, D. C. 8. Mary Sigourney, b. May 11, 1807; m. Moses P. Parish; lawyer. She d. ——; one child: Abbie, m. Aug. Wetmore, of New York.

IX. Eunice, b. March 12, 1783.

* Hon. Edward Atkinson is a well known writer upon topics of the day, and has given special attention to statistical and economic matters, food, fuel, etc. These subjects are treated by him in a thorough and exhaustive manner.

25.

(John 3, Stephen 2, Edmund 1.)

Children of **Benjamin⁴ Greenleaf** and Ann (Hale).

Child by 1st marriage :—

I. SUSANNA, b. Jan. 22, 1725; m. May 26, 1743, Timothy⁵ (570), son of John⁴ (27) and Abigail Greenleaf. She d. March 24, 1771 ; nine children.

Children by 2d marriage :—

II. ANNE, b. Nov. 14, 1727; m. Dec. 22, 1748, Matthew Perkins, of Newburyport, Mass., b. May 29, 1725, in Ipswich, Mass. She d. Aug. 28, 1762. He m. 2, Jan. 23, 1763, Jane (Noyes), widow of Jonathan Dole, b. Oct. 5, 1731. He d. May, 1815 ; res. Newbury, Mass. ; twelve children :—

i. Benjamin, b. Dec. 8, 1749; m. Mary ——. He d. March, 1797.
ii. John; b. Jan. 30, 1751; m. ——. He d. 1806.
iii. Nathan, b. April 9, 1752; d. Sept. 21, 1753.
iv. Ebenezer, b. Nov. 30, 1753; m. ——. He d. 1795.
v. Mary, b. April 22, 1755; m. —— Nicholas Johnson.
vi. Abigail, b. Sept. 21, 1756; m. —— Clough.
vii. Jane, b. April 14, 1758; m. —— Aaron Pardee.
viii. Esther, b. May 27, 1759; d. Oct. 19, 1759.
ix. Susanna, b. Sept. 9, 1760; d. Sept. 30, 1760.
x. Ruth, b. July 28, 1761; d. July, 1761.
xi. Sarah, b. July 28, 1761; d. July, 1761; twin.
xii. Elizabeth, b. June 2, 1762; d. June 22, 1762.

III. JUDITH, b. May 8, 1730; d. March 26, 1796; unmarried.

564. IV. EBENEZER,⁵ b. March 8, 1732; m. Dec. 21, 1760, Hannah Titcomb, b. about 1725; d. Sept. 4, 1790. He d. Sept. 2, 1796; five children :—

i. Ebenezer, b. Feb. 21, 1762; d. in infancy.

565. ii. Ebenezer,⁶ b. Oct. 4, 1763; m. Dec. 28, 1796, Jane, dau. of Capt. William and Jane (Greenleaf) Coombs (25), b. about 1766; d. May 15, 1851. He d. June 9, 1834; two children :—

566. 1. William Coombs,⁷ b. Oct. 6, 1797; m. Clara Parsons, dau. of Moses and Persis (Poor) Greenleaf (528). He d. July 22, 1851, in Springfield, Ill. ; a Presbyterian minister; no children. 2. Mary C., b. Jan. 31, 1800.

iii. Moses, b. Jan. 5, 1766; d. 1784, at sea.

BENJAMIN (25) GREENLEAF, CONTINUED :—
IV. Ebenezer.
   iv. Eunice, b. Aug. 31, 1768; m. Nov. 11, 1790, Benjamin Chadbourn, of South Berwick, Me.
   v. Hannah, b. Dec. 26, 1770; m. Nov. 11, 1790, Jacob Perkins, of Newburyport, Mass., b. July 9, 1766; d. July 11, 1849, in London, Eng.; nine children :—
   1. Hannah Greenleaf, b. Feb. 17, 1792. 2. Sarah Ann, b. Dec. 16, 1793; m. —— Bacon, in London, Eng. 3. Jane, b. Jan. 5, 1796; d. July 14, 1808. 4. Ebenezer Greenleaf, b. Dec. 29, 1797; d. Jan. 20, 1842. 5. Angier March, b. 1799; d. Jan. 20, 1872. 6. Louisa Jane, b. Sept. 11, 1801. 7. Elizabeth, b. May 7, 1804; m. —— Roy. 8. Henrietta, b. July 1, 1806; m. Henry Chubb, of London, Eng. 9. Mary, b. June 29, 1809; d. Oct. 24, 1810.

V. ABEL, b. Oct. 21, 1733; d. Jan. 27, 1799; unmarried.
VI. ELIZABETH, b. March 3, 1737; d. April 3, 1805; unmarried.
VII. JANE, b. July 5, 1739; m. July 17, 1760, Capt. William Coombs (565).

The two unmarried sisters, familiarly known as " Aunt Judy and Aunt Betty," and the bachelor brother, known as " Uncle Abel," made one family, and are well remembered in Newburyport. They died within a few years of each other.

26.
(John 3, Stephen 2, Edmund 1.)

Children of **Stephen**[4] **Greenleaf** and Eunice (Wallis).
   I. THOMAS, b. July 17, 1728; d. in infancy.
566a. II. THOMAS,[5] b. Sept. 10, 1729; m. Mrs. —— Harris; no children.
567. III. STEPHEN,[5] b. Feb. 14, 1730; m. Mrs. Mary (?) Soley, of Boston; one child :—
   A son, b. and d. in Boston; unmarried.
   IV. EUNICE, b. Feb. 2, 1732; m. Samuel Franklin, of Boston. She d. June 12, 1787; one child :—
   Hannah, m. Samuel Emmons, of Boston. She d. Dec., 1840, aged 83 years.
   V. GRACE, b. April 11, 1734; d. in infancy.
   VI. SARAH, b. Nov. 30, 1735; d. young.
   VII. ELIZABETH, b. Oct. 2, 1737; d. in infancy.
   VIII. ELIZABETH, b. Jan. 19, 1739; d. 1826; unmarried.

STEPHEN (26) GREENLEAF, CONTINUED :—

568. IX. JOHN,[5] b. July 13, 1741 ; m. ——; res. Portsmouth,
        N. H. ; two children :—

   i. Stephen, unmarried ; d. aged 32 years.
   ii. Mary, m. Enoch Moody, of Portsmouth, N. H.

The name of Greenleaf is extinct in this branch of the
        family.

X. MARY, b. March 16, 1742 ; m. John Roulstone, of
        Boston, Mass. She d. 1798 ; eight children :—

   i. Elizabeth Greenleaf, m. John Andrews.
   ii. Ruth, m. John Gray.
   iii. Jane Patterson, m. Paul Pritchard.
   iv. Eunice Wallace, m. Samuel Browning.
   v., vi., vii., and viii. died young.

XI. ABIGAIL, b. July 4, 1744 ; d. in infancy.

27.

(Samuel 3, Stephen 2, Edmund 1.)

Children of **John[4] Greenleaf** and Abigail——.

569. I. JOSHUA,[5] b. April 17, 1714 ; m. 1, Nov. 23, 1736,
        Judith Moody, b. Dec. 14, 1719 ; d. May 20, 1763 ;
        2, Dec. 1, 1763, Anna, widow of Stephen Kent. He
        d. Dec. 22, 1799 ; res. Newburyport, Mass. ; eight
        children.

II. ANNE, b. Nov. 2, 1716.

570. III. TIMOTHY,[5] b. June 23, 1719 ; m. May 26, 1743,
        Susanna, dau. of Benjamin[4] and Ann (Hale) Green-
        leaf (25). He d. July 20, 1764. She d. March 24,
        1771 ; res. Newburyport, Mass. ; nine children.

571. IV. CALEB,[5] b. April 15, 1722 ; m. Nov. 23, 1742, Mrs.
        Mary Pearson.

V. HANNAH, b. Oct. 30, 1724.

VI. SARAH, b. March 12, 1727 ; m. —— Boardman.

VII. ELIZABETH, b. July 22, 1734.

569.

(John 4, Samuel 3, Stephen 2, Edmund 1.)

Children of **Capt. Joshua[5] Greenleaf** and Judith
        (Moody).

I. SAMUEL, b. Sept., 1737 ; d. Jan. 18, 1744.

II. ABNER, b. June 10, 1740 ; d. July 2, 1740.

Capt. Joshua (569) Greenleaf, Continued :—

572. III. Abner,[6] b. Feb. 5, 1742; m. 1, Jan. 12, 1762, Elizabeth, dau. of Abner and Mary (Kent) Dole, b. Oct.
28, 1743. Abner Dole was b. May 11, 1706; 2,
Aug. 22, 1765, Elizabeth, dau. of Deacon James
Milk, of Portland, Me.; 3, Oct. 12, 1788, Anna,
dau. of Deacon Beck, of Newburyport, Mass. She d.
Feb. 15, 1818, aged 74 years. He d. March 31,
1805; res. Newburyport, Mass.; twelve children.

IV. Caleb, b. June 25, 1744; unmarried.

573. V. John,[6] b. March 31, 1747; m. Esther ——; d. Sept.
17, 1799, aged 50 years. He d. Oct. 18, 1803; res.
Newburyport, Mass.; eight children :—

573a. 1. Jacob,[7] b. Jan. 4, 1770; m. Feb. 10, 1799, Mary,
dau. of John Pettingill, A.M. He d. Dec. 4, 1838;
res. Newbury (Bellville); shipmaster; no children.

II. John, b. July 20, 1771; d. Aug. 29, 1802, at sea;
unmarried.

III. Judith, b. June 24, 1773; d. Feb. 1, 1802; unmarried.

IV. Esther, b. July 14, 1779; m. Dec. 23, 1804, 1,
Capt. Robert Park, who died at sea; 2, John Flanders, who first married Elizabeth. Esther d. 1854.

V. Elizabeth, b. Nov. 20, 1781; m. Dec. 30, 1804,
John Flanders, of Newburyport, Mass.

VI. Isaac Hall, b. Feb. 17, 1784; d. Aug. 15, 1802, at
sea; unmarried.

VII. Hannah Toppan, b. June 5, 1788; m. Nov. 16,
1807, Henry Greenleaf French, of Newburyport,
Mass.

VIII. Lydia Ingalls, b. May 20, 1790; m. March 27,
1808, Capt. Green Johnson.

The family name is extinct in this branch.

VI. Judith, b. Feb. 25, 1750; m. 1, Moses Kent; 2,
Rt. Rev. Edward Bass, the first Bishop of Massa-
chusetts. She d. about 1830; res. Newburyport,
Mass.

VII. Sarah, b. Oct., 1753; m. Nov. 13, 1780, Major
Jacob, son of Benjamin Coffin (b. 1710), b. June 11,
1756.

CAPT. JOSHUA (569) GREENLEAF, CONTINUED :—

VIII. ABIGAIL, b. Oct. 16, 1755 ; m. Capt. Philip Aubin, Superintendent of factories at Amesbury, Mass. She d. 1840; res. Newburyport, Mass.

572.

(Joshua 5, John 4, Samuel 3, Stephen 2, Edmund 1.)

Children of **Abner**[6] **Greenleaf** and Elizabeth (Dole).

Child by 1st marriage :—

574. I. SAMUEL,[7] b. 1764; m. Aug. 13, 1787, Susan, dau. of Capt. George Carroll, of New Jersey, b. January, 1767; d. December, 1842, in Campton, N. H. He d. 1815; res. Plymouth, N. H.; eight children.

Children by 2d marriage :—

575. II. JOSHUA[7] (Major), b. Jan. 1, 1767; m. 1, Oct. 21, 1789, Jane Ordway ; 2, March 4, 1790, Sarah Armstrong. He d. Nov. 3, 1852 ; res. Newburyport; eight children.

III. JAMES MILK, b. February, 1770; d. September, 1831 ; unmarried.

IV. ELIZABETH, b. May 6, 1775; m. Feb. 27, 1794, James Little, of Campton, N. H., b. Sept. 21, 1769; d. 1813. She d. Aug. 1, 1817, at Centre Harbor, N. H. ; res. Newburyport, Mass. ; nine children :—

i. George, b. December, 1794; d. Aug. 18, 1814.
ii. Elmira, b. May 20, 1796; d. Aug. 7, 1827.
iii. Harriet, b. March 27, 1798; d. March 16, 1857.
iv. Elizabeth Ann, b. April 26, 1800; d. Oct. 24, 1852.
v. Caroline, b. May 20, 1802; d. Aug. 4, 1864.
vi. Miranda, b. May 25, 1804; d. Jan. 20, 1853.
vii. Catherine Murray, b. April, 1806; d. Nov. 26, 1807.
viii. Catherine, b. Nov. 20, 1808; d. March, 1810.
ix. Emeline, b. July 24, 1812.

V. ABIGAIL, b. about 1780; d. about 1788.

576. VI. ABNER,[7] b. March 12, 1785; m. 1, Feb. 13, 1806, Betsey Flanders, of Salisbury, Mass., who d. Sept. 4, 1807; no children; 2, Oct. 1, 1808, at Portsmouth, N. H., Mariam, dau. of Matthew Bell, of Newcastle, N. H., b. Aug. 23, 1789; d. Sept. 23, 1873. He d. Sept. 28, 1868; res. Portsmouth, N. H.; twelve children.

VII., VIII., IX., X., XI., XII. d. in infancy.

574.

(Abner 6, Joshua 5, John 4, Samuel 3, Stephen 2, Edmund 1.)

Children of **Samuel**[7] **Greenleaf** and Susan (Carroll).

577. I. PHILIP,[8] b. 1790, at Plymouth, N. H.; m. May 26, 1811, Mary, dau. of James and Sarah Eaton, b. June 9, 1790; d. April 16, 1854. He enlisted in the war of 1812 with Capt. Smiley, of Haverhill. The last heard from him was at Greenbush, N. Y.; one child :—

578. Lewis,[9] b. Oct. 20, 1811; m. Jan. 1, 1840, Hannah Stewart, of Salisbury, Mass., b. Jan. 25, 1816; d. Jan. 12, 1894. He d. Nov. 21, 1893; res. Salisbury, Mass.; three children: 1. William Henry, b. April 11, 1841; unmarried. 2. Mary Sawyer, b. Feb. 1, 1846; m. April 26, 1870, Samuel J. Brown, of Salisbury, Mass.; one child: Fred C., b. March 11, 1875. 3. Ann Tracy, b. March 17, 1852; unmarried.

II. SAMUEL, b. 1792, in Plymouth, N. H.; d. 1824.

III. ABIGAIL, b. 1794, in Plymouth, N. H.; d. 1821; unmarried.

579. IV. JOHN,[8] b. April 15, 1796, in Plymouth, N. H.; m. April 10, 1820, Elizabeth Hutchinson Learned, of Boston, Mass., b. May 20, 1798; d. Nov. 20, 1891. He d. Dec. 15, 1865, at Cambridge, Mass.; res. Cambridge, Mass.; nine children :—

   I. Abigail Maria, b. April 7, 1821, at Woburn, Mass.; m. Oct. 7, 1847, Moses Smiley, of Reading, Mass. She d. Jan. 2, 1873; one child :—
A daughter, now living in Philadelphia, Penn.

   II. Elizabeth Richardson, b. Feb. 12, 1823, in Woburn, Mass.; m. Charles Dixon, of London, England; d. Feb. 8, 1853, in Troy, N. Y. She d. Feb. 8, 1853; three children, none now living.

   III. Sarah Carroll, b. Dec. 20, 1825; m. Jan. 20, 1851, Milo B. Abercrombie, of Macon Co., Ala., who d. Aug. 22, 1861. She d. Jan. 5, 1895; res. Worcester, Mass.; five children :—
1. Talulah, m. Charles H. Douglass, Principal of High School, Keene, N. H.; one child: Kenneth. 2. Daniel Webster, m.

SAMUEL (574) GREENLEAF, CONTINUED:—
IV. John.

> Emily Brainard, of St. Albans, Vt. He is Principal of Academy, Worcester, Mass.; four children. 3. Millard Fillmore, d. in infancy. 4. Wenonah, m. Dr. G. O. Ward, of Worcester, Mass.; one child: Otis. 5. Bolling G., m. Margaret Child, of Lynn, Mass.; two children: sons.

IV. Anna Maria Judson, b. Oct. 20, 1828; m. Robert Fulton Strean, of Washington, Penn. She d. Nov. 1, 1866; five children:—

> 1. Herbert, d. about 1890. 2. James G., married; res. Kansas City, Mo. 3. Helen D., m. Edward Shepperd; res. Cambridge, Mass.; two children. 4. Lizzie G., married; two children. 5. Maria, unmarried.

V. Susan Francis, b. Dec. 12, 1830; m. Aug. 12, 1851, Clarence C. Thayer, of Charleston, S. C. He d. several years ago; two children:—

> 1. Claude. 2. Clarence, res. Chicago, Ill.

VI. Mary Bird, b. May 12, d. Aug. 12, 1834.

VII. Ellen, b. July 30, 1835; m. Jan. 15, 1857, John Philemon, son of Col. William B. Paca, of Wye Hall, Queen Anne's Co., Md., and grandson of one of the signers of the Declaration of Independence. He d. June 23, 1871; res. Baltimore, Md.; five children:—

> 1. William, b. May 19, ——; d. June 27, 1859. 2. Juliana Tilghman, b. Aug. 29, 1861. 3. Elizabeth Greenleaf, b. Sept. 6, d. Nov. 27, 1865. 4. William Bennett, b. March 4, 1868. 5. Ernest, b. May 29, 1871; d. June 12, 1874.

VIII. John Edward, b. Sept. 13, 1836; d. Jan. 19, 1837.

IX. John Edward, b. March 10, d. March, 14, 1839.

579a. V. JAMES,[8] b. 1800; married; d. before 1828; no children.

VI. LEWIS, b. 1803, at Plymouth, N. H.; d. 1816.

VII. WILLIAM B., b. 1805; d. at sea, on his way to West Indies, 1840.

VIII. CATHERINE, b. January, 1808; m. 1834, William Blaisdell Bartlett, of Campton, N. H. She d. April 13, 1846; res. Toronto, Canada, and Plymouth, N. H.; two children:—

> i. Catherine.
> ii. William; both b. and d. at Toronto, Canada.

575.

(Abner 6, Joshua 5, John 4, Samuel 3, Stephen 2, Edmund 1.)

Children of **Major Joshua**[7] **Greenleaf** and Sarah (Armstrong).

580. I. CHARLES,[8] b. July 1, 1791; m. May 11, 1818, Hannah Follansbee; two children, both died young.
1. Sarah, d. June 19, 1822.
11. ———.

II. HENRY, b. June 25, 1792.

III. FRANKLIN, b. Sept. 21, 1793; d. young at sea.

IV. DOLLY, b. March 16, 1796; m. July 19, 1821, Capt. David Wood; one child :—
Charles G., res. Boston, Mass.; of the firm of Wetherell, Wood & Co.; d. April 21, 1894, in Boston.

V. ELIZA ANN, b. June 25, 1798.

VI. WILLIAM, b. Sept. 19, 1800.

VII. WILLIAM HENRY, b. Sept. 28, 1802; d. young; unmarried.

VIII. RUFUS, b. Feb. 15, 1805; d. about 1859.

576.

(Abner 6, Joshua 5, John 4, Samuel 3, Stephen 2, Edmund 1.)

Children of **Abner**[7] **Greenleaf** and Mariam (Bell).

I. A son, b. 1809; d. Aug. 17, 1809.

581. II. ALBERT,[8] b. Sept. 17, 1810, at Portsmouth, N. H.; m. 1837, Emily Ann, dau. of William Shaw, of Portsmouth, N. H. She d. May 31, 1892, in Baltimore, Md. He d. March 8, 1895; res. Baltimore, Md.; eight children :—
1. Albert William, b. Sept. 2, 1838; d. June 13, 1850.
11. Frances, b. June 23, 1840; d. Sept. 29, 1841.
111. Anne Elizabeth, b. Feb. 27, 1842; d. March 30, 1849.
1v. Edith Bell, b. Dec. 27, 1843; d. Feb. 10, 1861.
v. Abner, b. Sept. 30, 1845; res. Baltimore, Md.
vi. Emily Ann, b. July 29, 1847; d. June 10, 1850.
vii. Nancy Shaw, b. Nov. 11, 1850; d. April 8, 1858.
viii. Corinne Bell, b. July 24, 1856; res. Baltimore.

ABNER (576) GREENLEAF, CONTINUED :—

582. III. FRANKLIN,[8] b. July 23, 1812; m. Sarah Valentine.
He d. Sept., 1886; res. Brooklyn, N. Y.; four
children :—
    I. Isabella.
    II. Geraldine.
    III. Mary Dobson.
    IV. Sarah Lavinia.

583. IV. ABNER,[8] b. July 4, 1814; m. Jan. 8, 1837, Mary
Louisa, dau. of Hon. Daniel P. Drown, of Portsmouth, N. H.; res. Brooklyn, N. Y.; four children.

  V. LAVINIA, b. Sept. 26, 1816; d. Jan. 7, 1839; unmarried.

  VI. ANN ELIZA, b. Oct. 27, 1818; d. Jan. 3, 1821.

  VII. ELLEN, b. July 14, 1820; d. Jan. 3, 1867.

584. VIII. GEORGE,[8] b. Jan. 30, 1823; m. June 25, 1844, at
Greenland, N. H., Rhoda Ann, dau. of Joseph Fabian,
b. Jan. 20, 1823; d. April 26, 1852. He d. March 5,
1861, at Portsmouth, N. H.; three children :—
    I. Aletha, b. June 25, 1845; d. May 2, 1882, at Boston,
    Mass.
    II. Ellen, b. Aug. 1, 1846; res. Brooklyn, N. Y.
    III. Virginia, b. June 7, 1849; d. Dec. 13, 1864, at
    Portsmouth, N. H.

585. IX. JAMES FABIUS,[8] b. April 24, 1826; m. June 23,
1852, Almira H., dau. of Hiram and Mary (Duncan)
Locke, of Portsmouth, N. H. Hiram, b. Feb. 19,
1802; d. Jan. 27, 1843. Mary Duncan, b. April 10,
1807; d. Jan. 5, 1893. Almira H., b. Sept. 22,
1830. Hiram Locke owned and run two of the best
hotels at Portsmouth, N. H. James Fabius, res.
Beverly, Mass.; housebuilder; four children.

586. X. GARDNER JEFFERSON,[8] b. April 24, 1831; m. Nov.
23, 1858, Mary Elizabeth, dau. of John and Eliza
Ann (Foye) Hodgdon, b. Nov. 23, 1838; d. Oct.
27, 1893; res. Portsmouth, N. H.; two children :—
    I. William Hickman, b. Aug. 28, 1859; d. April 14, 1860.
    II. Clement, b. Jan. 28, d. May 10, 1864.

  XI. EMILY, b. July 13, 1833; d. Jan. 18, 1840.

  XII. ISABELLA, b. Nov. 10, 1834; d. Aug. 7, 1835.

583.

(Abner 7, Abner 6, Joshua 5, John 4, Samuel 3, Stephen 2, Edmund 1.)

Children of **Abner**[8] **Greenleaf** and Mary Louisa (Drown).

I. IDALIA DROWN, b. Jan. 31, 1838; res. Brooklyn, N. Y.

II. LAVINIA, b. Jan. 5, 1843; m. 1865, Stephen T. Bradford, of Brooklyn, N. Y.; res. Brooklyn, N. Y.; four children :—
    i. Edgar.
    ii. Mabel.
    iii. Ethel.
    iv. Vinnie, d. in infancy; twin.

587. III. HOWARD,[9] b. March 14, 1846; m. Sept. 2, 1867, Ida E. Francis, who d. Dec. 30, 1892; res. Middletown, N. Y.; one child :—
    Edwin Abner, b. Jan. 26, 1869; m. June 1, 1889, Gussie Winans, of New Hampton, N. Y.; one child: Kathleen, b. June 15, 1890; res. Brooklyn, N. Y.

IV. CARRIE LOUISE, b. Feb. 2, 1851; m. July 18, 1872, Isaac W. Carpenter, of Providence, R. I.; res. Whippany, N. J.; four children :—
    i. Daniel Greenleaf, b. Sept. 24, 1873, at Liberty Copper Mine, Frederick Co., Md.
    ii. Della Louise, b. Sept. 27, 1875, at Providence, R. I.
    iii. Ruth Evelyn, b. July 18, 1878, at Hays City, Ellis Co., Kan.; d. Jan. 18, 1891, at Rock Valley, Iowa.
    iv. Emilie Goodman, b. Jan. 16, 1883, at Hamilton Township, Ellis Co., Kan.

585.

(Abner 7, Abner 6, Joshua 5, John 4, Samuel 3, Stephen 2, Edmund 1.)

Children of **James Fabius**[8] **Greenleaf** and Almira H. (Locke).

588. I. JAMES ALBERT,[9] b. Feb. 19, 1856, at Portsmouth, N. H.; m. 1, Nov. 6, 1876, at Martinsburg, Penn., Jennie Eva Snyder, who d. April, 1879, at Roaring Springs, Penn.; 2, Sept. 15, 1880, at Huntingdon, Penn., S. Jennie Hatfield, b. June 3, 1860, at Huntingdon, Penn.; res. Huntingdon, Penn.; railroad business, Chief Assistant and Private Secretary to Superintendent Huntingdon & Broad Top Mountain R. R.; ten children.

JAMES FABIUS (585) GREENLEAF, CONTINUED :—
  I. James Albert.
    Child by 1st marriage :—
      1. James Albert, b. Dec. 23, 1877, at Riddlesburg,
         Penn. ; d. May 3, 1878.
    Children by 2d marriage, all born at Huntingdon, Penn. :—
      II. A child ; d. in infancy.
      III. Albert Hatfield, b. Feb. 17, 1883.
      IV. James Frederick, b. Sept. 1, 1884.
      V. Frank Locke, b. June 4, 1886.
      VI. Myra Catherine, b. Jan. 29, 1888.
      VII. Mary Duncan, b. Sept. 17, 1889.
      VIII. George Gage, b. April, d. July, 1891.
      IX. Helen May, b. Jan. 28, 1893.
      X. Martha Jeanette, b. Feb. 22, 1895.
589. II. FRANK MORDOUGH,[9] b. Dec. 10, 1859; m. July 12,
         1881, Julia Harrie, of Huntingdon, Penn. ; res. Hunt-
         ingdon, Penn. ; railroad business, General Freight
         Agent, H. & B. T. M. R. R. ; no children.
     III. MYRA BELLE, b. Jan. 29, 1864; m. Nov. 13, 1882,
         at Beverly, Mass., Arthur Cressy Wallis, of Beverly,
         Mass., b. Aug. 14, 1863 ; res. Beverly, Mass. ; shoe
         business ; three children :—
       i. Joseph Albert, b. May 23, 1884.
       ii. Helen Allston, b. Feb. 10, 1889.
       iii. Marion Greenleaf, b. March 29, d. Oct. 3, 1895.
     IV. FREDERICK, b. July 2, d. July 24, 1865, at Ports-
         mouth, N. H.

570.

(John 4, Samuel 3, Stephen 2, Edmund 1.)
Children of **Timothy**[5] **Greenleaf** and Susanna.
  I. ANNE, b. Nov. 25, 1744 ; m. *Woodbridge Hunt.   She
     d. Oct. 18, 1776 ; two children :—
   i. Woodbridge, b. Feb. 9, 1770; d. June 6, 1829.
   ii. Mary (Polly), b. March 20, 1774.
  II. SARAH, b. April 5, 1747 ; m. Capt. Offin Boardman.†
     She d. Aug. 29, 1796 ; five children :—
   i. Offin.
   ii. Hannah.

* Hist. and Geneal. researches in Merrimack Valley, p. 70, say Zebedee Hunt.

† Captain Boardman probably m. 2, Sarah, b. 1743, dau. of Richard Tappan. [N. E.
Hist. and Geneal. Reg., Vol. XXXIV. p. 52.] Sarah, widow of Capt. Offin Boardman,
Aug., 1820, aged 78 (*Essex Gazette*).

Timothy (570) Greenleaf, Continued:—

    II. Sarah.

    iii. Benjamin Greenleaf; res. Boston, Mass.

    iv. Susanna.

    v. Susanna.

    III. Woodbridge, b. Aug. 23, 1749; d. Oct. 18, 1769; unmarried.

590. IV. Timothy,[6] b. July 20, 1751; m. Joanna ——. He d. Feb. 1, 1786; one child:—

591.   Timothy,[7] b. about 1775, in Newburyport, Mass., where he lived a few years, and then moved to Salem, 1808, where he kept a boarding house; but becoming somewhat reduced in property he entered as steward on board of a privateer during the War of 1812, and was taken prisoner and carried to England. He m. Jan. 15, 1799, Sarah Rowe; res. Claremont, N. H., at one time, and had four children : 1. John, d. young. 2. Samuel, d. young.

592.   3. William O., b. in Claremont, N. H.; m. ——; d. May 30, 1829, in New York; two children : (1) Mary Eliza, b. July 10, 1825; m. Jesse B. Edwards, of Salem, Mass.; two children. (2) Sarah Howe, b. April 11, 1827. 4. Sarah Rowe, b. 1810; m. Oliver Weld, son of Simon Bailey, of Manchester, N. H.; three children.

    V. Susanna, b. April 9, 1753; d. in infancy.

    VI. Susanna, b. April 10, 1754; d. in infancy.

    VII. Elizabeth, b. July 10, d. Sept. 26, 1755.

    VIII. Benjamin, b. Nov. 6, 1756; d. Dec. 20, 1780; unmarried.

593. IX. Caleb,[6] b. Aug. 16, 1759, at Newburyport, Mass.; m. Dec. 13, 1785, Susanna, youngest dau. of William and Abigail (Patee) Emerson, of Methuen, Mass., b. July 23, 1762; d. March 29, 1835. He d. Jan. 28, 1836. He lived with his sister Hunt after his parents' decease (he being but nine years old when his mother died), in his earlier years, and settled on land owned before him by his maternal grandfather, where his son has lived, Haverhill, West Parish, Mass.; seven children.

593.

(Timothy 5, John 4, Samuel 3, Stephen 2, Edmund 1.)

Children of **Caleb**[6] **Greenleaf** and Susanna (Emerson).

594. I. BENJAMIN,[7] b. Sept. 25, 1786; m. Nov. 20, 1821, Lucretia, youngest dau. of Col. James Kimball, of Bradford, Mass., b. Feb. 28, 1794; d. Oct. 2, 1880. He d. Oct. 29, 1864; res. Bradford, Mass.; nine children :—

  I. Emily Anne, b. Sept. 13, 1822; m. Nov. 23, 1848, John Bartlett Tewksbury, of West Newbury, Mass. Real estate business; res. Bradford, Mass.; no children.

  II. Mary Abigail, b. June 24, 1824; d. in infancy.

  III. Benjamin, b. Oct. 4, 1825; d. Sept. 16, 1829.

  IV. Betsey Payson, b. March 19, 1827; d. in infancy.

  V. Betsey Payson, b. April 6, 1828; m. Oct. 19, 1854, Rev. S. C. Kendall, of Webster, Mass. He d. Oct. 2, 1895; res. Townsend, Mass.; three children :—

    1. Jennie Elizabeth, b. July 5, 1857; d. May 25, 1888. 2. James Greenleaf, b. May 19, d. Aug. 8, 1864. 3. George Burns, b. Feb. 21, 1867; d. Feb. 21, 1880.

  VI. Benjamin, b. July 11, 1830; d. in infancy.

  VII. Benjamin, b. July 31, 1831; d. Oct. 2, 1843.

  VIII. James Kimball, b. Dec. 31, 1832; d. March 7, 1834.

  IX. Lydia Kimball, b. May 14, 1836; m. July 12, 1859, Hon. Gilbert Mortier Sykes, b. Nov. 20, 1834. She d. Jan. 7, 1894; res. Dorset, Vt.; five children :—

    1. Emily Louise, b. Jan. 30, 1865. 2. Anna Gertrude, b. Dec. 12, 1867; m. Sept. 18, 1894, Edwin Burrage Child, of New York City; one child: Kathalyne Edwina, b. Aug. 7, 1895. 3. Bernard Greenleaf, b. Nov. 19, 1869. 4. Gilbert Kimball, b. Dec. 23, 1871; d. June 29, 1889, at St. Johnsbury, Vt. 5. James Edward, b. Oct. 24, 1874.

595. II. SAMUEL EMERSON,[7] b. May 7, 1788; m. Dec. 3, 1816, Sarah Hale, of Haverhill, Mass., b. 1797; d. July 8, 1867. He d. March 9, 1857; res. Haverhill, Mass.; six children :—

596.   I. Moses Poor,[8] b. Feb. 7, 1818; m. Susan M. Allen, b. 1825; d. Nov. 2, 1854. He d. Jan. 23, 1848; res.

CALEB (593) GREENLEAF, CONTINUED:—
  II. Samuel Emerson.
      West Newton, Mass.; physician; one child: Benjamin, d. Oct. 8, 1848,—an infant.
    II. Caroline, b. May 1, 1820; m. Nov. 22, 1849, Henry C., son of Benjamin Parker, who d. March 18, 1873. She d. Dec. 23, 1891.
    III. Mary Hale, b. March 15, 1823; m. Nov. 25, 1847, George Marston, b. 1821. He d. Jan. 11, 1894; two children:—
        1. Sarah. 2. Susan A.
    IV. Sarah Ann, b. Nov. 5, 1824; m. June 22, 1851, George L., son of Joseph and Phebe Hunt, b. 1822.
    V. Rebecca Jane, b. Aug. 20, 1830; d. Aug. 11, 1855.
597. VI. Samuel H.,[8] b. Jan. 25, 1835; m. Jan. 4, 1859, Cassendre T. Richardson; two children, both d. in infancy.
  III. SUSANNA, b. Nov. 22, 1790; d. in infancy.
  IV. ANNA, b. March 12, 1793; m. 1810, John Crowell, of Haverhill, Mass., b. 1789; res. Haverhill, Mass.; seven children:—
    i. Minerva, b. 1812; m. 1, Wilder Tilton, shoecutter, who d. 1834; 2, Cyrus Worthen. She d. Feb., 1893; res. Haverhill, Mass.; one child by 1st marriage: 1. Caroline Susan, b. June 17, 1836; m. 1, Jan. 16, 1858, James H. McPherson, of Francestown, N. H., enlisted in 1861 Civil War, and was killed before Petersburgh, Va.; two children by 1st marriage: (1) Carrie Minerva, b. Jan. 29, 1859. (2) James Harry, b. July 27, 1861; 2, 1868, Enoch R. Banks, of Portland, Me., upholsterer; res. Haverhill, Mass.; two children by 2d marriage: (3) Arthur Wilder, b. Aug. 27, 1869. (4) Gertrude May, b. Feb. 2, 1876. Children of Minerva by 2d marriage: 2. Franklin Lafayette. 3. Elizabeth Celesta. 4. Ellen Minerva. 5. Lydia Ann. 6. Louisa Maria. 7. John Cyrus.
    ii. Abel, d. in infancy.
    iii. William G., b. Dec. 20, 1816; m. Melinda Armstrong; farmer and timbering; res. Salem, N. H.; three children: a son and two daughters.
    iv. Susan G., b. 1818; d. 1859.
    v. Betsey, m. 1841, Andrew McCrillis. She d. Dec. 22, 1893; res. East Boston, Mass. Several children.
    vi. John, b. Sept. 28, 1823; m. 1, June 7, 1854, Sarah Bradley, dau. of Samuel Johnson. She d. Oct. 21, 1859. 2, Oct. 31, 1861, Caroline, dau. of Ephraim and Nancy Corliss, b. Sept.

CALEB (593) GREENLEAF, CONTINUED :—

IV. Anna.

> 20, 1829, in Haverhill, Mass. He d. April 28, 1890; res. Haverhill, Mass.; physician; one child by 1st marriage: William Henry, b. Oct. 6, 1857; d. Sept 16, 1858. One child by 2d marriage: William G.; res. Salem, N. H.

vii. Anne Dow, b. June 5, 1828, in Haverhill, Mass.; m. Andrew Jackson Chapman, b. Oct., 1827, of Petersboro, N. H.; d. many years ago; res. Haverhill, Mass.; five children: 1. George Andrew. 2. Alice Ann. 3. Albert Pierce. 4. Addie Pierce. 5. Belle Gertrude.

598. V. WILLIAM,[7] b. Dec. 7, 1795; m. May 12, 1818, Eliza Gordan, of Salem, N. H., who d. April 23, 1872. He d. Dec. 5, 1874; res. Haverhill, Mass.; two children :—

1. Lucretia Kimball, b. Aug. 13, 1821; m. Dec. 25, 1851, at Haverhill, Mass., David S., son of William and Lucinda Dickinson, b. May 31, 1818, at Swanzey, N. H.; d. Aug. 15, 1885; shoe stitcher; one child :—

> Benson Greenleaf, b. Aug. 18, 1863; m. Dec. 25, 1885, Harriet B. Langley; no children.

599. II. Benjamin William,[8] b. May 31, 1829; m. Sept. 1, 1853, Anna Y., dau. of Ephraim and Sally Northrop, of Vershire, Vt.; res. Haverhill, Mass.; no children.

VI. ABEL, b. April 22, 1799; d. Sept. 28, 1802.

VII. SUSANNA, b. Nov. 9, 1803; m. Jennes Hawkins. She d. Oct. 14, 1880; five children :—

i. Caleb Greenleaf.
ii. Eliza Ann Crowell, m. A. M. Cluff; res. Waltham, Mass.
iii. Sarah Jane Bartlett.
iv. Susan Abby.
v. Emily Sophia.

28.

(Samuel 3, Stephen 2, Edmund 1.)

Children of **Stephen[4] Greenleaf** and Mary (Gardner).

600. I. GARDNER,[5] b. Jan. 9, 1726; m. Jan. 21, 1748, Catherine Thompson, b. 1730; d. April 8, 1768. He d. Nov. 21, 1808; eight children.

II. ELIZABETH, b. Dec. 7, 1727; d. 1785–90.

III. STEPHEN, b. Jan. 4, 1731–32; d. Jan. 10, 1733.

IV. MARY, b. April 25, 1734; m. Dec. 24, 1761, A. Richardson.

STEPHEN (28) GREENLEAF, CONTINUED :—

601. V. STEPHEN,[5] b. Aug. 5, 1736; m. March 13, 1764, Maria Mason, who. d. Nov., 1802, at Haverhill, Mass. He d. 1812–15; two children :—
   I. Elias Mason, b. Dec. 1, 1764.
   II. Stephen.

   VI. REBECCA, b. March 19, 1739; d. June 2, 1749.

602. VII. ISAAC,[5] b. May 27, 1744; m. 1, Dec. 10, 1772, Mary Tufts, b. 1751; d. June 24, 1776; 2, April 30, 1778, Sarah, dau. of Jacob Rhoads, b. Dec. 1, 1756; d. Nov. 6, 1829. Mr. Rhoads was a shipbuilder. Isaac d. Feb. 19, 1807; res. Medford, Mass.; distiller; eight children.

600.

(Stephen 4, Samuel 3, Stephen 2, Edmund 1.)

Children of **Gardner**[5] **Greenleaf** and Catherine (Thompson).

   I. GARDNER, b. Aug. 20, 1748; d. ——.

   II. REBECCA, b. Sept. 25, 1750; m. April 30, 1770, Benjamin Floyd.

   III. MARY, b. Oct. 11, 1752; m. May 19, 1778, Samuel Kidder.

603. IV. JONATHAN,[6] b. June 9, 1754; m. May 5, 1778, Joanna Manning, who d. about 1797; res. Medford, Mass.; nine children.

   V. CATHERINE, b. May 23, 1756; m. May 21, 1778, E. Thomson.

   VI. HANNAH, b. March 3, 1758; m. June 12, 1785, Francis Tufts.

604. VII. GARDNER,[6] b. July 14, 1765; m. Oct. 1, 1786, Lydia Nickerson Hart, b. Oct. 7, 1763, in Lynn; d. April 12, 1863, in Boston. He d. June 27, 1801, at Medford, Mass.; seven children.

   VIII. ABIGAIL, b. April 1, 1768.

603.

(Gardner 5, Stephen 4, Samuel 3, Stephen 2, Edmund 1.)

Children of **Jonathan**[6] **Greenleaf** and Joanna (Manning).

   I. MARY, b. April 30, 1779; d. Nov. 11, 1784.

   II. JOANNA, b. March 20, 1780; d. ——.

JONATHAN (603) GREENLEAF, CONTINUED :—

    III. JOANNA, b. Dec. 28, 1781 ; m. Amos Locke.

    IV. JONATHAN, b. Feb. 16, 1784.

    V. MARY (POLLY) MANNING, b. Dec. 28, 1786; d. 1806 ; unmarried.

605. VI. WILLIAM,[7] b. March 13 or Oct. 7, 1788, in Medford, Mass.; m. Sally Hancock, of Otisfield, Me., b. April 24, 1784; d. March 21, 1869. He d. July 28, 1862, in Otisfield, Me. ; seven children.

606. VII. THOMAS,[7] b. Aug. 1, 1791; m. Oct. 2, 1822, Phebe, dau. of Joshua and Susanna (Leathers) Reed. He d. Sept. 29, 1862 ; three children.

    VIII. JOSEPH, b. Jan. 31, 1794; d. March 17, 1856; unmarried.

    IX. SARAH JONES, b. Oct. 25, 1797; married —— Upson.

605.

(Jonathan 6, Gardner 5, Stephen 4, Samuel 3, Stephen 2, Edmund 1.)

Children of **William**[7] **Greenleaf** and Sally (Hancock).

607. I. JOSEPH H.,[8] b. Oct. 22, 1810; m. Esther Turner, of Otisfield, Me. He d. June 17, 1886; no children.

    II. SALLY, b. March 4, 1812 ; m. Edmand H. Millett, of West Minot, Me. ; eight children :—

    i. William Greenleaf, b. April 8, 1832, in Otisfield, Me.

    ii. Sarah Abbie, b. July 29, 1834, in Otisfield, Me.

    iii. Frances Ellen, b. Sept. 4, 1836, in Minot, Me.

    iv. Harriet Elizabeth, b. April 22, 1838, in Minot, Me.

    v. Almeda Frances, b. Oct. 9, 1842.

    vi. Emma Florence, b. June 16, 1849.

    vii. Ella Jane, b. Dec. 17, 1850.

    viii. Mary Edith, b. Nov. 23, 1853.

    III. POLLY H., b. Nov. 1, 1814; m. Elbridge Millett; two children :—

    i. Joseph A., b. July 3, 1842.

    ii. Eliza J., b. Sept. 5, 1847.

    IV. JOANNA MANNING, b. Aug. 28, 1816; m. Cyrus Turner, of Otisfield, Me. ; five children :—

    i. Frances Ellen, b. July 10, 1841.

    ii. Sarah Abbie, b. Sept. 22, 1844.

    iii. Simeon Avery, b. May 3, 1849.

    iv. Harriet Merrow, b. Sept. 10, 1853.

    v. Clara Josephine, b. March 5, 1859.

WILLIAM (605) GREENLEAF, CONTINUED :—

V. ELIZABETH KNIGHT, b. Oct. 11, 1818; m. Roscoe
Attwood, of Minot, Me. ; four children :—
i. Joseph Lorenzo, b. Aug. 8, 1848.
ii. Stephen Merrill, b. Sept. 15, 1852.
iii. Frank Preston, b. March 19, 1854.
iv. Martha Elizabeth, b. July 23, 1858.

608. VI. SAMUEL KNIGHT,[8] b. Oct. 11, 1818; twin ; m. Eliza
S. Davis, b. July 19, 1822. He d. Sept. 4, 1878.
He lived on the home farm until the year 1866, when
he bought a farm in East Otisfield, Me., where he
spent the remainder of his days. The place is now
owned by his son Percival C. and his mother, who
lives with him ; ten children.

VII. MARTHA C., b. June 10, 1821 ; m. John Hill, of
Bridgton, Me. ; eight children :—
i. Mary Elizabeth, b. June 29, 1843.
ii. Charles William, b. July 9, 1845.
iii. John Franklin, b. Aug. 24, 1849.
iv. Sidney L., b. Nov. 3, 1851.
v. Ada Florence, b. Feb. 27, 1854.
vi. Ida Frances, b. Feb. 27, 1854; twin.
vii. Jessie Fremont, b. March 17, 1856.
viii. Annie Jane, b. Dec. 28, 1859.

608.

(William 7, Jonathan 6, Gardner 5, Stephen 4, Samuel 3, Stephen 2, Edmund 1.)

Children of **Samuel Knight**[8] **Greenleaf** and Eliza S.
(Davis).

I. ZEBULON D.,[9] b. Sept. 16, 1845 ; d. July 21, 1864.

II. MARY ETTA, b. March 16, 1847 ; m. Thomas Jackson. She d. Oct. 22, 1881 ; two children.

III. MARTHA VIRGINIA, b. Oct. 27, 1848; d. May 4,
1872.

IV. SARAH ELIZABETH, b. June 13, 1850; d. Feb. 22,
1853.

609. V. WILLIAM MANNING,[9] b. May 2, 1852, in Otisfield,
Me. ; m. Nov. 19, 1879, Mary C., dau. of C. R. and
Abby Pulsifer ; res. Auburn, Me. ; teller in National
Shoe and Leather Bank ; two children :—
i. Florence Abbie, b. Jan. 27, d. Aug. 14, 1884.
ii. Harry C., b. Dec. 16, 1886.

448 GENEALOGY.

SAMUEL KNIGHT (608) GREENLEAF, CONTINUED :—

610. VI. CHARLES EDWARD,[9] b. Feb. 28, 1854; m. Ellen A.
Dinsmore; res. Auburn, Me.; contractor and builder
in company with his father-in-law, Hon. Hiram
Dinsmore; two children :—

    I. Edna C.

    II. Elmer D.

611. VII. ELBRIDGE MILLETT,[9] b. Sept. 19, 1856; m. Sept. 5,
1883, Ellen F., dau. of Benjamin S. and Margaret
Farrow, b. Dec. 28, 1858; res. Auburn, Me.; master builder; four children :—

    I. Margaret F., b. July 23, 1884.

    II. Virginia G., b. July 18, 1886.

    III. Mabel, b. Aug. 11, 1887.

    IV. Florence E., b. March 27, 1893.

612. VIII. PERCIVAL CALVIN,[9] b. Oct. 17, 1858; m. Aug.
1, 1883, Hattie B., dau. of David R. and Louisa
(Lovejoy) Holden, b. April 22, 1862; res. Otisfield,
Me.; farmer; four children :—

    I. Henry Percival, b. Feb. 2, 1885; killed by light-
ning June 21, 1891.

    II. Ernest Lovejoy, b. Nov. 25, 1887.

    III. Francis Harrison Towne, b. Jan. 7, 1889.

    IV. William Henry, b. May 27, 1892.

    IX. CARRIE ELLEN, b. March 25, 1861; m. Robert H.
Union; res. Marblehead, Mass.; shoe manufacturer;
one child :—

    Chester H.

    X. AUGUSTA SPURR, b. Feb. 9, 1864; m. Harry L.
Haskell, of Auburn, Me.; two children :—

    i. Howard P., b. Dec. 19, 1887; d. March 19, 1891; drowned.

    ii. Helen P.

606.

(Jonathan 6, Gardner 5, Stephen 4, Samuel 3, Stephen 2, Edmund 1.)

Children of **Thomas**[7] **Greenleaf** and Phebe (Reed).

613. I. WILLIAM,[8] b. Oct. 25, 1825; m. Esther Horton, of
Gorham, Me.

    II. THOMAS R., b. Dec. 17, 1826.

    III. MARY, b. Sept. 12, 1831; d. May 17, 1848.

604.

(Gardner 5, Stephen 4, Samuel 3, Stephen 2, Edmund 1.)

Children of **Gardner**[6] **Greenleaf** and Lydia Nickerson (Hart).

I. LYDIA.

614. II. GARDNER,[7] b. May 5, 1789, at Medford, Mass.; m. 1, May 6, 1815, at Keene, N. H., Nancy Gaylord, b. Nov. 2, 1797, at Norwich, Conn.; d. May 21, 1837, in Boston; 2, Nov. 23, 1837, Rebecca Jane Caldwell, b. Dec. 22, 1814, in Truro, N. S.; d. Aug. 6, 1887. He d. March 24, 1864; res. Boston, Mass.

Child by 1st marriage :—

614a. 1. Gardner,[8] b. Jan. 19, 1824, in Boston; m. May 6, 1845, at Boston, Adaline Glynn. He d. Oct. 6, 1863; one child : Walter.

Children by 2d marriage :—

615. II. Lawrence Nichols,[8] b. Oct. 4, 1838; m. March 30, 1869, at Denver, Col., Jennie Sophia Hammond, b. Oct. 5, 1850, in Belvidere, Ill.; res. Denver, Col.; three children : 1. Gardner, b. Feb. 6, 1871. 2. Eugene L., b. Aug. 19, 1875. 3. Rebecca Jane, b. Sept. 10, 1877.

III. Rebecca Jane, b. March 12, 1840; m. March 18, 1863, Henry C. Lord. She d. May 17, 1877; three children :—

1. Henry G., b. May 30, 1865. 2. Albert T., b. Oct. 27, 1870. 3. Bertram, b. Feb. 25, 1873.

IV. Lucy Nichols, b. Oct. 5, 1841; m. Nov. 8, 1860, T. Albert Taylor. She d. March 31, 1890; one child :—

Grace Greenleaf, b. April 13, 1862.

V. Eugene Douglas,[8] b. Aug. 19, 1844; res. Boston, Mass.

615a. VI. Franklin Lewis,[8] b. Oct. 7, 1847; m. Jan. 13, 1875, Florence M. Cahill; proprietor Florence Mill Co.; res. Minneapolis, Minn.; two children : 1. Grace, b. April 1, 1876. 2. Gardner, b. Sept. 24, 1882.

615b. VII. Lyman Blanchard,[8] b. Sept. 19, 1851; m. April 20, 1892, Ellen M., dau. of Charles A. Browning,

GARDNER (604) GREENLEAF, CONTINUED :—

 II. Gardner.

  of Boston; res. Boston, Mass.; two children: 1.
  Browning, b. April 15, 1893; d. Dec. 30, 1894.
  2. Hilda, b. April 1, 1895.

 III. CATHERINE, b.——, 1794; d. May 26, 1883.

 IV. MARY.

 V. EUNICE.

 VI. ELIZA, b. 1798; d. Sept. 12, 1881.

 VII. OLIVER, b.——, d. Sept., 1883.

602.

(Stephen 4, Samuel 3, Stephen 2, Edmund 1.)

Children of **Isaac⁵ Greenleaf** and Sarah (Rhoads).

616. I. ISAAC,⁶ b. Feb. 3, 1779; m. Feb. 18, 1803, Hepzibah
  Shedd, b. April 6, 1780; d. Sept. 21, 1827; seven
  children :—

   I. Hepzibah, b. May 17, 1804, at Medford, Mass.; m.
    Dec. 28, 1823, Gardiner Fifield; seven children :—
    1. George G., b. Oct. 27, 1824; m. Sarah E. Richardson. 2. James
    F., b. Sept. 15, 1826; m. Tamzay Holbrook. 3. Frederick
    I., b. Oct. 31, 1828; d. April 16, 1830. 4. Frederick P., b.
    Oct. 24, 1831; d. May 23, 1851. 5. Georgianna I., b. Sept. 8,
    1836. 6. Winslow W., b. Oct. 2, 1840. 7. William E., b.
    March 19, 1845.

   II. Mary, b. Sept. 1, 1807; d. young.

   III. Sarah A., b. Nov. 13, 1808; m. Dec. 2, 1836,
    J. B. Mott.

   IV. George Gardner, b. Jan. 26, 1813.

   V. Lydia Spring, b. Dec. 16, 1816; m. Rufus C.
    Smith, b. July 13, 1817, in Hallowell, Me.

617.   VI. Edward Henry,⁷ b. Sept. 25, 1819, in Salem, Mass.;
    m. C. S. Colby, of Westport; res. Medford, Mass.

   VII. Manassah K., b. March 25, 1821, in Medford,
    Mass.; d. May 26, 1849.

 II. SARAH, b. Sept., 1780; d. Sept. 15, 1807; unmarried.

 III. MARY, b. Jan. 29, 1782; d. July 11, 1805; unmarried.

 IV. HANNAH HOPPIN, b. April 5, 1784; m. Aug. 23,
  1810, Henry Reed, b. Jan. 27, 1785; res. Medford,
  Mass.; five children :—

  i. Hannah, b. June 23, 1811.
  ii. Susanna, b. Feb. 15, 1813.
  iii. Henry F., b. June 15, 1818.

ISAAC (602) GREENLEAF, CONTINUED :—
IV. Hannah Hoppin.
   iv. Isaac R., b. Dec. 17, 1820; res. Boston, Mass.
   v. Rebecca G., b. Sept. 1, 1823.
V. REBECCA, b. Nov. 6, 1786; m. Feb. 13, 1812, John
    Burridge, Jr.
VI. ABIGAIL HOPPIN, b. Nov. 24, 1788; m. Dec. 18,
    1808, Thomas Shedd.
VII. ELIZA HOPPIN, b. Sept. 14, 1791; d. May 1, 1821;
    unmarried.
VIII. HARRIET, b. Nov. 14, 1794; m. Henry Rogers.

29.

(Tristram 3, Stephen 2, Edmund 1.)

Children of **Nathaniel**[4] **Greenleaf** and Judith (Coffin).

618. I. JOSHUA,[5] b. May 24, 1715; m. Annie, widow of Capt.
    Richard Kent, and dau. of Joseph and Mary Hale.
    She d. 1794.

II. JUDITH, b. Feb., 1716.

619. III. ABNER,[5] b. Nov. 9, 1718; m. May 19, 1757, Mary
    (Whittier?) Gutterson [Newbury, Mass., records], b.
    1736; d. 1812. He d. Jan. 10, 1810; res. Newbury,
    Mass.; eight children.

    Will probated March 8, 1810, Abner Greenleaf, joiner; names of
    daughters, Abigail and Elizabeth, appear in his will.

IV. SARAH, b. March 5, 1721; m. July 12, 1739, Joseph,
    youngest son of Joseph and Mary (Peasley) Whittier,
    b. March 31, 1716; d. Oct. 10, 1796, at Haverhill,
    Mass. She d. March 17, 1807; res. Haverhill,
    Mass.; eleven children, all born in Haverhill :—

   i. Stephen, b. April 6; d. April 15, 1740.
   ii. Thomas, b. July 29; d. Aug. 13, 1742.
   iii. Ruth, b. Dec. 26; d. Dec. 27, 1743.
   iv. Obadiah, b. Jan. 22, 1745-6; d. Oct. 3, 1754.
   v. Mary, b. Feb. 2, 1747-8; d. Sept. 5, 1802.
   vi. Joseph, b. Sept. 14, 1750; d. Sept. 21, 1754.
   vii. Nathaniel, b. July 13, 1753; d. Jan., 1839, at Hollis, Me.
   viii. Joseph, b. Sept. 20, 1755; m. Nov. 22, 1806, Mary, dau. of
    Amos Chase. He d. Feb. 20, 1833. She m. 2, Jonathan
    Taylor, of Biddeford, Me.; pub. at Biddeford, April 17, 1835.
    He d. 1836. She m. 3, ——— Hanson. Children of Joseph
    and Mary: 1. Sarah, b. Aug. 13, 1807; m. John Hilton. 2.
    Joseph, b. March 1, 1809; m. Mary A. Waterhouse. 3. Na-
    thaniel, b. Sept. 20, 1810; m. Mary Goodwin. 4. Elizabeth,

NATHANIEL (29) GREENLEAF, CONTINUED:—

IV. Sarah.

> b. March 14, 1812; d. July 19, 1816. 5. Amos, b. Feb. 14, 1815; m. Angelia R. Bastow. 6. William Penn, b. Jan. 27, 1817; m. Hannah Drew.

ix. Obadiah, b. Sept. 2, 1758; m. Dec. 7, 1786, at Dover, N. H., Sarah, dau. of Moses and Phebe (Hussey) Austin, b. July 9, 1765, at Rochester, N. H.; d. Aug. 11, 1844. Phebe, w. of Moses, was Aunt to Abigail, who m. John Whittier. Obadiah, d. July 29, 1814; res. Dover, N. H., where all the children were born: 1. Anna, b. Sept. 26, 1787; m. Isaac Wendall. 2. Moses, b. May 19, 1789; m. Gertrude Frye, and others. 3. Sarah, b. July 7, 1791; m. George D. Varney. 4. Joseph, b. Dec. 10, 1793; m. Nancy Locke. 5. John, b. Dec. 9, 1795; m. Hannah Hanson (Bemis). 6. Phebe Austin, b. March 11, 1798; m. Edmund Johnson. 7. Mary, b. July 14, 1800; m. Gideon C. Smith. 8. Ruth, b. Oct. 28, 1802; m. Samuel A. Shute. 9. Lydia, b. July 14, 1807; m. Leonard Smith.

x. John, b. Nov. 22, 1760; m. Oct. 3, 1804, at Haverhill, Mass., Abigail, dau. of Samuel and Mercy (Evans) Hussey, b. Sept. 3, 1779, at Somersworth, N. H.; d. Dec. 28, 1857, at Amesbury, Mass. He d. June 11, 1830. The family removed from Haverhill to Amesbury, July 6, 1836. It has been recorded by other authorities, that Abigail Hussey was the dau. of Joseph and Mercy (Evans), but Tates' records of Somersworth, N. H., say it was Samuel, and nothing is found concerning the marriage of Joseph; res. Haverhill, Mass., where all the children were born: 1. Mary, b. Sept. 3, 1806; m. Jacob Caldwell. 2. John Greenleaf, b. Dec. 17, 1807; d. Sept. 7, 1892, 4.30 A. M., at the residence of Miss Sarah Gove, in Hampton, N. H., where he had been passing two months. 3. Matthew Franklin, b. July 18, 1812: m. 1, Aug. 4, 1836, Abigail R. Poyen. She d. March 27, 1841, at Portland, Me.; two children: (1) Sarah, d. March 13, 1841, aged 8 months. (2) Joseph Poyen, d. Aug. 15, 1838. 2, Jane E. Vaughn, of St. John, N. B., b. April 27, 1819: three children: (3) Charles Franklin, b. Dec. 8, 1843. (4) Elizabeth Hussey, b. Aug. 10, 1845; m. S. T. Pickard, author of "Life and Letters of John Greenleaf Whittier," pub. 1894. Mr. Pickard is owner and editor of the Portland, Me., *Transcript.* Mrs. Pickard is the owner of the Amesbury Home; it is proposed to make it a memorial hall. (5) Alice Greenwood, b. Feb. 19, 1848; m. Wilbur Berry. 3, ———. He d. Jan. 7, 1883, at Boston, Mass. 4. Elizabeth Hussey, b. Dec. 7, 1815; d. Sept. 3, 1864, at Amesbury, Mass.

xi. Moses, b. Dec. 20, 1762; d. Jan. 23, 1824.

V. ELIZABETH, b. Nov. 22, 1723; m. —— Noyes.

VI. NATHANIEL, b. July 20, 1736; d. Aug. 10, 1755.

619.

(Nathaniel 4, Tristram 3, Stephen 2, Edmund 1.)

Children of **Abner**[5] **Greenleaf** and Mary Whittier [?] (Gutterson).

I. SARAH, b. April 25, 1758; m. —— Coffin.

II. NATHANIEL, b. Sept. 9, 1759.

620. III. ABNER,[6] b. Oct. 13, 1761; m. Nov. 27, 1783, Sarah Hale, of Salem, Mass. She d. 1853. He d. 1837; res. West Newbury, Mass.; nine children.

IV. JOSHUA,[6] b. Dec. 21, 1763; res. Newburyport, Mass.

621. V. SAMUEL,[6] b. March 14, 1766; m. Sept. 11, 1792, Miriam, dau. of Timothy and Mary (Bartlett) Pillsbury, b. Jan. 23, 1773; d. 1843, in Cincinnati, Ohio. He d. July, 1835; res. Cincinnati, Ohio; twelve children.

622. VI. JOSIAH,[6] b. March 22, 1773; m. Aug. 15, 1799, Mary Harvey. She d. 1849. He d. Nov. 21, 1848; res. Lowell, Mass.; four children :—

    I. Josiah, b. Feb. 4, 1804.

    II. Elizabeth, b. Sept. 15, 1805.

    III. Adeline, b. Nov. 29, 1811.

    IV. A dau., m. —— Fuller.

VII. ABIGAIL.

VIII. ELIZABETH.

620.

(Abner 5, Nathaniel 4, Tristram 3, Stephen 2, Edmund 1.)

Children of **Abner**[6] **Greenleaf** and Sarah (Hale).

I. MARY, b. about 1786; m. William Carr; six children.

II. SARAH, m. Moses Lancaster; five children.

III. MEHITABLE (HITTY), b. about 1790; d. Dec. 31, 1811.

IV. HARRIET, d. about 1845; aged about 40.

623. V. ABNER,[7] b. about 1795; m. Sophia Brown. He d. Dec. 1, 1834; three children :—

    I. Sophia Brown, b. about 1822.

    II. Abner, d. in childhood.

    III. Moses Brown.

624. VI. MATTHEW HALE,[7] m. Lydia, dau. of Ebenezer Hosum, a Revolutionary soldier; res. West Newbury, Mass.; no children.

ABNER (620) GREENLEAF, CONTINUED:—

VII. CHARLES How, d. Aug. 29, 1806.

625. VIII. ALFRED,[7] b. 1804; m. Nov. 27, 1830, in Salem, Mass.,
Lucy Lang Field. He d. Dec. 26, 1872. Educated at
Exeter Academy. Received honorary degree of A.M.
from Dartmouth College, also from the University of
New York; was principal of the Franklin School in
Salem, Mass., 1825–1837. For twenty-six years kept a
school for young ladies in Brooklyn, N. Y.; res.
Brooklyn, N. Y.; seven children:—

    I. Lucy Ann P.

    II. Sarah Ellen, b. October, 1833; d. October, 1851.

    III. Alfred.

    IV. Charles How.

    V. Eliza, d. in infancy.

    VI. Mary Catherine.

    VII. Emma Lucretia Latimer.

IX. CHARLES How, b. 1806; d. April 27, 1838, in
Brooklyn, N. Y.; graduated at Dartmouth College
and studied theology.

621.

(Abner 5, Nathaniel 4, Tristram 3, Stephen 2, Edmund 1.)

Children of **Samuel**[6] **Greenleaf** and Miriam (Pillsbury).

    I. LUCY, b. Dec. 2, 1793, in Newbury, Mass.; m. May
18, 1817, in Marietta, Ohio, William Holyoke; res.
Galesburg, Ill.; six children, one of whom was Rev.
W. E. Holyoke, of Elgin, Ill.

    II. GEORGE, b. Feb. 19, 1795; d. May 17, 1796.

    III. GEORGE, b. Oct. 26, 1796; d. Oct. 7, 1797.

625a. IV. SAMUEL,[7] b. July 8, 1798; married; d. 1848; no
children.

    V. CLEMENT, b. April 23, 1800, in Newbury, Mass.; d.
about 1827 at Natchez, Miss.; unmarried.

626. VI. EDWARD,[7] b. July 19, 1802; m. Jan. 25, 1825, at Cin-
cinnati, Ohio, Mary Jane, dau. of Joseph Allen, b.
March 27, 1808, at Bangor, Me.; d. Nov. 30, 1887.
He d. Oct. 29, 1873, at Indianapolis, Ind.; buried at
Crown Hill Cemetery. He moved in 1832 to Ten-
nessee, returned to Cincinnati in 1843, where he re-

SAMUEL (621) GREENLEAF, CONTINUED:—

VI. Edward.

sided until 1850, when he moved to Indianapolis, where he remained until his death. As a mechanical engineer he was not surpassed in the West; as a man, he was indeed " one of nature's noblemen," beloved and respected by all who knew him; eleven children.

VII. FRANCES, b. April 19, 1804; m. 1, Joseph Atwood; 2, Dr. W. C. White; 3, —— Irons. She d. 1863 at Memphis, Tenn.; no children.

VIII. MARY, b. Nov. 14, 1805; m. 1, Henry Coffin, of Cincinnati, Ohio; 2, Captain Butler, of Virginia. She d. about 1860 in Virginia; one child by 1st marriage :—

Frederick F.

IX. CAROLINE, b. March 13, 1808; m. 1827, Jesse O'Neil, of Cincinnati, Ohio; d. before 1876. She d. 1876, at Decatur, Ill.; two children :—

i. Julia, m. Hector Daniels, book dealer, of Cincinnati, Ohio.
ii. Clara, m. —— Wright, of Chicago, Ill.

X. MARTHA, b. Feb. 22, 1810; m. 1832, Joseph Drew, of Bolivar, Tenn. She d. 1832, at Bolivar, Tenn.

XI. CLARISSA, b. April 30, 1812; m. Jerome B. Williams, of Cincinnati, Ohio. She d. 1846, at Cincinnati, Ohio; no children.

XII. JULIA, b. March 22, 1815; m. 1836, D. S. James, of Bolivar, Tenn.; she d. 1886, at Fresno, Cal.; res. Fresno, Cal.; four children :—

i. Charles.
ii. Mary Agnes, married.
iii. ——, m. —— Beard; res. Fresno, Cal.
iv. ——.

626.

(Samuel 6, Abner 5, Nathaniel 4, Tristram 3, Stephen 2, Edmund 1.)

Children of **Edward**[7] **Greenleaf** and Mary Jane (Allen).

I. FRANCES ELIZABETH, b. Feb. 20, 1826, at Cincinnati, Ohio; m. 1, Nov. 18, 1856, at Indianapolis, Ind. Samuel Espy; 2, R. P. Lancaster; six children by 1st marriage :—

i. Jane, b. Feb. 24; d. July 20, 1858, Indianapolis, Ind.
ii. George, b. July 12, 1859; res. Chicago, Ill.

456 GENEALOGY.

Edward (626) Greenleaf, Continued :—

 I. Frances Elizabeth.

  iii. Edward Greenleaf, b. Jan. 17, 1861; m. Sept. 26, 1892, at Indianapolis, Ind., L. Gard, b. Dec. 1, 1865, Carroll Co., Ind.; one child : George Leland, b. July 7, 1893, at Indianapolis, Ind.

  iv. Samuel McClure, b. Sept. 19, 1862; m. May 3, 1892, Josephine Leach, b. Aug. 19, 1867, at Indianapolis, Ind.; one child : George Curtis, b. July 8, 1893.

  v. William, b. Feb. 15, 1864; d. July 14, 1865.

  vi. Mary Frances, b. Feb. 16, 1866; m. Sept. 9, 1891, William F. Wilfley, b. Feb. 12, 1865, near Mexico, Mo.; two children : 1. Frances Jane, b. Feb. 17, 1893. 2. Mary Edna, b. March 31, 1894.

 II. Edward Holabird, b. Dec. 14, 1827, at Cincinnati, Ohio; d. Aug. 11, 1830, at Cincinnati, Ohio.

627. III. Alvin Choate,[8] b. Dec. 14,1829, at Cincinnati,Ohio ; m. Jan. 3, 1855, at Indianapolis, Ind., Kate V. Pinkard. He d. Aug. 27, 1866, at Indianapolis, Ind. ; res. Pasadena, Cal.; four children :—

  I. Catherine St. Clair, b. March 8, 1856; m. Semour Locke, of Locke Haven; res. Pasadena, Cal.; one child :—

Preston.

  II. Annie, d. aged two years.

  III. Thomas Pinkard, b. about 1858; d. in infancy.

  IV. Margaret Lee, b. about 1863; res. Pasadena, Cal.

 IV. John Hancock, b. April 10, 1832, at Cincinnati, Ohio; d. Aug. 15, 1834, at Bolivar, Tenn.

 V. John Edward, b. Dec. 31, 1834, in Tennessee; d. June 22, 1842, at Whiteville, Tenn.

 VI. Mary Jane, b. Aug. 31, 1836, at Bolivar, Tenn.; m. Oct. 9, 1861, at Indianapolis, Ind., Leonidas Marion Phipps; res. Walla Walla, Wash., since 1888; nine children :—

  i. Ingram Allen, b. July 28, 1862; d. Feb. 11, 1890.

  ii. Edward Marion, b. Jan. 25, 1864; d. July 7, 1865.

  iii. Lucy, b. Nov. 1, 1865; d. Dec. 19, 1890.

  iv. Leon, b. July 3, 1867.

  v. Jane, b. Dec. 6, 1868.

  vi. Mary, b. July 16, 1871; m. Dec. 9, 1890, George Fitzhugh. She d. Oct. 9, 1894; res. Walla Walla, Wash.

  vii. Maurice Parvin, b. Oct. 25, 1872.

  viii. Hugh, b. Nov. 29, 1874.

  ix. Edna, b. Oct. 10, 1879.

EDWARD (626) GREENLEAF, CONTINUED:—

628. VII. CLEMENT ALLEN,[8] b. Sept. 26, 1838, at Whiteville, Tenn.; m. Aug. 6, 1862, at Indianapolis, Ind., Frances Caroline Phipps, b. Aug. 23, 1844; res. Greencastle, Ind.; ten children:—

629. I. Edward Timothy,[9] b. Aug. 27, 1865; m. Sept. 18, 1889, Jennie Boor, of Sandusky, Ohio; res. Lima, Ohio; in business with Lima Locomotive and Machine Works; two children: 1. Desdemona, b. July 7, 1890, at Indianapolis, Ind. 2. Marie, b. June 17, 1891, at Indianapolis, Ind.

630. II. Clement Allen,[9] b. Aug. 19, 1867; m. Sept. 10, 1891, at Mexico, Mo., Elizabeth Bert Wilfley; res. Indianapolis, Ind.; in business with Greenleaf Manfg. Co.; one child: Miriam Pillsbury, b. June 18, 1892, at Indianapolis, Ind.

III. John Leland, b. July 30, 1869.

IV. Harry, b. July 30, 1869; twin; d. at birth.

V. Mary, b. Jan. 14, 1872.

VI. Helen Milicent, b. April 12, 1874.

VII. Frances Jane, b. Dec. 5, 1877; d. Feb. 11, 1882.

VIII. Grace, b. May 16, 1881.

IX. May, b. May 16, 1881; twin.

X. Paul, b. March 25, 1884.

VIII. SOPHIA PILLSBURY, b. Sept., 1840, at Whiteville, Tenn.; d. June 14, 1844, at Cincinnati, Ohio.

IX. THOMAS NORMAN, b. July 26, 1842, at Whiteville, Tenn.; d. June 3, 1844, at Cincinnati, Ohio.

631. X. WILLIAM ALONZO,[8] b. Jan. 5, 1845, at Cincinnati, Ohio; m. Dec. 2, 1867, Hannah Anderson; res. Anderson, Ind.; three children:—

632. I. William Edward,[9] b. Sept. 8, 1868; m. Laura ——; res. Monmouth, Ill.; one child: Esther, b. 1892.

II. Mary Elizabeth, b. April 12, 1870; res. Indianapolis, Ind.

III. Francis Samuel, b. Nov. 2, 1872; res. Indianapolis, Ind.

633. XI. TIMOTHY PILLSBURY,[8] b. Dec. 14, 1847, at Cincinnati, Ohio; m. Dec., 1869, Sarah Jane Anderson. He d. May 27, 1890; res. Hagerstown, Ind. He removed

EDWARD (626) GREENLEAF, CONTINUED :—

    XI. Timothy Pillsbury.

      to Indianapolis with his parents in 1850; after his mar-
riage he went West, and was engaged in mining until his
death. He was killed by a fall of 300 feet, caused by the
cage cable breaking in the shaft of the Delz Mine, Park
City, Utah. He was a mechanical engineer of more
than ordinary ability and promise; two children :—

      I. Francis, b. March 9, 1872, at Indianapolis, Ind.

      II. Edward Noble, b. April 26, 1874.

32.

(Tristram 3, Stephen 2, Edmund 1.)

Children of **Tristram⁴ Greenleaf** and Dorothy (Rolfe).

634. I. SAMUEL,⁵ b. Aug. 15, 1729; m. Lois, dau. of Thomas
Rowell, of Amesbury, Mass. He d. April 3, 1778.
He held his Commission as Coronor from Governor
Phipps, 1756, and was sworn into office by John
Greenleaf and Nathan Hale, Justices of the Peace;
res. Amesbury, Mass.; five children :—

      I. Thomas R., b. 1755; d. Oct., 1781.

      II. Hannah, b. 1759; m. Benjamin Abbott, of Con-
cord, N. H. She d. March 15, 1831.

      III. Tristram, b. 1764; d. Oct., 1780; unmarried.

635.   IV. Stephen,⁶ b. April 11, 1766, in Newbury, Mass.;
m. 1791, Ruth Pettingill. She d. March 18, 1826.
He d. Dec. 26, 1845. He moved to Salisbury, N.
H., 1789; a farmer; nine children.

636.   V. Samuel,⁶ b. June, 1768; m. at Salisbury, N. H.,
Mary Wiggin. He d. Nov., 1845; merchant; res.
Boston, Mass.; one child: Sarah E., b. April,
1806; m. Sept. 26, 1826, in Boston, Charles J.
Cazenove. She d. 1871; res. Boston, Mass.

    II. MARTHA, b. Nov. 1, 1731; d. Dec. 3, 1735.

    III. STEPHEN, b. Jan. 13, 1733; d. Jan. 2, 1735.

    IV. MARTHA, b. June, 1736; m. Aug. 14, 1755, Obadiah
Horton.

    V. HANNAH, b. April 9, 1739; d. in infancy.

    VI. SARAH, b. July 11, 1741.

    VII. STEPHEN, b. Nov. 27, 1743; d. in infancy.

    VIII. HANNAH, b. July 16, 1746.

635.

(Samuel 5, Tristram 4, Tristram 3, Stephen 2, Edmund 1.)

Children of **Stephen**[6] **Greenleaf** and Ruth (Pettingill).

637. I. THOMAS ROWELL,[7] b. July 6, 1793; m. Mary Hawley. She d. May 3, 1873. In 1854 res. New Philadelphia, Ohio, in 1860 at St. Louis, Mo.; two children:—

638. I. George Henry,[8] b. Nov. 5, 1834, in Salisbury, N. H.; m. Oct. 4, 1870, Lou. Harrison, of Lebanon, Mo., b. Feb. 20, 1852. He d. Dec. 9, 1886; res. Galena, Ill.; four children: 1. May, b. March 8, 1872; m. Sept. 7, 1893, L. C. Mayfield, of Lebanon, Mo. 2. Lizzie Harrison, b. May 14, d. Nov. 13, 1874. 3. Annie Elmore, b. May 2, 1878. 4. George, b. March 18, 1885.

II. Andrew S., b. March 11, 1841; d. Nov. 27, 1870; unmarried.

II. HARRIET, b. March 17, 1795; d. in infancy.

III. HENRY, b. May 15, 1797; d. Nov. 27, 1832; unmarried.

IV. LOIS, b. June 9, 1799; m. Isaac Crane; d. 1882, in Salisbury, N. H.; res. Boscawen, N. H., in 1854.

V. EUNICE, b. May 15, 1801; m. James Colburn, of Franklin, N. H. She d. June 26, 1839; one child:—
A daughter, b. 1835.

VI. HARRIET, b. Aug. 25, 1803; m. Jotham Allds, of Claremont, N. H. She d. 1856.

639. VII. FRANCIS S.,[7] b. July 10, 1805; m. Charlotte Fowle Britton. He d. 1867. She d. 1885; res. Boston, Mass.; merchant; four children:—
I. Charlotte Maria, b. Feb. 14, 1836.
II. Henry Francis, b. Sept. 16, 1838; res. Boston, Mass.; merchant.
III. Ellen Britton, b. July 21, 1841; d. 1882.
IV. Mary Louise, b. Jan. 2, 1850; res. Boston, Mass.

640. VIII. TRISTRAM,[7] b. Nov. 27, 1807, in Franklin, N. H.; m. March 2, 1835, Ann Burleigh. She d. 1879. He d. Jan. 1, 1882, at Haverhill, Mass.; farmer; res. Salisbury, N. H.; five children:—
I. Louisa, b. April 2, 1836; d. April 5, 1843.

STEPHEN (635) GREENLEAF, CONTINUED:—
    VIII. Tristram.
      II. Charlotte B., b. Jan. 3, 1837; in Haverhill, Mass.

641.   III. Charles C.,[8] b. July 5, 1839; m. March 22, 1865, at Salisbury, N. H., Mary Susan Dimond, b. Nov. 10, 1840, at Salisbury, N. H.; res. Wauseon, Ohio; merchant miller, firm Lyon, Clement & Greenleaf: two children: 1. Anna Louise, b. March 19, 1868. 2. Carl Dimond, b. July 27, 1876, student at Chicago University.
      IV. William, d. in infancy.
      V. Helen L., b. July 12, 1848; d. July 25, 1880.
    IX. HANNAH, b. July 14, 1812; d. 1858, in Franklin, N. H.

33.

(Tristram 3, Stephen 2, Edmund 1.)

Children of **Enoch[4] Greenleaf** and Hannah (Bradshaw).
    I. HANNAH, b. Dec. 23, 1726; d. April 2, 1736.
642. II. JOHN,[5] b. Oct. 30, 1729; m. Bathsheba Milton, b. about 1732; d. Dec. 2, 1825; res. Hull, Mass.; one child :—
643.   Stephen[6], m. 1, June 5, 1766, Mehitable, dau. of Capt. Amos and Rebecca Binney, b. July 29, 1747; d. Oct. 26, 1767; 2, Jane, probably dau. of Elisha and Experience (Loring) Gould, b. 1748; d. Jan. 30, 1797; res. Hull, Mass.; one child by 1st marriage: Stephen, b. Oct. 2, 1767.
    III. EDMUND, b. Aug. 17, 1731; d. March 9, 1736.
    IV. JUDITH, b. July 26, 1733.
    V. SAMUEL, b. Oct. 24, 1735; d. 1741.
643a VI. EDMUND,[5] b. Jan. 21, 1740; m. Hannah ——. Will dated June 5, 1784; probated Aug. 30, 1784; res. Newbury; blacksmith [Newbury records]; four children :—
      I. Lydia Davis.
      II. Sarah Cooker.
      III. William.
      IV. Katharine.

34.

(Edmund 3, Stephen 2, Edmund I.)

Children of **Edmund**[4] **Greenleaf** and Mary (Hale).

644. I. WILLIAM,[5] b. Nov. 28, 1725; m. 1, Ruth Pearson, of Haverhill, Mass.; d. March 22, 1779; 2, April 11, 1784, Mary Soley, of Haverhill, Mass.; d. Nov. 7, 1802. He d. Jan. 7, 1800; res. Haverhill, Mass.; kept the "Sun" Tavern; eight children by 1st marriage.

II. MARY, b. April 30, 1729.

644.

(Edmund 4, Edmund 3, Stephen 2, Edmund 1.)

Children of **Capt. William**[5] **Greenleaf** and Ruth (Pearson).

645. I. DANIEL,[6] b. April 19, 1745; m. 1765, Ruth Dalton, of Newbury, Mass. He d. June 10, 1794; res. Haverhill, Mass.; ten children.

II. WILLIAM, b. June 16, d. Oct. 9, 1747.

III. HANNAH, b. July 30, 1748; d. July 1, 1749.

IV. EDMUND, b. Nov. 15, d. Nov. 25, 1749.

646. V. SAMUEL,[6] b. July 24, 1752, in Haverhill, Mass.; m. Dec. 9, 1779, Alice Ladd, of Haverhill, Mass.; d. 1842. He d. March 20, 1795. She m. 2, Captain Hoyt, of Epping, N. H. Mr. Samuel Greenleaf removed to Epping, N. H., July 20, 1783; kept an English and West India grocery store; three children :—

I. Sarah Ladd, b. Feb. 16, 1781; m. Henry Sanborn, of Epping, N. H.

II. Ruth Pearson, b. June 20, 1783; m. Jacob Swain, of Newburyport, Mass. She d. Oct. 31, 1847, at Newburyport, Mass.

III. Harriet Worthington, b. Aug. 6, 1785, at Epping, N. H.; m. Jonathan Moseley, of Lee, N. H.

647. VI. WILLIAM,[6] b. Nov. 9, 1754; m. March 16, 1788, Abigail Soley, dau. of his father's second wife, of Haverhill, Mass.; d. Feb. 4, 1804. He d. March 29, 1833; res. Haverhill, Mass.; kept the "Sun" Tavern; seven children.

VII. RUTH, b. July 17, 1758.

VIII. HANNAH, b. Sept. 14, 1762.

645.

Children of **Daniel**[6] **Greenleaf** and Ruth (Dalton).

648. I. JAMES,[7] b. Sept. 1, 1766; m. Sarah Townsend. He
    d. 1796; res. Haverhill, Mass.; four children :—

648a. 1. James,[8] b. Aug. 13, 1786; m. Sept. 1, 1811, Char-
    lotte Eaton. He d. Aug. 8, 1824; one child:
    Sarah T., b. May 3, 1812.

    II. Susanna Townsend, b. Feb. 11, 1790.

    III. John, b. Oct. 26, 1792.

    IV. Betsey Pettingill, b. May 7, 1795.

II. MARY PARSONS, b. July 1, 1768; m. —— Palmer.

III. DANIEL, b. Aug. 29, 1770; d. Oct. 8, —— in infancy.

IV. HANNAH, b. Aug. 18, 1771; m. Moses Kelly, b. Dec.
    28, 1767; res. Newton, N. H.; five children :—

    i. James, b. June 18, 1800; d. Oct. 11, 1803.

    ii. Emily, b. Nov. 18, 1802; d. Jan 30, 1862.

    iii. John, b. Nov. 13, 1806; m. Sarah Hills; res. Plaistow, N. H.;
    was a deacon in the Baptist Church. He d. July 24, 1884,
    at Plaistow; no children.

    iv. Greenleaf, b. Nov. 30, 1808; m. April 13, 1841, Louisa Flan-
    ders, of South Hampton, N. H. She d. Jan. 29, 1888. He d.
    Oct. 14, 1888; res. South Hampton, N. H., where he filled
    many of the town offices at different times. He was also Justice
    of the Peace for many years, and deacon in the Baptist Church;
    five children : 1. Myra Ann, b. June 26, 1842. 2. Lucina, b.
    June 17, 1845; m. Nov. 21, 1877, Isaac Hamilton Copeland;
    res. Amesbury, Mass.; one child: Charles Greenleaf, b.
    Sept. 8, 1879. 3. Louisa, b. June 17, 1845; d. Nov. 3, 1847,
    twin. 4. Elbridge Greenleaf, b. Sept. 16, 1846; d. Oct. 10,
    1847. 5. John Beaman, b. Sept. 1, 1849; d. Feb. 3, 1862.

    v. Edwin, b. May 14, 1811; m. Oct. 29, 1844, Jane B. Merrill,
    b. March 17, 1822. He d. July 3, 1880. She d. Feb. 23, 1896;
    res. Newton, N. H. He was a deacon in the Baptist Church;
    seven children : 1. Edwin Greenleaf, b. Oct. 7, 1845; m. Oct.
    27, 1867, Lizzie R. Smith; res. Newton, N. H.; eight chil-
    dren: (1) Elmer Howard, b. Sept. 29, 1868; m. March 5,
    1896, Mathilde Minot. (2) Edith Angela, b. July 4, 1870;
    m. June 6, 1894, Elwood S. Poore; one child: Edwin Spen-
    ser, b. May 23, 1895, in West Newbury, Mass. (3) Everett
    Leon, b. June 5, 1872. (4) Lula Belle, b. Nov. 10, 1876.
    (5) Mamie Augusta, b. Jan. 10, d. March 17, 1879. (6)
    Anna Laura, b. April 1, 1880; d. Jan. 9, 1895. (7) Clar-
    ence Edwin, b. Nov. 4, 1882. (8) Homer Flanders, b. Feb.
    28, d. July 7, 1886. 2. James Alvin, b. Aug. 30. 1847; d. Oct.

DANIEL (645) GREENLEAF, CONTINUED :—

IV. Hannah.

28, 1864. 3. Howard Malcolm, b. Nov. 7, 1848; d. Jan. 24, 1865. 4. Owen Dalton, b. Sept. 10, 1850; m. Aug. 1878, Ida Peaslee; children: (1) Lillian Viola, b. July 2, 1878; d. July 25, 1888. (2) Daisy Estelle, b. April 22, 1880; d. July 2, 1888. (3) Ida Violet, b. March 12, 1884. (4) Dora Adelaide, b. Oct. 12, 1885. (5) Stella May, b. March 29, 1888. (6) Everett Owen, b. Jan. 10, 1890. (7) Roscoe P., b. Nov. 8, 1892. (8) Angelia Elizabeth, b. Dec. 15, 1894. (9) Bernice Ardell, b. Nov. 13, 1895. 5. Milton Merrill, b. June 29, 1852; m. Oct. 13, 1875, Lola E. Bodwell. He d. Dec. 16, 1892; one child: Leon, b. Nov. 10, 1877. 6. Charles Sumner, b. March 29, 1856; m. March 29, 1874, Isabelle M. Stevens; one child: Blanche Lenore, b. April 10, 1875. 7. Lizzie Jane, b. Aug. 17, 1861; m. March 29, 1879, J. Albion Chase; five children: (1) Herbert Albion, b. May 2, 1880. (2) Annie Howard, b. July 12, 1882. (3) Mina Isabelle, b. April 2, 1885. (4) Clarence Reader, b. Dec. 13, 1887. (5) Raymond Temple, b. April 30, 1890.

V. ABIGAIL, b. Sept. 9, 1773; m. Nov. 25, 1801, John[6] Mitchell, b. Dec. 21, 1778; res. Haverhill, Mass.

VI. RUTH, b. July 31, 1775; m. William Hook, of Salem, Mass.; four children, of whom Elias and George G. were the celebrated church organ builders on Tremont Street, Boston, known of late years by the firm name of E. & G. Hook and Hastings.

VII. REBECCA, b. March 28, 1778; m. Sept. 3, 1797, Ephraim, son of Joseph Beaman, b. Nov. 17, 1770, at Lancaster, Mass.; d. May 6, 1822, at Boston, Mass. She d. Aug. 26, 1859, at Salem, Mass.; six children, all born in Boston, Mass. :—

i. Rebecca, b. December, 1798; d. Oct. 18, 1829.

ii. Charles Cotesworth (Rev.), b. Aug. 12, 1799, in Boston; m. July 10, 1839, Mary Ann, dau. of Nymphas and Martha (Babson) Stacy, of Wiscasset, Me., b. March 2, 1816, at Wiscasset, Me.; d. Feb. 22, 1875, in Cambridge, Mass. He d. July 4, 1883, in Boston.

Martha, wife of Nymphas Stacy, was b. in Gloucester, Mass., and d. in Wiscasset, Me., about 1850. She was the dau. of William and Anna (Rogers) Babson, both of Gloucester, Mass., and granddaughter of Rev. John Rogers, minister of Gloucester, Mass., from 1744 to 1782. She was a lineal descendant of John Rogers the fifth President of Harvard College, who married Elizabeth Denison, granddaughter of Gov. Thomas Dudley, and daughter of Major General Daniel

DANIEL (645) GREENLEAF, CONTINUED :—

    VII. Rebecca.

        Denison; four children: 1. Charles Cotesworth, b. May 7, 1840, in Houlton, Me.; m. Aug. 19, 1874, Hettie Sherman, eldest dau. of Hon. William M. Evarts; res. New York City; a partner of the law firm Evarts, Choate & Beaman. He was graduated at Harvard College, 1861; four children: (1) Mary Stacy, b. May 6, 1875. (2) Helen Wardner, b. Feb. 10, 1877. (3) Margaret, b. Sept. 21, 1878. (4) William Evarts, b. Jan. 25, 1881. 2. Nathaniel Parsons, b. March 25, 1843, at North Falmouth, Mass.; m. Dec. 18, 1884, Maria Fisher, dau. of Eben C. Stanwood, of Boston, Mass.; res. Boston, Mass. 3. George Herbert, b. July 27, 1845, at Edgartown, Mass.; m. Dec. 12, 1889, Anna E., dau. of George Sidney Lovett; res. Washington, D. C. 4. William Stacy, b. July 25, 1848, at Wellfleet, Mass.; res. New York City.

    iii. Mary Ann, b. Oct. 21, 1801; m. 1826, John Osborn. She d. Nov. 2, 1827.

    iv. Lucy Wheelock, b. Jan. 5, 1804; d. July 8, 1823.

    v. Caroline, b. April 20, 1808; d. Dec. 7, 1833.

    vi. Margaret Dalton, b. Nov. 20, 1811; d. Sept., 1833.

649. VIII. DANIEL,[7] b. May 5, 1780; m. May, 1803, Elizabeth W. Gale, of Concord, N. H.; d. June 8, 1847. He d. April 23, 1854; res. Washington, N. H.; eleven children.

650. IX. WILLIAM,[7] b. Sept. 3, 1782, in Haverhill; m. Ann Taylor, b. April 11, 1785, in Halifax, England. He d. Jan. 2, 1855; res. Wiscasset, Me.; eight children.

    X. SALLY, b. March 19, 1785; m. Joseph Brown, of Hampton, N. H.; res. Newbury, New Town, N. H.

649.

(Daniel 6, William 5, Edmund 4, Edmund 3, Stephen 2, Edmund 1.)

Children of **Daniel[7] Greenleaf** and Elizabeth W. (Gale).

    I. WILLIAM PITT, b. May 6, 1804; d. March 4, 1805, at Hebron, N. H.

651. II. WILLIAM PITT,[8] b. Aug. 16, 1805; m. Feb. 12, 1837, in Washington, N. H., Sarah H., dau. of Abijah and Sarah (Heald) Monroe (a carpenter), b. 1814, in East Washington, N. H.; d. Jan. 25, 1879. He d. Aug. 25, 1886, at Unity, N. H.; res. Washington, N. H.; six children :—

651a.   1. William Arthur,[9] b. Dec. 5, 1837, at Washington, N. H.; m. April, 1871, at Montgomery, Ala.,

Daniel (649) Greenleaf, Continued :—

II. William Pitt.

Mary E. Farlow, b. May, 1850, at Holly Springs, Miss. He d. 1874, at Montgomery, Ala.; Surgeon, U. S. A. The widow, res. Huntsville, Ala.; no children.

    II. Sarah, b. Nov. 12, 1840; m. Sept. 3, 1865, Benjamin F. Muzzey.

    III. John M., b. Dec. 1, 1842; res. Albuquerque, N. M.

652.   IV. Albert G.,[9] b. Feb. 14, 1847; m. Hannah L., dau. of Greeley Putney, of Washington, N. H.; two children: 1. Minnie M., b. June 16, 1871. 2. Nellie M., b. May 26, 1875.

    V. Mary A., b. Feb. 21, 1852; d. Feb. 16, 1864.

653.   VI. Edward E.,[9] b. Oct. 27, 1855; m. June 8, 1884, Mattie Coombs; res. Albuquerque, N. M.

    III. Mary Gibson, b. March 15, 1807; d. April 23, 1830; unmarried.

654. IV. Daniel G.,[8] b. Sept. 14, 1808; m. April 21, 1833, in Lowell, Mass., Rebecca, dau. of Ahaziah and Lucy (Hudson) Proctor; (a wheelwright), b. Oct. 27, 1812; d. Oct., 1880. He d. Jan. 12, 1888, at Lowell, Mass.; res. Lowell, Mass.; one child :—

Mary E., b. Aug. 28, 1836; d. June 11, 1859.

655. V. Oliver Peabody,[8] b. Nov. 1, 1810; m. Dec. 20, 1835, at Washington, N. H., Mary Jane, dau. of Charles and Hannah (Clark) French (a farmer), b. July 22, 1814; d. Jan. 22, 1883, in Hillsborough, N. H. He d. Feb. 15, 1877, at Hillsborough Bridge, N. H.; res. Hillsborough Bridge since 1849, formerly of Nashua, N. H.; four children :—

    I. Charles F., b. July 20, 1837; res. Hillsborough Bridge, N. H.

    II. Ellen M., b. April 2, 1841.

    III. Walter Scott, b. Sept. 27, 1846; d. Nov. 13, 1865.

    IV. Jenny, b. Sept. 24, 1854; d. June 1, 1857.

656. VI. Charles H.,[8] b. May 7, 1812; m. July 4, 1858, at Lempster, N. H., Mrs. Elizabeth B. Platt, dau. of Martin and Tirzah (Judd) Beckwith (a farmer), b.

DANIEL (649) GREENLEAF, CONTINUED :—
VI. Charles H.
Feb. 14, 1817, in Lempster, N. H.; d. Feb. 7, 1881.
He d. May 12, 1886, at Washington, N. H.; res.
Lempster, N. H.; no children.
VII. CHARLOTTE GREEN, b. March 7, 1814, at Concord,
N. H.; d. in infancy.
657. VIII. JAMES L.,[8] b. Oct. 13, 1815; m. Feb. 5, 1845, at
Manchester, N. H., Caroline R., dau. of Elijah and
Mary (Burnham) Farr (a farmer), b. Oct. 15, 1824,
in Littleton, N. H.; d. July 12, 1879, at Washington,
N. H. He d. Dec. 25, 1880, at Lowell, Mass.; res.
Washington, N. H.; three children :—
  I. Charles W., b. April 9, 1849, at Salmon Falls, N. H.;
    d. Sept. 17, 1873.
  II. Frank E., b. March 11, 1851, at Washington, N. H.;
    d. July 16, 1888; physician; res. New York City.
  III. Carrie Lizzie, b. Jan. 25, 1855, at Washington,
    N. H.; m. Sept. 20, 1876, Prof. Jasper T. Good-
    win, of Columbia College, New York City.
IX. ELIZABETH, b. Sept. 21, 1818, at Concord, N. H.;
res. New York City; unmarried.
658. X. GEORGE W.,[8] b. April 22, 1820; m. Aug. 6, 1846,
at Wardsborough, Ky., Mary Jane Keithley, b. 1828.
He d. Sept. 18, 1848, at Paducah, Ky.; res. Hop-
kinsville, Ky.; no children.
659. XI. HENRY,[8] b. March 6, 1822; m. Sept. 3, 1868, at
Bazaar, Kan., Mrs. Phebe Purcell, b. 1838. He d.
Nov. 8, 1888; res. Matfield Green, and Bazaar, Kan.;
teacher; three children, all b. at Bazaar.
  I. Marinda, b. June 19, 1869.
  II. Annie, b. Nov. 21, 1872.
  III. Elizabeth, b. Aug. 8, 1878.

650.

(Daniel 6, William 5, Edmund 4, Edmund 3, Stephen 2, Edmund 1.)

Children of **William**[7] **Greenleaf** and Ann (Taylor).
660. I. WILLIAM TAYLOR,[8] b. Sept. 6, 1807; m. Agnes R.
Milican. He d. Aug. 20, 1843; res. Newport, Ky.;
three children :—
  I. William.

WILLIAM (650) GREENLEAF, CONTINUED:—
  I. William Taylor.
    II. Joseph.
    III. Ann E. B., m. Samuel Morlidge; two children (sons).
  II. JAMES, b. March 17, 1810.
661. III. JOHN,[8] b. July 5, 1811; m. Louisa Poland. She d. Dec. 6, 1847; res. Wiscasset, Me.; four children:—
  I. Abigail D., b. Feb. 4, 1837; m. Hon. E. B. Bowman, of Council Bluffs, Iowa. She d. 1888.
  II. Charles Beaman, b. Nov. 26, 1838; d. April 10, 1893; apothecary; res. Portland, Me.
  III. Mary Louise, b. June 1, 1842; d. Dec. 26, 1862.
  IV. Edmund D.
662. IV. CHARLES T.,[8] b. January 28, 1815; m. Nov. 1, 1841, at Newport, Ky., Mary J. Wheeler, of Warwick, N. Y. She d. June, 1893. He d. Dec. 26, 1886, at Bath, Me.; seven children:—
663. I. Charles Henry,[9] b. Sept. 27, 1842; m. Emma C. Allen, of Bath, Me.; res. Bath, Me.; Treasurer Eastern Electric Construction Co., Agent American Express Co.; no children.
  II. William Franklin, b. Oct. 28, 1844; d. May 7, 1845.
664. III. Eugene,[9] b. Oct. 12, 1846; m. June 14, 1870, Emma J. Hartwell. He d. Nov. 26, 1892, at Bath, Me.; one child: Alice E., b. July 1, 1872; stenographer.
  IV. George Rogers, b. May 10, 1849; d. July 23, 1850.
  V. Albert, b. May 9, 1851; d. Nov. 14, 1851.
665. VI. Fred A.,[9] b. Nov. 27, 1853; m. Lillian S. Snow. He d. Oct. 23, 1885; res. Helena, Mont.; no children.
  VII. Annie T., b. Nov. 6, 1855; d. Oct. 7, 1865.
  V. SARAH ANN, b. Oct. 3, 1817; m. James William Fisher; both deceased; one child:—
James W. Fisher, Cashier Union National Bank, Brunswick, Me.
  VI. EDMUND D., b. Oct. 16, 1820.
  VII. FRANCIS, b. April 3, 1824.
  VIII. MARY, b. Oct. 19, 1825.

647.

(Capt. William 5, Edmund 4, Edmund 3, Stephen 2, Edmund 1.)

Children of **Lieut. William**[6] **Greenleaf** and Abigail (Soley).

I. ELIZA, b. June 18, 1788; m. Nov. 22, 1810, Hiram Plummer. She died Nov. 18, 1821; two children :—

  i. William Hiram, b. Sept. 22, 1811; d. April 21, 1832.

  ii. Harriott, m. Oct. 20, 1836, in Haverhill, Charles L. Bartlett; res. Boston, Mass.; five children: 1. Anna. 2. Florence. 3. Eliza, b. April 30, 1838; d. Aug. 3, 1839. 4. William Francis, b. June 6, 1840, in Haverhill, Mass.; m. Oct. 14, 1865, Mary Agnes Pomeroy. He d. Dec. 17, 1876, at Pittsfield; three children: (1) A dau., b. Sept. 16, 1866. (2) Edwin, b. Nov. 26, 1871. (3) Edith, b. Sept. 10, 1876. 5. Edith; one dau., m. a Manning.

General William F. Bartlett was in the Junior class at Harvard College early in 1861; on April 17, 1861, he joined the 4th Bat. M. V. M., and performed garrison duty at Fort Independence, Boston Harbor. July 2, 1861, Captain in 20th Regt. M. V. M.; Sept. 4 went to the front. Wounded April 24, 1862, at Yorktown, losing a leg. Sept. 6, 1862, in command of camp at Pittsfield, Mass. In 1863 he was in New Orleans. Wounded at Fort Hudson, May 27, 1863. Wounded May 6, 1864, at Wilderness. July 23, 1864, in command 1st Brigade, 9th Corps. A memoir of the General has been written by Francis William Palfrey.

II. AMEY, b. Feb. 25, 1790; d. Aug. 7, 1791.

III. WILLIAM, b. Jan. 31, 1794; d. Sept. 24, 1795.

666. IV. SAMUEL,[7] b. Sept. 11, 1795, in Haverhill, Mass.; m. 1, ———; 2, Dolly, dau. of Abel and Sarah Osgood, of Amesbury, Mass., b. July 20, 1796, in Amesbury, Mass. He d. Dec. 12, 1856, in Haverhill, Mass. She d. Jan. 25, 1870; res. Haverhill, Mass.; six children; all born in Haverhill, Mass.

V. SOPHIA, b. Oct. 14, 1797; d. Jan. 6, 1887, in Bradford, Mass.

VI. RUTH PEARSON, b. July 20, 1800; d. Oct. 5, 1891.

VII. ANN, m. Jan. 29, 1822, in Haverhill, Mass., Wesley, son of Wesley and Mary Balch, b. March 25, 1798, in Beverly, Mass. He d. July 30, 1851; res. Haverhill, Mass.; two children :—

  i. Eliza, m. 1. McCobb. 2. John A. Lowe. She d. Dec. 18, 1886; no children.

  ii. Harriott, m. May 2, 1854, in Haverhill, Mass., Jackson B., son of William and Dorothy Swett, b. Feb. 12, 1815, in Haverhill, Mass., his second wife. He d. Oct. 3, 1890.

666.

Children of **Samuel**[7] **Greenleaf** and Dolly (Osgood).

667. I. WILLIAM HOVEY,[8] b. Dec. 21, 1820; m. June 29, 1847, in Haverhill, Mass., Lucy Ann Jennings, b. April 22, 1825, in Methuen, Mass.; d. Oct. 23, 1891, in Haverhill, Mass.; res. Haverhill, Mass.; nine children :—

668. I. William Franklin,[9] b. June 20, 1850, in Haverhill, Mass.; m. Dec. 7, 1881, Ida F., dau. of Silas Tuttle, b. 1851.

II. Mary Elizabeth, b. Aug. 15, 1852, in Haverhill, Mass.; m. Nov. 27, 1879, Edward H., son of Obadiah and Mary Foster, b. 1839; one child :—
Wilbur Hazen, b. Aug. 29, 1880, in Bradford, Mass.

III. Anna Melissa, b. Nov. 14, 1854, in Haverhill, Mass.; d. Feb. 9, 1856.

IV. Alice A., b. Sept. 8, 1856, in Haverhill, Mass.; m. Oct. 13, 1880, George W., son of John and Hannah Edney, b. 1844; one child :—
Bessie Helen, b. July 19, 1882, in Haverhill, Mass.

V. George F., b. Dec. 22, 1857, in Haverhill, Mass.; d. Feb. 11, 1858.

VI. Susanna, b. Jan. 2, 1860, in Haverhill, Mass.; d. Oct. 29, 1862, in Boxford, Mass.

669. VII. Alva Mansfield,[9] b. Jan. 14, 1862, in West Boxford, Mass.; m. Annie S., dau. of Albert and Ellen Johnson, b. 1865, in Putnam, Conn.; one child : Harold Earl, b. April 29, 1885.

VIII. Carrie Helen, b. July 4, 1864, in West Boxford, Mass.; m. Dec. 24, 1891, Oliver C., son of Samuel and Isabel Frost, b. 1856; one child :—
Hilda Isabel, b. Feb. 21, 1894, in Haverhill, Mass.

IX. Inez Osgood, b. Sept. 10, 1866, in West Boxford, Mass.; unmarried.

II. CHARLES, b. Jan. 25, 1822; d. Nov. 15, 1824.

670. III. CHARLES E.,[8] b. Nov. 29, 1825, in Haverhill, Mass.; m. June, 1855, Sarah C., dau. of William and Dorcas Brown, b. Sept. 6, 1833, in Andover, Mass.

SAMUEL (666) GREENLEAF, CONTINUED :—
  III. Charles E.
      He. d. Dec. 14, 1888, in Lawrence, Mass.; four
      children :—
        i. Etta L., b. Nov. 10, 1856, in Saugus, Mass.; m. July
           4, 1874, in Lawrence, Mass., Arthur B., son of
           Robert and Agnes Heyworth, b. May 13, 1855, in
           Lawrence, Mass.; one child :—
         Agnes E., b. April 8, 1877, in North Andover, Mass.
       ii. Charles S., b. Sept. 3, d. Nov. 1, 1861, in Saugus,
           Mass.
      iii. Alice R. D., b. Nov. 19, 1867, in Saugus, Mass.;
           m. April 5, 1893, in Lawrence, Mass., Fred, son
           of George and Susan Knight, b. Dec. 27, 1861, in
           Somersworth, N. H.; no children.
       iv. James E., b. Sept. 14, 1870, in Lawrence, Mass.;
           d. Nov. 18, 1876, in North Andover, Mass.
   IV. RHODA C., b. March 11, 1831 ; m. March 13, 1851,
      Samuel A., son of Samuel and Betsey Hall, b. July
      16, 1828; res. Newton, N. H.; eleven children :—
        i. Charles M., b. March 19, 1852; d. March 18, 1858.
       ii. Henry A., b. Oct. 29, 1853; m. March 30, 1877, Elizabeth
           Rogers, dau. of Levi B. and Esther M. Webster, b. Aug. 23,
           1860, in Newton, N. H.; two children : 1. Clara Elizabeth, b.
           Nov. 29, 1878, at Newton, N. H. 2. Lura Kate, b. Feb. 25,
           1883, at Newton, N. H.
      iii. Rufus S., b. Dec. 23, 1855; d. April 10, 1858.
       iv. Mary E., b. Feb. 24, 1858, in Haverhill, Mass.; m. Dec. 25,
           1880, Edward H., son of Hiram Daniel and Ellen Frances
           (Mason) Kidder, b. Dec. 18, 1861, in Manchester, N. H.; three
           children : 1. Arthur E., b. Dec. 26, 1881. 2. Roscoe N., b.
           Sept. 27, 1884. 3. Helen M., b. May 11, 1892.
        v. Justin E., b. Aug. 30; d. Oct. 23, 1860.
       vi. Elmer Ellsworth, b. Aug. 8, 1861, in Plaistow, N. H.; m. July 2,
           1887, Mary Adelaide, dau. of Isaac Henry and Mary Jane
           Ward, b. Feb. 20, 1858, in Freeport, Me.; no children.
      vii. Allan L., b. June 17, 1865; d. Aug. 22, 1881.
     viii. Howard Wesley, b. Feb. 5, 1868, in Newton, N. H.; m. Sept.
           19, 1895, in Moncton, N. B., Isabella Maud, dau. of Chalmers
           and Huldah (Kelley) Kierstead, of Moncton, N. B., b. Nov.
           9, 1872.
       ix. Walter F., b. Nov. 23, 1870, in Newton, N. H.
        x. Ernest G., b. June 29, 1873, in Newton, N. H.
       xi. Karl M., b. Nov. 5, 1875, in Newton, N. H.

SAMUEL (666) GREENLEAF, CONTINUED:—

671. V. MATTHEW NOLAN,[8] b. April 12, 1834; m. June 28,
1860, at Haverhill, Mass., Mary Helen, dau. of Alfred and Mary Randall, of Exeter, N. H., b. July
17, 1841, in Exeter, N. H. He. d. June 17, 1873, in
Oakland, Me.; res. Haverhill, Mass.; one child.
His widow m. May 1, 1882, Albert Clinton, son of
John and Louisa Fowler, of Lowell, Mass., b. 1847;
no children.

Mr. Greenleaf's record of service in the Civil War being received
too late to appear in the section assigned to "Military and Naval Service,"
is as follows: April 16, 1861, private, Co. D, 5th Regt. Inf. Mass. Vols.,
enlisted at Haverhill, Mass. July 31, 1861, mustered out. Oct. 10, 1861,
re-enlisted. Nov. 27, 1861, mustered in as 1st Sergeant Co. C, 6th Regt.
Inf. N. H. Vols., at Exeter, N. H., for three years' service. April 29, 1862,
appointed 2d Lieut. Sept. 12, 1862, 1st Lieut., Co. E. July 1, 1863, Capt.
Co. H. July 30, 1864, wounded severely at the mine explosion Petersburg,
Va. Nov. 28, 1864, discharged for disability. March 1, 1865, restored to
rank. July 17, 1865, mustered out. He was in seventeen engagements
between 1862 and 1864 in Maryland, Virginia, North Carolina, and the
Siege of Vicksburg, Miss.

672.   Alfred Francis,[9] b. Oct. 19, 1861, at Boxford, Mass.;
son of Matthew Nolan[8] Greenleaf, and Mary H.
(Randall); m. Jan. 1, 1885, in Amesbury, Mass.,
Cora Isabella Smith, of Amesbury, b. Aug. 13, 1864;
res. Haverhill, Mass.; no children.

VI. FRANCES ANN, b. March 7, d. Sept. 7, 1836.

UNCONNECTED FAMILIES.

THE following records are given for the purpose of aiding others in tracing lines which the compiler could not further pursue without delaying indefinitely the publication of manuscripts already connected.

John Greenleaf (see page 193, also ancient records of Boston, New England Hist. Geneal. Register, Vol. 37, p. 287, Vol. 38, p. 300), probably son of Edmund and Sarah (Dole), b. about 1632; m. July 26, 1665, Hannah, dau. of William Veazie, of Braintree, Mass. (see Braintree records). His sister Mary is named in will of Eliza Robinson, as of kin to her. He resided in Boston; was a shipwright. Died Dec. 16, 1712, in Boston; nine children :—

I. ELIZABETH, b. July 19, 1666; d. Feb. 11, 1711.
II. HANNAH, b. Oct. 5, 1668.
III. MARY, b. Jan. 23, 1670.
IV. JOHN, b. Feb. 10, 1672; m. ———; one child :—

    John, b. about 1717; m., 1739, Mary, dau. of Joseph,* Jr., and Hannah (Binney) Gould, of Hull, Mass., b. April 25, 1718; five children :—

        I. Benjamin, b. Jan. 13, 1769; m. Abigail Rhoades, of Dorchester, Mass. He d. Jan. 10, 1821, at Weymouth, Mass.; no children.

        II. Mary (Polly), b. July 24, 1770; m. Nov. 17, 1793, Samuel, son of Samuel and Mary Reed, b. Sept. 16, 1765; d. Feb. 28, 1853. She d. 1856; res. Hull, Mass. (Reed geneal.) ; nine children :—

        1. Mary, d. in infancy. 2. Mary, b. Feb. 21, 1797. 3. Elizabeth, b. March 17, 1809. 4. John. 5. Thomas. 6. Sarah. 7. William. 8. Philip. 9. Samuel.

---

*Joseph was son of Joseph, Sr., son of Robert and Mary (Prince) Gould. Robert Gould, common ancestor, from England, was nephew of John Stone, first settler of Hull (or Nantasket), Mass. Hannah, wife of Joseph Gould, Jr., was dau. of John and Hannah (Paine) Binney, of Hull, Mass. Mary, wife of John Greenleaf,[3] m. 2, June 12, 1781, Nicholas Phillips, of Weymouth, Mass.

John Greenleaf, Continued:—

    iii. Lydia, b. Sept. 6, 1773; m. May 28, 1797, Benjamin, son of Benjamin Binney, of Hull, Mass., b. May 4, 1744; d. July 16, 1844, at East Cambridge, Mass. She d. Jan. 22, 1858, at East Cambridge, Mass.; res. Boston, Mass.; eight children:—

        1. Lydia, b. July 3, 1798; m. Noah Blanchard, of Boston. She d. July 16, 1871. 2. Jane, b. April 7, 1800; m. Barnabas Binney (her cousin). 3. Benjamin, b. July 12, 1801; m. Nov. 3, 1830 or 31, Sarah, dau. of William and Mary (Williams) Greenleaf (189), of Stockbridge, Mass. He d. Jan. 3, 1877; tinman; res. Boston (Binney geneal.); five children: (1) Sarah E. Frances, b. Nov. 27, 1832; d. Sept. 25, 1833. (2) Harriet Jane, b. Sept. 3, 1834; d. Oct. 19, 1835. (3) Benjamin, b. July 15, 1836; d. May 27, 1857. (4) William H., b. Nov. 9, 1837; d. Dec. 16, 1841. (5) Deodat Williams, b. Oct. 4, 1847; m. Joseph Morse; divorced. 4. Matthew, b. Oct. 8, 1803; m. Sarah R. Ellis; umbrellas; res. Boston. 5. Mary Phillips, b. April 24, 1805; m. 1, S. H. Springer; 2, G. P. Learned. 6. Sarah Spear, b. Dec. 13, 1806; d. Oct. 29, 1819. 7. Elizabeth, b. Feb. 26, 1809; d. April 18, 1817. 8. Susan Tidd, b. March 12, 1811; m. Robert P. Tuton.

    iv. John, b. June 6, 1775; m. Sarah Adams, of Boston. He d. Dec. 23, 1829. Buried at Hull, Mass., in same inclosure with Bathsheba; four children: 1. John. 2. Adeline. 3. Sarah. 4. Lydia.

    v. Bathsheba, b. Aug. 7, 1777; m. John Norwood. She d. Sept. 12, 1851. Buried in Hull, Mass.; two children:—

        1. Elizabeth G. 2. Bathsheba, d. in infancy.

V. William, b. 1675; d. young.

VI. Stephen, b. March 5, 1677; m——. It appears probable that he was the father of Stephen Greenleaf whose son Stephen married Emma Blowers.

VII. Samuel, b. Feb. 26, 1680; d. Aug. 7, 1737 (Granary Epitaph, Boston).

VIII. Sarah, b. Sept. 3, 1683.

IX. William, b. Nov. 4, 1687; d. Aug. 9, 1690.

Children of **Stephen Greenleaf**, the son of Stephen, who came from England and settled in Boston, Mass., and Emma (Blowers). He d. ——, 1782. She b. 1740; d. Jan., 1786; they lived and died in Boston, Mass.; four children :—

I. SALLY, m. —— English; res. Boston, Mass.
II. NABBY, m. —— Bennett; res. Boston, Mass.
III. BETSEY, m. —— Webber.
IV. STEPHEN, b. Jan. 27, 1779, in Boston; m. Jan. 24, 1804, in Yarmouth, Me., Mary, dau. of James and Mercy (Burbank) Savery, of Plymouth, Mass., b. May 22, 1784; d. Nov. 18, 1858. He d. July 4, 1854, at Norway, Me.; res. Yarmouth, Me.; removed 1805 to Norway, Me.; ten children :—

    i. Fanny Ordway, b. Aug. 4, 1804; m. Jeremiah Wellington Hobbs, of Norway, Me., b. June 8, 1812. She d. Dec. 14, 1888; three children :—

    1. Jeremiah W., b. Dec. 25, 1844; d. Oct. 24, 1864; shot while on picket duty, Civil War. 2. George Washington, b. Nov. 30, 1845; m. May 16, 1876, Emma Wardwell, of Otisfield, Me.; res. Norway, Me.; three children: (1) Mary Emma, b. Sept. 10, 1879; d. Sept. 6, 1880. (2) Savery Greenleaf, b. Dec. 30, 1880. (3) Oscar Wardwell, b. April 27, 1890. 3. Catherine Sophronia, b. May 25, 1847; d. Nov. 30, 1863.

    ii. Sally English, b. June 24, 1806; d. Sept. 2, 1828.
    iii. Mary, b. Aug. 24, 1807; m. 1830, Cyrus S. Cushman, b. Oct. 27, 1802; d. July 30, 1830. She d. July 30, 1836; res. Norway, Me.; four children :—

    1. Cyrus. 2. Frances. 3. Sarah Elizabeth, m. Alfred Noyes, of Georgetown, Mass.; one child: Alfred, m.; res. West. 4. Louisa Jane, d. Boston, Mass.

    iv. Stephen, b. May 16, 1809; m. Jane H. Hill, b. May 9, 1809; d. Nov. 19, 1846. He d. April 5, 1884, in Brighton, Mass.; res. Norway, Me.; one child: Mark Hill, b. April 24, 1840; m. Annie Sawyer; res. Brighton, Mass.; no children.

    v. Emma Blowers, b. May 11, 1811; m. April 3, 1831, John Hatch, of New Gloucester, Me., b. Sept. 16, 1800; d. Feb. 9, 1869, at Norway, Me.; res. Norway, Me.; six children :—

    1. James Lewis, b. Feb. 13, 1832, at New Gloucester, Me.; m. 1856, Mary Jane, dau. Dr. Solomon Cushman, of Brunswick, Me. He

STEPHEN GREENLEAF, CONTINUED :—

 d. Sept. 25, 1858; grad. Bowdoin College 1854; asst. ed. Charleston *Courier* at time of his death; res. Charleston, S. C.; one child: John Edwin, d. March, 1858. 2. Isabella Bennett, b. Nov. 2, 1833; m. March 3, 1857, Henry A. Whitney, of Portland, Me. She d. May 23, 1861, at Montreal, Can.; no children. 3. Olive Cushman, b. Jan. 6, 1836; res. Norway, Me. 4. Stephen Greenleaf, b. July 12, 1839; m. Ida Bradbury, of Norway, Me.; res. Norway; one child: John Osgood, b. April 1, 1869; d. Oct. 6, 1887. 5. Ivah Tenney, b. Aug. 18, 1842; m. Oct. 27, 1861, William H. Whitcomb, of Norway, Me.; res. Norway; three children: (1) Henry Eugene, b. June 26, d. July 25, 1862. (2) Mary Emma, b. Oct. 15, 1864; d. Sept. 24, 1865. (3) Isabella Hatch, b. July 27, 1866. 6. Izah Tenney, b. Aug. 18, 1842, twin; m. April 25, 1864, Ozias Whitman, of Buckfield, Me.; res. Red Wing, Minn.; no children.

VI. James Savery, b. Feb. 5, 1814; m. 1838, Jane T., dau. of William C. Whitney. He d. Dec. 13, 1880; carpenter and builder in Norway, Me., until 1864, when he moved to South Abington, Mass., where he died; six children: 1. Charles Franklin, b. Sept. 20, 1839, at Norway, Me.; m. 1, March 10, 1864, Euphemea J. Bradbury; 2, ———; res. Norway, Me. 2. Helen, b. Oct. 28, 1841; m. Nov. 5, 1859, Philo S. Cherry, of South Paris, Me.; res. Red Creek, N. Y.; six children. 3. Solomon Cushman, b. Jan. 17, 1846; m. April 15, 1871, in Savannah, Ga., Susan Compton, b. Sept. 19, 1844, in Hampton Co., S. C., near Gifford's Station. He d. Nov. 2, 1882, at Gifford's Station, S. C.; two children: (1) Charles Henry, b. June 17, 1873, in Hampton Co., S. C. (2) James Savery, b. Sept. 21, 1879, in Barnstable Co., near Matthew's Bluffs, on Savanna River. 4. Mary Jane, b. April, 25, 1848; res. Norway, Me. 5. Flora, b. Oct. 15, 1850; res. Sedalia, Mo. 6. James, b. March 23, 1853, in Norway, Me.; d. May 20, 1884, at Boston, Mass.

Children of Philo S. Cherry and Helen :—

 (1) Charles Howard, b. Sept. 5, 1860; m. May 1, 1890, Viola Ardee; one child: Henry, b. April 22, 1891; res. West. (2) George, b. Oct. 10, 1862; d. Jan. 27, 1866. (3) Fanny, b. March 17, 1864; d. 1879. (4) Nellie, b. June 29, 1865; m. Nelson W. Smith; res. Montreal, Can. (5) Myron, b. May 13, 1878; res. Red Creek, N. Y. (6) Willard, res. Red Creek, N. Y.

STEPHEN GREENLEAF, CONTINUED:—

 VII. Priscilla Churchill, b. Dec. 30, 1817; m. 1842, Jacob
  Smith Cushman, of Massachusetts, b. July 13, 1819;
  res. Wakefield, Mass.; three children :—

1. Emma Jane, m.—— Perkins; res. Wakefield, Mass.; Post Office
Address, North Rochester, Mass. 2. Hannah. 3. Horatio, twin.

 VIII. Martha Bartlett, b. July 17, 1819; m. William
  Mills, of Great Falls, N. H.; res. Lawrence, Mass.;
  six children :—

1. Mary Frances, m. at Great Falls, N. H., Timothy Conklin; res.
Harlem, N. Y. 2. William Greenleaf, m. at Great Falls, N. H.,
Georgie Allard, of N. H.; res. Portland, Me.; five children.
3. Abby Jane, m. at Great Falls, N. H.; two sons living at
Dover, N. H. 4. Oscar, m. Caddie Lufkin, of Portland, Me.;
res. Lawrence, Mass. 5. George W., m. Mary ——; res.
Brighton, Mass. 6. Martha, m. at Portland, Me., Charles
Peasley; res. Chicago, Ill.; one child: a son.

 IX. Mercy Elizabeth, b. May 23, 1823; d. Sept. 5, 1825.

 X. George Washington, b. Oct. 10, 1825; m. March 8,
  1855, Ruth Ann Glines, of Kingston, N. H. She d.
  Oct. 9, 1864, at Portland, Me. He d. Oct. 15, 1868;
  five children: 1. Ivah Jane, b. Aug. 30, 1854; m.
  March 27, 1883, Fred Everett, of Norway, Me.
  She d. July 27, 1883. 2. Emma Frances, b. March
  17, d. July 16, 1859. 3. Edward Ivan, b. July 16,
  1860; d. Aug. 8, 1864. 4. Emma Frances, b. Dec.
  31, 1862; d. July 29, 1880. 5. Oscar, b. Aug. 23,
  1864; d. March 11, 1880.

Children of **Paul Greenleaf** and ———; shipsmith, b. in
Newburyport, Mass., about 1736; res. and d. in Seabrook,
N. H., where all of his children were born.

I. SAMUEL, b. May 8, 1758; m. 1, Dec. 1789, Hannah Rowe,
of Nottingham, N. H., sister of Capt. Elijah Rowe, b.
Aug. 13, 1765; d. Feb. 11, 1835; 2, Dec., 1835, Mrs.
Anna Smith, his wife's sister. She d. Nov. 4, 1852, at
Keene, N. Y. He. d. Dec. 20, 1840; shoemaker; res.
Bradford, Vt., 1790 until 1836, thence removed to Wash-
ington, Vt.; nine children by 1st marriage.

II. NATHAN, b. Oct. 16, 1761; m. Jan. 2, 1786, Mary Clifford,
b. Jan. 12, 1763; d. Aug. 12, 1849, at Salem, N. H. He
d. June 30, 1831; farmer; res. Weare and Henniker,
N. H. A Revolutionary pensioner; eight children.

III. ENOCH, m. Betsey Merrill, of Seabrook, N. H.; lost at
sea; five children.

IV. PAUL.

V. WILLIAM, died at sea.

VI. SARAH.

VII. LYDIA.

VIII. HANNAH.

IX. ABIGAIL.

X. NANCY.

I. Children of **Samuel Greenleaf**, son of Paul, and Hannah
(Rowe).

I. DOLLY, b. March 10, 1790; m. Nov. 10, 1823, John Mc-
Duffee, of Bradford, Vt., b. about 1766; d. May 4, 1851.
She d. May 7, 1874 (his second wife); res. Bradford,
Vt.; six children :—
  i. Daniel, b. Sept. 15, 1824; d. July 29, 1835.
  ii. Mansfield, b. Sept. 12, d. Sept. 14, 1826.
  iii. Charles, b. Nov. 19, 1827.
  iv. Henry C., b. June 21, 1829; d. March 16, 1831.
  v. Henry C., b. Oct. 3, 1831.
  vi. Horace, b. Dec. 23, 1833.

II. POLLY, b. July 8, 1792; d. July 24, 1807.

III. LOWELL, b. March 30, 1794; m. 1, Jan. 6, 1817, Betsey
Davis, of Bradford, Vt. She d. Sept. 10, 1826; 2, June
3, 1828, Anna Wyman, of Montpelier, Vt.; res. Bradford, Vt.

SAMUEL GREENLEAF, CONTINUED :—

Children by 1st marriage :—

 I. Melissa, b. Sept. 15, 1817; m. May 28, 1838, Sargent T. George; two children.

 II. Julia, b. June 21, 1822; m. May 8, 1833, Richard D. Harris, Lewiston, Me.

Children by 2d marriage :—

 III. Betsey Ann, b. Aug. 26, 1830; m. Nov. 14, 1865, John B., son of David Rollins, of Bradford, Vt.; res. Bradford, Vt., until 1870, then San Francisco, Cal.; no children.

 IV. Emilyette, b. Feb. 15, 1836.

 V. Lowell F., b. Nov. 23, 1837.

IV. HANNAH, b. Jan. 4, 1796; m. Dec. 28, 1824, Jacob Corliss, of Bradford, Vt. He d. Oct. 24, 1830; res. Charlestown, Mass., and Topsham, Vt.; two children :—

 i. Hannah Maria, b. July 27, 1827.

 ii. Gilbert Lafayette, b. July 9, 1829; d. Sept. 20, 1846.

V. PHILLIPS, b. Sept. 4, 1797; m. 1, March 20, 1825, Sarah Stevens, of Bradford, Vt. She d. Sept. 13, 1832; 2, July 21, 1835, Eliza, dau. of Robert and Elizabeth (Varnun) Barnett, or Burnett, of Newbury, Vt., b. April 28, 1802, at Goffstown, N. H.; d. May, 1883.

Children by 1st marriage :—

 I. Sarah H., b. Oct. 8, 1826, at Bradford, Vt.

 II. Nicholas S., b. Nov. 22, 1827; m. July 6, 1854, Mary W. Carter, of Newbury, Vt.; one child : Sarah Eliza, b. May 10, 1855.

Children by 2d marriage :—

 III. A son, b. March 8, 1842.

 IV. Charles W., b. Oct. 7, 1844; d. Dec. 28, 1849.

 V. Lowell, m. July 12, 1869, Susan, dau. of David and Susan (Corliss) Eastman. She d. May 31, 1888; no children.

VI. SILVER, b. March 5, 1799; m. June 23, 1846, Rhoda Freeman, of Vassalboro, Me.; res. Freedom, Me.; returned to Bradford September, 1868; three children, all born at Freedom :—

 I. Olive Jane, b. June 4, 1848, at Freedom, Me.; d. June, 1871.

 II. Mary Hannah, b. Feb. 20, 1850; d. 1864.

SAMUEL GREENLEAF, CONTINUED :—

    III. Charles Henry, b. May 20, 1854; d. 1864.

VII. SALLY R., b. Aug. 9, 1802; m. Sept. 22, 1847, Reuben M. Kent, of Piermont, N. H.

VIII. LUVINIA, b. May 21, 1808; m. Dec. 15, 1836, John Celley, of Corinth, Vt. ; one child :—

    Nancy Jane, b. March 13, 1844.

IX. MELISSA, b. Oct. 28, 1811; m. March 14, 1832, Amos White, of Topsham, Vt. ; four children; all born at Topsham :—

    i. Lydia E., b. Jan. 15, 1834.
    ii. Hannah G., b. Sept. 25, 1836.
    iii. Carlos, b. June 9, 1842.
    iv. Noel Byron, b. Nov. 10, 1844.

II. Children of **Nathan Greenleaf,** son of Paul, and Mary (Clifford).

I. MOSES, b. April 11, 1786; m. Lois Dow. He d. Nov. 14, 1853; moved from Moultonboro, N. H., about 1812 to Henniker, N. H.; lived there many years; children :—

    I. Louis, d. at South Antrim, N. H.
    II. Lois.
    III. Abigail.
    IV. A son ; res. North Weare, N. H., 1856.

II. WILLIAM, b. Sept. 4, 1787; m. 1, Jan. 2, 1816, Mary (Polly) Leslie, of Henniker, N. H. She d. Jan. 18, 1832; 2, Charlotte Cumber, of Bolton, Lower Canada. He d. at Salem, N. H., 1863; was in the War of 1812; res. New Salem, N. H.

Children by 1st marriage :—

    I. Susan, b. Oct. 28, 1818; m. Levi Perry; res. Dorchester, Mass., 1850–60; two children : 1. Cornelia. 2. ———.

    II. George Leslie, b. Sept. 18, 1820, at Henniker, N. H.; m. 1, Mary Blythe Scott. She d. March 7, 1863; 2. Oct. 28, 1863, Rosanna Scott; child by 1st marriage : 1. George Sumner, b. May 3, 1842, in Methuen, Mass.; m. Feb. 25, 1869, Ada How-

NATHAN GREENLEAF, CONTINUED:—

> ard; two children: (1) Leslie Henshaw, d. in in-
> fancy. (2) Ada May, b. May 4, 1872; m. L.
> Eugene Sessions. Mr. Geo. S. Greenleaf is a manu-
> facturing jeweler; res. Minneapolis, Minn. Child
> by 2d marriage: 2. Lennie, b. Aug. 20, 1865; m.
> June 18, 1884, Alba Markey; three children: (1)
> Daisy Estella, b. Aug. 12, 1885. (2) Alice Ger-
> trude, b. April 27, 1887. (3) Ida Josephine, b.
> April 18, 1889.

> III. Elvira, res. Henniker or Hopkinton, N. H.; unmar-
> ried.

> IV. Abraham Clifford, b. Feb. 26, 1822; res. Charlotte,
> Mich.; known as A. C. Green; has three or four
> children.

> V. A son, b. Feb. 24, 1824.

> VI. A son, b. March 4, 1827.

> VII. Lozina, b. March 4, 1828, in Henniker, N. H.;
> m. Isaac James Alexander[7] Hastings, b. Dec. 22,
> 1822, in Derry, N. H.; res, Salem, N. H.

Children by 2d marriage:—

> VIII. Mary.

> IX. Sophia.

> X. Clarinda.

> One of these daughters married Amos Tappan; res. Bradford, Mass.

III. LYDIA, b. Oct. 18, 1790; m. David Dunlap, of New
Salem, North Village, N. H. She d. April 7, 1847; two
children:—

> i. Jacob Patterson, b. May 13, 1823.
> ii. David, b. Dec. 28, 1828.

IV. ABIGAIL, b. Feb. 24, 1792; unmarried; res. Deering, N.
H., at Rob. Goodale's.

V. ENOCH, b. Nov. 26, 1795; m. Dec. 12, 1816, Lydia With-
ington, of Henniker, N. H.; moved from Henniker, 1840;
res. Haverhill, Mass., 1856. He d. March 26, 1860, at
Haverhill, Mass.; four children:—

> I. Edna Melissa, b. July 10, 1818, at Henniker, N. H.;
> m. Jan. 22, 1856, Benjamin Brown, of Haverhill,
> Mass. She d. May, 1867.

> II. Ozias Worcester, b. Sept. 18, 1820; m. Dec. 25,
> 18—, Luna Oakes, of Lowell, Mass., b. Feb. 4,

NATHAN GREENLEAF, CONTINUED:—

    1807–10. He d. Nov. 21, 1887; four children: 1. Rodney W., b. Oct. 31, 1841; m. Sept. 17, 1865, at Woburn, Mass., Louisa Fowle, b. Oct. 12, 1842; five children: (1) Louis A., b. June 14, 1866. (2) Francis E., b. Oct. 25, 1871. (3) Albert R., b. Oct. 19, 1874. (4) Laura L., b. May 18, 1876. (5) Warren F., b. March 2, 1884. 2. Charles H., b. Dec. 31, 1842; m. Hattie M. Porter. He d. Sept. 2, 1885; no children. 3. Eleanora A., b. Aug. 11, 1844; m. Sept. 11, 1865, Pulaski M. Church, b. Nov. 1, 1841; no children. 4. Frank A., b. May 21, 1849; m. June 5, 1883, Annie Nash, b. April 5, 1855, in Boston; res. Boston; fire department; no children.

   III. Isaac Proctor, b. Aug. 13, 1823; m. Dec. 30, 1851, Olive Davis, of Nashua, N. H. He d. Aug. 11, 1884, at Onset Bay; organ builder; res. Massachusetts.

   IV. Nathan Stillman, b. Nov. 4, 1826, in Hillsboro, N. H.; m. Sept 26, 1847, at Haverhill, Mass., Charlotte E., dau. of Samuel and Sarah Woods, of Bradford, Mass. He d. March 19, 1896; three children: 1. Frank Leroy, b. July 17, 1849; d. Sept. 2, 1850. 2. Francis S., b. March 24, 1852; d. Sept. 9, 1855. 3. George E., b. Aug. 31, 1855; m. ——. He d. July 1, 1881; one child, d. in infancy. His widow has since died.

VI. MARY, b. Oct. 25, 1797; m. David Dunlap, b. about 1797; d. April 11, 1889. She d. Aug. 26, 1873; res. Salem, N. H., North Village, 1856; no children.

VII. SUSANNA, b. July 23, 1803; d. April 7, 1804.

VIII. PLUMA, b. March 14, 1808; d. Sept. 11, 1879; res. Lawrence, Mass., or Manchester, N. H., 1856; unmarried.

III. Children of **Enoch Greenleaf,** son of Paul, and Betsey (Merrill).

I. CHARLES W., b. June 10, 1826, in Newburyport, Mass.; m. Nov. 27, 1848, Elizabeth J. Southwell, of Middlebury, Vt.

ENOCH GREENLEAF, CONTINUED:—

He d. Feb. 23, 1887, in Newburyport, killed by a fall in a barn; six children:—

    I. Mary, b. Sept. 22, 1849; d. Oct. 3, 1869.

    II. John, b. Jan. 7, 1854; m. Elizabeth Waldo, of Brookfield, Vt.

    III. Ida, b. Oct. 5, 1858; m. George F. Kibling, of Norwich, Vt.

    IV. Harriet, b. April 19, 1865; m. George Thompson, of Bradford, Vt.

    V. Charles A., b. Jan. 29, 1868; res. Newbury, Vt.; creamery; unmarried.

    VI. Sarah, b. May 15, 1870.

II. ALBERT.

III. SARAH.

IV. HANNAH.

V. JANE.

Children of **David Greenleaf** and Mary (Bickford) ; m. May
22, 1705, at Boston, Mass.; res. Haverhill, Mass. He
sailed for England; his wife not hearing from him married
again.
BICKFORD, son of David and Mary, b. Feb. 10, 1706; m. 1,
Jan. 4, 1727, Judith Marvel; 2, Elizabeth Middleton.
He d. about 1753; res. Haverhill, Mass.

Children of **Bickford Greenleaf** and Judith (Marvel).
I. MARY (Mercy), b. April 29, 1730.
II. DAVID, b. Nov. 9, 1731.
III. THOMAS, b. Sept. 10, 1733.
IV. SARAH, b. July 29, 1735.
V. THOMAS, b. May 21, 1737.
Child by 2d marriage :—
VI. DAVID, b. April 29, 1753, in Haverhill, Mass. When a
small boy he went with his mother to live at Lancaster,
N. H.; m. 1, Betsey Beedel; 2, 1788, Sarah Rogers;
3, Lois Gould; 4, Mrs. Ruth Stockwell Hutchins, b. Sept.
21, 1778, in Lancaster, N. H. He d. March 28, 1835, in
Lancaster, N. H.
Children by 1st marriage :—
I. Richard, m. ——; res. Groton, Mass., or N. H.
II. John, b. Dec. 10, 1775, in Port Sea, England; m.
——; d. 1834, at Port Sea, England. Impressed
by British man-of-war while living in Nova Scotia,
and afterwards lived in England. Had several children.
III. Phebe, b. Aug. 12, 1777; m. Samuel Stone, of Stratford, N. H.; res. Stratford, N. H. Had several
children.
Children by 2d marriage :—
IV. Sarah, b. Dec. 2, 1789; m. 1, Ephraim Stockwell, b.
Oct. 25, 1774; 2, William H. Prentiss; res. Lancaster, N. H.; nine children by 1st marriage :—
1. Sarah Ann, m. Joseph Wilder, of Lancaster, N. H. 2. Juliette,
m. William Lovejoy. 3. Jeanette, m. Edward McIntire. 4.
Elizabeth, m. Dr. Curtis, of Cincinnati, O. 5. Lucy, m. Dr.
James Whittemore, of Cambridge, Mass. 6. William, m.

BICKFORD GREENLEAF, CONTINUED:—

Sophia Savage, of Lancaster, N. H. 7. Charles, m. ——, of Ohio. 8. Emmons, physician; unmarried; d. in Cincinnati, Ohio. 9. Ephraim; unmarried; d. in Cincinnati, Ohio.

Children by 3d marriage :—

v. William R., b. April 10, 1791; d. June 11, ——, at Lancaster, N. H.

vi. Henry, b. April 28, 1793; married. He d. 1822, at Orford, N. H.; res. Orford, N. H.; one child: a daughter. His widow married again, probably, and lived in Connecticut.

vii. Nancy, b. Jan. 30, 1795; m. George Andros. He res. and d. at Orford, N. H.; lived also at Norwich, Vt.

viii. David, b. Dec. 7, 1797; went West.

ix. Elijah, b. Dec. 7, 1797; twin; d. March 1, 1822, at Lancaster, N. H.

x. Hamilton, d. at Lancaster, N. H.

xi. Eunice, b. Aug. 26, 1799; m. Alpheus Hutchins. She d. May, 1850, at Northumberland, N. H.; res. Lancaster, N. H.; children :—

Frank Sylvester, two daughters, and others.

xii. Franklin, d. at Lancaster, N. H.

xiii. Mary, b. June 28, 1801; m. Andrew Derby. She d. at Lancaster, N. H.; res. Lancaster, N. H.; three children :—

1. Edwin Ruthven, res. Cedar Rapids, Iowa. 2. John, res. Lancaster, N. H. 3. Augusta.

xiv. Elisha.

Children by 4th marriage :—

xv. Joseph Parsons, b. Aug. 31, 1809, in Lancaster, N. H.; m. 1, March, 1836, Sarah McCoy, b. Feb. 6, 1815; d. Sept. 1, 1853. 2, Cyrene (Hunt) Sherman; res. West Medford, Mass. Three children by 1st marriage: 1. Charles Henry, b. Jan. 31, 1837; m. June 18, 1862, Sarah Kimball Reed, b. May 3, 1840; d. Nov. 6, 1888. He d. March 23, 1873; five children: (1) Mary Eliza, b. April 21, 1863; m. June 8, 1887, D. Fraser McIntosh, b. Jan. 1, 1857; res. Woburn, Mass. (2) William Reed, b. June 18, 1864; m. March 3, 1889, Maggie

BICKFORD GREENLEAF, CONTINUED :—

McMurray, b. Feb. 7, 1864. (3) Flora Clark, b. Feb. 14, 1867; m. June 16, 1887, Fred. S. Nichols, b. Sept. 19, 1862; d. Sept. 1, 1889; res. Woburn, Mass.; one child: Chauncey Greenleaf, b. March 17, 1888. (4) Emma Betsey, b. March 4, 1869; m. Oct. 23, 1889, Fred E. Cottle, b. June 23, 1867; res. Woburn, Mass.; one child: Edmund Charles, b. June 17, 1892. (5) Charles Henry, b. Dec. 2, 1872. 2. Mary Frances, b. Sept. 23, 1838; m. Feb. 23, 1869, Thomas Kent Hale, b. Sept. 13, 1829; two children: (1) Alice Crosby, b. Feb. 22, 1870; res. Cambridge, Mass. (2) Mabel Greenleaf, b. Aug. 8, 1880. 3. William Franklin, b. Sept., 1840; d. Nov., 1842.

XVI. Lucinda Maria, b. March 19, 1811; m. Feb. 24, 1830, William Pearson, of Lancaster, N. H., b. March 8, 1807, in Orford, N. H.; d. June 12, 1887, in Boston, Mass. She d. Oct. 16, 1887; three children :—

1. William Henry, b. July 31, 1832, in Lancaster, N. H.; m. Feb. 21, 1861, Nancy Delia Benjamin, b. June 24, 1833, in North Whitefield, Me.; collector of taxes; res. Boston, Mass.; three children, born in Boston, Mass.: (1) Seth Greenleaf, b. Aug. 20, 1862; d. March 31, 1864. (2) Nella Jane, b. Dec. 31, 1864. (3) Arthur Emmons, b. Jan. 9, 1869. 2. Edward Asher, b. Jan. 21, 1840, at Lancaster, N. H.; m. 1, July 22, 1862, Addie Crocker. She d. July 12, 1865; 2, Sept. 5, 1868, Sophia Downing Owens; 3, Annie A. Lowry, b. July 22, 1857; m. Dec. 23, 1879; res. New York; one child by 2d marriage: (1) William Edward, b. Oct. 24, 1869; children by 3d marriage: (2) Edward Lowry, b. Nov. 16, 1880. (3) Annie May, b. May 13, 1882. (4) Maxwell John, b. Feb. 24, 1885. (5) Alice Le Baron, b. Nov. 14, 1888. 3. Nella Jane, b. Sept. 3, 1842; m. 1, June 7, 1860, Ansel G. Foss, of Auburn, Me., b. Feb. 28, 1836; d. March 28, 1871; 2, Aug. 1, 1883, Col. Jonas Harrod French, b. Nov. 4, 1829, in Boston, Mass.; res. Bay View, Gloucester, Mass.

XVII. Seth, b. June 28, 1812; m. Nov. 13, 1836, Lydia Hall Burnham, b. May 15, 1810. He d. Sept. 3, 1880; res. Concord, N. H.; three children : 1. Harriet Newell, b. Sept. 3, 1837; d. Feb. 23, 1840. 2. Charles Henry (Col.), b. July 23, 1841; m. May 2, 1867, Abigail Burnham, b. Jan. 17, 1841. Proprietor

BICKFORD GREENLEAF, CONTINUED :—

Hotel Vendome, Boston, Mass.; no children.   3,
William Harvey, b. July 24, 1843; m. Lucy Courser,
b. April 3, 1840; res. Nashua, N. H.; two children: (1) Hattie, b. Nov. 12, 1866; m. George
Smith, b. Oct. 26, 1865; two children: [1]Abigail
Greenleaf, b. April 21, 1891; [2]Seth Greenleaf, b.
March 5, 1893. (2) Caroline Thurber, b. March
29, 1873; m. May 15, 1895, Arthur Nathaniel Richardson, b. May 11, 1866, of Portland, Me. (Richardson Land Co., of Deering, Me.)

XVIII. Jane, b. July 9, 1814; m. Charles Pearson, an
older brother of William, above named; res. Bakers-
field, Vt.; ten children :—

1. Hiram G., b. May 5, 1833; d. July 9, 1842. 2. Charles Franklin,
b. Aug. 14, 1835; d. Sept. 10, 1854. 3. Amos, b. Aug. 4, 1837;
d. Aug. 11, 1842. 4. William Henry, b. June 8, 1839; d. Sept.
4, 1851. 5. Seth, b. March 27, 1841; d. July 27, 1842. 6. Hiram
Greenleaf, b. Jan. 28, 1843; m. Dec. 7, 1865, Armida Kellogg;
served in the Civil War (cavalry); one child: a daughter. 7.
Jane Emma, b. Nov. 25, 1845; d. Nov. 18, 1865. 8. William
Edward, b. Sept. 5, 1851; m. May 10, 1876, Annie P. Hubble;
two children, a son and daughter. 9. Lucinda M., b. May 17,
1853; d. April 25, 1888, in Boston. 10. Harriet, b. Oct. 26,
1855; m. Feb. 27, 1878, W. R. Parker; res. Enosburg Falls,
Vt.; no children.

XIX. Mercy (Nella), b. Feb. 23, 1818; m. John Cowles
Flower, b. July 20, 1815; d. Jan. 18, 1861. She
d. Sept. 18, 1889; res. Burke, Vt.; two children :—

1. Sarah Ellen, b. Dec. 15, 1847; m. 1, George Lincoln, b. Dec. 14,
1844; d. Oct. 10, 1871; 2, Isaiah Warren Black, b. Aug. 31,
1853; res. West Medford, Mass.; one child by 2d marriage:
Alice, b. Sept 30, 1879. 2. John Asher, b. Nov. 28, 1853; m.
Emma Evans, b. May 18, 1852; two children: (1) Marion
Evans, b. Aug. 28, 1885. (2) Ida May, b. May 18, 1888.

XX. Betsey, b. 1825; d. 1842; res. Ithaca, N. Y.; unmarried.

Children of **Robert Greenleaf**, b. about 1738, d. 1812, and
Elizabeth (Earl), of Secaugus, N. J.
I. POLLY, b. about 1760; m. William Earl.
II. ENOCH, m. Maria Rikeman.
III. ROBERT, JR., m. Sarah Earl.
IV. CORNELIUS, d. in Canada.
V. JOHN, m. Rachel Sickles.
VI. PETER, d. unmarried.
VII. CHARITY, m. William Howard.
VIII. PEGGY, m. Silas Perwin.
    Some of the families descending from Robert Greenleaf resided at
    New Durham, and other parts of Hudson County, N. J., and
    some few at South Amboy.

Children of **Enoch Greenleaf**, son of Robert, Sen., and Maria
(Rikeman).
I. SARAH, m. James Howell.
II. ELIZABETH, m. Henry Howell.
III. EVERT, m. Jane Danielson.
IV. ROBERT, m. Margaret Reily.
V. TOBIAS, m. Susan Latorette.
VI. DANIEL, m. Sarah Saxton.
VII. SAMUEL, m. Margaret Swanier.

Children of **Robert Greenleaf, Jr.**, son of Robert, Sen., and
Sarah (Earl).
I. A son, d. in infancy.
II. NATHANIEL, unmarried.
III. ELIZABETH, m. 1, Mich. M'Closkey; 2, James Randall.
IV. ROBERT.
V. JAMES.
VI. CORNELIUS, m. Catherine Fitener.
VII. PHILIP, m. Eliza Wooley.
VIII. PETER.

Children of **John Greenleaf**, son of Robert, Sen., and Rachel
(Sickles).
I. JACOB, m. Eliza Van Houghton.
II. ABRAHAM, unmarried.
III. JOHN.

Martin Greenleaf, b. in Germany; came to America when quite a young man, and settled near Churchtown, Lancaster Co., Penn. He m. a Miss —— Gibbs; nine children :—

I. MARTIN, unmarried; d. when quite a young man.

II. JOHN, unmarried; killed by a wagon running over him.

III. A SON, d. quite young.

IV. A SON, d. quite young.

V. JACOB, b. Jan. 14, 1759, at Churchtown, Penn.; m. 1792, Fronica (Frances), dau. of Ulrich* and Fronica (Gross) Bruner, b. Oct. 13, 1765; d. Aug. 21, 1858. He d. Oct. 14, 1824, in Salisbury Gap; eight children.

VI. BARBARA, d. young.

VII. ANNA, d. young.

VIII. AGNES, unmarried.

IX. MARY, m. Her husband died; no children.

Children of **Jacob Greenleaf**, son of Martin, and Frances (Gross).

I. JOHN, b. Feb. 7, 1792, in Berks Co., Penn.; m. Jan. 21, 1819, Anna Worrest, d. 1874. He d. 1874; a farmer. They died of pneumonia, seven weeks apart; res. Lancaster Co., Penn., until 1850, then moved to Juniata Co.; four children :—

    I. ——, d. in infancy.

    II. Frances, b. Aug. 30, 1823; d. July 26, 1892; unmarried.

    III. Annie B., b. Dec. 9, 1828; unmarried; res. Thompsontown, Penn.

    IV. Peter Lednum, b. March 25, 1830; d. 1876; physician; grad. 1854, and commenced practice in partnership with his preceptor, Dr. E. D. Crawford, in Thompsontown, Penn. In three years Dr. Crawford sold out to him, and he practiced until his death.

---

* Ulrich Bruner, b. June 4, 1730; m. April, 1755, Fronica Gross, b. in Curpfalz (the Palatinate) in the town of Nebersheim. Her father was Isaac Gross, and her mother was Magdalena; maiden name, Rotsen. He d. Feb. 19, 1821. She d. Feb. 27, 1796. They had eleven children: ¹Maria, d. young. ²John. ³Isaac, d. young. ⁴Fronica, d. young. ⁵Ulrich. ⁶Fronica. ⁷Barbara. ⁸Isaac. ⁹Jacob, d. young. ¹⁰Jacob. ¹¹Magdalena. In 1813 there were living John, Ulrich, Fronica, Barbara, Isaac, Jacob, and Magdalena.

JACOB GREENLEAF, CONTINUED:—

II. JACOB, b. Nov. 30, 1793; d. young.

III. MARIA, b. Nov. 17, 1795.

IV. ELIZABETH, b. Oct. 1, 1797.

V. JACOB, b. Dec. 23, 1799; m. Feb. 8, 1827, Annes, dau. of
John and Martha Stewart (?), of Oxford, Chester Co., Penn.,
b. Feb. 23, 1803; d. June 20, 1871. He d. Feb. 25, 1885;
nine children:—

  I. S. Handford, b. March 3, 1828; res. Honey Brook,
    Chester Co., Penn.

  II. Martha J., b. Sept. 10, 1829; m. James Ogden, of
    Lancashire, Eng. He d. Jan. 13, 1894; seven chil-
    dren:—

1. Ellen E., b. Jan. 4, 1856; unmarried. 2. Annes F., b. June 30,
1857; m. Jan. 6, 1886, James H. Ferron; three children: (1)
Martha. (2) Lillian. (3) Charles. 3. Victoria, b. July 22,
1859; m. April 5, 1888, William Mullin; two children: (1)
Raymond. (2) Clifford. 4. Jacob G., b. Jan. 13, 1861; m.
May 11, 1887, Viola E. Cunningham; one child: Anna. 5.
James E., b. June 1, 1863; m. Oct. 31, 1893, Emma Null; no
children. 6. John S., b. May 9, 1868; m. March 17, 1892,
Annie Smiley; one child: James. 7. Arthur H., b. April 17,
1871; d. June 3, 1880.

  III. Jacob O. B., b. Aug. 17, 1831; unmarried; d. ——.

  IV. John J., b. May 6, 1833; m. June 10, 1874, Mary
    E. Bemsole. He d. July 18,1889; res. Altoona, Penn.;
    four children: 1. Mary M., b. March 13, 1875. 2.
    Frank B., b. June 29, 1877. 3. Bessie M., b. June
    4, d. June 7, 1882. 4. Nellie A., b. May 8, 1887.

  V. Samuel H., b. March 17, 1835; res. Gap, Lancaster
    Co., Penn.

  VI. Frances E., b. July 17, 1837; unmarried; d. April
    4, 1881.

  VII. Sarah A., b. July 1, 1839; m. Sept. 1, 1870, Isaac
    N. Townsend; six children:—

1. Ella A., b. Oct. 31, 1871. 2. Jacob N., b. July 5, 1873. 3. Samuel H., b. Jan. 22, 1874. 4. Edgar J., b. April 23, 1877. 5.
Chester A., b. March 7, 1879. 6. Charles G., b. July 27, 1885.

  VIII. Martin S., b. July 31, 1841; res. McKees Gap,
    Blair Co., Penn.

  IX. Isaac B., b. Sept. 14, 1844; res. 353 Broomall Street,
    Chester, Penn.

JACOB GREENLEAF, CONTINUED:—

VI. FRONICA (Frances), b. Nov. 25, 1802.

VII. MARTIN, b. June 1, 1805; m. Margaret, dau. of Robert
Patterson, b. 1805. He d. May, 1876. She d. Jan. 16,
1884; seven children:—

   I. Robert Patterson, b. Dec. 14, 1830; m. Nov. 20,
1855, 1, Esther F. Turner; d. May 27, 1868; 2,
Nov. 11, 1869, Laura Elizabeth Atkinson, of
Thompsontown, Penn.; physician; graduated in
1855, and practiced in Oxford, Chester Co., Penn.,
until 1865, then moved to Wilmington, Del., where
he now resides; three children by 1st marriage: 1.
Martin, Jr., b. Feb. 17, 1859; m. Laura Swisher;
two children: (1) Carrol. (2) Etta. 2. Anna
Margaret, b. May 7, 1864; unmarried. 3. Infant,
b. April 30, d. May 12, 1867. Child by 2d marriage:
Louis Evans Atkinson, b. April 3, 1871; d. June 17,
1890, drowned by the accidental upsetting of his boat.

   II. Jacob Raymond, b. Dec. 8, 1833; m. April 14, 1859,
Elizabeth Johnson; five children: 1. May Bell, b.
Dec. 31, 1859. 2. John. 3. Frank Martin. 4.
Margaret. 5. Louisa.

   III. Martin Yates, b. March 26, 1835; m. Feb. 24,
1863, Hannah Rea; two children: 1. May Ida, b.
Feb. 21, 1864. 2. Anne, b. Nov. 1, 1867.

   IV. Isabella Elizabeth, b. June 30, 1837.

   V. Frances Lucinda, b. Feb. 25, 1840; m. John Walker;
no children.

   VI. Sarah Maria, b. Dec. 12, 1843.

   VII. John Timlow, b. Dec. 11, 1846.

VIII. BARBARA, b. April 13, 1808; m. Nov. 15, 1832, Jacob
Brackbill. She d. Feb. 24, 1846.

Joseph Greenleaf, m. Feb. 13, 1758, Susanna, dau. of Amos
Pearson and Mary (Morse), b. Feb. 8, 1739; d. Dec. 22,
1816. He was appointed, by Gen. George Washington,
keeper of Portland Light, the first lighthouse established on
our seacoast, Jan. 7, 1791. The lighthouse was 72 feet
high; the lantern, 15 feet; the whole, 87 feet. He died
suddenly while taking a boat into Portland Harbor, Oct. 3
1795; six children:—

    i. Joseph, b. June 22, 1759; d. June 19, 1770; drowned.
    ii. Amos, b. Sept. 19, 1765; m. Jan. 10, 1787, Polly
        Lowell. He d. Sept. 20, 1789, in West Indies.
    iii. Susanna, b. Jan. 17, 1768; m. Jan. 23, 1785, Josiah,
        son of John Cox (3d), b. 1756. He d. Dec. 17,
        1850. She d. Dec. 17, 1850; ten children:—

1. Susan, b. Nov. 8, 1785; m. Aug. 17, 1806, Abel Vinton; moved
to Marietta, Ohio. 2. Eliza, b. Feb. 1, 1788; m. Sept. 27, 1807,
Dea. John Harrod, or Joseph. She d. May, 1843. 3. Fanny,
b. May 1, 1790; living in Chelsea, Mass., 1870; unmarried. 4.
Caroline, b. Sept. 11, 1792; m. Sept. 22, 1818, Elisha Vinton.
5. John, b. Feb. 27, 1794; d. in infancy. 6. John, b. Feb. 13,
1795; m. 1, Thankful Gore; 2, Adeline Preble. He d. Jan. 25,
1871. 7. Mary, b. Dec. 26, 1797; d. in infancy. 8. Josiah, b.
Jan. 26, 1799; d. 1826; unmarried. 9. Emily, b. June 11, 1801.
10. Mary, b. Nov. 15, 1804; m. June 30, 1830, Enoch Ilsley.

    iv. Mary, b. Dec. 20, 1773; d. April 25, 1834; un-
        married.
    v. Joseph, b. Dec. 9, 1776; m. Sally Stevens. He d.
        Dec. 26, 1851; four children: 1. Mary Jane, b.
        April 25, 1811; m. Solomon T. Shirley, of Deering.
        She d. April 23, 1886, at Deering; five children.
        2. Joseph P., b. July 27, 1815; m. Susan Russell,
        of Conway, N. H. He d. April 10, 1893; no chil-
        dren living. 3. Amos, b. May 5, 1818, in Port-
        land, Me.; m. June 3, 1845, at Portland, Mary D.
        Mitchell; res. Yarmouth, Me.; four children: (1)
        William Henry, b. April 29, 1846; d. June 28,
        1846. (2) Susan Augusta, b. June 10, 1850; m.
        Walter B. Allen, Yarmouth, Me.; no children. (3)
        Henry Clark, b. Aug. 25, 1852; d. May 28, 1858.
        (4) Mary Louise, b. Dec. 9, 1863; m. James D.
        Rogers, Yarmouth, Me.; three children. 4. Henry

JOSEPH GREENLEAF, CONTINUED:—

> C., b. Nov. 25, 1822; m. Susan Bisbee, of Yar-
> mouth, Me. He d. June 19, 1876; no children
> living.
>
> VI. Sally, b. Aug. 30, 1778; d. 185–, at Portland.

Children of Mary Jane and Solomon T. Shirley :—

> 1. Abby, b. ——; m. Frank Fowler, Malden, Mass.; no children.
> 2. Murilla, b. ——; m. Andrew Geyer, Brooklyn, N. Y.; no
> children. 3. Elizabeth L., b. ——; unmarried; res. Deering,
> Me. 4. ——. 5. ——.

Children of **Samuel Greenleaf** b.——, and Martha (Bull), b.
1679; m. Oct. 14, 1708, at Boston, Mass. She d. Feb.
22, 1759; six children :—

I. HANNAH, b. Jan. 7, 1709.

II. ELIZABETH, b. Aug. 8, 1711.

III. SAMUEL, b. July 28, 1712.

IV. JOHN, b. Dec. 10, 1714.

V. JONATHAN, b. Sept. 22, 1716; m. Feb. 26, 1738, Mary
Cunningham. He d. Dec. 23, 1758; res. Boston; three
children :—

> 1. Mary, b. Nov. 22, 1739.
> II. Samuel, b. Oct. 28, 1740; m. Nov. 17, 1763, Mehita-
> ble Snoden; four children.
> III. Hannah, b. Dec. 17, 1741.

VI. STEPHEN, b. July 22, 1719.

Children of **Levi Greenleaf** and Mary.

I. LEVI DOUGLASS, b. about 1851, in Hallowell, Me.

II. JAMES FRANKLIN, b. Nov. 20, 1853, in Hallowell, Me.; m.
June 21, 1876, Olive C., dau. of James H. Rand, of
Standish, Me.; five children :—

> 1. Nina Belle, b. Aug. 28, d. Oct. 11, 1883.
> II. Elton Brackett, b. July 1, 1885.
> III. Frank Delbert, b. June 21, 1887.
> IV. Sarah Mabel, b. Jan. 22, 1890.
> V. Eugene Levi, b. May 29, 1892.

III. WILLIAM, b. about 1855.

NEWBURY RECORDS.

BIRTHS.

Mary Greenleaf, of Samuel and Hannah	July 19, 1731.
Richard Greenleaf, of Thomas and Susanna . . .	Sept., 1764.
Keturah Greenleaf, of Richard and Lois	Dec. 1, 1790.
Thomas Greenleaf, of Richard and Lois	April 25, 1793.
Susanna Greenleaf, of Richard and Lois	Dec. 24, 1797.
Eunice Greenleaf, of Richard and Lois	Aug. 22, 1800.
Richard Greenleaf, of Richard and Lois	Feb. 11, 1802.
Elizabeth Greenleaf, of Thomas and Elizabeth . .	Aug. 8, 1792.
Mary Connell Greenleaf, of Joseph and Elizabeth . .	Jan. 6, 1806.
Abigail Greenleaf, of Joseph and Susan	Aug. 27, 1811.
Joseph Greenleaf, of Joseph and Susan	Sept. 16, 1813.
Edmund Greenleaf, of Joseph and Susan	June 14, 1814.
Edmund Greenleaf, of Joseph and Susan	Feb. 14, 1818.
Chester Allen Greenleaf, of Joseph and Susan . . .	March 28, 1826.
Sarah Greenleaf, of Charles and Hannah	June 19, 1820.
Benjamin F. Greenleaf, of Benjamin and Elizabeth . .	Feb. 9, 1827.
Benjamin Franklin Greenleaf, of Benjamin and Elizabeth,	June 1, 1829.
Benjamin Greenleaf, of Benjamin and Esther . . .	Jan. 6, 1829.

MARRIAGES.

Sarah Greenleaf and Tristram Knight	June 9, 1719.
Abigail Greenleaf and William Ripp	Dec. 22, 1720.
Samuel Greenleaf and Mary Moody	Oct. 3, 1721.
Mary Greenleaf and Nathan Noyes	Dec. 27, 1725.
Benjamin Greenleaf and Annie Woodbridge . . .	Sept. 23, 1724.
Elizabeth Greenleaf and Ebenezer Choate . . .	Sept. 3, 1730.
Mary Greenleaf and Abraham Davis	Jan. 10, 1733.
Ruth Greenleaf and Mark Moors, Jr.	July 24, 1735.
Deborah Greenleaf and Moses Swett	Nov. 27, 1735.
Joshua Greenleaf and Sarah Pettingill . . .	May 11, 1738.
Elizabeth Greenleaf and Nathaniel Atkinson, Jr. . .	Nov. 30, 1738.
Mrs. Hannah Greenleaf and Josiah Titcomb, Jr. . .	Dec. 10, 1745.
Mrs. Jane Greenleaf and Thomas Clark	Nov. 10, 1747.
Mrs. Sarah Greenleaf and Thomas Woodbridge . .	Nov. 21, 1749.
Mary Greenleaf and Nathaniel Plumer	Oct. 5, 1750.
Anna Greenleaf and Joseph Spiller	Sept. 7, 1756.
Judith Greenleaf and Richard Dummer	June 6, 1754.
Abigail Greenleaf and Jonathan Plummer	Nov. 27, 1760.
Thomas Greenleaf and Susanna Brown	March 9, 1762.
Mary Greenleaf and Caleb Toppan	April 14, 1762.
Hannah Greenleaf and William Woodman . . .	May 13, 1766.
Sarah Greenleaf and Wingate Newman	June 17, 1769.
Lydia Greenleaf and Thomas Davis	Dec. 28, 1778.
Thomas Greenleaf and Elizabeth Hidden	Jan. 6, 1779.

Sarah Greenleaf and Thomas Coher	May 3, 1781.
William Greenleaf and Mary Dean	June 18, 1782.
Elizabeth Greenleaf and Benjamin Pike	April 1, 1783.
Sarah Greenleaf and Joseph Pearson	Oct. 19, 1783.
Anna Greenleaf and Edward Brock	Feb. 1, 1787.
Hannah Greenleaf and James Duncan	Sept. 5, 1786.
Tamson Greenleaf and Levi Shacford	Aug. 30, 1787.
Richard Greenleaf and Lois Rogers	Dec. 1, 1789.
Elizabeth Greenleaf and John Greenleaf	Jan. 5, 1794.
Thomas Greenleaf and Lydia Griffin	Nov. 9, 1796.
Joanna Greenleaf and Daniel Giddings	Nov. 2, 1797.
Sally Greenleaf and James Kettell, Jr.	May 22, 1798.
Joseph Greenleaf (p. 336) and Elizabeth Hills	Nov. 25, 1801.
Abigail Peverly Greenleaf (p. 336) and Benjamin Hale	Dec. 12, 1802.
Mary Greenleaf (p. 336) and William Stickney Dodge	Sept. 16, 1804.
Sally Greenleaf and Edward Farling (or Phelan)	Oct. 9, 1806.
Joseph Greenleaf and Susan Purvier	Nov. 20, 1810.
Mary Greenleaf and Stephen Bailey, Jr.	1811.
Susan Dennis Greenleaf and David Cloutman	April 21, 1811.
Edmund Greenleaf, of Canterbury, N. H., and Lydia Bartlett	June, 1810.
Elizabeth Greenleaf and Reuben Brown	June, 1810.
Mary Greenleaf and Moses Pettingell	Nov. 27, 1811.
James Greenleaf and Charlotte Little	July 15, 1813.
Catherine Greenleaf and Joseph Stanwood	Oct. 22, 1815.
Thomas Greenleaf and Charlotte Bailey	March 2, 1817.
Mrs. Polly Greenleaf and Thomas Pettingell	July 29, 1822.
Mary Greenleaf and Daniel Tarr	Oct. 17, 1822.
Richard Greenleaf and Eliza Ackerman	Jan. 12, 1825.
Mary C. Greenleaf and Alexander Smith, Jr.	Dec. 7, 1826.
Henrietta Greenleaf and Chester Allen	May 23, 1827.
Sophia B. Greenleaf and Andrew M. Paul	Nov. 24, 1845.

DEATHS.

Mary Greenleaf, widow of ——	April 4, 1776.
Susanna Greenleaf, dau. of Richard and Lois	Feb. 13, 1802.
Eunice Greenleaf, dau. of Richard and Lois	Oct. 11, 1801.
Abigail Greenleaf, dau. of Joseph and Susan	Aug. 30, 1812.
Benjamin F. Greenleaf, son of Benjamin and Elizabeth	Nov. 6, 1828.
Sarah Greenleaf, dau. of Charles and Hannah	June 19, 1822.

IPSWICH RECORDS.

MARRIAGES.

Mrs. Margaret Greenleaf and John Lull	Feb. 14, 1734.
Joseph Greenleaf and Susanna Annable	Nov. 11, 1789.

HAVERHILL RECORDS.

BIRTHS.

George A. Greenleaf, of Albert H. and Augusta . . Jan. 8, 1860.
Albert H. Greenleaf, b. in Maine. Augusta Greenleaf, b. in Haverhill.

MARRIAGES.

Albert H. Greenleaf (22), son of Joshua and Margaret, and Augusta, dau. of Greenleaf and Analine George; July 17, 1859.

Sophie A. Greenleaf (32), dau. of William and Mary, and Amos C. (36), son of Amos and Mary Toppan; April 16, 1868.

Clara S. Greenleaf (34), dau. of William and Mary, and Thomas W. (37), son of John and Dorcas Peasley; Dec. 13, 1871.

James C. Greenleaf (23), son of John and Catherine, and Eunice B., dau. of J. and Emma Boult (20); Nov. 26, 1884.

DEATHS.

Nathaniel Greenleaf, d. Dec. 28, 1836.

Abigail Greenleaf (74), d. Dec. 19, 1844; cancer; b. 1770, in West Newbury, Mass.

Lydia Greenleaf (67 yrs. 3 mos. 19 ds.), dau. of William and Almira (Lovering), d. May 9, 1866.

Sarah H. Greenleaf (70 yrs. 2 mos. 7 ds.), dau. of Samuel and Rebecca (Hale), d. July 7, 1867.

Ida M. Greenleaf (12 yrs. 8 mos. 26 ds.), dau. of Edward and Mary (Littlefield), d. Jan. 24, 1876.

Anna Greenleaf (71), dau. of Joseph and Mary (Burleigh), d. Oct. 14, 1879.

Samuel H. Greenleaf (1 m. 20 d.), son of Samuel and Hattie, d. March 26, 1881.

BOSTON RECORDS.

BIRTHS.

John Greenleaf, of Stephen and Mary . . . . July 12, 1708.
Stephen Greenleaf, of Stephen and Mary . . . March 17, 1709-10.
Mary Greenleaf, of Stephen and Mary . . . . Jan. 9, 1711.
Simon Greenleaf, of John and Elizabeth . . . . Jan. 9, 1715.
Sarah Greenleaf, of John and Elizabeth . . . . Aug. 21, 1725.

NOTES.

William White. In the year 1635 he landed. The General Court ordered the bounds of Ipswich and Quascacunquan (now Newbury) to be laid out, when some of the chief (people) of Ipswich desired leave to remove to Quascacunquan to begin a settlement, which was granted them. Among those who removed to Newbury were Rev. Thomas Parker, Nicholas Noyes, Henry Sewall, William White, William Moody, and Richard Kent.—[Phillip's Geneal., Appendix I., p. 886.]

Nathan Piper came from England to Massachusetts about 1653. Settled in Ipswich, Mass., before 1658, and died in 1676. After his death his wife Sarah married Ezekiel Woodward, of Wenham, and was living April 10, 1696.—[Boston *Transcript*, Notes and Queries 4729, Dec. 23, 1893.] Calender number 15, page 200.

"In the year 1730, William Shattuck sells land in Watertown to his son-in-law, William Greenleaf, of Boston, felt maker." The felt making was probably for felt hat bodies.—[Jona. Greenleaf papers, No. 197.] Calender number 5, page 195.

Judge Benjamin Greenleaf was appointed executor of the will of (Sir) William Pepperell, and in joint with his will, Mary Pepperell. The will probated July 24, 1759 (or 1757). July 14, Mr. Greenleaf declined the trust. Calender number 559, page 426.

The following persons served as Sheriffs of Suffolk County under the Province Charter, and under the Constitution, etc. List follows with names of Stephen Greenleaf, Jan. 3, 1757, and William Greenleaf, 1775.—[Prof. and Industrial History of Suffolk County, Vol. I. page 99.] Calender number 38, page 206; 40, page 207.

1770. Stephen Greenleaf, Sheriff of Suffolk County, under the king. During the Colonial period there was no officer bearing the title of sheriff until the time of Andros (1687), when James Sherlock acted in that capacity and officiated in the Superior Court of Indication in 1688, over which Joseph Dudley presided as Chief Justice with William Stoughton and Peter Buckley as associates.—[Town Records.] Calender number 38, page 206.

New London *Gazette*, Feb. 17, 1775. Stephen Greenleaf. "Cash given by Stephen Greenleaf, at his shop in Windham, for good hair: where he still continues his business and where all gentlemen may be supplied with wigs of any kind very cheap for the ready cash—and all favors shall be thankfully received." Calender number 273, p. 329.

Essex Gazette.

1772. From Boston *Gazette*, January 13. Communication from Joseph Greenleaf, two columns.

1773. Boston, Thursday, April 1. Last Lord's Day (March 28) a son of Mr. Oliver Greenleaf was baptized by Rev. Dr. Cooper, by the name of Oliver Cromwell.

1773. Newburyport, April 8. Samuel Greenleaf, Innholder, Commissioner on Estate.

1774. October 10. Died at Boston, Mr. William Greenleaf, aged 82.

1775. Hollis, July 20. Amory & Greenleaf advertise all who are indebted to said company that Enoch Greenleaf resides at Hollis in the County of Hillsboro, and Province of New Hampshire. Said Greenleaf has for sale New England and West India rum, sugar, and molasses, rice, etc.

Salem Gazette.

1783. Salem, June 10. The collector of excise for the County of Essex, gives notice that he shall attend in the several towns in said county to collect the duty on carriages as follows: at the office of Capt. Moses Greenleaf in Newburyport, etc.

1785. Boston, December 26. Died at New Haven, Mr. Stephen Greenleaf, late of this town.

Massachusetts Gazette.

1786. Boston, Monday, January 30. Died on Wednesday last, Mrs. Emma Greenleaf, aged 46, widow of the late Mr. Stephen Greenleaf of this town.—[See "Unconnected Families."]

February 13. Advertisement of mail stage from Boston to Portsmouth. Stage puts up at Mr. John Stevens' noted tavern in Portsmouth. John Stevens Senior. John Greenleaf. (Calendar number 568.)

Salem Mercury.

1788. September 30. Married at Boston, Mr. Charles Sigourney, merchant, to Miss Polly Greenleaf, of Newburyport.

Salem Gazette.

1793. January 22. Died at Bolton, of a paralytic, William Greenleaf, Esq. May 7. Died at Newburyport, Mr. Samuel Greenleaf.

1795. October 3. Died suddenly, Capt. Joseph Greenleaf, of Cape Elizabeth. He had been keeper of the lighthouse on Portland Point from the time of its first establishment.

1798. New York, September 15. Yesterday died Mr. Thomas Greenleaf, editor of the *Argus* and *Patriotic Register*. (Calender number 8.)

1800. Salem, September 12. In list of deaths by yellow fever on board U. S. Ship "Warren" from the Havanna, dated thence August 22. Jonathan Greenleaf, midshipman, June 30, forty-three names. (Calender number 524.)

1802. February 19. Died at Welton, Mrs. Judith Greenleaf, consort of Enoch Greenleaf, Esq.

1803. Salem, October 21. Died at Newburyport, Mr. John Greenleaf, aged 56.

1805. Salem, May 21. Died in Boston, Miss Eunice Greenleaf.

1809. Salem, July 18. Died at Newburyport, Mr. Joseph Greenleaf, aged 71, formerly of Boston.

1811. Salem, June 7. Died in this town, widow Joanna Greenleaf, aged 54.

1814. Salem, June 10. Died at Sandwich, Mr. Joseph Greenleaf, bookseller, of Boston, by the bursting of a fowling piece.

1816. Salem, October 18. Died at Newburyport, Mrs. Elizabeth Greenleaf, wife of Col. John Greenleaf.

1817. Salem, March 7. Married at Newburyport, Mr. Thomas Greenleaf to Miss Charlotte Bailey.

1818. Salem, February 10. Died at Boston, Mr. George K. Greenleaf, aged 49. Salem, February 13. Died at Newburyport, Mrs. Anna Greenleaf, aged 74.

1820. Salem, August 18. Died at Newburyport, Miss Jane Greenleaf, aged 83.

1821. July 3. Died at Newburyport, Col. Charles Greenleaf, aged 30.

1824. April 6. Married in Gloucester, Mr. George T. Barrett to Miss Abigail W. Greenleaf. July 6. Drowned near Dover, N. H., Mr. Timothy Greenleaf, of Salem, aged about 50 years. Calendar number 591.

1826. September 12. Died in Boston, Mass., Dorcas Greenleaf, aged 45.

1827. January 5. Died on board ship "Suffolk," on her passage from Batavia for Antwerp, Mr. John Greenleaf, carpenter, aged 26.

1829. February 27. Died in Newburyport, suddenly, Col. John Greenleaf, aged 69. He was found dead sitting in his armchair at his counting room, and probably died in a fit. Calendar number 560.

1831. April 22. Died in Charlestown, Richard Greenleaf, formerly of Newburyport, aged 20.

1838. December 18. Married in Gloucester, Mr. Joseph G. Greenleaf to Miss Eliza Priestly.

Petition of inhabitants of Whiscasset and Mounsweg to form a town. Dec. 17, 1754, Richard Greenleaf, Samuel Greenleaf.—[N. E. Hist. and Geneal. Reg. Vol. xxvii. p. 411. Mass. Arch., Book 116, pp. 736, 738.] Calender number 295, 296, pages 336, 337.

Middlesex Gazette, Middletown, Conn.

Oct. 12, 1798. Report of Health Committee, New London. October 9. Deaths since last report (October 2), Joseph Greenleaf, aged 20.

Aug. 30, 1821. Married in Danbury, Mr. Levi G. Porter of this town to Miss Betsey Greenleaf, of Danbury.

Joseph Greenleaf, whose wife Elizabeth, appointed administratrix April 15, 1806, appears at Salem Probate Rec. office, Vol. ccclxxiii. p. 489.

"Here lyes the body of Samuel Greenleaf; d. Aug. ye 7th, 1737, aged 56 years; and Martha, his wife, d. Feb. 22, 1757, aged 78. Also Jonathan Greenleaf, d. Dec. 23, 17—, aged 42 (603); and Moses Greenleaf, son to Capt. Stephen Greenleaf of Newbury, died March 8, 1753, aged 55" (12).—[Old Granary Burial Ground, Boston. See Bridgman History of Pilgrims of Boston.]

Died, Feb. 9, 1896, Ann Greenleaf, widow of James Butler, 84 years; res. 90 Elm Hill Ave., Boston Highlands.—[Boston *Herald.*]

Transcript, Notes and Queries, 6413, April 18, 1896.

The "*Royal American Magazine*, a Universal Repository of Instruction and Amusement," was the last magazine established previous to the Revolution. Its first number, January, 1774, bore this imprint: "America; Boston. Printed and sold at Greenleaf's Printing Office, in Union Street near the conduit, where subscriptions continue to be taken in." It was published for six months, and then suspended; but Joseph Greenleaf revived and continued it until the following April, when "the war put a period to the magazine." Each number was embellished with two copper-plate engravings, most of which were designed and engraved as indicated by the imprint, "Paul Revere, Sculp." Some were crude, but most of them have an historical value. He produced for the magazine several portraits of historic personages. Then follows a list of the different engravings which appeared in this magazine, and for the last number, March, 1775, his "America in distress," for the engraving of which appears this charge in his day book: April 1, 1775. Joseph Greenleaf, Esqr., Dr. To engraving plate for March Mag'e, £3-0s-0d.—["Life of Paul Revere," by Elbridge H. Goss.] Calendar number 6, and personal history page 77.

The Gazetteer of Maine.

Mr. William Dodd, of Boston, early purchased of the State the township which is now Williamsburg in Piscataquis County, which was afterwards named after his Christian name. Moses Greenleaf (528), Mr. Dodd's agent and surveyor, settled there in 1810. The town has a noted pre-eminence in its locality in one respect, for it is the first map of Maine was plotted, and the first book of the County written. The work was "Greenleaf's Statistics of Maine," issued as early as 1816, intended to explain his map—previously published. This book he afterward enlarged and amended, issuing it in 1829 as the "Survey of Maine." The first mentioned book had 154 pages, the last 468. He issued a new map, enlarged and improved, at the same time with the latter volume. The plantation was organized in 1819, and Eben Greenleaf (529) being chosen first plantation clerk. The highest elevation of lands in the town is "Greenleaf's Hill," named in honor of one of its first and most distinguished settlers, viz., Moses Greenleaf.

Legal changes of name, approved Feb. 6, 1839. "John Greenleaf Cloutman, Jane Cloutman, Elizabeth Cloutman, and Charles Cloutman of Portland, be severally allowed to take the name of Greenleaf for their surnames."—[Private and Special Laws of the State of Maine, 1839.] Perhaps others unaccounted for may have had their names changed to Greenleaf.

The Greenleaf Law Library, incorporated February, 1867.

The Law Library belonging to the Cumberland Bar Association of Portland, Maine, came to an end in the great fire of that city, July 4, 1866. Soon after Mrs. Mary Longfellow, widow of Mr. James Greenleaf (547), of Cambridge, Mass., hearing of the loss, tendered the law library of her late husband, which had descended from his father, Professor Simon Greenleaf, formerly of Portland, as a gift to the Bar, which was gratefully accepted. It consisted of 1,269 volumes. This has been increased by the purchase of many other volumes, so that the Greenleaf Law Library of the Cumberland Bar is now one of the finest and most useful in the State.

Enoch Greenleaf.

"Original settlers of Salisbury, Mass. The first or original list of ye townsmen of Salisbury in ye book of Records." Here follows the names and number. "No. 58, Enoch Greenleaf. The whole number of settlers was 68." "This is a true copy as they were first listed in ye book of Records, as attests. Thos. Bradbury, Rec'r." "At a general meeting of ye town of Salisbury, 3rd 12mo. 1650 (Feb. 3, 1651). Also it was ordered at ye same meeting that all those whose names are hereunder written shall be accompted comonors and none but y to this p'sent yt is to say. (Enoch Greenleaf's name does not appear in the list.) A true copy, etc. Thomas Bradbury." In the tax rate of Dec. 25, 1650, the name of Enoch Greenleaf does not appear, neither does it appear in the rate made 18 5th mo. 1652. He may have removed from Salisbury to Malden about this time. Salisbury, Conn., was not divided into settler's rights until 1732. Salisbury, Mass., was incorporated in 1640.—[See N. E. Hist. Reg., Vol. iii. p. 55.] July, 1695. John Morton *et als.*, to Enoch Greenleaf, 100 acres and meadows at Dunes, Scarborough.—[York County, Maine, Rec. Book, 136.] May 18, 1636. John Greenleaf, of St. Andrews, Undershaft; dyer. Bachelor, aged 24, at his own government. Hester Hoste, maiden, aged 21, dau. of James Hoste, of Stephany, who consents at St. Augustines near Pauls Gate.—[Vol. xxviii., General Gleanings in England. Essex Inst. Coll. p. 141.]

Robert Greenleaf, perhaps a brother of Edmund. In a MS. preserved at the State Paper Department of Her Majesty's Public Record Office, England, where the name of Greenleaf is not found among the emigrants to any of the New England States, or other northern American Plantations, but the name of Robert Greenleaf is given as having emigrated to Virginia in 1610, in the ship "Wyall," and settled in Charles City Neck. He was aged 43 years, and Susan, his wife, followed him there in 1620 in the ship "Jonathan," together with his son Thomas and daughter Ann. In the same record the name of William Greenleaf is given as a passenger in the ship "William and John" to the Island of St. Christophers in September, 1635, from the port of London. William died September, 1635. —[See also Hotten's Edition "Original list of Emigrants from Gt. Britain to the American Plantations," pub. by J. W. Bouton, 706 Broadway, N. Y., 1874.] Sept. 2, 1635. "Theis underwritten names are to be transported to St. Christopher's imbarqued in the 'William and John.'" William Greenleaf, 26 years of age, and others.— [N. E. Hist. and Geneal. Register, Vol. xiv. p. 355.]

John Greenleaf.

"Old Churches and Families of Virginia," p. 284, Vol. ii. Frederick Co., 1744, church organized. (1) McCoy's Chapel, known as the "Old Chapel." Thomas, Lord Fairfax, and others. (2) Cunningham's Chapel. (3) Two on North and South branches of Shenandoah (one at Winchester, and one at Bunker Hill), called Morgan's Chapel. (4) Wood's Chapel, between Winchester and Charlestown. (5) One at Shepardstown, called Mecklenburg Chapel, and (6) 1772, church at Carney's Spring, near Berryville; neither built, because of a quarrel. War came on, and funds were given to the Overseers of the Poor. 1762, a new stone church at Winchester. Vestrymen from 1764-1780. County and Parish of Frederick, in 1769, divided into the Counties of Dunmore, afterward changed to Shenandoah, Frederick, and Berkley, and into the Parishes of Beckford, Frederick, and Norbone.—Isaac Hite, John Hite, and John Greenleaf.

Richard Greenleaf.

In July and August, 1894, Prof. Ernest A. Congdon, of Philadelphia, while on a visit in London, examined the Calendar of State Papers (Colonial), 1534-1674, in 4 vols., and the Calendar of State Papers (Domestic), 1635-1668, 44 vols., with the following result: The only mention of any of the name of *Greenleaf* therein appears Sept. 29, 1652. Lessee of the estate of John Smith, Wingall County, Hereford.

Richard Greenleaf, of Kilpeck, petitions that Smith leased to him before the wars lands in Wernegeuny, and he sold the reversion to petitioner's son *Thomas (Greenleaf)*, but now the estate is sequestered for recusancy and delinquency of John Smith, the lease and sale notwithstanding. Begs to enjoy the lease, or to be tenant to the state of the premises. Referred to the Co. Com.

Nov. 5, 1652.—To grant Letters of Marque to *Richard Greenleaf*, Commissioner of the West India merchant.

Sept. 9, 1653.—Information of Joan, wife of Richard Greenleaf, of Kilpeck. That she was taken to the palace prison by the king's soldiers as an intelligencer, when the Marquis of Hereford got her exchanged. Her son was also taken prisoner as a suspected intelligencer of Parliament, Aug. 1, 1646.

June, 1636.—Calendar of State papers, 96, II., 1627: *Richard Greenleaf.* Detailed statement of the evidence by which petitioner brought home acts complained of to Moses Cowley, Lawrence Hall, "Richard Greenleaf, and others."

Nov. 9, 1652.—Order of the Council of State. For a warrant to permit *Richard Greenleafe* to export fifty dozen of shoes to Barbadoes, for the use of that plantation. Petitions of the wives of Captains Stagg and Dennis, both castaways in the "John," in her voyage to Virginia in the States' service, to be referred to Committee of Admiralty for their report upon what may be done for the relief of the petitioners.

Newburyport Public Library. Title Deeds of the Parsonage lot. The identity between the Public Library lot and the Old Parsonage is established by the following conveyances: (I.) William Dole to Stephen Greenleaf, 2 March, 1719, 2 acres. [Essex Reg., Book xxi. leaf 192]. (II.) Stephen Greenleaf to Edmund Greenleaf, 2 acres (8 rods broad on Greenleafe Lane). [Book xxi. leaves 192, 193.] (III.) Edmund Greenleaf to John Cheyney (1723). [Book xli. leaf 80.] (IV.) John Cheyney to Thomas Brown, Jun. [Book xlvii. leaf 81.] (V.) Thomas Brown, Jr., to John Lowell, clerk, for £320, May 23, 1726. (VI.) John Lowell, counsellor, inherits from his father, John, the pastor, 1767, and with Elizabeth Lowell, widow, and Sarah Lowell, wife to Patrick Tracy, for £920, July 21, 1771. [Book cxxviii. leaf 257.] (VII.) Patrick Tracy's will, dated Oct. 16, 1788. [Rec. Book lx. leaf 50; Probate Rec. (O. Ser.)]; also, Inventory of Patrick Tracy's estate, April 7, 1791. [Book lxi. leaf 117, Probate Records.] Thomas Russell and Elizabeth, *ux.*, to (VIII.) Timothy Dexter. Quit Claim, April 8, 1791. [Book cliii. leaf 76.] Witness, John Lowell, Esq., and John Lowell, Jr. Undoubtedly written by the former, who also takes the acknowledgment. Dudley Atkins Tyng, administrator, with will annexed of Patrick Tracy. Patrick Tracy to Timothy Dexter. Quit claim, April 6, 1791. [Book cliii. leaf 76.] (IX.) Timothy Dexter, of Chester, Rockingham Co., N. H., and Elizabeth, his wife, to John Greenleaf, dated April 9, 1796. Acknowledged in Connecticut. Consideration, $8,400. [Book cxxxix. leaf 273.] (X.) John Greenleaf and wife Elizabeth to James Prince, dated March 11, 1800, for $9,000. [Book clxvi. leaf 220.] (XI.) Sarah Doane, wife of Samuel D. Doane, of Boston. Mary L. Prince, single woman. Ann L. Jewett, wife of Nathaniel Jewett, of Washington City. William H. Prince, heirs and devises of James Prince, to William Manning for $5,000; date, June 16, 1830. [Book cclvii. leaf 91.] (XII.) William Manning to Jeremiah Coleman, Sept. 4, 1830. [Rec. Essex Reg., Book cclvii. leaf 202. (XIII.) Jeremiah Coleman, conveyed to Moses Coleman an undivided half of the premises (?). (XIV.) Moses Coleman and wife to William Ashby, Nov. 5, 1850, for $3,000, undivided half of 63 89-100 rods. (XV.) William Ashby and Ann Ashby, Jeremiah Coleman and Mary Coleman, to Edward S. Moseley, Joshua Hale, and Charles M. Bayley, trustees, for $6,000. Date, April 16, 1864. [Rec. Book dclxvii. leaf 115.] (XVI.) Edward S. Moseley, Joshua Hale and Charles M. Bayley, trustees, to the Mayor and Aldermen of the city of Newburyport, Sept. 22, 1865.

Hartford Daily Times, Saturday, June 22, 1895.

In referring to a letter from Mr. James E. Greenleaf as to the authorship of the famous campfire and marching song, "John Brown's Body," the *Times* says:—

"It seems the 'Glory, Glory, Hallelujah,' was originally an old Methodist refrain; but Mr. Greenleaf's inspiration put the refrain and the tune to a sudden use and almost world-wide popularity."

(The song was originated by the compiler when at Fort Warren, in 1861. The music was an old hymn. The words, as sung, were applied by the soldiers in a spirit of frolic to a comrade by the name of Brown, who had met with a slight mishap. Mr. Greenleaf started the singing, and the soldiers added fresh verses as they marched around the grounds. The words and air were so strikingly martial that he wrote them out from memory the same night, and they were shortly after played by the garrison, P. S. Gilmore's 2d Battalion of Infantry, Band, from whence the song spread throughout the army.)

Governors of Massachusetts, 1631.

The governors were elected in England prior to 1631; from 1631 to 1679 they were chosen here by the people.

1631. John Winthrop.	1646. John Winthrop.
1634. Thomas Dudley.	1649. John Endicott.
1635. John Haynes.	1650. Thomas Dudley.
1636. Henry Vane.	1651. John Endicott.
1637. John Winthrop.	1654. Richard Bellingham.
1640. Thomas Dudley.	1655. John Endicott.
1641. Richard Bellingham.	1665. Richard Bellingham.
1642. John Winthrop.	1673. John Leverett.
1644. John Endicott.	1679. Simon Bradstreet.
1645. Thomas Dudley.	

The government was administered for a time, after the first charter was dissolved, by a president.

In 1687 Sir Edmund Andros acted as governor, by authority of a royal commission.

In 1689 he was deposed by the people, who elected Simon Bradstreet president, and afterwards made him governor.

The governors under the second charter from 1692 to 1774 were appointed by the king.

1687. Edmund Andros.	1728. William Burnett.
1691. Simon Bradstreet.	1730. Jonathan Belcher.
1692. William Phipps.	1741. William Shirley.
1694. William Stoughton.	1749. Spenser Phipps.
1699. Earl Bellamont.	1753. William Shirley.
1700. William Stoughton.	1756. Spenser Phipps.
1702. Joseph Dudley.	1757. Thomas Pownal.
1715. William Tailer.	1760. Francis Bernard.
1716. Samuel Shute.	1769. Thomas Hutchinson.
1722. William Dummer.	1774. Thomas Gage.

In 1780 the present line of State Executives commenced :—

1780. John Hancock.	1836. Edward Everett.
1794. Samuel Adams.	1840. Marcus Morton.
1797. Increase Sumner.	1841. John Davis.
1800. Caleb Strong.	1843. Marcus Morton.
1807. James Sullivan.	1844. George N. Briggs.
1809. Christopher Gore.	1851. George S. Boutwell.
1810. Elbridge Gerry.	1853. John H. Clifford.
1812. Caleb Strong.	1854. Emery Washburn.
1816. John Brooks.	1855. Henry J. Gardner.
1823. William Eustis.	1858. Nathaniel P. Banks.
1826. Levi Lincoln.	1861. John A. Andrew.
1834. John Davis.	

ERRATA.

PAGE

2.   75.   Enoch Greenleaf, for Salisbury, Conn., read Mass.

     85.   Line 34, for Lempriere, 145, read 745.

     86.   Line 34, for Magnolia, read Magnalia.

     88.   Line 16, [7]Solomon, for died 1754, read 1654.

    100.   Line 13, for (7) Francis B., b. Aug. 26, 1798, read Francis B., b. Aug. 21, 1764, of Duncan and Susanna (Blake).

60.   111.   Lucinda, fifth line, for Hull, Eng., read Wiltshire; next line read "emigrated to Boston, Mass., thence to New Haven, Conn., in 1635, where they bought 500 acres of land at a penny an acre."

576. 151.   Abner Greenleaf, for Miriam, read Mariam.

    168.   Andrew Peterson, for **515**, read **517**.

    169.   Calvin Whitcomb, for **253**, read **254**.

    175.   James Leeds, for **54**, read **51**.

    191.   VII. Judith, for Nantucket, read Newbury, Mass.

34.   205.   Edmund,[4] for b. Feb. 27, read Feb. 10.

    211.   For Margaret G. Dawes, d. June 15, read June 25.

    248.   XVI. Louisa, for Melville, read Charles Melville.

    259.   For Monroe Carpenter, read J. Monroe Carpenter.

    276.   II. Martha Ann Buell, for b. May 13, read May 31.

    301.   For m. Frank Gaspie, read Frank Glaspie.

222. 307.   For Esther Calkins, read Esther Calkins Broughton.

    308.   IV. For William Josephus, read William James.[9]

    316.   Last line but one, for he d. Jan. 15, 1882, read she d.

    335.   For Lucinda (Porter), read Lucinda (Stevens).

    336.   VI. Catherine, b. June 11, for 1796, read 1795.

311. 340.   V. Westbrook,[7] for res. Edgecomb, read Westport.

    355.   iii. George F. Jewett, for b. in China, Me., read China Sea.

343. 355.   IV. W. Scott,[9] for res. Westport, Me., read Brockton, Mass.

    357.   VIII. Edward J., b. 1860, d. Aug. 8, 1864, an error.

349. 357.   For Naomi Barter (Abbot), read Loama A. (Barter).

367. 362.   For Witcher, read Whitcher.

    364.   III. James Baker Greenleaf, for b. Oct. 30, read Oct. 25. V. Fred Stinson Greenleaf, for detective, read draughtsman.

    379.   For J. E. Shurard, read J. E. Sherrard. VI. Ana Greenleaf, for Colorado, read California.

430.   III. For Jone, read Ione.

433. 380.   I. Horatio N.[8] Greenleaf, m. March 14, for 1843, read 1849.

446. 384.   VII. For Rhoda, dau. of William, read John.

ADDENDA.

301. XIV. Charlotte, dau. of John[7] Greenleaf and Martha (Tooker), m. Feb. 11, 1867, Henry Cuddeback, at Ovid, Mich., b. April 14, 1834; two children: 1. Blanche, b. Aug. 21, 1869. 2. Kate, b. July 12, 1871; d. May 4, 1877.

305. IV. Mary Ann, m. Daniel H. Bassett; six children: 1. Harriet. 2. William. 3. Mary. 4. Almond. 5. James. 6. Susan.

217. 306. II. Chester A.,[10] son of William H.[9] Greenleaf, d. Feb. 9, 1896.

308. IV. William James,[9] b. Nov. 13, 1824, son of William Josephus[8] Greenleaf and Esther Calkins (Broughton); m. July 4, 1847, Nancy E., dau. of James F. and Experience Maria (Drake) Green, of Wysox, Bradford Co., Pa., b. March 16, 1829. He d. April 22, 1862; a carpenter; res. Alba, Pa.; four children: 1. Ida Brunett, b. Oct. 4, 1850; m. Aug. 1, 1867, Dayton E. Stull, of Elmira, N. Y.; res. Canton, Pa. 2. Estella Lafrank, b. May 16, 1852, at Alba, Pa.; d. Dec. 28, 1862. 3. Nathan Lee, b. Sept. 12, 1856; res. Emporia, Texas. 4. William James,[10] b. March 25, 1862; m. Feb. 19, 1889, Ida A. Gleason, of Osceola, Pa., b. July 13, 1872; painter and paper hanger; res. Osceola, Pa.; two children: (1) Andrew Lee, b. Jan. 21, 1890. (2) Henry B., b. Aug. 22, 1891.

239. 312. I. William H. S. Greenleaf, m. Myra Joselyn, Oct. 25, 1825.

313. II. Mary Elizabeth Greenleaf, m. Tyler Gibbs, April 12, 1825.

320. viii. Sarah Jane, m. Francis S. Cramer; five children: two daughters and three sons.

320. xi. Catherine L., m. Nov. 3, 1893, George M. Gray; one child: G. Merrill, b. Sept. 2, 1894.

329. V. To Woodbridge[7] Greenleaf and Mary (Holman), Enoch Dummer, b. June 3, 1799.

329. V. Lydia Greenleaf, m. Samuel Fowler, Aug. 28, 1800.

294. 336. II. Abel,[6] m. Catherine Peverly, Dec. 23, 1778.

343. viii. Rev. Benjamin F. Parsons, d. Feb. 3, 1896.

322. 348. II. Joseph L., son of William C. Greenleaf, d. Nov. 21, 1895.

353. V. Mary Spring, dau. of Pamelia P. (Greenleaf) and Joshua R. Trevett, d. Oct. 12, 1895.

356. I. Emily A., m. Cornelius Rairdon; eleven children.

357. IV. Abbie L., m. Joseph McDonald; two children: 1. George. 2. Harry L.

357. IX. Lizzie B., m. George Gove; three children: 1. Lizzie May. 2. Georgia A. 3. Emma P.

350. 358. VI. Silas Payson[8] Greenleaf, m. Mary Pinkham.
356. 359. II. George Freeman[9] Greenleaf, m. Mary J. Gerry.
357. 359. III. Elwell[9] Greenleaf, m. Aurelia Day.
358. 359. VI. Payson S.[9] Greenleaf, m. Susan Harding.

362. Wallace D. Williams, m. Isabel Platt, of West Medford, Mass., Nov., 1894.

362. V. Rachel Arnold Greenleaf, widow of James Baker, d. Mar. 26, 1896.

372. 364. I. Harriet F., m. 1885, George White; res. Latah, Washington; one child: Francis G., b. 1894.

II. Harry W., m. Oct. 25, 1895, Annie Jackson; res. Roxbury, Mass.

402. 372. IV. Thomas Y.[8] Greenleaf, d. Dec. 18, 1895, buried Anson Cemetery.

412. 374. III. Melvin A.[10] Greenleaf, m. Nettie C., dau. James M. Story, Aug. 11, 1878.

380. I. Walter N. Greenleaf, m. B. M. Prinkle, of Veedersburgh, Ind.; three children, daughters.

380. II. Mary J. Greenleaf (dau. of Horatio N.[8] Greenleaf), m. Henry T. Allen; six sons.

380. IV. Avenah C. (dau. of Horatio N.[8] Greenleaf), m. Cyrus F. Wilson; one son.

446. 380. For dau. of William, read John.

624. 453. Mrs. Lydia H., widow of the late Matthew H. Greenleaf, d. in West Newbury, Mass., April 5, 1887; aged 79 yrs. 10 mos. 23 ds.

Betsey Greenleaf, m. Josiah, son of Stephen Goodrich, b. Aug. 13, 1793; d. Feb. 13, 1862. She d. April 12, 1869; res. Ithaca, N. Y.; three children: 1. Harvey, b. May 3, 1817; m. Lydia Hallett. 2. Stephen, b. May 3, 1817; twin. 3. Minerva E., b. ——; d. Aug. 9, 1852.

—— Greenleaf, m. Hannah, dau. of Edward Hazen, b. about 1703; res. Rowley, Mass.—(N. E. Hist. and Geneal. Register, Vol. xxxiii. p. 231.)

Stephen, b. Sept. 12, 1812, in Westport, Me.; m. Oct. 3, 1844, Catherine Stone, b. in Boothbay, Me., Feb. 2, 1822; d. Dec. 2, 1870. He d. Feb. 19, 1883. Their son, Woodbury D., was b. March 16, 1847, in Wiscasset, Me.; m. April 27, 1881, Mrs. Mary E. Smith, dau. of John and Rebekah Sheldon, of Wiscasset, Me., b. Dec. 27, 1851; no children.

BIRTHS.

MARRIAGES.

DEATHS.

GENERAL INDEX.

Peake, Rev. John, 58.
Pearson, Amos, 23; Benjamin, 25; David, 26.
Pemberton, Samuel, 68.
Penniman & Cutler, 103.
Pepperell, Sir William, 151, 162.
Perkins, Capt. Benj., 23, 24.
Perley, Chief Justice, 153.
Perry, John, 26.
Pettingell, Joseph, 24; Nathaniel, 58.
Phelps, Lydia, 148.
Phillips, William, 91.
Plant, Rev. Matthias, 54.
Pidgeon, Moses, 24.
Pierce, Enoch, 25; Franklin, 53; Joshua, 82.
Pike, Daniel, 24, 59; Robert, 5, 80; William, 79.
Pile, William, 79.
Pilsbury, Christopher, 25; Increase, 5.
Powell, Jeremiah, 53; William, 53.
Prescott, Harriet E., 61; Jonathan, 76.
Price-Greenleaf Fund, 98.
Quincy, Josiah, 66.
Rawson, Edward, 3.
Richardson, Enoch, 26.
Roberts, John C., 26.
Robertson, Daniel, Jr., 93.
Robinson, Elizabeth, 68; Nathaniel, 67.
Robson, Thomas, 93.
Roche, de la, Geo. H. F. F., 149.
Rogers, David, 26; Edmund, 24; Moses, 21, 26.
Rolfe, Hannah, 74.
Rooksby, Major, 76.
Rowe, John, 63.
Ruddock, John, 63.
Ruggell, Geo., 73.
Russell, Thomas, 69.
Sargent, Edwin, 67.
Sargent & Greenleaf, 115.
Saunders, Thomas, 68.
Savage, Habijah, 88; Mrs. Hannah (Tyng), 88.
Sawyer, Manasseh, 166; Dr. Micajah, 21, 53.
Sawyer, Nathaniel, 163.
Schell, Augustus, 102.
Schell & Slossen, 102.
Schell, Slossen & Hutchins, 103.
Schulze, Hon. Johann, 117.
Sedgwick, Theodore, 46.
Sewall, Mrs. Elizabeth L., 83; Stephen, 19, 34.
Seward, Secretary Wm. H., 101.
Shackford, John, 26; William, 26.

Shays, Daniel, 36, 166.
Shirley, Governor, 162.
Sleeper, John, 26.
Sloat & Greenleaf, 119.
Slossen, John, 102.
Smith, Mrs. E. Vale, 39; Rev. Isaac, 54; Jeremiah, 24; John, 26, 85; Nathaniel, 26; Rev. Thomas, 68.
Somerby, Anthony, 74; Richard, 74.
Somersby, Daniel, 24; Joseph, 24.
Spooner, Bartholomew, 26.
Sprague, Dr. John, 21.
Spring, Rev. Samuel, 26, 57.
Springfield Paper Co., 110.
Stanwood, Joseph, 34.
Stearns, Col. Ephraim, 167.
Stevens, B. F., 68, 165; Paul, 24.
Steele, Nancy, 101.
Stickney, Jonathan, 26; Joseph, 24; Samuel, 26; William, 23.
St. John, Elizabeth, 147; Lord Chief Justice, 147; Rt. Hon. Sir Oliver, 147; William, 147.
Stone, John, 21.
Strong, Governor, 44.
Sullivan, General John, 30, 165, 166.
Surratt, Mrs., 101.
Swain, Edward, 24.
Swayne, John, 79; Richard, 79.
Sweetzer, Seth, 77.
Swett, Dr. J. B., 24; Samuel, 24.
Talleyrand, 30.
Tarbox, Rev. Increase N., 69.
Taylor, Israel, 163; Lewis H., 109.
Teal, Josiah, 24.
Teel, William, 21.
Temple, Abigail, 146; Sir William, 65.
Tench, Francis, 101.
Thomas, Isaiah, 78; Thomas, 21.
Thompson, Rev. William, 86.
Tillman, Andrew P., 109.
Titcomb, Enoch, Jr., 21, 32, 34; George, 32; Jonathan, 32; Joshua, 34; Major Gen., 37; Margaret T., 32; Michael, 24; Moses, 32; Nicholas, 24; Richard, 21, 34; Selina J., 32; William, 32; Zebulon, 24.
Toppan, Abraham, 24; Benjamin H., 24.
Tracy, Hannah, 28, 45; James, 27; James J., 164; Nathaniel, 26, 28, 31, 34, 37, 42, 45, 53, 69; Nicholas, 21; Patrick, 21, 24, 28, 31, 45, 60.
Treat, Eunice, 77; Governor, 77; Rev. Samuel, 77.

INDEX TO GENEALOGY.

Calendar number in heavy figures; page number in light figures.

GREENLEAF NAMES.

(518)

Marie, 457.
Marietta, 253, 376, 377.
Marie J. W. M., 218.
Marinda, 466.
Marion Constance, 224.
Marion E., 351.
381 Mark,[9] 366.
Mark, 251.
Mark J., 357.
Marohn T., 389.
539 Marshfield P.,[8] 415.
Martha, 202, 258, 323, 367, 404, 455, 458.
Martha A., 346, 377.
Martha A. B., 276, 278.
Martha C., 447.
Martha E , 256.
Martha J., 254, 361, 392, 440.
Martha L., 413.
Martha M., 230, 269.
Martha N., 311.
Martin Luther, 302.
Mary, 55, 193, 194, 195, 196, 200, 204, 205, 206, 209, 213, 218, 237, 238, 241, 247, 252, 262, 274, 280, 288, 293, 299, 327, 329, 334, 336, 337, 340, 347, 349, 365, 403, 406, 426, 428, 432, 444, 445, 450, 453, 455, 457, 461, 467.
Mary A., 249, 287, 305, 332, 335, 346, 352, 388, 393, 414, 423.
Mary Ann R., 295.
Mary Ann Wroe, 96, 210.
Mary C., 275, 279, 313, 430, 454.
Mary D., 438, 440.
Mary E., 224, 242, 275, 313, 324, 327, 339, 345, 397, 441, 447, 457, 465, 469.
Mary F., 370.
Mary Flora B., 267.
Mary G., 331, 465.
Mary H., 268, 371, 379, 381, 443.
Mary J., 276, 282, 283, 308, 380, 456.
Mary J. Waring, 287.
M. Jane, 292.
Mary Knight, 270.
Mary L., 230, 250, 324, 333, 459.
Mary M., 259.
Mary P., 421, 462.
Mary S., 265, 378, 435.
Mary T., 320, 322.
Mary W., 230, 240, 419.
624 Matthew H.,[7] 453.
Matthew H., 354.
671 Matthew Nolan,[8] 471.
Mattie J., 374.
Mattie L., 387.
Mattie M., 373, 359.
Maud D. J., 382.
Maud E., 285, 327.
Maud G., 382.
Maud M., 350.
May, 457, 459.
May E., 358.
270 336 Mayo,[5] 328.
Mayo, 26, 178, 336.
Mehitable Coats, 427.
Melinda, 246, 373, 375.
Mellen E., 321.
Melville, 379.
430 Melville,[9] 379.
Melville T., 356.
412 404 Melvin A.,[10] 374.
510 Melvin G.,[8] 404.
363 Menzies B.,[9] 361.
Mercy, 207, 337, 347, 348.
Mercy Ellen, 353.
Mercy Jennie, 378.
Merrill L., 359.
Mignon, 379.
Mildred C., 373.
139 267 Miller Thaddeus,[9] 114, 265.
227 309 Milton Perry,[10] 308.
Minerva, 256.
Minerva E., 285.
Minerva U., 259.
Minnie E., 241, 351.
Minnie M., 380, 465.
Miriam P., 457.
Mitty, 365.
M. Lillian, 378.
Mona M., 404.
Morris D., 252.
244 325 Moses,[7] 314.
525 411 Moses,[6] Capt., 133, 134, 135, 178, 410.
528 412 Moses,[7] Judge, 136, 411.
533 Moses,[8] 412.
535 Moses,[9] 179, 413.
Moses, 55, 201, 413.
Moses B., 453.
596 Moses P.,[8] Dr., 442.
Myra Bell, 440.
Myra C., 440.
Nabby (Abigail), 337.

OTHER NAMES.

Abercrombie, M. B., 435.
Abbott, Benjamin, 458; Edith L., 407; Luther W., 407.
Abrams, Anna A., 333; Carrie, 297; Mary E., 343.
Acker, James W., 302.
Ackley, Betsey E., 406.
Adair, Elizabeth, 343.
Adams, Edith, 353; John W., 363; Henry, 361; Hattie E., 317; Katie E., 233; Mary R., 276; Pamela, 362; Warren, 347; William, 224.
Albee, E. W., 276.
Alcorn, Loie, 286.
Aldworth, Elizabeth, 194; John, 194; Sir Richard, 194; Robert, 194.
Alexander, Wm. L., 413.
Alger, Marcia J., 223.
Allds, Jotham, 459.
Allen, 259; Ann Penn, 101, 217; Alonzo N., 243; Benjamin M., 402; Emma C., 467; George W., 311; Henry T., 380; James, 217; John, 243; Marcus W., 243; Martha E., 392; Mary J., 454; Nathan, 319; Sumner D., 319; Susan M., 442; William, 101, 218; William H., 222.
Alley, Maggie M., 394.
Almy, James G., 211.
Alverson, K. D., 228; Willard, 228; W. N., 228; W. W., 228.
Ames, Charles G., 252; Clarissa, 317; James G., 252; Timothy H., 401.
Anderson, F. C., 241; Hannah, 457; Pollina, 227; Sarah J., 457.
Andrews, H., 240; Isaac P., 240; John, 432; Rev. Otis, 392; Trueman L., 316.
Apthorp, Charles, 209; East, 209; John, 209.
Appleton, C. H., 217; Charlotte D., 222; John, 216; Dr. Nathan W., 216; William G., 210.
Arms, Alfred, 268.
Armstrong, Melinda, 443; Sarah, 434.
Arnette, R. M. J., 232.
Arnold, Benjamin, 367; Ellen, 240; Hannah, 222; James F., 381; N. J., 323; Rachel, 339.
Arthur, Hannah S., 298; Samuel D., 300.
Athearne, Frank, 390.

Atkinson, Amos, 429; Annie, 429; Hon. Edward, 429; George, 429; Helen, 200; Sarah, 203; William P., 429.
Attwood, Roscoe, 447.
Atwood, Joseph, 455.
Aubin, Capt. Philip, 434.
Austin, Moses, 452; Sarah A., 452; W. S., 278.
Averill, Susan, 229.
Avery, Ruth, 210.
Babbitt, J. J., 276.
Babcock, J. C., 326; Louisa, 319.
Babson, Martha, 463.
Bacon, 431; David, 206; Josiah, 385.
Badger, Elizabeth B., 74, 190; Giles, 74, 190; Nathaniel, 74, 190.
Bagley, Stephen, 392.
Bahr, John, 266.
Bailey, Arad., 330; Clemence, 407; George, 356; Oliver W., 441; Simon, 441.
Baird, John B., 250.
Baker, A. B., 279; B. R., 247; Alice J., 319; Emma J., 293; Chauncy, 227; James, 362; Josephine C., 299; Samuel P., 341.
Balch, Wesley, 468.
Balding, Hester J., 295.
Baldwin, C. A., 375; Fred. H., 230.
Ball, Louisa, 388.
Ballou, Elizabeth J., 308; John, 423.
Baltimore (Lord), 220.
Bancroft, Howard, 334.
Bangs, Lemuel, 403.
Banks, Enoch R., 443.
Barber, Isabella, 249.
Barclay, Elizabeth, 243; George W., 248.
Barnes, ——, 284.
Barnum, Alexander M., 261.
Barstow, Mabel, 323.
Barter, Casselda, 348; Loami A., 357.
Bartlett, Charles C., 399; Charles L., 468; David H., 74, 192; Edward K., 242; Greenleaf C., 192; Lydia, 205; Mary, 453; Thomas, 74, 192; William B., 436; General William F., 468.
Barr, Rev. Hugh, 255; Martha L., 255.
Barrett, Adelaide M., 280; Harriet L., 280.
Bass, Rt. Rev. Edward, 48, 55, 433.
Bassett, Daniel H., 305; Roxy (or Rozy), 369.

542 INDEX TO GENEALOGY.

Herrick, Nathaniel, 265.
Herring, Noah, 276.
Hersey, Lois J., 368.
Hescock, E. T., 339.
Heyworth, Arthur B., 470; Robert, 470.
Higby, Anne E., 259; Cassius M., 259; Marvin S., 259.
Higgins, Isaiah, 368; Nettie, 383; Warren M., 395.
Hildbolt, Fanny, 236.
Hill, Deborah, 147; Effie A., 272; Rev. George E., 219; Harvey, 301; James, 274; John, 447; Levi, 320; Sarah, 72, 190, 462; William, 72, 190.
Hills, C. T., 317; Elizabeth, 82, 199; Joseph, 199.
Hilton, Elizabeth, 72, 190; John, 451; Moses, 337; William, 190.
Hinds, Emma M., 382.
Hinkley, Helena, 384; Samuel, 367.
Hires, Martha, 376.
Hirst, Judge, 427.
Hiscock, Mrs. E. T., 338.
Hitchcock, Chas. H., 246; Hiram, 111, 245; James L., 112, 245; Mary F., 423; Mary O., 250.
Hoadly, Sally, 226.
Hobson, Mary, 376.
Hobbs, Almira, 383; George, 383.
Hodgdon, Abigail, 345; Cyrus, 346; John, 438; Mary E., 438; Stephen G., 353; Thomas, 344.
Holbrook, Bradford, 363; Charles A., 402; Peter, 367, 384; Rhoda, 384; Tamzay, 450.
Holden, David R., 448; Dellia B., 318; Hattie B., 448; Louise T., 271.
Holman, Calvin J., 317; Charles T., 317; David S., 317; John G., 316; Jonathan, 316; Jonathan L., 316; Joshua, 315; Leonard S., 316; Mary, 329.
Holmes, Clarence, 407; Mary A., 275.
Holt, Dr., 426; Peter, 330.
Holyoke, Rev. W. E., 454; William, 454.
Hollister, Dency, 226.
Homer, Adeline, 419; Rev. Dr. Charles W., 419; Frances P., 419; Henry G., 419; Margaret, 419.
Hook, Elias, 463; George G., 463; William, 463.
Hopkins, Huldah, 263.
Horton, Esther, 448; George P., 261; Ida, 325; Obadiah, 458; Timothy K., 268.

Hostetter, Mary I., 416.
Hosum, Ebenezer, 453; Lydia, 453.
Hotchkiss, ——, 294; Henry L., 222; Maria L. F., 296.
Houghton, Frank L., 370; Gracia, 267; Martin, 314; Thomas, 370.
House, Daniel, 253.
Houston, Mary, 248.
How, Frank G., 342.
Howard, Daniel, 366; Hannah, 305; Judge, 209; Mrs. Matilda, 324; Susan P., 389.
Howe, Lottie, 224.
Howell, Charles, 320.
Howes, Alvin, 369; Betsey, 369; Cordelia A., 368; Eleanor, 324; George K., 404; Helen, 370; William K., 404.
Hoxie, Alice, 262.
Hubbard, Burton, 293; Charles F., 291; Mina L., 270.
Hughes, James M. L., 241.
Hull, Pauline A., 261.
Humastun, Isaac, 263.
Hunt, Alonzo C., 264; Benjamin F., 287; Frederick S., 287; George L., 443; Joseph, 443; Woodbridge, 440; Zebedee, 440.
Huntress, Mrs. Betsey, 130, 396; Jennie F., 396; Robert, 396.
Hurlburt, Clara, 293; Samuel E., 293.
Huse, Mrs. ——, 423.
Hussey, Abigail, 452; Phebe, 452; Samuel, 452.
Huston, Hugar H., 270.
Hutchins, Augustus S., 222; Julia S., 222; Hon. Waldo, 102, 219, 222; William E., 222.
Hutchings, Frederick, 345.
Hutchinson, Bessie D., 234; James, 237.
Hynes, Alvin, 334.
Ingalls, L., 393.
Ingersoll, Antoinette De F., 344; Dorothy (Dolly), 410; Mary A., 344.
Ingraham, Anna K., 214; Charlotte, 212; Duncan, 100, 212, 214, 215; Duncan N., 98, 99; Duncan G., 340; George, 215; Henry E., 215; James S., 267; Susan I., 214.
Ingram, Manship, 248.
Ireland, Willis C., 374.
Irons, ——, 455.
Irvine, W., 231.
Iseman, John E., 298.
Jackman, Dorothy L., 331.
Jacques, Mary, 191, 202.

Lancaster, Moses, 453; R. P., 455.
Land, Leroy, 292.
Lander, Sally, 367.
Lane, Fraisilette C., 427; Francis, 427; Rhoda A., 391.
Lang, Charles, 283.
Langley, Harriet B., 444.
Lapham, Rev. Dr., 426.
Lasky, Mrs. Phebe A., 274.
Laughton, John, 399.
Laurence, Elizabeth, 218.
Lawrence, Isaac, 214; Jane, 317; Maria E., 214; Napoleon B., 265.
Laylor, Diana, 277.
Laythe, Edson H., 275; Fred. S., 275.
Lea, Elizabeth A., 228.
Leach, Josephine, 456.
Leal, Eleanor, 197.
Learned, Abbie M., 370; Elizabeth H., 435.
Leavitt, Emma, 363; Ida F., 353; Moses, 425; Sophia, 425.
Le Claire, Edgar, 250.
Lee, John, 133, 412; John A., 321; Joseph, 412; Lucy, 229; Mary, 412; Martha L., 412; Mrs. Robert E., 220.
Leeds, ——, 225.
Leeman, Jacob, 236; Samuel C., 236.
Lemon, Hattie, 243.
Leigh (see Lee), John, 412; Silas P., 410.
Leigher, Wm., 366.
Leonard, Israel, 231; Israel G., 232; Joseph, 231.
Lessingham, Clara, 213.
Lester, Henry, Jr., 293; James G., 293; Josephine B., 417.
Leverett, John, 195; Knight, 195; Thomas, 195.
Lewis, Allen, 345; Colonel, 220; Daniel, 225; David, 358; Emma, 358; Rebecca, 225; Silas, 346.
Libby, Hattie M., 387; William H., 387.
Lighthipe, L. C., 215.
Lincoln, Jane, 224.
Lindsey, H. H., 231.
Ling, Phebe, 322.
Lipscomb, Emma, 233.
Little, Eben, Jr., 331; Henry B., 409; Henry Willard, 331; James, 434; Joseph, 192; Lucy E., 410; Moses, 25, 192; Sarah J., 410.
Livingston, Walter C., 218.

Lobeck, Henry C., 245.
Locke, Almira H., 438; Amos, 446; Hiram, 438; Nancy, 452; Semour, 456.
Long, Joanna, 405.
Longfellow, Jonathan, 74, 192; Mary, 418; Stephen, 418.
Lord, Henry C., 449; Nellie, 351; Thomas, 412.
Lorens, ——, 422.
Lorey, Louise, 313.
Loring, Experience, 460.
Lovell, Ada E., 389; George, 278; Jonathan, 337; Sarah B., 313; Sewell, 383.
Lovett, Anna E., 464; George S., 464; Richmond, 288.
Lowell, Abigail G., 362; John, 362; Rebecca, 191; Richard, 191; Wilmot L., 364.
Lucas, Ira H., 267; Lucinda, 236.
Luce, Nannie W., 370.
Ludd, Nellie, 355.
Lunt, Alden B., 273; Ann, 200; Arabella, 426; Daniel, 428; Henry, 428; Joseph, 426.
Lyman, Augustus J., 221.
Lynde, Sarah A., 269; Thomas, 269.
Lynn, David, 221; Fanny, 220.
Mack, Henrietta R., 212; Dr. John, 295.
Mackcres, Mary, 201.
Maconnell, Richard, 260; Walter G., 260.
McBride, Alice M., 246; Emma L., 401; Lottie L., 401.
McCann, Admiral W. P., 265.
McCarty, B. Frank, 347, 353; Howard, 335; James, 347.
McClintock, Frances, 362.
McComber, Franklin, 228.
McConkin, Agnes, 257.
McCoy, Allen H., 244.
McCrillis, Andrew, 443.
McDonald, Joseph, 357; Wiley S., 232.
McDougall, Alexander, 373.
McFarland, John M., 394.
McFarlin, Aurilla, 259.
McFerren, Sarah A., 271.
McGraw, Martin, 250.
McIntire, Charles, 297; Mary C., 372.
McIntosh, R. M., 315.
McKay, John, 237.
McKenney, Alice, 385.
McKenzie, Angus, 422; Donald, 422; George S., 421; John D., 421; Malcolm, 422; Spencer G., 422.

Payson, Sarah, 424.
Peabody, Abigail, 329; Mary, 328;
    Nathan, 328.
Pearson, Augustus, 410; George
    H., 423; Green, 428; Henry
    S., 423; Mrs. Mary, 432;
    Moses, 405; Ruth, 461; Wil-
    liam H., 395.
Peaslee, Ida, 463; Josiah, 365.
Peasley, Mary, 156, 451.
Peck, Benona, 247; Homer, 247.
Pell, William A., 258.
Penn, William, 265.
Penney, Edgar, 301; Henry, 301.
Pennington, Rebecca, 334.
Pentland, W., 330.
Percival, Rev. C. H., 349.
Perkins, Angier M., 431; Ebenezer
    G., 431; Elizabeth, 431; Han-
    nah G., 431; Henrietta, 431;
    Jacob, 431; John, 412; Matthew,
    430; Sally, 383; Sarah A., 431;
    Susan B., 414.
Perry, Mary J., 344; Nelson W.,
    419; Dr. Samuel, 98, 214.
Peterson, Rebecca, 122, 300; Rulif,
    122, 300.
Pettengill, Anna, 205; John, 433;
    Lucy G., 331; Mary, 433;
    Moses, 332; Peabody, 332;
    Ruth, 458.
Petite, A. H., 316.
Phelps, Jason, 286.
Philbrick, Caleb, 238; Clymene, 238.
Philbrook, Emeline, 331.
Phillips, Colonel, 195.
Phinney, Theresa, 242.
Phipps, David, 209; Frances C.,
    457; Leonidas M., 456.
Pickard, S. T., 452.
Pickering, A., 403.
Pierce, Benjamin, 53, 199; Cather-
    ine, 405; Daniel, 6, 81, 82, 405;
    Mrs. Lydia, 199; Martha, 10,
    81, 82, 199; Mary, 74, 191, 201;
    Sarah, 82, 200.
Pierson, Henry J., 250; Josephine,
    422.
Pike, Abbie M., 332; Helen F.,
    343; John, 3, 192; Sherman
    B., 257.
Pillsbury, Hon. E. F., 383; Miriam,
    453; Timothy, 453.
Pinkard, Kate V., 456.
Pinkham, Alden, 358; Asanath,
    239; Hannah A., 239; Martha
    J., 358; Mary, 358; Minerva,
    349.
Piper, Isabel N., 330; John, 369;
    Margaret, 200; Nathaniel, 200.

Plant, James C., 275.
Platt, Mrs. Elizabeth B., 465;
    Judge, 341.
Plummer, Hiram, 468; Joshua, 199.
Poland, Louisa, 467.
Polk, Alva W., 364; William J.,
    280.
Pollard, F. A., 326.
Polley, Laura, 296.
Pomeroy, Jane, 371; Mary A., 468:
    Rebecca J., 381.
Pool, Gertrude, 304.
Poor, Ebenezer, 410; Persis, 411.
Poore, E. S., 462.
Pope, Edward, 211, 212, 215.
Porter, Albert S., 308; Rev. W.
    H., 308.
Pottle, Jennie, 364.
Potts, Bertha, 198; George H., 198;
    Rev. Francis H., 150, 416.
Potwin, Mary A., 109, 249.
Powell, Stephen C., 222.
Powers, John G., 378; Richard K.,
    330.
Poyen, Abigail R., 452.
Pratt, John M., 388; Norton E.,
    321.
Preble, Hephzibah, 337; Mary, 337.
Prentiss, Caleb, 197; William, 196;
    William H., 197.
Presbury, Edward, 132, 405; Mary,
    132, 405.
Presey, Alice, 194.
Pressey, Hannah, 369; Moses, 388;
    Nancy, 361.
Preston, J. H., 396.
Price, Ezekiel, 95, 210; Mary D.,
    95, 210.
Pritchard, Mary, 219; Paul, 432.
Proctor, Ahaziah, 465; Rebecca,
    465.
Prouty, Elizabeth W., 307.
Pulsifer, C. R., 447; Mary C., 447.
Pultz, Elmer, 254.
Purcell, Mrs. Phebe, 466.
Purdy, D. J., 280; Ralph, 280;
    William A., 380.
Purse, Laura, 342.
Putnam, ——, 403.
Putney, Greeley, 465; Hannah L.,
    465.
Quackenbos, Anna, 196.
Quimby, Asa, 381; Martha A., 381;
    Phœbe, 294.
Quincy, Edmund, 63, 94, 96, 208;
    Sally, 94, 208.
Rackliff, Mary E., 398.
Radz, Jacob, 236.
Rairdon, Cornelius, 356.
Raisch, Carl, 309.

380; Sophia F., 242; Susan, 390.

Weare, Nathaniel, 193.

Weatherhead, Sarah, 267.

Weaver, Edward L., 378.

Webb, Lucy, 329.

Webster, ——, 385; Eliza S. G., 221; Elizabeth R., 470; Frances J., 219; Harriet, 219; Lester, 282; Levi B., 470; Mary, 219; Dr. Noah, 101, 102, 218; Rosalia, E. S., 220; William E., 220; William G., 220.

Weed, Mrs. Helen L., 341.

Weeks, Levi H., 231.

Weld, Rev. Ezra, 196.

Weller, Anna C., 276.

Wellington, Hattie, 322.

Wells, John, 71, 193; Roderick, 229.

Welsh, Dorcas, 196; Frank J., 301; Jeff, 379; H. K. W., 219.

Weitzell, Agnes M., 246.

Wendall, Isaac, 452.

Wentworth, Frances, 323.

West, Helen L., 221; Sarah J., 245.

Weston, James E., 323.

West & Greenleaf, 196.

Wetherby, Edmund, 236.

Wetmore, Aug., 429.

Weymouth, Rufus, 383; Timothy, 366.

Wheeler, E. E., 417; Eliza J., 321; Rev. Joseph, 209; Joshua, 314; Lydia, 365; Mrs. Mary B., 326; Mary J., 467.

Wheelwright, Capt. Abraham, 422; Elizabeth C., 422.

Wheildon, Grace, 241.

Whipple, Addie S., 230; Carrie E., 241; Mary J., 212.

Whiston, Dr. E. A., 424.

Whitaker, William, 322.

Whitcher, Sargent C., 362; Levi, 362.

Whitcomb, Prudence, 208; Rebecca, 208.

White, Dr. Albert, 307; Elizabeth, 410; Ferdinand E., 306; Florence L., 378; Gilman, 410; Hulbert F., 317; Thomas H., 318; Dr. W. C., 455.

Whitehead, Irwin, 309.

Whitehouse, Izzie M., 378.

Whitman, Peter, 411.

Whitney, Charles A., 415; Emily, 247; Joseph, 310; Julia, 313; Mary P., 224; Olive E., 415; Rev. Peter, 224; Thaddeus, 268; W. G., 228.

Whitted, H. I., 311.

Whittemore, Rev. Aaron, 205; Henry, 424; Joseph, 23, 273; William T., 424.

Whittier, Abigail, 294; Alice G., 452; Anna, 452; Elizabeth H., 452; Horatio, 294; John, 452; John Greenleaf, 156, 452; Joseph, 451, 452; Levi, 362; Lydia A., 452; Matthew F., 452; Mary, 451, 452 (see Mary Gutterson); Moses, 452; Obadiah, 452; Phebe A., 452; Sarah, 452.

Whitwell, Virginia, 344.

Wickwire, Mrs. Elizabeth, 226.

Widdifield, Georgiana, 274.

Wiggin, Mary, 458.

Wight, Margaret A., 396; Timothy, 395.

Wilbur, Emeline, 311; Harris, 277; Dr. Henry D., 278; Sally, 389.

Wilcox, George, 111, 245; Julius, 245.

Wilder, Anna E., 330; Rufus L., 415; Samuel J., 412; Silas A., 326; Susanna A., 373; Sylvia E., 373; Theodore, 373.

Wiley, Charles, 400; Eliza, 399.

Wilfley, Elizabeth B., 457; William F., 456.

Wilkins, Anna, 343; Evaline, 273; Zena, 324.

Willard, ——, 399; Abbie G., 417; Augustus, 319; Edwin A., 417; Joseph, 70, 418; Martha, 368; Mary (Polly), 226; Mary E., 419; Mrs. Mary H., 238; Judge Paul, 146, 147, 148, 419; Simon, 70, 77, 146, 226.

Willcox, Samuel S., 322.

Williams, Avery, 273; Charles, 272; Mrs. E. C., 315; Harriet H., 372; Henry, 272; Jerome B., 455; John, 362, 372; Mary, 289; Patty, 227; Rachel, 308; Royal S., 228.

Williamson, Almira L., 396; Eben, 396; Flora A., 401; Granville B., 369; Hannah, 131, 367; John L., 368; Margaret, 400; Mary, 237, 256; Rev. Stephen, 338; Sylvia, 368.

Wills, Pressie J., 285.

Wilson, ——, 72, 190; Caroline, 290; Content, 215; Cyrus F., 380; David, 335; William, 215; William K., 329, 330; William M., 300.

Winans, Gussie, 439.

Unconnected Families not Indexed.

www.ingramcontent.com/pod-product-compliance
Lightning Source LLC
Chambersburg PA
CBHW060948280326
41935CB00009B/653